36: *British Novelists, 1890-1929: Modernists*, edited by Thomas F. Staley (1985)

37: *American Writers of the Early Republic*, edited by Emory Elliott (1985)

38: *Afro-American Writers After 1955: Dramatists and Prose Writers*, edited by Thadious M. Davis and Trudier Harris (1985)

39: *British Novelists, 1660-1800*, 2 parts, edited by Martin C. Battestin (1985)

40: *Poets of Great Britain and Ireland Since 1960*, 2 parts, edited by Vincent B. Sherry, Jr. (1985)

41: *Afro-American Poets Since 1955*, edited by Trudier Harris and Thadious M. Davis (1985)

42: *American Writers for Children Before 1900*, edited by Glenn E. Estes (1985)

43: *American Newspaper Journalists, 1690-1872*, edited by Perry J. Ashley (1986)

44: *American Screenwriters*, Second Series, edited by Randall Clark, Robert E. Morsberger, and Stephen O. Lesser (1986)

45: *American Poets, 1880-1945*, First Series, edited by Peter Quartermain (1986)

46: *American Literary Publishing Houses, 1900-1980: Trade and Paperback*, edited by Peter Dzwonkoski (1986)

47: *American Historians, 1866-1912*, edited by Clyde N. Wilson (1986)

48: *American Poets, 1880-1945*, Second Series, edited by Peter Quartermain (1986)

49: *American Literary Publishing Houses, 1638-1899*, 2 parts, edited by Peter Dzwonkoski (1986)

50: *Afro-American Writers Before the Harlem Renaissance*, edited by Trudier Harris (1986)

51: *Afro-American Writers from the Harlem Renaissance to 1940*, edited by Trudier Harris (1987)

52: *American Writers for Children Since 1960: Fiction*, edited by Glenn E. Estes (1986)

53: *Canadian Writers Since 1960*, First Series, edited by W. H. New (1986)

54: *American Poets, 1880-1945*, Third Series, 2 parts, edited by Peter Quartermain (1987)

55: *Victorian Prose Writers Before 1867*, edited by William B. Thesing (1987)

56: *German Fiction Writers, 1914-1945*, edited by James Hardin (1987)

57: *Victorian Prose Writers After 1867*, edited by William B. Thesing (1987)

58: *Jacobean and Caroline Dramatists*, edited by Fredson Bowers (1987)

59: *American Literary Critics and Scholars, 1800-1850*, edited by John W. Rathbun and Monica M. Grecu (1987)

60: *Canadian Writers Since 1960*, Second Series, edited by W. H. New (1987)

61: *American Writers for Children Since 1960: Poets, Illustrators, and Nonfiction Authors*, edited by Glenn E. Estes (1987)

62: *Elizabethan Dramatists*, edited by Fredson Bowers (1987)

63: *Modern American Critics, 1920-1955*, edited by Gregory S. Jay (1988)

64: *American Literary Critics and Scholars, 1850-1880*, edited by John W. Rathbun and Monica M. Grecu (1988)

65: *French Novelists, 1900-1930*, edited by Catharine Savage Brosman (1988)

66: *German Fiction Writers, 1885-1913*, 2 parts, edited by James Hardin (1988)

67: *Modern American Critics Since 1955*, edited by Gregory S. Jay (1988)

68: *Canadian Writers, 1920-1959*, First Series, edited by W. H. New (1988)

69: *Contemporary German Fiction Writers*, First Series, edited by Wolfgang D. Elfe and James Hardin (1988)

70: *British Mystery Writers, 1860-1919*, edited by Bernard Benstock and Thomas F. Staley (1988)

continued on back endsheets

Restoration and Eighteenth-Century Dramatists
First Series

Restoration and Eighteenth-Century Dramatists
First Series

8040

Edited by
Paula R. Backscheider
University of Rochester

A Bruccoli Clark Layman Book
Gale Research Inc. • Book Tower • Detroit, Michigan 48226

Manufactured by Edwards Brothers, Inc.
Ann Arbor, Michigan
Printed in the United States of America

Copyright ©1989
GALE RESEARCH INC.

**Library of Congress Cataloging-in-
Publication Data**

Restoration and eighteenth-century dramatists, first series/
edited by Paula R. Backscheider
    p. cm.–(Dictionary of literary biography; v. 80)
"A Bruccoli Clark Layman book."
Includes index.
ISBN 0-8103-4558-7
    1. English drama–18th century–Dictionaries 2. English
drama–Restoration, 1660-1700–Dictionaries. 3. English
drama–18th century–Bio-bibliography. 4. English drama–
Restoration, 1660-1700–Bio-bibliography. 5. Dramatists,
English–18th century–Biography–dictionaries. 6. Drama-
tists English–Early   modern,   1500-1700–Biography–
Dictionarys. I. Backscheider, Paula. II. Series.
PR701.R4   1989
822'.009–dc19
[B]   89-1070
                                        CIP

To Jacob H. Adler in the year of his retirement

Contents

Plan of the Series

. . . Almost the most prodigious asset of a country, and perhaps its most precious possession, is its native literary product—when that product is fine and noble and enduring.

Mark Twain*

The advisory board, the editors, and the publisher of the *Dictionary of Literary Biography* are joined in endorsing Mark Twain's declaration. The literature of a nation provides an inexhaustible resource of permanent worth. We intend to make literature and its creators better understood and more accessible to students and the reading public, while satisfying the standards of teachers and scholars.

To meet these requirements, *literary biography* has been construed in terms of the author's achievement. The most important thing about a writer is his writing. Accordingly, the entries in *DLB* are career biographies, tracing the development of the author's canon and the evolution of his reputation.

The purpose of *DLB* is not only to provide reliable information in a convenient format but also to place the figures in the larger perspective of literary history and to offer appraisals of their accomplishments by qualified scholars.

The publication plan for *DLB* resulted from two years of preparation. The project was proposed to Bruccoli Clark by Frederick G. Ruffner, president of the Gale Research Company, in November 1975. After specimen entries were prepared and typeset, an advisory board was formed to refine the entry format and develop the series rationale. In meetings held during 1976, the publisher, series editors, and advisory board approved the scheme for a comprehensive biographical dictionary of persons who contributed to North American literature. Editorial work on the first volume began in January 1977, and it was published in 1978. In order to make *DLB* more than a reference tool and to compile volumes that individually have claim to status as literary history, it was decided to organize volumes by topic, period, or genre. Each of these freestanding volumes provides a biographical-bibliographical guide and overview for a particular area of literature. We are convinced that this organization—as opposed to a single alphabet method—constitutes a valuable innovation in the presentation of reference material. The volume plan necessarily requires many decisions for the placement and treatment of authors who might properly be included in two or three volumes. In some instances a major figure will be included in separate volumes, but with different entries emphasizing the aspect of his career appropriate to each volume. Ernest Hemingway, for example, is represented in *American Writers in Paris, 1920-1939* by an entry focusing on his expatriate apprenticeship; he is also in *American Novelists, 1910-1945* with an entry surveying his entire career. Each volume includes a cumulative index of subject authors and articles. Comprehensive indexes to the entire series are planned.

With volume ten in 1982 it was decided to enlarge the scope of *DLB*. By the end of 1986 twenty-one volumes treating British literature had been published, and volumes for Commonwealth and Modern European literature were in progress. The series has been further augmented by the *DLB Yearbooks* (since 1981) which update published entries and add new entries to keep the *DLB* current with contemporary activity. There have also been *DLB Documentary Series* volumes which provide biographical and critical source materials for figures whose work is judged to have particular interest for students. One of these companion volumes is entirely devoted to Tennessee Williams.

We define literature as the *intellectual commerce of a nation:* not merely as belles lettres but as that ample and complex process by which ideas are generated, shaped, and transmitted. *DLB* entries are not limited to "creative writers" but extend to other figures who in their time and in their way influenced the mind of a people. Thus the series encompasses historians, journalists, publishers, and screenwriters. By this means readers of *DLB* may be aided to perceive litera-

*From an unpublished section of Mark Twain's autobiography, copyright © by the Mark Twain Company.

ture not as cult scripture in the keeping of intellectual high priests but firmly positioned at the center of a nation's life.

DLB includes the major writers appropriate to each volume and those standing in the ranks immediately behind them. Scholarly and critical counsel has been sought in deciding which minor figures to include and how full their entries should be. Wherever possible, useful references are made to figures who do not warrant separate entries.

Each *DLB* volume has a volume editor responsible for planning the volume, selecting the figures for inclusion, and assigning the entries. Volume editors are also responsible for preparing, where appropriate, appendices surveying the major periodicals and literary and intellectual movements for their volumes, as well as lists of further readings. Work on the series as a whole is coordinated at the Bruccoli Clark Layman editorial center in Columbia, South Carolina, where the editorial staff is responsible for accuracy of the published volumes.

One feature that distinguishes *DLB* is the illustration policy–its concern with the iconography of literature. Just as an author is influenced by his surroundings, so is the reader's understanding of the author enhanced by a knowledge of his environment. Therefore *DLB* volumes include not only drawings, paintings, and photographs of authors, often depicting them at various stages in their careers, but also illustrations of their families and places where they lived. Title pages are regularly reproduced in facsimile along with dust jackets for modern authors. The dust jackets are a special feature of *DLB* because they often document better than anything else the way in which an author's work was perceived in its own time. Specimens of the writers' manuscripts are included when feasible.

Samuel Johnson rightly decreed that "The chief glory of every people arises from its authors." The purpose of the *Dictionary of Literary Biography* is to compile literary history in the surest way available to us–by accurate and comprehensive treatment of the lives and work of those who contributed to it.

The *DLB* Advisory Board

Foreword

This volume of the *Dictionary of Literary Biography: Restoration and Eighteenth-Century Dramatists*, First Series, includes eighteen playwrights born between 1621 and 1666. They practiced their art in difficult and tumultuous circumstances, coped with situations no dramatists before or since have faced, and produced some of the best–and strangest–plays in English literature.

After years of conflict, a civil war had broken out between the supporters of the English Parliament and those of King Charles I. On 30 January 1649 Charles had been executed, and England became a commonwealth, governed as a republic and dominated by Puritans. The country's first written constitution, the Instrument of Government, established that legislative authority should be vested in Parliament and executive power in council; the head of the government would be the lord protector, and that was Oliver Cromwell. The Commonwealth and the Cromwell years meant that the theaters, seen as places of licentious corruption, had been officially closed since 1642 and were dismantled by soldiers in 1649. After Cromwell's death in 1658 and the unsettled two years that followed, Parliament invited the executed king's son to resume the English throne.

In 1660, when Charles II issued patents to open two theaters a scant three months after he landed in England, playwrights faced problems that not even the king's enthusiasm could solve. In spite of scattered performances throughout the Interregnum and the perseverance of the Red Bull Theatre, there were few trained performers and no established audiences. In the eighteen years the theaters had been closed, the actors had found new occupations, died, or at least grown old. An entire generation had grown up almost without public performances and had found other leisure activities. It would be the 1662-1663 season before newly written plays would be ready; they included a hit, Samuel Tuke's *Adventures of Five Hours*, and John Dryden's *Wild Gallant*. Consequently the managers faced serious problems. They brought back some of the aging actors and opened "nurseries"

to train new players. In fact, the two new companies were managed by Caroline dramatists, Sir William Davenant (the Duke's Company), who had been appointed master of the company at the Cockpit, Drury Lane, in 1640, and Thomas Killigrew (the King's Company), and both revived their own pre-Commonwealth plays in the first season. So small was the audience that personal satire could flourish in the plays. For instance, Shadwell ridiculed Robert Howard in *The Sullen Lovers* (1668), George Villiers, duke of Buckingham, added a scene attacking William Coventry and John Duncomb to Howard's *The Country Gentleman* (1669), and William Cavendish, duke of Newcastle, portrayed Charles Sedley in *The Heiress* (1669).[1]

The king had seen actresses on the French stage, and he wanted women on the London stage; therefore, the managers and their friends began to train the pretty, but often illiterate, girls they could recruit from London and the surrounding areas. Audiences were often harder to get than actresses, even in a time when no woman with even slight pretensions to modesty would stand on a public stage. The managers did what they could to attract an audience. They revived the tried-and-true plays from the Elizabethan and Jacobean era; they performed Shakespeare, Beaumont and Fletcher, Jonson, Massinger, Dekker, and lesser lights like William Berkeley, Henry Glapthorne, William Rowley, and Richard Brome; they revived their own plays, and Davenant put on part 2 of *The Seige of Rhodes*, the sequel to the play often considered the model for the many heroick tragedies that followed and the continuation of the first English opera, which Davenant had staged in 1656; they used elaborate costumes and scenery–Sir Fopling Flutter, for instance, strolled about the stage in the latest French fashions, and plays were set in Peru, Mexico, China, Russia, Cuba, and Africa. Playbills show that an ordinary ticket typically paid for a full evening of entertainment: three musical selections, act 1, a piece of music (often performed by a child), acts 2 and 3, a peasant dance, act 4, a national dance (Scottish were popular), act 5, music, and, in addition, an afterpiece. Moreover, managers and their playwrights learned to turn ordinary drama into spectacle. Thomas Shadwell's *Psyche* featured in the prologue Venus descending from heaven "in a large Machine, with Love her Son and two little Graces." In the play some of the special effects included Zephyrs descending and carrying Psyche into the clouds, Cupid flying on stage to give a speech, Venus being lost in the clouds, Jupiter riding his eagle through the air accompanied by thunder and lightning, and, at the end, a palace breaking in half.

Samuel Pepys occasionally commented on the poor attendance in the theaters that had been filled before the Interregnum, but, as time passed, the theater again became a popular pastime for groups of Londoners. Many of those who came, however, came to see and be seen. Anecdotes tell us that the movement and chatter often drowned out the performers, and it was far from unusual for a man to call across the theater to a friend regardless of what was happening on the stage. In fact, until David Garrick's time, some assured that they would be seen by sitting on the stage. Drawn by the king's patronage, members of the court, the rich, the witty, the fops, the idle young, their mistresses, and their servants and footmen came in large numbers. As Harold Love, Emmett Avery, Pierre Danchin, and others have pointed out, ordinary citizens, merchants and their apprentices, and even children attended too. Sailors and other riffraff took the cheapest seats; prostitutes and sharpers came to make contacts. And, of course, the older people who remembered the great plays of the seventeenth century bought tickets.

Because of the relatively small number of theatergoers, managers needed huge repertories. During the Restoration about ten new plays a year appeared, and the rest were the safer revivals. Throughout the age, repertory theater reigned. Some actors knew over one hundred parts, and every player knew twenty or thirty and was expected to be able to perform them after an afternoon's rehearsal of selected scenes. These playwrights, then, had to compete with the greatest plays written in the greatest period of English drama, had to appeal to a fickle and extremely diverse audience, and had the king as their chief critic. Some of Charles II's tastes were not as salutary for the theater as his encouragement of actresses and his eye for adaptable continental comedies; for instance, he loved bombastic, heroick

drama and preferred rhymed dialogue. One guide to his taste is the fact that he honored John Dryden's *Secret Love; or, The Maiden-Queen* with "the Title of His Play."[2] Those few who know Restoration drama in detail can name a number of plays suggested by the king, as *The Adventures of Five Hours* was to Samuel Tuke and *Sir Courtly Nice* to John Crowne. The adaptations of Molière and other French plays also point to Charles's influence, direct or felt.

As if the problems endemic to reopening the theater were not enough, other circumstances beyond the managers' control affected drama. In January 1672 the Theatre Royal on Bridges Street burned, and the King's Company had to move into Lisle's Tennis Court, Lincoln's Inn Fields, the playhouse recently abandoned by the Duke's Company when they moved into Dorset Garden. In 1682 the King's Company collapsed, and the so-called United Company controlled London theater until Thomas Betterton and other chief actors rebelled against the low salaries and miserly benefits. From 1682, then, until 1695, when the Lincoln's Inn Fields theater opened in what had formerly been a tennis court, playwrights had but one venue for their plays. Charles's death in 1685 meant the end of comfortable patronage, and the scramble to make plays profitable intensified.

King Charles's interest in the theater naturally resulted in its assuming a political hue. Whether this element was as slight as a flattering prologue mentioning the king or a dedication to one of his favorite courtiers (or mistresses) or as great as the Tory themes in the plays of John Crowne, Aphra Behn, Thomas Southerne, and Thomas Durfey, it was there. When Charles died and the country writhed over James's policies and perceived ambitions, this political dimension increased, and the stage became a place for the exploration of political themes of the most serious kind. Play after play explored forms of government, the authority of rulers, and the responsibilities of subjects, especially to tyrants. King William and Queen Mary, who assumed the throne in 1689, brought a measure of stability to the country, but William was never popular and, more important, never interested in the theater. With the death of Charles II, then, the English theater was catapulted into the market economy of the modern world.

During Charles's reign, the theater had attracted the greatest literary men of the time, and many of them were courtiers. Their effort to achieve wit, high seriousness, and elevation produced a theater alienated from large segments of the population. Dryden defined heroick drama as "an imitation, in little of an Heroick Poem" and went on to explain that "an Heroick Poet is not ty'd to a bare representation of what is true, or exceeding probable: but that he may let himself loose to visionary objects, and to the representation of such things, as depending not on sence . . . may give him a freer scope for imagination."[3] Tragedy came to be characterized by bombastic speeches, extravagant action, hysterical emotion, trumpets, drums, ghosts, and giant headdresses. The language that was their attempt to invent diction for the elevated sentiments of the stage was equally extravagant. Dryden's Berenice, for instance, tells her love that if she dies first, she will "Stop short of Heav'n, and wait you in a Cloud; / For fear we lose each other in a crowd."

Yet the theater had to build an audience. In efforts to make theater a popular in addition to high-culture entertainment, playwrights tried some of the same appeals we see in movies. Sex, violence, and special effects abounded. Their extravagance can be seen in two examples: the stage directions for the blood oath in Nathaniel Lee's *Lucius Junius Brutus* (1680) reads, "The Scene draws, showing the sacrifice: One Burning and another Crucify'd: the Priests coming forward with Goblets in their hands, fill'd with human blood." The conclusion of Charles Gildon's *Phaeton* (1698), which borrows from *Medea*, has the children torn to pieces by the mob and several characters melted when Lybia puts on a poisoned crown. The description of the deaths occupies two full pages and includes such gory details as "The blazing Crown belch[ed] out a fiery Deluge, / That prey'd upon her Hair, her Head, her Face; / From whence her Flesh like melting Wax ran down, / Mingl'd with Fire and Blood."

And then Jeremy Collier published his notorious essay, *A Short View of the Immorality and Profaneness of the English Stage* (1698). Moral reform was in the air. The active and growing Societies for the Reformation of Manners, royal proclamations, and threats of prosecution provided a dangerous climate for Collier's identification of the chief culprit responsible for national decline. Already struggling to increase its audience and just beginning to attract the middle class, the theater could hardly afford to be branded immoral. It had to respond. Collier had used the greatest living dramatists as his most prominent examples of the debauched and corrupting nature of the

stage: John Dryden, Thomas Durfey, John Vanbrugh, William Congreve, and William Wycherley. All but Wycherley answered quickly, Dryden in "To My Friend, The Author [Peter Motteux]," Durfey in the preface to his *Campaigners*, Vanbrugh in *A Short Vindication of "The Relapse" and "The Provoked Wife,"* and Congreve in *Amendments of Mr. Collier's False and Imperfect Citations*. In addition, Charles Gildon, Peter Motteux, John Dennis, George Farquhar, and many others published objections and refutations. Collier quickly published *A Defence of the Short View of the Profaneness and Immorality of the English Stage*, and many people, including a number of influential bishops, took his side. F. T. Wood counted sixty-two pamphlets siding with Collier and thirty-four defending the stage.[4] The controversy raged for years, but the effect on the theater was immediate. Dryden's moving poem begins,

> 'Tis hard, my Friend, to write in such an Age,
> As damns not only Poets, but the Stage.
> ....
> But, when to common sense they give the Lie,
> And turn distorted Words to Blasphemy,
> *They* give the Scandal. . . . (lines 1-2, 11-13)

In the same year Dryden had lamented the mutilation of plays in "To Mr. Granville, on his Excellent Tragedy, call'd *Heroick Love*": " . . . Murd'ring Plays, which they miscal Reviving. / Our Sense is Nonsense, through their Pipes convey'd; / Scarce can a Poet know the Play He made; / 'Tis so disguis'd in Death: Nor thinks 'tis He / That suffers in the Mangled Tragedy" (lines 24-28). In an attempt to purge "immorality and profaneness," plays succumbed to "mangling" aimed at reform. During the 1698-1699 season, Nathaniel Lee's *Rival Queens* became the tamer *Alexander* and John Fletcher's *Night Walker "The Little Thief."* Playwrights worried about legal prosecution produced new plays, often hasty and mediocre efforts, anonymously, and carefully included moral elements. In *Feign'd Friendship* (May 1699), for instance, Eugenia lectures all around her and reforms Lord Frolicksome and Lady Generous. Durfey's *Campaigners* (June 1698) was one of the few serious new plays, and John Dennis's *Rinaldo and Armida* (November 1698) sidestepped the controversy and took advantage of the audience for opera.

When Collier's attack came, the theaters were already in trouble. As Robert D. Hume says in *The Development of English Drama in the Late Seventeenth Century*, Rich's "ragtag and bobtail company" had barely survived its first seasons after the players' secession, and Betterton's company was old, disorganized, and working in cramped quarters. Concerts continued to compete vigorously, and the theaters invested in expensive spectacles like *The Island Princess.* The playwrights, then, had to appeal to a broad–and often rowdy–audience, stay out of trouble with the reformers, include music and spectacle, and still satisfy the expectations for good plays: well-designed plots, good characters, lively dialogue, pleasing settings, and engrossing incidents. In 1707, citing their economic straits, the Lord Chamberlain ordered a new union of companies, and, until 1714, London would have but a single company again. The conservative management of Rich and his successors made the blow to practicing and aspiring playwrights even greater.

For those who know only one or two of Wycherley's comedies and Dryden as a poet, the sheer number of plays and the variety of their forms, themes, and techniques may be a surprise. Recognition of the quality of plays like Vanbrugh's *Provoked Wife* and Southerne's *Wives' Excuse,* the fascination of the dark themes of the plays of Lee, Otway, and Pix, and the continued vigor of acting parts like Shadwell's eccentrics, Banks's queens, and Dryden's flirts may awaken a new interest in the drama of the Restoration and early eighteenth century.

This book is the first of the three *Dictionary of Literary Biography* volumes on *Restoration and Eighteenth-Century Dramatists;* its eighteen essays are to be followed by thirty-six more in the second and third series, representing playwrights born between Susannah Centlivre and William

Congreve in 1670 and George Colman the Younger and James Boaden in 1762. In addition to giving lively accounts of the career and significance of each playwright, contributors have put additional effort into recovering the canons of their playwrights' dramatic writings. Long-forgotten prologues, epilogues, poems, and periodical essays join plays in filling out the picture of this rather incompletely understood and underappreciated theatrical period.

When I think of this book, I remember the generosity, diligence, experience, knowledge, and even humor of the contributors. I want to express my gratitude to them, to Rob Hume who has been a willing resource for me and a number of them, and to the graduate assistant who worked on the project with creativity, efficiency, and intelligence from beginning to end, Laurie A. Sterling.

–Paula R. Backscheider

1. Robert D. Hume, *The Development of English Drama in the Late Seventeenth Century* (Oxford: Clarendon Press, 1976), pp. 259-260.

2. Preface to *Secret Love,* in volume 9 of *The Works of John Dryden,* edited by John Loftis and Vinton A. Dearing (Berkeley: University of California Press, 1966), p. 115.

3. "Of Heroique Plays," prefixed to *The Conquest of Granada,* in volume 2 of *The Works of John Dryden,* edited by John Loftis, David S. Rodes, and Vinton A. Dearing (Berkeley: University of California Press, 1978), pp. 10, 12.

4. "The Attack on the Stage," *Notes and Queries,* 163 (25 September 1937): 218-222.

Acknowledgments

This book was produced by Bruccoli Clark Layman, Inc. Karen L. Rood, senior editor for the *Dictionary of Literary Biography* series, was the in-house editor.

Production coordinator is Kimberly Casey. Art supervisor is Susan Todd. Penney L. Haughton is responsible for layout and graphics. Copyediting supervisor is Joan M. Prince. Typesetting supervisor is Kathleen M. Flanagan. William Adams, Laura Ingram, and Michael D. Senecal are editorial associates. The production staff includes Brandy H. Barefoot, Rowena Betts, Charles D. Brower, Joseph M. Bruccoli, Amanda Caulley, Teresa Chaney, Patricia Coate, Mary Colborn, Sarah A. Estes, Brian A. Glassman, Cynthia Hallman, Judith K. Ingle, Kathy S. Merlette, Sheri Beckett Neal, and Virginia Smith. Jean W. Ross is permissions editor.

Walter W. Ross and Jennifer Toth did the library research with the assistance of the reference staff at the Thomas Cooper Library of the University of South Carolina: Daniel Boice, Cathy Eckman, Gary Geer, Cathie Gottlieb, David L. Haggard, Jens Holley, Dennis Isbell, Jackie Kinder, Marcia Martin, Jean Rhyne, Beverly Steele, Ellen Tillett, Carol Tobin, and Virginia Weathers.

Dictionary of Literary Biography • Volume Eighty

Restoration and Eighteenth-Century Dramatists
First Series

Dictionary of Literary Biography

John Banks

(circa 1653-April 1706)

David Wykes
Dartmouth College

PLAY PRODUCTIONS: *The Rival Kings*, based on a translation of Gauthier de Costes de la Calprenède's *Cassandre*, London, Theatre Royal in Drury Lane, June 1677;

The Destruction of Troy, based on a translation of Raoul Lefèvre's *Recueil des histoires de Troyes*, London, Dorset Garden Theatre, November 1678;

The Unhappy Favourite, based on a translation of *Le Comte d'Essex. Histoire Angloise*, London, Theatre Royal in Drury Lane, May 1681;

Virtue Betrayed, based on a translation of *Nouvelles d'Elisabeth, reyne d'Angleterre*, London, Dorset Garden Theatre, March 1682;

Cyrus the Great, based on a translation of Madeleine de Scudéry's *Artamenès, ou Le Grand Cyrus*, London, Lincoln's Inn Fields, December 1695;

The Albion Queens, Banks's revision of his unperformed play *The Island Queens*, based on William Camden's *History of . . . Princess Elizabeth*, London, Theatre Royal in Drury Lane, 6 March 1704.

BOOKS: *The Rival Kings: or The Loves of Oroondates and Statira, a Tragaedy. Acted at the Theater-Royal* (London: Printed for L. Curtis, 1677);

The Destruction of Troy, a Tragedy, Acted at His Royal Highness the Duke's Theatre (London: Printed by A. G. & J. P., sold by C. Blount, 1679);

The Unhappy Favourite: or The Earl of Essex. A Tragedy. Acted at the Theatre Royal By their Majesty's Servants (London: Printed for R. Bentley & M. Magnes, 1682; facsimile edition, New York: Columbia University Press, 1939);

Vertue Betray'd: or, Anna Bullen. A Tragedy. Acted at his Royal Highness the Duke's Theatre (London: Printed for R. Bentley & M. Magnes, 1682; facsimile edition, Los Angeles: Clark Memorial Library, 1981);

The Island Queens: or, The Death of Mary, Queen of Scotland. A Tragedy. Publish'd only in Defence of the Author and the Play, against some mistaken Censures, occasion'd by its being prohibited the Stage (London: Printed for R. Bentley, 1684);

The Innocent Usurper; or, The Death of the Lady Jane Gray. A Tragedy (London: Printed for R. Bentley, 1694);

Cyrus the Great: or, The Tragedy of Love. As it is Acted at the Theatre in Little-Lincoln's-Inn-Fields, By His Majesty's Servants (London: Printed for R. Bentley, 1696);

The Albion Queens: or, The Death of Mary queen of Scotland. As it is acted at the Theatre-Royal, by Her Majesties servants (London: R. Wellington, 1714?).

Between 1677 and 1696 five tragedies by John Banks were staged and printed in London. Two further tragedies were prohibited performance but were printed, in 1684 and 1694 respectively. A revised version of one of the prohibited plays was staged in 1704 and printed some time later. Banks's œuvre comprises these eight tragedies and constitutes most of what is known about him.

Banks's earliest plays, *The Rival Kings, The Destruction of Troy*, and *Cyrus the Great*, are restless variations on the heroic mode, centered on the conflicts of love, friendship, and greatness experienced by heroes of antiquity. With his fourth play, however, *The Unhappy Favourite* (produced in May 1681), Banks originated and developed a type of pathetic tragedy on a subject from English history with a female protagonist–invariably a queen–that Allardyce Nicoll, adapting and backdating a term Nicholas Rowe coined in 1714, named the "she-tragedy" and that has some importance in the evolution of late-seventeenth-century drama.

Banks's professed ambition was to make himself the protégé of the female audience for serious drama. Six of his plays are formally dedicated to titled ladies. In the prologue he wrote for *The Unhappy Favourite*, he says: "To all the shining Sex this Play's addresst," and "If you are pleas'd, we will be bold to say, / This modest Poem is the Ladies Play." In the lexicon of Restoration drama, this feminine emphasis is glossed as an overriding interest in the griefs of love and a general movement of the play toward the tender or pathetic or sentimental end of the tragic spectrum. The plays that followed *The Unhappy Favourite* all share this coloring, but *The Unhappy Favourite* was not Banks's only plea for female interest. His prologue to *The Rival Kings* (1677) contains these lines:

> To th' Ladies now the Author by me speaks,
> A just admirer of your gallant Sex;
> He is your Poet, and a Lover too,
> For chiefly he designed this Play for you.

In his letter of dedication to *The Innocent Usurper*, dated 1693, he says that his heroine "will draw tears from the fair Sexes eyes." Indeed, not only the she-tragedies but Banks's earlier attempts at the heroic mode reveal his efforts to produce a "feminine" style of Restoration tragic drama.

Banks's plays received more than three hundred performances on the London stage between 1677 and 1779. More than half of these performances were of *The Unhappy Favourite;* performances of *The Albion Queens* (the revised and only performed version of *The Island Queens*) and the slightly less popular *Virtue Betrayed* together account for more than a hundred. These three tragedies were frequently chosen as vehicles for the ben-efit performances of leading actresses. Frequency of theatrical performance, however, was no defense against critical hostility. Alexander Pope names Banks in both editions of *The Dunciad* as a writer with appeal to coarse tastes, and in his notes to the poem he follows the established tradition of attacking Banks's style, "a sort of *Beggars Velvet*, or a happy mixture of the *thick Fustian* and *thin Prosaic*." Richard Steele had established this tradition in 1709 (*Tatler*, no. 14) when he described a performance of *The Unhappy Favourite* "in which there is not one good line, and yet a play which was never seen without drawing tears from some part [some female part, one presumes] of the audience." The habit of denigrating Banks's style for its "most dry discourses, and expressions almost ridiculous with respect to propriety" completely dominated whatever critical discussion was extended to him over the next two centuries, culminating in Edmund Gosse's *Dictionary of National Biography* entry of 1885: "Banks is a dreary and illiterate writer, whose blank verse is execrable. It appears, however, that his scenes possessed a melodramatic pathos which appealed to vulgar hearers, and one or two of his pieces survived most of the Restoration drama upon the stage." Banks had to wait for the twentieth-century work of James Sutherland, Eric Rothstein, and Robert D. Hume for more discriminating critical justice.

Of Banks's life we have only the barest outline. F. S. Tupper and T. M. H. Blair have found evidence that a John Banks, very likely the dramatist, received a marriage license on 21 February 1691, his age being stated as "abt. 38." He married Elizabeth Thompson at St. Paul's, Covent Garden, and in 1693 was residing in Charles Street (now Charles II Street), between Piccadilly and Pall Mall, the house having possibly been inherited by his wife. The *Survey of London* states that John Banks, dramatist, was a ratepayer in Charles Street from 1696 to 1700. The parish register of St. James, Westminster, shows that John Banks was buried there on 9 April 1706.

Gerard Langbaine, in *An Account of the English Dramatick Poets* (1691), gave Banks's profession as that of attorney-at-law, "a member of the Honourable Society of New-Inn." Later, Langbaine and Charles Gildon revised the entry on Banks to say that he "quitted the more profittable Practice of the Law, for some Years, in pursuit of the Bays, till experience convinced him of his Error." Banks may be referring to this withdrawal from the theater in his dedication to *The In-*

nocènt Usurper (dated "Charles St., Oct. 5th, 1693"), where he speaks of his "*quondam* brothers of the Chime (for now I own myself not one)." General experience with the lives of playwrights seems, however, to have created and sustained the idea that Banks's was a career of dire poverty. There is certainly no evidence that he profited much by his plays, and the possession of a freehold in Westminster need indicate no particular prosperity, since several of the houses in Charles Street "were probably mean in character." Moreover, on his death, commissions were issued to creditors.

Some lines, albeit conventional ones, in his prefatory poem to Charles Saunders's *Tamerlane the Great* (1681) seem to indicate that Banks in mid career had no expectations of gaining much by his works.

Not, *Spencer*, dead, nor *Spencer* now alive
Cou'd ever find a way by wit to thrive:
It is a Dream of Wealth, a Fairy Land,
A fickle Treasure grasp'd like Golden Sand,
Which, as 'tis held, does vanish through the
    Hand.

Yet these clues do not quite establish that Banks went "in tatters," as the satirical tradition claimed. Neglect of the law, pursuit of the bays, and subsequent squalor is a formulaic sequence of events, and even though there are no facts to controvert it, there are none to verify it either.

Banks's debut as a dramatist was made in the shadow of Nathaniel Lee. In March 1677 the King's Company at Drury Lane had produced one of the greatest successes of the Restoration theater, Lee's *The Rival Queens, or The Death of Alexander the Great*. In late June the company ventured on Banks's *The Rival Kings,* apparently hoping that a second play on the topic would repeat the success of the first. Both plays draw on Gauthier de Costes de la Calprenède's huge romance *Cassandre* (1642-1645) for characters and plots, and one of the romantic triangles–that of Lysimachus, Parisatis, and Ephestion–is common to both plays. *The Rival Kings* got a few performances and nevermore appeared on the stage. In his epilogue Banks is evidently embarrassed at his play's resemblance to "your loved Alexander" and can offer only "this excuse upon the author's score, / This though come last was writ a year before."

The implicit denial of indebtedness to Lee is sustained on examination of the plays. Despite the same source, many characters in common, and shared conventions of heroic drama, Banks's play differs from Lee's, principally in being closer to the expected type of the heroic play employing such material. Where Lee had chosen blank verse in the main, Banks's play is entirely rhymed, though he does employ variations such as quatrain verse extensively. Banks's Statira is impressively heroic, particularly in her debates with Alexander, but she does not approach Lee's Roxana in dramatic impact.

In one important respect, however, it is *The Rival Kings* that challenges orthodox expectation more vigorously. Heroic virtue, magnanimity, is conventionally embodied in Alexander. Banks writes of Alexander in his dedication as the greatest of men, but the play does not unambiguously endorse this verdict until Alexander's death scene in the fifth act, when he bestows his beloved Statira on his now undisguised rival king, Oroondates, after returning to her the kingdom of her father, Darius. One of Alexander's captains, Cassander, who feels his honor has been mortally slighted by the emperor, poisons Alexander. Cassander's speeches and those of other captains describe a mixture of greatness and growing tyranny in Alexander, including some murderous acts. The play, in fact, debates the concurrence of empire and tyranny, using the occasion of Cassander's disaffection. In the theater Cassander could be presented as an unambiguously evil conspirator, but the page, developing suggestions found in la Calprenède, permits Cassander his case and questions–until the denouement–the glory of Alexander.

Oroondates, in contrast, seems closer to the form of greatness possessed by Banks's later heroines, displaying magnanimity and amorous fidelity while hemmed in oppressively by circumstance. Though Alexander threatens his life and plans to marry Statira, Oroondates will not join Cassander's plot and earns his liberty by his fortitude in the face of Alexander's absolute power.

Banks's second play, *The Destruction of Troy,* is drawn from Raoul Lefèvre's *Recueil des histoires de Troyes,* the first book printed in English (1475), which in Caxton's translation, much modernized, was often reprinted in the Restoration as *The Destruction of Troy.* The play was staged at Dorset Garden in November 1678, with no success, and was printed in 1679. It has fourteen roles, the part of Achilles having been created by Thomas Betterton. It begins as a blank-verse play, with eruptions of rhyme at heightened moments, becoming predominantly rhymed in the later acts.

The Greeks are striving to end their siege of Troy. After Ulysses steals the Palladium (the statue of Pallas Athena believed to ensure the city's safety), Patroclus is killed in the course of a three-on-three combat, and the vengeful Achilles kills Troilus. Polyxena, mourning her brother Troilus, is left onstage with Achilles, lamenting over the body of Patroclus. Achilles, alone, indicates that he is falling in love with Polyxena but intends to take his revenge on Hector. The next day, when Achilles has departed for this duel, Ulysses announces the wooden-horse scheme. After Hector is slain by Achilles comes the scene that Eric Rothstein has indicated as definitive of Banks's "stupid" heroes. Achilles, over the body of Troilus, is "thunderbolted" by love for Polyxena. He lies down next to the body, offers his own body to be dragged like Hector's, and finally offers to end the siege if Hecuba, to whom he sends Troilus's body, will permit him to marry Polyxena. This conversion to love, with its extravagant body language, certainly engrosses the audience's attention, but it does not erase the magnanimous side of Achilles' character. He has despised the plot to steal the Palladium and knows nothing of the horse scheme. His separate peace with the Trojans is mendaciously accepted by his fellow Greeks, who will use the horse (containing a thousand men) to "surprise both Trojans and Achilles" during his wedding to Polyxena.

In act 5 Achilles becomes the target of both Greek and Trojan conspirators. Urged on by the vengeful Andromache, Paris wounds Achilles at the moment of his marriage to Polyxena. The Greeks emerge from the horse, and Troy is overwhelmed. Achilles asks Polyxena if she is not really glad that he is dying and gets from her a brief but forceful acknowledgment of her love for him. He calls for Troy's utter destruction, asking that Polyxena alone be spared. Held upright by Agamemnon and Ulysses, he kills Paris and dies "like the King of Slaughter" watching "the Pageantry of Death."

In his verse dedication published in *Cyrus the Great* (1696), Banks describes the play as "Writ and design'd . . . /Ere my then happier Favourite took place." Since *The Unhappy Favourite* was first staged early in 1681, Banks can be assumed to have composed *Cyrus* about 1679 or 1680. Something occurred, however, to prevent its performance for fifteen years. In the dedication Banks associates the play with "two labours" of his muse's brain which "Through Spite and Envy were the stage debarr'd." *The Island Queens* and *The Innocent Usurper* were undoubtedly banned for political reasons, but it seems fairly unlikely that *Cyrus the Great* was stopped by the Master of the Revels. No record of such intervention exists, nor is it possible to detect in the play the kind of statement or event that would obviously alarm the censor. Neither of these circumstances is conclusive, of course, but the possibility that it was the players who decided against performing *Cyrus the Great* is increased by the comments of Gildon in 1699. He says that the play "had been formerly refus'd the Action," a phrase that seems more likely to describe a theatrical than a political rejection, especially since he goes on to say, "yet it held up its Head about six days together" in 1695. (The *Oxford English Dictionary* includes an obsolete meaning of *action*, with an instance from 1679, defining it as "a theatrical performance, a play.") Later theatrical historians unhesitatingly took the phrase to mean that *Cyrus the Great* was initially damned by the players.

Critics of the earlier twentieth century attributed the failure of *Cyrus the Great* (a relative failure; it got a handful of performances) to its having been staged after the vogue for heroic plays had passed, but, as Robert D. Hume points out, in the 1690s "serious drama enjoys a considerable resurgence–in quantity if not in quality," and the new companies' suddenly increased appetite for fresh plays is presumably what led to revival of *Cyrus the Great*.

The chief source material for this play was Madeleine de Scudéry's *Artamenès, ou Le Grand Cyrus* (1649-1653), a long prose romance which appeared in an English translation in 1653. Banks augmented this source with material from Herodotus, and, if he did not overflow with Greek, he either used B. R.'s 1584 translation of books 1 and 2 or drew on some intermediary. The play is in blank verse with infrequent passages heightened by rhyme, and there are scenes with songs, scenes depicting supernatural events (a reanimated prophetic corpse, for example, in act 1), and a mad scene (with Lausaria, in act 4). Lausaria's ghost plays a considerable part in the action.

Cyrus the Great is subtitled *The Tragedy of Love* and is in fact a love-and-greatness play in which the greatness, though repeatedly invoked, is curiously secondary, and love is not asserted as a counter value; the only lover left alive is Cyrus, whose love has been reshaped into pitiful mourning for Lausaria, who has died of the shock of pub-

Illustration for act 5, from the 1735 edition of Cyrus the Great

licly avowing her love for him. Most of the vivid action involves problems of love, and Cyrus's oft-proclaimed status (he is said to have "The most Heroick Mind that ever was") is really a backdrop for the love dilemmas. Banks does show Cyrus in heroic action, but always in a reactive manner. He wins two great battles without spectacular leadership. He spares Craesus from execution and "defeats" his uncle, Cyaxeres, who envies his greatness, by showing how much Cyaxeres is indebted to him. He forgives a sexual rival, releases the lovers who are his prisoners, and spares Thomyris–yet all this is strangely distant and unemphatic. In love with Panthea, Cyrus becomes eloquent, but his chief action concerning love is to reject it for himself because of Lausaria's madness and death, and it is hard not to feel that Cyrus is the principal spectator of the agonies of Lausaria and Panthea, rather than a participant in the main activity of the play. His standing in the audience's eyes is perhaps summarized when he encounters Panthea, who has stabbed herself and is dying over the corpse of her dismembered husband, Abradatus. Cyrus begs Panthea to speak on his behalf to Abradatus in the next life.

And tell him how I took his hand in mine,
....
And put it to my eager lips, and ask'd
His pardon thus–Ha! Horror! Worse than Horror

> [Cyrus taking Abradatus's hand, offering to put it to his mouth, it comes from the Body. . . .]

Banks took this incident from Scudéry; it has a place in the general effort he was making in *Cyrus the Great* to include visual spectacle of the supernatural and horrific. But the effect is bathetic, the most striking instance of Cyrus as the suffering spectator whose passion is largely reaction. The imperial promises Cyrus makes to his troops in the play's last speech seem far less characteristic than the arrangements for Lausaria's funeral—the ultimate spectacle—with which the speech ends.

Despite the critics who have so often excoriated it, Banks's blank verse is a more successful idiom than his rhyming couplets. In *Cyrus the Great* the verse is unexciting but workmanlike, allowing for the fact that Banks always felt free to depart from the ten-syllable iambic pattern. He does not here, nor ever did, write incompetent blank verse. He rather wrote it with freedoms and variations that brought no particular increase in eloquence, and thus left him open to the accusation that he could not count. All the plays from *Cyrus the Great* to the end of his career are in blank verse with passages heightened by heroic couplets.

The Unhappy Favourite (produced in May 1681) is Banks's first play on a theme from Tudor history, and its success encouraged him to continue with such subjects for the rest of his career. Matters of history, however, could imply analogies to current politics, and two of Banks's last four plays were prohibited.

The principal source of *The Unhappy Favourite* was *The Secret History of the Most renowned Queen Elizabeth and the Earl of Essex* (1680), a translation of an anonymous French *nouvelle historique* published in Paris in 1678: *Le Comte d'Essex. Histoire Angloise.* (T. M. H. Blair and David Wykes have studied closely the relationship of the play to its sources.) Banks's reliance on this French novel helps define the particular contribution he made to English drama with his first two she-tragedies, for he was drawing on French fiction for the concept of "secret history," whereby public events—war and peace, rebellions, revolutions, the breaking and making of alliances, the rise and fall of favorites—are motivated "in reality" by the concealed amorous entanglements of the principal characters. It is the "Cleopatra's nose" and "cherchez la femme" version of history, and the most marked shift of direction that Banks imparted to English drama was to base the tragedy of political intrigue on a structure of hidden sexual motivation. In fact, he sentimentalized the history play.

Banks's four she-tragedies come much closer to making a homogeneous group than do his three heroic plays. After *The Unhappy Favourite*, Banks was working within a convention he himself had established. The she-tragedies have a purposefulness and confidence that the earlier plays lack. They are never subtle; characters, even the main ones, tend to be one-dimensional, and emotions are established at once on a uniformly high-pitched level. But the emotional effects are not bogus. Theirs is a lurid presentation of history, but the characters are not abstractions, and the torments to which Banks subjects them find a genuinely correspondent resonance in the audience.

One aspect of Banks's design in the she-tragedies went swiftly out of fashion, even though three of the plays stayed in the repertory well into the second half of the eighteenth century. Banks universally employs a rhetoric of nimiety. Characters, in the general fashion of Restoration tragedy, describe their emotions, and do so in Banks's plays at a length and with a rhetorical fervor and elaboration that seemed ridiculous in the eighteenth century. To this taste Banks's characters say too much too often (and on the eighteenth-century stage much was omitted), but clearly Banks regarded such elaboration as essential to his conception of tragedy, based partly upon the belief that his characters should possess feelings and expression ostentatiously above those of lesser mortals.

The Unhappy Favourite describes the sentimental circumstances of the earl of Essex's rebellion of 1601 and the consequent execution of the earl. Queen Elizabeth is deeply in love with Essex, but her regal dignity and female modesty prevent her declaring her love, except in soliloquies and frequent asides. The queen's minister, the hunchbacked Machiavel Burleigh, is in love with the countess of Nottingham, whose rejected sexual advances to Essex have transformed her into a vengeful virago, bent on Essex's destruction. His return against orders from Ireland, where he has failed to end Tyrone's rebellion, gives his enemies their opportunity. The audience learns in the second act that Essex has secretly married the countess of Rutland. Essex defends himself heroically (that is, with considerable huffing) against charges of treason and disrespect, and the queen initially supports him. When Essex's self-assertion becomes excessive, however, Elizabeth slaps him. His attempted

London rebellion, whose motives are carefully passed over, means that he must go to trial, but the queen secretly gives him a ring with which at need he can claim his life of her. The countess of Rutland then reveals her marriage to Essex. Condemned and imprisoned in the Tower of London, Essex is visited by the countess of Nottingham, emissary of the queen, to ask if he has any request to make of her majesty. Essex tells her of Elizabeth's gift of the ring and asks her to bear it back to the queen. Nottingham takes it but does not deliver it, substituting a lying account of Essex's haughty unrepentance. He is executed, but a letter conveyed by his wife reveals the plot of his enemies.

Banks's modifications of his source indicate the imperatives of the form of tragedy he was writing. Elizabeth's dilemma is the impasse presented by her love and her royal status. She loves and pities Essex equally, but she can never make an avowal of her feelings for him as she does in the novel. Essex's heroic status maintains its theatrical form. Since the queen does not declare her love for him openly, he is not tempted to see his secret marriage as having robbed him of a crown. His amorous feelings are focused without complication on Rutland. He makes a successful oratorical defense of his conduct in Ireland, clearing himself in the audience's view of any taint of disloyalty. The opportunities for complex motivation offered by *The Secret History* are discarded in favor of simpler, heroic delineation. Banks simplified character motivation and simultaneously overlaid it with an ornate fabric of heavily affective rhetoric, and henceforth this was to be his formula.

The second she-tragedy, *Virtue Betrayed*, repeated the formula almost exactly. Again, Banks went to an English translation of a French novel for source material: *The Novels of Elizabeth, Queen of England, containing the History of Queen Ann of Bullen* (1680), a translation of *Nouvelles d'Elisabeth, reyne d'Angleterre* (1674), an anonymous work often erroneously attributed to Marie Catherine, comtesse d'Aulnoy.

From the novel Banks takes the secret history of Anna Bullen's fall. The queen herself is utterly innocent, of saintly and Protestant innocence, in fact. She has been betrothed to Piercy, son of the earl of Northumberland, but the father has contrived to make Anna believe that Piercy has married someone else. She has reluctantly married the king. In doing so, Anna has unwittingly made an enemy of Lady Blunt, who, con-

spiring with the Machiavellian Cardinal Wolsey, seeks to destroy and replace the new queen. As the misunderstandings between Anna and Piercy are explained, the now jealous and furious king, in love already with Jane Seymour, traps them in conversation together, and letters Rochford has written to Blunt, addressing her as "sister," are produced as evidence of the incest of Anna and Rochford. Piercy has been pardoned at his father's request but has been wounded. Despite eloquent appeals, including one from the infant Princess Elizabeth (at the play's beginning Anna seems newly wed, so the appearance of this well-spoken child in act 5 is quite a surprise), all the innocent victims are put to death. Hearing of Anna's death, Piercy reopens his wound and dies in the arms of Diana, who hopelessly loves him. Then the plots that betrayed the victims are revealed and establish their innocence.

Heroism in *Virtue Betrayed* is the power of the innocent to suffer in eloquence. The self-assertion and defiance of Essex in *The Unhappy Favourite*, which maintain a connection with the heroic play, are now gone. *Virtue Betrayed* completed the movement toward the sentimental that had been increasing throughout Banks's career, and it displays all the limited resources of his primary-colored rhetoric in the speeches of characters caught helplessly but most self-consciously in the toils of inevitable, undeserved destruction. The mournful duet of Piercy and Diana at the end of act 3 is unlike anything Banks had done before, but the course of his career clearly predicts his arrival at that point. With the success of *Virtue Betrayed*, Banks seemed poised to profit from the happy continuation of the type of drama he had established. Censorship, however, would thwart him.

The Innocent Usurper was never acted. In a letter of dedication, dated 5 October 1693, Banks says that it was written "Ten years since." As *The Island Queens* was printed in 1684, it seems likely that *The Innocent Usurper* was composed first, in about 1682 or 1683. *The Gentleman's Journal* of April 1692 wrote: "Mr. Banks hath writ a Tragedy call'd the *Innocent Usurper*. . . . However, there being some reasons which hinder it from appearing on the Stage, he designs to submit it to the Judgement of every Impartial Reader, and it will very speedily appear in print." The newspaper speaks as if the play were recently composed and recently prohibited. The play may have been submitted to the theater in the early 1680s; some form of political objection was likely raised, and

Princess Elizabeth begging Henry VIII to spare her mother's life, an illustration from the 1734 edition of Virtue Betrayed

it was declared to be unstageable. In the 1690s the play was again proposed for performance, and this time was both cast and rehearsed before being again prohibited because of perceived "parallels" to contemporary political situations, whereupon Banks decided to sell it to Bentley. The cast list published with the 1694 edition is of the United Company and could be for 1683 or 1693, but the latter date is slightly more probable.

This conjecture gets some support from Banks's dedication. He says that it was initially forbidden "by a Capricio and hard-heartedness of some of the Civil Powers of the Stage," but thereafter he speaks as if to defend the play against par-

allels detected in it with the current reign, that of William III and Mary II: "In it I have follow'd nicely the Truth, and it cannot be judg'd in that Age, when it was written [the early 1680s], that I have interwoven any thing with an intent to pattern with these Times [the early 1690s], unless I had been a Conjurer." As to parallels recently detected: "It is suppos'd the Lady Jane wore Petticotes, and can any one be so foolish as to think her Majesty will for that Reason put them off?" These remarks could indicate that someone had whispered in the ear of authority that a parallel existed between Jane Grey, the Protestant claimant pushed forward to keep the throne from a Catholic successor, Mary I, and Mary II, Protestant daughter of James II, advanced in the line of succession to prevent the throne going to her Catholic half brother, "James III." Whatever the cause–and perhaps, as Banks says, it was no more than that the play was said to have "a scurvy Title"–*The Innocent Usurper* was never staged, and in the next generation the sentimental possibilities of the Lady Jane Grey story were exploited instead by Nicholas Rowe.

The source material for *The Innocent Usurper* is the life of "Queen Jane" included in Peter Heylyn's *Ecclesia Restaurata, or The history of the reformation of the Church of England* (editions of 1660, 1670, 1674). Heylyn was not writing "secret history" on the French model, and Banks's play does not pretend to reveal secret amorous motives. But Heylyn was a historian who described characters in ways that Banks found congenial, offering the kind of assistance Banks had found earlier in the French nouvelles.

Lady Jane Grey is an innocent but, even more emphatically, a reluctant usurper. Her taking the crown is the plot of her wicked father-in-law, Northumberland, and her termagant mother, the duchess of Suffolk, both moved by desire of personal aggrandizement. Northumberland's son, Gilford Dudley, has recently married Jane, and his ecstatic love for her is matched by his grovelingly subservient filial gratitude. The thought of Jane's elevation delights Gilford, and in the big second act scene where her conspiratorial relations and their associates kneel and beg Jane to mount the throne, it is Gilford's pressure, his threat of suicide, that determines her to take the fatal step. During the rest of the play Jane–as much in love with Gilford as he with her–shapes his attitudes. She leads him to see the wickedness of what they have done, and later, when she is deposed, he shares her joy at being disburdened of guilt and also her eager desire to plead guilty at their trial. When Northumberland, who has tried to save himself by converting to Catholicism, endeavors to convert Jane and Gilford, it is again Jane who stiffens Gilford to resist (his filial obedience tempts him to transgress to save his father) and to accept death.

Jane's character is cut from the same cloth as that of Anna Bullen. Circumstances, set in place by the machinations of the wicked, trap her in a situation where she can only suffer as she maintains her integrity. Conspiracy crashes around her (Northumberland is executed, and the duchess goes mad), but nothing can save her.

Her heroism is asserted in behaving aright, and the actions of her character consist principally in resisting the temptation to compromise and in bringing Gilford to an identity of sentiment with her. Gilford's character, pulled about by his love for Jane and his duty to Northumberland, has more superficial dynamism, but in fact his internal conflict–gushingly verbalized–is vacillation, and he comes close to justifying the accusation that Banks creates stupid heroes and "womanish" ones. Gilford's character is sacrificed so that Jane may be seen to have something to do other than be the victim of her circumstances.

That *The Innocent Usurper* was prohibited should not nullify an appreciation of the considerable tact Banks displays in handling the Catholic element. Until late in the play, the Catholicism of Mary, who does not appear, is carefully deemphasized, and it is not until the attempts to undermine Jane's Protestantism in the last act that the issue becomes prominent. Even then, the Catholic party is represented by Northumberland and the devious Bishop Gardner, and the prospect of the kingdom coming under the reign of Bloody Mary is quite subordinated to the firm declarations of Jane's conscience. But tact did no good, and Banks's play is still awaiting its premiere.

It is likely that Banks's last written play was *The Island Queens*, printed in 1684. Knowledge that this play was banned comes solely from Banks himself, on the title page and in the dedication, where he speaks of it as "forbidden the Stage." Arthur F. White could find no particular reasons for the suppression, and it must be assumed that the subject of a Protestant monarch with a possible Catholic successor was sufficiently alarming in the early 1680s to arouse the censors, although Mary of Scotland's Catholicism is alluded to with the lightest of emphasis.

In writing *The Unhappy Favourite*, Banks had, as Blair has shown, supplemented his main source, *The Secret History*, with information drawn from William Camden's history of Queen Elizabeth. For his play about Mary, Queen of Scots, Banks seems to have gone back to Camden for characters and situations, and to have contrived his own plot with no specific fictional model to copy. The absence of a fictional model of secret history–the absence in fact of a jealous female antagonist, a Nottingham or a Blunt–meant in the outcome that *The Island Queens* (like *The Innocent Usurper*) is not secret history as *The Unhappy Favourite* and *Virtue Betrayed* are. Love and sentiment abound in the play, but the prime movers of

Mary's downfall are policy and personal ambition, motives identified in standard, rather than secret, history.

Mary, quite like Anna Bullen and Jane Grey, has a saintly innocence that Banks never hints at compromising. Amid conspiracies and concealed animosities, she continues pure and suffering, adored by the duke of Norfolk, who pays with his life for his love, and by the page Dowglas, a choral voice proclaiming Mary's limitless virtues. Elizabeth's secretaries, Cecil and Davison, conspire with Morton, villainous regent of Scotland, to bring about Mary's fall, implicating her in Babington's plot.

Elizabeth in *The Island Queens* is Banks's most accomplished major character, and the preference of actresses for her role rather than that of Mary is easily understood. Mary has the one-note eloquence of the she-tragedy, but Elizabeth's emotions vary widely with the turns of the plot. She is sometimes imperious, almost tyrannical, as when receiving the advice of her parliament. Her personal affection for Mary leads to sisterly reconciliations. She experiences horror at evidence of Mary's implication in plots, envy at hearing of Mary's popularity with Londoners, and nearly disabling pity when she is half tricked into signing the death warrant. Mary is undoubtedly the focal character–she has the affecting interviews from which Banks draws his most characteristic sentiment (as when Mary, en route to prison, meets Norfolk, en route to the scaffold)–but Elizabeth competes successfully with her by virtue of her moral and emotional complexity.

Banks's career as an author had been dormant for about ten years, since the publication of *The Island Queens* in 1684, but the printing of *The Innocent Usurper* in 1694 signaled his return to public life. In the following year *Cyrus the Great* finally appeared onstage, and it was published in 1696. Banks seems to have composed nothing new after 1684, but these previously written plays demonstrate his continued interest in the stage. After another interval, this time of eight years, a revised version of *The Island Queens*, retitled *The Albion Queens*, was staged at Drury Lane on 6 March 1704 and printed about ten years later. It became a stock play and was frequently reprinted, always in the revised form.

According to the bibliographical probabilities, *The Albion Queens* should be accepted as Banks's own revision of *The Island Queens*. It was staged during his lifetime and was always attributed unambiguously to him alone. The eight-year silence had precedent in the ten-year interval between 1684 and 1694. Colley Cibber, in his *Apology* (1740), gives a circumstantial account of how Banks managed to get a noble supporter to intervene with Queen Anne to permit the production on 6 March 1704. These factors combine to compel an editor to include *The Albion Queens* as one of Banks's works, although it is reasonable to be both surprised and impressed by the extent to which Banks, a couple of years before his death and after a long hiatus in his career, was able to reshape his style to conform to post-Restoration standards.

The revisions of *The Albion Queens* are almost entirely stylistic. Events and motivation are largely unaltered. The only change in event is that the page Dowglas, who throws himself to the floor in an agony of grief at Mary's condemnation in *The Island Queens*, is made to poison himself in *The Albion Queens*. Overwhelmingly the rewriting is designed to prune and regulate the excesses of Banks's rhetoric, though the substitution is usually banality for brutal vigor. There is an overall proliferation of gentility. For example, biblical references are cut or muted. "The sacred host of heaven" becomes "The pow'rs above." "Moses" becomes "Aeolus." Norfolk's soliloquy at the beginning of act 2 offers a telling instance:

> Rejoyce all living Creatures that have Breath,
> Through this vast City let your Noises joyn,
> And Eccho all ye Lands and Seas, she comes.
> The distant Shouts and wafted sounds of Bells
> Proclaim to *Londons* Walls Queen *Mary's* come.
> Winds bear it into *France* to glad her Friends,
> Winds waft it into *Scotland* to her Foes,
> Till with the News they blast, with envy die.

In *The Albion Queens* this passage becomes:

> Shout the Loud world, sound all the vast Creation,
> Let proud *Augusta*, clad in Robes of Triumph,
> Through her glad Streets, with Golden Trumpets sound
> And Ecchoe to the Ocean that She comes;
> *Maria* comes proclaim it to the clouds,
> Let the four winds from distant corners meet,
> And on their wings first bear it into *France*,
> Then back agen to *Edina's* proud walls,
> 'Til victim to the sound th' aspiring city falls.

The crude strength of Banks's earlier style is here replaced by the routine of stock poetical diction. It seems that Banks in this revision made his style safer by accepting a standard that drained from his play much of the strength and originality it possessed. If *The Albion Queens* is Banks's last writing, it is a sorry epitaph for a playwright who made a small but distinctive contribution to Restoration drama.

References:

Thomas Marshall Howe Blair, Introduction and notes to *The Unhappy Favourite* [facsimile text] (New York: Columbia University Press, 1939);

James J. Devlin, "The Dramatis Personae and the Dating of John Banks's *The Albion Queens*," *Notes and Queries*, 208 (1963): 213-215;

Diane Dreher, Introduction to *Vertue Betray'd* [facsimile text] (Los Angeles: Clark Memorial Library, 1981);

Robert D. Hume, *The Development of English Drama in the Late Seventeenth Century* (Oxford: Clarendon Press, 1976);

Eric Rothstein, *Restoration Tragedy: Form and the Process of Change* (Madison, Milwaukee & London: University of Wisconsin Press, 1967);

James Sutherland, *English Literature of the Late Seventeenth Century* (Oxford: Clarendon Press, 1969);

Fred Salisbury Tupper, "John Banks: A Study in the Origins of the Pathetic Tragedy," Ph.D. dissertation, Harvard University, 1935;

Arthur F. White, "The Office of Revels and Dramatic Censorship during the Restoration Period," *Western Reserve University Bulletin*, new series 34 (September 1931): 5-45;

David Wykes, "The *barbinade* and the She-Tragedy: On John Banks's *The Unhappy Favourite*," in *Augustan Studies: Essays in Honor of Irvin Ehrenpreis*, edited by Douglas Lane Patey and Timothy Keegan (London & Toronto: Associated University Presses, 1985), pp. 79-94.

Aphra Behn

(1640?-16 April 1689)

Katharine M. Rogers
American University

See also the Behn entry in *DLB 39: British Novelists, 1660-1800.*

PLAY PRODUCTIONS: *The Forced Marriage; or, The Jealous Bridegroom*, London, Lincoln's Inn Fields, 20 September 1670;

The Amorous Prince, London, Lincoln's Inn Fields, 24 February 1671;

The Dutch Lover, London, Dorset Garden Theatre, 6 February 1673;

Abdelazer; or, The Moor's Revenge, London, Dorset Garden Theatre, 3 July 1676;

The Town Fop; or, Sir Timothy Tawdry, based on George Wilkins's *The Miseries of Enforced Marriage*, London, Dorset Garden Theatre, circa September 1676;

The Debauchee, probably by Behn, adapted from Richard Brome's *A Mad Couple Well Matched*, London, Dorset Garden Theatre, February 1677;

The Rover; or, The Banish't Cavaliers, adapted from Thomas Killigrew's *Thomaso; or, The Wanderer*, London, Dorset Garden Theatre, 24 March 1677;

The Counterfeit Bridegroom; or, The Defeated Widow, probably by Behn, adapted from Thomas Middleton's *No Wit, No Help Like a Woman's*, London, Dorset Garden Theatre, circa September 1677;

Sir Patient Fancy, London, Dorset Garden Theatre, 17 January 1678;

The Feigned Courtesans; or, A Night's Intrigue, London, Dorset Garden Theatre, circa March 1679;

The Young King; or, The Mistake, derived from Gauthier de Costes de la Calprenède's *Cléopâtre*, London, Dorset Garden Theatre, circa September 1679;

The Revenge; or, A Match in Newgate, probably by Behn, adapted from John Marston's *The Dutch Courtesan*, London, Dorset Garden Theatre, circa June 1680;

Aphra Behn, engraving by Fittler

The Second Part of The Rover, London, Dorset Garden Theatre, circa January 1681;

The False Count; or, A New Way to Play an Old Game, London, Dorset Garden Theatre, November 1681;

The Roundheads; or, The Good Old Cause, London, Dorset Garden Theatre, circa December 1681;

Like Father, Like Son, London, Dorset Garden Theatre, circa March 1682;

The City Heiress; or, Sir Timothy Treat-all, London, Dorset Garden Theatre, late April 1682;

The Lucky Chance; or, An Alderman's Bargain, London, Theatre Royal in Drury Lane, April 1686;

The Emperor of the Moon, London, Dorset Garden Theatre, March 1687;

The Widow Ranter; or, The History of Bacon in Virginia, London, Theatre Royal in Drury Lane, 20 November 1689;

The Younger Brother; or, The Amorous Jilt, London, Theatre Royal in Drury Lane, February 1696.

BOOKS: *The Forc'd Marriage, Or The Jealous Bridegroom, A Tragi-Comedy, As it is Acted at His Highnesse The Duke of York's Theatre* (London: Printed by H. L. & R. B. for James Magnus, 1671);

The Amorous Prince, or, The Curious Husband. A Comedy, As it is Acted at his Royal Highness, the Duke of York's Theatre (London: Printed by J. M. for Thomas Dring, 1671);

The Dutch Lover: A Comedy, Acted At The Dukes Theatre (London: Printed for Thomas Dring, 1673);

Abdelazer, or The Moor's Revenge. A Tragedy. As it is Acted at his Royal Highness the Duke's Theatre (London: Printed for J. Magnes and R. Bentley, 1677);

The Town-Fopp: Or Sir Timothy Tawdrey. A Comedy. As it is Acted at his Royal Highness the Duke's Theatre (London: Printed by T. N. for James Magnes and Rich Bentley, 1677);

The Rover. Or, The Banish't Cavaliers. As it is Acted At His Royal Highness the Duke's Theatre (London: Printed for John Amery, 1677); modern edition, edited by Frederick M. Link (Lincoln: University of Nebraska Press, 1967; London: Arnold, 1967);

The Debauchee: Or, The Credulous Cuckold, A Comedy. Acted at His Highness The Duke of York's Theatre (London: Printed for John Amery, 1677);

The Counterfeit Bridegroom: Or The Defeated Widow. A Comedy, As it is Acted at His Royal Highness The Duke's Theatre (London: Printed for Langley Curtiss, 1677);

Sir Patient Fancy: A Comedy. As it is Acted at the Duke's Theatre (London: Printed by D. Flesher for Richard Tonson & Jacob Tonson, 1678);

The Feign'd Curtizans, Or, A Nights Intrigue. A Comedy. As it is Acted at the Dukes Theatre (London: Printed for Jacob Tonson, 1679);

The Revenge: Or, A Match In Newgate. A Comedy. As it was Acted at the Dukes Theatre (London: Printed for W. Cademan, 1680);

The Second Part Of The Rover. As it is Acted by the Servants of His Royal Highness (London: Printed for Jacob Tonson, 1681);

A Farce Call'd The False Count, Or, A New Way to play An Old Game. As it is Acted at the Duke's Theatre (London: Printed by M. Flesher for Jacob Tonson, 1682);

The Roundheads Or, The Good Old Cause, A Comedy As it is Acted at His Royal Highness the Dukes Theatre (London: Printed for D. Brown, T. Benskin & H. Rhodes, 1682);

The City-Heiress: Or, Sir Timothy Treat-all. A Comedy. As it is Acted at his Royal Highness his Theatre (London: Printed for D. Brown, T. Benskin & H. Rhodes, 1682);

Prologue to Romulus [single sheet with epilogue on verso] (London: Printed by Nath. Thompson, 1682); republished in *Romulus and Hersilia; or, The Sabine War. A Tragedy Acted at the Dukes Theatre,* anonymous (London: Printed for D. Brown & T. Benskin, 1683);

The Young King: Or, The Mistake. As 'tis acted at his Royal Highness The Dukes Theatre (London: Printed for D. Brown, T. Benskin & H. Rhodes, 1683);

Poems upon Several Occasions: with A Voyage to the Island of Love (London: Printed for R. Tonson & J. Tonson, 1684);

Prologue [to John Fletcher's *Valentinian,* altered by John Wilmot, earl of Rochester] [single sheet] (London: Printed for Charles Tebroc, 1684);

Love-Letters Between a Noble-Man And his Sister, three volumes in two (London: Printed & sold by Randal Taylor, 1684, 1687);

La Montre; or, The Lover's Watch, Behn's translation of a work by Balthazar de Bonnecorse (London: Printed by R. H. for W. Canning, 1686);

The Luckey Chance, or An Alderman's Bargain. A Comedy. As it is Acted by their Majesty's Servants (London: Printed by R. H. for W. Channing, 1687);

The Emperor of the Moon: A Farce. As it is Acted by Their Majesties Servants, At the Queens Theatre (London: Printed by R. Holt for Joseph Knight & Francis Saunders, 1687);

The Fair Jilt: Or, The History of Prince Tarquin and Miranda (London: Printed by R. Holt for Will. Canning, 1688);

Oroonoko: Or, The Royal Slave. A True History (London: Printed for Will. Canning, 1688);

The History of Oracles and the Cheats of the Pagan Priests, Behn's translation of Bernard Le Bovier Fontenelle's French adaptation of A. van Dale's *De oraculis ethnicorum* (London, 1688);

A Discovery of New Worlds. From the French. Made English by Mrs. A. Behn. To which is prefixed a preface, by way of essay on translated prose; wherein the arguments of Father Tacquet, and others, against the System of Copernicus ... are likewise considered, and answered, Behn's translation of, and preface to, a work by Fontenelle (London: Printed for William Canning, 1688);

Agnes de Castro or, The Force of Generous Love. Written in French by a Lady of Quality. Made English by Mrs. Behn, Behn's translation of a novel by J. B. de Brilhac (London: Printed for William Canning, 1688);

Lycidus: Or The Lover in Fashion. Being an Account from Lycidus to Lysander, of his Voyage from the Island of Love. From the French. By the Same Author Of the Voyage to the Isle of Love. Together with a Miscellany Of New Poems. By Several Hands, Behn's translation of a work by Paul Tallemant, with poems by Behn and others (London: Printed for Joseph Knight & F. Saunders, 1688)–contains the following poems by Behn: "Song. On Occasion"; "On the Honourable Sir Francis Fane, on his Play call'd the Sacrifice"; "To Damon. To inquire of him if he cou'd tell me by the Style, who writ me a Copy of Verses that came to me in an unknown Hand"; "To Alexis in Answer to his Poem against Fruition. Ode"; "To Alexis, On his saying, I lov'd a Man that talk'd much"; "A Pastoral Pindarick. On the Marriage of the Right Honourable the Earle of Dorset and Midlesex, to the Lady Mary Compton"; "On Desire A Pindarick."; "To Amintas, Upon reading the Lives of some of the Romans"; "On the first discovery of falseness in *Amintas*"; "To the fair Clarinda, who made Love to me, imagin'd more than woman";

The History of the Nun: Or, The Fair Vow-Breaker (London: Printed for A. Baskerville, 1689);

The Lucky Mistake: A New Novel (London: Printed by R. Bentley, 1689);

The Widdow Ranter or, The History of Bacon in Virginia. A Tragi-Comedy, Acted by their Majesties Servants (London: Printed for James Knapton, 1690);

The Younger Brother: Or, The Amorous Jilt. A Comedy, Acted at the Theatre Royal, By His Majesty's Servants (London: Printed for J. Harris & sold by R. Baldwin, 1696);

The Histories And Novels of the Late Ingenious Mrs. Behn: In One Volume. . . . Together with The Life and Memoirs of Mrs. Behn (London: Printed for S. Briscoe, 1696);

The Lady's Looking-Glass, to dress herself by; or, The Whole Art of Charming (London: W. Onley for S. Briscoe, 1697);

Histories, Novels, and Translations, written by the most ingenious Mrs. Behn; the second volume (London: Printed by W. O. for S. B. & sold by M. Brown, 1700).

Collection: *The Works of Aphra Behn*, 6 volumes, edited by Montague Summers (London: Heinemann / Stratford-upon-Avon: Bullen, 1915).

Aphra Behn was one of the best and most successful comic writers in a great age of English comedy. If her plays are less polished than those of George Etherege and William Wycherley, it must be remembered that, unlike them, she had to support herself: she produced eighteen to twenty-one plays, in contrast to Etherege's three and Wycherley's four. Most of them were successful, and two, *The Rover* and *The Emperor of the Moon*, held the stage for three quarters of a century. She competed on such equal terms with men that, speaking from the purely literary point of view, one could say her sex was irrelevant to a consideration of her achievement. It is, however, significant that she was the first English woman to make her living as a writer. A highly competent professional, she held her own in the tough world of the Restoration theater. She did not modestly conceal her authorship, and, when attacked as a writer or as a woman, she defended herself with vigorous counterattacks.

Little is known of Behn's early life, not even her maiden name (which may have been Amis, Johnson, or Cooper). She probably did spend a few months in Surinam in her twenties, as she claimed in her novella *Oroonoko* (1688), presumably because her father had some kind of appointment there. On her return to England she probably married a man named Behn, for even hostile contemporaries did not question her marriage; but he seems to have died soon afterward (perhaps 1665), since he is not mentioned in any records of her life. The suppositions that he was Dutch and a merchant seem to be based simply

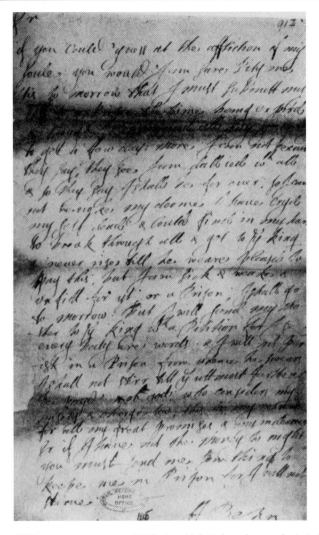

Letter to Thomas Killigrew, circa autumn 1668, in which Behn—about to be imprisoned for debt—
asks for help in obtaining payment for her services as a spy in Antwerp during the
Second Dutch War (by permission of the Public Record Office)

on inferences from satiric butts in her plays. The first definite records, state correspondence of 1666, show Behn acting as a spy in Antwerp during the Second Dutch War. Like many Crown employees, she could not get paid; she returned to London penniless and was actually imprisoned for debt. She wrote pathetic letters to government officials, including Thomas Killigrew, who was also manager of the Theatre Royal on Bridges Street, one of the two licensed theaters.

Perhaps this connection influenced her to turn to play writing to support herself. There was a voracious demand for new plays, and contemporaries may have greeted a female playwright as an agreeable novelty (as they did another novelty, actresses). Somehow she learned the necessary stagecraft, and, by the 1670s, she was part of the Restoration world of playwrights,

actors, and court wits. Her friends included the earl of Rochester, the leading actress Elizabeth Barry, and the writers John Dryden, Thomas Otway, and Edward Ravenscroft. Behn seems to have been an attractive woman, a witty conversationalist, and a warm friend. According to the author of the memoir that prefaces the 1696 collection of her *Histories and Novels* (probably Charles Gildon), "She was of a generous and open temper, something passionate, very serviceable to her friends in all that was in her power, and could sooner forgive an injury than do one. She had wit, honor, good humor, and judgment. She was mistress of all the pleasing arts of conversation, but used 'em not to any but those who loved . . . plain dealing. She was a woman of sense, and by consequence a lover of pleasure, as indeed all . . . are; but only some would be thought to be above the conditions of humanity, and place their chief pleasure in a proud, vain hypocrisy." Behn attracted her full share of her period's characteristically ferocious lampoons, which were infused with particular venom because of her sex. She was attacked, in Matthew Prior's *A Satyr on the Modern Translators* (1685) and elsewhere, for "the ruine of her Face" (at forty-five), for sexual promiscuity, and for getting her lovers to write her plays. Actually, her only proven love affair was a long, unhappy one with a cold, bisexual lawyer named John Hoyle.

The prologue to her first play, *The Forced Marriage; or, The Jealous Bridegroom* (1670), makes the most of its author's sex, coupling an ambivalent defense of women's wit with a coy appeal to men's gallantry. Erminia, the heroine, is bestowed by the King and her father upon Alcippus as a reward for his success in battle, but she and Philander love each other, while Alcippus is loved by Galatea. Erminia marries Alcippus in obedience to her father, but persuades him not to consummate the marriage, although she promises to be faithful to him. Nevertheless, he suspects her with Philander and strangles her. The situation is saved when it turns out that she is not dead and her marriage is declared invalid, so the true lovers can pair off. Although the play does show the painful consequences of enforced marriage, Behn's treatment is not original or profound enough to be significant; *The Forced Marriage* is a standard tragicomedy with the plot complications and emotional appeals traditional in its genre.

Behn's second play, *The Amorous Prince* (1671), is also a tragicomedy in verse. Frederick, son of the Duke of Florence, has seduced Cloris under promise of marriage and goes on to attempt to seduce Laura, the love of Curtius, his best friend. Ultimately, on finding out that Cloris is Curtius's sister, Frederick repents and proposes to her, leaving Laura to Curtius, who is very grateful. Loyalty to royal persons is laid on thickly in both *The Forced Marriage* and *The Amorous Prince*. There is a little more humor in the second play, centering on Lorenzo, Frederick's worthless friend, who voices in passing a criticism of the double standard (V.i). Both these tragicomedies were moderately successful.

Behn made better use of her talents in *The Dutch Lover* (1673), an intrigue comedy written mostly in prose. Euphemia, engaged by her father to the loutish Haunce van Ezel, in desperation offers herself to Alonzo. Although he would

rather have an affair with her, he consents to marriage because she is so beautiful. He disguises himself as Haunce, so they can marry under her father's nose. Although Behn did question the double standard in occasional speeches of various plays, in general she presented it without criticism. She idealized rakes like Alonzo, who want to possess every pretty woman they see and to exploit women as much as they can, and she apparently noticed no incongruity when these very men expect sisters to be models of chastity and mistresses, of constancy: Marcel does his best to seduce fifteen-year-old Clarinda; yet he feels honor requires him to kill his sister for letting herself be seduced. *The Dutch Lover* failed on its first performance, because, Behn charged, of poor acting and costuming and—more significant—of prejudice against a woman's work. The female playwright had become a threatening competitor instead of an entertaining novelty.

Provoked by this undeserved failure, Behn added a vigorously feminist "Epistle to the Reader" to the published play (1673). After roundly abusing a fop who parroted at the play's opening that it could not be any good because it was a woman's, Behn went on to argue, not only that women could equal men in learning if they had equal opportunities for education, but that learning is not necessary for composing entertaining comedies. This was a radical challenge to the general assumption of her time that good writing must be based on a sound knowledge of critical principles, which could be derived only from a classical education, unavailable, of course, to women. Even more radical was her attack on the belief, piously maintained by every other playwright of the time, that the purpose of drama is moral teaching; she disproved it simply by looking at the plays. Although she mocked the excessive claims made for entertaining literature, she was not awed by more solemn types of composition: a good play is worth more than volumes of pedantic scholarship, and plays have done less harm than sermons. Writing with the insight of an outsider, she deflated pretensions on all sides.

Behn's next play, *Abdelazer; or, The Moor's Revenge* (1676), is a bloody tragedy of revenge and lawless love, suited to contemporary taste and, accordingly, popular. Abdelazer, the villainous Moor, conspires with the Queen of Spain, his paramour, to kill her husband and to declare her virtuous son illegitimate; then he has her killed. The murders add up until seven people are dead out of a cast of fifteen. Incongruously, the play

Aphra Behn, portrait attributed to Sir Peter Lely (Montague Summers, ed., The Works of Aphra Behn, *volume 1, 1915)*

opens with Behn's best lyric, "Love in fantastick Triumph sat."

With *The Town Fop; or, Sir Timothy Tawdry* (1676), her first play set in London, she found her style. The fop Sir Timothy, who prides himself on his sophistication, prefers whoring to marriage and ineptly schemes to exploit women. He intends to neglect his wife while spending her fortune, but he is in abject subjection to his domineering mistress Betty Flauntit. The serious part of the play, founded on George Wilkins's *The Miseries of Enforced Marriage* (1605-1606), centers on Bellmour, who is forced by his uncle to marry Diana, although he loves and is engaged to Celinda. Immediately after his marriage he is consumed with remorse, refuses to consummate his union with Diana, and flings himself into debauchery. In the end this marriage is unrealistically annulled, so that he can marry Celinda.

The Rover; or, The Banish't Cavaliers (1677) was Behn's most successful play; after several seventeenth-century revivals, it was acted in every season but one between 1703 and 1743. Revived in 1757, it was again successful. A 1790 bowdlerized version, *Love in Many Masks*, did not last; but a slightly adapted one, produced in Stratford in 1986, proved that *The Rover* can still be highly effective in the theater. Willmore is a rover both because he is sexually inconstant and because he is a follower of Charles II, banished from his country by the Commonwealth government. He is in Naples at Carnival time with his friends Frederick, Belvile (who is in love with Florinda), and Blunt (a rich but boorish squire). Florinda has been promised by her father to a rich old man and by her brother to his friend Antonio; both she and her sister, Hellena, who is destined to become a nun, resolve to make their own life choices.

Willmore is charming and irresponsible, irresistibly attractive to women and eager to bed them all. "What the Devil should I do with a virtuous Woman?" he asks. "Virtue is but an Infirmity in Women," an annoyance in attractive ones and a self-delusion in those too ugly to be solicited (IV. ii). He is effectively played off against Belvile, who is seriously intent on marrying Florinda; because Willmore cannot take anything seriously, he repeatedly blunders into and ruins their carefully planned schemes to elope. He is involved chiefly with two women, Angelica Bianca and Hellena. Angelica Bianca, a beautiful and expensive courtesan who prides herself on her professional coldness of heart, falls helplessly in love with him. He reproaches her for selling love; she counters by telling him that men who marry for money are equally prostituting themselves. He concedes she is right, but this point, like several interesting issues raised in the play, is not further developed. And in the end Willmore will marry a rich woman and enjoy her money. Angelica gives herself to Willmore for nothing and is enraged to find that this sacrifice does not ensure his constancy; she threatens to shoot him but cannot force herself to do so and ultimately goes off with a paying lover. Angelica is a remarkably perceptive and sympathetic portrayal of a character generally stereotyped in Restoration literature. Apparently hardened by her professional success, she becomes vulnerable by falling in love and is forced for the first time to understand the emotional destitution of a prostitute's life. In her soliloquy at the end of IV.ii she recognizes that a woman who has lost her chastity cannot expect to be beloved or respected, no matter what other qualities she has: "Nice Reputation, tho it leave behind / More Virtues than inhabit where that dwells, / Yet that once gone, those virtues shine no more." Behn demonstrated her seriousness by making Angelica speak in verse.

Hellena is lively and delightful, if not quite so witty as Etherege's young women. She pursues and wins Willmore in spite of his inconstancy and her brother's restrictiveness. In one of Behn's few attempts at the witty sparring between lovers that was a distinctive feature of the comedy of wit, she has Hellena and Willmore debate the issue of marriage versus free love, responsible love versus irresponsible self-indulgence. In their final negotiation in act 5, Hellena holds out for marriage, despite Willmore's argument that love requires no vows and that marriage is its certain bane. She points out what the result would be for her: "A Cradle full of Noise and Mischief, with a Pack of Repentance at my Back." When he offers to "teach thee to weave a true Love's Knot," she answers, "So can my Dog." Nevertheless, they do agree; and we are left to assume that Hellena will be happy with her man and Willmore with his woman and her three hundred thousand crowns. She will, at least, be allowed more freedom than in Italy. When her brother consoles himself for her marriage with the thought that he will no longer be "a Slave" to preserving her honor intact, Willmore answers, "I am of a Nation, that are of opinion a Woman's Honour is not worth guarding when she has a mind to part with it."

Behn is probably the author of *The Debauchee* (1677), a close adaptation of Richard Brome's *A Mad Couple Well Matched* (1639), and *The Counterfeit Bridegroom; or, The Defeated Widow* (1677), a highly improved version of Thomas Middleton's *No Wit, No Help Like a Woman's* (1611). Her next play, *Sir Patient Fancy* (1678), is another comedy using contrasting pairs of lovers. Isabella, daughter to Sir Patient Fancy, and her next-door neighbor Lucretia, daughter to Lady Knowell, lament the custom that denies women free choice in marriage and the parental preference for rich fools. Isabella loves Lodwick Knowell, and Lucretia loves Leander Fancy; but their parents intend to marry them to others for money. Lucretia deplores her mother's conceit in her learning, but Isabella points out that male pedants can be at least as prolix and foolish as any woman.

Old Sir Patient Fancy, a Puritan fanatic and a hypochondriac, dotes on his young wife, who is scheming to enjoy her lover, Wittmore. When Fancy announces his intention of leaving London, which would separate the lovers, the families join in convincing him that he is deathly ill. In act 3 Lodwick and Wittmore have arranged to enter Fancy's house at night, Lodwick to make honest love to Isabella and Wittmore to go to bed with Lady Fancy. The lovers are mismatched in the dark, with amusing results; Lady Fancy's and Wittmore's overtures, which would be appropriate to each other, respectively disgust and alarm Lodwick and Isabella. Behn uses the situation to illustrate contrasting kinds of love. As Wittmore acts on his belief that he has met Lady Fancy, Isabella indignantly asks, "Do you love me?"; for she assumes that love would preclude an attempt at seduction. Wittmore's idea of love, on the other hand, is "a good substantial Passion, without any design but that of right-down honest Injoyment" (IV.i). It is characteristic of Behn and her age that she can accept both attitudes while making a clear distinction between them.

Lady Knowell is treated with significantly more sympathy than the stock learned lady of seventeenth-century drama. Unlike Molière's *femmes savantes* and their innumerable English imitations, she is genuinely learned and genuinely enthusiastic about learning: it would be a real treat for her to laugh over Martial's epigrams with Leander. He, meanwhile, cannot wait to get away from her to court her daughter. But, having set her up as an amorous old woman, Behn softens the picture by letting her graciously hand over Leander to Lucretia, saying she was only testing his love for her daughter. She also promotes her son's marriage to Isabella. The only character to dislike her seriously is sour Sir Patient, and it is not the learned lady who is humiliated, but her antifeminist opponent.

Sir Patient is a stock but amusing Puritan, who values "not whether there be Love between 'em or not. Pious Wedlock is my Business" (IV.ii). His wife points to the hypocrisy of his religion: "a Psalm is not sung so much out of Devotion, as 'tis to give notice of our Zeal and pious Intentions: 'tis a kind of Proclamation to the Neighbourhood" (IV.ii). In the end Lodwick arranges for Sir Patient to be distracted by a comic council of doctors while the desirable marriages take place; Lady Fancy openly tells Sir Patient that she married him because she and her lover had no other means of support; and Sir Patient resolves to make the best of the situation and to become a man of the town himself. The epilogue, spoken by Lady Knowell, argues woman's right to write

Angelica threatening to shoot Willmore in act 5, part 1, of The Rover, *illustration from the 1735 edition*

comedy; and, in an epistle, "To the Reader," Behn defended herself against the charge of bawdiness. Although the play is not so innocent as she claims, she was certainly justified in asserting that bawdiness that would pass unnoticed in a man's work was condemned in hers. She also points out that bawdy, demanded by popular taste, is more excusable in an author who writes to support herself than in men who write only for fame.

Sir Patient Fancy was successful, as was Behn's next play, *The Feigned Courtesans; or, A Night's Intrigue* (1679). Here she reworked several elements from *The Rover.* The principal young women, Marcella and Cornelia, flee their home to escape, respectively, a forced marriage and the convent. Marcella is in love with an Englishman, Fillamour, who wishes to marry her. His friend, Galliard, is a rover ever seeking sexual adventure, but he ultimately agrees to marry the lively Cornelia. The complicated plot overworks Behn's favorite devices of disguise and mistaken identity. To give just a partial summary: Marcella and Cornelia are living in Rome disguised as courtesans, but they also frequently dress as boys. Fillamour visits a woman who, he thinks, is Marcella and who *is* Marcella, but she is pretending to be Euphemia, a courtesan; he is attracted to her because she is Marcella, but flees her because she tells him she is Euphemia. Then Marcella, disguised as a boy, reproaches him for visiting Euphemia instead of meeting Marcella. The ladies' servant, Petro, keeps appearing in various guises—as fencing master, etiquette master, guide to antiquities, and pimp—in order to fleece two foolish English travelers, Sir Signal Buffoon and his tutor, Parson Tickletext.

Behn took the opportunity to capitalize on her success by bringing out an early work, *The Young King; or, The Mistake* (1679), a high-flown tragicomedy derived from Gauthier de Costes de la Calprenède's romance *Cléopâtre* (1647-1656). This play did not succeed on the stage, but it went into two editions. Cleomena, the Dacian princess, falls in love with Thersander, prince of Scythia, while he is serving in the Dacian army, even though the two countries are at war. Because of various misunderstandings, they fight and wound each other, but they are ultimately reconciled. Cleomena has been raised as a warrior so that she can succeed to the throne instead of her brother, whose reign, according to an oracle, would ruin the country. Finally, a way is found for him to reign without disaster; and Cleomena willingly resigns the Dacian throne to become queen consort of Scythia. Like most of Behn's fighting women, Cleomena combines warlike prowess and bravery with a soft womanly heart, preferring love to all else. After this, Behn probably wrote *The Revenge; or, A Match in Newgate* (1680), an adaptation of John Marston's *The Dutch Courtesan* (1605), which humanizes the title character.

In *The Second Part of The Rover* (1681), Willmore, still a banished cavalier, is in Madrid, along with Blunt. Hellena died only a month after their marriage–a loss that he manages to bear "with a christian Fortitude"; he regrets rather more the loss of her fortune, much of which he has spent on the courtesan La Nuche (I.i). He is still pursuing her, but she discarded him when his money ran out. His friend Beaumond, who has money, is also courting La Nuche; and the situation is further complicated by Beaumond's fiancée, Ariadne, who sees Willmore as a more exciting lover. Meanwhile La Nuche cannot repress her love for Willmore, although she realizes that it will destroy her career. Looking at her bawd, Petronella, she sees the fate of a prostitute who has lost youth and beauty and lacks money. Nevertheless, she renounces self-interest for love and ultimately assures Willmore: "I am yours, and o'er the habitable World will follow you, and live and starve by turns, as Fortune pleases" (V.iii). Ariadne and Beaumond agree to marry. Much fun is generated by the contest among some secondary characters over who will marry two rich female "Monsters," a giant and a dwarf; for the seventeenth-century audience, the comedy is increased by their being Jewish.

Aphra Behn, engraving based on a portrait by Riley

Willmore is even more exploitative of women here than he was in part 1. It is true that he can be attractively lively, carefree, and candid, as in his courtship scene with Ariadne in IV.i. But he is the Restoration rake at his most selfish and destructive, taking women's bodies as he likes, without any thought about their needs. He is not even interested in knowing a woman's name, only whether she is pretty and available. And there is no evidence of criticism in Behn's presentation of him. She does offer a balanced view of La Nuche's dilemma, as the courtesan recognizes that it is unnatural to barter love for money and base to cheat and jilt men but also recognizes how disastrous it would be for her to lose control of her feelings (IV.i). Nevertheless, when she hands herself and her money over to Willmore, although she must realize that he will use and discard her, her self-destructive decision is presented as womanly and right.

The Second Part of The Rover was enthusiastically received, although it did not last in the repertory. One reason for its inferiority to the first part is that Behn had already used the best things in her source for that play. Like most Restoration playwrights, Behn took inspiration from earlier plays; but in most cases she remade them to the extent that they became original works. *The Rover* is a vastly improved version of a ten-act closet drama by Thomas Killigrew, *Thomaso; or, The Wanderer* (1664).

The False Count; or, A New Way to Play an Old Game, first produced in November 1681, was often presented during the period and revived as late as 1730. Though Behn in her epilogue called it a "slight Farce," it is not only amusing but pointed. Carlos complains furiously to his friend Antonio that his Julia has been forced to marry rich old Francisco. Antonio is supposed to marry Francisco's daughter, Isabella, but loves Clara. Isabella is ridiculously conceited of her beauty and rank, considering that her father started life as a shoemaker. She sneers at Antonio, although he is handsome and gentlemanly, because he is a merchant. To punish her the young men set up a clever chimney sweep, Guiliom, as a count and have him woo Isabella. She is enchanted by his rude arrogance, which she mistakes for aristocratic breeding, and his burlesque of heroic courtship, which she takes at face value. Besides being funny, Guiliom serves as a vehicle for satire on aristocratic pretensions; for it is suggested at the end, after his marriage to Isabella and his exposure, that, given plenty of money, he will be able to pass very well for a lord. The last lines of the play, too, remonstrate against despising the merchant class.

Carlos and Antonio get the women they love through an elaborate scheme by which they convince Francisco he is imprisoned in the sultan's seraglio; he is so terrified that he actually orders his wife to yield to Carlos, whom he believes to be the sultan. There are fine comic effects when Julia insists on keeping her dear honor and not robbing her husband of his rights, while he, who has been repressively jealous, insists that she cuckold him with her lover.

The years 1678 to 1682 were a period of intense party feeling in England, and the Tory playwrights took the opportunity to express their loyalty in political plays, such as John Dryden and Nathaniel Lee's *The Duke of Guise* (1682), Thomas Otway's *Venice Preserved* (1682), and John Crowne's *City Politiques* (1683). Behn's contributions were *The Roundheads; or, The Good Old Cause* (1681) and *The City Heiress; or, Sir Timothy Treat-all* (1682). Both were very successful. *The Roundheads* is set in the last days of the Commonwealth,

as the surviving Puritan leaders are contending for power. In Behn's version, Lambert and Fleetwood are competing to become king. Lady Lambert already sees herself as queen. Loveless, a cavalier whose estate has been sequestered, is put off by her pride and her politics but cannot help loving her beauty. His friend, Freeman, is an old lover of Lady Desbro, wife of another republican leader. There is some amusing satire on Puritan hypocrisy and self-righteousness, as when Fleetwood, offered the crown, says he will "go seek the Lard in this great Affair; and if I receive a Revelation for it, I shall with all Humility espouse the Yoke, for the Good of his People and mine" (I.ii). Behn's comedy *Like Father, Like Son* (1682) is the only one of her plays that was not successful enough to be printed.

Tom Wilding, the hero of *The City Heiress* and the nephew of Sir Timothy Treat-all, is a rake adored by the three principal women in the play: Lady Galliard, a rich widow; Charlot, who is heiress to a rich businessman and has eloped with Wilding; and Diana, his kept mistress. His friend Sir Charles Meriwill loves Lady Galliard and hopes to marry her, but she is indifferent to him because he is modest and respectful. Wilding's boldness and assertiveness are irresistible to the women, although his inconstancy distresses them. In the end, Sir Charles persuades Lady Galliard to accept him by pushing into her house when drunk and threatening to rape her. Charlot marries Wilding, and Diana marries Sir Timothy, who thinks she is the heiress. Sir Timothy, a caricature of Shaftesbury, is a zealous Whig who keeps open house for Commonwealthsmen and true-blue Protestants in order to foster their seditious views. He disinherits Wilding partly for his extravagance and debauchery but mostly for his Tory politics.

However, Behn let her Tory enthusiasm carry her too far in an epilogue that she wrote for an anonymous tragedy, *Romulus and Hersilia* (1682), which plainly glanced at the disloyalty of King Charles's Whiggish but beloved illegitimate son, the Duke of Monmouth. Behn was taken into custody and evidently frightened into avoiding political writing in the future. Indeed, for the next four years she did not write for the stage at all. She turned to scandalous fiction, *Love-Letters Between a Noble-Man And his Sister* (1684, 1687), and poetry, *Poems upon Several Occasions* (1684).

In April 1686 she came back with another successful comedy, *The Lucky Chance; or, An Alderman's Bargain.* Leticia, engaged to Bellmour, has agreed to marry Sir Feeble Fainwou'd because she was destitute and because he told her Bellmour was dead. Bellmour's friend Gayman loves Julia, who has married Sir Cautious Fulbank for his money. Julia repents her marriage and still loves Gayman, but she refuses to commit adultery with him, although he has spent all his fortune in trying to persuade her. She makes a distinction, unusually sharp for the time, between chastity, which she values, and reputation, which she scorns: she does not hesitate to avow her love for Gayman, her wish that she could please herself sexually, her scorn for "the Censures of the Croud," and her refusal to "change my Freedom and my Humour, / To purchase the dull Fame of being honest" (V.iv). Gayman wins three hundred pounds from Sir Cautious and then bets his winnings against a night with Julia; he wins again, and Sir Cautious is only too eager to keep his bargain rather than lose the three hundred pounds. When Julia discovers this, she renounces him. Meanwhile, Bellmour has prevented Sir Feeble from consummating his marriage with Leticia by pretending to be his own ghost. Finally the two old men resign their wives to their lovers, philosophically acknowledging that they could not keep them anyway.

The Emperor of the Moon, a farce, was Behn's most popular play after *The Rover*. First produced in March 1687, it had at least 130 performances by 1749 and was mentioned in the *Spectator* (number 22). Doctor Baliardo has become so obsessed with his astronomical studies that he takes literally the romances of moon voyages and believes there is a world on the moon. The lovers of his daughter and niece plot to gain his consent to their marriages by playing on his delusion: they make him believe that the Emperor of the Moon and the Prince of Thunderland have fallen in love with the girls, come disguised as these mythical personages, fool the doctor with an elaborate show, and have the marriages performed before his eyes. The proceedings are enlivened by three comic servants: Scaramouch and Harlequin compete ingeniously for the hand of the third, the duenna Mopsophil. This farce probably owed its success to its combined attractions of singing, dancing, slapstick humor, rich pageantry, and ingenious special effects.

The next year Behn published three prose tales, of which the best is *Oroonoko*, the first treatment of black slavery in English literature. It is a fascinating combination of Enlightenment ideas on the noble savage and exotic local color, of realis-

tic detail and the fustian of heroic drama. Behn's tales suffer from the immaturity of fiction in her time but often show originality and presage the down-to-earth realism of Daniel Defoe. She also did some translation, notably of scientific and philosophical works by Bernard Le Bovier, Sieur de Fontenelle.

Behn died in 1689 after several years of illness and poverty. Nevertheless, she was buried in Westminster Abbey. Two of her comedies were produced posthumously, *The Widow Ranter; or, The History of Bacon in Virginia* (in November 1689) and *The Younger Brother; or, The Amorous Jilt* (in February 1696). Both failed–*The Widow Ranter* because it was badly miscast and injudiciously cut; *The Younger Brother* probably because of inherent weakness. *The Widow Ranter* is set in Virginia and derides colonial administrators, as Behn had already done in *Oroonoko*. Its serious plot shows Bacon, a valiant soldier, defending Jamestown against the Indians; his principal motive, however, is love for the Indian queen, whom he hopes to gain by killing her husband in war. His efforts are impeded by a cowardly, dishonest council (resembling Behn's London aldermen), who envy and fear him and are using the pretext that he waged war without proper authorization. Bacon wins his war but accidentally kills the Indian queen and therefore poisons himself.

Daring, one of Bacon's officers, is loved by the Widow Ranter, who had been transported from England and sold but soon married her master and is now a rich widow. She blusters, drinks, and fights like a man but is nevertheless attractive and good-natured. Although she loves him, she does not pine for Daring: "Pox on't no; why should I sigh and whine, and make my self an Ass, and him conceited?" (IV.iii). Daring at first prefers the more conventionally feminine Chrisante, but Ranter wins his heart by dressing as a man and pursuing him onto the battlefield. He presses her to marry him immediately, promising her he "will never–be drunk out of thy Company" and telling her, "I never lik'd thee half so well in Petticoats" as in breeches (IV.iii).

George Marteen, the "Younger Brother" of Behn's last play, returns to London to see his beloved Mirtilla, the amorous jilt. Olivia, his sister, whom he has placed, disguised as a page, to watch Mirtilla, tells him that the amorous jilt has married a rich fool and is also wooing Olivia herself, whom she believes to be a boy. George leads a double life, as an apprentice businessman to please his father and as a gallant beau. In the lat-

Anne Bracegirdle as Semernia, the Indian queen in The Widow Ranter
(Montague Summers, The Restoration Theatre, *1934)*

ter role he has become friendly with Prince Frederick, who is also in London pursuing Mirtilla, whom he fell in love with abroad. When she sees him, she cannot resist his high station. George overhears them together in her bedroom and is enraged, but when fire breaks out, love and friendship overcome revenge, and he risks his life to save them. Finally, George disgraces Mirtilla by arranging for Frederick to see her courting the supposed page Olivia.

Not only did Behn achieve great success as an author but she never felt obliged to conceal her sex or her identity. Nine of the prologues or epilogues to her plays indicate her sex, and she published seven plays with signed dedications. (That of *The Young King* is signed Astera, presumably a misprint for Astrea, her well-known pseudonym.) Three of them have feminist prefaces. Behn demonstrated conclusively that a woman could openly succeed as an author if she was suffi-

ciently tough. Although she complained of antifeminist prejudice, she was able to oppose it without the inhibitions of her eighteenth-century successors: she boldly–and rightly–claimed that she had written "as many good Comedies, as any one Man that has writ in our Age," and also that she wrote for ego satisfaction as well as need–"I value Fame as much as if I had been born a *Hero*," she declared in the preface to *The Lucky Chance.*

Behn's creative works, however, do not show the feminism so apparent in the outward aspects of her career. She wrote not only as well as a man but as a man; there is little evidence of a distinctively female point of view or sensibility in her plays, tales, or poems. All too accurately, she described her literary talent, in the preface to *The Lucky Chance*, as "my Masculine Part." She was, of course, writing to support rather than to express herself; and if she had radically challenged contemporary assumptions and literary conventions, she would hardly have succeeded in the theater.

It has been argued that Behn's repeated and eloquent protests against forced, loveless marriages are distinctively feminist. But in fact they are equally characteristic of her male contemporaries; her treatment of the theme is neither more serious nor more perceptive than theirs. Restoration comedy–like comedy in most ages– consistently pits young people against repressive elders and argues that the young should choose each other for love, regardless of money or family interest. Almost all the Restoration comic writers portray independent, resourceful heroines, well aware of what they want and prepared to go after it in defiance of the wishes of their elders. Here, as in her satire of Whig Puritan businessmen, Behn may have been expressing personal conviction, but she was also following the dominant trend among comic dramatists of her time.

Behn's calls for emotional and sexual freedom for women have been hailed as feminist protest against the double standard, and so, in a way, they are. The song that opens *The Emperor of the Moon* proclaims that woman was "Born free as Man to Love and Range, / Till nobler Nature did to Custom change, / Custom, that dull excuse for Fools, / Who think all Virtue to consist in Rules." Again, however, this attitude was not peculiar to Behn. The class for which she wrote delighted in outraging the conventions of respectable sexual behavior and prided itself on exposing the hypocrisy of repressing people by defining one's own self-interest as their duty. Moreover, in view of seventeenth-century social conditions, to say nothing of biology, free love is not necessarily a glorious liberation for women. In the Restoration world, where the strong exploited the weak, members of the weaker group who abandoned caution and calculation would destroy themselves. Wilding of *The City Heiress* sounds attractively free when he counters Lady Galliard's objections to sex without marriage by claiming that "All the Desires of mutual Love are virtuous. / Can Heav'n or Man be angry that you please / Your self, and me, when it does wrong to none?" (IV.i). But, in fact, she would be doing wrong to herself, because of consequences that he does not acknowledge and that Behn rarely did either. Lady Galliard risks not only pregnancy but loss of her chances for marriage. If she were not rich, she would face destitution as well by having no husband to support her when

she was too old to attract lovers. Possibly Behn half-realized that urging women to give themselves without reserve when they faced such disastrous consequences was a cruel deception; for her female characters who abandon law and calculation for love are not carefree rovers, but slaves to love such as Lady Galliard (for most of *The City Heiress*) and La Nuche of *The Second Part of The Rover*. Behn idealizes this type (as did another otherwise liberated contemporary woman, Delarivière Manley), but it is hardly a model of liberation.

Behn's presentation of the rake-hero betrays a similar insensitivity to exploitation of women. Alonzo of *The Dutch Lover* and Willmore the Rover bully women, value them only as sexual objects, and unblushingly take all they can get without a thought for the woman's rights and feelings– and yet they are presented as irresistibly charming and, apparently, as ideals of virility. *The City Heiress* makes much of the contrast between Sir Charles, a modest, considerate wooer, who bores the woman he loves, and Wilding, who charms all the women by rude boldness and overbearing of their wishes. Wilding needs ready money, but when his friend suggests he marry one of the heiresses who love him, he demurs on the grounds that his uncle may die soon, leaving him six thousand pounds per year–"and who the Devil cou'd relish these Blessings with the clog of a Wife behind him?" (II.ii). The play's plot supports what Charles's uncle tells him: "You shou'd have huft and bluster'd at her door, / Been very impudent and saucy . . . courted at all hours and seasons; / Let her not rest, nor eat, nor sleep, nor visit . . . Women love Importunity" (I.i). Behn's rakes are both more brutal and more dominant than those of Wycherley and Etherege. Sparkish of Wycherley's *The Country Wife* (1675) shares Willmore's impatience with virtue in women (III.ii)–but Sparkish is presented as a contemptible fop. Etherege's Dorimant is as hard to catch as Willmore, but Harriet induces him not only to propose marriage but to agree to conditions that (symbolically, at least) indicate some reformation of his behavior (*The Man of Mode*, V.ii, 1676).

What is distinctive in Behn is her sympathetic representation of mature, unconventional women. Generally, when such characters appear in Restoration comedy, they are humorously satirized, like Wycherley's Widow Blackacre (in *The Plain Dealer*, 1676), or totally denigrated, like Thomas Shadwell's Lady Fantast (in *Bury Fair*, 1689). Behn's Widow Ranter, on the other hand, is likable and attractive even though she unabashedly smokes, drinks, speaks without restraint, and wins her man through a bold assault. Lady Knowell, too, is treated with unusual sympathy for her type. Moreover, she is ridiculed for such foibles as conceit, not for her intellectual interests themselves; such characters were used by other dramatists to demonstrate that women should not attempt to acquire learning, because they were not capable of it. Behn's prostitutes are remarkable for being presented as real women with serious problems: she realistically portrays them as hardened but also reveals their motivation, their vulnerability, their self-contempt, and the painful insecurity of their position. She has been criticized for not resolving Angelica's situation at the end of *The Rover*, but actually there could be no solution for Angelica; letting her relapse into her accustomed way of life, however unsatisfying she now finds it, is honest and realistic, unlike the sentimentalized ending of *The Second Part of The Rover*, which sends La Nuche after Willmore without any thought of what will happen to her.

It is obvious that Behn shared the intellectual interests of Lady Knowell (although, unlike her, she did not know Latin) and the assertiveness and plain-speaking of the Widow Ranter. As a woman who had lost her reputation, she had something in common with the courtesans as well. Their uncontrollable love for Willmore is like her own for Hoyle, as expressed in her "Love Letters to a Gentleman," which are believed to be slightly fictionalized versions of her actual letters to him and were first published in *The Histories And Novels of the Late Ingenious Mrs. Behn* (1696). Like Angelica and La Nuche, Behn was in a weak bargaining position, and she was appealing desperately for the love of a man who she knew would not return it.

Behn was celebrated in her own time for her humor and her representation of love. Her warm temperament and bohemian life-style would have confirmed the stereotype that love was woman's subject. However, it is her comedy that has lasted—her manipulation of intrigue and her humorous characterization. She makes the most of the standard Restoration comic plot—bringing together three or four young couples despite obstacles and hairbreadth escapes. If her mistaken identity gambits sometimes become pointlessly complicated, they are more often developed with delightful ingenuity, such as the nocturnal confusion in Sir Patient Fancy's house and the series of disguises under which Petro gulls

the fools in *The Feigned Courtesans*. She develops the typical characters with originality and vitality—the rake Willmore, for example, the lively young woman Hellena, the courtesan Angelica, the fop Sir Timothy Tawdrey, the Puritan Sir Patient Fancy. She effectively plays off serious lovers against rovers, repressive elders against exuberant permissive ones (as in *The City Heiress*). If her works lack the polish of the highest comedy, they have more contact with practical reality, as when Hellena points out that free love produces bastards for their mother to look after or when Wittmore justifies Lady Fancy's marriage on the grounds that she had no other means of support. Behn was less successful when she attempted to dramatize high-flown romances in tragicomedy.

Behn's reputation has been influenced overwhelmingly by her sex. Absurdly, she is not represented in either of the large standard anthologies of Restoration and eighteenth-century drama: that of Dougald MacMillan and Howard Mumford Jones (twenty-five plays) or that of George H. Nettleton, Arthur E. Case, and George Winchester Stone (twenty-four). (Neither is any other woman, despite the number of female playwrights active in the period.) The allegations of particular bawdiness that Behn protested in her own time pursued her well into the twentieth century. Scholarship has concerned itself mostly with the more colorful aspects of her life, and there is still very little criticism of her plays. Insights generated by the women's movement have led to a more balanced and sympathetic view of Behn as a woman. Two recent books, by Angeline Goreau and Maureen Duffy, appreciate her importance as a feminist precursor and her difficulties as a woman competing in a man's world.

Bibliography:

Mary Ann O'Donnell, *Aphra Behn: An Annotated Bibliography of Primary and Secondary Sources* (New York: Garland, 1986).

Biographies:

George Woodcock, *The Incomparable Aphra* (London: Bordman, 1948);

William J. Cameron, *New Light on Aphra Behn* (Auckland, N.Z.: University of Auckland Press, 1961);

Maureen Duffy, *The Passionate Shepherdess: Aphra Behn* (London: Cape, 1977);

Angeline Goreau, *Reconstructing Aphra: A Social Biography of Aphra Behn* (New York: Dial, 1980).

References:

Douglas J. Canfield, "The Ideology of Restoration Tragicomedy," *ELH*, 51 (Fall 1984): 447-464;

Jones DeRitter, "*The Gypsy, The Rover,* and *The Wanderer*: Aphra Behn's Revision of Thomas Killigrew," *Restoration*, 10 (1986): 82-92;

Angeline Goreau, "Aphra Behn: A Scandal to Modesty," in *Feminist Theorists: Three Centuries of Key Woman Thinkers*, edited by Dale Spender (New York: Pantheon Books, 1983), pp. 125-229;

George Guffey, "Aphra Behn's *Oroonoko*: Occasion and Accomplishment," in *Two English Novelists Aphra Behn and Anthony Trollope: Papers Read at a Clark Library Seminar, May 11, 1974* (Los Angeles: William Andrews Clark Memorial Library, U.C.L.A., 1975), pp. 3-41;

Robert D. Hume, "The Myth of the Rake in Restoration Comedy" and "Marital Discord in English Comedy from Dryden to Fielding," in his *The Rakish Stage: Studies in English Drama, 1660-1800* (Carbondale: Southern Illinois University Press, 1983), pp. 138-213;

Cheri Davis Langdell, "Aphra Behn and Sexual Politics: A Dramatist's Discourse with Her Audience," in *Drama, Sex and Politics*, edited by James Redmond (Cambridge: Cambridge University Press, 1985), pp. 109-128;

Frederick M. Link, *Aphra Behn* (New York: Twayne, 1968);

John Loftis, *The Spanish Plays of Neo-classical England* (New Haven: Yale University Press, 1973);

Fidelis Morgan, "Aphra Behn and 'The Lucky Chance,'" in *The Lucky Chance; Or, the Alderman's Bargain*, edited by Morgan, The Royal Court Writers Series (London: Methuen, 1984);

Joseph F. Musser, Jr., "'Imposing Nought But Constancy in Love': Aphra Behn Snares *The Rover*," *Restoration*, 3 (1979): 17-25;

Katharine M. Rogers, "Fact and Fiction in Aphra Behn's *Oroonoko*," *Studies in the Novel*, 20 (Spring 1988): 1-15;

A. H. Scouten and Robert D. Hume, "'Restoration Comedy' and Its Audience, 1660-1776," in *The Rakish Stage: Studies in English Drama, 1660-1800*, by Hume (Carbondale: Southern Illinois University Press, 1983), pp. 48-81.

Papers:

The Bodleian Library at Oxford University houses a copy of Behn's *The Younger Brother;* information and letters concerning Behn's spy mission in Holland can be found in the Public Record Office.

Roger Boyle, Earl of Orrery

(21 April 1621-16 October 1679)

Robert F. Bode
Tennessee Technological University

PLAY PRODUCTIONS: *The General*, probably the play performed as *Altemera*, Dublin, Thomas Court (Orrery's Dublin residence), 18 October 1662; performed as *The General*, Theatre Royal on Bridges Street, 14 September 1664;

Henry the Fifth, London, Lincoln's Inn Fields, 4 August 1664;

Mustapha, London, Lincoln's Inn Fields, 3 April 1665;

The Black Prince, London, Theatre Royal on Bridges Street, 19 October 1667;

Tryphon, London, Lincoln's Inn Fields, 8 December 1668;

Guzman, London, Lincoln's Inn Fields, 15 April 1669;

Mr. Anthony, London, Dorset Garden Theatre, between January and July 1672.

BOOKS: *Parthenissa* (Waterford: Printed by Peter de Pienne, 1651);

Parthenissa. The Fifth Part (London: Printed by T. R. & E. M. for Henry Herringman, 1656);

The History of Henry the Fifth. And the Tragedy of Mustapha, Son of Solyman the Magnificent. As they were Acted at his Highness the Duke of York's Theater (London: Printed for H. Herringman, 1668);

Parthenissa. The Sixth Part (London: Printed for Henry Herringman, 1669);

Two New Tragedies: The Black Prince, and Tryphon: the first Acted at the Theatre-Royal, by his Majestie's Servants; The Other By his Highness the Duke of York's Servants (London: Printed by T. N. for H. Herringman, 1669);

English Adventures, probably by Orrery (London: Printed by T. Newcomb for Henry Herringman, 1676);

A Treatise of the Art of War (London: Printed by T. N. for Henry Herringman, 1677);

Poems on Most of the Festivals of the Church (London: Printed for Henry Herringman, 1681);

Mr. Anthony. A Comedy, As it is Acted by Their Majesty's Servants (London: Printed for James Knapton, 1690);

Guzman. A Comedy. Acted at the Theatre-Royal (London: Printed for Francis Saunders, 1693);

Herod the Great. A Tragedy (London: Printed by Tho. Warren for Francis Saunders & Thomas Bennet, 1694);

The Tragedy of King Saul (London: Printed for Henry Playford, 1703);

A Collection of the State Letters of the Right Honourable Roger Boyle, The First Earl of Orrery (London: Printed by J. Bettenham, sold by C. Hitch, 1742);

The Dramatic Works of Roger Boyle, Earl of Orrery, 2 volumes, edited by William Smith Clark II (Cambridge, Mass.: Harvard University Press, 1937)–comprises *The Generall, Henry the Fifth, Mustapha, The Black Prince, Guzman, Mr. Anthony, Herod the Great, The Tragedy of Zoroastres,* and *The Tragedy of King Saul.*

OTHER: *The Generall*, in *A Brief Description of the Ancient and Modern Manuscripts Preserved in the Public Library, Plymouth: To which are added, Some Fragments of Early Literature Hitherto Unpublished*, by J. O. Haliwell-Phillipps (Plymouth: Privately printed, 1853), pp. 55-175.

First a soldier and only afterward a literary figure, Roger Boyle, earl of Orrery, gave the bulk of his time and energy to the fulfillment of his many military obligations under both Oliver Cromwell and Charles II and pursued his literary interests mainly during periods of leisure forced upon him by illness. Even when he was not engaged in literary pursuits, however, he was a prolific writer of letters, and at the conclusion of his military career he distilled all of his experience as a general into *A Treatise of the Art of War* (1677), which proposed many innovations in the care and training of common soldiers that are accepted as commonplace today. As a literary fig-

Roger Boyle, earl of Orrery, and his wife, Margaret, countess of Orrery (collection of Patrick Reginald Boyle)

ure he is credited with introducing rhymed heroic plays onto the Restoration stage, and his early heroic plays were popular and influential in his own time. He also wrote a heroic romance, *Parthenissa* (1651-1669), noted for being the first of its kind in English, and may have written another, nonheroic, romance titled *English Adventures* (1676), but his literary reputation rests on his plays rather than the romance.

The son of Richard Boyle, first earl of Cork, and his second wife, Katherine Fenton, Roger Boyle was born on 21 April 1621 at Lismore Castle, Waterford, Ireland. He was given the title Lord Boyle, baron of Broghill, on 30 November 1627. He entered Trinity College, Dublin, on 9 May 1630 and remained there for four or five years, not working toward a degree because of his age. In 1636 he and his brother Lewis, Viscount Kinalmeaky, began a journey around Europe which lasted until 1639; during this period they lived for a year and a half in the house of Giovanni Diodati, a renowned scholar and professor at the University of Geneva and a preacher in the Swiss Reformed church. It was

after their departure from Geneva that Broghill was introduced to the reading of romances and plays; near the end of the journey in Paris both brothers acted in private performances of plays, and during their time in Paris "heroic" drama was introduced onto the French stage. After their return to England, Broghill became part of the group of younger courtiers who frequented Whitehall palace, where he became intimate with Sir John Suckling and Sir William Davenant, the poet laureate. He may have seen performances of Davenant's court masques while there, and he was certainly introduced to the court fashion of platonic love as it was imported into England by Queen Henrietta Maria. After this initiation he never fully abandoned his appreciation for the idealism of this noncarnal type of love, which provided a portion of the plot in each of his early heroic plays. In 1641 Broghill returned to Ireland, where he fought for the next several years to suppress the revolt of the Irish Catholics. Before he left for Ireland, Broghill married Margaret Howard (1623-1689), the third daughter of Theophilus Howard, second earl of Suffolk.

Over the next two and a half decades they had seven children: Roger (1646-1682), Henry (died 1693), Elizabeth (died 1709), Katherine (1652-1681), Margaret (died 1683), an unidentified daughter, and Barbara (1664-1682).

After the execution of Charles I, Broghill secretly maintained a correspondence with Charles II which was eventually to lead to a planned meeting with the exiled king under the cover of a visit to a Continental spa for his health. When Oliver Cromwell discovered this relationship and confronted him with it, however, Broghill agreed to return to Ireland under Cromwell in 1649 to fight against the non-Parliamentary forces. Between that time and 1653 Broghill wrote the first four parts of *Parthenissa*, a heroic romance. Although this work imitates the style of the French heroic narratives that were becoming quite popular at this time, it was not itself a popular work because of its tedious and convoluted plot. It did, however, earn a sizeable reputation for both itself and its author because it was the first work of its kind by an English author.

Broghill held several administrative and military posts under Cromwell as a result of his service in Ireland. He became a trusted intimate of Cromwell's and an influential member of his cabinet. In 1657 Broghill, who had a reputation as a persuasive speaker, served as one of the chief spokesmen for a committee which Parliament sent to urge Cromwell to accept the crown and, failing that, to marry his daughter Frances to Charles II as a means of restoring the monarchy. Toward the end of Cromwell's life, however, Broghill associated himself with the people who were working directly for the restoration of Charles II to the throne, and as a result the king named him earl of Orrery on 5 September 1660.

Orrery also gained Charles II's personal favor during this period. He became a part of the group of wits who often met with the king in private, and, as a result of discussions as to whether the rhyme which they enjoyed in French plays could be used to good effect in English ones, the king asked Orrery to compose a play in rhyme as an experiment. Orrery undertook the task.

By this time the gout which had periodically afflicted Orrery began to recur more frequently and for periods of greater duration. The gout was and continued to be the illness which forced upon him the leisure to write, and the connection between his attacks of gout and his play writing became well known among London literary figures. He had an attack shortly after the king asked him to compose a play in rhyme, and by the end of 1661 this play, *The General*, was complete. The play, with a Mediterranean background, concerns the love triangle of Clorimum, a general who at first serves and later rebels against a usurping tyrant called only "King," Lucidor, the leader of the rebels against the usurper, and Altemera, a princess who is in love with Lucidor and who has promised herself to him before the beginning of the play. The working out of this relationship is set against the action and intrigue generated by the removal of the usurper and the restoration of the rightful king, Melizer. In her biography of Orrery, Kathleen Lynch sees this aspect of the play as Orrery's interpretation of his own position in the politics of the time. There is also a strong element of platonic love in the play, with Clorimum and Altemera strongly bound by the conflicting demands of love, honor, duty, and valor. All decisions affecting the love relationships of the three characters are preceded by lengthy disputations reminiscent of the précieuse debates of the earlier part of the century. At the end Clorimum must resign his claims on Altemera before she will accept Lucidor.

The verse form of the play was considered one of Orrery's main contributions to the drama of the period. The French verse form that had appealed to the king, and that he had had in mind when he commanded Orrery to experiment with rhyme in an English play, consisted of iambic-hexameter lines. Orrery, however, altered the form of the lines to rhymed couplets consisting of five iambic-pentameter feet, thereby producing the pattern of language that John Dryden described as so graceful and suitable for repartee in his letter to Orrery, which serves as a preface to the published edition of *The Rival Ladies* (1664). Until recently this innovation had been credited to Orrery himself; however, Ted-Larry Pebworth has suggested that Orrery may have been influenced by the rhymed iambic-pentameter verse Abraham Cowley used in his unfinished *Davideis*, which Orrery had read and praised in a poem addressed to Cowley in 1656.

The king was so pleased with the result of Orrery's experiment in *The General* that he gave the play to Thomas Killigrew, manager of the King's Company, who produced it on 14 September 1664; although *The General* was not the first play by Orrery to be produced in London, this

John Webb's 1665 design for Solyman's tent in act 1, scene 1, of Mustapha *(William Smith Clark II, ed.,*
The Dramatic Works of Roger Boyle, Earl of Orrery, *volume 1, 1937)*

play was in order of composition the first of the new species called the "rhymed heroic play" and had undoubtedly circulated among the court wits in manuscript for some time prior to its production. The general popularity of the heroic subject matter and the clear approbation of the king for both the content and the form made the play very influential. Its disputative scenes or "debates" on love versus honor and its use throughout of heroic couplets were immediately and widely imitated.

On 18 October 1662 Orrery presented a play to a large gathering at his Dublin residence, Thomas Court. The title of that play was *Altemera*, but although no copy of that play survives, evidence suggests that it was virtually identical with *The General*. This, then, would have been the first performance of an English rhymed heroic play.

When Sir William Davenant, longtime friend of Orrery, heard that the rival company had and planned to produce a play by Orrery written in rhymed heroic verse, he asked for another for his company. According to his letters, Orrery wrote this unnamed play in a matter of a few weeks, and he sent copies to the duke of Ormonde, lord lieutenant of Ireland, and later to the king. This play never reached Davenant and

has subsequently been lost; not even its title has survived. However, Orrery did send Davenant his *Henry the Fifth*, which was produced at the Lincoln's Inn Fields theater on 4 August 1664. This play inaugurates the kind of heroic play considered typical of Orrery. It is very loosely based on historical events which Orrery alters to suit his need. The pattern of action is much the same as that of *The General*, with a love triangle consisting of King Henry V, Owen Tudor, and Princess Katherine of France. However, King Henry wins the princess's hand after Tudor selflessly resigns his love as a result of his friendship for the king. Until he turned to comedy, Orrery used love-friendship as the primary conflict in his heroic plays. Typically in Orrery's early heroic plays the friendship of the rivals is a strong bond which makes the two equal; however, when one of the friends is a king, the friendship gives way to king worship, as it does here. *Henry the Fifth* relies less on action and more on speech than did its predecessor, another element of the style of Orrery's early heroic plays.

Orrery's next play, *Mustapha*, followed quickly on these successful productions and was in many ways similar to *Henry the Fifth;* Davenant's company performed *Mustapha* on 3 April 1665. In this play Roxolana plots to remove

Mustapha, Solyman's eldest son by another wife, from the succession to make way for her own son, Zanger. Mustapha and Zanger, however, are sworn friends who both love the Queen of Hungary, to whose capital Solyman has laid siege. Because of their friendship, each brother argues the other's case before the queen, but the love triangle differs from that of *Henry the Fifth* in that both lovers die, Mustapha executed by Solyman as the result of a plot against him by Zanger's mother, Roxolana, and Zanger by his own hand because of his friendship for Mustapha. Although Dryden criticized the play in his preface to *Troilus and Cressida* (1679) for going on beyond the death of Zanger to show the punishment of Roxolana, the play was extremely popular; it was performed at court on 18 October 1666 and often revived on the stage during the next two decades.

In 1665 Orrery began *The Black Prince*, again as a result of a request by Charles II. The subject of the play seems to have been suggested by the imminence of war between England and France. Killigrew's company, however, did not perform the play until 19 October 1667. The play differs from *Henry the Fifth* only in the degree of complexity of the love interest. Samuel Pepys notes in his diary entry for the date of the first performance that he recognized "the same points and turns of wit" he had seen in Orrery's previous two plays.

Tryphon, performed 8 December 1668, was not as popular as Orrery's previous plays had been. Although the play is again loosely based on history (the story of the Syrian tyrant), Kathleen Lynch sees this play as similar to *The General* in its somewhat autobiographical nature. She says, "The central issue of *Tryphon* is the vexatious question, provoked by Orrery's own troubled experience: Is it right to serve an usurper?" Pepys in his diary entry for the opening date noted that the sameness of Orrery's plays had begun to wear out London's taste for them, and William S. Clark in the critical preface to his edition of Orrery's plays has traced patterns of repeated lines and ideas in these plays. This play was the last Orrery wrote on his particular model, the last of his heroic plays to be performed, and the last of his plays to be printed in his lifetime.

Orrery's contemporaries still considered him in the front rank of dramatists, however, and Davenant's company quickly produced his farcical comedy *Guzman* on 15 April 1669. Although the play is set in Spain, the action follows patterns readily found in English comedy of the period and the recent past. The main line of action is supplied by Guzman's rather independent servant Francisco, who, disguised as Alcanzar the Astrologer, manipulates a group of people into a series of real marriages and into a few fake ones, which are revealed to be tricks at the end of the play. The rest of the play is made up of the largely recognizable humourslike actions of Guzman himself, described in the list of characters as "an old, covetous, rich, amorous, cowardly buffoon." In his diary entry for the opening day Pepys notes that he was told by Thomas Shadwell that Orrery had changed genre because he thought that "his heroic plays could do no more wonders," but that the new play is nevertheless "a mean thing."

Undaunted, Orrery soon afterward produced *Mr. Anthony*, another farcical comedy, which was performed at the Dorset Garden Theatre during the first half of 1672. The setting for this play is apparently England of the recent past, but otherwise it repeats the patterns and devices of *Guzman*. It was the last of his plays to be performed during his lifetime.

In 1671 Orrery went back to the rhymed heroic play with *Herod the Great*. As is usual in his heroic plays, Orrery retells a series of historical episodes, this time certain events of Jewish history originally recorded by Flavius Josephus, and alters them according to his dramatic needs. Beyond that, however, he changes his pattern considerably. There is no love-friendship conflict of noble suitors here; instead all the chief characters with the exception of Mariamne are studies in evil. The action consists of a series of deaths, efforts by Antipater to fulfill his desire for an incestuous relationship with his stepmother Mariamne, and Salome's manipulation of Herod's jealousy of his wife to the point that he murders her. Mariamne alone exhibits the heroic virtue found in characters in the previous plays. Critics differ on the precise source which influenced Orrery's interest in such characters, but there is general agreement that in producing them he is writing to contemporary taste. The play is all action and theatrical effect; there is virtually no debate, and the language of the couplets surpasses anything Orrery had done before in sustained naturalness and smoothness. The play had been written to rely heavily on the "special effects" available at the King's company theater in Bridges Street, including the temple that, according to the stage direction at the beginning of the

Page from the manuscript for Zoroastres, tentatively attributed to Orrery (Sloane MS. 1828, fol. 77ʳ; by permission of the British Library) second act, "appears [with] Herod seated on a throne within it"; however, the theater burned on 25 January 1672 and, as a result, *Herod the Great* was never performed. Critics agree that it would have been a major success in performance and the highlight of Orrery's dramatic career.

After his final return to Ireland, Orrery may have written a heroic play entitled *The Tragedy of Zoroastres;* but there is some doubt as to whether he completed the play or, in fact, had any hand in its writing at all. In his edition of Orrery's plays William S. Clark attributes the play to Orrery on the basis of its being ascribed to him on the only extant manuscript and on the probability that the handwriting of much of the manuscript is Orrery's. Kathleen Lynch accepts his conclusions in her biography. However, Antony Hammond in his 1975 article on the manuscript of the play questions both the trustworthiness of the ascription and the identification of the handwriting. *Zoroastres* is similar to *Herod the Great* in its heavy reliance on theatrical effects but very inferior in plotting and verse. If the play was indeed written by Orrery in 1676, as the title page of the manuscript states, then it signals the beginning of the degeneration of his talent. It was never produced.

About this time he may also have written another romance, *English Adventures*, which was published anonymously in 1676. The work proceeds on a basis contrary to *Parthenissa*, being a story of infidelity rather than the idealized chastity of platonic love. In her biography Kathleen Lynch conjectures that it was written to please Charles II and notes that the work is remembered because part of its action was Thomas Otway's source for the plot of *The Orphan* (1680).

In 1678 Orrery began *Poems on Most of the Festivals of the Church*, which was published after his death. His final dramatic work was the rhymed heroic play *King Saul*, apparently written between 1677 and his death on 16 October 1679 and subsequently found among his papers. The play dramatizes the events of the biblical story of David and Saul, which was once considered the play's only source since, contrary to his earlier practice, Orrery did not make major changes in the events as they were recounted in the original story to suit the development of his plot. However, Ted-Larry Pebworth has shown that Orrery's recently recovered poem on the 1656 edition of the incomplete *Davideis* praises the same characteristics in Cowley's poem that he incorporates into *King Saul* and has consistently emphasized in his other

heroic plays: valor, duty, friendship, and love. Also, similarity of plotting and conception of character as well as echoes and parallels of language suggest that Cowley's *Davideis* was the major nonbiblical source for the play. The play itself, however, is considered by other critics to be a perfunctory treatment of the subject couched in some very mediocre verse and thus, if *Zoroastres* was actually written by Orrery, a further indication of his degenerating talents. *King Saul* was never produced, although it was prepared for production at the beginning of the eighteenth century and finally published in 1703.

Roger Boyle, earl of Orrery, has been, as both his twentieth-century editor and his biographer have noted, a much-neglected writer. He was considered by many of his contemporaries to be influential and a popular writer whose early plays were financially and critically successful. However, most of his plays were written in the rhymed-heroic style, which had a very short popular stage life, and his two comedies were not successes in his own time. The influence which he exerted came from two sources: he was the first to write a rhymed heroic play, one that received the immediate approbation of the king and was therefore quickly imitated, and he was an important nobleman in an age when that was still a strong recommendation for the value of his work. His most imitated innovation, his use of heroic couplets, was imitated immediately, before his own first play was even performed. Thereafter his talent developed or improved in only one direction, his skill in writing heroic couplets, until he finally achieved a level of competence which could be called "good" in *Herod the Great*, the work which several critics consider his best. Only a tiny body of criticism discusses his works as its main subject, and more general studies of the drama and the period have relegated both the man and his plays to the occasional brief reference.

Biography:

Kathleen Lynch, *Roger Boyle, First Earl of Orrery* (Knoxville: University of Tennessee Press, 1965).

References:

Antony Hammond, "The Manuscript of *Zoroastres,*" *Library*, fifth series 30 (March 1975): 34-40;

Kathleen Lynch, "Conventions of Platonic Drama in the Heroic Plays of Orrery and Dryden," *PMLA*, 44 (June 1929): 456-471;

L. J. Mill, "The Friendship Theme in Orrery's Plays," *PMLA*, 53 (September 1938): 795-806;

Ted-Larry Pebworth, "The Earl of Orrery and Cowley's *Davideis*: Recovered Works and New Connections," *Modern Philology*, 76 (November 1978): 136-148.

Papers:

The National Library, Dublin, the British Library, Chatsworth, and Petworth house collections of Orrery papers. Oxford University, the Huntington Library, and the British Library have manuscript copies of various plays.

John Crowne
(April 1641-April 1712)

Beth S. Neman
Wilmington College

PLAY PRODUCTIONS: *Juliana; or, The Princess of Poland*, London, Lincoln's Inn Fields, summer (probably June) 1671;

The History of Charles the Eighth of France; or, The Invasion of Naples by the French, London, Dorset Garden Theatre, late November 1671;

Andromache, translated from Jean Racine's *Andromaque*, London, Dorset Garden Theatre, late summer 1674;

Calisto, at Court, 15 February 1675;

The Country Wit, London, Dorset Garden Theatre, on or before 10 January 1676;

The Destruction of Jerusalem by Titus Vespasian, part 1, London, Theatre Royal in Drury Lane, on or before 12 January 1677; part 2, 18 January 1677;

The Ambitious Statesman, Or The Loyal Favourite, London, Theatre Royal in Drury Lane, March(?) 1679;

The Misery of Civil War (later *Henry the Sixth: The Second Part*), adapted from William Shakespeare's *Henry VI*, part 2 and part 3, London, Dorset Garden Theatre, February(?) 1680;

Thyestes, London, Theatre Royal in Drury Lane, March(?) 1680;

Henry the Sixth: The First Part, With the Murder of Humphrey Duke of Gloucester, adapted from Shakespeare's *Henry VI*, part 2, London, Dorset Garden Theatre, April(?) 1681;

City Politiques, London, Theatre Royal in Drury Lane, 19 January 1683;

Sir Courtly Nice; or, It Cannot Be, London, Theatre Royal in Drury Lane, 9 May 1685;

Darius, King of Persia, London, Theatre Royal in Drury Lane, late April 1688;

The English Frier; or, The Town Sparks, London, Theatre Royal in Drury Lane or Dorset Garden Theatre, mid March(?) 1690;

Regulus, London, Theatre Royal in Drury Lane, early June 1692;

The Married Beau; or, The Curious Impertinent, adapted from a story in part 1 of Miguel de Cervantes's *Don Quixote*, London, Theatre Royal in Drury Lane, April 1694;

Caligula, London, Theatre Royal in Drury Lane, early March(?) 1698;

Justice Busy; or The Gentleman Quack, London, Lincoln's Inn Fields, 1700(?).

BOOKS: *Pandion and Amphigenia: or, The History of the Coy Lady of Thessalia* (London: Printed by I. G. for R. Mills, 1665);

Juliana or the Princess of Poland. A Tragicomedy. As it is acted at His Royal Highness the Duke of York's Theatre (London: Printed for Will. Cadman & Will. Birch, 1671);

The History of Charles the Eighth of France, Or The Invasion of Naples by the French. As it is acted at his Highnesses the Duke of York's Theatre (London: Printed by T. R. & N. T. for Ambrose Isted, 1672);

Notes and Observations on the Empress of Morocco. Or, Some few Errata's to be Printed instead of the Sculptures with the Second Edition of that

Manuscript for a song by Crowne, with music by Henry Purcell (Egerton M S. 2960, p. 54; by permission of the British Library)

Play, by Crowne, John Dryden, and Thomas Shadwell (London, 1674);

Andromache. A Tragedy. As it is Acted At the Dukes Theatre (London: Printed by T. Ratcliffe & N. Thompson for Richard Bentley, 1675);

Calisto: Or, The Chaste Nimph. The Late Masque At Court, As it was frequently Presented there, By several Persons of Great Quality. With the Prologue, and the Songs Betwixt the Acts (London: Printed by Tho. Newcomb for James Magnes & Richard Bentley, 1675);

The Countrey Wit. A Comedy: Acted at the Dukes Theatre (London: Printed by T. N. for James Magnes & Richard Bentley, 1675);

The Destruction of Jerusalem by Titus Vespasian. In Two Parts.–As it is Acted at the Theatre Royal (London: Printed for James Magnes & Richard Bentley, 1677);

The Ambitious Statesman, Or the Loyal Favourite. As it was Acted at the Theatre Royal, By His Majesties Servants (London: Printed for William Abington, 1679); modern edition, edited by Shivaji Sengupta, Ph.D. dissertation, Columbia University, 1979;

The Misery of Civil-War. A Tragedy, As it is Acted at the Duke's Theatre, By His Royal Highnesses Servants (London: Printed for R. Bentley & M. Magnes, 1680); republished as *Henry the Sixth. The Second Part. Or The Misery of Civil War* (London: Printed for R. Bentley & M. Magnes, 1681);

Henry the Sixth, The First Part. With The Murder of Humphrey Duke of Glocester. As it was Acted at the Dukes Theatre (London: Printed for R. Bentley & M. Magnes, 1681; facsimile, London: Cornmarket Press, 1969);

Thyestes A Tragedy. Acted at the Theatre-Royal, By their Majesties Servants (London: Printed for R. Bentley & M. Magnes, 1681);

City Politiques. A Comedy. As it is Acted By His Majesties Servants (London: Printed for R. Bentley & Joseph Hindmarsh, 1683); modern edition, edited by John Harold Wilson (Lincoln: University of Nebraska Press, 1967; London: Arnold, 1967);

Sir Courtly Nice: or, It cannot Be. A Comedy. As it is Acted by His Majesties Servants (London: Printed by H. H. Jun. for R. Bentley & Jos. Hindmarsh, 1685); modern edition, edited by Charlotte Bradford Hughes (The Hague & Paris: Mouton, 1966);

A Poem, on The Lamented Death of our Late Gratious Soveraign, King Charles the II. Of ever Blessed Memory. With a Congratulation to the Happy Suc-

cession of King James the II (London: Printed for John Smith, 1685);

Darius King of Persia. A Tragedy, As it is Acted by Their Majesties Servants (London: Printed for R. Bentley, 1688);

The English Frier: Or, The Town Sparks. A Comedy, As it is Acted by Their Majesty's Servants (London: Printed for James Knapton, 1690);

Daeneids, Or The Noble Labours of the Great Dean of Notre-Dame in Paris, For the Erecting in his Quire a Throne for his Glory, and the Eclipsing the Pride of an Imperious, Usurping Chanter. An Heroique Poem in Four Canto's. Containing a true History, and shews the Folly, Foppery, Luxury, Laziness, Pride, Ambition, and Contention of the Romish Clergy (London: Printed for Richard Baldwin, 1692); republished as *The Church Scuffle, or the Noble labours of the great dean of Notre Dame . . .* , in *The Third Part of Miscellany Poems*, fourth edition, by John Dryden and others (London: Printed for Jacob Tonson, 1716);

The History of the Famous and Passionate Love, Between A Fair Noble Parisian Lady, And a Beautiful Young Singing-Man; A Chanter in the Quire of Nôtre-Dame in Paris, And A Singer in Opera's. An Heroic Poem. In Two Canto's. Being in Imitation of Virgil's Dido and Æneas; and shews all the Passions of a Proud Beauty, compell'd by Love, to abandon her self to her Inferiour; and being forsaken, how she Reveng'd her self, and recovered her Honor (London: Printed for R. T., 1692);

The Married Beau: Or, The Curious Impertinent, A Comedy: Acted at the Theatre-Royal, By Their Majesties Servants (London: Printed for Richard Bentley, 1694);

Regulus: A Tragedy. As it is Acted by Their Majesties Servants (London: Printed for James Knapton, 1694);

Caligula. A Tragedy, As it is Acted at the Theatre Royal By His Majesty's Servants (London: Printed by J. Orme for R. Wellington, 1698).

Collections: *The Dramatic Works of John Crowne*, 4 volumes, edited by James Maidment and W. H. Logan (Edinburgh: William Paterson/London: H. Sothern, 1872-1874);

The Comedies of John Crowne: A Critical Edition, edited by B. J. McMullin (New York: Garland, 1984).

Although three centuries have lapsed since most of John Crowne's plays were produced, he remains worth remembering, not only because some of his songs and at least one of his comedies, *Sir Courtly Nice* (1685), continue to offer literary delight, but also because, like Samuel Pepys, both his life and works in their typicality offer genuine insight into Restoration living. His life helps us to understand that most politicized of all times because, no less than the king's ministers (or mistresses) or Pepys himself, Crowne led a life of politic compromise, "a career of loyalty" as John Genest terms it in his *Some Account of the English Stage, from the Restoration in 1660 to 1830* (1832). And his works, besides the varying degree of pleasure they still provide, are historically valuable because of the ways their plots and characters reflect political events. Furthermore, since Crowne was not of independent means and, therefore, wrote less to express himself than to please his audience, his works offer a rather precise calibration of what was in vogue during his time.

Crowne was baptized on 6 April 1641 at St. Martins-in-the-Fields, London, and grew up in that parish, the eldest of the three Crowne children–John, Henry, and Agnes–who survived their father. His family maintained their chief residence there at least from the 1638 baptism of his elder brother, William (who may have been the model for Crowne's striking metaphor about "witless elder brothers, [kept] out of company, for fear of shaming their parents"). They were still in the parish when Crowne and his father left for America in 1657, Crowne's father, William, having described himself then as "late of the Parish of Martins in the field in the Countie of Middlesex."

Crowne's father's life was a model of political prudence that surely set an example for his son. From his youth, he was adept at sensing the political wind and setting his sails accordingly. For example, the flattering account that he wrote in 1637 about Thomas Howard, second earl of Arundel's 1636 ambassadorial mission to Ferdinand II, which he observed while serving as a tutor in the household, won him the prestigious appointment of Rouge Dragon, Pursuivant of Arms to the King. Even the setting of the Royalist sun found William Crowne prepared. He became, in fact, one of only a handful of Knights Pursuivant who continued active in the College during Cromwell's time. For in 1637 or 1638 Crowne married Agnes Mackworth Watts, widow of the son of a former lord mayor of London and daughter of the most prominent Parliamentarian family in Shropshire. With the help of the

Mackworths, and especially the considerable influence of his brother-in-law Humphrey, William and his family prospered during Cromwell's ascendancy. Among the major Shropshire offices he held in the Parliamentary cause were secretary to Denbigh, commander of the Parliamentarian forces there; lieutenant colonel for delinquent estates; commissioner, Shropshire Militia; member of Parliament, Bridgnorth. Through such service, William Crowne had by 1656 garnered enough wealth and influence with Cromwell to buy the patent for Nova Scotia.

In the summer of 1657, perhaps already scenting the changing political winds, William Crowne sailed to America with his sons, John and Henry. Once in America, John Crowne matriculated at Harvard, studying there from September 1657 through December 1660 but not taking his degree. In 1661 he returned to England with his father so the elder Crowne might take his place as Rouge Dragon at the coronation of Charles II and, more important, so he might argue for his rights to his American property, which, having been procured by Cromwell's decree, were invalidated by the Restoration.

When his father returned to America, however, John Crowne did not go with him but stayed on in England and made it his home. Although his family had been associated with Dissenting causes during Crowne's boyhood, he found New England Puritanism oppressive–especially, perhaps, that of the theologically rigorous Harvard. Or, at least, such was the reason Crowne gave for not returning to America. As critic John Dennis remembered it in 1719, "The vivacity of [Crowne's] Genius made him soon grow impatient of that sullen and gloomy Education, and soon oblig'd him to get loose from it and seek his Fortune in *England*." In any case, shortly after Crowne's repatriation he ingratiated himself with his monarch and separated himself forever from the old defeated cause by publicly denouncing his Harvard teachers and the family who had sheltered him while he was a student there. He swore in a deposition:

That two of the execrable murderers of his majesty's royal father, of blessed memory, landed [at Boston]. . . . That the deponent then boarded in the house of Mr. Norton and was present when they visited him, and that he received them with great demonstrations of tenderness; that, after this the said [regicides] went and resided in Cambridge, (the university of New England, of which the deponent was a member,) and that, having acquaintance with many of that university, he inquired of them how the said [regicides] were received; and that it was reported to him by all persons, that they were in exceeding great esteem.

The young Crowne at first had difficulty earning his living. In 1664, in fact, his poverty exempted him from the two-shilling hearth tax. Dennis describes those early days: "[Crowne's] necessity, upon his first Arrival here, oblig'd him to become a Gentleman-Usher to an old Independant lady. But he soon grew as weary of that precise Office, as he had been before of the Discipline of [America]." Amid what Crowne calls the "hurry of business and travel . . . [and of] many importunate, not to say insolent affairs," he turned to writing.

His first effort was *Pandion and Amphigenia: or, The History of the Coy Lady of Thessalia* (1665), a prose romance of some 307 pages. Although it has both the defects of youth–since Crowne was "scarcely 20 years of age when [he] fancied it"– and the defects of that prolix, diffuse genre with its abundance of "fungous words and lame conceits," as Crowne himself termed them, it supplied enough of what the 1665 reading public sought for its unknown author to find it a publisher; and George Villiers, second duke of Buckingham, and Elkanah Settle, as well as other court wits and writers, knew the book well.

Crowne began his career as a dramatist in 1671 with *Juliana; or, The Princess of Poland*. Even with this first effort he was well aware that ingratiating himself with king and court was of primary importance. Consequently, he subtly flattered the king by choosing as the play's hero the duke of Curland, a putative ancestor of the current duke, whose claim to Tabago Island Charles was presently championing. Dedicating his play to Roger Boyle, earl of Orrery was also an act of political savvy. This figure of almost universal regard had, like Crowne, given his support alternatively to both Protector and king and now commanded considerable financial and political influence.

Juliana is a combination of heroic tragedy and comedy-romance and has all the crowd-pleasing elements of both genres. Written in heroic couplets, tragic blank verse, and comic prose, it concerns a (fictitious) struggle for succession in the royal house of then-exotic Poland. Its plot is filled with mistaken identity, spirited damsels dressed in masculine garb, jealousy, approaching madness, thwarted–then requited–love, court

intrigue and betrayal, swordplay, and blood. Yet it includes the broad comedy of the picaresque-inn convention, which gives the play its most memorable character, the comic Landlord.

Crowne complained that *Juliana* was not as well received as he had hoped because he was forced to have it produced while the court was away for the summer; yet it must have been a fairly impressive initial effort, for the Dorset Garden Theatre chose his next work, *The History of Charles the Eighth of France; or, The Invasion of Naples by the French*, as the first new play to be staged there after its opening on 9 November 1671.

In *Charles the Eighth* Crowne gives a dramatic interpretation of events in 1496 surrounding that youthful French king's conquest of Naples and his subsequent returning it to its former ruling family, with honor accruing to all sides. In choosing this historic episode for his heroic drama, Crowne is able to support his own King Charles in his recent alliance with France and to sound that most royally flattering of all strains: the divine right of kings. He states frankly in the epilogue that he hopes to make:

> heroic virtue shine
> In royal breasts, where it shews most divine.
> And so does Kings and Monarchy advance,
> Nay, guarded with the names of Charles and
> 　　France,
> Names that now shake the world. . . .

By the time Crowne wrote *Charles the Eighth*, his political prudence was already bearing fruit, and he began to attract the notice of the powerful and influential. His dedication to John Wilmot, second earl of Rochester, with whom he admits he yet had "not the Honour of much acquaintance," still makes clear that "favours" had already been "bestow[ed]."

With *Charles the Eighth*, which played "six days together" at its opening "and now and again afterward," according to prompter John Downes, in his *Roscius Anglicanus* (1708), Crowne had sufficiently established himself among the modish playwrights to be given the recognition of satire. Crowne was among the targets of *Timon* (by Buckingham, or Rochester, or both; 1674), an imitation of Nicolas Boileau's third satire (1666):

> Kickum for Crown declar'd; said in romance
> He had outdone the very wits of France:
> Witness *Pandion* and his *Charles the Eight*.

Whilst sporting waves smil'd on the rising sun.
Waves smiling on the sun? I'm sure *that's* new,
And 'twas well thought on, give the Devil his
    due.

Further evidence of Crowne's acceptance into the inner circles occurred not long afterward when John Dryden enlisted his efforts along with Thomas Shadwell's to write a satire on Elkanah Settle's *The Empress of Morocco* (1673), which had attacked Dryden in the preface. Together they wrote the devastating *Notes and Observations on the Empress of Morocco. Or, Some few Errata's to be Printed instead of the Sculptures with the Second Edition of that Play* (1674). Years later, in recalling that "three parts of every four were written by me," Crowne regretted the incident and admitted that "I gave vent to more ill nature . . . than I will do again." But at the time, one supposes, the young Crowne was flattered by the laureate's attentions and eager to make one with his cause.

Crowne's next dramatic effort was a translation of Jean Racine's *Andromaque* (1667). Crowne's *Andromache* played during the vacation period of 1674 and so, according to the author, "deserved a better liking than it found." The play is an almost verbatim rendering of Racine's interpretation of the Pyrrhus-Andromache myth, with the single exception of the final three scenes where Racine's wording is rearranged so that most of the violent events with which the play concludes are presented onstage rather than simply narrated in the Greek fashion. In the epistle to the reader Crowne denies even the translator's role and claims only to have changed most of another author's "not very fortunate . . . Verse" to prose.

Although Crowne had not yet produced a major success, he must have shown sufficient promise for Rochester to risk recommending him to the royal family to author a projected court masque featuring the princesses, Mary (age thirteen) and Anne (age eleven). Even granting that Rochester's recommendation of a relative unknown was motivated largely by "malice," as Dennis put it, "to mortify Mr. Dryden," still Rochester's choice must have been well considered, for his own critical reputation was at stake. Crowne was given the commission by royal command, and Rochester's reputation was safe; the masque succeeded admirably.

The project, however, was not without difficulty. Crowne's hasty selection of the Calisto myth from Ovid's *Metamorphoses* presented the for-

midable problem he describes in the preface: "to write a clean, decent, and inoffensive play on the story of a rape." In that myth Jupiter, in the shape of Calisto's protector, Diana, violates the nymph and fathers her child. Crowne solves his dilemma and writes a play appropriate for little princess-actresses by having Calisto stand firm against all attacks. Thus, like Milton's masque *Comus* (1634), Crown's *Calisto* (1675) is a celebration of chastity.

We can guess some of the excitement of the presentation from Crowne's description in his preface to the published play:

> The dancing, singing, music, which were all in the highest perfection, the most graceful action, incomparable beauty, and rich and splendid habit of the Princesses, whose lustre received no moderate encrease from the beauty, and rich habits of the ladies who had the honor to accompany 'em, and share in the performance, . . . an entertainment . . . honoured and adorned, followed at innumerable rehearsals, and all the representations by throngs of persons of the greatest quality, and designed for the pleasures and divertisements of their Majesties, and Royal Highnesses, and, accordingly, very often graced with their presences. . . .

That Crowne's description is no hyperbole is well supported by detailed bills still extant for costumes, sets, musicians, singers, dancers, wardrobe masters, and refreshments–more than six thousand pounds in all. John Evelyn, commenting upon the magnificence of the spectacle in his well-known diary, noted that "the principals . . . were all covered with Jewels." The masque–which, according to Crowne, was "rehearsed and acted" some twenty or thirty times–firmly established Crowne as a court favorite.

This preference was not diminished by Crowne's next play, *The Country Wit* (1676), which, as he acknowledges in the dedication, was also "honour'd with the King's favour." The main plot is based on the standard comic conflict between an overbearing father and a spirited daughter desiring to choose her own husband:

> SIR THOMAS RASH: . . . Maid! you shall love him, I'll make you love him. What cannot you love £2000 a year, and a fair mansion house, and all conveniences, as fine as any in all Cumberland? . . .
>
> CHRISTINA: Have you forgot already, sir, you have as good as engag'd me to Mr. Ramble?

Pages from inventory of goods for costumes worn in Calisto *(Add. MS. 27588, pp. 3, 16; by permission of the British Library)*

16   A Memorandom off all sorts of stufs Reserud
      ffor the womans habits

Madam   Jmiwin Reserud ffor the habit off juice off   yd
Enyght   silver taby of yards — — — — — 21 La qu²
peice   a yard and quarter of whyt Lutstring for it —
     ffor hir habitt off shyeardis of ~~gould~~ shlade tinsel 9 yds
     off yallou tinsell ffor it — — — — 2 yds

Mis butler ffor the habit of plenty Reserud of gald Colored
plenty   silver taby — — — — — — 17 yards
     off flouwer silk and silver stuff for hir — 9 yds & a half
     three quarters of a yard of sky colored Lutstring
     a yard and half of pink Colored Lutstring

Mis butler
attreane   Reserud of black sattin 4 yards for tofts and sliues
     of silver ~~and gould~~ tinsell for lyning and lambertin 8 yd & half

Mis hunt ffor hir Reserud of black satin 4 yds
attrean off silver and gold tinsell — — — — 8 yds & a half
     of green damask — 5 yards
     of tinsel lace 24 yards whyt and scarlet

Mis butler Reserud a yard and half of sky colored satin
shepardis of Chiry colored taby — 4 yards and a half
     of Chiry Colored a winion sesnett — 4 yards
     of silver and gold tinsell 8 yards and a half

Mis hunt a yard and half of sky Colored Sattin
shepardis 4 yard and a half of Chiry colored taby
     of Chiry colored a winion 4 yards
     of silver and gold tinsell 8 yards and a half

Mis Marstew
shepardis ffor hir of Chiry Colored satin on yard and half
     greene taby 5 yards
     Chiry Colored a winion 2 yards
     silver and gold tinsell 8 yds and a half

Mis peives
shepardis of Chiry colored satin on yard and a half
     greene taby 5 yards
     Chiry Colored a winion 2 yards
     of silver and gold tinsell 8 yards and a half

     Reserud of Mr butts ~~theart~~ 30 and 40 strings of perl

In making the Cumberland suitor, Sir Mannerly Shallow, a country booby, and his rival, Mr. Ramble, a city rake, Crowne is able to satirize the excesses of both country and town. Crowne takes his subplot from Molière's *Le Sicilien* (1667), borrowing scenes and occasionally dialogue directly. Also French is the play's important emphasis on roughhouse, mistaken identity across class lines, and sexual intrigue–what Crowne apologetically concedes is "low comedy, . . . almost sunk into farce." Nevertheless, thematically *The Country Wit* honors sexual virtue as well as wit. When the play's values are made explicit in the end, not only is Sir Mannerly's foolishness punished by a misalliance with the porter's daughter, but Ramble, now reformed and repentant–however improbably–is rewarded with the hand of the chaste heroine. With Charles's patronage, the play was moderately successful in its first run and continued to be revived fairly regularly into the 1720s.

Crowne turned again to heroic tragedy with his next play, *The Destruction of Jerusalem*, parts 1 and 2, and with it achieved his first smash hit. According to a contemporaneous letter, it "met with as wild and unaccountable Success as Mr. Dryden's *Conquest of Granada*." In a two-afternoon extravaganza, first produced in January 1677, Crowne combines Josephus's account of events leading to the sacking of Jerusalem with Racine's rendering of the love of Roman Emperor Titus and Judaic Queen Berenice to produce a drama of extraordinary spectacle and pageantry. The play opens to the sound of music within "the brazen gates of the Temple" and "the women's court, behind gilded lattices"; then "the gates open" as "loud musique plays" and a double procession of splendidly garbed priests and Pharisees "come out of the sanctuary." Later, while "wind, thunder, rain, and lightning strive, . . . a noise is heard like an earthquake," and an unseen voice "groans here tormented, . . . the veil flies open and shews the Sanctum Sanctorum," and an angel, "all clad in robes of fire . . . descends over the altar." The climactic scene brings to the stage a representation of the temple in flames and a noisy simulation of the destruction of the city.

In the midst of this spectacle Crowne presents a conflict of love and honor, typical of heroic drama. He leaves its resolution ambiguous, however. Honor would seem to triumph when in the final scene Titus, conscious of his duty to his people, renounces personal happiness and sends away the brokenhearted Queen Berenice. But Berenice has the last word in an incongruously comic epilogue where she invites to court all who, like herself, are "forsaken slighted mistresses" and wryly concludes, "But if [only] half resort,/Queen Berenice will have a crowded court."

The popularity of this play justified the Duke's Company's considerable expense in buying the property from the King's Players, for whom Crowne had been under regular contract. Not only was it an immediate success but it was published three times during Crowne's lifetime and frequently revived well into the eighteenth century. This popularity, however, lost Crowne the patronage of Rochester, whose temper, according to social arbiter and critic Charles Saint-Evremond, was habitually clouded by "malice . . . when heated by a debauch." Rochester's attempt to ruin Crowne with Charles by vilifying his character did not succeed, however, and served only to ingratiate Crowne with his monarch. When the play was published, Crowne, having already discounted any possibility of Rochester's continuing sponsorship, wrote a flattering dedication to the duchess of Portsmouth–Rochester's enemy but Charles's most influential mistress–thus further securing himself in the king's regard.

Even so, Crowne was not able to exploit the royal esteem to his father's advantage in America. In 1667 the Treaty of Breda had ceded territory in North America to the French, including the Crowne properties in Nova Scotia. In 1679 the Crownes saw a means of compensation for their loss in the New England colonies' acquisition of Indian lands after their victory in King Philip's War. Consequently, they petitioned first for Mount Hope and then for Boston Neck, but, although Charles wrote a letter of endorsement calling John Crowne his "well beloved subject," the colonists remained adamant that "no part of those lands be given to Mr. Crowne, whatever his pretensions to the King's favor on some other occasion." The colonists argued that "they fought and paid and bled for it," and "earnestly beg[ged]" with such determination that they persuaded the various boards and commissions considering the case. Eventually they prevailed with the king himself.

The years during which his petition pended, 1679-1681, were exceptionally productive ones for Crowne, who wrote four plays, saw them produced, and prepared eight books for publication. They were not, however, good years

Record of the king's request for a recommendation on John Crowne's petition to be granted a tract of land in New England (Document SP 44/55; by permission of the Public Record Office, London)

for playwrights. Dryden, Shadwell, Aphra Behn, among others, complained about what Behn called "this cursed plotting Age / [that] has ruin'd all our Plots upon the Stage." While Titus Oates was actually believed to have uncovered a "Popish Plot" to kill Charles and replace him with his more overtly Catholic brother, James–and the Whigs plotted to replace James in the succession with Charles's illegitimate son, Monmouth–political and religious discord was rampant and occasionally violent; civil war seemed imminent; and Londoners were not in the mood for theater.

Crowne blamed "this miserable time ... [when] the whole State seems out of tune" for the poor reception in spring 1679 of *The Ambitious Statesman, Or The Loyal Favourite,* the work he believed "the most vigorous of all my foolish labours." *The Ambitious Statesman* was designed to be thematically comforting. Ending as it does with heroic lovers finally united in the grave, the downfall of its insidiously ambitious protagonist, and the secure continuity of the state, it leaves the message that evil can triumph only for a

time. More specifically, Crowne responds to his society's desire for stability by supporting his king. In act 5 his dying hero speaks with topical import:

> Princes are sacred!
> Whate'er religion rebels may pretend,
> Murderers of Kings are worshippers of devils.

He provides subtler reassurance in dedicating the play to the duchess of Albemarle, whose father and father-in-law were among the most instrumental in securing Charles's throne amid even more turbulent times. This tragedy in blank verse reads well, so well in fact, that despite the disappointing stage reception, the book was republished in a second edition in 1681 (and the play may even have been revived at that time).

Crowne adapts Shakespeare for his next plays, *The Misery of Civil War* (1680; later titled *Henry the Sixth: The Second Part*) and *Henry the Sixth: The First Part, With the Murder of Humphrey Duke of Gloucester* (1681). In doing so he followed the same strategy to which Dryden, Shadwell, Thomas Otway, Edward Ravenscroft, and

Nahum Tate all resorted during this time "so unhealthy to poetry," as Crowne termed it. Shakespearean adaptations not only offered a still potent audience appeal but also could supply useful framework for polemic. Although Crowne never seems to have held strong personal, political, or religious convictions, his plays condemned the policies he believed a threat to his king (and patron)–at this time, the Catholic threat exemplified by the Popish Plot, and the Whiggish threat to royal prerogative. In Shakespeare's *Henry VI*, part 2 (acts 4 and 5) and part 3, on which Crowne based his *The Misery of Civil War*, and in Shakespeare's *Henry VI*, part 2 (acts 1, 2, and 3), of which Crowne's *Henry the Sixth: The First Part, With the Murder of Humphrey Duke of Gloucester* is a close rendering, Crowne not only found literary vehicles for both these condemnations but analogies to current positioning of brother against brother (Charles against James) and son against father (Monmouth against Charles). In addition, Shakespeare's depiction of the Wars of the Roses gave Crowne the opportunity to demonstrate the anguished futility of civil war. He added speeches justifying the divine right of kings, such as these lines from Edward's thematic summary that concludes *The Misery of Civil War*: "A Monarch's Right is an unshaken Rock. / No storms of War nor time can wear away." And Crowne incorporated "a little vinegar against the Pope" by making the Cardinal the major instigator of the Duke of Gloucester's murder in part 1 and including anti-Catholic innuendoes in both parts.

Between his two Henry VI plays, Crowne wrote and produced (in spring 1680) *Thyestes*, which should be considered with them. Like them, it is derived from a genre of proven crowd pleasers–here Senecan revenge tragedies–modified to appeal to Restoration audiences and to reflect current concerns. This grim tale of a king forcing his brother to banquet on his murdered son as revenge for his having raped the queen seems hardly topical, but to an audience steeped in discord and whose Parliament threatened passage of exclusionary laws compelling their king to renounce his brother in favor of his illegitimate son, *Thyestes*–with its emphasis on the unnaturalness of brotherly betrayal–conveyed an applicable warning. To the final thematic speech on the agony of being human, which rang as true to Crowne's audience as it did to Seneca's, Crowne adds the question of the hour, which he asks rhetorically: "Can baseborn bastards, lawful sovereigns be?" Like Crowne's Shakespeare adapta-

tions, *Thyestes* also derides the other perceived threat to the established stability, Catholicism. Crowne explains his symbolism in the epilogue: "Pagan and popish priests / Are but two names for the same bloody beasts."

All three plays were well received. Sources for the editors of *Biographia Dramatica* (1812) report that *Thyestes* "met with good success"; and Gerard Langbaine says both Shakespeare adaptations were "acted with good applause," but added "at first" to his note on *Henry the Sixth: The First Part*. Crowne, unaware of Charles's private predilection for Catholicism, had overplayed his anti-Catholic strategy so that, in Langbaine's words, "at length, the Romish faction opposing *Henry the Sixth: The First Part*, by their interest at Court, got it supprest."

Crowne made a similar misjudgment with *City Politiques* (1683) that almost prevented this distinguished comedic satire on Whig politics and poetics from reaching the stage. In assessing the division of parties following the Popish Plot, Crowne correctly understood the Tories to be the court party, but he did not have the political foresight to discern the emerging parliamentary democracy and thus realize the dangers in offending important Whigs. *City Politiques* was suppressed for six months until Charles himself intervened, and it could begin a run that lasted well into the next century.

City Politiques is a masterpiece of satiric diminution. To persuade his audience that the Whigs, who controlled London–and through it, the courts and often Parliament–were unprincipled and reckless reprobates, willing to disrupt the established order for personal gain, Crowne placed the action in the turbulent political climate of 1540s Naples, identified the characters as Whigs, and set them up as the conventional butts of traditional scatological farce. The irresponsible politicians in the political plot are the cuckolds and cuckolders, dupes and witlings, of the farce. A typical example is Craffy, a poetic hack, who says in I.i, "I come to beg of thee, as ever thou wouldst save the life of an honest young fellow of thy own party, and true Whig as I hope to be saved, to lend me a little of thy assistance, for thou art a rare fellow at wenching." *City Politiques* succeeded dramatically, and its satire hit home–perhaps too well. Five days after it opened, Crowne was "cudgeled" by an irate theatergoer.

The rejection of Crowne's American claim in 1682 dissolved his hopes of financial security from that source. Although he was at the height

Illustration from the 1735 edition of Sir Courtly Nice *(courtesy of Archives and Rare Books Department, University of Cincinnati Libraries)*

of his dramatic powers, he was so disillusioned about the vagaries of theatrical success and so dismayed by the enemies his writing had made him, both on the left and on the right, that he was ready to abandon the theater. He thus turned to the king himself, whose favor he still enjoyed. According to Dennis, Crowne "desir'd his Majesty to establish him in some Office, that might be a Security to him for Life. The King had the Goodness to assure him he should have an Office, but added that he would first see another Comedy." That comedy, which Charles forced on the reluctant playwright, dismissing his pleas that "he plotted slowly and awkwardly" by insisting he base it on the Spanish *Non pued Esser*, became Crowne's masterpiece, *Sir Courtly Nice; or, It Cannot Be* (1685).

Sir Courtly Nice is a drama of universal interest because, notwithstanding its topical references, it is a comic commentary on the war between the sexes. In this perpetual war for domination, Crowne identifies with the position of women. He introduces the play from the point of view of its two spirited and witty heroines, Leonora, confined and guarded by her brother Bellguard, and Violante, who would gladly marry Bellguard except "so fond am I of Liberty." Crowne postpones Bellguard's appearance to the close of act 1.

By then the audience has been charmed by the ladies and chilled, though amused, by Leonora's imprisoners: her aunt who brags about her "perpetual displeasure . . . at all sort of youthful Follies" ["or any sort o' youth"]; her cousin Hothead, "so fierce an Enemy to Fanaticks [Dissenters], that he cou'd eat no other meat"; and the hypocritically pious Dissenter Testimony, who worries about "the great–great sinfulness of sin, that sin is one of the sinfullest things in the whole World." When Bellguard first appears, the audience is already eager for Leonora to escape the effete clutches of her approved suitor, Sir Courtly Nice–who is described as "so respectful to every thing belongs to a Gentleman, he stand's bare to his own Perewig"–so that she can marry her loyal Mr. Farewel. They are ready also for Bellguard to be outwitted and to be humbled enough to make him a worthy husband for Violante. Crowne contrives to have all happen as the audience wishes, mainly through the complex and hilarious agency of Crack, a consummate impersonator of fantastic characters.

Throughout the merriment Crowne aims some devastating satire at the hypocrisy and vicious foolishness of his time. He ridicules extremes in thought and manners: Testimony and Hothead (sanctimonious Dissenter and Dissenter baiter), Sir Courtly Nice and Surly (fop and boor). But his strongest condemnation is reserved for attitudes that see love only as appetite and women as chattel.

Although *Sir Courtly Nice* was universally acclaimed and became a staple of the English stage for more than a century, Charles's death just before the anticipated first performance extinguished, in Dennis's words, Crowne's "Hope of being made happy for the rest of his Life, by the Performance of the King's Promise." Crowne, therefore, was forced to continue writing and conforming his views to those from whom he sought favor. The prologue to *Sir Courtly Nice* itself offers an example of such conformity in its eagerness to blame his earlier anti-Catholicism on "a Turn-coate Doctor's lying Creed," to welcome James: "How greatly Heaven has our great loss supplyed," and even to extol the spiritual power of the new Catholic king and queen, "that Illustrious paire . . . Who both Reform and Grace Us by their sway."

The flattery made its impact. James's household warrants record twenty-pound payments to Crowne for *Sir Courtly Nice* and for his next play, *Darius, King of Persia* (first produced in late April 1688). Although *Darius* had a short run and was less than a critical success, James's patronage on author's night made it economically profitable.

This rather ponderous tragedy combines a historical main plot derived from Curtius's *De Gestis Alexandri Magni*, a subplot of thwarted love roughly based on Euripides' *Hippolytus*, and a luxury of blood and spectacle. By exemplifying a good king surrounded by treachery, Crowne used *Darius*, only months before William's revolution, to support James with such lines as "Leave the dispose of Crowns to Kings and Gods."

With the Revolution of 1688, however, divine right was dead, the Stuarts replaced by William of Orange, and the court party changed from Tory to Whig; Crowne perforce changed too. Not only is each of his four surviving plays from William's reign dedicated to an influential instigator of the revolution, and not only do they all contain flattering references to the new regime, but they also attack those administrations to which Crowne once was so loyal–most explicitly perhaps in the dedication to *Caligula* (1698): "What a glorious figure does England now make in comparison of what it did some years ago! It lay one reign becalm'd in luxury, in another fettered." But these works received no patronage comparable to that of the past, and each effort met with some disappointment.

Crowne had thought to ride the wave of anti-Catholic, anti-Jacobite sentiment with *The English Frier; or, The Town Sparks* (1690), a satiric comedy against the preceding "vicious, degenerate age, . . . where men were thought great politicians, that had no more policy than what serv'd the Court's ambition or their own . . . and Treachery to our country was called fidelity to the King." But he had underestimated Jacobite ferocity. Despite the play's acknowledged comic freshness and wit, Jacobite drumming and catcalling in the pit dramatically shortened its run.

In 1692, shortly after William's "late victorious day" at La Hogue, Crowne wrote a heroic tragedy, *Regulus*, glorifying another military hero, whom he describes as "[without] fault . . . approach[ing] near gods in excellence." Crowne based his play on Nicolas Pradon's French historic tragedy of the same name (1688), adding a love-honor conflict, songs by Henry Purcell, a set of comedic characters, and spectacle such as a mad scene, two ghosts, and a bloody body upon the rack. But, as Langbaine wrote, it too "met with no good success, though the Design [was] Noble." In 1692 Crowne also wrote two mock heroic poems against Catholics and Jacobites, *Daeneids* and *The History of the Famous and Passionate Love*.

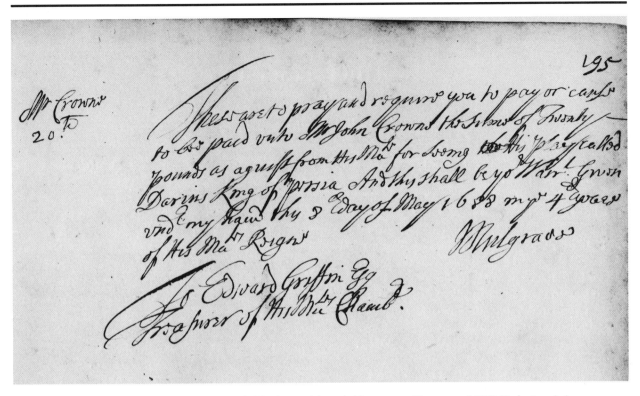

The king's bonus for Darius, *as recorded in the royal household warrants (Document LC5/148; by permission of the Public Record Office, London)*

Early in 1694 Crowne staged *The Married Beau; or, The Curious Impertinent*, a comedy which he cleverly developed from Miguel de Cervantes's tragic novella of the subtitle (in *Don Quixote*, part 1, 1605). With *The Married Beau* Crowne caught the transitional mood of his audience by adding to the brittle wit of Restoration comedy some of the real emotion and "good nature" of eighteenth-century sentimental comedy; as Langbaine writes, it was "often Acted with General Approbation." Even so, Crowne was bitter about William's lack of artistic interest and patronage; he writes in its dedication: "Alas! how barren and miserable is [Poetry] now; No ray from Court shines on us."

Discouraged, Crowne applied in 1695 for the position of King's Waiter with the Customs Department. Following his application, he obtained several fifty-pound grants, but whether he actually assumed the position is unknown. Although Crowne acknowledged receiving "a large share of [Mary's] princely bounty," except for those 1695-1696 moneys, William seems to have ignored him.

In 1697 England entered into the Peace of Ryswick, which in part provided for a commission to settle North American land disputes.

Crowne naturally renewed his petitioning for his father's property in Nova Scotia, a process which continued frustratingly until 1703.

In spring 1698 Crowne staged his final tragedy, *Caligula*, whose horrors and gross injustices may have mirrored his frame of mind and whose theme was admittedly calculated to flatter the king and to win him to his cause:

> In this play, I set tyranny before the eyes of the world, and the dreadful consequences of lawless and boundless power.... The favour, or rather authority, which a mighty neighbouring kingdom had in our court some years ago, got my inheritance, which, tho' it lay in the deserts of America would have enabled me, if I cou'd have kept it, to have liv'd at my ease.... No wonder then if I am pleas'd with the successes of our wise and valiant king, who was born to free and do justice to opprest mankind; and I hope, to myself.

Although Langbaine is correct in saying that Crowne "has very nicely follow'd the character" of Caligula drawn by Suetonius, the play suffers from weak plotting and the monotony and bombast characteristic of heroic-tragic verse. Nor did it succeed politically. Crowne's suit dragged on until 1701, when the commissioners, although recognizing the justice of his claim, gave England the land; William then awarded Crowne only fifty pounds compensation.

During these years Crowne also experienced a serious illness–perhaps a recurrence of the "tedious sickness" he complained of in 1687. In justifying defects in *Caligula*, he says he was incapacitated by "a distemper, which seated itself in my head, threatened me with an epilepsy, and frequently took from me not only all sense, but almost all signs of life." Possibly Crowne never enjoyed completely good health again. At any rate he wrote only one more play, *Justice Busy* (1700?), a comedy that was never printed although some of its charming songs are still extant. Downes tells us, "Twas well acted, but proved not a living play."

Anne's ascent to the throne in March 1702 found Crowne with no hope of regaining his American property, unable to write, and in reduced circumstances. In June he petitioned for relief. As secretary of state Daniel Finch, second earl of Nottingham summarized:

> Petitioner proved his right & title before the Lords Commissioners of Trade who made their report accordingly. That he received 50£ from ye Treas'ry last Summer, but is now in great want and Prays the restoration of his Lands & some relief from his present necessities.

On 3 July he also petitioned "to be employed in some of . . . the Commissioners of Prizes . . . agencies abroad." Whether moved by the justice of his appeal or by nostalgia for the author of her childhood masque, Anne ordered Crowne paid fifty pounds, a bounty she repeated once or twice a year until his death–although sometimes only after a reminding petition from Crowne.

All we know of Crowne's life in retirement is that he lived in St. Giles Parish, home to many theatrical and literary people, where he was buried on 27 April 1712. His pension of fifty or one hundred pounds was not lavish, but since it more than matched the average annual salary of British clergy at that time, it must have supplied his basic needs. In fact, in 1695 Crowne had an apartment on fashionable Great Russell Street. Our final picture of him is the fond recollection of an octogenarian (W. O.) in a 1745 issue of *Gentlemen's Magazine* of "many a cup of metheglin have I drank with little starch'd *Johnny Crown*."

Yet "little starch'd Johnny Crowne" with his fastidious, near-foppish dress and manner, his wit, and his gift for comedy, is a near-tragic figure because he spent his whole life as a reluctant sycophant. He was what Dryden calls a "Weathercock of Government: that when the Wind blows for the Subject, point'st to Priviledge; and when it changes for the Soveraign, veers to Prerogative." He spent his life flattering courtiers, yet he despised the court. Dennis reports: "The Promise of a Sum of Money made him sometimes appear there to solicit the Payment of it: But as soon as he had got it, he vanish'd, and continued a long time absent from it." But although Crowne had "adversions to some things I saw acted there by great men," he was "fixt . . . in a dependence on that Court, for I could have my compensation no where else."

If Crowne's necessity caused him anguish and, perhaps, shame, it also provided the essential spur for his dramaturgy. And the Restoration stage was the brighter for his work. Crowne's writing rarely reaches inspired heights, but he says truly that "Few of my contemporaries have pleas'd the world much more than I have done, both in tragedy and comedy." As a court playwright, he was fortunate that Charles II's love of witty comedy and farce permitted him to develop his comic gift. But like other Restoration dramatists, he was fettered by Charles's predilection for the pompous posing of heroic tragedy and its pretentious heroic rhyme. Crowne was, however, especially skilled at blank verse, and, when liberated from what he called "this obstinate incorrigible rhyme," he exhibits a good ear for dialogue.

He is strongest in his handling of language and in the dramatizing of short scenes. Weakest in overall plotting, he excelled at adaptation. In revising Shakespearean and classical material to appeal to Restoration audiences, he reduced the number of characters and tightened plots to give more unified focus, increased spectacle, shortened speeches into realistic dialogue, and strengthened love interest–often adding female characters.

Crowne was professional at his craft, a creator of tragedies with theatrical appeal and of comedies offering the pleasures of wit, farce, and satiric bite and, in *Sir Courtly Nice*, writer of at least one play of which, in Dennis's words, "the greatest Comick Poet that ever liv'd in any Age might have been proud to have been the Author."

Bibliography:

George Parker Winship, *The First Harvard Playwright: A Bibliography of the Restoration Drama-*

tist (Cambridge, Mass.: Harvard University Press, 1922).

Biographies:

John Dennis, Letter "To Mr. * * * In which are some Passages of the Life of Mr. John Crown, Author of *Sir Courtly Nice*" (23 June 1719), in *The Critical Works of John Dennis*, 2 volumes, edited by Edward Niles Hooker (Baltimore: Johns Hopkins University Press, 1939, 1943), II: 404-406;

Arthur Franklin White, *John Crowne: His Life and Dramatic Works* (Cleveland: Western Reserve University Press, 1922);

Richard Leonard Capwell, "A Biographical and Critical Study of John Crowne," Ph.D. dissertation, Duke University, 1964.

References:

David S. Berkeley, "Sentiment in Crowne's *The Married Beau*," *Notes and Queries*, 199 (April 1954): 179;

Eleanore Boswell, *The Restoration Court Stage (1660-1702) With a Particular Account of the Production of "Calisto"* (Cambridge, Mass.: Harvard University Press, 1932);

Antony Hammond, " 'Beau' Hewyt and John Crowne," *Notes and Queries* (December 1973): 466-467;

Anthony Kaufman, "Civil Politics–Sexual Politics in John Crowne's *City Politiques*," *Restoration: Studies in English Literary Culture*, 6 (Fall 1982): 72-80;

Michael de L. Landon, "John Crowne's *City Politiques*," *Theatre Notebook*, 31, no. 2 (1977): 38;

Gerard Langbaine, "John Crown," in his *The Lives and Characters of the English Dramatick Poets*, revised and augmented by Charles Gildon (London: Printed for W. Turner, 1699);

Archibald McMechan, "John Crowne: A Biographical Note," *Modern Language Notes*, 6 (May 1891): 278-286;

B. J. McMullin, "Sargeant Maynard's Teeth," *Notes & Queries*, 226 (June 1981): 211-212;

McMullin, "The Songs from John Crowne's *Justice Buisy, or the Gentleman-quack*," *Review of English Studies*, 28 (May 1977): 168-175;

Robert Gayle Noyes, "Mrs. Bracegirdle's Acting in Crowne's *Justice Busy*," *Modern Language Notes*, 43 (June 1928): 390-391;

William M. Peterson, "Sentiment in Crowne's *The Married Beau*," *Notes & Queries*, 198 (November 1953): 483-485;

Shivaji Sengupta, "Biographical Notes on John Crowne," *Restoration: Studies in English Literary Culture*, 6 (Spring 1982): 26-30;

Patricia M. Seward, "An Additional Spanish Source for John Crowne's *Sir Courtly Nice*," *Modern Language Review*, 67 (July 1972): 486-489;

James L. Thorson, "Authorial Duplicity; A Warning to Editors," *Analytical and Enumerative Bibliography*, 3 (March 1979): 79-96;

Adolphus William Ward, "John Crowne, His Place in Restoration Comedy," in *Representative English Comedies*, volume 4: *Dryden and his Contemporaries: Cowley to Farquhar*, edited by Charles Mills Gayley and Alwin Thaler (New York: Macmillan, 1936), pp. 243-255.

John Dryden

(9 August 1631-1 May 1700)

James A. Winn
University of Michigan

PLAY PRODUCTIONS: *The Wild Gallant,* revised from an older play, possibly by Richard Brome, London, Vere Street Theatre, 5 February 1663;

The Indian Queen, by Dryden and Sir Robert Howard, London, Theatre Royal on Bridges Street, January 1664;

The Rival Ladies, London, Theatre Royal on Bridges Street, early months of 1664;

The Indian Emperor, London, Theatre Royal on Bridges Street, early months of 1665;

Secret Love, London, Theatre Royal on Bridges Street, final days of January 1667;

Sir Martin Mar-All, by Dryden and William Cavendish, duke of Newcastle, London, Lincoln's Inn Fields, 15 August 1667;

The Tempest, revised from William Shakespeare's play by Dryden and Sir William Davenant, London, Lincoln's Inn Fields, 7 November 1667;

An Evening's Love; or, The Mock Astrologer, London, Theatre Royal on Bridges Street, 12 June 1668;

Tyrannic Love, London, Theatre Royal on Bridges Street, 24 June 1669;

The Conquest of Granada, part 1, London, Theatre Royal on Bridges Street, December 1670; part 2, January 1671;

Marriage A la Mode, London, Theatre Royal on Bridges Street, probably late November or early December 1671;

The Assignation; or, Love in a Nunnery, London, Lincoln's Inn Fields, not later than early autumn of 1672;

Amboyna, London, Lincoln's Inn Fields, possibly February 1673;

Aureng-Zebe, London, Theatre Royal in Drury Lane, 17 November 1675;

All for Love, London, Theatre Royal in Drury Lane, probably 12 December 1677;

The Kind Keeper; or, Mr. Limberham, London, Dorset Garden Theatre, 11 March 1678;

Oedipus, by Dryden and Nathaniel Lee, London, Dorset Garden Theatre, autumn 1678;

John Dryden (portrait attributed to Sir Godfrey Kneller; Charles E. Ward, ed., The Letters of John Dryden, *1942)*

Troilus and Cressida, revised from Shakespeare's play, London, Dorset Garden Theatre, not later than April 1679;

The Spanish Friar, London, Dorset Garden Theatre, 1 November 1680;

The Duke of Guise, by Dryden and Lee, London, Theatre Royal in Drury Lane, 30 November 1682;

Albion and Albanius, an opera with text by Dryden and music by Louis Grabu, London, Dorset Garden Theatre, 3 June 1685;

Don Sebastian, London, Theatre Royal in Drury Lane, 4 December 1689;

Amphitryon, London, Theatre Royal in Drury Lane, probably early October 1690;

King Arthur, an opera with text by Dryden and music by Henry Purcell, London, Dorset Garden Theatre, early June 1691;

Cleomenes, by Dryden and Thomas Southerne, London, Theatre Royal in Drury Lane, on or before 16 April 1692;

Love Triumphant, London, Theatre Royal in Drury Lane, probably late January 1694;

"The Secular Masque," inserted into *The Pilgrim*, revised from John Fletcher's play by Sir John Vanbrugh, London, Theatre Royal in Drury Lane, late April or early May 1700.

SELECTED BOOKS: *Astræa Redux. A Poem On the Happy Restoration & Return Of His Sacred Majesty Charles the Second* (London: Printed by J. M. for Henry Herringman, 1660);

To His Sacred Maiesty, A Panegyrick On His Coronation (London: Printed for Henry Herringman, 1661);

To My Lord Chancellor, Presented on New-years-day, By J. Driden (London: Printed for Henry Herringman, 1662);

The Rival Ladies. A Tragi-Comedy. As it was Acted at the Theatre-Royal (London: Printed by William Wilson for Henry Herringman, 1664);

Annus Mirabilis: The Year of Wonders, 1666. An Historical Poem: Containing The Progress and various Successes of our Naval War with Holland, under the Conduct of His Highness Prince Rupert, and His Grace the Duke of Albermarl. And describing The Fire Of London (London: Printed for Henry Herringman, 1667);

The Indian Emperour, Or, The Conquest of Mexico by the Spaniards. Being the Sequel of the Indian Queen (London: Printed by J. M. for H. Herringman, 1667);

Secret-Love, Or The Maiden-Queen: As it is Acted By His Majesties Servants, at the Theater-Royal (London: Printed for Henry Herringman, 1668);

Of Dramatick Poesie, An Essay (London: Printed for Henry Herringman, 1668);

Sr Martin Mar-all, Or The Feign'd Innocence: A Comedy. As it was Acted at His Highnesse the Duke of York's Theatre (London: Printed for H. Herringman, 1668);

The Wild Gallant: A Comedy. As it was Acted at the Theater-Royal, By His Majesties Servants (In the Savoy: Printed by Tho. Newcomb for H. Herringman, 1669);

The Tempest, Or The Enchanted Island. A Comedy. As it is now Acted at his Highness the Duke of York's Theatre (London: Printed by J. M. for Henry Herringman, 1670);

Tyrranick Love, Or The Royal Martyr. A Tragedy. As it is Acted by his Majesties Servants, at the Theatre Royal (London: Printed for H. Herringman, 1670);

An Evening's Love, Or The Mock-Astrologer. Acted at the Theater Royal, By His Majesties Servants (In the Savoy: Printed by T. N. for Henry Herringman, 1671);

The Conquest of Granada by the Spaniards: In Two Parts. Acted at the Theater-Royall (In the Savoy: Printed by T. N. for Henry Herringman, 1672);

Marriage A-la-Mode. A Comedy. As it is Acted at the Theatre-Royal (London: Printed by T. N. for Henry Herringman, 1673);

The Assignation: Or, Love in a Nunnery. As it is Acted, At the Theatre-Royal (London: Printed by T. N. for Henry Herringman, 1673);

Amboyna: A Tragedy. As it is Acted At the Theatre-Royal (London: Printed by T. N. for Henry Herringman, 1673);

Aureng-Zebe: A Tragedy. Acted at the Royal Theatre (London: Printed by T. N. for Henry Herringman, 1676);

The State of Innocence, and Fall of Man: An Opera. Written in Heroique Verse, And Dedicated to Her Royal Highness, The Dutchess (London: Printed by T. N. for Henry Herringman, 1677);

All for Love: Or, The World well Lost. A Tragedy, As it is Acted at the Theatre-Royal; And Written in Imitation of Shakespeare's Stile (In the Savoy: Printed by Tho. Newcomb for Henry Herringman, 1678);

Oedipus: A Tragedy. As it is Acted at His Royal Highness The Duke's Theatre. The Authors Mr. Dryden, and Mr. Lee (London: Printed for R. Bentley & M. Magnes, 1679);

Troilus and Cressida, Or Truth Found too Late. A Tragedy As it is Acted at the Dukes Theatre. To which is Prefix'd, A Preface Containing the Grounds of Criticism in Tragedy (London: Printed for Jacob Tonson & Abel Swall, 1679);

The Kind Keeper; Or, Mr. Limberham: A Comedy: As it was Acted at the Duke's Theatre By His Royal Highnesses Servants (London: Printed for R. Bentley & M. Magnes, 1680);

The Spanish Fryar Or, The Double Discovery. Acted at the Duke's Theatre (London: Printed for Richard Tonson & Jacob Tonson, 1681);

His Majesties Declaration Defended: In a Letter to a Friend. Being An Answer To A Seditious Pam-

An anonymous portrait of Dryden, probably circa 1662 (by permission of the Bodleian Library, Oxford University)

phlet, *Called A Letter from a Person of Quality to his Friend: Concerning The Kings late Declaration touching the Reasons which moved him to Dissolve The Two Last Parliaments At Westminster and Oxford,* anonymous, usually attributed to Dryden (London: Printed for T. Davies, 1681);

Absalom and Achitophel. A Poem (London: Printed for J. T., 1681);

The Medall. A Satire Against Sedition (London: Printed for Jacob Tonson, 1682);

Mac Flecknoe, Or A Satyr Upon the True-Blew-Protestant Poet, T. S. (London: Printed for D. Green, 1682);

Religio Laici Or A Laymans Faith. A Poem (London: Printed for Jacob Tonson, 1682);

The Duke of Guise. A Tragedy. Acted By Their Majesties Servants. Written By Mr. Dryden, and Mr. Lee (London: Printed by T. H. for R. Bentley & J. Tonson, 1683);

The Vindication: Or The Parallel Of The French Holy-League, And The English League and Covenant, Turn'd into a Seditious Libell against the King and his Royal Highness, By Thomas Hunt and the Authors of the Reflections upon the Pretended Parallel in the Play called The Duke of Guise (London: Printed for Jacob Tonson, 1683);

Miscellany Poems. Containing a New Translation Of Virgills Eclogues, Ovid's Love Elegies, Odes of Horace, And Other Authors; With Several Original Poems. By the Most Eminent Hands, by Dryden and others (London: Printed for Jacob Tonson, 1684)–includes twenty-six works by Dryden;

The History of the League. Written in French By Monsieur Maimbourg. Translated into English According to His Majesty's Command (London: Printed by M. Flesher for Jacob Tonson, 1684);

Sylvae: Or, The Second Part Of Poetical Miscellanies, by Dryden and others (London: Printed for Jacob Tonson, 1685)–includes seventeen works by Dryden;

Threnodia Augustalis: A Funeral-Pindarique Poem Sacred to the Happy Memory Of King Charles II (London: Printed for Jacob Tonson, 1685);

Albion and Albanius: An Opera. Perform'd at the Queens Theatre, in Dorset Garden (London: Printed for Jacob Tonson, 1685);

A Defence Of The Papers Written by the Late King Of Blessed Memory, And Duchess of York, Against The Answer made to Them. By Command, anonymous, often attributed at least in part to Dryden (London: Printed by H. Hills, 1686);

The Hind And The Panther. A Poem, In Three Parts (London: Printed for Jacob Tonson, 1687);

A Song for St Cecilia's Day, 1687. Written By John Dryden, Esq; and Compos'd by Mr. John Baptist Draghi (London: Printed for T. Dring, 1687);

Britannia Rediviva: A Poem On The Birth Of The Prince (London: Printed for J. Tonson, 1688);

The Life Of St. Francis Xavier, Of The Society Of Jesus, Apostle of the Indies, and of Japan. Written in French by Father Dominick Bohours, of the same Society. Translated into English By Mr. Dryden (London: Printed for Jacob Tonson, 1688);

Don Sebastian, King of Portugal: A Tragedy Acted at the Theatre Royal (London: Printed for Jo. Hindmarsh, 1690);

Amphitryon: Or, The Two Socia's. A Comedy. As it is Acted at the Theatre Royal (London: Printed for J. Tonson & M. Tonson, 1690);

King Arthur: Or, The British Worthy. A Dramatick Opera. Perform'd at the Queens Theatre By their Majesties Servants (London: Printed for Jacob Tonson, 1691);

Eleonora: A Panegyrical Poem: Dedicated to the Memory Of the Late Countess Of Abingdon (London: Printed for Jacob Tonson, 1692);

Cleomenes, The Spartan Heroe. A Tragedy, As it is Acted at the Theatre Royal (London: Printed for Jacob Tonson, 1692);

The Satires Of Decimus Junius Juvenalis. Translated into English Verse. By Mr. Dryden, And Several other Eminent Hands. Together with the Satires Of Aulus Persius Flaccus Made English by Mr. Dryden. With Explanatory Notes at the end of each Satire. To which is Prefix'd a Discourse concerning the Original and Progress of Satire. Dedicated to the Right Honourable Charles Earl of Dorset, &c. (London: Printed for Jacob Tonson, 1693);

Examen Poeticum: Being The Third Part Of Miscellany Poems. Containing Variety of New Translations Of The Ancient Poets. Together with Many Original Copies, By The Most Eminent Hands, by Dryden and others (London: Printed by R. E. for Jacob Tonson, 1693)–includes fifteen works by Dryden;

Love Triumphant; Or, Nature will Prevail. A Tragi-Comedy. As it is Acted at the Theatre Royal, by Their Majesties Servants (London: Printed for Jacob Tonson, 1694);

An Ode, On The Death Of Mr. Henry Purcell; Late Servant to his Majesty, and Organist of the Chapel Royal, and of St. Peter's Westminster. The Words by Mr. Dryden, and Sett to Musick by Dr. Blow (London: Printed by J. Heptinstall for Henry Playford, 1696);

The Works Of Virgil: Containing his Pastorals, Georgics, And Aeneis. Translated into English Verse; By Mr. Dryden. Adorn'd with a Hundred Sculptures (London: Printed for Jacob Tonson, 1697);

Alexander's Feast; Or The Power Of Musique. An Ode, In Honour of St. Cecilia's Day (London: Printed for Jacob Tonson, 1697);

Fables Ancient and Modern; Translated into Verse, From Homer, Ovid, Boccace, & Chaucer: With Original Poems (London: Printed for Jacob Tonson, 1700);

The Pilgrim, A Comedy: As it is Acted at the Theatre-Royal, In Drury-Lane. Written Originally by Mr. Fletcher, and now very much Alter'd, with several Additions. Likewise A Prologue, Epilogue, Dialogue and Masque, Written by the late Great Poet Mr. Dryden, just before his Death, being the last of his Works (London: Printed for Benjamin Tooke, 1700).

Collections: *The Works of John Dryden,* 18 volumes, edited by Walter Scott (London: William Miller, 1808); revised by George Saintsbury (London & Edinburgh: W. Patterson, 1882-1893);

Dryden: The Dramatic Works, 6 volumes, edited by Montague Summers (London: Nonesuch Press, 1931-1932);

The Works of John Dryden, edited by Edward Niles Hooker, H. T. Swedenberg, and others (Berkeley: University of California Press, 1955-   ).

OTHER: "Upon the Death of Lord Hastings," in *Lachrymae Musarum; The Tears of the Muse: Exprest in Elegies; Written By diverse persons of Nobility and Worth, Upon the death of the most hopefull, Henry Lord Hastings, Onely Sonn of the Right Honourable Ferdinando Earl of Huntington Heir-generall of the high born Prince George Duke of Clarence, Brother to King Ed-*

Dryden's brother-in-law and collaborator on The Indian Queen. *This engraving by R. White is based on a portrait by Sir Godfrey Kneller and was published as the frontispiece to Howard's* Five New Plays *(1692).*

ward the fourth. Collected and set forth by S. B. (London: Printed by Tho. Newcomb, 1649);

"To his friend the Authour, on his divine Epigrams," in *Sion and Parnassus, Or Epigrams On severall texts of the Old and New Testament. To which are added, A Poem on the Passion. A Hymn on the Resurrection, Ascension, And feast of Pentecost,* by John Hoddesdon (London: Printed by R. Daniel for G. Eversden, 1650);

"Heroique Stanza's, Consecrated to the Glorious Memory of his most Serene and Renowned Highnesse Oliver Late Lord Protector of this Common-Wealth, &c.," in *Three Poems Upon the Death of his late Highnesse Oliver Lord Protector of England, Scotland, and Ireland. Written By Mr Edm. Waller. M^r Jo. Dryden. M^r*

Sprat, of Oxford (London: Printed by William Wilson, 1659);

Sir Robert Howard, *Poems. Viz. I. A Panegyrick to the King. 2. Songs and Sonnets. 3. The Blind Lady, a Comedy. 4. The Fourth Book of Virgil. 5. Statius his Achilleis, with Annotations. 6. A Panegyrick to Generall Monck,* edited, with an introduction ("To my Honored Friend, Sr Robert Howard, On his Excellent Poems"), by Dryden (London: Printed by Henry Herringman, 1660);

The Indian-Queen, by Dryden and Howard, in *Four New Plays, Viz: The Surprisal, The Committee, Comedies. The Indian-Queen, The Vestal-Virgin, Tragedies. As they were Acted by His Majesties Servants at the Theatre-Royal. Written by the Honourable Sir Robert Howard* (London: Printed for Henry Herringman, 1665);

Ovid's Epistles, Translated By Several Hands, includes a preface, and translations of two epistles, by Dryden (London: Printed for Jacob Tonson, 1680);

"The Life of Plutarch," in volume 1 of *Plutarchs Lives. Translated From the Greek by Several Hands,* 3 volumes (London: Printed for Jacob Tonson, 1683);

"A Parallel, Of Poetry and Painting," in *De Arte Graphica. The Art of Painting,* by C. A. Du Fresnoy. *With Remarks. Translated into English, Together with an Original Preface containing A Parallel betwixt Painting and Poetry. By Mr. Dryden. As also a Short Account of the most Eminent Painters, both Ancient and Modern continu'd down to the Present Times, according to the Order of their Succession. By another Hand* (London: Printed by J. Heptinstall for W. Rogers, 1695);

The Annals and History Of Cornelius Tacitus: His Account of the Antient Germans And The Life of Agricola. Made English by several Hands. With The Political Reflections And Historical Notes of Monsieur Amelot De La Houssay, and the Learned Sir Henry Saville. In Three Volumes, book 1 of volume 1 translated by Dryden (London: Printed for Matthew Gillyflower, 1698);

"To My Friend, the Author," in *Beauty in Distress. A Tragedy. As it is Acted at the Theatre in Little Lincolns-Inn-Fields. By His Majesty's Servants,* by Peter Motteux (London: Printed for Daniel Brown & Rich. Parker, 1698);

"Life of Lucian" and other front matter, in *The Works of Lucian, Translated from the Greek, by several Eminent Hands. The First Volume. With*

The Life of Lucian, A Discourse of his Writings, And A Character of some of the present Translators (London: Printed for Sam. Briscoe, 1711).

Although better known today for his poetic satires, classical translations, and critical prose, John Dryden was the dominant dramatist of his generation. His twenty-seven plays include farces, comedies, tragicomedies, operas, and heroic tragedies in rhyme and blank verse. More than any other figure, he shaped the emerging style of the English drama after the eighteen-year hiatus enforced by the civil wars and the Interregnum. His theoretical writings on the drama, which began with the dedication to his first published play (1664) and continued into the last years of his life, are the first sustained body of serious dramatic criticism in English. In this as in other aspects of his career Dryden was a restless thinker, changing his positions in response to the development of his own talents and a rapidly changing political and intellectual world.

Dryden's parents came from prominent Northamptonshire families linked by landholding, Puritanism, intermarriage, and opposition to the personal government of Charles I. His father, Erasmus Dryden, was a younger son of the Drydens of Canons Ashby; his mother, Mary Pickering, was a daughter of the Reverend Henry Pickering, rector of Aldwincle All Saints. Born in Aldwincle in 1631, the poet was probably named for his uncle John Pickering, who died in 1628 of an illness contracted while in prison for defying the King's Forced Loan of 1626. The Pickerings owned much of the land around Titchmarsh, the village where Dryden was reared; they also controlled the advowson of his parish church, St. Mary Virgin Titchmarsh. In 1633 a Presbyterian named Thomas Hill, who had known Dryden's father at Emmanuel College, Cambridge, came to the pulpit; Hill's preaching, described by an admiring contemporary as "plain, powerful, spiritual, frequent, and laborious," was John Dryden's first experience with the formal spoken word, and probably the beginning of his lifelong hostility to the clergy.

When the Short Parliament began its momentous proceedings in 1640, the two members for Northamptonshire were the poet's uncle Sir John Dryden and his first cousin Sir Gilbert Pickering; Thomas Hill followed them to London in 1641 to join a committee opposing the liturgical innovations of William Laud, archbishop of Canter-

bury, and stayed to participate in the work of the Westminster Assembly. Not much later, perhaps in 1644, young John Dryden came to Westminster School, where he encountered the powerful schoolmaster Richard Busby, who also taught Christopher Wren, John Locke, Robert South, Robert Hooke, and Matthew Prior. From Busby, Dryden learned Latin, Greek, history, astronomy, and other advanced subjects in an atmosphere stressing memory, competition, facility in translation, and the invention of poetic conceits. Busby told Thomas Hill that he wanted members of the Parliamentary committee supervising the school to reward his students with money for composing extemporaneous verses because that exercise would "incredibly *whet* up and *raise* their *Phansies*," and Dryden's first poem, on the death of his schoolmate Lord Hastings (1649), is a pastiche of Cowleian conceits, an extravagant display of his youthful "fancy." The public theaters had been shut down before the boy arrived in London, but he might have seen illegal performances at the Red Bull, and he surely read plays while at Westminster: Busby's library included the dramatic works of Ben Jonson and William Cartwright, both of whom were old Westminsters, and the imagery of the Hastings elegy owes much to the language of the Caroline masque. Public events during Dryden's years at Westminster were spectacularly theatrical: the execution of Laud (1645), Pride's Purge of the Long Parliament (1648), and the execution of Charles I (1649). Unlike Dryden's Puritan relatives, who presumably approved of these events, Busby was a defiant high-church Royalist, and his ideas had a telling impact on Dryden, whose poem on Hastings, written in the summer of 1649, also obliquely laments the death of the king.

In the Puritan effort to reform the universities, Thomas Hill became Master of Trinity College, Cambridge; Dryden, still following a path marked out by his family, matriculated there in 1650, along with four other King's Scholars from Westminster, and took his B.A. in 1654. Political and theological controversy was urgent at Cambridge during these years, but we know little about Dryden's opinions or his literary development. His tutor, John Templer, was one of the new fellows appointed to replace those purged by the Parliamentary visitation, but later became a defender of the Restoration Anglican settlement. The two scraps of Dryden's poetry we possess from these years–a prefatory poem for a collection of epigrams by his Westminster friend

Illustration for The Wild Gallant *in the 1735 edition of* The Dramatick Works of John
Dryden, Esq. *(engraving by van der Gucht, after H. F. B. Gravelot)*

John Hoddesdon (1650) and a conceited poetic
compliment to his pretty cousin Honor (in a letter written in 1653 or 1655)–are utterly conventional. He was discommonsed and gated on 19
July 1652 for "his disobedience to the vicemaster
& his contumacy in taking of his punishment in-
flicted by him," but we are not even sure which
of two men was the insulted vice-master on this occasion, and the incident appears to have been
minor. A contemporary said that "Dryden . . .
was reckoned a man of good parts & Learning
. . . [and] had to his knowledge read over & very
well understood all yᵉ Greek & Latin Poets."
Dryden's rank at graduation confirms this estimate: the future laureate stood third in his college.

Erasmus Dryden died in June of 1654, leaving his son a part of the rents of a small piece of
land in Blakesley, worth well under one hundred
pounds a year. The poet, who had taken his B.A.
a few months earlier, may have returned to Trinity after his father's death, but he had left the college for good before April of 1655, and we next
encounter him in London on 19 October 1657,
signing a receipt for fifty pounds paid to him by
John Thurloe, secretary of state to Oliver Cromwell. This was probably a payment for clerical
work performed in the office of the Latin Secretary, where John Milton and Andrew Marvell
were employed; the three poets marched together in the funeral procession for Cromwell on
23 November 1658, an occasion for which Dry-

den also composed a poem. His first cousin, Gilbert Pickering, had risen to the post of lord chamberlain under the protector and therefore supervised the arrangements for the funeral, a fact doubtless relevant to Dryden's elegy, a task he referred to as "our duty and our interest too."

Dryden made many important contacts in the London of the late 1650s. His later references to Sir William Davenant's *The Siege of Rhodes* sound as if he managed to see the first production of that "opera" in 1658. A later attack by Thomas Shadwell says that Dryden lived for a time in the home of the bookseller Henry Herringman, later his publisher, for whom he "Writ Prefaces to Books for Meat and Drink"; in this capacity, he may have written prefaces for one or two treatises by Dr. Walter Charleton, who nominated him for membership in the Royal Society a few years later. His friendship with Sir Robert Howard, the amateur poet and playwright whose poems he edited and introduced to the public in 1660, also clearly antedated the Restoration. In his poem in praise of Howard, Dryden seized the opportunity to praise the new king, and in *Astræa Redux,* a full-dress panegyric published in the same month, he welcomed Charles II to England and deftly apologized for his own complicity with the previous regime:

> For by example most we sinn'd before
> And glass-like, clearness mixt with frailty bore.
> But since reform'd by what we did amiss
> We by our suff'rings learn to prize our bliss.

Astræa Redux marks the beginning of Dryden's successful campaign to secure the attention of the restored court; he followed it with a poem on the coronation (1661) and a poem in praise of Edward Hyde, earl of Clarendon, lord chancellor to the new king (1662). At least as important as these public gestures of fealty was the poet's courtship of Elizabeth Howard, sister to Sir Robert and daughter of the impoverished earl of Berkshire. According to a manuscript note scribbled by the king, Clarendon was a "great favourite" of Elizabeth's mother; Dryden's marriage on 1 December 1663 therefore brought him within the orbit of James, duke of York, who had recently married Clarendon's daughter, Anne Hyde. James was already under suspicion of being a Roman Catholic, and Elizabeth Howard's family included many recusants: her eldest brother Charles, viscount Andover, for whom the

Drydens later named their own first son, was unquestionably a Catholic.

Even before his marriage Dryden became active in the restored theater, Charles II's favorite form of entertainment. Sir Robert Howard was artistically and financially involved with the troupe headed by Thomas Killigrew, which became the King's Company; Dryden, who shared lodgings in Lincoln's Inn Fields with Howard before marrying his sister, quickly became involved as well. His first play, *The Wild Gallant*, was a revised version of an earlier English play, now lost, perhaps the work of Richard Brome. When the King's Company staged this rough-hewn humors comedy at Vere Street in February of 1663, it was in direct competition with Sir Samuel Tuke's smash hit, *The Adventures of Five Hours*, written at the suggestion of the king and staged by Davenant and the Duke's Company at their new theater in Lincoln's Inn Fields. Dryden's prologue, which glances pointedly at the success of the rival play, also reveals his sense of his position in dramatic history. Well-read in earlier English theater, the young dramatist wonders whether he can invent "any thing that's new," and refers to "*Fletcher* and *Ben*" as "Elder Brothers, . . . that vastly spent" the "estate" of "wit." Superficially less "new" than Tuke's play, *The Wild Gallant* failed, both at Vere Street and in a later court performance, but Dryden learned much from this first attempt: after the court failure, he wrote an elegant paper of verses thanking Barbara Palmer, countess of Castlemaine and chief mistress to the king, for her "encouragement"; and, as his next entry into theatrical competition, he composed a "Spanish" tragicomedy on the model of Tuke's success, *The Rival Ladies* (1664), which includes several scenes in rhyming couplets and quatrains. In collaboration with Howard, who was well informed about the king's stated preference for rhyming plays in the French fashion, he also wrote *The Indian Queen* (1664), the first completely rhymed heroic play staged in London after the Restoration.

Dryden dedicated *The Rival Ladies* to Howard's kinsman Roger Boyle, earl of Orrery, who was also composing rhymed plays at the king's command. In the dedication he articulated for the first time the arguments for rhymed drama that he would repeat steadily for the next thirteen years:

> Rhyme so Knits up [Memory] by the Affinity of Sounds, that by remembering the last Word in one Line, we often call to Mind both the Verses.

Illustration for The Indian Queen *in the 1735 edition of* The Dramatick Works of John Dryden, Esq. *(engraving by van der Gucht, after H. F. B. Gravelot)*

Then in the quickness of Reparties, (which in Discoursive Scenes fall very often) it has so particular a Grace, and is so aptly Suited to them, that the suddain Smartness of the Answer, and the Sweetness of the Rhyme, set off the Beauty of each other. But that benefit which I consider most in it, because I have not seldome found it, is, that it Bounds and Circumscribes the Fancy. For Imagination in a Poet is a faculty so Wild and Lawless, that, like an High-ranging Spaniel it must have Cloggs tied to it, least it out-run the Judgment.

There are three essential claims here. Ever the practical craftsman, Dryden first notes that rhyme aids memory, and in a theater world where plays had short runs and rotated frequently in repertory, the actors had to carry thousands of lines in their memories; Samuel Pepys witnessed some occasions where they suffered lapses. In his comments on quickness, smartness, and sweetness, Dryden applauds the usefulness of rhyme in pointing up sallies of wit, either by satisfying or deceiving our expectations. He recognizes the potential for witty parallelism and antithesis in rhyming verse, but his poetic satires are more memorable for instances of such technique than his rhyming plays. The third claim is more complex: the Dryden who had been taught to "*whet* up and *raise* [his] *Phansie*" at Westminster was now praising the discipline of rhyming because "it Bounds and Circumscribes the Fancy." This interest in controlling the poetic imagination is an early instance of a tension that runs throughout Dryden's literary criticism: at times he rises to an almost Longinian fervor in "preferr[ing] the sublime Genius that sometimes erres, to the midling or indifferent one which makes few faults, but seldome or never rises to any Excellence"; at other times he argues with equal intensity for the importance of judgment, restraint, cool correctness.

Dryden's theory is more applicable to some of his rhymed plays than to others. *The Indian Queen,* a collaborative effort for which Howard must bear some of the blame, is stiff and stylized, but *The Indian Emperor* (1665), a sequel entirely by Dryden, is much more subtle. Drawing on historical accounts of the conquest of Mexico by the Spaniards, Dryden saw the rich moral and literary possibilities in that clash of cultures, and wrote full, complex roles for Cortez and Montezuma, roles that challenged the talents of Charles Hart and Michael Mohun. The play dramatizes a conflict between Art and Nature to which he had already referred in his early poems, and to which he would return in the great poems and critical essays of his maturity. In the very first scene Cortez declares his admiration for the "natural" Indians in a striking speech:

Wild and untaught are Terms which we alone
Invent, for fashions differing from our own:
For all their Customs are by Nature wrought,
But we, by Art, unteach what Nature taught.

Modern readers may find Dryden's sympathy for the culture of the Aztecs particularly impressive; a scene in which the greedy Spaniards attempt to torture Montezuma for his gold gives the title character enormous stature and dignity.

But just as he was beginning to find his voice as a playwright, Dryden had an enforced vacation from the theater. A few weeks after *The Indian Emperor* opened, the Second Dutch Naval War began, and the bubonic plague, which started to spread during the same winter, was raging in London by the spring. The lord chamberlain closed the theaters in June of 1665, and they stayed dark until December of 1666. Dryden used these eighteen months, which he spent at the Howard family estate in Wiltshire, to write an extraordinary piece of dramatic criticism, the *Essay of Dramatick Poesie;* a two-plot tragicomedy, *Secret Love;* and a heroic poem on current events,

Annus Mirabilis (1667). In the *Essay,* cleverly set in the context of the naval battle of Lowestoft, four sophisticated speakers debate the relative merits of ancient and modern drama, French and English plotting, rhymed and unrhymed dialogue. Dryden's own preferences for modern authors, English "mixed" plots, and rhyming dialogue carry the day in each of the three debates, but much of the continuing interest of the *Essay* lies in its slightly oblique treatment of some more general issues. Dryden was essentially arguing for a heightened mimesis, "Nature wrought up to an higher pitch," a theory that would give the drama a kind of grandeur more normally associated with epic. He evidently believed that such grandeur, gained by borrowing some but not all of the conventions of French serious drama, might allow the writers of new English plays to differentiate themselves from Jonson, Fletcher, and Shakespeare, whom he later called "the Gyant Race, before the Flood."

When Dryden returned to London in the winter of 1666-1667, he began to claim a large share of public attention. His new play, *Secret Love,* starring Charles Hart and Nell Gwyn, was so successful that the king claimed it as "his play." This is the first of several dramas by Dryden in which a comic plot involving a "gay couple" speaking prose comments ironically on a high plot involving courtly figures speaking blank verse. Pepys was rapturous about Nell Gwyn's performance as Florimell, particularly praising the scene where "she comes in like a young gallant; and hath the motions and carriage of a spark the most that ever I saw a man have. It makes me, I confess, admire her." Dryden was clearly taking advantage of the talents of his players. Revivals of *The Indian Emperor* and a revised version of *The Wild Gallant* followed immediately, and the Duke's Company also bid for Dryden's services: he helped the duke of Newcastle with *Sir Martin Mar-All,* a slapstick farce starring the comedian James Nokes; and he helped Davenant revise *The Tempest* for an autumn premiere, adding several new characters and much bawdy dialogue. Both these plays had long lives. *Sir Martin Mar-All,* a perennial favorite with the king, was revived throughout the century; five years after the premiere, for example, the Duke's Company chose that play to open their new playhouse at Dorset Garden. *The Tempest,* which strikes most modern readers as a cheap travesty of Shakespeare's play, was one of the most-popular plays

Nell Gwyn, who played Florimell in Secret Love, *Donna Jacinta in* An Evening's Love, *Valeria in* Tyrannic Love, *and Almahide in* The Conquest of Granada *(portrait from the studio of Peter Lely, circa 1675; by permission of the National Portrait Gallery, London)*

of the later seventeenth century; it was frequently revived as a semi-opera.

Dryden's other major publication of 1667 was his poem on the recent naval campaign and the Great Fire, *Annus Mirabilis*, a demonstration of his skills at political polemic and an effective defense of the court against those who blamed disaster on royal immorality. Not surprisingly, Charles named Dryden his poet laureate when Davenant died in April of 1668 and arranged for the poet to receive an M.A. by dispensation. In the same spring the new laureate signed an unprecedented agreement with the King's Company, promising to write three plays a year in return for a share in the company comparable to those held by the leading actors. He never technically fulfilled the terms of the contract, which proved profitable for the next several years, and in the prologue to the first play he wrote under the new arrangement, a ribald comedy called *An Evening's Love* (1668), he described his efforts at play writing as "ungrateful drudgery." The working metaphor of that prologue is that of a husband bored with his wife, and Dryden's close connection with the King's Company did lead to at least one sexual adventure, an affair with Anne Reeves, a minor actress for whom he wrote several small roles.

Dryden's success did not go unchallenged. The *Essay of Dramatick Poesie*, first published late in 1667 (with 1668 on the title page), sparked an intense debate. Sir Robert Howard, who had already questioned Dryden's position in favor of dramatic rhyme, repeated his arguments with a renewed intensity that may be partially explained by some personal and political animosities that had now grown up between the brothers-in-law. Thomas Shadwell, who thought Dryden insufficiently respectful toward Ben Jonson, also attacked him in prefaces and prologues and brought a character called "Drybob" on stage in his comedy *The Humourists* (1670) carrying a dog that made Dryden's metaphor of imagination as a "High-ranging Spaniel" ludicrously literal. The Court Wits, especially Rochester and Buckingham, resented Dryden's incursions into literary and social areas they regarded as their own territory.

Dryden made himself vulnerable to attack through the bombastic excesses of such rhyming plays as *Tyrannic Love* (1669) and *The Conquest of Granada* (two parts, 1670 and 1671). *Tyrannic Love,* written to honor Queen Catharine, pits the queen's patron saint, an early Christian martyr, against the Roman emperor Maximin; it includes torture, bloodshed, and much hyperbolic verbal rant. Particularly notorious is the speech in which Maximin orders Catharine tortured on the wheel:

> Go, bind her hand and foot beneath that Wheel:
> Four of you turn the dreadful Engine round;
> Four others hold her fast'ned to the ground:
> That by degrees her tender breasts may feel,
> First the rough razings of the pointed steel:
> Her Paps then let the bearded Tenters stake,
> And on each hook a gory Gobbet take;
> Till th'uppr flesh by piece-meal torn away,
> Her beating heart shall to the Sun display.

Nor is such excess confined to language. In the final scene, furious at his inability to turn back time and countermand his own orders, Maximin kills the soldier who comes to report the execution of Saint Catharine and her mother; the stage direction specifies a ludicrous action: *"Kills him, then sets his foot on him, and speaks on."* When Porphyrius, who loves Maximin's wife, Berenice, attempts unsuccessfully to rescue the empress, Maximin orders them both executed. Valeria, Maximin's virtuous daughter who loves Porphyrius, stabs herself; Placidius, who loves Valeria, stabs Maximin, who wrests away the knife, sits down upon his victim, and stabs him repeatedly in a scene in which tragic rant turns into comedy. Porphyrius and Berenice, who have escaped execution, arrive in time to declaim over three corpses, one of whom, Valeria, comes to life in her real identity as Nell Gwyn to speak an explicitly comic epilogue. Cursing the soldier

who means to carry off her body, Nell breaks the frame of the play: "Hold, are you mad? you damn'd confounded Dog,/I am to rise, and speak the Epilogue." Addressing the "kind Gentlemen" and "Sweet Ladies" of the audience, she explains that she is the "Ghost of poor departed *Nelly*"; "trust[ing] no Poet," she provides her own epitaph: "Here *Nelly* lies, who, though she liv'd a Slater'n/Yet dy'd a Princess, acting in S[aint] *Cathar'n*."

While altogether more complex and serious than *Tyrannic Love, The Conquest of Granada,* a ten-act drama staged in two parts, is an uneasy blend of epic and romance elements. The descriptions of offstage acts of impossible bravery by the hero Almanzor rise to moments of poetic grandeur; an evil female character, Lyndaraxa, displays a hypnotic sexual power analogous to Almanzor's physical prowess; and the complexities of party treachery among the various factions in Granada demonstrate the fullness of Dryden's understanding of the politics of his own world. Nonetheless, the play remains extreme. One contemporary witness, the wife of the diarist John Evelyn, admired it, but thought it "designed for an Utopia rather th[a]n our stage." If the physical action of the play displays nothing quite so absurd as Maximin sitting on his victim, the imagery of many of Almanzor's speeches comes close: claiming that he has "that Soul which Empires first began," for example, he issues this impossible boast: "The best and bravest Souls I can select,/And on their Conquer'd Necks my Throne erect." Again, the excess is a part of Dryden's meaning; men in the grip of Almanzor's vaunting pride, he insists, will believe they can erect their thrones on conquered necks. But the politics behind Almanzor's rant are at least as important as the psychology; his claim to force as the only source of political legitimacy is a reductive version of the theory of natural law developed in Thomas Hobbes's *Leviathan* (1651).

While there are excellent reasons for believing that Dryden read *Leviathan* with care and skepticism soon after its publication, this play makes a more sustained use of Hobbesian ideas and categories than his earlier works, and since Hobbes was popularly considered a dangerous and atheistical thinker, some of Dryden's contemporaries seized on his use of Hobbesian ideas as another reason to criticize him, failing to recognize that his use of Hobbes was both skeptical and creative. When Almanzor first strides onto the stage, a street brawl between the Zegrys and the Abencerrages

OF
HEROIQUE PLAYES.

An Essay.

Hether Heroique verse ought to be admitted into serious Playes, is not now to be disputed: 'tis already in possession of the Stage: and I dare confidently affirm, that very few Tragedies, in this Age, shall be receiv'd without it. All the arguments, which are form'd against it, can amount to no more than this, that it is not so near conversation as Prose; and therefore not so natural. But it is very clear to all, who understand Poetry, that serious Playes ought not to imitate Conversation too nearly. If nothing were to be rais'd above that level, the foundation of Poetry would be destroy'd. and, if you once admit of a Latitude, that thoughts may be exalted, and that Images and Actions may be rais'd above the life, and describ'd in measure without Rhyme, that leads you insensibly, from your own Principles to mine: You are already so far onward of your way, that you have forsaken the imitation of ordinary converse. You are gone beyond it; and, to continue where you are, is to lodge in the open field, betwixt two Inns. You have lost that which you call natural, and have not acquir'd the last perfection of Art. But it was onely custome which cozen'd

a 2   *us*

First page of Dryden's preface to The Conquest of Granada, *from the 1672 quarto edition*

is in progress; instinctively taking the weaker side, he disobeys King Boabdelin's order to desist, kills his man, and is condemned to death. The defiant speech he addresses to Boabdelin at this juncture is a dramatic caricature of Hobbes's ideas about the "state of nature":

> No man has more contempt than I, of breath;
> But whence hast thou the right to give me death?
> Obey'd as Soveraign by the Subjects be,
> But know, that I alone am King of me.
> I am as free as Nature first made man

> 'Ere the base Laws of Servitude began
> When wild in woods the noble Savage ran.

But Dryden knew how to learn from his sources, even those sources with which he had fundamental disagreements, and his frequent use of political and military language to describe the interior strife between passion and reason reveals his complex intellectual engagement with Hobbes, whose challenging theory of politics begins with a theory of psychology. A particularly striking example comes early on, when the king's brother Abdalla, entranced by the temptress Lyndaraxa, decides to attempt a revolt, refusing what he knows to be the good advice of Abdelmelech:

> Your Councels, noble *Abdelmelech,* move
> My reason to accept 'em; not my Love.
> Ah, why did Heav'n leave Man so weak defence
> To trust frail reason with the rule of Sence?
> 'Tis over-pois'd and kick'd up in the Air,
> While sence weighs down the Scale; and keeps it
>   there.
> Or, like a Captive King, 'tis born away:
> And forc'd to count'nance its own Rebels sway.

Three successive couplets offer three related metaphors. "Frail reason," like a weak king, is unable to rule over "Sence," which Hobbes had already called the "Originall" of all human thoughts. Heavy and physical, "sence" will inevitably "over-pois[e]" the nebulous reason. Outweighed and disarmed by "sence," reason is finally led away like a captive king, an image sure to remind Dryden's audience of Charles I. By employing these metaphors Dryden is describing three usurpations at once: the usurpation of Abdalla's reason by the force of "sence," in this case the powerful sexuality of Lyndaraxa; the consequent usurpation of the kingdom of Granada, which Abdalla seeks in order to win her hand; and the usurpation of the kingdom of England by Cromwell, still the chief bugbear of official mythology. Although the character here describing his own yielding to "sence" is eventually killed as a result of his stage Hobbism, the essential metaphor upon which his speech depends, equating civil disorder within the body politic and psychological disorder within one man's mind, comes straight from Hobbes.

If Mrs. Evelyn was responding to this kind of intellectual complexity when she praised Dryden's play for being "full of ideas," that phrase was acute criticism indeed. But what finally sets *The Conquest of Granada* apart from Dryden's earlier plays is his success in integrating materials drawn from political philosophy, prose romance, and epic poetry into a coherent dramatic whole. If we compare the stylized exchanges between Saint Catharine and Maximin in *Tyrannic Love* with such powerful scenes as Lyndaraxa's attempted seduction of Almanzor, or Almanzor's attempted seduction of Almahide, we can only conclude that the time Dryden devoted to *The Conquest of Granada* was well spent. The play is indeed "full of ideas," but part of its greatness lies in Dryden's dramatization of the limits of ideology. When Almanzor approaches

Almahide in the second of those scenes, she appeals to his "Vertue":

> ALMAHIDE. Remember the great Act you did this
>   day:
> How did your Love to Vertue then give way?
> When you gave freedom to my Captive Lord;
> That Rival, who possest what you ador'd.
> Of such a deed what price can there be made?
> Think well: is that an Action to be paid?
> It was a Myracle of Vertue shown:
> And wonders are with wonder paid alone.
> And would you all that secret joy of mind
> Which great Souls only in great actions find,
> And that, for one tumultuous Minute loose?
> ALMANZOR. I would that minute before ages
>   choose.
> Praise is the pay of Heav'n for doing good;
> But Love's the best return for flesh and blood.

Almanzor's reply powerfully acknowledges the psychological reality of sexual desire; thanks to his interest in Anne Reeves, Dryden was freshly aware of that reality. By choosing "that minute before ages," Almanzor objects to the absurd ideology of romance, which imposed upon heroes the duty of chivalric behavior without the "return" of fleshly love. But he is willing to lose everything for that "one tumultuous Minute," a passionate and irrational refusal of the cynical pragmatism of Hobbes, who had claimed in *Leviathan* that "the object of mans desire, is not to enjoy once onely, and for one instant of time; but to assure for ever, the way of his future desire."

A decade later Dryden said he had known these plays were "bad enough to please, even when I writ them." At the time, the most effective of many attacks and parodies was *The Rehearsal* (1671), a hilarious burlesque of the conventions of heroic drama by George Villiers, duke of Buckingham, in which a fussy, self-important poet called Mr. Bayes brings two gentlemen to the theater to watch a rehearsal of his new play, a pastiche of mangled couplets parodying heroic dramas by Dryden and others. *The Rehearsal* may have been one factor leading to Dryden's eventual change of opinion about rhymed heroic drama, but it did not threaten his livelihood. As a sharer in the King's Company, which produced *The Rehearsal,* Dryden actually stood to make money from this attack, and there is no evidence that it compromised the success of his own new comedy, *Marriage A la Mode,* which probably came on stage a few weeks before Buckingham's farce. Among Dryden's finest plays, this spar-

John Dryden, circa 1683 (portrait by John Riley; David Piper, The Development of the British
Literary Portrait up to Samuel Johnson, *1968)*

kling performance shows how much he had
learned about the possibilities of the double plot:
the high plot concerns usurpation, birth mystery,
and the claims of class; the comic plot, this time
with two "gay couples," leads us to expect a double adultery that never quite happens. The amorous songs in this play, like those in *The Conquest
of Granada* and several other plays, demonstrate
Dryden's skill at the lyric eroticism valued by the
court. As the curtain goes up, for example, two
women sing this libertine lyric:

> Why should a foolish Marriage Vow
>   Which long ago was made,
> Oblige us to each other now
>   When Passion is decay'd?
> We lov'd, and we lov'd, as long as we cou'd,
>   Till our love was lov'd out in us both:
> But our Marriage is dead, when the Pleasure is
>   fled:·
>   'Twas Pleasure first made it an Oath.

Stylish at every level, *Marriage A la Mode* may

stand as further evidence of Dryden's confidence
at this stage of his career, when he had, in his
own appropriate metaphor, "swept the stakes," enjoying fame, steady income, a place at court, and
the favors of a beautiful actress.

A sudden break in Dryden's string of successes came with the fire of 25 January 1672,
which destroyed the Bridges Street theater and
forced the King's Company to take refuge in
Lincoln's Inn Fields, recently left vacant by the
Duke's Company when they moved to their splendid new theater at Dorset Garden. Dryden's en-
vied status as a sharer in the company now became a liability: he had to contribute toward the
construction of a new theater and scene house at
Drury Lane, and his company was at a serious disadvantage while waiting for those facilities to be
constructed. The plays he wrote for the King's
Company during their residence at Lincoln's Inn
Fields are among his least distinguished: *The Assignation* (1672), set in an Italian nunnery, was his

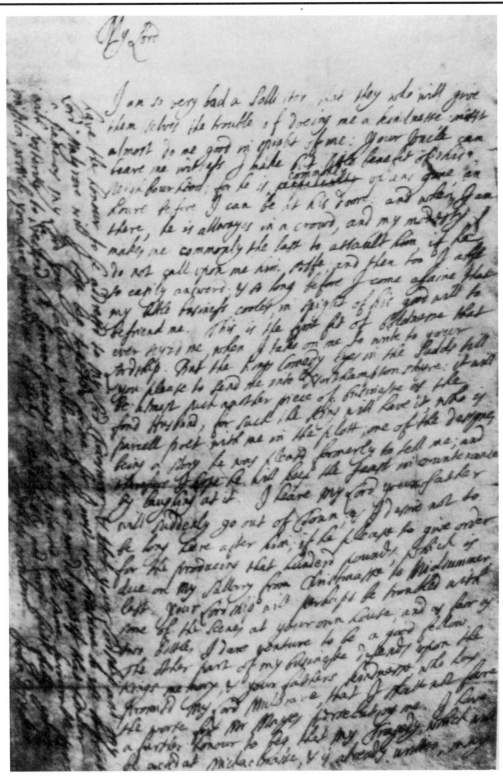

*Letter to Edward Osborne, viscount Latimer, son of the lord treasurer, Thomas Osborne, earl of Danby. Probably written in late June 1677, this letter mentions Dryden's intention to work on "the Kings Comedy" (*The Kind Keeper*), for which Charles II "is parcell poet with me in the plott." Dryden then asks Latimer to remind his father that Dryden is owed one hundred pounds of his laureate's stipend and that he has been promised a raise. The "Tragedy, which will be acted at Michaelmasse" is most likely* All for Love, *though its first performance was probably in December 1677, not on 29 September. Finally Dryden requests that Latimer join John Sheffield, earl of Mulgrave, in convincing Danby to allow* All for Love *to be dedicated to him (by permission of the Historical Society of Pennsylvania).*

first failure in years; *Amboyna* (1673), a shoddy piece of propaganda in support of the Third Dutch Naval War, is even worse.

For the opening of the new house, Dryden planned to compete directly with the operatic spectaculars being staged at Dorset Garden: he wrote a rhyming adaptation of *Paradise Lost* called *The State of Innocence*, but staging this elaborate semi-opera was beyond the resources of the King's Company, and it was never performed. Dryden's first new play for Drury Lane was his last and best rhyming tragedy, *Aureng-Zebe* (1675). Framed by a prologue and epilogue announcing the author's intent to abandon rhymed drama, this psychologically subtle tragedy of character eschews the onstage violence and verbal rant of the earlier tragedies. Though courageous in offstage battles and passionately devoted to his wife, Indamora, who must withstand the advances of her brother-in-law and her father-in-law, Aureng-Zebe is a more reflective hero than any of his predecessors; his soliloquies dramatize such issues as the futility of virtue:

> When I consider Life, 'tis all a cheat;
> Yet, fool'd with hope, men favour the deceit;
> Trust on, and think to morrow will repay;
> To morrow's falser than the former day;
> Lies worse; and while it says, We shall be blest
> With some new joys, cuts off what we possess.
> Strange couzenage! none would live past years
>   again,
> Yet all hope pleasure in what yet remain;
> And, from the dregs of Life, think to receive,
> What the first sprightly running could not give.
> I'm tir'd with waiting for this Chymic Gold,
> Which fools us young, and beggars us when old.

Unjustly neglected, *Aureng-Zebe* justifies comparison with the plays of Jean Racine, and deserves a modern production. Its most impressive scenes are a series of variations on the theme of reconciliation, with proud characters forced to beg the forgiveness of those they have wronged or misunderstood.

When he published *Aureng-Zebe*, Dryden included a revealing dedication in which he expressed his weariness with writing for the stage:

> If I must be condemn'd to Rhyme, I should find some ease in my change of punishment. I desire to be no longer the *Sisyphus* of the stage; to rowl up a Stone with endless labour (which to follow the proverb, gathers no Mosse) and which is perpetually falling down again. I never thought myself very fit for an Employment, where many of my Predecessors have excell'd me in all kinds; and some of my Contemporaries, even in my own partial Judgment, have out-done me in *Comedy*. Some little hopes I have yet remaining, and those too, considering my abilities, may be vain, that I may make the world some part of amends, for many ill plays, by an Heroique Poem.

Hoping to secure the leisure in which to write an epic poem, Dryden successfully sought to have his salary from the crown increased and hinted that he would like to retire to a sinecure at Oxford. But little came of these plans: political turmoil promptly put both Dryden's regular salary and his additional pension in arrears; the approach to Oxford was fruitless; and financial survival, therefore, meant writing more plays. Mindful of his financial situation, Dryden now worked his way free of his troublesome contract with the King's Company: he successfully sought to receive a regular third day's profits for *All for Love* (1677), his first blank-verse tragedy, and he sold his next two plays to the Duke's Company over the feeble protests of his former colleagues, who struggled on for a few more years before joining their rivals in the United Company, founded in 1682.

All for Love, now the most frequently read and produced of Dryden's plays, is a reworking of *Antony and Cleopatra*. The title page informs us that the play is "*Written in Imitation of Shakespeare's Stile*," but Dryden's supple, enjambed blank verse owes much to Milton, and his dramatic structure follows French models. He adheres to the unities, bringing Antony's wife Octavia from Rome to the besieged Alexandria in order to do so; he stringently limits the number of characters, shrinking Shakespeare's cast of thirty-four to ten; he stages no battles, structuring his play as a series of emotional confrontations between various pairs and triads of characters. With the added naturalism of blank verse, this tragedy continues the developments begun in *Aureng-Zebe;* taken on its own terms, it has great strengths, including psychological complexity and densely metaphorical language. Years later Dryden said it was the only play he had ever written to please himself.

The two plays Dryden sold to the Duke's Company in 1678, by contrast, were attempts to please the public: *The Kind Keeper* (11 March 1678), a sexual farce that was quickly closed down, was an imitation of Thomas Durfey suggested by the king; Dryden spoke disparagingly of it in a private letter and a public prologue. The semi-operatic version of *Oedipus* (autumn

Illustration for All for Love *in the 1735 edition of* The Dramatick Works of John Dryden, Esq. *(engraving by van der Gucht, after H. F. B. Gravelot)*

1678), on which Dryden collaborated with Nathaniel Lee, was a typical Dorset Garden spectacular; Dryden's cynical epilogue admits that the play provides "what your Pallats rellish most, / Charm! Song! and Show! a Murder and a Ghost!" But by this time, the laureate had other worries besides popularity: much of his energy in the next few years was taken up with political controversy. These concerns are already apparent in *Oedipus*, where the physical description of the character of Creon ("This ill-shap'd body with a daring soul") is clearly meant to insult Anthony Ashley Cooper, earl of Shaftesbury and leader of the Whig op-

position in Parliament. Dryden's antagonism to Shaftesbury, which led to his most important satirical poems, was not merely a matter of abstract loyalty to the crown. The Popish Plot hysteria of 1678 and 1679 threatened his wife's family, and the plan to exclude the duke of York from the succession threatened his livelihood as the laureate. Elizabeth Dryden's brother Charles Howard, now earl of Berkshire, died in exile, having fled for his life, and her aged cousin William Howard, viscount Stafford, was among the Catholic peers executed as a result of the alleged plot. Dryden's patron York, supposedly implicated in the plot, spent long months in exile in Scotland during these years, and his absence probably increased Dryden's sense of vulnerability: the laureate had long been associated with the successor, and had dedicated the published version of *The State of Innocence* (1677) to Maria of Modena, York's Catholic second wife.

Dryden's one play of 1679 was a cautious adaptation of Shakespeare's *Troilus and Cressida*, for which he wrote one powerful scene, a quarrel and reconciliation between Hector and Paris suggested by Betterton. In the general flatness of this play, we may perhaps detect an avoidance of the shrill language of controversy, though the dynamic scene between the Trojan brothers probably owes something to Dryden's observation of the troubled relations between Charles and James. But even cautious writers were vulnerable, as Dryden learned on the evening of 18 December 1679, when he was beaten senseless by hired thugs in Rose Alley. The responsibility for this violent punishment remains uncertain: the most likely theory is that Dryden was beaten up for a poem he did not write, "An Essay on Satire" by his friend the earl of Mulgrave, but a political motive is also a possible explanation. By the next fall Dryden had partially recovered his health and definitely strengthened his satirical resolve. When Parliament convened to discuss the Exclusion Bill, which would have barred James from the succession on the grounds of his being a Catholic, the Duke's Company had a new play ready to entertain them, a spirited tragicomedy by Dryden called *The Spanish Friar* (1680). Here the low plot defuses the issue of Catholicism, venting resentment of Catholic corruption on a harmlessly comic figure, "a reverend fat, old gouty Fryar" played by the talented Anthony Leigh, but the high plot delivers a conservative Tory message about the holiness of the succession: "let the bold Conspirator beware / For Heaven makes Princes its peculiar Care."

In this Parliament the Exclusion Bill passed the Commons but was rejected by the Lords; in the next Parliament, held at Oxford, the same issues returned with added urgency, and Charles had to resort to a dramatic dissolution to retain control. During the remaining years of Charles's reign, Dryden devoted himself to effective propaganda on behalf of the crown. His most-famous poem, *Absalom and Achitophel* (1681), retells the Exclusion Crisis in terms of the "throne narrative" of Second Samuel. Dryden casts James Scott, duke of Monmouth, Charles's illegitimate Protes-

tant son and the successor proposed by the Whigs, as King David's beautiful, rebellious son Absalom; he casts Shaftesbury as the evil counselor Achitophel. Published a week before Shaftesbury was to stand trial for high treason, the poem had an unprecedented sale. When Shaftesbury was acquitted by a Whig jury, Charles asked Dryden for another poem, and the laureate responded with a cutting satire called *The Medal* (1682). During the same winter he was collaborating with Lee on *The Duke of Guise*, which was widely (and correctly) regarded as a "parallel play" aimed at Monmouth. Delayed for several months by the continuing political crisis, this historical play was finally staged on 30 November 1682, by which time Charles had broken the opposition: a few days before the delayed premiere, Shaftesbury fled to Holland, where he died on 21 January 1683.

The Duke of Guise, which Dryden unwisely sought to "vindicate" from the charge that it was an attack on Monmouth, was his last regular play for some years. His time was increasingly devoted to poetry; he moved from *Religio Laici* (1682), a serious statement of his Anglican faith, to the varied classical translations published in the miscellanies of 1684 and 1685. With little enthusiasm, he collaborated with the composer Louis Grabu on a fully sung opera for the king. *Albion and Albanius*, originally conceived as a mere prologue to a semi-operatic version of the King Arthur story, eventually swelled to three acts, and was in rehearsal when the monarch died in February of 1685. With an added "apotheosis," the opera was finally staged in June, but its run was spoiled by Monmouth's rebellion. During the remaining years of James II's reign, Dryden wrote no plays at all. He converted to Catholicism, defending that controversial choice in his longest original poem, *The Hind And The Panther* (1687), and undertook a number of tasks in propaganda and translation for the king, including a long life of Saint Francis Xavier (1688) and *Britannia Rediviva* (1688), a poem on the birth of Prince James Francis Edward. Since James, unlike Charles, was reliable about paying the laureate's salary, Dryden now had less financial incentive to write for the theater.

In the allegedly Glorious Revolution of December 1688, however, Dryden lost his positions as poet laureate and historiographer royal; necessity forced him back into dramatic writing. *Don Sebastian*, which he had ready within a year of the revolution, was his first new play in six years; bru-

Anthony Leigh as Friar Dominic in The Spanish Friar *(engraving by John Smith, based on a painting by Sir Godfrey Kneller)*

tally censored in performance, though published complete, it is Dryden's longest, most complex, most mature tragedy. *Don Sebastian* (4 December 1689) contains some ironic political material, but ultimately moves from the particular to the general, focusing on the moral and psychological issues implicit in the recent political struggle. In his artful preface Dryden lists the many "discouragements [that] had not only wean'd me from the Stage, but had also given me a loathing of it." In a tone much like that he had used fourteen years earlier, when he complained of being "the *Sisyphus* of the stage," he explains that his "bad circumstances" have "condemn'd [him] to dig in [the] exhausted Mines" of the theater, but he actually found rich ore in his own earlier plays, ex-

pertly refining material from *An Evening's Love, Tyrannic Love, The Conquest of Granada, Marriage A la Mode,* and *Oedipus,* among others. In all those plays Dryden had presented characters who changed their minds, and Dorax in *Don Sebastian* is his finest study in the psychology of inconsistency, a part worthy of the skills of Betterton. Before the play begins, this rough Portuguese soldier has become a Moslem out of anger at Don Sebastian; he protects Don Sebastian from the Moors in hope of slaying his king himself in a duel, but his better nature wins out in a supremely dramatic scene of reconciliation. The dilemma of Dorax is not a simple allegory of the Revolution, which would have been a dangerous and futile gesture, yet by creating Dorax, Dryden chan-

Thomas Betterton, who played the title role in Oedipus, *Troilus in* Troilus and Cressida, *Torrismond in* The Spanish Friar,
the title role in The Duke of Guise, *Dorax in* Don Sebastian, *and Jupiter in* Amphitryon *(portrait from the studio of Sir
Godfrey Kneller, circa 1690-1700; by permission of the National Portrait Gallery, London)*

neled the tension between loyalty and self-interest that many Englishmen felt during and after the Revolution into a richly human drama. When Benducar tries to tempt Dorax to take part in a conspiracy against the emperor, for example, the old soldier's reply appeals to the feudal values of honor and loyalty that Dryden associated with the Stuarts:

> He trusts us both; mark that, shall we betray him?
> A Master who reposes Life and Empire
> On our fidelity: I grant he is a Tyrant,
> That hated name my nature most abhors;
> ....
> But, while he trusts me, 'twere so base a part
> To fawn and yet betray, I shou'd be hiss'd
> And whoop'd in Hell for that Ingratitude.

The next play, *Amphitryon* (1690), is one of Dryden's funniest comedies, full of sexual humor, physical farce, and political stings. Jupi-

ter descends from the clouds complaining that "All subjects will be censuring their Kings." Mercury describes "Arbitrary Power" as "a knockdown argument" and accuses his "Brother Phoebus" of being "a meer Country Gentleman, that never comes to Court . . . drinking all Night, and in your Cups . . . still rayling at the Government." The servant Sosia complains that great lords refuse to pay wages, invoking the "Priviledge of their Honour," yet "stand up for Liberty and Property of the Subject," a speech immediately glossed by Mercury as having "something of the Republican Spirit." Political innuendo was by no means Dryden's only game in this deft reworking of Plautus and Molière, but the political dimension does often deepen and complicate the jokes.

The success of *Amphitryon*, according to Dryden, had much to do with songs written for the production by Henry Purcell. During the winter of 1690-1691 Dryden was hard at work revis-

John Dryden, 1693 (portrait by Sir Godfrey Kneller; by permission of the National Portrait Gallery, London)

ing the operatic *King Arthur*, which he had first written before the death of Charles, for a production with music by Purcell; it came on stage in June. Woefully neglected and virtually never performed as its makers intended, this fascinating reworking of the Arthur legend has sometimes been mounted as a grand opera, with much of Dryden's text pared away and bogus recitatives written in; more commonly, one hears concert performances of the music, with the parts Dryden wrote for Betterton and the other nonsinging actors entirely omitted. Like the Dorset Garden *Tempest*, the unperformed *State of Innocence*, and most other English "operas" of its period, *King Arthur*

is actually a semi-opera, with the plot carried forward by scenes of spoken dialogue, which frame several special scenes featuring singing, dancing, and spectacular scenic effects. Eschewing the version of the Arthur legend involving Launcelot and Guinevere, Dryden places the legendary king in a battle with the Saxons, and gives him a blind sweetheart, Emmeline. Magic plays a large role, as Merlin and his good spirits struggle against the power of the evil enchanter Osmond. Properly understood, this play is an allegory in which Arthur seeks to gain moral vision and Emmeline recovers her physical vision. There was undoubtedly a political allegory in the origi-

Illustration for Love Triumphant *in the 1735 edition of* The Dramatick Works of John
Dryden, Esq. *(engraving by van der Gucht, after H. F. B. Gravelot)*

nal, lost version that Dryden had prepared for
Charles, and although he insisted that he had
wholly altered the play, elements of that original
can be detected by those alert to the Jacobite innuendo that Dryden slipped into all of his late writings.

Although it was a splendid spectacle, *King Arthur* did little to relieve the poverty that Dryden
was suffering. Even before the premiere of *King
Arthur* in the late spring of 1691, he had probably begun working on *Cleomenes*, a formal,
Racinian tragedy based on a story from Plutarch.
Slowed down by illness but hoping to have the
play ready for a fall or winter opening, the old
poet asked his young friend Southerne to help
him finish the last act, and Southerne quickly
obliged. But the play was delayed by the machina-

tions of Shadwell; not until April of 1692 was a
censored version performed. After experiences
of this sort, Dryden's dramatic energy naturally
flagged, especially since he was finding his way toward a more reliable source of income in the
work he was now performing toward his translation of Juvenal and Persius, the forerunner of
the great Virgil project of the later 1690s. Early
in 1694 London audiences saw (and damned) a
work Dryden self-consciously declared his last
play, a mixed-plot tragicomedy called *Love Triumphant*. Stubbornly old-fashioned, these last two
plays might be mistaken for early works if we did
not know the dates of their composition. *Cleomenes*, largely in blank verse, includes one extensive
scene in rhyme, an echo of Dryden's first tragic

John Dryden, circa 1695, painted by James Maubert for bookseller Jacob Tonson (by permission of the National Portrait Gallery, London)

idiom; *Love Triumphant* has much in common with *Secret Love*.

Determined to write no more dramas, Dryden cast the prologue to *Love Triumphant* as the comic last will and testament of Dryden the playwright, and he remained more or less detached from the theater for the next six years, during which he translated all of Virgil and large selections from Ovid, Homer, Boccaccio, and Chaucer. Nonetheless, he evidently continued to think about the drama. His "A Parallel, Of Poetry and Painting" (in *De Arte Graphica*, 1695) devotes considerable space to a discussion of the unities, with references to William Shakespeare, Thomas Otway, John Fletcher, and Sir Robert Stapylton, and self-critical examples from five of his own plays. He put considerable time into arranging a performance (probably in 1696) of *The Husband his own Cuckold*, a comedy by his second son, John, who was now living in Rome, where both he and Charles were employed in the papal household; the youngest son, Erasmus-Henry, had become a priest and was also in Italy. This episode led to a partial reconciliation with his old antagonist Sir Robert Howard, uncle to the fledgling author and dedicatee of the published play. Like more-active playwrights, Dryden was offended by Jeremy Collier's *Short View of the Immorality and Profaneness of the English Stage* (1698), and used a poem in praise of his friend Peter Motteux to reply obliquely to Collier's charges of obscenity ("To My Friend, the Author"). He groused about badly performed revivals of his earlier plays, and frequently mentioned new plays by Congreve and others in letters to his cousins in the country.

Second page of Dryden's last surviving letter. Writing to a young cousin, Mrs. Elizabeth Steward, Dryden mentions "The Secular Masque" that he has written for John Vanbrugh's revision of John Fletcher's The Pilgrim *and refers to a falling-out with Thomas Betterton's acting company at Lincoln's Inn Fields, perhaps because—as he had written to Mrs. Steward earlier—he felt that the company could have given a better performance to* The Way of the World, *a new play by his friend William Congreve (MA 130; by permission of the Pierpont Morgan Library).*

John Dryden, circa 1698 (portrait by Sir Godfrey Kneller; by permission of Trinity College, Cambridge University)

It is one of the charming accidents of history that the last words Dryden wrote were for a theatrical occasion. As a favor to Sir John Vanbrugh, he composed "The Secular Masque," an allegory summing up the century now drawing to a close, for insertion in Vanbrugh's revised version of an old play by John Fletcher called *The Pilgrim*. Janus, Chronos, Momus, Venus, Diana, and Mars appear to banter briefly about the century; scoffing at love and war, Momus, the god of laughter and criticism, carries the day. Set to music by Daniel Purcell, Dryden's rollicking and irreverent verses on the passing of the century were first

heard as the poet lay dying: although one tradition reports that he died on the third night, we are not even certain that he saw "The Secular Masque" performed.

Very few of Dryden's plays are now read, let alone staged, and this omission distorts dramatic, intellectual, poetic, and cultural history. Playgoers who derive their view of "Restoration" attitudes toward sexuality from *The Country Wife* and *The Man of Mode* would have a more complex view if they could see *Marriage A la Mode* or *Aureng-Zebe*. Political historians and theorists who imagine that Dryden and his contemporaries embraced a complacent nationalism or an unthinkingly Eurocentric perspective should read *The Indian Emperor* and *Don Sebastian*. Students of later poetry who admire the passionate language of heroines in Pope or Keats may be surprised to discover that the source is actually Dryden. Musicologists who persist in the notion of England as a cultural backwater would profit by hearing a proper performance of the Dryden-Purcell *King Arthur*. To be sure, few of Dryden's plays can bear comparison with Shakespeare's; neither can Shaw's or Stoppard's. But this rich, uneven, complicated body of writing by the dominant literary man of the later-seventeenth century does not deserve its current place at the margin of the canon.

Letters:
The Letters of John Dryden, edited by Charles E. Ward (Durham, N.C.: Duke University Press, 1942).

Bibliographies:
Hugh Macdonald, *John Dryden: A Bibliography of Early Editions and Drydeniana* (Oxford: Oxford University Press, 1939);

John A. Zamonski, *An Annotated Bibliography of John Dryden: Texts and Studies, 1949-1973* (New York: Garland, 1975);

David J. Latt and Samuel Holt Monk, *John Dryden: A Survey and Bibliography of Critical Studies, 1895-1974* (Minneapolis: University of Minnesota Press, 1976).

Biographies:
Samuel Johnson, "Dryden," in his *Lives of the English Poets* (1779-1781), edited by G. B. Hill (Oxford: Clarendon Press, 1905);

Edmond Malone, volume 1 of *The Critical and Miscellaneous Prose Works of John Dryden,* 4 volumes, edited by Malone (London: Cadell & Davis, 1800);

Walter Scott, volume 1 of *The Works of John Dryden,* 18 volumes, edited by Scott (London: William Miller, 1808);

Charles E. Ward, *The Life of John Dryden* (Chapel Hill: University of North Carolina Press, 1961);

James M. Osborn, *John Dryden: Some Biographical Facts and Problems,* revised edition (Gainesville: University of Florida Press, 1965);

George McFadden, *Dryden the Public Writer, 1660-1685* (Princeton, N.J.: Princeton University Press, 1978);

James A. Winn, *John Dryden and his World* (New Haven, Conn.: Yale University Press, 1987).

References:
John M. Aden, *The Critical Opinions of John Dryden: A Dictionary* (Nashville: Vanderbilt University Press, 1963);

Gilbert Spencer Alleman, *Matrimonial Law and the Materials of Restoration Comedy* (Philadelphia: University of Pennsylvania Press, 1942);

Ned Bliss Allen, *The Sources of Dryden's Comedies* (Ann Arbor: University of Michigan Press, 1935);

Anne T. Barbeau, *The Intellectual Design of John Dryden's Heroic Plays* (New Haven, Conn.: Yale University Press, 1970);

Eleanor Boswell, *The Restoration Court Stage* (Cambridge, Mass.: Harvard University Press, 1932);

Louis I. Bredvold, *The Intellectual Milieu of John Dryden* (Ann Arbor: University of Michigan Press, 1934);

John Russell Brown and Bernard Harris, eds., *Restoration Theatre* (London: Arnold, 1965);

David Bywaters, "Dryden and the Revolution of 1688: Political Parallel in *Don Sebastian,*" *Journal of English and German Philology,* 85 (July 1986): 346-365;

J. Douglas Canfield, "The Ideology of Restoration Tragicomedy," *ELH,* 51 (Fall 1984): 447-464;

Canfield, "The Jewel of Great Price: Mutability and Constancy in Dryden's *All For Love,*" *ELH,* 42 (Spring 1975): 38-61;

Pierre Danchin, *Prologues and Epilogues of the Restoration,* 3 volumes to date (Nancy: Presses Universitaires, 1981-);

John Downes, *Roscius Anglicanus (1708),* edited by Judith Milhous and Robert D. Hume (London: Society for Theatre Research, 1987);

T. S. Eliot, *John Dryden: The Poet, the Dramatist, the Critic* (New York: Holliday, 1932);

Michael Foss, *The Age of Patronage: The Arts in England, 1660-1750* (Ithaca, N.Y.: Cornell University Press, 1972);

John Freehafer, "The Formation of the London Patent Companies in 1660," *Theatre Notebook,* 20 (Autumn 1965): 6-30;

William Frost, *Dryden and the Art of Translation* (New Haven, Conn.: Yale University Press, 1955);

James D. Garrison, "Dryden and the Birth of Hercules," *Studies in Philology,* 77 (Spring 1980): 180-201;

George R. Guffey, "Politics, Weather, and the Contemporary Reception of the Dryden-Davenant *Tempest*," *Restoration,* 8 (Spring 1984): 1-9;

Jean H. Hagstrum, *Sex and Sensibility from Milton to Mozart* (Chicago: University of Chicago Press, 1980);

Paul Hammond, "Dryden and Trinity," *Review of English Studies,* new series 36 (February 1985): 35-57;

Alfred Harbage, "Elizabethan-Restoration Palimpsest," *Modern Language Review,* 35 (July 1940): 287-319;

Phillip Harth, *Contexts of Dryden's Thought* (Chicago: University of Chicago Press, 1968);

Harth, Alan Fisher, and Ralph Cohen, *New Homage to John Dryden* (Los Angeles: Clark Library, 1983);

Leslie Hotson, *The Commonwealth and Restoration Stage* (Cambridge, Mass.: Harvard University Press, 1928);

Derek Hughes, "Dryden's *Don Sebastian* and the Literature of Heroism," *Yearbook of English Studies,* 12 (1982): 72-90;

Hughes, *Dryden's Heroic Plays* (London: Macmillan, 1981);

Robert D. Hume, *The Development of English Drama in the late Seventeenth Century* (Oxford: Clarendon Press, 1976);

Hume, *Dryden's Criticism* (Ithaca, N.Y.: Cornell University Press, 1970);

Hume, "Securing A Repertory: Plays on the London Stage 1660-5," in *Poetry and Drama 1570-1700: Essays in Honour of Harold F. Brooks,* edited by Antony Coleman and Antony Hammond (London: Methuen, 1981), pp. 158-172;

D. W. Jefferson, "The Significance of Dryden's Heroic Plays," *Proceedings of the Leeds Philosophical and Literary Society,* 5 (1940): 125-139;

Bruce King, *Dryden's Major Plays* (Edinburgh: Oliver & Boyd, 1966);

King, ed., *Dryden's Mind and Art* (Edinburgh: Oliver & Boyd, 1969);

King, ed., *Twentieth Century Interpretations of "All for Love": A Collection of Critical Essays* (Englewood Cliffs, N.J.: Prentice-Hall, 1968);

James and Helen Kinsley, eds., *Dryden: The Critical Heritage* (London: Routledge & Kegan Paul, 1971);

Arthur C. Kirsch, *Dryden's Heroic Drama* (Princeton: Princeton University Press, 1965);

Richard Law, "The Heroic Ethos in John Dryden's Heroic Plays," *Studies in English Literature,* 23 (Summer 1983): 389-398;

John Loftis, "The Hispanic Element in Dryden," *Emory University Quarterly,* 20 (Spring 1964): 90-100;

George DeForest Lord, ed., *Poems on Affairs of State,* 7 volumes (New Haven, Conn.: Yale University Press, 1963-1975);

Katharine Eisaman Maus, "Arcadia Lost: Politics and Revision in the Restoration *Tempest*," *Renaissance Drama,* 13 (1982): 189-209;

Michael McKeon, *Politics and Poetry in Restoration England: The Case of Dryden's Annus Mirabilis* (Cambridge, Mass.: Harvard University Press, 1975);

Judith Milhous, *Thomas Betterton and the Management of Lincoln's Inn Fields, 1695-1708* (Carbondale: Southern Illinois University Press, 1985);

Milhous and Robert D. Hume, "Dating Play Premières from Publication Data, 1660-1700," *Harvard Library Bulletin,* 22 (October 1974): 374-405;

Milhous and Hume, "Lost English Plays, 1660-1700," *Harvard Library Bulletin,* 25 (January 1977): 5-33;

Milhous and Hume, *Producible Interpretation: Eight English Plays 1675-1707* (Carbondale: Southern Illinois University Press, 1979);

Earl Miner, *Dryden's Poetry* (Bloomington: Indiana University Press, 1967);

Miner, ed., *John Dryden* (Athens: Ohio University Press, 1972);

Guy Montgomery, *Concordance to the Poetical Works of John Dryden* (Berkeley: University of California Press, 1957);

F. H. Moore, "The Composition of *Sir Martin Mar-All*," *Studies in Philology,* extra series 4 (January 1967): 27-38;

Frank Harper Moore, *The Nobler Pleasure: Dryden's Comedy in Theory and Practice* (Chapel Hill: University of North Carolina Press, 1963);

John Robert Moore, "Political Allusions in Dryden's Later Plays," *PMLA,* 73 (March 1958): 36-42;

Richard L. Oden, ed., *Dryden and Shadwell, The Literary Controversy and Mac Flecknoe (1668-1679): Facsimile Reproductions* (Delmar, N.Y.: Scholars' Facsimilies, 1977);

H. J. Oliver, *Sir Robert Howard (1626-1698): A Critical Biography* (Durham, N.C.: Duke University Press, 1963);

Annabel Patterson, *"The Country Gentleman:* Howard, Marvell, and Dryden in the Theatre of Politics," *Studies in English Literature,* 25 (Summer 1985): 491-509;

Curtis A. Price, *Henry Purcell and the London Stage* (Cambridge, U.K.: Cambridge University Press, 1984);

Alan Roper, *Dryden's Poetic Kingdoms* (London: Routledge & Kegan Paul, 1965);

Roper, "Dryden's 'Secular Masque,' " *Modern Language Quarterly,* 23 (1962): 29-40;

Arthur H. Scouten, "The Premiere of Dryden's *Secret Love,"* *Restoration,* 9 (Spring 1985): 9-11;

Peter Skrine, *The Baroque: Literature and Culture in Seventeenth-Century Europe* (London: Methuen, 1978);

Gunnar Sorelius, "The Early History of the Restoration Theatre: Some Problems Reconsidered," *Theatre Notebook,* 33, no. 2 (1979): 52-61;

Susan Staves, *Players' Scepters: Fictions of Authority in the Restoration* (Lincoln: University of Nebraska Press, 1979);

H. T. Swedenberg, Jr., ed., *Essential Articles for the Study of John Dryden* (Hamden, Conn.: Archon, 1966);

Eugene M. Waith, *The Herculean Hero in Marlowe, Chapman, Shakespeare and Dryden* (New York: Columbia University Press, 1962);

Waith, *Ideas of Greatness: Heroic Drama in England* (New York: Barnes & Noble, 1971);

Waith, "The Voice of Mr. Bayes," *Studies in English Literature,* 3 (Summer 1963): 335-343;

John Harold Wilson, *Mr. Goodman the Player* (Pittsburgh: University of Pittsburgh Press, 1964);

David Wykes, *A Preface to Dryden* (London: Longmans, 1977).

Papers:
There exists only one poetic manuscript by Dryden, the fair copy of his elegy for Cromwell, on display at the British Library. There are no holograph manuscripts of his plays or criticism. Some of his letters do survive in manuscript; Ward's edition lists their current locations, including the Houghton Library at Harvard, the Beinecke Library at Yale, and the Clark Library at U.C.L.A., which recently acquired one more letter.

Thomas Durfey
(1653-26 February 1723)

Carolyn Kephart

PLAY PRODUCTIONS: *The Siege of Memphis: Or, The Ambitious Queen*, London, Theatre Royal in Drury Lane, circa September 1676;

Madam Fickle: Or, The Witty False One, London, Dorset Garden Theatre, November 1676;

The Fool Turn'd Critic, London, Theatre Royal in Drury Lane, circa November 1676;

A Fond Husband: Or, The Plotting Sisters, London, Dorset Garden Theatre, May 1677;

Trick for Trick: Or, The Debauch'd Hypocrite, adapted from John Fletcher's *Monsieur Thomas*, London, Theatre Royal in Drury Lane, circa March 1678;

Squire Oldsapp: Or, The Night-Adventurers, London, Dorset Garden Theatre, circa June 1678;

The Virtuous Wife: Or, Good Luck at Last, London, Dorset Garden Theatre, circa September 1679;

The Royalist, London, Dorset Garden Theatre, June 1681;

Sir Barnaby Whigg: or, No Wit Like a Woman's, London, Theatre Royal in Drury Lane, October 1681;

The Injured Princess: Or, The Fatal Wager, adapted from William Shakespeare's *Cymbeline*, London, Theatre Royal in Drury Lane, circa March 1682;

A Commonwealth of Women, adapted from Fletcher's *The Sea Voyage*, London, Theatre Royal in Drury Lane, circa August 1685;

The Banditti; Or, A Ladies Distress, London, Theatre Royal in Drury Lane, circa January 1686;

A Fool's Preferment: Or, The Three Dukes of Dunstable, adapted from Fletcher's *Noble Gentleman*, London, Dorset Garden Theatre, circa April 1688;

Love for Money: Or, The Boarding School, London, Theatre Royal in Drury Lane, circa January 1691;

Bussy D'Ambois: Or, The Husband's Revenge, adapted from George Chapman's *Bussy D'Ambois*, London, Theatre Royal in Drury Lane, circa March 1691;

The Marriage-Hater Match'd, London, Theatre Royal in Drury Lane, circa January 1692;

The Richmond Heiress; Or, A Woman Once in the Right, London, Theatre Royal in Drury Lane, April 1693;

The Comical History of Don Quixote, part 1, London, Dorset Garden Theatre, May 1694; part 2, London, Dorset Garden Theatre, circa May 1694; part 3, London, Theatre Royal in Drury Lane, circa November 1695;

A Wife for Any Man, London, unknown theater, 1696 or 1697;

Cinthia and Endimion: Or, The Loves of the Deities, London, Theatre Royal in Drury Lane, circa December 1696;

The Intrigues at Versailles: Or, A Jilt in All Humours, London, Lincoln's Inn Fields, circa May 1697;

The Campaigners: Or, The Pleasant Adventures at Brussels, London, Theatre Royal in Drury Lane, circa June 1698;

The Famous History of the Rise and Fall of Massaniello, parts 1 and 2, London, Theatre Royal in Drury Lane, circa May 1699;

The Bath: Or, The Western Lass, London, Theatre Royal in Drury Lane, 31 May 1701;

The Old Mode and the New: Or, Country Miss with her Furbeloe, London, Theatre Royal in Drury Lane, 11 March 1703;

Wonders in the Sun: Or, The Kingdom of the Birds, London, Queen's Theatre, 5 April 1706;

The Modern Prophets: Or, New Wit for a Husband, London, Theatre Royal in Drury Lane, 3 May 1709.

BOOKS: *Archerie Reviv'd, Or The Bow-Man's Excellence: An Heroick Poem*, by Durfey and Robert Shotterel (London, 1676);

The Siege of Memphis; or, The Ambitious Queen. A Tragedy, Acted at the Theatre-Royal (London: Printed for W. Cadman, 1676);

Madam Fickle: Or The Witty False One. A Comedy. As it is Acted at his Royal Highness the Duke's Theatre (London: Printed by T. N. for James Magnes & Rich. Bentley, 1677);

Thomas Durfey (portrait by van der Gucht; Cyrus Lawrence Day, ed., The Songs of Thomas D'Urfey, *1933)*

A Fond Husband: or, The Plotting Sisters. A Comedy: As It Is Acted at His Royal Highness the Duke's Theatre (London: Printed by T. N. for J. Magnes & R. Bentley, 1677);

The Fool Turn'd Critick: A Comedy: As It Was Acted at the Theatre-Royall. By His Majesties Servants (London: Printed for J. Magnes & R. Bentley, 1678);

Trick For Trick: Or The Debauch'd Hypocrite. A Comedy, As It Is Acted at the Theatre-Royal, by His Majestie's Servants (London: Printed for L. Curtiss, 1678);

Squire Oldsapp: Or, The Night-Adventurers. A Comedy: As it is Acted at His Royal Highness The Duke's Theatre (London: Printed for J. Magnes & R. Bentley, 1679);

The Virtuous Wife; or, Good Luck at Last. A Comedy. As It Is Acted at the Duke's Theater, by his Royal Highness His Servants (London, in the Savoy: Printed by T. N. for R. Bentley & M. Magnes, 1680);

Sir Barnaby Whigg: or, No Wit Like A Womans. A Comedy. As It Is Acted by Their Majesties Servants at the Theatre-Royal (London: Printed by A. G. & J. P. for J. Hindmarsh, 1681);

The Progress of Honesty, or A View of Court and City: A Pindarique Poem (London: Printed for J. Hindmarsh, 1681);

Butler's Ghost: or, Hudibras. The Fourth Part. With Reflections upon These Times . . . (London: Printed for J. Hindmarsh, 1682);

The Royalist. A Comedy; As It Was Acted at the Duke's Theatre (London: Printed for J. Hindmarsh, 1682);

The Injured Princess, Or The Fatal Wager: As It Was Acted at the Theater-Royal, by His Majesties Servants (London: Printed for R. Bentley & M. Magnes, 1682; facsimile, London: Cornmarket Press, 1970);

A New Collection of Songs and Poems (London: Printed for J. Hindmarsh, 1683);

Choice New Songs Never Before Printed (London: Printed by J. Playford for J. Hindmarsh, 1684);

Several New Songs (London: Printed by J. Playford for J. Hindmarsh, 1684);

The Malecontent, a Satyr: Being the Sequel of The Progress of Honesty, or A View of Court and City (London: Printed for J. Hindmarsh, 1684);

A Third Collection of New Songs, Never Printed Before (London: Printed by J. P. for J. Hindmarsh, 1685);

An Elegy Upon the Blessed Monarch King Charles II. And Two Panegyricks Upon Their Present Sacred Majesties, King James and Queen Mary (London: Printed for J. Hindmarsh, 1685);

A Common-Wealth of Women. A Play: As It Is Acted at the Theatre Royal, by Their Majesties Servants (London: Printed for R. Bentley & J. Hindmarsh, 1686);

The Banditti, Or, A Ladies Distress. A Play, Acted at the Theatre-Royall (London: Printed by J. B. for R. Bentley & J. Hindmarsh, 1686);

A Compleat Collection of Mr. D'Urfey's Songs and Odes, Whereof the First Part Never Before Published (London: Printed for J. Hindmarsh, 1687);

A Poem Congratulatory on the Birth of the Young Prince, Most Humbly Dedicated to Their August Majesties King James, and Queen Mary (London: Printed for J. Knight & F. Saunders, 1688);

A Fool's Preferment, or, The Three Dukes of Dunstable. A Comedy. As It Was Acted at the Queens Theatre in Dorset-Garden, by Their Majesties Servants. Written by Mr. D'Urfey. Together, With All the Songs and Notes to 'Em, Excellently Compos'd by Mr. Henry Purcell (London: Printed for J. Knight & F. Saunders, 1688); modern edition, in *A Study of the Plays of Thomas D'Urfey*, by Robert S. Forsythe, 2 volumes (Cleveland, Ohio: Western Reserve University Press, 1916, 1917), II: 13-99;

New Poems, Consisting of Satyrs, Elegies, and Odes: Together with a Choice Collection of the Newest Court Songs, Set to Musick by the Best Masters of the Age (London: Printed for J. Bullord & A. Roper, 1690);

Collin's Walk Through London and Westminster, A Poem in Burlesque (London: Printed for R. Parker & A. Roper, 1690);

Love for Money: or, The Boarding School. A Comedy. As It Is Acted at the Theatre Royal (London: Printed for J. Hindmarsh & A. Roper, sold by R. Taylor, 1691);

Bussy D'Ambois, or The Husbands Revenge. A Tragedy: As It Is Acted at the Theatre Royal (London: Printed for R. Bently, Jo. Hindmarsh & A. Roper, 1691); facsimile, in *Five Restoration Theatrical Adaptations*, edited by Edward A. Langhans (New York & London: Garland, 1980);

A Pindarick Ode on New-Year's-Day, Perform'd By Vocal and Instrumental Musick, Before Their Sacred Majesties K. William and Q. Mary (London: Printed for A. Roper, 1691);

A Pindarick Poem on the Royal Navy. Most Humbly Dedicated to Their August Majesties, K. William, and Q. Mary (London: Printed & sold by R. Taylor, 1691); republished as *A Pindarick*

Poem upon the Fleet (London: Printed & sold by R. Taylor, 1692);

The Marriage-Hater Match'd: A Comedy. Acted at the Theatre Royal by Their Majesties Servants (London: Printed for R. Bentley, 1692);

The Richmond Heiress: or, A Woman Once in the Right. A Comedy, Acted at the Theatre Royal, by Their Majesties Servants (London: Printed for S. Briscoe, 1693);

The Comical History of Don Quixote. As It Was Acted at the Queen's Theatre in Dorset Garden, by Their Majesties Servants. Part I (London: Printed for S. Briscoe, 1694);

The Comical History of Don Quixote, As It Is Acted at the Queen's Theatre in Dorset Garden. By Their Majesties Servants. Part the Second (London: Printed for S. Briscoe & H. Newman, 1694);

The Songs To the New Play of Don Quixote. As They Are Sung at the Queen's Theatre in Dorset Garden. Part the First Sett by the Most Eminent Masters of the Day (London: Printed by J. Heptinstall for S. Briscoe, 1694);

The Songs to the New Play of Don Quixote. As They Are Sung at the Queen's Theatre in Dorset Garden. Part the Second Sett by the Most Eminent Masters of the Age (London: Printed by J. Heptinstall for S. Briscoe, 1694);

Gloriana. A Funeral Pindarique Poem: Sacred to the Blessed Memory of That Ever-Admir'd and Most Excellent Princess, Our Late Gracious Soveraign Lady Queen Mary (London: Printed for S. Briscoe, 1695);

The Comical History of Don Quixote. The Third Part. With the Marriage of Mary the Buxome (London: Printed for S. Briscoe, 1696);

New Songs in the Third Part of the Comical History of Don Quixote Written by Mr. D'Urfoy. And Sung at the Theatre Royal. With Other New Songs by Mr. D'Urfoy (London: Printed for S. Briscoe, 1696);

A New Opera, Call'd, Cinthia and Endimion: or, The Loves of the Deities. As It Was Designed to Be Acted at Court, Before the Late Queen; and Now Acted at the Theatre Royal, by His Majesty's Servants (London: Printed by W. Onley for S. Briscoe & R. Wellington, 1697);

The Intrigues at Versailles; or, A Jilt in All Humours a Comedy, Acted by His Majesty's Servants, at the Theatre in Lincolns-Inn-Fields (London: Printed for F. Saunders, P. Buck, R. Parker & H. Newman, 1697);

Albion's Blessing: A Poem Panegyrical On His Sacred Majesty King William the III. And on His Happy Return, and the Publishing the Late Glori-

ous Peace (London: Printed by W. Onley for R. Battersby & T. Cater, 1698);

The Campaigners: or, The Pleasant Adventures at Brussels. A Comedy. With a Familiar Preface Upon a Late Reformer of the Stage. Ending With a Satyrical Fable of the Dog and the Ottor (London: Printed for A. Baldwin, 1698);

A Choice Collection of New Songs and Ballads. The Words Made to Several Pleasant Tunes (London: Printed by W. Pearson for H. Playford, 1699);

The Famous History of the Rise and Fall of Massaniello, In Two Parts (London: Printed for J. Nutt, 1700 [the second part dated 1699 as *The Famous History and Fall of Massaniello: Or A Fisherman a Prince*]);

An Ode, For the Anniversary Feast Made in Honour of St. Cæcilia. Nov. 22. Anno Domini, 1700 (London: Printed for H. Playford, 1700);

The Bath, Or, The Western Lass. A Comedy, As It Is Acted at the Theatre Royal in Drury-Lane (London: Printed for P. Buck, 1701);

The Old Mode & the New; or, Country Miss With Her Furbeloe. A Comedy as It Is Acted at the Theatre Royal by Her Majesty's Servants (London: Printed for B. Lintott, 1703);

Tales Tragical and Comical ... From the Prose of Some Famous Antique Italian, Spanish and French Authors. Done into Several Sorts of English Verse, with Large Additions and Improvements (London: Printed for Bernard Lintott, 1704);

Wonders in the Sun, or, The Kingdom of the Birds; A Comick Opera. With Great Variety of Songs in All Kinds, Set to Music by the Most Eminent Masters of the Age (London: J. Tonson, 1706; facsimile, Los Angeles: William Andrews Clark Memorial Library, 1964);

Stories Moral and Comical (London: Printed by F. Leach, 1707);

The Trophies: Or, Augusta's Glory, A Triumphant Ode, Made in Honour of the City, and upon the Trophies Taken from the French at the Battle of Ramellies, May the 23d, 1706. By His Grace the Duke of Marlborough and Monsieur d'Auverquerque, and Now Fix'd in the Guild-Hall, London. Most Humbly Dedicated to the Right Honourable, the Lord Mayor, the Honourable, the Court of Aldermen and Sheriffs, and Also, the President and Court of Managers for the United Trade to the East-Indies (London, 1707);

Honor and Opes, or The British Merchant's Glory: A Poem (London, 1708);

Modern Prophets: or, New Wit for a Husband. A Comedy. As It Is Acted at the Theatre-Royal in Drury-Lane, by Her Majesty's Servants (London: Printed for B. Lintott, 1709?);

Songs Compleat, Pleasant and Divertive, 5 volumes, edited by Durfey; volumes 1 and 2 by Durfey (London: Printed by W. Pearson for J. Tonson, 1719);

Wit and Mirth: Or Pills to Purge Melancholy, 6 volumes (London: Printed by W. Pearson for J. Tonson, 1719-1720; facsimile, New York: Folklore Library, 1959)–volumes 1-5: same contents as *Songs Compleat, Pleasant and Divertive;* volume 6: new material, edited by Durfey;

New Opera's, With Comical Stories and Poems, On Several Occasions, Never Before Printed. Being the Remaining Pieces, Written by Mr. D'Urfey (London: W. Chetwood, 1721; facsimile, New York: Blom, 1968);

Collection: *Two Comedies by Thomas D'Urfey: Madam Fickle; or, the Witty False One. A Fond Husband; or, the Plotting Sisters*, edited by Jack A. Vaughn (Rutherford, Madison & Teaneck, N.J.: Fairleigh Dickinson University Press, 1976).

The origins and early years of Thomas Durfey are obscure; even his surname is equivocal, having been variously spelled in his day and this. Durfey himself preferred to Gallicize it as D'Urfey, the better to support his claims of kinship to the French romancier Honoré d'Urfé, author of *L'Astrée* (1607-1627); such claims, however, seem to have been the product of wishful thinking rather than actual fact, although Durfey's early biographers have generally taken such hearsay at face value. Durfey's father, Severinus, was probably a descendant of French Protestant emigrants, but there is no evidence that his mother, Frances, was related to the Elizabethan dramatist Shackerley Marmion, as is sometimes held. What is known for certain is that Durfey was born in Devonshire in 1653 and that he had moved to London by 1676, when his first play, *The Siege of Memphis*, was produced at the Drury Lane theater. Unfriendly contemporary sources state that he originally had been apprenticed as a scrivener, although Durfey himself claimed to have studied law before becoming a playwright.

Yet whatever the uncertainties of his origins, it can be established without question that few literary figures have enjoyed a career as long, as varied, and as successful as did Tom

To the Right Honourable
EDWARD *Earl of* CARLISLE,
Viscount Howard of Morpeth *&c.*

My most Honoured Lord,

THough the Subject of these Dramatick Sheets, has the Misfortune to be a Frenchman, and consequently his History the less esteemed by our Nation, to whom in the present Juncture they appear so obnoxious; yet I well knowing that your Lordships impartial Judgment will set the right Value upon Merit, and prize the Jewel as it deserves, let the Country from whence it came be never so barbarous, have presumed to introduce him to kiss your Lordships Hand, with this Excuse, that though he is himself a Native of *France*, yet he has left none behind him to equal his Character , or that dare pretend to half the Honour, Bravery or Justice.

About Sixteen Years since, when first my good or ill Stars ordained me a Knight Errant in this Fairy Land of Poetry, I saw the *Bussy D' Ambois* of Mr. *Chapman* Acted by Mr. *Hart*, which in spight of the obsolete Phrases and intolerable Fustian , with which a great Part of it was cramm'd, and which I have altered in these new Sheets) had some extraordinary Beauties, which sensibly charmed me ; which being improved by the graceful Action of that eternally Renowned, and Best of Actors, so attracted not only me, but the Town in general, that they were obliged to pass by and excuse the gross Errors in the Writing, and allow it amongst the Rank of the Topping Tragedies of that Time.

For a long time after it lay buried in Mr. *Harts* Grave, who indeed only could do that noble Character Justice, till not willing to have it quite lost I presumed to revise it, and writ the Plot new, mending the Character of *Tamira*, whom Mr. *Chapman* had drawn quite otherwise, he making her lewd, onely for the sake of lewdness; which I have here altered, and in the first Act mentioned a former Contract between her and *D' Ambois*,

A 2   which

The Epistle

which gives some Excuse for her Love afterwards, and renders the Distress in the last Act to be much more lyable to Pity.

Amongst the rest of your Lordships extraordinary Favours, for which I can never enough express my Gratitude, you did me the Honour at my reading this Play to you particularly to commend that Alteration, which, I confess, encouraged me to get it Acted, though without Success, till Mr. *Mounfort* did me the Favour; who, though he was modestly very diffident of his own Action, coming after so great a Man as Mr. *Hart*, yet had that Applause from the Audience, which declared their Satisfaction, and with which I am sure he ought to be very well contented.

I have great hopes (my Lord) that the Play, altogether as I have now written it, will in some measure answer your Expectation : your Lordship is so well read amongst the Poets, and so great a Patron of them, that you are capable of making a Distinction between a Judge and a Critick (especially as Criticks go now a days) that decry without Weighing, and judge without Examination, who are so greedy of that Title, that they would not change it for a Knighthood ; and take more pains to dissect an unhappy piece of Poetry though with loss Skill, than a Novice in Surgery would in the Hall, if he were put to read upon a Malefactor just beg'd for an Anatomy.

The Age grows more poignant every day than other ; and as immortal *Shakespear* says, the Toe of the Peasant treads so near the Heel of the Courtier, that it galls his Kibe. Some gradually aspire to Fame by Merit and Qualification ; but there are another Sort in Town here, that will be Wits and Criticks in spight of Providence and Nature, who are learned in nothing but a good Memory ; and if every Saying were restored to the right Owner, would appear as contemptible, as the deplumed Crow in the Fable, Alluding to the Satyr.

In this vile Age each raw, pert, callow Chit
Drunk with the fumes of indigested wit,
As much by wine inspir'd to play the Fool ;
One, that a month before was whip't at School,
For groveling dulness with inervate Force,
Shall dare to back the Muses soaring Horse :
So Magots, bred by the Suns genial Eye,
In th' Morning crawl, and before Evening fly.

These

Dedicatory.

These few Verses falling in this place so pat I beg your Lordships Pardon for inserting, who to my knowledge are so little an Incourager of all false Pretenders to Wit and Learning, that you always weigh the Merit of the Position, before you grant it proper ; and will rather silently smile at a young Critick, who is erroniously noysy, and consequently often impertinent , than be of his opinion for your own sake, or explode him before Company for his.

Into the unmerciful Claws of such Tyrants as these 'tis my Misfortune to fall, and without doubt should be worsted, if I had not your Lordships Patronage and Approbation, but *Momus* snarls not, when *Apollo* sings ; Envy must be appeased and Prejudice disarmed, when you, my Lord, appear in my defence: the Character of a true English Noble man, so well maintained in every Action of your Life, secures that Love and Admiration, which every one pays, that has the Honour to know you. The Critick veils to your more powerful Judgment in Wit ; your fellow Peers honour you for your stanch Loyalty to the King, and generous Candour for your Country, and for your admired Humility, uncommon Justice and generous Charity, three renowned Qualities, that hold the Mirrour, where may be seen the bright Visage of true Nobility : You are beloved by all in general, as you are, and deserve to be, admired by,

My most Honoured Lord,

Your Lordships devoted, faithful

and most humble Servant,

Tho. D'Ursey.

Dramatis

Dedication to Durfey's revision of George Chapman's Bussy D'Ambois *(from the 1691 quarto edition)*

Durfey. Of the seventy years Durfey lived, forty-five were spent in experimenting with virtually every literary form then in vogue: stage works encompassing tragedy, dramatic opera, comedy, masque, and musical comedy (a genre that Durfey himself created); songs ranging from solemn elegies to bawdy ditties; poems of every description from political satire to panegyrics; and English translations of French and Italian tales. Most of his works were well received by audiences and readers, if not by critics and rivals; indeed, his popular fame and aristocratic patronage inspired less fortunate writers to sneeringly envious satires against Poet Stutter. Yet, although Durfey's speech impediment was a matter of ridicule, it had no effect on his singing voice (which was, according to contemporary sources, a fine baritone that Durfey often accompanied with his bass viol) or his fortunes, as was proven by "Advice to the City," a duet which Durfey sang at court with none other than Charles II. Indeed, it was as much Durfey's songs as his plays that established his reputation in his own time; his six-volume collection *Wit and Mirth: Or Pills to Purge Melancholy* (1719-1720) has continued to be our best source for popular song of the late-seventeenth and early-eighteenth centuries.

Durfey's career as a dramatist began in 1676, in which year three of his plays, a tragedy and two comedies, were produced. *The Siege of Memphis*, his maiden effort, weakly imitated John Dryden's heroic style. Robert Forsythe considered it "an excellent example of a bad heroic play"; Durfey himself admitted that it was ill-conceived, ill-written, and ill-acted. He enjoyed surprising success, however, with the farcical *Madam Fickle*, which played to full houses, enjoyed the "particular applause" of Charles II, and was revived as late as 1711. Not as fortunate was *The Fool Turn'd Critic*, a satire on the would-be wits of the town, which was performed at about the same time and promptly failed despite its abundance of song clearly intended to charm an audience known for its music-loving predilections. *The Fool Turn'd Critic* is the first English play to have been published along with the musical accompaniment to its songs; significantly, many of those songs are performed by the fool of the title, Tim, a brainless but self-important young fop who constantly boasts of his musical knowledge.

The extremely successful *A Fond Husband* (1677), a bawdy romp that immediately became one of Charles II's favorite plays, quickly followed these two comedies. Thomas Shadwell, irked by what he considered the undeserved good fortune of Durfey's comedy, wrote a blistering preface for his own comedy *A True Widow* (1678) that railed against farce; in Shadwell's play, *A Fond Husband* is praised only by witless fops, and Durfey is pilloried as Young Maggot, "An Inns of Court Man, who neglects his Law, and runs mad after Wit, pretending much to Love, and both in spight of Nature, since his Face makes him unfit for one [Durfey was notoriously hard-favored], and his Brains for the other." Despite these drawbacks, Maggot is described by one of the characters as "the darling of the Ladies, they dote on him for his songs, and fear him for his Lampoons, and the men think no Debauch perfect without him"–an early indicator of Durfey's popularity. *A Fond Husband* was continually revived, its last known performance taking place in 1740.

After *A Fond Husband*, Durfey's next plays–seven in all from 1678 to 1686–were less favorably received: *Trick for Trick* (1678), *Squire Oldsapp* (1678), *The Virtuous Wife* (1679), *The Royalist* (1681), *Sir Barnaby Whigg* (1681), *The Injured Princess* (1682), *The Banditti* (1686) and *A Fool's Preferment* (1688) enjoyed little success. Only *A Commonwealth of Women* (1685) and *Love for Money* (1691) did well. However, from 1688 to 1695 Durfey was fortunate in having the assistance of Henry Purcell, his frequent collaborator and constant friend, in setting the songs in his new plays to music–particularly those of *The Marriage-Hater Match'd* (1692), *The Richmond Heiress* (1693), and the three-part *Comical History of Don Quixote* (1694 and 1695)–which greatly enhanced their good fortune with the London audience. Earlier, in 1681, Purcell had set a song for Durfey's *Sir Barnaby Whigg;* "Blow, Boreas, Blow" was the composer's first work for the comic stage. Purcell, better than any other musician of the period, was able to furnish Durfey's songs with settings that fit the lyrics, the context, and the performer; he continued to assist the playwright from the outset of his career as a theater composer until his abrupt ending. Indeed, Purcell's last musical work, composed just before his early death in 1695, was the setting of the well-known mad aria "From rosy bowers" for the second part of *Don Quixote*, sung by Letitia Cross in the role of Quitteria. Durfey undoubtedly felt the loss keenly, but he continued to experiment with musical theater, collaborating with popular, if decidedly lesser, composers such as John Eccles, Jeremiah Clarke, and Purcell's brother Daniel.

First two pages and chorus for a song in the first part of The Comical History of Don Quixote;
from The Songs To the New Play of Don Quixote *(1694)*

All of Durfey's thirty-two plays contain music. Inclusion of songs into dramatic works was typical of this period, initially influenced by earlier French plays, particularly the comedies of Molière; but Durfey went further than any of his contemporary countrymen in making his songs not only fit a play's action but advance it. This technique can be seen from the start, in the otherwise undistinguished heroic-rhymed tragedy *The Siege of Memphis* (where the song "Begone dull fear" inspires the hero and heroine to remain true to one another despite the machinations of their enemies); the extremely musical *Fool Turn'd Critic* prefigures Durfey's later extensive and influential use of the actor-singer.

The London in which Durfey began his career as a dramatist had only two theater companies, the King's Company at Drury Lane and the Duke's Company at Dorset Garden; the two companies joined in 1682 and continued their alliance until 1695, when Thomas Betterton and other seasoned performers fomented an "Actors' Rebellion" and seceded to form their own company at Lincoln's Inn Fields. These developments were carefully followed by Durfey, who like every experienced playwright of the period wrote his stage works around the talents of available players and tailored leading roles to best fit an actor's special "line." More than any of his counterparts, Durfey scouted for and made use of a performer's singing ability. Having found that the actor William Mountfort possessed, in addition to good looks and histrionic talent, a "clear, warbling Counter-tenor" voice, Durfey gave him eight highly functional mad songs to sing as the deranged hero Lyonel in *A Fool's Preferment*, all of them set by Henry Purcell; one of them, "I'll sail upon the dog-star," endures as a concert favorite. For Anne Bracegirdle, Durfey wrote *The Richmond Heiress*, which made full use of the actress's arch wit, vivacious youth, and fine singing voice. Indeed, *The Richmond Heiress* was the first play in which Bracegirdle sang, and to good purpose: rumor accused her of having been Mountfort's mistress and implicated her in his violent death by ambush (December 1692), but Durfey gave her a song in which she could proclaim that she was "still of Vesta's train, a maid . . . in thought and deed, as so will die"—words that her later reputation seems, from appearances at least, to have borne out. Bracegirdle sang this song as a duet with the comedian Thomas Doggett, for whom Durfey would write many comic songs; the role of Sancho in the first two parts of *The Comical His-*

tory of Don Quixote was specifically intended for Doggett's particular brand of buffoonery and his way with a ribald ditty. Doggett had begun his onstage singing career a year before *The Richmond Heiress* as the "dull softly fool" Solon in Durfey's *Marriage-Hater Match'd*, a highly successful farce in which the "Beauties and delightful Entertainment of the Lyric part" were praised by Durfey's contemporary Charles Gildon in the play's preface and evidently were much appreciated by the audience. In this play no fewer than six of the actors either develop their characters or further the plot through song—a tactic Durfey had previously employed in *Love for Money*, a popular comedy satirizing the then-fashionable girls' boarding schools and inspired by Durfey's firsthand observations during a brief stint as a music instructor at a girls' academy.

Durfey's characteristic style of frenetic town farce studded with well-placed functional songs—typically performed by the actors themselves rather than by the customary professional singers—proved very popular and soon attracted followers: by the mid 1690s many Durfey-style song-rich comedies came to the London stage. But the tremendous audience approval of Durfey's *Comical History of Don Quixote* was a response to something entirely new—comic semi-opera. Earlier semi-operas (or dramatic operas) by other hands were high-minded productions with serious plots, or adaptations of Shakespeare (Dryden's *Albion and Albanius* and *King Arthur*, Dryden and Sir William Davenant's *The Tempest*, Elkanah Settle's *The Fairy Queen*), embellished with essentially detachable masques; with *The Comical History of Don Quixote*, however, Durfey promulgated what can only be considered the first musical comedy, ingeniously altering Cervantes to fit the scope of the stage and the talents of the players and interspersing the action with highly pertinent songs. The third part suffered from reorganization of theater personnel after the "Actors' Rebellion" of 1695, but the first two parts played to packed houses and inspired a multitude of imitations. Among Durfey's disciples were Peter Anthony Motteux (*Love's a Jest*, 1696), the actor George Powell (*The Cornish Comedy*, 1696), Thomas Dilke (*The Lover's Luck*, 1695), Edward Ravenscroft (*The Anatomist*, 1696), and Elkanah Settle (*The World in the Moon*, 1697). Unfortunately, Durfey's trend setting was nipped in the bud by Jeremy Collier, whose *Short View of the Immorality and Profaneness of the English Stage* (1698) pilloried *The Comical History of Don Quixote* for its purported indecency and put a stop to simi-

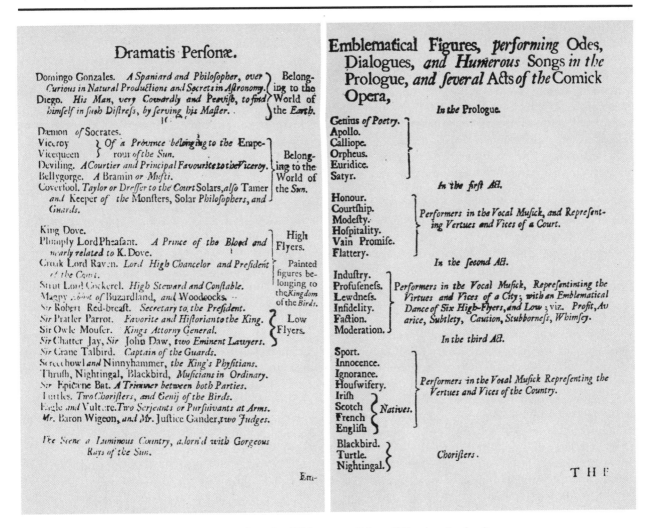

Dramatis personae from the 1706 quarto edition of Wonders in the Sun

lar efforts by other playwrights.

In happier times Durfey might have further influenced trends with his masque *Cinthia and Endimion: Or, The Loves of the Deities*, performed in the winter of 1696-1697. Durfey claimed that the work was originally intended for the entertainment of his royal patroness Queen Mary before her untimely death by smallpox, but evidence suggests that he actually wrote it a decade earlier, perhaps as an entertainment for Charles II, who apparently also had inconveniently died before the masque could be staged. *Cinthia and Endimion* was an unusual mingling of high-flown sentiment and acerbic social commentary, chiefly expressed in courtly songs for the amorous gods and in earthy anti-establishment ballads for the rustics who wish to overthrow Olympus. The masque seems to have met with some success—a contemporary account notes that it was "acted with applause," and it was revived in 1697; one observes that simi-

lar efforts by other playwrights immediately followed, such as Motteux's masque of Hercules and Iole in *The Novelty* (1697) and his *Acis and Galatea* (1701), Settle's lavish lunar/pastoral masque in *The World in the Moon*, Powell's *Imposture Defeated* (1697), which ended with a masque of "Endimion, the Man in a Moon," Charles Gildon's *Phaeton* (1698), and John Oldmixon's *The Grove* (1700). However, audience tastes were undergoing unamusing changes because of the stage-reform movement, which Durfey mocked in *Cinthia and Endimion* with a defiantly unmoral epilogue, spoken by Doggett in the role of the rebellious bumpkin Colin.

Collier's denunciation of the theater had a deadening effect on the repertoire. Durfey attempted to defend his style of comedy in his preface to his comedy *The Campaigners* (1698), but his argument was as much a failure as was his play. The sickly post-Collier tendency toward morally irreproachable comedies and tediously unamusing dramatic operas may have pleased the righteous but hardly made for full houses. Durfey seems to have endeavored to shake the status quo with *The Famous History of the Rise and Fall of Massaniello* (1699), a two-part tragedy of surprising power and originality that makes fascinating use of music and song to depict the ideological gulf separating the Neapolitan aristocracy from the rebellious rabble. *Massaniello*, however, was not a success onstage. The London audience longed for a more genteel type of variety and began to look to the Continent for entertainment, finding the novelty it sought in imported foreign singers (introduced by Betterton's company in 1695) and in the newest craze, all-sung opera based on Italian models.

As Curtis A. Price has noted, the period from 1700 to 1710 was a critical decade for the London musical theater; Durfey's *Wonders in the Sun: Or, The Kingdom of the Birds* (1706), a semioperatic extravaganza of real, albeit eccentric genius, fits into the middle of this period of upheaval. Durfey despised Italian opera; his prologue to a 1704 revival of his comedy *Madam Fickle* made contemptuous reference to the newly built Haymarket theater destined for imported operatic performances and bitterly observed that "Wit and Sence,/and pleasing Humour is quite gone from hence,/And foreign *Sol fa* grubbles up the Pence." Durfey wrote *Wonders in the Sun* to dazzle, amaze, irritate, and shock his audience with something even more innovative than *The Comical History of Don Quixote*: satirical semi-opera. By then fifty-three years old, looking back on a career that spanned four monarchies, Durfey could state authoritatively how much he considered England to have altered for the worse since the good old days of Charles II. Instead of enshrining England as the best of all possible worlds through elaborate tributes of song, dance, and spectacle, Durfey used the semi-opera format to portray a nation in decline, corrupt with factional strife, loose in moral fiber, shorn of the glory that had been hers in years past—a depiction greatly at variance with conservative and self-satisfied public opinion. In *Wonders in the Sun* the philosopher Gonzales and his servant Diego travel to the sun and meet its bizarre denizens, who offer their terrestrial guests musical entertainments that pour scorn on English politics and morals—as well as on Durfey's personal anathema, Italian music. That *Wonders in the Sun* was expressly intended to be performed at the new Haymarket theater only added to the irony. Not surprisingly, the work was a failure (a very expensive one, according to a contemporary source), all the more so because its competition at the rival theater was George Farquhar's latest comedy, *The Recruiting Officer*. Only one other play of Durfey's was produced after *Wonders in the Sun*—*The Modern Prophets* (1709), a flat failure.

Durfey's insular attitudes, so satirically expressed in *Wonders in the Sun*, informed all his works. A life spent exclusively in England showed its good side in Durfey's patriotic songs and poems in praise of monarch and country and its blind side in his political comedies (*Sir Barnaby Whigg*, *The Royalist*, *The Compaigners*, *The Modern Prophets*), which ridicule foreign governments and fashions, as well as members of the rival party (usually the Whigs, but Durfey tended to shift his loyalties according to prevailing trends). Durfey also played to his audiences by constant references to the latest town scandals and theater gossip. His works were calculated to entertain and were hence mostly comedies; they are characterized by rapid movement, full employment of available actors' powers, and solid, often farcical action. The usual Restoration fops, fools, and flirts are well in evidence. In most respects Durfey's plays are typical of the period; their use of music, however, is unusual and innovative. Durfey's most important contribution to the theater of his time was his use of functional song employed to advance the action of both comedy and tragedy. The effect of the songs is, of course, assisted by the musical settings provided by various composers; however, the lyrics are of paramount importance in achieving the desired dramatic effect. Through the lyrics—comical, witty, satirical, melancholy, amorous, or a combination thereof—Durfey develops characters, enhances key scenes, reinforces plot lines, and underscores thematic elements. Song is made to serve either as an extension of speech or as an intensifier of events within the play; in either case it is organic to the action.

Durfey's dual career as playwright and songwriter kept him in the public eye throughout his long life. Contemporary references are frank and plentiful, detailing in often invidious fashion Durfey's egregious vanity, pretensions to fashion, ulterior politics, inability to live within his means, predilections for social climbing and name dropping, penchant for dissipation, resilience in adversity, and smugness in success. His later years seem to have been full ones. Although Durfey

Frontispiece to Wit and Mirth

had fallen out of favor under James II, royal patronage resumed with the accession of Queen Anne, for whom Durfey frequently sang at court; George II and Queen Caroline attended the theater to see revivals of Durfey's plays and hear the annual rhyming orations that Durfey, apparently cured at last of his stammering, delivered in June of 1715, 1716, and 1717. The notoriously profligate young dukes of Dorset and of Wharton were generous patrons who included the playwright in their revels at Knole and at Winchendon. Always convivial, Durfey cultivated a wide range of acquaintances and was a familiar and conspicuous figure in the London scene, making his appearances at the theaters, coffeehouses,

and fashionable haunts followed by his servant Jack, sporting his song-won gold watch and diamond ring and otherwise playing the gentleman, to the intense spite of his less fortunate fellow writers. Among his many friends were Joseph Addison and Richard Steele, who advertised benefit performances of his plays in *The Guardian* (nos. 67 and 82, 1713) and *The Lover* (no. 40, 1712). Equally obliging although less appreciative was Alexander Pope, whose prologue to the 1713 revival of *A Fond Husband* ambiguously observed that Durfey "scorn'd to borrow from the Wits of yore;/ But ever writ, as none e'er writ before."

Durfey's last book, *New Opera's* (1721), published two years before his death, would seem to bear out Pope's apparent sarcasm. The book's three unstaged plays–*The Two Queens of Brentford, The Grecian Heroine,* and *Ariadne, or the Triumph of Bacchus*–range from the ridiculously eccentric to the wildly gory to the arguably estimable. *The Two Queens,* an ill-conceived parody of George Villiers, duke of Buckingham's *The Rehearsal* (1671), was apparently written around 1714, then subsequently revised with the addition of a great deal of song; *The Grecian Heroine* is bloody, bombastic, and dull. But *Ariadne* can be seen as the culmination of Durfey's many-faceted career, in which Durfey incorporated virtually all of the genres of lyric that he had explored during his nearly half-century of creativity. An operatic libretto in the Italian style, *Ariadne* synthesizes the Italianate all-sung format of recitative and aria with English-inspired comedy and song forms. The special pains Durfey took with *Ariadne* to prove his native language and music superior to those of Italy resulted in his best-written stage work; unfortunately, it has remained his most undervalued and undiscussed.

Two portraits of Durfey survive, each revealing widely differing but well-attested characteristics of the man's personality: one, the frontispiece engraving to *Wit and Mirth,* is a flattering full-face depiction of a brisk and good-humored man-about-town; the other, painted at about the same time by van der Gucht, grotesquely exaggerates Durfey's aquiline craggy features, unkindly intimating the touchy pride and hardened impudence resented and derided by enemies such as Tom Brown.

Durfey died at the age of seventy on 26 February 1723 and was interred in St. James's Church–London's most fashionable church at the time, which would have pleased him–at the expense of the duke of Dorset. Considering his roistering tendencies and well-known alcoholic excesses, he attained a ripe old age indeed: Richard Burridge in 1702 had described him as "old Tipple-pitcher Durfey, such a true Bacchanalian Priest, that he holds there is no such Sanity, as to be Sick with the Staggers, and the sweetest Life is to be Dead Drunk." Durfey had never married; a lampoon of 1692 mocked his unsuccessful wooing of a rich widow, who had refused him because of his atheism, and twitted his predilection for "the Ladies," who persisted in admiring him more as a singer than a suitor; a satire of 1704 taxed him with keeping a mistress. He left little save debts to the friends he made his heirs; however, legend avers that he kept his famous watch

and ring to the end and bequeathed them to Steele.

Durfey's hitherto neglected stage works have been receiving increased attention with the rise of scholarly interest in Restoration and early-eighteenth-century theater. Written expressly to divert an audience that knew what it liked, his plays are often immediate, topical, tuneful, and vivacious, and, at their best, exhibit a remarkable, forward-looking originality.

References:

Richard Burridge, *A Scourge for the Play-Houses: or, The Character of the English-Stage* (London: Printed for the author, 1702; New York: Garland, 1974);

Cyrus Lawrence Day, *The Songs of Thomas D'Urfey* (Cambridge, Mass.: Harvard University Press, 1933);

Edward J. Dent, *Foundations of English Opera* (Cambridge: Cambridge University Press, 1940);

William D. Ellis, Jr., "Thomas D'Urfey, the Pope-Philips Quarrel, and *The Shepherd's Week,*" *PMLA,* 74 (June 1959): 203-212;

Roger Fiske, *English Theatre Music in the Eighteenth Century* (London: Oxford University Press, 1973);

Robert Stanley Forsythe, *A Study of the Plays of Thomas D'Urfey,* 2 volumes (Cleveland: Western Reserve University Press, 1916-1917);

Cary B. Graham, "The Jonsonian Tradition in the Comedies of Thomas D'Urfey," *Modern Language Quarterly,* 8 (March 1947): 47-52;

Lucyle Hook, "Anne Bracegirdle's First Appearance," *Theatre Notebook,* 13 (Summer 1959): 133-136;

Robert D. Hume, *The Development of English Drama in the Late Seventeenth Century* (Oxford: Clarendon Press, 1976);

Hume, "Opera in London, 1695-1706," in *British Theatre and the Other Arts,* edited by Shirley Strum Kenny (Washington, D.C.: Folger Books, 1984), pp. 67-91;

Carolyn M. Kephart, "Actors as Singers in the Early Restoration Theatre," *Essays in Theatre,* 4 (November 1985): 61-76;

Kephart, "New Light on the Theatre from *Wit and Mirth, or, Pills to Purge Melancholy,*" *Theatre Notebook,* 38, no. 1 (1984): 4-10;

Kephart, "Thomas Durfey's *Cinthia and Endimion:* A Reconsideration," *Theatre Notebook,* no. 3 (1985): 134-139;

Kephart, "The Uses of Song in English Drama, 1690-1710," *Theatre Studies*, 33 (Winter 1988): 59-78;

Kathleen M. Lynch, "Thomas D'Urfey's Contribution to Sentimental Comedy," *Philological Quarterly*, 9 (July 1930): 249-259;

J. S. Manifold, *The Music in English Drama* (London: Rockliffe, 1956);

Judith Milhous, "The Multimedia Spectacular on the Restoration Stage," in *British Theatre and the Other Arts, 1660-1800*, pp. 41-66;

Milhous, *Thomas Betterton and the Management of Lincoln's Inn Fields, 1695-1708* (Carbondale: Southern Illinois University Press, 1979);

Robert Etheridge Moore, *Henry Purcell and the Restoration Theatre* (Cambridge: Harvard University Press, 1961);

Allardyce Nicoll, "Italian Opera in England: The First Five Years," *Anglia*, 34 (1922): 257-281;

Robert Gale Noyes, "Conventions of Song in Restoration Tragedy," *PMLA*, 53 (March 1938): 162-188;

Poeta Infamis: or, A Poet Not Worth Hanging, anonymous (London: Printed for B. C., 1692);

Curtis A. Price, "The Critical Decade for English Music Drama, 1700-1710," *Harvard Library Bulletin*, 26 (January 1978): 38-76;

Price, *Henry Purcell and the London Stage* (London: Cambridge University Press, 1984);

Price, *Music in the Restoration Theatre* (Ann Arbor, Mich.: UMI Research Press, 1979);

Eric Rothstein, *Restoration Tragedy* (Madison: University of Wisconsin Press, 1967);

Jack A. Vaughn, " 'Persevering, Unexhausted Bard': Tom D'Urfey," *Quarterly Journal of Speech*, 53 (December 1967): 342-348;

Visits from the Shades, anonymous, part 1 (London, 1704; New York: Garland, 1972);

J. A. Westrup, *Purcell* (London: Dent, 1937);

Wit for Money: or, Poet Stutter, anonymous (London: Printed for S. Burgis, 1691);

Franklin B. Zimmerman, *Henry Purcell, 1659-1695: His Life and Times* (New York: St. Martin's Press, 1967).

George Etherege

(1636-circa May 1692)

Frederick M. Link
University of Nebraska–Lincoln

PLAY PRODUCTIONS: *The Comical Revenge; or, Love in a Tub,* London, Lisle's Tennis Court at Lincoln's Inn Fields, March 1664;

She Would If She Could: A Comedy, London, Lisle's Tennis Court at Lincoln's Inn Fields, 6 February 1668;

The Man of Mode; or, Sir Fopling Flutter, London, Dorset Garden Theatre, 11 March 1676.

BOOKS: *The Comical Revenge; or, Love in a Tub. Acted at His Highness the Duke of York's Theatre in Lincoln's-Inn-Fields* (London: Printed for Henry Herringman, 1664);

She wou'd if she cou'd, A Comedy. Acted at His Highness the Duke of York's Theatre (London: Printed for Henry Herringman, 1668);

The Man of Mode, or, Sʳ Fopling Flutter. A Comedy. Acted at the Duke's Theatre (London: Printed by J. Macock for Henry Herringman, 1676).

Collections: *The Works of Sir George Etherege: Containing His Plays and Poems* (London: Printed for H. H. & sold by J. Tonson and T. Bennet, 1704);

The Works of Sir George Etheredge: Plays and Poems, edited by A. Wilson Verity (London: Nimmo, 1888);

The Dramatic Works of Sir George Etherege, 2 volumes, edited by H. F. B. Brett-Smith (Oxford: Blackwell, 1927);

The Poems of Sir George Etherege, edited by James Thorpe (Princeton, N.J.: Princeton University Press, 1963);

The Plays of Sir George Etherege, edited by Michael Cordner (Cambridge, U.K.: Cambridge University Press, 1982).

George Etherege has usually been grouped with John Dryden, William Wycherley, and William Congreve as one of the significant writers of Restoration high comedy. *The Man of Mode* (1676), his best play, is still familiar to readers, although not as well known as Wycherley's *The Country Wife* (1675) or Congreve's *The Way of the World* (1700). Its author is less known; most of our infor-

mation comes from letters written between 1685 and 1688, long after he ceased writing for the stage, and for some periods of his life contemporary references are few and scattered. Etherege was not a professional writer like Dryden; he wrote only three plays and a handful of unremarkable poems, spent more time as a minor diplomat than as a dramatist, and more time as a court wit than as anything else. Although *The Comical Revenge* (1664) and *She Would If She Could* (1668) are interesting, Etherege's reputation rests primarily on his masterpiece, *The Man of Mode.* Critics and historians have tended to follow his contemporaries in identifying him with the society depicted in the play and that depiction with the reality of Restoration court life. The play, although arguably atypical of comedy from 1660 to 1700, has come to epitomize for later readers and audiences the work of that mob of gentlemen who wrote with ease.

Much of our information about Etherege's life comes from registers and scattered legal documents. His grandfather was a London vintner who retired to Maidenhead, Berkshire, some time after 1628. His father, also named George, is a shadowy figure. Born in 1607, he spent several years on his father's land in Bermuda, returned to England in 1634, and married Mary Powney of old Windsor in October of that year. In 1636 he purchased a place at court worth two hundred pounds "before the troubles," probably fled to France in 1644, and died there in 1650.

Etherege was the second child and eldest son of this marriage. Born around the middle of 1636, probably in his grandfather's house, he was left dependent on his grandfather when his father died. William Oldys records the rumor that he "had some education at the university of Cambridge," but neither this report nor that connecting him with Lord William's Grammar School at Thame has ever been confirmed. To provide for him, his grandfather in 1654 apprenticed him to George Gosnall, a Beaconsfield attorney with connections to Clement's Inn, one of the London

Inns of Chancery. Legal documents bearing Etherege's signature suggest that he remained with Gosnall about four years; he was admitted to study law as a member of Clement's Inn on 19 February 1659 and was in London in connection with the aftermath of a lawsuit between his uncle and his grandfather in June of that year.

By the winter of 1663, however, he had left the law, made friends with Lord Buckhurst, and begun work on his first play. Since his plays and letters show him fluent in French, master of enough Latin to quote Horace, and possessed of the manners required at court, he must have begun to acquire these skills as a law student and perfected them in the intervening years. The four-year gap in the record strongly suggests the accuracy of Oldys's report that he "travelled into France, and perhaps Flanders also, in his younger years," possibly on the strength of having seen his uncle's lawsuit settled mostly in his favor. Frederick Bracher has plausibly reconstructed the kind of life Etherege probably led as a law apprentice, stressing the easy access between the Inns of Court and the playhouses. Although we do not know precisely how he managed his entrée into the society Oldys describes as comprising "those leading Wits among the Quality and Gentry of chief rank and distinction, who made their pleasure the chief business of their lives," it seems clear that the Restoration provided the incentive for the move from a sober career Etherege probably did not enjoy much into the lively and hedonistic circle surrounding Charles.

The Comical Revenge, Etherege's first play, was dedicated to his young friend Charles Sackville, then Lord Buckhurst and after 1677 earl of Dorset, and first produced at the Duke of York's theater in Lincoln's Inn Fields, probably in March of 1664. A strong cast, headed by Thomas and Mary Betterton as Beaufort and Graciana and including Henry Harris as Sir Frederick and the great comedian James Nokes as Sir Nicholas Cully, presented what the prompter John Downes later recalled as a production more successful than "any preceding Comedy; the Company taking in a Months time at it 1000 *l*." Its success was fairly lasting; Gerard Langbaine remarked in 1691 that the play had "always been acted with general approbation," and the number of performances recorded in *The London Stage 1660-1800* suggests the truth of his observation. The play was entered in the Stationers' Register on 8 July 1664; two quartos were printed in that

year, and five more appeared before the century's end.

The play's four loosely connected plots involve characters on three social levels. The high plot, presented largely in rhymed couplets, rings changes on upper-class love-honor and love-friendship conflicts familiar to theater audiences since Jacobean times. J. H. Wilson sums it neatly: "A loves B, B loves A; C also loves A, and D loves C. With much hocus-pocus, fine sentiment, and honor debates, the letters are jumbled about until the author comes up triumphantly with AB and CD. Multiplication, of course, is expected to follow." Audiences would have seen a parallel to the conflicts among Colonel Bruce, Lord Beaufort, and Lovis over Graciana and Aurelia a year or so earlier in Sir Samuel Tuke's *The Adventures of Five Hours*, a play which includes some comic elements.

Etherege's other three plots all involve gulling. In one, Wheadle, played by Samuel Sandford, recruits Palmer to help him fleece Sir Nicholas Cully, a well-named knight, puritan in politics only. After Etherege exploits the taste of the early 1660s for antipuritan satire, Wheadle's plot to marry his mistress to the knight and thereby control his money is foiled by Sir Frederick. The less-elevated characters and situations of this plot look backward to Ben Jonson and Thomas Middleton as much as the high plot does to Francis Beaumont and John Fletcher, but contemporary parallels in plays such as Dryden's *The Wild Gallant* (1663), James Howard's *The English Monsieur* (1663), and John Wilson's *The Cheats* (1663) are also plentiful. No rhyme and meter here; Etherege relies on racy and often slangy prose at the greatest possible remove from the abstractions and love "wounds" of the high plot.

The low plot, also in prose, features Dufoy (Joseph Price), a valet tagged by broken English who provides farcical relief and hits at the French. The play's title comes from IV.vi, in which Betty the maid gets her revenge on Dufoy for earlier pretending love for her by drugging him and putting him in a tub with the top and bottom cut out for his head and legs, thus publicly announcing that he has the pox. This strand is slight, involving only a few scenes.

These three plots are clearly subordinated to that which pits Sir Frederick Frollick against the widow Rich (Jane Long) in the game of love. They are one of J. H. Smith's gay couples, although here the man dominates the overall action. Lord Beaufort is Sir Frederick's cousin, and

Dufoy in his tub, in act 4, scene 6, of The Comical Revenge; or, Love in a Tub *(frontispiece to the 1715 edition)*

Mrs. Rich is Lord Bevil's sister; these relationships connect the lovers with the high plot. Dufoy is Sir Frederick's valet, and Betty is Mrs. Rich's maid; these relationships connect the lovers with the low plot. Sir Frederick's interest in Wheadle's women connects him to the main gulling plot, which he exposes in V.ii. Such connections are largely fortuitous; Etherege tries to unify his materials by creating parallels in language and situation and by using music and dance to establish a dominant tone. Both techniques have been studied by modern critics, especially Dale Underwood, Norman H. Holland, Jocelyn Powell, Virginia O. Birdsall, and Rose Zimbardo. Their work confutes the older view that the play merely jumbles together high heroics, low humours, farce, and intrigue.

Some parallels are obvious. Genuine affection leads to honorable marriage (Beaufort, Bruce, Sir Frederick); affectation leads to outwitting (Sir Nicholas and the sharpers are married to cast mistresses); vulgar appetite leads to disease (Dufoy). The high-plot characters are so constrained by convention that their plight approaches the ludicrous; Sir Frederick is so extravagantly devoted to the unconventional that he runs the risk of seeming perpetually adolescent. Specific actions are also contrasted. The duel between Beaufort and Bruce follows the parody duel between Sir Nicholas and Palmer (III.v and IV.iv). Wheadle baits Sir Nicholas with a "civil Message" (I.iii); in the next scene Graciana rejects Aurelia's message from Bruce. Bruce literally almost dies for love (IV.iv); Sir Frederick merely pretends death (IV.vii); in both cases, women are led to make and then retract a declaration of love. The tricks of the sharpers are paralleled by Sir Frederick's ruses, and the revenge of Betty on Dufoy is linked with that of the widow on Sir Frederick.

Patterns of action and character are reinforced by imagery, mostly of predation and aggression. Beaufort's love is made so ethereal that he cannot speak of it except in verse. Sir Frederick's is more earthy, but both lovers use conventional metaphors equating love with war. Sir Frederick's fishing images in I.ii are converted downward by Wheadle (I.iii); the metaphoric "wounds" of love in the high plot become the actual wounds of the pox in the low. Birdsall argues that contrasting images of illness or disease, warfare and death, and pastoralism set up an "essential contrast between a vital and an effete way of life," but one can notice these patterns without accepting a particular interpretation of their significance. Some critics suggest that these parallels attack both the high and low worlds in the play in order to set up the contest between Sir Frederick and the widow as the via media of the play. Others, like Zimbardo, argue that Etherege uses them as ways of replaying the same conceptions; in the replaying on different levels "the ideas of love and honor are not canceled out" but "enriched in texture and made more complex as well as funny." This more subtle view takes better account of the ending of the play, which affirms the marriages of the high-plot lovers as well as that of Sir Frederick and his lady.

Powell conceives of *The Comical Revenge* as a "dramatic fantasy of sheer exhilaration and enjoyment" which uses spectacle rather than plot or thematic parallels to present experience. He contrasts the stylized gestures of the high plot with the burlesque ones of the low, the antimasque of the servants dancing around Dufoy's tub with the masquerades of Sir Frederick and his band of fiddlers. The play becomes a "comedy-ballet" unified by its songs, dancing, and shows. Certainly several scenes have this quality, notably those in the tavern (II.iii) and in Covent Garden (III.ii). Powell and Robert Jordan are right in stressing the vitality of Sir Frederick as a key to the success of the play; attempts to fit him into a tripartite scheme of true wit, witwoud, and witless simply do not work.

Nevertheless, *The Comical Revenge* raises a question that has troubled many critics of *The Man of Mode:* how is one to interpret Sir Frederick Frollick? His name suggests harmless fun; to

frolic is to be merry, even joyful. But joy and mirth here are the acknowledged result of drunkenness and include crowning one's valet, breaking the heads and instruments of hired musicians, creating a public disturbance, fighting a "bloody war" with the constable, and breaking windows. Since Sir Frederick is probably past thirty, these can hardly be excused as adolescent pranks. Jenny pretends to be offended by them, referring with obvious irony to "heroic actions" and "most honourable achievements," but her anger is as easily appeased as that of the other characters. Sir Frederick has the grace to call his night's work "ill done," but no one seems to think it especially serious; boys will be boys even at his age. His view of women is equally childish. Having dined on Mrs. Grace, Mrs. Lucy, and perhaps Jenny, he has no qualms about Mrs. Rich. Her ruin, he thinks, will be her problem: " 'twas none of my seeking." Beaufort, one notes, neither admonishes his cousin for his past behavior nor hesitates to introduce him to the table of the man he hopes to make his father-in-law; yet this same Beaufort is fanatic about honor.

To take proper account of the way in which the plots of the play are resolved, Sir Frederick must be played as a wild but good-natured man more inclined to criminal conversation with "civil" ladies than to civil conversation with "ceremonious" ones. Arthur Huseboe points out that he serves "to moderate some of the excesses in the upper and lower plots," although whether he is also "clearly a force for social good" whom marriage will thoroughly reform is more problematic. The play's action, as Harold Weber notes, shows instinct and eroticism in conflict with the social need for order and stability; in these terms, "the metamorphosis of the rake is thus a necessary part of his dramatic character and function; his movement from sexual adventure to domesticity qualifies his initial sexuality but does not deny it." In this play the resolution of the plot does not undercut such an interpretation, and the moral issue is muted as long as the character of Sir Frederick is seen as consistent with the reward the denouement confers on him. In *The Man of Mode*, the issue is less easily avoided.

Robert Hume remarks that in *The Comical Revenge* Etherege tried to combine in "a sure-fire formula" four of "the most popular distinguishable modes of the time." Paradoxically, that fact suggests why the play is rarely read and never performed today. Modern readers expect generic decorum. We do not take easily to high-flown verse, certainly not when it is mixed with racy prose, or to high romance jostling con games and farcical gulling. We do not expect episodes from *Animal House* in *As The World Turns*, even if incidents and themes in the two can be paralleled. Confronted with such a range of tones, we tend to see the serious plot of Etherege's play either as distracting or as satiric. The former view destroys its unity; the latter turns its weak construction into a potential asset at the expense of historical probability and of the response of the ordinary reader.

In the dedication to the first quarto Etherege reminds Buckhurst that writing the play "was a means to make me known to your lordship." The two had exchanged bawdy letters in crude octosyllabic verse during the winter of 1663-1664, and Buckhurst may well have been the key figure in Etherege's initial preferment. The success of *The Comical Revenge*, however, opened other doors; its author was soon established as one of the group of court wits that included Sir Charles Sedley and John Wilmot, earl of Rochester. King Charles himself attended the opening of *She Would If She Could* on 6 February 1668. This play, although superior to *The Comical Revenge*, generated considerably less interest. Samuel Pepys's diary gives a lively account of the premiere:

and my wife being gone before, I to the Duke of York's playhouse, where a new play of Etheriges called *She would if she could*. And though I was there by 2 a-clock, there was 1000 people put back that could not have room in the pit; and I at last, because my wife was there, made shift to get into the 18*d* box–and there saw; but Lord, how full was the house and how silly the play, there being nothing in the world good in it and few people pleased in it. The King was there; but I sat mightily behind, and could see but little and hear not all. The play being done, I into the pit to look my wife; . . . and among the rest, here was the Duke of Buckingham today openly sat in the pit; and there I found him with my Lord Buckhurst and Sidly and Etherige the poett–the last of whom I did hear mightily find fault with the Actors, that they were out of humour and had not their parts perfect, and that Harris did do nothing, nor could so much as sing a Ketch in it, and so was mightily concerned: while all the rest did though the whole pit blame the play as a silly, dull thing, though there was something very roguish and witty; but the design of the play, and end, mighty insipid.

The poorly prepared production may well account for the indifferent reception of a play later popular with audiences and critics alike. Thomas Shadwell, with similar reason for complaint, praises the play in the preface to his play *The Humourists* (1671) as "the best Comedy that has been written since the Restauration," also citing "imperfect representation" as the cause of its poor reception.

Pepys's strictures notwithstanding, *She Would If She Could* has a more unified structure than *The Comical Revenge* and also a more consistent tone. Etherege replaces the multiple-plot-intrigue structure of his first play with a single plot involving pairs of characters and plot strands connected by the constant interaction of the characters rather than primarily by family relationships. The social range is restricted by the omission of con artists like Wheadle and Palmer; the action largely concerns upper-class characters and focuses more exclusively on one kind of intrigue, the battle of the sexes. Farcical materials are sharply curtailed; the sophisticated banter of Courtall and Freeman replaces Sir Frederick's fighting and window breaking; and prose replaces the verse and prose alternation in *The Comical Revenge*. The widow Rich develops into a pair of unmarried ladies, Gatty and Ariana; Sir Frederick is transformed into the gallants Courtall and Freeman. Courtall and Gatty are the "madcap" lovers, Freeman and Ariana the fainter and more subdued pair. The antipuritan satire and ridicule of folly evident in the gulling plot of the earlier play are retained but integrated with the other concerns of the new play in the persons of Sir Oliver and Lady Cockwood. The high spirits of Sir Frederick are also retained, but embodied in a new character, Sir Joslin Jolly.

In creating a better plot and establishing a dominant tone, Etherege does not sacrifice dramatic interest. Nor does he abandon themes and devices used in his first effort. Instead, he makes better use of them. *She Would If She Could* shows his continuing interest in theatrical effects such as music, singing, and dance; here, however, they have more frequent thematic interest even though they are still often fortuitously introduced. The imagery still identifies love and sex with hunting, gaming, eating, and warfare, but Etherege makes more subtle use of it, and of political imagery in particular. Strong contrasts are retained, but here between characters and scenes rather than between plots. Intrigue formulas still underlie the action, but *She Would If She Could* focuses as much on character as on action; except for Rakehell and Sentry, the characters also tend to be more interesting than those of *The Comical Revenge*. Conversation is better balanced with incident too. Wheadle and Palmer, and Sir Nicholas Cully in large part, are no more than their names; Sir Oliver and Lady Cockwood are much more than theirs.

The action of *She Would If She Could*, like that of other comedies of the period–and especially of those now most read–requires its lovers to come to some compromise between the individual's love of freedom and society's need for restraint, between the individual's need to gratify immediate appetites and her or his need to create a stable life which will survive the chaos of conflicting and transitory desires. The play uses sex and marriage in polite society as the vehicle for exploring this theme. Heroes and heroines are so in part because they understand and accept the oppositions involved. The action involves them in witty, often apparently frivolous banter which addresses the polarities, ambiguities, and ironies facing such couples and terminates in some kind of provisional accommodation which usually is to be sealed by marriage. These pairs are contrasted to other characters and relationships which represent the uncompromising or unaware, and, therefore, wrong or impossible "solutions" to the problem.

Robert Hume has recently exploded the myth of the rake in Restoration comedy. All too few critics distinguish between the libertine talk of plays such as *She Would If She Could* and libertine behavior. True, images of predation and conquest dominate that talk, but the talk leads to the altar and to the comic affirmation of dance. The elaborate discussions of Epicureanism, Hobbesian naturalism, and libertinism which have occupied many critics of Etherege since Thomas H. Fujimura in 1952 are as misleading in their way as was the presentation in an early period of the world of Etherege's plays as a sort of fantasyland unrelated to the real world. Such critics try to refute the moral objections of Richard Steele and Thomas Babington Macaulay by transforming stage comedy into philosophy; some earlier critics try to do so by making it irrelevant to life. Most of these plays, including *She Would If She Could*, are conventionally moral in basic theme and structure, a fact which irritates those critics who valorize social revolt and irreconcilable intellectual conflicts.

The strong thematic interest of *She Would If She Could* would be subliminal in production, at least for most audiences. Nevertheless, what is presented can be apprehended at some level by an interested playgoer, and the play presents contracts that would be noticeable in any coherent production. One of the most obvious of these identifies the city with freedom and sexual license and the country with convention and restraint. For example, Gatty is played off against Ariana in these terms in I.ii:

> ARIANA. But we have left the benefit of the fresh air, and the delight of wandering in the pleasant groves.
> GATTY. Very pretty things for a young gentlewoman to bemoan the loss of indeed, that's newly come to a relish of the good things of this world.
> ARIANA. Very good, sister!
> GATTY. Why, hast not thou promised me a thousand times, to leave off this demureness?
> ARIANA. But you are so quick.
> GATTY. Why, would it not make anyone mad to hear thee bewail the loss of the country? speak but one grave word more, and it shall be my daily prayers thou may'st have a jealous husband, and then you'll have enough of it I warrant you.

Another contrast, and one of Etherege's triumphs in the play, is between the Cockwoods and Sir Joslin Jolly. Sir Oliver and his lady suggest repression and the hypocrisy and subterfuge that accompany it. Lady Cockwood's denial of instinct is expressed in the castle or fortress imagery used about her home, in her inability to admit her sexual desires even to herself, and in her insistence on cloaking them in the outmoded language of *préciosité*. She is the quintessential equation of honor with new brocade. Sir Oliver is impotent, especially with her but perhaps with all women; he talks of his exploits, but his talk seems especially cheap. The play implies that she would be different if he were, and expresses this topsy-turvy relationship in political imagery that puts the woman at the helm of this particular matrimonial ship. It is hard to find the comic resolution convincing in their case even though Etherege clearly does not treat them as harshly as a more satirical dramatist, such as Wycherley, would have done.

At the other extreme is Sir Joslin Jolly, whose name recalls Sir Frederick Frollick's. He is lord of misrule, Birdsall's "eternal fertility spirit, the Dionysian reveler." Powell remarks that he is

The unmasking of Lady Cockwood in act 3, scene 3, of She Would If She Could *(frontispiece to the 1715 edition)*

entirely fictional; his antics "have no literal reference to reality." Like Dionysus, he is inevitably associated with wine, women, and song, and he ends the play by inviting the other characters to join the final dance which signifies, at least for the time being, the restoration of social harmony.

Between the symbolic representations of repression and impotence on the one hand and fecundity and license on the other, the two pairs of lovers find their way to a reasonable compromise worked out in repeated witty exchange. Both couples clearly realize the difficulty of their task and the tentativeness of any solution, but it seems wrong to read the play as a defeat for either men or women, as the triumph of convention over freedom, or as a satiric attack on conventional values

spoiled by a tacked-on ending paying lip service to social form. The characters get something for what they give up; how long they retain what they get, Etherege implies, is uncertain but at least partially under their control.

As Dale Underwood and Peter Holland have noted, the sets for *She Would If She Could* can be made to express the basic contrasts of the play. Lady Cockwood, and to some extent Sir Oliver, are associated with private interiors, Sir Joslin with public places of amusement and adventure: the Bear tavern, the New Exchange, the Mulberry Garden, New Spring Garden. Fewer scene changes are required than in *The Comical Revenge*, and scenes tend to alternate between repressive interiors and the fashionable locations which, by contrast, celebrate the openness and freedom which the couples seek.

Although not as popular as *The Comical Revenge, She Would If She Could* was not a failure, either. Entered in the Stationers' Register on 24 June 1668, it went through five editions in some fifty years. It was performed throughout its century and into the next and has been produced at least twice in this century; Michael Cordner records British performances in 1976 and 1979, for example.

The Comical Revenge could not succeed on the modern stage because modern audiences would not accept a "straight" rendering of the high plot, and any production which played that plot for laughs (as the Guthrie production [June 1980] played the sentimental plot of John O'Keeffe's 1791 play *Wild Oats*) would still lack a coherent tone. *She Would If She Could*, on the other hand, can still be successfully produced. Although Fujimura is right in noting that "the courtship is left pretty much to chance, and the final agreement among the lovers is due principally to accident and opportunity," modern audiences are more accustomed to plays in which "*talk* has become an important kind of action."

Most critics who do not see *The Comical Revenge* as the first comedy of manners accord that honor to *She Would If She Could*. One need not accept their definitions of Restoration comedy or their accounts of dramatic history in the late-seventeenth century to agree at least that Etherege's second play offered something new to its initial audiences. Hume sees "resemblances in the parts, but no parallel to the nature of the play as a whole. . . . *She wou'd* is unique: its combination of refinement and a London setting, and its emphasis on wit and character instead of intrigue are unparalleled." The originality of Etherege's contribution was also noted by his contemporaries, not always approvingly. Alexander Radcliffe's "News from Hell" (1682) places the playwright there

    for writing superfine,
With words correct in every Line:
And one that does presume to say,
A Plot's too gross for any Play:
Comedy should be clean and neat,
As Gentlemen do talk and eat.
So what he writes is but Translation
From Dog and Pa[r]tridge conversation.

Since the Dog and Partridge was a fashionable tavern, Radcliffe seems to be suggesting that

Etherege merely records rather than creates (through heightening and judicious selection) his language. This, like H. F. B. Brett-Smith's conclusion that in these plays audiences "were suddenly confronted with the world they knew," suggests a stark naturalism careful examination will hardly confirm. Nevertheless, Etherege brings to dramatic life both the fashionable shops and pleasure gardens of London and its environs and also, in his characters, those who sought diversion there, integrating such scenes and characters into a traditional, highly artificial and stylized dramatic form.

Etherege's standing at court, established by two plays and a group of aristocratic friends, was further confirmed by his appointment in 1668 as a Gentleman of the Privy Chamber in Ordinary and secretary to Sir Daniel Harvey, England's ambassador to Turkey. He accompanied Harvey to Constantinople late in 1668 and remained there until 1671, returning to London in the fall after a stay in Paris. Little is known of his stay abroad except for one shrewd letter dating from early 1670, written to Joseph Williamson in the office of the secretary of state.

Upon his return to London, Etherege seems to have taken up the easy, directionless life he had left. His graceful but undistinguished songs and lyrics were widely circulated in manuscript and frequently printed in collections of occasional verse. These he continued to produce, and they exemplify his life as well as do his plays. Some adopt the pastoral mode, addressing a Celia or a Cloris or offering a dialogue between a Phillis and her Strephon. He tries his hand at the "imperfect enjoyment" poems so much in vogue, at dramatic monologue; he writes in praise of basset and of the poetry of Margaret Cavendish; he enjoys "rambles" and a bawdy exchange of verse letters. He is best at love songs, songs not as good as Dryden's or Matthew Prior's, perhaps, but polished, tonally secure, and elegant in their use of the formulas of the day. In "To a Lady, Asking Him How Long He Would Love Her," for example, he tries the carpe diem theme:

Cloris, it is not in our power
To say how long our love will last,
It may be we within this hour
May lose those joys we now may taste;
    The blessed that immortal be
    From change in love are only free.
....
Then since we mortal lovers are,
Let's question not how long 'twill last,

But while we love let us take care
Each minute be with pleasure past;
   It were a madness to deny
   To live because we're sure to die.

As many poems are no doubt lost as are preserved, but enough exist to prove that poetry, like drama, was a casual interest, not a vocation. Indeed, Etherege pursued women and the gaming table more avidly. Both interests are referred to nostalgically in a much later (1688) letter to Henry Jermyn, Lord Dover: "Had I spent my time as wisely as Dick Brett, Sir Patrick Trant, and many others, I might discover misteries which wou'd deserve your favour, but I need not tell you I have preferr'd my pleasure to my profit and have followed what was likelier to ruin a fortune already made than make one: play and women. Of the two the Sex is my strongest passion." In the same letter he reports having given up "the very thought of play," but he seems never to have given up his carnal pursuits for more lasting emotional attachments.

Oldys reports that "it was ascribed to his indolence, or too great an indulgence in his pleasures, rather than any close engagement at that time to more serious applications in the affairs of State, that his ingenuity was so alienated from the exercise of his pen," and adds that he was apparently "too free of his purse in gaming, and of his constitution with women and wine; which embarrassed his fortune, impaired his health, and brought some satirical reflexions upon him." From John Bowman, an old actor, Oldys had the report that "Sir George was, in his person, a fair, slender, genteel man; but spoiled his countenance with drinking, and other habits of intemperance; and in his deportment, very affable and courteous, of a sprightly and generous temper. . . ."

The contemporary "reflexions" Oldys mentions include several poems which conferred on Etherege the sobriquet "gentle George," and at least one rather more acerbic one cited by Oldys from a manuscript copy "found among the Earl of Arlington's papers, in 1739":

Eth'rege by Knight and Lords united club,
Pickled his *Play*, and *Person* in a *Tub*:
For *Comical Revenge*, the Lord thought fit
To have a single Trial of his Wit;
In which the Title, if well understood,
Does shew, he *wou'd* write better *if he cou'd*:
But he and 's Play have different mishaps;
One's purg'd to cure, t'other to get more claps.

His meagre face did his bad fate fortell;
That, like himself, 'twoud not be cout'nanc'd well:
Instead of sense, he welcomes you with sound;
For his Fee-simple was two hundred pound:
Yet let us not at this great bounty scoff;
He's the first Fire-ship e'er was well paid off.
Ovid to *Pontus* sent, for too much Wit;
Eth'rege to *Turkey*, for the want of it.

Warned by the careless productions of *She Would If She Could*, Etherege seems to have taken pains to ensure that his third and last play, *The Man of Mode*, fared better. Dryden himself contributed the epilogue, Sir Car Scroope the prologue. The first recorded performance, probably the premiere, took place at Dorset Garden theater on 11 March 1676, with King Charles II in the audience. Betterton acted Dorimant and Mrs. Betterton, Bellinda; William Smith, who had created the roles of Bruce in *The Comical Revenge* and Courtall in *She Would If She Could*, acted Sir Fopling Flutter. Downes lists Elizabeth Barry as having played Loveit; Betterton's casting here, as Huseboe suggests, may have been designed to encourage the audience to identify Dorimant with the earl of Rochester. Barry was then Rochester's mistress; Rochester was as fond of quoting Edmund Waller as is Dorimant; and Betterton is said to have "dressed himself to resemble Rochester." Oddly, Downes lists no actress for Harriet. The play was entered in the Stationers' Register on 15 June 1676; quarto 1 was published shortly thereafter. Its success was immediate and lasting; Downes tells us that, being "well Cloath'd and well *Acted*," it "got a great deal of Money." The duchess of York accepted the dedication of the printed text, which Etherege calls "the first thing I have produced in your service."

Many critics have agreed with W. B. Carnochan that each of Etherege's earlier plays "is apprentice work for *The Man of Mode*." Perhaps so, at least in the sense that one can see parallels and a certain line of development: each successive play, for example, is clearly superior to its predecessor. In the eight years following *She Would If She Could* theater in London changed considerably. Libertine and fop remained, as did the contrasts between city and country, young and old, wits and would-be wits, and bold and more staid pairs of lovers. These elements attest to the continuing reliance of comic drama on formulaic characters and plots. In important ways, however, *The Man of Mode* is unlike the earlier comedies. In the first place, it focuses on Dorimant, centering every part of the action on him. The

(1)

THE
Man of Mode,
O R,

Sr Fopling Flutter.

ACT I. SCENE I.

*A Dreſſing Room, a Table Covered with a Toilet,
Cloaths laid ready.*

Enter Dorimant *in his Gown and Slippers, with a Note in
his hand made up, repeating Verſes.*

Dor. NOW for ſome Ages had the pride of Spain,
       Made the Sun ſhine on half the World in vain.
                          [*Then looking on the Note.*

             For Mrs. Loveit.
What a dull inſipid thing is a Billet doux written in
Cold blood, after the heat of the buſineſs is over?
It is a Tax upon good nature which I have
Here been labouring to pay, and have done it,
Put with as much regret, as ever Fanatick paid
The Royal Aid, or Church Duties ; 'Twill
Have the ſame fate I know that all my notes
To her have had of late, 'Twill not be thought
Kind enough. Faith Women are i'the right
When they jealouſly examine our Letters, for in them
              B   We

First page of act 1, scene 1, in the 1676 quarto edition of Etherege's third play. After quoting the first two lines from Edmund Waller's Of a War with Spain, *Dorimant speaks in prose, but the printer set his speech as though it were verse.*

emphasis on talk as action is obvious. Dorimant, Harriet, Loveit, Bellinda, Sir Fopling–all are more fully realized and individuated than similar types in the earlier plays. The language is more obviously witty and polished and exhibits greater nuance and subtlety. The tone is distinctly harder. In keeping with theatrical trends in the mid 1670s, the play emphasizes sex and the risqué far more than did *The Comical Revenge* or *She Would*

If She Could. In those plays, for example, the hero merely talks of sexual adventures; Courtall in the latter play goes to some trouble to avoid Lady Cockwood's advances. By 1676 a servant can enter "*tying up linen*" after his master's sexual encounter (IV.ii), and it is possible to stage the china scene in *The Country Wife.*

The plot of *The Man of Mode* is slight and uncomplicated. Dorimant occupies himself escaping

Mrs. Loveit, a mistress he has tired of, while simultaneously trying to seduce Bellinda and persuade Harriet to marry him. Medley is his confidant, Young Bellair and Emilia the more conventional couple. Loveit and Old Bellair's effort to marry Young Bellair to Harriet provide some block to the Dorimant-Harriet plot, and Old Bellair provides the conventional block to the marriage of his son and Emilia. The important block to Dorimant's capture of Harriet, however, is the lady herself; Old Bellair's infatuation with Emilia is as easily disposed of as his wish that his son marry Harriet. That the blocking action is so casually handled and that Sir Fopling is largely irrelevant to the plot suggest the subordination of action to character and dialogue characteristic of the play. Even John Dennis admits "there is no great Mastership in the Design of it."

Etherege's plays have never been fertile ground for source hunting, and this play is no exception. The possible debt of *The Comical Revenge* to *The Adventures of Five Hours* has been noted, but the conventional and formulaic character of most comic plots of the period make borrowing difficult to establish. Jean Auffret and others have argued that *The Man of Mode* owes something to Molière's *Les Précieuses ridicules* (1659), but the careful reader will see only Sir Fopling's calling the roll of his servants as a likely debt. Scholars have recorded very few specific borrowings. Even Langbaine, notorious for recording "plagiaries," is silent about Etherege.

In characterization *The Man of Mode* goes well beyond Etherege's earlier achievements. Dorimant, Sir Fopling, Mrs. Loveit, Bellinda, and Harriet are the most remarkable of his creations, but nearly every character is vivid except the conventional pair of lovers and Lady Townley, whose roles suggest formula presentation. Etherege is successful not only with these major characters but also with those who take the minor roles–the orange woman and the shoemaker in I.i, for example. The former's disgust at the "filthy trick these men have got of kissing one another!" (I.i) and her apt remark to Dorimant and Medley, "what you gentlemen say it matters not much . . ." (I.i), go well beyond necessary exposition, as does the shoemaker's confidence in I.i that his marital relations are those of gentlemen:

> 'Zbud, there's never a man i' the town lives more like a gentleman, with his wife, than I do. I never mind her motions, she never inquires into mine, we speak to one another civilly, hate one another heartily, and because 'tis vulgar to lie and soak together, we have each of us our several settle-bed.

In Lady Woodvill's few lines, to take another example, Etherege makes good his implicit promise to present "a great admirer of the forms and civility of the last age" (I.i). Thomas Otway might have made Old Bellair's pursuit of Emilia disgusting. Etherege makes it comical, reserving for the old man the remnants of Sir Frederick's and Sir Joslin's exuberance; it is Old Bellair who calls for the dance at the end of the play.

Sir Fopling Flutter has always been admired and had many descendants, the best known of them George Farquhar's Lord Foppington. Although neither he nor his female counterpart Lady Woodvill appears until act 3, both have been announced and described in act 1. Sir Fopling is "the pattern of modern foppery" (I.i). In the plot he serves to give Dorimant the excuse he wants for abandoning Loveit. Thematically, he presents shadow without substance, the ultimate danger to which Dorimant, Harriet, and all others who must concern themselves with social appearances inevitably expose themselves. He is characterized in terms of conventional surfaces, of clothing especially, and his identification of people with things is everywhere emphasized, whether in Dorimant's "I would fain wear in fashion as long as I can, sir, 'tis a thing to be valued in men as well as baubles" and "Truly there is a *bel air* in galleshes as well as men" (III.ii), in the catalog of Sir Fopling's clothes in the same scene, or in his fondness for masks (IV.i). Although he says "my clothes are my creatures" (IV.i), in truth he is no more than equipage. Caricature or condemnation would have been easy, but Etherege instead gives his character unfailing good humor and a capacity for sublime self-satisfaction which fascinate and amuse rather than disgust.

Dorimant and the three women he involves himself with have elicited far more ambivalent responses. Although acknowledging in *Spectator* no. 65 (1711) that the play is widely considered the pattern of genteel comedy, Richard Steele cited a generous selection of incidents and speeches to argue Dorimant considerably less than "a fine Gentleman . . . honest in his Actions, and refined in his Language." Rather, he is "a direct Knave in his Designs, and a Clown in his Language" and "this whole celebrated Piece is a perfect Contradiction to good Manners, good Sense, and common Honesty; . . . there is nothing in it but what is

Elizabeth Barry, the actress who played Mrs. Loveit in the first production of The Man of Mode
(engraving by R. B. Parkes, based on a 1689 painting by Sir Godfrey Kneller)

built upon the Ruin of Virtue and Innocence. . . . I allow it to be Nature, but it is Nature in its utmost Corruption and Degeneracy."

To this Collieresque attack John Dennis replied that corrupt and degenerate nature were proper subjects of ridicule and ridicule the proper subject of comedy. Comedy does not exhibit moral patterns; it invites laughter. Dorimant pleases because he is true to life; "a young Courtier, haughty, vain, and prone to Anger, amorous, false, and inconstant. He debauches *Loveit*, and betrays her; loves *Belinda*, and as soon as he enjoys her is false to her." The play gives "a true Resemblance of the Persons both in Court and Town, who liv'd at the Time when that Comedy was writ," as is proved by everyone then having remarked that Dorimant was a true picture of the earl of Rochester.

The issues argued by those involved in the Collier controversy dominated the discussion of Restoration comedy at least through the middle of the present century. In that discussion the character of Dorimant figures prominently, partly be-

cause he and his creator have been seen as exemplars of Restoration court life. It is important to note that Steele and Dennis, who are fairly typical representatives of the two sides, agree on several fundamental points. Both think that Dorimant is an accurate representation of a court wit of the period—the play "mirrors" its age. Both think Dorimant morally reprehensible. Both agree that plays can and do seriously influence the behavior of audiences and readers. They disagree primarily about whether comedy should be exemplary or satiric, about whether it presents patterns for emulation or characters which provoke corrective laughter.

Charles Lamb's contribution to the debate is often unfairly maligned. Although few would agree with his notion that Restoration comedy has "no reference whatever to the world that is," he does insist that a mistaken theory of effect underlies the attacks of the moralists:

All that neutral ground of character, which stood between vice and virtue; or which in fact was indifferent to neither, where neither prop-

Dramatis personae from the 1684 edition of The Man of Mode, *annotated with the cast for a seventeenth-century production (by permission of the Harvard Theatre Collection)*

erly was called in question; that happy breathing-place from the burthen of perpetual moral questioning . . . is broken up and disenfranchised, as injurious to the interests of society. . . . We dare not dally with images, or names, of wrong. We bark like foolish dogs at shadows. We dread infection from the scenic representation of disorder; and fear a painted pustule. . . . I could never connect those sports of a witty fancy in any shape with any result to be drawn from them to imitation in real life.

Lamb's observation that "we cling to the painful necessities of shame and blame" and "would indict our very dreams," is more profound than the words of many of the moralists who have ridiculed him. Unfortunately, Macaulay and his successors set the terms of the debate, and later criticism focuses on Lamb's mistaken attempt to disconnect Restoration comedy from everyday morality rather than on the more interesting aspects of his essay.

Samuel Johnson and Macaulay are surely right in saying that the moral issue is relevant; to argue otherwise both trivializes the work in question and contradicts the experience of readers and audiences. Thus John Palmer—who states that Etherege never gives us "the corrective laugh of the intellectual satirist" or shows any "grave purpose and intentness of mind," as Molière does—does neither Etherege nor his work any service. Similarly, when Bonamy Dobrée, as late as 1924, remarks that Etherege espoused no views and took no positions, that his plays are "pure works of art" rarely appealing to the intellect and not to be taken seriously, that their sex comedy is "like the frolicking of lambs," and that "the solemn motto on the sundial is hidden beneath the roses," serious readers are apt to conclude that Etherege is not worth their time.

Palmer and Dobrée defended plays such as *The Man of Mode* on the basis of their accurate reflections of contemporary life and their stylistic ex-

Medley and Dorimant (center), in act 1, scene 1, of The Man of Mode *(frontispiece to the 1715 edition)*

cellence. Palmer summarizes a century of defense when he calls Etherege an artist who "accurately reflected this period in his personal character, and received a sincere impulse to reflect it artistically in his comedies. . . . His plays are morally as well as artistically sound. He felt and saw the comedy of contemporary life; and he honestly sought and found the means to express it." Palmer's insistence that the writer's impulse "is not the impulse of a moralist to improve the world: it is the impulse of an artist to express it" sounds quite modern; Johnson's insistence that no man was ever the better for reading Restoration comedy sounds old-fashioned indeed. Both sides, however, oversimplify theoretical issues that seem to current critics extremely complex.

A considerable body of criticism, beginning in the 1950s, responded to the attacks of the moralists–including William Archer, L. C.

Knights, and John Wain–by showing that plays such as *The Man of Mode* indeed have considerable intellectual interest. Fujimura, Underwood, Norman Holland, Birdsall, and many others have stressed the influence of contemporary philosophy, particularly that of Thomas Hobbes and neo-Epicurean thought, on the plays. Dorimant, for example, becomes the typical libertine; plays such as *The Man of Mode* express typical libertine or hedonistic values. Although these writers sometimes confuse the intellectual and social context of a play with its literary significance, their work provides a useful corrective to the "fairyland" view which decontextualizes the plays altogether.

Most contemporary critics would respond to the controversy which Etherege's play so perfectly illustrates by arguing that, while there is certainly a connection between art and life, plays are complex constructions which we may set beside other complex constructions, of which our conception of reality is one. All such constructions are distorted, whether or not they are reflections of some objective reality. For many modern readers, the traditional terms of the argument seem hardly more than historical curiosities. Etherege's play is one reality, Steele's essay on it another; the concatenation of many such realities with readers and audiences not only enlarges our experience but associates literature and culture far more intimately and indissolubly than earlier critics could have believed.

Thus, it is possible to see Dorimant as an admirable figure or as one the play condemns, to see him either as hero or as antihero, possible even to see him as a character combining the virtues and vices of courtiers of his day–or of ours. Etherege does not include obviously normative characters or speeches, as Congreve does in *The Way of the World*. One cannot easily take Young Bellair, Emilia, or Lady Townley as such exemplars because they are not central enough; they have too few lines. One can take Dorimant as hero and Harriet as heroine if one also takes wit, style, and aggressive mastery of social forms to be the chief and proper business of life, or if one is convinced that beneath their surfaces is genuine feeling and commitment. On the other hand, the two become antihero and antiheroine if one sees no depth in them to admire or regards as reprehensible their behavior toward those who are less hard, controlled, brilliant, and successful. Finally, one can take the middle view: on the whole, they are to be admired, but Etherege's vision does not always allow him to transcend the moral limitations of his world and create characters whose final accommodation can be fully accepted by the variety of audiences which great drama must eventually please.

Readers may identify themselves with Dorimant and Harriet and yet feel sympathy for Loveit and Bellinda, though such views may not seem consistent. A successful production, however, must choose from the many potential interpretations one which can be made convincing on the stage. If Dorimant is to be hero, Loveit and Bellinda must not be acted as to make audiences respond too sympathetically to them, and Dorimant's feeling for Harriet must be made explicit and convincing. If he is to be Don Giovanni, he may indeed be charming, but he must seem a hard and brittle creature when the curtain comes down, incapable of a humane response either to Loveit's passion or Bellinda's frailty. The usual,

and probably the best, approach is to present Dorimant as the rake who meets his match in Harriet. Having found a woman he cannot manipulate, he has also found one who may be a worthy partner. Since overt expressions of love are suspect in a world of surfaces, the lovers' feelings for each other are wittily and indirectly expressed. Since social pressure is relentless, all promises are conditional, all relationships fragile.

Far from being the quintessential comedy of manners, *The Man of Mode* is a most unusual play for its period. Superficially, it invites us to believe that it will represent for us what we know to be a small segment of Restoration life. After all, contemporary audiences "saw" Dorimant as Rochester or some other courtier like Rochester, even Etherege himself. But the play in fact presents us with that selection and structuring of materials characteristic of all art, formulaic or not. It is representational only as representational art is. It will not, finally, satisfy readers who expect a play to announce its own unequivocal criteria of value; if it did, interpretations would not differ as radically as they do.

A successful production, as Hume has noted, must offer a coherent interpretation within the limits set by the text. Some readers and directors may construct an interpretation without much regard for dramatic history or social context. Others will try to construct that interpretation most consistent with all other evidence from genre and period, trying for fidelity to a history inevitably altered by the perspective from which it is viewed. A play like *The Man of Mode* is of special interest precisely because it is more ambiguous than Etherege's other plays and those of most of his contemporaries, because it lends itself to controversy and will not be exhausted by interpretation.

One might suppose that the success of *The Man of Mode* would have inspired Etherege to further writing for the stage. After all, two of his three plays were distinct successes, and each shows steady progress toward mastery of comic form and increasing control of a brilliant style. But his greatest triumph turned out also to be his farewell to the stage; he wrote no more plays. He is next heard of in June of 1676 at Epsom, in the company of Rochester and others; Charles Hatton reports him "tossing some fiddlers in a blanket for refusing to play," first brawling with the constable and then momentarily appeasing him with "a submissive oration." The affair left one man dead. Some eighteen months later, he was involved in a tavern brawl. Two years later, on 15 January 1680, Hatton wrote his brother that the collapse the previous day of the tennis court near Clare market had injured "Sr George Etheridge." The scant data from these years suggest that "easie Etheridge" was an all too appropriate appellation.

The second of the Hatton references is the first known to Etherege's knighthood, which must have been conferred about 1679. Contemporary gossip suggests that he purchased the honor as a prelude to marrying money, and that he married to ameliorate pressing gambling debts. Whatever the reason, he married Mary Arnold, née Sheppard, widow of a successful London lawyer, sometime after 1676 and before 1680. A contemporary poem refers to his "flux in *Tongue* and *Purse*" as having led him to exchange one snare for a worse. *An Answer to the Satyr on the Court Ladies* (1680), is even more explicit:

> Yet there's Sr George, that honest Man ne're fails;
> Always of Women writes, & always Rails;
> For which, the Gods have plagu'd him to the
>   height,
> And for his Comfort sent him such a Wife:
> A Wife that represents all Forms; a Bitch,
> A Wizard, wrincled Woman, & a Witch.

The marriage may well have been unsuccessful, but one cannot firmly conclude this either from the contemporary gossip to that effect or from the fact that Etherege went to Ratisbon alone in 1685. He may have owed his appointment as Resident to the Diet of the Holy Roman Empire in part to his earlier connection with Henrietta Maria, who had become queen; in his letterbook he gives the credit to the earl of Sunderland, to whom his earlier diplomatic experience, good connections, and easy manners may have recommended him. He may also have desired to escape gambling debts in England. In any case, he took leave of the court at the end of August 1685 and traveled to Ratisbon by way of The Hague and Cologne, arriving at his new post in November. A diplomatic resident, although lower in rank than an ambassador, was paid well for the duties required; Etherege received three pounds per day plus an allowance for unusual expenses and entertainment. Payments totaling more than three thousand pounds over the period from November 1685 through May 1688 are recorded–a considerable sum despite the heavy expenses entailed by the position.

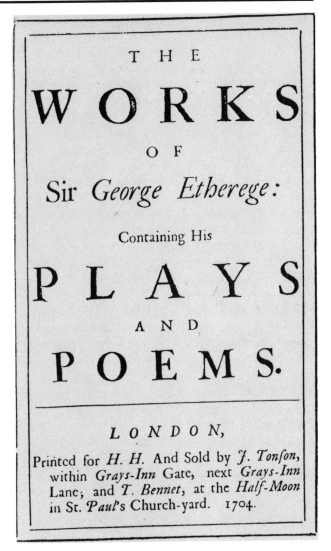

THE

WORKS

OF

Sir *George Etherege*:

Containing His

PLAYS

AND

POEMS.

LONDON,

Printed for *H. H.* And Sold by *J. Tonson*, within *Grays-Inn* Gate, next *Grays-Inn* Lane; and *T. Bennet*, at the *Half-Moon* in St. *Paul's* Church-yard. 1704.

Title page for the first collected edition of Etherege's writings, published twelve years after his death

Of Etherege's four hundred or so extant letters, all but thirty-odd date from the Ratisbon residency. There is no complete edition. Some letters remain in manuscript; Bracher's edition omits about one hundred fifty letters entirely and prints only the most interesting passages from many others. Sybil Rosenfeld's collection includes only those letters in the British Library letterbook. From the two collections, however, one can get a good picture of the dramatist, then about fifty. He indulged his passion for gambling in the early months of his stay and his passion for women until the end. He had dancing and fencing instructors and enjoyed what opera and other music were available. He gave some time to tennis and more to hunting. How much he gave to business is debatable. The post was not an especially sensitive one. Etherege reported the ponderous machinations between the Holy Roman Empire and the Turks in the east and between the Empire and France, Brandenburg, and other European powers in the west. He was not a subtle or patient man; both the clumsy governance structure of the Empire and the political goals of the key figures making policy far from Ratisbon led to seemingly endless moves and countermoves which amused and irritated him by turns. Used to the comparatively informal manners of London, he was also unprepared for the stuffy forms of a provincial city and took apparent pleasure in flouting social conventions, especially in the early months of his stay.

Many of his letters are detailed accounts of trivia, of little interest to anyone, and Bracher wisely omits much of these in his edition. Some letters are chatty, amusing, and witty. Occasionally Etherege is the shrewd political analyst; more often he is gossip and raconteur even of personal affairs not much to his credit. He was handicapped not only by his easy disposition but by a treacherous and puritanical secretary who lost no opportunity to discredit him and whom he seems not to have suspected until the latter part of his stay. Although Rosenfeld notes that many of his correspondents were old acquaintances who expected to be amused as well as informed, the letters do not much advance Etherege's status either as diplomat or writer. Their biographical interest, however, is considerable. They suggest, for example, that he often preferred not to exercise his abilities if he could satisfy his appetites instead. On the other hand, he seems to have taken his duties more seriously as the years passed, and his allegiance to the cause of James never wavered. He writes with growing anger and dismay about William's preparations for invading England and when James "abdicated" he followed him to France.

Etherege's last years are even more obscure than his first. He left Ratisbon for Paris early in 1689, but his few letters from the French capital do not indicate what he did there. He may have joined James's court at Saint-Germain, but no record of his presence has been found. The list of benefactors of the Benedictine monastery at Ratisbon records that he died a Roman Catholic; this also is plausible but unconfirmed. Nor is the place and date of his death known. George Bradbury, his former attorney, reports him dead in a letter dated 3 February 1691; the Ratisbon monks record 28 July 1699, altered to 1691 in

the manuscript; and Narcissus Luttrell mentions having heard of his death in February 1691. On the other hand, Gerard Langbaine in 1691 hopes "this great Master would oblidge the World with more of his Performances," and Etherege's nephew, in legal testimony, gives circa 10 May 1692 as the date of death. This last would seem the most reliable date.

Neither his poems nor his letters are of much literary significance, but Etherege is rightly known as an important and innovative dramatist. Until recently, he has often been considered the inventor or one of the principal inventors of what has been variously called the comedy of manners, comedy of wit, intellectual comedy, or high comedy; that invention, exemplified most perfectly in *The Man of Mode*, has been used to define Restoration comedy. More careful attention to theatrical history in the period has undercut such a definition, the inaccuracy of which will be obvious to anyone who reads a representative selection of plays written and produced between 1660 and the end of the century. No one comic type dominates, certainly not the so-called comedy of manners. Instead, one finds an astonishing variety of forms, most of them using conventional themes, characters, and plot structures. In the 1660s many of these forms hark back to Jacobean and Caroline drama, but they soon developed contemporary features. Theatrical taste changed rapidly in the years following the Restoration; playwrights wrote not only for specific acting companies but often (if not usually) for specific theaters and actors. Political events, especially in the turbulent 1680s, effected considerable changes in repertory and audiences. It is now clear that the comedy of manners, far from being the characteristic or defining type of comedy in the era, consists of a small number of plays crystallized from a matrix much less pure stylistically and much more diverse than earlier literary history supposed.

Etherege's three plays are, indeed, very different from each other despite their common features and themes. Each reflects its period and the theatrical taste of that period. Like his contemporaries, Etherege is a formulaic dramatist. Unlike most of them, he created characters and character interactions which still interest readers and, to some extent at least, would still interest audiences. It may be that he is still widely read, in part, because he was the only one of the court wits of a celebrated (or notorious) age who really succeeded as a dramatist; we surely retain our fascination with the connections between life and art. In the final analysis, however, it is Etherege's superior command of the language and style available to him, and his ability to use that language to create meaningful comic structures, which distinguish him and give *The Man of Mode* its enduring place in English drama.

Letters:

The Letterbook of Sir George Etherege, edited by Sybil Rosenfeld (Oxford: Oxford University Press, 1928);

Letters of Sir George Etherege, edited by Frederick Bracher (Berkeley: University of California Press, 1974).

Bibliographies:

"Bibliography of the Plays," in *The Dramatic Works of Sir George Etherege*, edited by H. F. B. Brett-Smith (Oxford: Blackwell, 1927), I: xciii-cviii;

David D. Mann, *Sir George Etherege: A Reference Guide* (Boston: G. K. Hall, 1981).

Biography:

William Oldys, "Sir George Etherege," *Biographia Britannica*, volume 3 (London, 1750), pp. 1841-1849;

Dorothy Foster, "Sir George Etherege," *Times Literary Supplement*, 16 February 1922, p. 108; 23 February 1922, p. 124; "Concerning the Grandfather and Father of Sir George Etherege," *Notes & Queries*, 142 (6 May 1922): 341-344; (13 May 1922): 362-365; "Addenda et Corrigenda," *Notes & Queries*, 142 (27 May 1922): 414; "Sir George Etherege: Collections," *Notes & Queries*, 153 (10 December 1927): 417-419; (17 December 1927): 435-440; (24 December 1927): 454-459; (31 December 1927): 472-478; "Addenda," *Notes & Queries*, 154 (14 January 1928): 28; "Sir George Etherege," *Times Literary Supplement*, 31 May 1928, p. 412;

H. F. B. Brett-Smith, Introduction to *The Dramatic Works of Sir George Etherege*, edited by Brett-Smith (Oxford: Blackwell, 1927), I: xi-xcii;

Eleanore Boswell, "Sir George Etherege," *Review of English Studies*, 7 (April 1931): 207-209; response by Dorothy Foster, 8 (October 1932): 458-459;

Sybil Rosenfeld, "Sir George Etherege in Ratisbon," *Review of English Studies*, 10 (April 1934): 177-189;

John W. Nichol, "Dame Mary Etherege," *Modern Language Notes*, 64 (June 1949): 419-422;

Thomas H. Fujimura, "Etherege at Constantinople," *PMLA*, 71 (June 1956): 465-471;

Frederick Bracher, "Sir George Etherege and His Secretary," *Harvard Library Bulletin*, 15 (October 1967): 331-344;

Bracher, "Etherege as Diplomat," *Harvard Library Bulletin*, 17 (January 1969): 45-60;

Arthur Huseboe, "The Mother of Sir George Etherege," *Notes & Queries*, 220 (June 1975): 262-264;

Bracher, "Etherege at Clement's Inn," *Huntington Library Quarterly*, 43 (Spring 1980): 127-134.

References:

John Barnard, "Point of View in *The Man of Mode*," *Essays in Criticism*, 34 (October 1984): 285-308;

Andrew Bear, "Restoration Comedy and the Provok'd Critic," in *Restoration Literature: Critical Approaches*, edited by Harold Love (London: Methuen/New York: Barnes & Noble, 1972), pp. 1-26;

Ronald Berman, "The Comic Passions of *The Man of Mode*," *Studies in English Literature*, 10 (Summer 1970): 459-468;

Virginia O. Birdsall, *Wild Civility: The English Comic Spirit on the Restoration Stage* (Bloomington: Indiana University Press, 1970);

Purvis E. Boyette, "The Songs of Etherege," *Studies in English Literature*, 6 (Summer 1966): 409-419;

Frederick Bracher, "The Letterbooks of Sir George Etherege," *Harvard Library Bulletin*, 15 (July 1967): 238-245;

Brian Corman, "Interpreting and Misinterpreting *The Man of Mode*," *Papers in Language and Literature*, 13 (1977): 35-53;

Paul C. Davies, "The State of Nature and the State of War: A Reconsideration of *The Man of Mode*," *University of Toronto Quarterly*, 39 (October 1969): 53-62;

John Dennis, *A Defence of Sir Fopling Flutter* (London: Printed for T. Warner, 1722); republished in *The Critical Works of John Dennis*, volume 2, edited by E. N. Hooker (Baltimore: Johns Hopkins University Press, 1943), pp. 241-250;

Bonamy Dobrée, *Restoration Comedy 1660-1720* (Oxford: Oxford University Press, 1924);

Thomas H. Fujimura, *The Restoration Comedy of Wit* (Princeton, N.J.: Princeton University Press, 1952);

Jean Gagen, "The Design of the High Plot in Etherege's *The Man of Mode*," *Restoration and 18th Century Theatre Research*, second series 1, no. 2 (Winter 1986): 1-15;

Edmund Gosse, "Sir George Etherege: A Neglected Chapter of English Literature," *Cornhill Magazine*, 43 (March 1881): 284-304; republished in *Seventeenth-Century Studies* (London: Kegan Paul, Trench, 1883), pp. 231-265;

Harriett Hawkins, *Likenesses of Truth in Elizabethan and Restoration Drama* (Oxford: Clarendon Press, 1972);

John G. Hayman, "Dorimant and the Comedy of a Man of Mode," *Modern Language Quarterly*, 30 (June 1969): 183-197;

Norman H. Holland, *The First Modern Comedies: The Significance of Etherege, Wycherley, and Congreve* (Cambridge, Mass.: Harvard University Press, 1959);

Peter Holland, *The Ornament of Action: Text and Performance in Restoration Comedy* (Cambridge: Cambridge University Press, 1979);

Derek Hughes, "Play and Passion in *The Man of Mode*," *Comparative Drama*, 15 (Fall 1981): 231-257;

Robert D. Hume, *The Development of English Drama in the Late Seventeenth Century* (Oxford: Clarendon Press, 1976);

Hume, "Elizabeth Barry's First Roles and the Cast of *The Man of Mode*," *Theatre History Studies*, 5 (1985): 16-19;

Hume, "The Myth of the Rake in Restoration Comedy," in *The Rakish Stage: Studies in English Drama, 1660-1800* (Carbondale: Southern Illinois University Press, 1983), pp. 138-175;

Hume, *Producible Interpretation* (Carbondale: Southern Illinois University Press, 1985);

Hume, "Reading and Misreading *The Man of Mode*," *Criticism*, 14 (Winter 1972): 1-11;

Arthur R. Huseboe, *Sir George Etherege* (Boston: Twayne, 1987);

Robert Jordan, "The Extravagant Rake in Restoration Comedy," in *Restoration Literature: Critical Approaches*, pp. 69-90;

David Krause, "The Defaced Angel: A Concept of Satanic Grace in Etherege's *The Man of Mode*," *Drama Survey*, 7 (Winter 1968-1969): 87-103;

Charles Lamb, "On the Artificial Comedy of the Last Century" [1822], *The Works of Charles and Mary Lamb*, volume 2, edited by E. V. Lucas (London: Methuen, 1903), pp. 141-147;

Gerard Langbaine, *An Account of the English Dramatick Poets* (Oxford: Printed by L. L. for G. West & H. Clements, 1691; Los Angeles: William Andrews Clark Memorial Library, 1971);

Thomas Babington Macaulay, "Comic Dramatists of the Restoration," *Edinburgh Review*, 72 (January 1841): 490-528;

David D. Mann, comp. and ed., *A Concordance to the Plays and Poems of Sir George Etherege* (Westport, Conn.: Greenwood Press, 1985);

Leslie H. Martin, "Past and Parody in *The Man of Mode*," *Studies in English Literature*, 16 (Summer 1976): 363-376;

Frances S. McCamic, *Sir George Etherege: A Study in Restoration Comedy (1660-1800)* (Cedar Rapids, Iowa: Torch Press, 1931);

Vincenz Meindl, *Sir George Etherege, sein Leben, seine Zeit, und seine Dramen* (Vienna: Braumüller, 1901);

John Palmer, *The Comedy of Manners* (London: Bell, 1913);

Jocelyn Powell, "George Etherege and the Form of a Comedy," in *Restoration Theatre*, edited by J. R. Brown and B. Harris (London: Arnold, 1965), pp. 43-69; republished in *Restoration Dramatists: A Collection of Critical Essays*, edited by Earl Miner (Englewood Cliffs, N.J.: Prentice-Hall, 1966), pp. 65-85;

Powell, *Restoration Theatre Production* (London: Routledge, Kegan Paul, 1984);

Nadia J. Rigaud, *George Etherege: Dramaturge de la Restauration anglaise*, 2 volumes (Lille: Atelier reproduction des thésès Université de Lille, III; dist. Paris: Librarie H. Champion, 1980);

Elkanah Settle, *A Defence of Dramatick Poetry* (London: Printed for E. Whitlock, 1698); republished in *The English Stage*, volume 25A, edited by Arthur Freeman (New York: Garland, 1972);

Arthur Sherbo, "A Note on *The Man of Mode*," *Modern Language Notes*, 64 (May 1949): 343-344;

Irene Simon, "Restoration Comedy and the Critics," *Revue des langues vivantes*, 29 (1963): 397-430;

John H. Smith, *The Gay Couple in Restoration Comedy* (Cambridge, Mass.: Harvard University Press, 1948);

Richard Steele, *Spectator* no. 65 for 15 May 1711 and no. 75 for 26 May 1711; republished in

Everyman's Library, volume 1, edited by G. G. Smith (London: Dent, 1907), pp. 245-248, 284-287;

John Traugott, "The Rake's Progress from Court to Comedy: A Study in Comic Form," *Studies in English Literature*, 6 (Summer 1966): 381-407;

Dale Underwood, *Etherege and the Seventeenth-Century Comedy of Manners* (New Haven: Yale University Press, 1957);

Harold Weber, *The Restoration Rake-Hero: Transformation in Sexual Understanding in Seventeenth-Century England* (Madison: University of Wisconsin Press, 1986);

D. R. M. Wilkinson, *The Comedy of Habit: An Essay on the Use of Courtesy Literature in a Study of Restoration Comic Drama* (Leiden: Universitaire Pers, 1964);

John Harold Wilson, *The Court Wits of the Restoration* (Princeton: Princeton University Press, 1948);

Rose Zimbardo, *A Mirror to Nature: Transformations in Drama and Aesthetics 1660-1732* (Lexington: University of Kentucky Press, 1986);

Zimbardo, "Of Women, Comic Imitation of Nature, and Etherege's *The Man of Mode,*" *Studies in English Literature*, 21 (Summer 1981): 373-377.

Papers:

Two volumes of holograph letters are part of the Middleton papers in the British Library (Add. MSS 41836 and 41837); they contain almost two hundred letters. The Houghton Library at Harvard University owns two letterbooks (fMS Thr 11 and 11.1) in the hand of Hugo Hughes, Etherege's secretary. They include transcripts, summaries, and lists of letters, with many corrections by Etherege. The British Library has a manuscript copy of part of the first of the Houghton letterbooks (Add. MS 11513) which includes copies of additional letters not found elsewhere. Manuscripts of Etherege's poems are scattered: see the Thorpe edition for locations.

Nathaniel Lee
(circa 1645-1652 - spring 1692)

Richard E. Brown
University of Nevada, Reno

PLAY PRODUCTIONS: *The Tragedy of Nero, Emperour of Rome*, London, Theatre Royal in Drury Lane, 16 May 1674;

Sophonisba, or Hannibal's Overthrow. A Tragedy, London, Theatre Royal in Drury Lane, 30 April 1675;

Gloriana, or the Court of Augustus Caesar, London, Theatre Royal in Drury Lane, circa 29 January 1676;

The Rival Queens, or the Death of Alexander the Great, London, Theatre Royal in Drury Lane, 17 March 1677;

Mithridates King of Pontus, A Tragedy, London, Theatre Royal in Drury Lane, circa February 1678;

Oedipus: A Tragedy, by Lee and John Dryden, London, Dorset Garden Theatre, autumn 1678;

Caesar Borgia; Son of Pope Alexander the Sixth: A Tragedy, London, Dorset Garden Theatre, spring or summer 1679;

Theodosius: or, The Force of Love, A Tragedy, London, Dorset Garden Theatre, late summer or September 1680;

Lucius Junius Brutus; Father of his Country. A Tragedy, London, Dorset Garden Theatre, December 1680;

The Duke of Guise. A Tragedy, by Lee and Dryden, London, Theatre Royal in Drury Lane, 30 November 1682;

The Princess of Cleve, London, Dorset Garden Theatre, December 1682 or January-February 1683;

Constantine the Great; A Tragedy, London, Theatre Royal in Drury Lane, November 1683;

The Massacre of Paris: A Tragedy, London, Theatre Royal in Drury Lane, 7 November 1689.

BOOKS: *The Tragedy of Nero, Emperour of Rome: As It Is Acted at the Theatre-Royal, by His Majesties Servants* (London: Printed by T. R. & N. T. for James Magnes & Richard Bentley, 1675);

Sophonisba, or Hannibal's Overthrow. A Tragedy, Acted at the Theatre-Royall, by Their Majesties Servants (London: Printed for J. Magnes & R. Bentley, 1676);

Gloriana, or the Court of Augustus Caesar. Acted at the Theatre-Royal, by Their Majesties Servants (London: Printed for James Magnes & R. Bentley, 1676);

The Rival Queens, or the Death of Alexander the Great. Acted at the Theatre-Royal. By Their Majesties Servants (London: Printed for James Magnes & R. Bentley, 1677; facsimile, Menton, U.K.: Scholar, 1971); modern edition, edited by P. F. Vernon (Lincoln: University of Nebraska Press, 1970);

Mithridates King of Pontus, A Tragedy: Acted at the Theatre Royal, by Their Majestie's Servants (London: Printed by R. E. for James Magnes & Rich. Bentley, 1678);

Oedipus: A Tragedy. As it is Acted at His Royal Highness The Duke's Theatre. The Authors Mr. Dryden, and Mr. Lee (London: Printed for R. Bentley & M. Magnes, 1679); modern edition, in *The Works of John Dryden*, volume 13, edited by S. Edward Niles Hooker, H. T. Swedenberg, Jr., and others (Berkeley, Los Angeles & London: University of California Press, 1984);

Cæsar Borgia; Son of Pope Alexander the Sixth: A Tragedy Acted at the Duke's Theatre by Their Royal Highnesses Servants (London: Printed by R. E. for R. Bentley & M. Magnes, 1680);

Theodosius: or, The Force of Love, A Tragedy. Acted by Their Royal Highnesses Servants, at the Duke's Theatre (London: Printed for R. Bentley & M. Magnes, 1680);

Lucius Junius Brutus; Father of his Country. A Tragedy. Acted at the Duke's Theatre, By Their Royal Highnesses Servants (London: Printed for Richard Tonson & Jacob Tonson, 1681); modern edition, edited by John Loftis (Lincoln: University of Nebraska Press, 1967);

The Duke of Guise. A Tragedy. Acted By Their Majesties Servants. Written By Mr. Dryden, and Mr. Lee (London: Printed by T. H. for R. Bentley & J. Tonson, 1683);

Nathaniel Lee, engraving by John Watts

Constantine the Great; A Tragedy. Acted at the Theatre-Royal, by Their Majesties Servants (London: Printed by H. Hills Jun. for R. Bentley, 1684);

The Princess of Cleve, As It Was Acted at the Queens Theatre in Dorset-Garden (London: Printed for Abel Roper, 1689);

On the Death of Mrs. Behn [broadside] (London: Printed for Abel Roper, 1689);

The Massacre of Paris: A Tragedy. As It Is Acted at the Theatre Royal by Their Majesties Servants (London: Printed for R. Bentley & M. Magnes, 1690).

Collection: *The Works of Nathaniel Lee,* 2 volumes, edited by Thomas B. Stroup and Arthur L. Cooke (New Brunswick, N.J.: Scarecrow Press, 1954-1955).

OTHER: "To Mr. Dryden, on his Poem of Paradice," in *The State of Innocence, and Fall of Man: An Opera,* by John Dryden (London:

Printed by T. N. for Henry Herringman, 1677);

"To the Unknown Author Of this Excellent Poem, 'Take it as Earnest,'" in *Absalom and Achitophel. A Poem,* by Dryden, second London edition (London: Printed for J. T. & sold by W. Davis, 1681).

One of the three leading tragedians of his day, Nathaniel Lee, as J. M. Armistead observes, led the move away from "awe-inspiring characters and happy endings–typical of tragi-comedies and heroic plays of the 1660s–to the more vulnerable and pathetic figures, and to the homicidal or suicidal conclusions, which characterized the tragedies of the later 1670s and 1680s." In the process, Lee preceded John Dryden in turning from heroic couplets to blank verse as the medium for serious drama. The most-notable quality of Lee's dramatic language, however, is what Armistead calls its "impassioned lyricism," which enables the playwright to express the torment of his self-destructive heroes and the desperate passion of his yearning lovers.

Lee's life is not heavily documented. After attending Cambridge, and earning a B.A. in 1669, young Nathaniel, the son of Richard and Elizabeth Lee, was attracted to the London stage, beginning as an actor in 1672. He soon shifted to the writing of tragedies; his first, *The Tragedy of Nero*, was performed at Drury Lane on 16 May 1674. Over the next nine years he composed or collaborated on a dozen more plays, at least four of them smash hits. His dedications and occasional verse suggest that he was warmly patronized by the nobility ("Dedicating *Lee*," sneered Matthew Prior). Another sign of his eminence is that he collaborated with John Dryden on two plays, *Oedipus* and *The Duke of Guise*. But this working friendship must have been even more complex than the collaborations suggest, for Dryden supplied Lee with prologues, epilogues, and a poem in praise of *The Rival Queens*, while Lee responded with verses praising *The State of Innocence* (1677)–in which he urged Dryden to write a poem comparing King Charles II to King David–and another poem puffing *Absalom and Achitophel* (1681), which appeared in the second London edition (also 1681). Lee's one other clearly documented friendship was with Aphra Behn, for whom he wrote a broadside eulogy following her death in 1689. Lee acquired a reputation for heavy drinking (contemporary satirists mention his paunch and carbuncled, ruby face), and this habit may have contributed to the deterioration which resulted in his admission to "Bedlam" (Bethlem Royal Hospital) on 11 November 1684. Though he was discharged in 1688 and wrote verses thereafter, he resumed drinking and was found dead in a London street in the spring of 1692.

Nero portrays a corrupt Roman court dominated by a depraved emperor, whose atrocities punctuate the plot. Nero sentences his mother to death, forces the philosopher Seneca to commit suicide, seduces the beautiful Poppea, and kills his wife, Octavia, for refusing to murder her brother. The ghost of Caligula incites Nero to burn Rome, and the play ends with the city in flames, while several characters, including the emperor, die in quick succession. The villain-hero's flashing couplets and exuberance of spirit are amazing to contemplate. *Nero* treads the border between conventional heroic villainy (exemplified by Dryden's Maximin) and campy parody of vil-

lainous clichés. Roswell Gray Ham explains the play's excesses as a mingling of Renaissance tragic elements with the rakish distortion of Hobbism popular at the court of Charles II. Indeed, the mixture of prose and blank verse with heroic couplets suggests that Lee's first play is a complicated hybrid.

Nero enjoyed some popularity as late as 1736, although Lee complains in his dedication that it was "sufficiently censur'd" by the critics. The ranting protagonist and lurid imagery have long been regarded as evidence of Lee's lack of artistic discipline, although Armistead argues for a serious study of the psychology and impact of evil. David S. Kastan suggests a political reading based on parallels between Nero's Rome and Restoration England: in both cases, people of honor confronted political and social chaos because of their leaders' corruption. Personifying this desperation is the emperor's brother-in-law Britannicus, an idealist who cannot adjust to the stark fact of Nero's horrors and exhibits the gentler madness of disorientation.

First produced on 30 April 1675, *Sophonisba* proved to be one of Lee's most popular plays and was revived as late as 1775. It depicts the careers of Hannibal and Massinissa, two African leaders destined to fall before the invading Roman general, Scipio. Hannibal, a gloriously ranting hero, loves Rosalinda jealously and is vouchsafed wild omens from the gods. Massinissa is more vulnerable, torn between his military alliance with the Romans and his fatal love. "O Sophonisba, oh!" he sighs famously. Meanwhile the Roman Scipio embodies efficiency and self-discipline. He emerges from the plot victorious over Hannibal but is bewildered to find that his ally Massinissa has disobeyed his instructions to abandon Sophonisba, and the two lovers have drunk poison together.

Armistead argues that the play depicts the decline of conventional stage heroism in the face of a new order. If the audience is meant to admire displays of the vaunting heroic temperament in early scenes, it should later shed sympathetic tears for the devastation that dooms the race of giants. Eric Rothstein notes two specific ways Lee has altered the heroic formulas: Massinissa commits suicide (an act which would be unthinkable for a hero such as Dryden's Almanzor), and the hero's role is split into three, so that all the principal actors of the King's company–Charles Hart, Michael Mohun, and Edward Kynaston–could play heroic parts. The

To Mr. *Lee*, on his *Alexander*.

THE Blast of common Censure cou'd I fear,
   Before your Play my Name shou'd not appear ;
For 'twill be thought, and with some colour too,
I pay the Bribe I first receiv'd from You :
That mutual Vouchers for our Fame we stand,
To play the Game into each others Hand ;
·ind as cheap Pen'orths to our selves afford
As Bessus, and the Brothers of the Sword.
Such Libels private Men may well endure,
When States, and Kings themselves are not secure :
For ill Men, conscious of their inward guilt,
Think the best Actions on By-ends are built.
And yet my silence had not scap'd their spight,
Then envy had not suffer'd me to write :
For, since I cou'd not Ignorance pretend,
Such worth I must or envy or commend.
So many Candidates there stand for Wit,
A place in Court is scarce so hard to get ;
In vain they croud each other at the Door ;
For ev'n Reversions are all beg'd before :
Desert, how known so e're, is long delay'd ;
And, then too, Fools and Knaves are better pay'd.
Yet, as some Actions bear so great a Name,
That Courts themselves are just, for fear of shame :
So has the mighty Merit of your Play
Extorted praise, and forc'd it self a Way.
'Tis here, as 'tis at Sea ; who farthest goes,
Or dares the most, makes all the rest his Foes ;

a   *Yet,*

Yet, when some Virtue much out-grows the rest,
It shoots too fast, and high, to be opprest ;
As his Heroic worth struck Envy dumb
Who took the Dutchman, and who cut the Boom :
Such praise is yours, while you the Passions move,
That 'tis no longer feign'd ; 'tis real Love :
Where Nature Triumphs over wretched Art ;
We only warm the Head, but you the Heart.
Always you warm ! and if the rising Year,
As in hot Regions, bring the Sun too near,
Tis but to make your Fragrant Spices blow,
Which in our colder Climates will not grow.
They only think you animate your Theme
With too much Fire, who are themselves all Phle'me :
Prizes wou'd be for Lags of slowest pace,
Were Cripples made the Judges of the Race.
Despise those Drones, who praise while they accuse
The too much vigour of your youthful Muse :
That humble Stile which they their Virtue make
Is in your pow'r ; you need but stoop and take.
Your beauteous Images must be allow'd
By all, but some vile Poets of the Crowd ;
But how shou'd any Sign-post-dawber know
The worth of Titian, or of Angelo ?
Hard Features every Bungler can command ;
To draw true Beauty shews a Masters Hand.

JOHN DRYDEN.

Commendatory verse by John Dryden, in the 1677 quarto edition of The Rival Queens. *Lee had just written a poem in praise of* Dryden's The State of Innocence *(1677).*

implication of this second change is that heroism is no longer being conceived of as monolithic strength and ego but is beginning to exhibit emotional diversity.

Gloriana (1676) also suggests that Lee was uncovering new tensions in the heroic personality. The godlike Augustus feels the painful limitations of old age and the burden of past follies; the young Caesario and Julia share the emperor's lack of self-control, and their enormous passions create a similarly morbid self-consciousness. However, the promising psychological conflicts implicit in heroism are buried within the dizzying plot of *Gloriana*, which contains the usual political rivalries and love triangles, but is marred by a surprising number of unresolved relationships and cases of unexplained motivation.

In his dedicatory epistle Lee describes himself as "blasted in my hopes, and press'd in my growth by a most severe if not unjust fortune." Presumably he refers to the dismal reception afforded *Gloriana*, which has been regarded at least

from Joseph Addison's criticism onward as Lee's worst play. Essentially it lacks the appealing characterizations and clear conflicts that forcibly recommend *Sophonisba*.

By contrast Lee's next play proved to be his most popular. First produced on 17 March 1677, *The Rival Queens* was revived for the queen's birthday in 1681 and was performed before the court on other occasions as well. P. F. Vernon notes that three other plays of 1677 were indebted to it; among them, Dryden's *All for Love* followed *The Rival Queens* in employing blank verse, and its even better-known meeting between Cleopatra and Octavia is based on the confrontations between Lee's queens. Dryden's soldier Ventidius, who advises Mark Antony, is also modeled on Lee's Clytus. Colley Cibber paid Lee's play the ultimate compliment with his parody, *The Rival Queans* (1703?); and there were at least five other dramatic burlesques, plus a burlesque opera. The remarkable endurance of *The Rival Queens* on London and American stages until the mid-nineteenth century may be explained not only by the fact that it is written in blank verse rather than couplets, but also by its use of bombast to characterize the hero's weakness rather than as a device to glorify him and by the excellent handling of the conflict between Roxana and Statira, the queens of the title.

Armistead proposes that this play contains Lee's most "convincing plot insofar as motivation is concerned," portraying the psychological dangers of heroism and its impact on society. Alexander the Great follows his passions to the point of madness, breaking faith with his wife, violating promises to his retainers, and executing competitors. The emperor is justly criticized for impulsiveness, boasting, and sensuality by a blunt old soldier, Clytus; but in a typical cycle of action and remorse, the hero repays such honesty by killing Clytus and then weeps over him inconsolably. A different view of the play is offered by Laura Brown, who contends that Alexander's psychology should not be termed coherent: rather, Lee betrays the transitional nature of his drama by oscillating between Alexander's heroic monstrosity and his pathos, unable to create the necessary transitions between extremes which would suggest a unified personality.

Sometimes Lee makes plain that he means to distance himself from the tired clichés of heroic rant which Alexander employs. When the emperor boasts that "Jove made my Mother pregnant" and calls himself "a God" who gives life to his followers, Clytus replies piercingly, "When Gods grow hot, where is the difference/'Twixt them and Devils?" Yet the hero is not always corrected by a satiric interlocutor, and then the play unintentionally leaves itself open to laughter. In Alexander's climactic fit of madness, he utters one of the play's best-known, inadvertently funny lines, addressed to his horse: "Bear me, Bucephalus, amongst the Billows." Statira's remark about Alexander–"Then he will talk, good Gods, how he will talk!"–became another standard eighteenth-century joke. Incidentally, the play also gave birth to the famous saying, "When Greek meets Greek," based upon Clytus's line, "When Greeks joined Greeks, then was the tug of war."

Mithridates (1678) reworks a conflict favored by seventeenth-century dramatists: a royal household is split when two princes and their kingly father become rivals in love and political intrigue, thereby endangering the state. Mithridates is torn between two selves, represented by the virtuous prince Ziphares and the bestial, scheming prince Pharnaces. Counseled by plotters who support Pharnaces' ambition for the throne, Mithridates gives in to his lust and rapes Ziphares' beloved, Semandra; the king also credits lies accusing his good son of disloyalty. But this king is racked by guilt and longs for the purity embodied by the son he has betrayed. If most of the play is devoted to portraying the dark psychology of royal self-indulgence, it also includes moments of pathos. Semandra, already violated by the king, is accidentally stabbed by her lover, Ziphares; the young man then joins her in death by drinking poison. Expiring, she forgives Mithridates and imagines wedding Ziphares in heaven, where she may become "The smiling Mother of some little Gods."

With *Mithridates* Lee began to perfect his conception of blank-verse tragedy. In an important passage of the dedication he declares, "I have endeavour'd in this Tragedy to mix Shakespear with Fletcher; the thoughts of the former, for Majesty and true Roman Greatness, and the softness and passionate expressions of the latter." The vigor of the blank verse and the intelligence with which the imagery is executed make this one of Lee's most satisfying plays to read, although Robert D. Hume complains, "Alas, he cannot resist pumping the majesty too hard and swooning too lyrically over the passionate beauties, thus dehumanizing his characters. Lee comes so close to being a great tragic writer that his failures are somewhat infuriating."

In his dedication of *Mithridates*, Lee mentions the "particular praises" of the queen. Princess Anne portrayed Semandra twice in court theatricals. Dryden honored the 1681 Drury Lane revival with a new prologue and epilogue. The play's great popularity until 1738 is evidenced by numerous reprints. Lee himself declared it to be his favorite child.

Acts 1 and 3 of *Oedipus* are Dryden's; acts 2, 4, and 5 are Lee's, composed to Dryden's scenario. Dryden's emotional level is cooler, more ironic, while Lee's blank verse is exceptionally lurid. Alan Roper, in his commentary for the California Dryden edition of the play, follows the tradition of assuming that Dryden dominated Lee in this project; though Lee was surely allowed free rein to produce his characteristic poetic effects, which were highly applauded. As Roper mentions, Addison "noted that the audience for *Oedipus* typically let pass in silence the couplets with which Dryden closed the third act, . . . whereas the same audience would salute with

Act II. RIVAL QUEENS. *Scene 2.*

Design for a costume worn by William Smith in the title role of Alexander the Great, *an adaptation of* The Rival Queens
*(by permission of the Henry E. Huntington Library and Art Gallery). Smith played the lead in productions of the play
at the Theatre Royal in Drury Lane during 1778-1780.*

'Thunder-claps of Applause ... the Impieties and Execrations' that close Lee's Act IV." The play's initial run lasted ten days, and it was frequently revived until the middle of the eighteenth century. In its day, as Hume observes, it "was considered one of the major monuments of Carolean tragedy," even though it does not come very close to Sophocles, instead borrowing many of its ideas from Seneca, Corneille, and the conventions of English Renaissance tragedy. Both Lee and Dryden were still under obligation to the Theatre Royal in 1678 when they allowed *Oedipus* to be performed at Dorset Garden, signaling their intention to switch to the rival Duke's company. Both continued to write for that company until the two companies were joined in 1682.

John Dryden recorded that Lee's *Massacre of Paris* was banned at the request of the French ambassador; it was not performed until 7 November 1689, after the Protestant accession. Armistead contends that the play must have been composed in 1679, in which case its anti-French, anti-Catholic bias was a response to public excitement over the Popish Plot. Hume proposes a date of 1681, when Lee's immediate stimulus would have been the Exclusion Crisis then raging. Either way, this treatment of the St. Bartholomew's Day Massacre of the Huguenots (24 August 1572) makes a more sharply topical statement than any of Lee's earlier plays, reflecting the politicizing of the London audience that began in 1678. Here Charles IX of France stands for England's Charles II, an indecisive monarch surrounded by scheming Catholics as well as innocent Protestants who require defending. The wicked queen mother, the calculating duke of Guise who leads the massacre, and the patiently suffering Huguenot admiral of France may seem nothing more than props for Lee's propaganda. Armistead points out, however, that the French horror was surely intended to warn a weak English king that he must bring about a reconciliation between extremes to prevent a similar bloodbath. Hence the true message of the play is moderating rather than incendiary.

Armistead also argues that the admiral's passivity, arising from his faith in predestination, makes the play tragic; for, if he had resisted, he might have overturned his persecutors. However, Richard E. Brown proposes that Lee's earlier investigations of the psychopathology of violent, self-indulgent heroes are reversed in the laudatory portrait of the admiral's patient resignation. Lee's advocacy of self-control is also seen in his portrait of Princess Marguerite, who loves Guise violently until she learns that he will command the massacre. Then repugnance cools her ardor, suggesting that the clichéd behavior of amorous excess can and should be suppressed in the face of more serious moral demands.

Thomas B. Stroup and Arthur L. Cooke note that after an impressive first run, *The Massacre of Paris* was revived in 1715-1716 and again in 1745 to coincide with the anti-Protestant excitement generated by the Old Pretender and then the Young Pretender. Earlier critics praised the simple energy of the play's blank verse, calling it among Lee's best, but perhaps the play has attracted less interest in recent times because its obvious topicality seems to date it more than the classical subjects Lee often chose.

In the dedication of *Caesar Borgia; Son of Pope Alexander the Sixth,* Lee complains that he has been "so harshly handl'd by [the critics], that my courage quite fail'd me." The theory that *The Massacre of Paris* was banned in 1679 has led some commentators to speculate that Lee hurriedly patched together his tragedy about Borgia to offer as a substitute that year. Many critics have found the play excessively bloody. Hume records

the following totals: "three poisonings (with two deaths on stage); five stranglings (all on stage); a death by sniffing poisoned gloves; and finally a little boy, Borgia's son Seraphino, is led on stage to die, 'with his Eyes out, and Face cut.' " Part of the point of these Italian horrors is surely to encourage the antiforeign, anti-Catholic fervor of the audience, though without the specific parallels to contemporary English politics found in *The Massacre of Paris.* The only direct application of the play to England comes in Borgia's dying vow to live on and "act/New mischiefs," including the murder of two French kings and an attempt on Britain, which will be foiled by "her most watchful Angel." Armistead, however, finds a larger moral idea behind Borgia and Machiavelli's faith that bestial cunning and violence can lead to the achievement of absolute power. Lee's Machiavelli is a pagan surprised to discover, in the aftermath of Borgia's raging death, that he has lived in a Christian universe after all.

The palpably Elizabethan-Jacobean flavor of *Caesar Borgia* is anticipated in several of Lee's earlier plays. *Nero* recalls the old villain tragedies; *The Rival Queens* contains a gang of malcontents who thirst for bloody revenge; *Mithridates* and *The Massacre of Paris* feature Machiavellian schemers who manipulate complex plots to ruin their victims. Lee had regularly employed ghosts and portents, fits of madness, poisonings, and suicides, and he had already discovered the emotional expressiveness of blank verse. However, the Italian setting, Machiavelli's thoughtful soliloquies on the nature of power, and the reminiscences of the Othello-Iago relationship in Borgia's dependence on his counselor make *Caesar Borgia* Lee's strongest evocation of Renaissance stage traditions.

Following a series of bloody tragedies, Lee turned to his "softest" subject, *Theodosius.* In his dedication the author observes that he has previously been criticized for "ungovern'd Fancy" but implies that his "Sallies of Youth" are now over. The centrality given to love in both the play's plots was a surefire recipe for popularity, and fitted the play to survive in the succeeding age of sentiment. First produced in late summer or early autumn of 1680, *Theodosius* was revived regularly until the very end of the eighteenth century and played in several American cities during the period.

Richard E. Brown argues that the play's unifying idea is to condemn the self-dramatizing excesses of clichéd heroism in both politics and

love. The general Marcian, intemperate critic of
his emperor, Theodosius, must learn humility
and self-discipline before the emperor's sister
will marry him. By contrast, the self-indulgent
Varanes insists on acting out the part of the
doomed lover when he cannot have his beloved
Athenais. Before committing suicide, Varanes
carefully instructs his servant to "bear me with
my blood distilling down/Straight to the Temple,
lay me! O Aranthes!/Lay my cold Coarse at
Athenais Feet,/And say, O why, why do my eyes
run o're!/Say with my latest gasp I groan'd for pardon." This behavior is corrected when the melancholy but temperate Theodosius, contemplating
the suicides of Varanes and his own betrothed
(the same Athenais), remembers he is a Christian
and decides that he must live.

Theodosius does resign the throne to his sister and her new husband, Marcian, however—
shadowing the hope that a weak, love-distracted
King Charles II might also give way, not to the
blustery James, duke of York (later James II), but
to that well-qualified pair, William and Mary. Although in other respects *Theodosius* is not a bla-
tantly topical work (Lee retreats from modern
Catholic France and Italy to fifth-century Byzan-
tium and the safer contrast between Christianity
and paganism), the play's conclusion provides an
unmistakably political image reflecting opinions
common during the Exclusion Crisis. Characteristically, Lee seems intent on inciting partisan feelings while at the same time offering a pattern of
moderation to calm them.

It was Lee's misfortune that *Lucius Junius Brutus*, now regarded as his masterpiece, was banned
after either three or six nights for "very Scandalous Expressions & Reflections vpon yᵉ Government" at the height of the Exclusion Crisis. The
play was never revived, though Charles Gildon
adapted it under the title *The Patriot, or the Italian
Conspiracy* (1702). The excellence of Lee's play
springs from the consistency with which Lee
evokes a sense of Roman civilization, the subtlety
with which he analyzes republican politics, and
the balance he achieves between the tragic claims
of Brutus and his son Titus. As John Loftis remarks, "the ideal of Roman decorum dominates
the play. Its success derives finally from the sustained grandeur of the tragic hero, Brutus, in
whom a sense of duty enforces a suppression of
private emotion." Lee's verses often achieve a superb dignity, yet are "untainted by the emotional
frigidity which was endemic in neoclassical tragedy."

Modern critics are evenly divided over the
question of whether the play's political tendency
favors Whigs or Tories. Any depiction of the republican overthrow of the Roman King Tarquin
must appear Whiggish on its face, especially
since Lee stresses Tarquin's licentiousness and excessive leniency–charges that were leveled against
Charles II by his detractors. Moreover, Brutus delivers memorable speeches defending what Laura
Brown calls the bourgeois ideology of liberty and
mercantilism, while the play contains no comparable spokesman for the Tory side. On the other
hand, since Brutus executes both his sons, Tiberius and the beloved Titus, for their roles in a
plot against the new republic, the hero may
seem, in Armistead's words, a dangerous "constitutional enthusiast," unyielding before the legitimate appeal of human nature. Further, the play's
parallels with contemporary English events grow
extremely complicated. Brutus's resolve to execute his sons recalls Charles II's failure to discipline his illegitimate son, James Scott, duke of
Monmouth, who was the Whigs' primary hope to
supplant the Catholic duke of York and succeed
his father. So Brutus's decisive act appears to criticize the English king; yet it also offers a model
which the king might still follow to achieve mastery over his child (a double-edged parallel recalling Dryden's *Absalom and Achitophel*). At the same
time, the scheme which threatens Brutus's fledgling republic also recalls the alleged Popish Plot
against the king's life (1678). In Lee's play grisly
human sacrifice and the drinking of blood are
practiced by a macabre priesthood in order to satirize the Catholic party. Therefore, Brutus's victory over them should seem like a triumph for
the English monarch–except that Brutus himself
is no king, but merely a successful rebel. Finally,
it is possible the parallels favoring Whigs and Tories cancel each other out. Richard E. Brown concludes that the chief political lessons implied by
the play are not partisan but general: "domestic
morality and self-restraint are required for political order; . . . stable government requires an
open and pacific temperament; . . . the mob . . .
must be controlled or no institution can stand."

Quite apart from its political argument, *Lucius Junius Brutus* has been praised as a profound
tragedy of character. The complexity of Lee's design is indicated by the fact that both Brutus and
Titus have been identified as the play's tragic consciousness. Brutus is a tragic figure, according to
Antony Hammond, because "his belief in himself
outruns what we can accept as right or just, and

his moral nature becomes deeply flawed without his growing aware of it." Titus is a "man by degrees consumed by the 'contagious air' of intellectual and moral uncertainty and disorder," writes Gerald D. Parker, until he finds peace by accepting his role as his father's sacrificial lamb. The competing claims of these two archetypal figures have suggested to David M. Vieth the deepest power of psychological myth.

The Duke of Guise was composed at Lee's instigation, with John Dryden contributing the opening scene, act 4, and "the first half or a little more" of act 5. Lee wrote the rest. Both men already had on hand material from which they could draw. Lee's *Massacre of Paris,* banned in 1679 or 1681, depicts the same duke of Guise earlier in his career and explores related political issues. Lee was able to reuse 150 lines of argumentation from *The Massacre of Paris,* here assigned to new speakers. Dryden had also composed a play about Guise in 1660 (never produced), and he confessed that one of his scenes (V.i) was lifted from that earlier work.

The Duke of Guise derives nearly all its meaning from political parallels interpreting recent events in England. As Richard E. Brown summarizes:

> The portrait of Henry [III of France], a mixture of vacillation and anger, generosity and calculation, provides a not wholly flattering type for Charles II. Guise, who wishes to rule while retaining the king as his puppet, signifies the ambitious Duke of Monmouth. Guise's Council of Sixteen, their brains seething with sedition, recalls "the sixteen Whig peers who petitioned Charles in February 1680/1 not to hold a Parliament at Oxford." Malicorne, Guise's advisor in the play, who has sold his soul to the devil, is thought to resemble Monmouth's prominent Whig supporter, the Earl of Shaftesbury.

The action consists of confrontations between supporters and opponents of the king that demonstrate the types of personalities found in both camps. Although the arguments are pointed, they are pitched at a far more reasonable level than the dialogues in Lee and Dryden's *Oedipus.*

Roswell Gray Ham, Frances Barbour, and Robert D. Hume interpret the defense of the king's prerogative in *The Duke of Guise* as a sign Lee changed his allegiance from Whig to Tory late in his career. J. M. Armistead, David M. Vieth, and Richard E. Brown, however, argue from different viewpoints that Lee's output be-

fore 1682 is not consistently Whiggish but shows a deep concern over the social chaos that results from an absence of authority. Thus it is possible that Lee's contributions to *The Duke of Guise* required no great sacrifice of earlier principles.

The play's premiere was postponed by the lord chamberlain from July to November 1682; when it was finally performed, the queen attended as a sign of official support. During its first season it was repeated often, but afterward was never revived. When the Whiggish press attacked its promonarchical implications, Dryden replied with a partisan and devious pamphlet, *The Vindication* (1683), that describes the play's composition.

The vengeful tone of *The Princess of Cleve* (1682 or 1683) is suggested by Lee's statement that "this Farce, Comedy, Tragedy, or meer Play, was a Revenge for the Refusal of [*The Massacre of Paris*]; for when they expected the most polish'd Hero in Nemours, I gave 'em a Ruffian reeking from Whetstone's-Park [a prostitutes' hangout]." The play's remarkable bitterness must explain its failure to catch on during the first season, though it was revived in 1689. Hume's essay treating this long-ignored work as a major social satire surely came as a surprise when it appeared in 1976, but the case for Lee's artistic seriousness has since been supported by Armistead and Richard E. Brown.

Hume categorizes *The Princess of Cleve* as Lee's only split-plot tragicomedy. Nemours pursues two upper-class women, the princesses of Cleve and of Jainville, while at the same time he is chasing a married bourgeoise. Nemours is thought to signify John Wilmot, earl of Rochester (who had died in 1680); Armistead also identifies other parallels between figures in the play and conspicuous members of Restoration society. The play's satire works by deliberately exaggerating the amoral edge of libertine comedy to such a degree that what should be wickedly funny becomes disgusting. The attack becomes especially disagreeable when it is directed against the naiveté of excessively sensitive characters such as the Prince and Princess of Cleve. Nemours mocks their heroic speech so cleverly that they assume his motives are honorable. Nemours's knowing command of the heroic manner demonstrates that Lee remained a master of poetic subtleties as late as 1682. Yet the playwright does not endorse Nemours's hypocrisy or sexual rapacity any more than he approves of the dumb heroes or licen-

Nathaniel Lee, a nineteenth-century engraving by A. W. Warren

tious cits who are being deceived. All are condemned in this panorama of rottenness.

First produced in November 1683, *Constantine the Great* contains Lee's most optimistic portrait of an absolutist ruler. Previously Lee's point has generally been that power encourages excess, and at the beginning of his last play the Emperor Constantine is just as self-indulgent and tyrannical as Nero, Alexander, Mithridates, Borgia, or Tarquin. Moreover, he has a wicked counselor, Arius, to encourage his darker passions. But Constantine is also surrounded by influences which eventually save him from wrong–his brother Dalmatius, his tender son Crispus, and most of all his spiritual adviser, Sylvester. Hence tragedy is averted when the emperor suddenly comprehends Arius's evil and rejects his own worst impulses.

Stroup and Cooke demonstrate that *Constantine the Great* contains numerous topical allusions. The emperor represents Charles II; Dalmatius is his brother, the duke of York; Crispus recalls the duke of Monmouth; the wicked Arius corresponds with Anthony Ashley Cooper, earl of Shaftesbury; and the Rye House Plot against the lives of the king and his brother is figured in the action. The drift of these parallels has proven controversial, however. The play may be interpreted as proof of Lee's conversion to Toryism after *Lucius Junius Brutus* was banned from the stage, since the emperor vanquishes Arius/Shaftesbury, escapes the plot against him, and is reconciled with his son. But Richard E. Brown argues that while Arius may be killed in a poison bath, "fulfilling a Tory fantasy," nevertheless the emperor and his brother are unpleasant representatives of royal power in their suppression of dissent and their interference in young love. The play creates far more sympathy for Crispus than for his father. Brown concludes, "The very necessity of submitting Constantine to a last-act conversion is curious, if Lee's motive throughout the play is to praise the behavior of Charles II." Perhaps Lee employs topical references only to add interest to the worn-out heroic bombast with which he ends his career; or the political parallels may constitute a bitter acknowledgment of King Charles's victory over the Whigs in 1682.

The fame of Lee's hospitalization in Bedlam, the rhetorical extravagance of his early plays, and his use of spectacular staging, all supported his contemporary reputation as a mad playwright. In "A Parallel of Poetry and Painting" (1695) Dryden refers to his recently deceased colleague:

> Another, who had a great genius for tragedy, following the fury of his natural temper, made every man and woman too in his plays stark raging mad; there was not a sober person to be had for love or money. All was tempestuous and blustering; heaven and earth were coming together at every word; a mere hurricane from the beginning to the end, and every actor seemed to be hastening on the day of judgment.

Claims for a more disciplined and profound artistry have been substantiated by Armistead's careful attention to Lee's shaping of source materials and his creation of imagery patterns. Hume has discovered that the neglected *Princess of Cleve* is a major satire against Restoration libertinism. Philip Parsons, in his survey of Restoration stagecraft, has concluded, "[i]n his command of the resources of the baroque Restoration stage, Lee is the outstanding creative figure." Parsons cites the ironic use of spectacular backdrop to shed light on Alexander's character in *The Rival Queens*, the symbolic opening tableau in *Theodosius*, and the repeated sacrificial images in *Lucius Junius Brutus* to illustrate Lee's mastery of stage effects. Richard E. Brown has argued for Lee's equal partnership in his collaborations with Dryden and has joined Armistead in proposing that Lee's later political dramas chart an intelligent course among partisan positions.

Perhaps the most surprising revelation has been that Lee was a skilled manipulator of dramatic tone. Contemporaries identified two strains in his work: the wild, bombastic exclamations described by Dryden and "softer" love scenes which especially pleased the ladies in the audience. Now Lee is also seen as a satirist of heroic clichés, a writer of rich, vigorous blank verse, a sensitive psychologist whose poetry is capable of reflecting the madness of Nero, the dignity of Brutus, the pathos of Brutus's son, Titus, or the argumentativeness of the politicians in *The Duke of Guise*. If he is still recognized as a pivotal figure in the transition from heroic to pathetic drama by such critics as Eric Rothstein and Laura Brown, his oeuvre is also beginning to be recognized as far more diverse than the heroic-pathetic axis might suggest. If his early reputation suffered from the suppression of his masterpiece, *Lucius Junius Brutus*, now Lee's reputation would undoubtedly be enhanced by a wider reading of *The Princess of Cleve*, a play unpalatable to former ages but well suited for late-twentieth-century tastes.

Bibliography:

J. M. Armistead, *Four Restoration Playwrights, a Reference Guide to Thomas Shadwell, Aphra Behn, Nathaniel Lee, and Thomas Otway* (Boston: G. K. Hall, 1984), pp. 167-259.

Biography:

Roswell Gray Ham, *Otway and Lee: Biography from a Baroque Age* (New Haven: Yale University Press, 1931).

References:

J. M. Armistead, *Nathaniel Lee* (Boston: Twayne, 1979);

Frances Barbour, "The Unconventional Heroic Plays of Nathaniel Lee," *Studies in English*, no. 20 (1940): 109-116;

Laura Brown, *English Dramatic Form, 1660-1760* (New Haven & London: Yale University Press, 1981);

Richard E. Brown, "The Dryden-Lee Collaboration: *Oedipus* and *The Duke of Guise*," *Restoration*, 9 (Spring 1985): 12-25;

Brown, "Heroics Satirized by 'Mad Nat. Lee,'" *Papers on Language and Literature*, 19 (Fall 1983): 385-401;

Brown, "Nathaniel Lee's Political Dramas, 1679-1683," *Restoration*, 10 (Spring 1986): 41-52;

Arthur L. Cooke and Thomas B. Stroup, "The Political Implications in Lee's *Constantine the Great*," *Journal of English and Germanic Philology*, 49 (1950): 506-515;

Antony Hammond, "The 'Greatest Action': Lee's *Lucius Junius Brutus*," in *Poetry and Drama: Es-

says in Honor of Harold F. Brooks, edited by Antony Coleman and Hammond (London & New York: Methuen, 1981), pp. 173-185;

Robert D. Hume, *The Development of English Drama in the Late Seventeenth Century* (Oxford: Clarendon Press, 1976);

Hume, "The Satiric Design of Nat. Lee's *The Princess of Cleve,*" *Journal of English and Germanic Philology,* 75 (January-April 1976): 117-138;

David S. Kastan, "*Nero* and the Politics of Nathaniel Lee," *Papers on Language and Literature,* 13 (Spring 1977): 125-135;

Geoffrey Marshall, *Restoration Serious Drama* (Norman: University of Oklahoma Press, 1975), pp. 155-179;

George McFadden, *Dryden the Public Writer 1660-1685* (Princeton: Princeton University Press, 1978), pp. 208-222;

Gerald D. Parker, " 'History as Nightmare' in Nevil Payne's *The Siege of Constantinople* and Nathaniel Lee's *Lucius Junius Brutus,*" *Papers on Language and Literature,* 21 (Winter 1985): 3-18;

Philip Parsons, "Restoration Tragedy as Total Theatre," in *Restoration Literature: Critical Approaches,* edited by Harold Love (London: Methuen, 1972), pp. 27-28, 32-33, 59-64;

Eric Rothstein, *Restoration Tragedy: Form and the Process of Change* (Madison, Milwaukee & London: University of Wisconsin Press, 1967), pp. 77-86, 91-96;

William Van Lennep, "The Life and Works of Nathaniel Lee, Dramatist (1648?-1692): A Study of Sources," Ph.D. dissertation, Harvard University, 1933;

David M. Vieth, "Psychological Myth as Tragedy: Nathaniel Lee's *Lucius Junius Brutus,*" *Huntington Library Quarterly,* 39 (November 1975): 57-76;

Eugene M. Waith, *Ideas of Greatness: Heroic Drama in England* (New York: Barnes & Noble, 1971), pp. 235-242.

Delarivière Manley
(1672?-11 July 1724)

Linda R. Payne
University of Delaware

See also the Manley entry in *DLB 39: British Novelists, 1660-1800.*

PLAY PRODUCTIONS: *The Lost Lover; or, The Jealous Husband*, London, Theatre Royal in Drury Lane, March 1696;

The Royal Mischief, London, Lincoln's Inn Fields, April-May 1696;

Almyna; or, The Arabian Vow, London, Queen's Theatre, 16 December 1706;

Lucius, the First Christian King of Britain, London, Theatre Royal in Drury Lane, 11 May 1717.

BOOKS: *Letters Written by Mrs. Manley, to Which Is Added a Letter from a Supposed Nun in Portugal to a gentleman in France in imitation of the nun's five letters in print by Colonel Pack* (London: Printed for R. Bentley, 1696); republished as *A Stage-Coach Journey to Exeter* (London: Printed for J. Robert, 1725);

The Lost Lover; or, The Jealous Husband: A Comedy. As it is Acted at the Theatre Royal By His Majesty's Servants (London: Printed for R. Bentley, F. Saunders, J. Knapton & R. Wellington, 1696);

The Royal Mischief: A Tragedy. As it is Acted By His Majesties Servants (London: Printed for R. Bentley, F. Saunders & J. Knapton, 1696); modern edition, in *The Female Wits*, edited by Fidelis Morgan (London: Virago Press, 1981);

The Secret History, of Queen Zarah, and the Zarazians; Being a Looking-glass for --------- in the Kingdom of Albigion, 2 volumes (London, 1705);

Almyna; or, The Arabian Vow: A Tragedy. As it is Acted at the Theatre Royal in the Hay-Market, by her Majesty's Servants (London: Printed for W. Turner, 1707);

Secret Memoirs and Manners of Several Persons of Quality, of Both Sexes from the New Atalantis, an Island in the Mediterranean, 2 volumes (London: John Morphew & J. Woodward, 1709);

Memoirs of Europe, towards the Close of the Eighth Century, 2 volumes (London: Printed for John Morphew, 1710);

The D. of M-----h's Vindication: in answer to a pamphlet lately published call'd (Bouchain, or a Dialogue between the Medley and the examiner.) (London: Printed for J. Morphew, 1711);

Court Intrigues, in a Collection of Original Letters, from the Island of the New Atalantis, &c. (London: Printed for John Morphew & James Woodward, 1711);

The Adventures of Rivella; or, the History of the Author of the Atalantis (London, 1714);

Lucius, the First Christian King of Britain: A Tragedy. As it is Acted at the Theatre-Royal in Drury-Lane. By His Majesty's Servants. (London: Printed for J. Barber, 1717).

OTHER: Commendatory verse, in *Agnes de Castro, A Tragedy. As it is Acted at the Theatre Royal, By His Majesty's Servants*, by Catharine Trotter (London: Printed for H. Rhodes, R. Parker & S. Briscoe, 1696);

Poems signed Melpomene and Thalia, in *The Nine Muses. Or, Poems Written by Nine severall Ladies Upon the Death of the late Famous John Dryden, Esq.*, nine poems, possibly compiled by Manley (London: Printed by Richard Basset, 1700);

"The Lady's Pacquet of Letters, Taken from Her by a French Privateer in Her Passage to Holland," in *Memoirs of the Court of England*, by Marie Catherine d'Aulnoy (London: B. Bragg, 1707);

"The Remaining Part of the Unknown Lady's Pacquet of Letters," in *The History of the Earl of Warwick*, by d'Aulnoy (London: J. Woodward, 1708);

The Power of Love. In Seven Novels, adapted by Manley from William Painter's *The Palace of Pleasure* (London: Printed for John Barber, 1720).

(1)

THE

Secret History

OF

Queen *ZARAH*, &c.

OF all the Kingdoms in the World *Albigion* is now reckoned the fulleſt of Adventures, there being ſcarce any Nation in the Habitable Earth but what it hath ſome Commerce or Communication with, inſomuch that the People are become as Famous Abroad for Politicks, as the *Muſ-*

B   *covites*

(2)

covites are at Home for Love and Gallantry. The Youth of that Country, encourag'd by their Parents Examples, Aſpire to be Privy Counſellors before they get rid of the Rod of their Schoolmaſters; and Prentice Boys aſſume the Air of Stateſmen e'er yet they have learn'd the Myſtery of Trade.

Mechanicks of the Meaneſt Rank plead for a *Liberty* to abuſe their Betters, and turn out Miniſters of State with the ſame Freedom that they ſmoke *Tobacco*. *Carmen* and *Coblers* over Coffee draw up Articles of Peace and War, and make Partition Treaties at their Will and Pleaſure; In a Word, from the Prince to the Peaſant every one here enjoys his Natural Liberty, whether it proceed from the Nature of the Climate

(3)

Climate or the Temper of the People I cannot reſolve you; I rather think Subjects are ſuch as the Rules and Laws of the Government make them.

This Renowned Lady *Zarah*, (tho' of Obſcure Parents) was Born in the Reign of *Rollando* King of *Albigion*, one of the moſt Gallant Princes the World ever had when Gallantry was ſo much in Vogue, that it was almoſt as Natural to be a Gallant as to Live: In thoſe Happy Days it was ſhe firſt receiv'd the Breath of Life common to all other Creatures as well as her, but which none has improv'd to that vaſt Advantage; her Mother's Name was *Janiſa*, a Woman who mov'd in a low Sphere, but had a large Occupation, was one who knew the World well, and was

B 2   ſtudi-

(4)

ſtudious of her own Intereſt; and though ſhe was not admir'd for her Wit, that defect was ſupply'd by ſome little Arts ſhe had peculiar to ſome Sort of Women, by which Means ſhe gain'd the Hearts of all the Men who convers'd with her.

In a few Years *Zarah* grew up to the Admiration of all that knew her Birth and Education, for her Mother had inſtructed her in ev'ry Art that was neceſſary to engage and charm Mankind, ſo that ſhe ſoon became the Object of their Wiſhes and Deſires, as well for the Excellency of her Wit as the Agreeableneſs of her Beauty; about that Time there was One *Hippolito*, a Handſome Gentleman, Well Born, Young and Vigorous, who had pleas'd other Women, and was

Opening pages of text from the 1705 edition of one of the earliest romans à clef in English. Set in Albigion (England), the novel focuses on the rise of Zarah (Sarah Churchill, duchess of Marlborough) and the Zarazians (Whigs) and their challenge to the rightful power of Rollando (Charles II) and his heirs. Also mentioned in these pages are Janisa (Frances Jennings, Lady Sarah's mother) and Hippolito (John Churchill, duke of Marlborough).

As a playwright, hack author, panegyrist, and political satirist, Delarivière Manley gained a curious combination of respect and contempt that has characterized her reputation to the present day. Cut off by an early false marriage from the decorum and security of her genteel cavalier upbringing, she used the pen as weapon and tool to vindicate herself and even attempt to reform the society by which she felt herself victimized. She is best known for her secret histories, especially the *New Atalantis–Secret Memoirs . . . from the New Atalantis* (1709) and *Memoirs of Europe* (1710)– which are only now being taken seriously as important contributions to the development of the English novel. Her contemporaries would have further identified her as a highly effective Tory pamphleteer and propaganda writer and editor for Jonathan Swift's *Examiner*.

Yet Manley first garnered fame as a "petticoat author" in the playhouse. Three of her four extant plays might best be described as heroic tragedies and achieved modest success. She manipulated the genre in interesting ways, playing on some of its expectations and deflating others, perhaps calling into question the moral ambiguity inherent in the traditional superman protagonists. At the very least she exploited it to its fullest degree by revealing a far greater fascination with extraordinary evil than extraordinary good that suggested a kinship as well to revenge or horror tragedy. The failure of Manley's lone comedy discouraged her from developing what may have been a genuine gift for characterization and lively dialogue.

While one tragedy was notorious for the same lurid eroticism and violence (or "warmth," as Manley euphemized) that caused her *New Atalantis* to be vilified, the other plays were far more "respectable" and aspire to art rather than mere sensationalism. Furthermore, all four plays demonstrate the same concern for the wrongly oppressed and the same interest in the psychology of political and moral seduction that characterize her better-known fictions. And they provided her the means to develop with unusual depth and complexity a number of heroines characterized by great strength and resourcefulness, whether in conventional virtue or in corruption induced by society's victimization. Her work as a dramatist also enriched her work as a novelist, preparing her to use dialogue more extensively and effectively than was common in contemporary novels and romances. More important, she developed a flair for graphic scene painting that greatly enlivened her narratives. While her fiction more obviously influenced the writing of others, her work in both genres advanced the acceptance of women writers and helped to open up new perceptions of women both as creators and characters.

Preceded only by Aphra Behn in writing professionally, Manley debuted in the 1695-1696 theatrical season along with Catharine Trotter and Mary Pix. To pursue a public career was in itself considered immodest and immoral in a woman. Lack of formal education put women writers at a further disadvantage, and most were forced to work for very little remuneration as Grub Street hacks. Those, like Manley, who achieved any degree of fame found their private lives under constant scrutiny, with inferences made about their lives from their works and vice versa, and constant accusations that any writing worthy of note had been plagiarized.

Although some information about Manley is available from public records, letters, and contemporary reports, many gaps have been filled in from her own *Adventures of Rivella* (1714) and the "Delia" episodes in the *New Atalantis*, both now considered basically autobiographical but undoubtedly heightened and enhanced. While this makes objectivity problematic, in some respects it is appropriate since much of the passion in her works proceeds from the intimate connection between their issues and motifs and her own day-to-day struggle for survival.

Questions exist even about her name and birth date, because of confusion in the *Dictionary of National Biography* between Manley and her older sister, Mary Elizabeth, born in 1663. Although for years scholars referred to the author as Mary Delarivière Manley, she appears in contemporary sources only as Delarivière or Dela. The preface to *Rivella* indicates that she was born "at Sea, between Jersey and Guernsey" and hence christened "De la Rivière Manley," but she may also have been named for the wife of her father's commanding officer. Her most likely birth date is 1672, established by correlating the verifiable events of her father's career with those recollected in *Rivella*. Reconstructing this chronology, however, is made more difficult by her obvious attempts in *Rivella* to obscure her true age. Her mother died some time before 1680, when Manley's father, Sir Roger Manley, moved his three daughters and son from Portsmouth to Suffolk.

Manley's upbringing was unusually literary; her father, a former cavalier and military governor, published translations from the Dutch, a history of the English rebellion, and a continuation of a Turkish history. Manley also credited him as author of an early novel, *The Turkish Spy* (1687-1693), although she may have been remembering his historical work since her attribution is not generally accepted. Her recollections in *Rivella* include schooling by a household governess and, at about age twelve, "conducting an extensive correspondence with a young suitor without being unduly influenced by 'the many Romances she daily read.'"

A year or two later Manley was sent away to study languages with a Huguenot minister. Although she learned to "read, speak and write French with a Perfection truly wonderful," her health forced her back home before she could master Latin, Spanish, and Italian as planned. Her father died in 1687, and the events in the next year leading up to the Glorious Revolution and flight of James II dashed her hopes for court preferment, where she had been promised a place as maid of honor to Queen Mary. Manley and her younger sister, Cornelia, were made the charges of a cousin, John Manley, whom their father had educated and treated as a son. An elderly aunt further indulged Manley in reading "Books of Chivalry and Romances," which made her "fancy every Stranger . . . in what Habit soever, some disguis'd Prince or Lover."

Upon the aunt's death, John Manley posed as a widower and married his young ward, secluding her and quickly squandering her inheritance before she could discover that his wife was indeed alive. Pregnant and perpetually ill, she was totally dependent on him and continued to live with him for at least three years. In 1693-1694 she joined the household of Barbara Villiers, duchess of Cleveland, and some biographers place her years with John Manley before that date. Others have suggested that the letters in her first literary work, *Letters Written by Mrs. Manley* (1696; republished in 1725 as *A Stage-Coach Journey to Exeter*), may date from a trip to join Manley in the country after the duchess accused her of seducing her son.

As retainer to the aging duchess, a former mistress to Charles II, Manley was exposed firsthand to all the glittering decadence of the fading Restoration world and probably gained the contacts for the rich gossip which later filled her scandal chronicles. During her subsequent exile from the city, she apparently resolved to make her own way in the world, returning to London in 1696 with her first two plays as well as the epistolary narrative of her trip and sojourn.

Quickly gaining two patrons, the duke of Devonshire and Sir Thomas Skipwith, master of the Theatre Royal in Drury Lane, Manley had the two London theaters competing to produce her plays. In a commendatory verse for Catharine Trotter's first play she issued a bold challenge to "Aspiring Mankind" who since the death of Aphra Behn had "quite regained the sway,/Again had taught us humble to obey," giving notice that she longed to compete "in the poetic race,/To loose the reins and give their glory chase." Her comedy, *The Lost Lover; or, The Jealous Husband*, was produced in March 1696 at Drury Lane. It is most interesting for the way in which it combined the Restoration tradition with the sentimental. While Colley Cibber's *Love's Last Shift*, generally considered the first sentimental comedy, had just appeared, Manley claimed to have written hers two years prior. Although critics have labeled the play an intrigue comedy, none of the intrigues that are hinted at are actually executed.

Manley's two heroes, Wilmore and Wildman, are fairly typical Restoration rakes. Wilmore is in love with Marina, whose mother, Lady Young Love, controls her fortune. The widowed mother fancies Wilmore for herself and matches her daughter with his country-squire father. Wilmore plans to effect a switch at some point, but he is crossed by Belira, Marina's pretended friend and Lady Young Love's confidante. Wilmore's cast-off lover, Belira, still scrambles for some means to get him for herself but overtly promotes the marriage to Lady Young Love, preferring to be mistress to a young man with a rich old wife than to be cut off entirely should he marry his true love. His plots and counterplots foiled when the old lady overhears him arguing with Belira, Wilmore eventually gains his desired bride when her mother grants her freedom of choice. He does not really repent or reform, having bargained with Belira about keeping her if she would help him to marry Marina.

The second rake, Wildman, pursues Olivia, who has been forced into marrying a jealous old miser. Wildman is crushed when Olivia announces her resolve to remain a dutiful wife, refusing to hear or read any further overtures from him despite her affection for him. He carries on, however, in characteristic rakish self-service, courting the poet Orinda.

The Lost Lover most notably breaks with tradition in the handling of the heroine Olivia and the villainess Belira. Olivia is quite unusual: attractive, witty, and spirited, when trapped in a bad situation she determines to make the best of it and maintain her self-respect. Belira, though a bit melodramatic as the woman scorned, is treated with more sympathy than was normally accorded a fallen woman. Wilmore admits, "My Pity is due to an unhappy Woman, who had never bin [*sic*] such, if She had not known me." Both Lady Young Love and the fortune-hunting fop Sir Amorous Courtall are allowed more complexity than many of their comedic counterparts and also escape the harsher fates accorded the butts of crueler deceptions.

Faults in this play are obvious: the structure is flimsy, plotting threadbare, motivation underdeveloped. The very little real action is confined to a few scenes, leaving the rest quite unbalanced—stiff bits of clumsy exposition. The two rakes are stock characters of little interest, and the love interest character, Marina, is a mere paper doll. In her preface, however, Manley calls the play "the Follies of seven days (for barely in that time this Play was wrought)" and herself "so great a Stranger to the Stage, that . . . had lived buried in the Country, and in the six foregoing years had actually been but twice at the House." Examined in this light, *The Lost Lover* is not a negligible first effort. She herself asserted that "the bare Name of being a Woman's Play damned it beyond its own want of merit."

Olivia and Belira are much better drawn than the stock lovers and demonstrate Manley's interest in women who attempt to gain control of their own lives. A few scenes of dialogue—particularly the two between Wilmore and Belira—move briskly, crackling with feeling and spirit. Had she not been thoroughly discouraged "by the little success it met with in the Acting" and the greater financial rewards that she reaped from her tragedies and scandal chronicles, Manley might have developed her comedic thrust and turned the potential shown here to good account either in political or social satire.

As it was, in the preface she declared herself convinced that "Writing for the Stage is no proper Way for a Woman, to whom all Advantages but mere Nature are refused." She assured her "Offended Judges" that she would appear before them again only because she already had a tragedy in rehearsal which was too late to recall. That was *The Royal Mischief* (1696), which enjoyed a run of at least six performances, with two author's benefits. Manley cited influences both

from John Dryden's heroic dramas and from John Dennis's *Essay on the Operas after the Italian Manner* (1706) and made effective use of the pomp and spectacle of the heroic style.

Although Manley commended herself for distributing poetic justice to the villainess more carefully than did her historical source, Jean Chardin's *Travels* (1686), the energy of the play is all focused on the evil princess Homais. This focus reflects a vogue in the 1690s for villain tragedies, but further evidences Manley's particular fascination with strong women. Perhaps the greatest weakness of *The Royal Mischief* is a serious shortage of likable characters. The Prince of Libardian, husband to Homais, maintains his rule and survives her schemes, restoring order in the end, but he is not developed with any depth or feeling, and his values seem equivocal. His public governance reflects wisdom and justice; yet he has acted the tyrant with Homais. Manley obliquely suggests that his confinement of Homais—first in an impotent marriage, then within actual guarded walls—contributes to if not initiates her corruption.

Prince Levan is set forth as a romantic hero, but his vaunted honor and virtue are shaky as well. He believes hearsay accusations against his virtuous wife, Bassima, and offers very little resistance as Homais seduces him. With no more justification than his wounded pride, he becomes Homais's dupe and indulges his lust by ruthlessly seeking the deaths of Bassima and her alleged lover, Osman, ultimately turning traitor and attempting regicide against his own uncle.

The wronged couple Osman and Bassima also fail to arouse much pity. Osman is innocent only because of Bassima's virtue, which he continuously assaults from the time they meet until the guards are coming to execute them. He urges that there is yet time for her to make him "blest" as the guards have several more doors to break down before reaching them. She, on the other hand, is cloyingly pious in her refusals to consummate the adultery yet is too weak to honor her husband with real faithfulness.

As for the monster Homais, in the first act Manley does create some interest in her motivation, attempting both in the princess's own speeches and in those whereby her pimps represent her to Prince Levan to portray her as wronged by her husband. But this strain of justification is largely lost in the lies, seductions, murders, and rebellions she subsequently wreaks. She is responsible for the other offensive element of

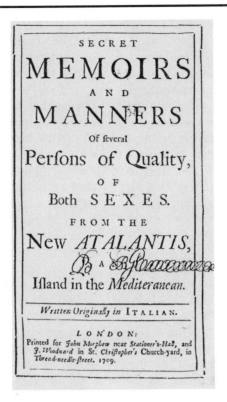

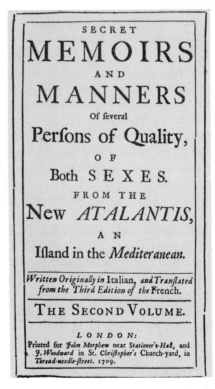

Title page for part 1, with frontispiece and title page for part 2, of Manley's four-part anti-Whig satire, New Atalantis, notorious among her contemporaries for its depictions of orgies, incest, rape, and homosexuality (by permission of the Beinecke Rare Book and Manuscript Library, Yale University)

The Royal Mischief, the excessive violence and luridness of the last act. After Osman's failed assault, Bassima is fairly gently poisoned by Homais; she dies onstage. Osman, according to the graphic description of a guard, is fired from a cannon, his charred remains scattered over the horrified crowd and then collected by his distracted wife, who singes her hands on them. Homais, stabbed by her wronged husband, deliberately bespatters him with "her gore," confesses all, and tries to strangle her young lover as she dies so that he will join her in hell. Finally, Prince Levan falls on his own sword and leaves the Protector standing alone to lament the "mischief two fair Guilty Eyes have wrought."

The Royal Mischief opened at Lincoln's Inn Fields in April or May of 1696, after being pulled from the rival Drury Lane company mid-rehearsal because of Manley's squabbles with the management and players. The play and the defection provided the main comic action for the anonymous satire, *The Female Wits*, at Drury Lane the next season. Manley was the main butt as the affected author of a ludicrous tragedy, which becomes even more ridiculous in the spoof as the Osman and Bassima characters escape in a rocket ship and become emperor and empress of the moon. Despite the facility with which it lent itself to parody, *The Royal Mischief* was a crowd pleaser, and even contemporary critics wrote of its "force and fire" and "just" "Metaphors and Allegories."

Manley's reaction to the parody is not known. She wrote no more plays for the next ten years, as she had indeed promised in the preface to *The Lost Lover*, but her silence may have had as much to do with other circumstances of her life as with the criticism she received. At about that time she met John Tilly, a lawyer and deputy warden of the Fleet Prison; although he was married, they lived together openly. Her biographers have asserted that having failed as a writer, she turned to the only other available livelihood–being a kept mistress. But there is no evidence to indicate that their relationship was a result of financial necessity; all of her autobiographical reflections point to Tilly as her great love, and she is believed to have borne him at least one child. It seems likely, in fact, that her domestic projects brought on her hiatus as a writer. In addition to home and family, she was actively involved in Tilly's many dubious lawsuits and get-rich-quick scams, which invariably failed. The only writing she apparently undertook during this period was two poems for *The Nine Muses* (1700), a collection

of nine elegies for Dryden. The poems representing the dramatic muses Melpomene and Thalia were signed by Manley, and it has been suggested that she compiled the book's contents.

In 1702 Tilly's wife died, and Manley reported that, although he quickly suggested marriage, she burst into tears, saying, "I am undone from this Moment! I have lost the only Person, who secured to me the Possession of your Heart!" Realizing that they were destitute on their own, she offered him his freedom to marry well. He repaired his fortune with a rich widow that very year. Manley left London for two years in order to regroup her economic and emotional forces.

On her own again, Manley began to write. Whether motivated more by hardship or political feeling, she published one of the first English romans à clef, *The Secret History, of Queen Zarah, and the Zarazians*, during the campaign for the parliamentary elections of 1705. In this and her subsequent scandal chronicles she attempted simultaneously to safeguard her libels by distancing them and to establish credibility as a historian by claiming the novels to be translations of actual records of ancient, faraway kingdoms. In the *New Atalantis* she heightened the satire by using as narrators outsiders from another culture. At the same time she attempted recognizable portraits of actual people and established detail in setting and circumstance.

In addition, Manley prefaced *Queen Zarah* with one of the earliest apologies for realistic fiction, drawing important distinctions between the extravagant foreign romances in fashion and what she called history writing, although to the modern eye she did not achieve those distinctions to a great degree. As her audience recognized *Queen Zarah* as a thinly masked attack on the personal and political doings of Sarah, duchess of Marlborough, and the Whigs, the book was an immediate popular success. Criticism, of course, and moral outrage were also harsh.

In 1706 Manley brought out the tragedy *Almyna; or, The Arabian Vow.* It was unsigned, perhaps because politically motivated riots in the playhouse were not unusual and she feared Whig reprisals in reaction to *Queen Zarah*. Or it may have been an artistic decision: still reaping the commercial success of *Queen Zarah*, Manley may have felt she could afford to separate her play from the sensation and allow it to succeed or fail on its own merits. It seems unlikely, however, that she would have been able to resist trying to profit from her infamy, and, in fact, the play's title is an anagram of her own name. This action may have been a coy way of exposing herself while appearing to desire modest anonymity.

Manley admitted taking "something of a Hint" from Antoine Galland's *Arabian Nights' Entertainments* (1704), then recently translated. The resulting work is still largely original, however, and features the most coherent plot of any of Manley's plays, one unified by a strong, overtly feminist theme. At its heart is the determination of Caliph Almanzar to avenge on womankind in general the unfaithfulness within his own family. Supported by the holy writings of the Alcoran, which place women in a class with animals in possessing no immortal souls, he resolves never to trust another woman but to wed and bed as many as he chooses, killing each in the morning. There are also very strong statements condemning education in women, who are "born to obey, to know they nothing knew," for making them contradictions to their own nature, attempting to usurp the male "just Prerogative." These criticisms merely serve as opportunities for Almyna, who "Join'd Art to Nature, and improv'd the Whole/What ever Greek or Roman Eloquence/ Egyptian Learning, and Philosophy can teach;/ She has, by Application made her own."

Manley's characteristic charismatic evil and seething eroticism are absent from this play. In order for it to achieve its designed effect the caliph must be sympathetic—mistaken but not inherently malicious—as must the second male lead, his brother and heir Abdalia, who has dishonorably jilted one beautiful sister for another. Manley handles the caliph quite skillfully, making him just and honorable in every other way, courageous and heroic. The love which the virtuous and passionate Almyna bears him seems quite convincingly motivated.

Almyna rejects her engagement to Abdalia when she learns what he has done to her sister, seizing the opportunity to seek marriage to the caliph instead. She determines to risk martyrdom in order to gain a night with the ruler wherein she might save the other women of her kingdom and save him as well from his own destructive obsession. Her nobility, aided somewhat by her beauty, does indeed win his love and convince him of the fineness of her soul. He therefore foreswears subsequent marriages, although further testing her by pretending to proceed with her own execution, which he has no intention of carrying out.

Manley is much less successful in developing any sympathy for the caliph's brother. Although she claimed in the preface to be rewriting the last act in order to spare and reunite the doomed former lovers, such a revision would not have strengthened audience sympathy and would have eliminated most of the onstage action. Too much of the plot has already taken place in the past or takes place offstage. The final act, in which the brother stages the rebellion where he and Almyna's sister are accidentally killed, provides the only real action, except for the all-important music and dancing.

The blank verse, on the other hand, is grand and stirring, helping to render Almyna a splendid heroine. Quite modern in her outlook and revolutionary in her ambitions, she nevertheless shows the requisite reverence for both father and husband. She attempts to effect change through persuasion rather than force. While she and Homais may share the same potential for greatness, having similar attributes and accomplishments, Manley never allows Almyna to think herself above the law or even mores of her society— the key distinction between her virtue and Homais's evil.

The next year was a busy one for Manley, again destitute, according to a letter she wrote Elizabeth Montagu, countess of Sandwich, asking for patronage for the printing of *Almyna*. She published another modestly successful epistolary collection, "The Lady's Pacquet of Letters," in a translation of work by Marie Catherine d'Aulnoy. The series was continued in 1708 with more letters appended to a work by d'Aulnoy. In none of the various circumstances of her life, however, were the greatest benefits available to a writer of her class sufficient to prevent her being hungry and debt-ridden.

In 1709 she refocused her energies on the Tory cause, bringing out her greatest scandal chronicle, *Secret Memoirs and Manners of Several Persons of Quality, of Both Sexes from the New Atalantis, an Island in the Mediterranean*, to help topple the Whigs in 1710. The anonymous publication was an overnight cause célèbre, outdoing even *Queen Zarah* in depicting orgies, incest, rapes, and homosexuality. Manley spent at least a week in jail when she admitted authorship of the second volume in order to gain the release of the printer and publisher. Upon her release she quickly produced volumes 3 and 4 of the *New Atalantis, Memoirs of Europe* (1710).

Frontispiece and title page for the autobiographical novel that is an important source of information about Manley's life

The same year Manley also turned to journalism, creating the *Female Tatler* and its colorful persona Mrs. Crackenthorpe, "a Lady that knows every thing." She sent a copy of the *New Atalantis* to Tory minister Robert Harley, offering further services to the party. Her contributions over the next four years included writing for and editing the *Examiner* with Jonathan Swift and producing several pamphlets, both independently and in collaboration with Swift.

By 1711 Manley was living with printer John Barber. It is generally believed that Barber kept Manley, although one Barber biographer asserted that the author merely maintained an apartment at Barber's house to be near the press. She was already ill with the dropsy which plagued her the rest of her life. That year the letters of "The Lady's Pacquet of Letters" were republished as *Court Intrigues, in a Collection of Original Letters, from the Island of the New Atalantis, &c.*, either as an attempt by Manley to turn a quick dollar or as a pirated edition capitalizing on her fame.

Following Queen Anne's death and the fall of the Tories in 1714, Manley again retired briefly from London, writing to Harley that she was too impoverished to maintain suitable mourning. It was in that year that she published *The Adventures of Rivella* in order to forestall a biography underway by hack writer Charles Gildon for rival printer Edmund Curll, and to demonstrate that "Her Vertues are her own, her Vices occasion'd by her Misfortunes."

Manley's relations with Swift and Sir Richard Steele testify that her seemingly grubbing existence usually came to earn grudging admiration from those who knew her well. Swift had deprecated her personally and professionally, characterizing her writing "as if she had about two thousand epithets and fine words packed up in a bag, and that she pulled them out by handfuls, and strewed them on her paper, where about once in five hundred times they happen to be right." But not only did he go on to hire her and collaborate with her on the *Examiner* and Tory tracts, he described her "Vindication" of the duke of Marlborough (1711) as superior to his own efforts at that time. Similarly, late in Manley's life Steele patched up a feud they had kept running in print for many years, recommending her last play and providing the epilogue for it.

In choosing her subject for *Lucius, the First Christian King of Britain* (1717), Manley may have had in mind Steele's well-known essay *The Christian Hero* (1701) as she sought to make another sordid and bloody story amenable to the mellowing tastes of the century's second decade. It opened at Drury Lane on 11 May 1717 for a run of at least three nights, and perhaps as many as fifteen, with a revival and another author's benefit in 1720.

But if Manley's intention was indeed to glorify Lucius, she was again overtaken by her zest for creating riveting villains. The British usurper Vortimer completely overshadows his heir, Lucius, wreaking horror wherever he conquers, attempting several times to rape the conquered Queen Rosalinda, once as part of the execution he has fashioned to keep her from her beloved prince. Meanwhile, Iagoan schemer Arminius convinces the gullible Lucius that Rosalinda, his untainted love, is a virtual whore.

Lucius never really does anything through the first four acts, although we hear secondhand of an unconvincing conversion to Christianity to please Queen Rosalinda. Only in the final act does he qualify as a hero by killing a coarse ravisher to save Rosalinda, not knowing that the man is Vortimer in disguise. Horrified by his patricide, he prepares to commit suicide until advised in the nick of time that he had actually been conceived before Vortimer murdered the rightful king and raped Lucius's mother. Lucius is in reality the heir to the throne and no kin to the heathen he has just dispatched.

Two villainous princesses also complicate the almost-hopelessly confusing proceedings. They are far less compelling than the male villains, but the heroine Rosalinda provides considerably more interest than does the titular hero. Her virtue is better delineated. More fully dimensioned, she shows much greater strength of character—with far more honorable reasons for shunning her marriage bed than Lucius—and more believable motivation for Christian martyrdom, some of her impassioned speeches suggesting Lear. Manley's writing for the queen is unmistakably rant, but first-rate rant in the midst of impenetrable intrigue and wooden expository dialogue.

During her last seven years Manley published only one work, *The Power of Love. In Seven Novels* (1720), a collection of tales adapted from William Painter's *Palace of Pleasure* (1566-1567) and supplemented by two similar, original stories. *The Court Legacy*, fragments of a ballad opera, was published in 1733 as a product of the author of the *New Atalantis*, but modern scholars have found no similarity to her other works and point out internal evidence indicating composition after Manley's death. In her will she mentioned two plays, "one Tragedy call'd the *Duke of Somerset* and one Comedy named *the double Mistress* which I hope may perhaps turn to some account," instructing all her other papers to be burned. Unfortunately, there is no trace of these plays.

Although Barber prospered, aided in great measure by the income from Manley's popular works, the author was still hounded by debts. Apparently his treatment of her, though kind at first, became a source of great humiliation. When he was exiled in Calais because of contacts with the "Pretender," the companion he sent for to relieve his distress was not Manley but a coarse woman he had ostensibly hired as her maid. Manley died shortly thereafter on 11 July 1724 in London. She was buried in the middle aisle of the Church of St. Benet at Paul's-Wharf, with an epitaph generously describing her as "acquainted with several parts of knowledge, and with the most polite writers, both in the French and English Tongue," which, "together with a greater Natural Stock of Wit, made her Conversation agreeable to all who knew Her, and her Writings to be universally Read with Pleasure."

While Manley's plays drew positive reviews, the attention of her own century focused primarily on the supposed looseness of her life and her fiction. Within a few years her plays, unrevived and out of print, were nearly forgotten. The nineteenth-century stage histories tended to characterize her writing by her fiction, although the few discussions devoted to critical analysis of the plays credited them with liveliness and passion. The general condemnation of Manley and censure of her work carried over well into this century, with moral condescension coloring even those major studies of the novel which began to give her histories their due. It is only very recently that critics have evaluated her fictions for considerations of art and style rather than as types for popular hackwork. Her drama has received even less such scholarship.

Although Manley's fictions are now available in facsimile reprints, her plays are not. Only *The Royal Mischief* is available in a modern edition but remains unannotated. The themes of Manley's works, as well as her commanding use of metaphor and the motif of persecuted innocence, are perhaps of greatest interest to the modern reader. All of her tragedies turn on issues of order, governance, succession, and rebellion as she seeks to uphold Tory principles. Images of government and family are intertwined, as in each case regicide is also presented as some sort of parricide. Sexual seduction and corruption serve as powerful metaphors for political degeneracy and social victimization in the Whig regime, and perhaps in patriarchy.

Manley's fascination with the roles and choices available to women, and with the consequences to those women who seek to govern their own lives rather than allowing themselves to be passively bartered among men, makes her work particularly vital today. Although the moral order she represents in her plays reinforces certain boundaries beyond which women dare not tread, punishing and rewarding accordingly, she shows a far greater creativity in envisioning options within those boundaries than did most of her contemporaries. She also dramatized the fall of those women who transgressed as majestic and tragic, helping to call into question the very order she depicts.

Furthermore, *The Lost Lover* and *Lucius* can be profitably read as specimen pieces: the former reflects an early tendency to sentimentality and the latter an attempt to impose the vogue for the "Christian hero" on heroic drama. *Almyna* can stand alongside any tragedy from the early eighteenth century and has the most to offer in terms of characterization and feminism. A modern edition could help attract more serious attention to

Manley's work other than the *New Atalantis;* it would demonstrate that her writing merits study and continues to stimulate and entertain even outside the context of the author's racy life and times.

Biographies:

Walter and Clare Jerrold, *Five Queer Women* (London: Brentano's, 1929), pp. 83-138;

Paul B. Anderson, "Mistress Delarivière Manley's Biography," *Modern Philology*, 33 (February 1936): 261-278;

Dolores Diane Clark Duff, "Materials toward a Biography of Mary Delarivière Manley," Ph.D. dissertation, Indiana University, 1965;

Fidelis Morgan, ed., *A Woman of No Character: An Autobiography of Mrs. Manley* (London: Faber & Faber, 1986).

References:

Constance Clark, *Three Augustan Women Playwrights* (New York: Peter Lang, 1986);

Nancy Cotton, *Women Playwrights in England c. 1363-1750* (Lewisburg, Pa.: Bucknell University Press, 1980), pp. 84-88, 97-102;

Fidelis Morgan, Introduction and notes to *The Royal Mischief*, in *The Female Wits: Women Playwrights of the Restoration*, edited by Morgan (London: Virago Press, 1981), pp. 32-43, 209-210;

Gwendolyn B. Needham, "Mary de la Rivière Manley, Tory Defender," *Huntington Library Quarterly*, 12 (May 1949): 253-288;

Needham, "Mrs. Manley: An Eighteenth-Century Wife of Bath," *Huntington Library Quarterly*, 14 (May 1951): 259-284;

Dolores Palomo, "A Woman Writer and the Scholars: A Review of Mary Manley's Reputation," *Women and Literature*, 6, no. 1 (1978): 36-46;

John J. Richetti, *Popular Fiction Before Richardson: Narrative Patterns 1700-1739* (Oxford: Clarendon Press, 1969), pp. 119-152;

Philip Sergeant, *Rogues and Scoundrels* (London: Hutchinson, 1924), pp. 171-209.

Peter Anthony Motteux

(25 February 1663-18 February 1718)

Carolyn Kephart

PLAY PRODUCTIONS: *The Rape of Europa by Jupiter*, London, Dorset Garden Theatre, 1694?;

The Taking of Namur, and His Majesty's Safe Return, London, Lincoln's Inn Fields, August/September? 1695;

Love's a Jest, London, Lincoln's Inn Fields, June 1696;

The Loves of Mars and Venus, interlude performed with Edward Ravenscroft's *The Anatomist*, London, Lincoln's Inn Fields, November 1696;

The Novelty, Every Act a Play, by Motteux and others, London, Lincoln's Inn Fields, June 1697;

Europe's Revels for the Peace, London, at Court, 4 November 1697;

Beauty in Distress, London, Lincoln's Inn Fields, April/May 1698;

The Island Princess, adapted from Nahum Tate's adaptation of an anonymous adaptation of John Fletcher's *The Island Princess*, London, Dorset Garden Theatre, 7 February 1699 (perhaps performed a few days earlier at the Theatre Royal in Drury Lane);

Acis and Galatea, London, Lincoln's Inn Fields, November/December? 1701;

Britain's Happiness, London, Theatre Royal in Drury Lane, and Lincoln's Inn Fields, 1704;

Arsinoe, Queen of Cyprus, London, Theatre Royal in Drury Lane, 16 January 1705;

Farewell Folly, or The Younger the Wiser, London, Theatre Royal in Drury Lane, 18 January 1705;

The Temple of Love, London, Queen's Theatre, 7 March 1706;

Thomyris, Queen of Scythia, London, Theatre Royal in Drury Lane, 1 April 1707;

Love's Triumph, London, Queen's Theatre, 26 March 1708.

BOOKS: *The Gentleman's Journal; or The Monthly Miscellany* (London: R. Baldwin, January 1692-November 1694);

The Works of Mr. Francis Rabelais, Doctor in Physick: Containing five Books of the Lives, Heroick Deeds and Sayings of Gargantua, And his Sonne Pantagruel, books 4 and 5, translated by Motteux (London: Printed for R. Baldwin, 1693, 1694);

The Rape of Europa by Jupiter. A Masque; As it is Sung at the Queens Theatre, in Dorset-Garden. By Their Majesties Servants (London: Printed by M. Bennet, 1694); facsimile in *The Rape of Europa by Jupiter (1694) and Acis and Galatea (1701)* (Los Angeles: William Andrews Clark Library, 1981);

The Present State of the Empire of Morocco, translated from the French of Pidou de Saint Olon (London, 1695);

Maria. A Poem Occasioned by the Death of Her Majesty. Addrest to Three Persons of Honour (London: Printed for P. Buck, 1695);

Words for a Musical Entertainment at the New Theatre, in Little Lincoln's Inn-Fields; on the Taking of Namur, and His Majesty's Safe Return [single sheet] (London, 1695?);

Words for an Entertainment at the Music Feast (London, 1695);

Love's a Jest. A Comedy, As It Is Acted at the New Theatre in Little Lincolns Inn-Fields. By His Majesties Servants (London: Printed for P. Buck, J. Sturton & A. Bosvil, 1696);

The Loves of Mars & Venus. A Play Set to Music, As It Is Acted at the New Theatre, in Little Lincolns Inn-Fields, by His Majesty's Servants (London, 1696);

Single Songs, and Dialogues, in the Musical Play of Mars & Venus (London: Printed by J. Heptinstall & sold by J. Hare & J. Welch, 1697);

Europes Revels for the Peace, and His Majesties Happy Return. A Musical Interlude. Performed at the Theatre in Little Lincolns-Inn Fields, by His Majesties Servants. With a Panegyrical Poem Spoken There, on the Same Occasion (London: Printed for J. Tonson, 1697);

The Novelty. Every Act a Play. Being a Short Pastoral, Comedy, Masque, Tragedy and Farce after the Italian Manner. As It Is Acted at the New-Theatre in Little Lincolns Inn-Fields, by His Majesty's Ser-

vants. *Written by Mr. Motteux, and Other Hands* (London: Printed for R. Parker and P. Buck, 1697);

Beauty in Distress. A Tragedy. As It Is Acted at the Theatre in Little Lincolns Inn-Fields. By His Majesty's Servants (London: Printed for D. Brown & R. Parker, 1698);

The Island Princess, or The Generous Portuguese. Made into an Opera. As It Is Performed at the Theatre Royal (London: Printed for R. Wellington & sold by B. Lintott, 1699); facsimile of manuscript, with music, in *Five Restoration Theatrical Adaptations*, edited by Edward A. Langhans (New York & London: Garland, 1980); modern edition, edited by Curtis A. Price and Robert D. Hume (Tunbridge Wells: Richard Macnutt, 1985);

The Words of a New Interlude, Called The Four Seasons, or Love in Every Age. And of all the Musical Entertainments, in the New Opera, Called the Island Princess, or the Generous Portuguese (London: Printed for R. Basset, 1699);

The History of the Renown'd Don Quixote, 2 volumes, translated by Motteux and others (London: Printed for S. Buckley, 1700-1703);

The Masque of Acis and Galatea, With the rest of the Musical Entertainments, in a New Opera Call'd The Mad Lover (London: Printed for R. Parker and H. Newman, 1701); facsimile in *The Rape of Europa by Jupiter (1694) and Acis and Galatea (1701)* (Los Angeles: William Andrews Clark Library, 1981);

Britain's Happiness, A Musical Interlude. Perform'd at Both the Theatres. Being Part of the Entertainment Subscrib'd for by the Nobility (London, 1704);

Arsinoe, Queen of Cyprus. An Opera, After the Italian Manner. As It Is Perform'd at the Theatre Royal in Drury-Lane, by Her Majesty's Servants (London: J. Tonson, 1705);

The Temple of Love: A Pastoral Opera. English'd from the Italian. All Sung to the Same Musick. By Signior J. Saggione. As It Is Perform'd at the Queen's Theatre in the Haymarket. By Her Majesty's Sworn Servants (London: J. Tonson, 1706);

Thomyris, Queen of Scythia. An Opera, As It Is Perform'd at the Theatre-Royal in Drury-Lane (London: Printed for Jacob Tonson, 1707);

Farewel Folly, or The Younger the Wiser (London: J. Round, 1707);

Love's Triumph. An Opera. As It Is Perform'd at the Queen's Theatre in the Hay-Market (London: Printed for J. Tonson, 1708);

A Poem in Praise of Tea (London: Printed for J. Tonson, 1712); also published as *A Poem upon Tea* (London: J. Tonson, 1712).

OTHER: "To The King on His Majesty's Landing in Holland," in *A Collection of State Songs, Poems, etc.* (London, 1716).

Peter Anthony Motteux, of eventful life and unsavory death, was during his career as a playwright (1694?-1708) known chiefly for his continual strivings for novelty in the interest of financial gain: most of his dramatic works are characterized by extensive use of music and range from short masques to translations and imitations of Italian opera. It is to his operas that Motteux owes the attention of the student of theater, because he swayed public taste in such a manner as to pave the way for G. F. Handel.

Born Pierre Antoine le Motteux in Rouen, France, in 1663, son of a well-to-do Huguenot merchant, Antoine le Motteux, Motteux seems to have received a wide and thorough education that emphasized letters and languages. In his early twenties he was forced to immigrate to London during the religious oppression which ensued after the revocation of the Edict of Nantes in 1685. Thus deprived of what he himself called "a handsome Patrimony," he lived for a time with one of his relations, a tradesman. He was made a London citizen in March 1685 and married his first wife, Elizabeth, an Englishwoman, in 1691. The marriage lasted only three years and apparently was childless.

A man of many talents and congenial personality, Motteux quickly and perfectly assimilated the English language, became acquainted with London's literary circle, and by 1692 he was singlehandedly editing *The Gentleman's Journal; or The Monthly Miscellany*, an innovative magazinelike omnium-gatherum of town gossip, criticism, poetry, and essays written by Motteux himself, with verse contributions by friends such as Matthew Prior, Aphra Behn, Thomas Durfey, and John Dennis; also provided was inside information on play productions at London's two theaters. Here Motteux reflected an interest that would soon burgeon into a career. Patterned after the fashionable French *Mercure Galant, The Gentleman's Journal* ran from January 1692 to November 1694. Besides this undertaking, Motteux also repub-

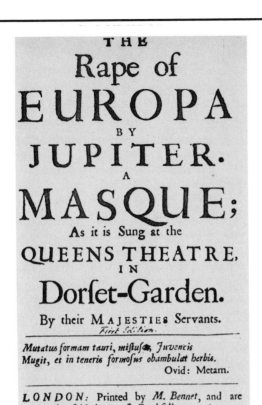

THE

Rape of EUROPA

BY

JUPITER.

A

MASQUE;

As it is Sung at the

QUEENS THEATRE,

IN

Dorſet-Garden.

By their MAJESTIES Servants.

First Edition.

Mutatus formam tauri, miſtuſæ, Juvencis
Mugit, et in teneris formoſus obambulat herbis.
                                    Ovid: Metam.

LONDON: Printed by *M. Bennet*, and are
to be ſold by moſt Bookſellers. 1694.
Price Sixpence. *2. Octob*

The Names of the Perſons that Sing.

Jupiter.	Mr. *Bowman.*
Mercury.	Mr. *Magnus.*
Europa.	Mrs. *Bracegirdle.*
Herſe.	} Two Nymphs { Mrs. *Hodgſon.*
Aglaura.	Mrs. *Cibber.*
Coridon.	Mr. *Doggett.*

Dancers.

Mr. *Doggett.*
Mr. *Phillboy.*
Mr. *Prince.*
Mr. *Bray.*
Mrs. *Knight.*
Mrs. *Lucas.*
Mrs. *Temple.*

ARGU

ARGUMENT.

Europa *Siſter of* Cadmus, *and Daughter of* Agenor *King of* Phœnicia, *was Sollicited by her Father to marry a Nobleman of* Tyre. *But She being a Nymph of* Diana's *train, was averſe to the Importunities of her Lover, and commands of her ſevere Father; In vain was her Averſion, for he ſtrictly commanded her to prepare her ſelf for the performance of his will. But* Death *being a more acceptable choice, ſhe gets leave for a ſhort time, (by the intercesſion of her Brother and a promiſe of compliance upon her return, to her Father's orders) with a few Companions to retire to the Country:* Jupiter *being cloy'd with the Fruition of his late Miſtreſs* Io, *Reſolves*

Argument.

ſolves upon a New Amour, and Deſcending with his Son Mercury, *ſees the diſcontent* Europa, *and loves her. But finding her Inclination contrary to his Deſires, transforms himſelf into the Figure of a Bull, and ſo by Artifice, Endeavours to Enjoy his Love. The Nymph being pleas'd with the beauty of the Metamorphoz'd Deity, Adorns the Beaſt with Ribbons and Flowers, and by degrees is Encourag'd to get upon him, when the God taking the Hint, conveys her thro' the Helleſpont, and raviſhes her, and to Recompence her Loſt Virginity makes her a Star.*

S C.

Title page, dramatis personae, and argument from the unique copy of a brief masque attributed to Motteux through internal evidence (by permission of the Henry E. Huntington Library and Art Gallery) lished Sir Thomas Urquhart's translation of the first three books of François Rabelais's works, along with his own translations of books 4 (1694) and 5 (1693).

Motteux's involvement with the London stage may have begun in 1694 with *The Rape of Europa by Jupiter*, a short, anonymous masque that Lucyle Hook contends was written by Motteux to be included in a revival of John Wilmot, earl of Rochester's adaptation of John Fletcher's tragedy *Valentinian* (circa 1612). Although this claim cannot be established with certainty, *The Rape of Europa* possesses several characteristics often found in Motteux's stage works: brevity, a classical theme undercut by broad vernacular comedy, extensive use of the actor-singer, and musical settings by theater composer John Eccles. Although the exact performance dates are not known, the printed version reveals that it was performed at Dorset Garden Theatre and featured as its principals Anne Bracegirdle and John Bowman, important performers whose singing ability equaled their acting–a teaming of talents that Motteux was to employ in several other productions.

Shortly after King William's victory at Namur in August 1695, Motteux wrote (in French) a pro-English parody of Nicholas Boileau's "Ode sur la Prise de Namur" (1693); he also composed a brief musical entertainment, produced at the Lincoln's Inn Fields theater, to celebrate the event. In this song-filled bagatelle Motteux did everything possible to cater to his audience's patriotic zeal, jostling high-flown allegorical figures with the lowest comic characters, all of whom proclaim William's martial virtues in fulsome fashion. *The Taking of Namur, and His Majesty's Safe Return* was short, strictly topical, and had only a brief run. Motteux later wrote the words to two other musical entertainments similar to *The Taking of Namur* in their grandiloquently overwrought allegory and coarse rusticity: *Europe's Revels for the Peace*, performed at court on 4 November 1697 to celebrate the Peace of Ryswick; and *Britain's Happiness*, a flattering trifle addressed to Queen Anne, mounted at both Drury Lane and Lincoln's Inn Fields in 1704.

Love's a Jest (1696), Motteux's first full-length play, enjoyed a popularity that came as a surprise even to the author, who confessed in his preface to the printed version, "I am almost asham'd to mention the extraordinary Success of a Play which I my self must condemn." With its stress on urban satire and concatenated intrigue, *Love's a Jest* is typical post-Restoration comedy,

earthy, bawdy, and fast moving, interlarded with dollops of gratuitous sentiment, every bit of it calculated to please its audience and realize a profit. Following the fashion set by Thomas Durfey of having able-voiced actors double as singers, a practice much appreciated by London theatergoers, Motteux stuffed his play full of song, making sure to include a duet (set by John Eccles) for Bowman and Bracegirdle, who played the flirtatious couple Airy and Christina.

Motteux's next effort was another brief musical work written in collaboration with Eccles, *The Loves of Mars and Venus* (1696), an interlude for Edward Ravenscroft's comedy *The Anatomist*. The racy wit and frank eroticism of *The Loves of Mars and Venus* show Motteux at his best: gods and goddesses are transformed into Olympian beaux and ladies who engage in intrigue as energetically as any of their London counterparts. Venus was played and sung by Anne Bracegirdle, now at the height of her beauty and charm; Paris by John Bowman, famed for his fine bass-baritone and for his devotees among the ladies of the audience. Contemporary sources state that the masque was a considerable factor in the play's initial popularity. Motteux's last interlude featuring Bowman and Bracegirdle was *Acis and Galatea* (produced in 1701), one of three musical entertainments set by Eccles and performed with a revival of Fletcher's circa 1616 play *The Mad Lover* (the other two were Motteux's short "Martial Welcome" in the second act and his skitlike "Wine and Love" in the third). For *Acis and Galatea* Motteux conceived of another novel twist in his casting: Bowman played the cyclops Polyphemus and Bracegirdle (known, as Colley Cibber relates, for her "handsome legs and feet") took the breeches part of the shepherd Acis, with comic and highly successful results.

Emboldened by the good fortune of *The Loves of Mars and Venus*, Motteux went out on a dramatic limb with *The Novelty, Every Act a Play* (1697). This odd potpourri strung together pastoral, masque, comedy, tragedy, and farce; Motteux himself wrote the masque, *Hercules* (as usual, set to music by Eccles), revamped the last act of an unsuccessful tragedy by Edward Filmer, and "scribbled over a Farce after the Italian Manner, and an Imitation of part of a diverting French Comedy" to fill out his dramatic sampler; John Oldmixon contributed the pastoral, *Thyrsis*. A contemporary satire summarized its inspiration and its fate onstage as "Every Word stolen, and then Damn'd," but Motteux reported that it did well, considering the summer season and the resultant diminished audience.

Beauty in Distress (1698) was Motteux's sole attempt at seriousness; an overwrought blood-thirsty tragedy of horror and revenge, it found its author uncomfortably out of his element (as Motteux observed, it had "no Singing, no Dancing, no mixture of Comedy, no Mirth, no change of Scene, no Rich Dresses, no Show"), and promptly failed onstage. Afterward Motteux would concentrate on creating musical drama ranging from masques to song-stuffed adaptations of English plays and "Englishings" of Italian opera. His topical farce, *Farewell Folly* (1705), reflects the decline of the actor-singer and the audience's growing infatuation with professional singers; in the play the majority of the songs were performed by Richard Leveridge, a popular concert basso.

A full-blown example of his adaptations is *The Island Princess* (1699), Motteux's semi-operatic adaptation of Fletcher's circa 1621 tragicomedy as altered in 1687 by Nahum Tate. Motteux's radical reworking required a great deal of music, both vocal and instrumental, most of which was composed by Daniel Purcell and Jeremiah Clarke; this music was cast in the form of discrete, detachable masques placed at the end of each act. Although Motteux previously had been allied with the company at Lincoln's Inn Fields, *The Island Princess* was concocted for the Drury Lane theater expressly to combat the success enjoyed by John Dennis's musical tragedy *Rinaldo and Armida* at the rival playhouse, and *The Island Princess* seems to have achieved its aim very satisfactorily. However, the artistic merits of Motteux's version of *The Island Princess* are exceedingly small: the play itself was drastically cut to accommodate large amounts of garish spectacle and undistinguished, often coarse and inane, song. Its extreme popularity seems to have owed more to its music than to Motteux's ingenuity.

Motteux's first wife had died in 1694, an event which seems to have brought about the cessation of *The Gentleman's Journal;* by 1699 Motteux had remarried; by his second wife, Priscilla, he had seven children, only three of whom survived him, between 1700 and 1710. In 1700 he accepted a position with the post office, which by 1702 was paying him forty pounds a year. Between 1695 and 1708 Motteux wrote, in addition to dramatic works, various poems, songs, and translations, as well as prologues and epilogues for other authors' plays. Perhaps most important,

in 1700 and 1703 Motteux published his fine and still highly regarded English translation of Miguel de Cervantes's *Don Quixote*. How long Motteux stayed with the post office and how enriched he was by *Don Quixote* are not known, but in 1705 he was casting about for more money and began to establish himself in business. By 1711 he was described in *The Spectator* (no. 288) as a prosperous East India merchant with a flourishing trade in silk, lace, tea, and china, whose warehouse in Leadenhall Street was a favorite haunt of London's fashionable ladies. Once he became a tradesman, Motteux ceased writing for the theater, but between the years 1700 and 1708 he produced several stage works, most notably translations of Italian operas.

The "foreign invasion" of French and Italian performers on the London stage at the turn of the seventeenth century had come about as a result of the 1695 breakup of the United Company (formed in 1682), which created intense and bitter competition between the young—or inexperienced—actors at Drury Lane and the seceding group of seasoned performers, headed by Thomas Betterton, at Lincoln's Inn Fields. After 1695 all kinds of stratagems were employed to attract audiences, and entr'acte entertainments featuring French and Italian singers and dancers increasingly swelled the bills; the obvious next step was full-fledged opera, which Motteux was happy to provide.

Motteux had praised Italian opera in *The Gentleman's Journal* before he began to write for the stage; years later, in January 1705, he realized a long-held goal by bringing to the London stage its first Italianate opera (that is, all sung, as opposed to the native English semi-opera's combination of play with interpolated musical scenes). *Arsinoe, Queen of Cyprus* was produced at Drury Lane with music by Thomas Clayton, Nicolino Hyam, and Charles Dieupart; the cast was all English. Motteux translated Tomaso Stanzani's 1677 libretto in no especially poetic or faithful manner; modern critics have damned *Arsinoe* for its inanity and mediocrity, but the most vociferous critic was Motteux's contemporary Colley Cibber, whose biased—and isolated—opinion was given in his *Apology* (1740): "The *Italian* Opera began first to steal into *England;* but in as rude a Disguise, and unlike it self, as possible; in a lame, hobling Translation, into our own Language, with false Quantities, or metre out of Measure, to its original Notes, sung by our own unskilful Voices,

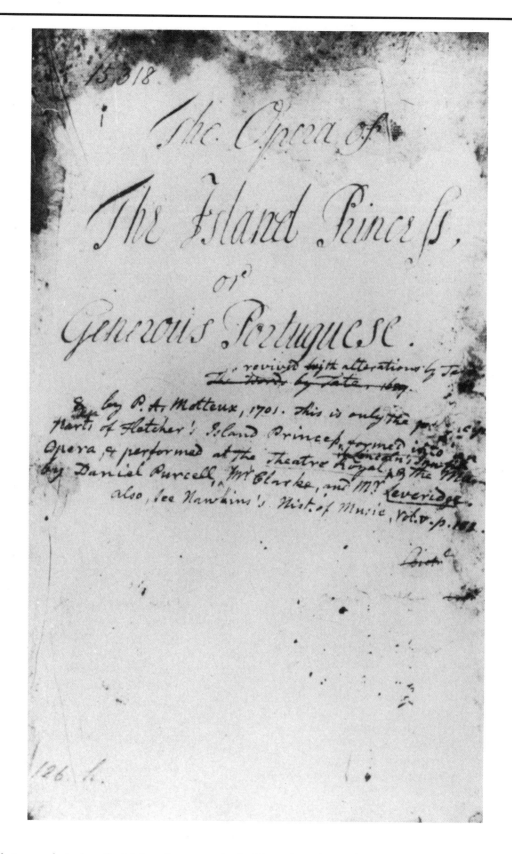

Title page and opening of act 1 from the manuscript for Motteux's semi-operatic version of a tragicomedy by John Fletcher
(by permission of the British Library)

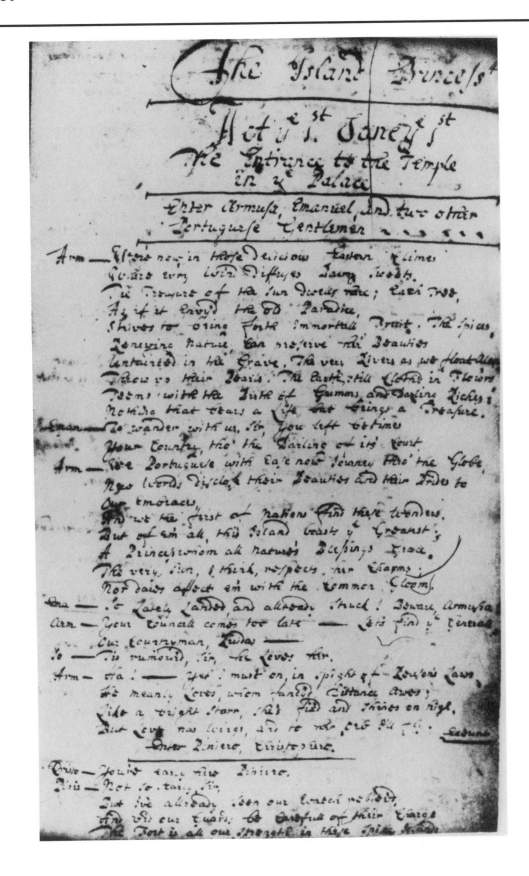

The M A S Q U E
O F

Acis and Galatea,

With the reft of the
MUSICAL ENTERTAINMENTs,
In a New

OPERA

CALL'D

The Mad Lover.

The *Mufick* by Mr. *John Eccles*, Ma-
 fter of his *Majefty's Mufick*.

The Words by Mr. *MOTTEUX*.

L O N D O N,

Printed for *R. Parker* at the *Royal Exchange*, and *H. Newman* in the *Poultry*. 1701.

---

(3)

THE

Martial Welcome

I N T H E

Second Act.

Enter Mars *and* Bellona, *with Attendants to a Warlike
Symphony, and come forwards through* Trophies *and a*
Triumphal-Arch, *keeping Time with the Mufick*.

Mars *and* Bellona.

THE loud Alarms of War muft ceafe,
Hufh'd by the fofter Charms of Peace.
Peace, the Conqu'ror's trueft gain,
With him returns to blefs his Native Plain:
Yet fee with *Mars*, *Bellona* here;
To grace his Triumph we appear.
Uncommon Souls uncommon Honours claim,
Thus now Immortal Pow'rs own his Immortal Fame.

Since Peace to his Ardor at laft is a Bar,
Sound Trumpets, joyn Warriors, with Harmony jar,
Thus pleafe him in Peace with an Image of War.
　　　The Chorus repeat the three foregoing Lines.
Mars. When the whole World amaz'd
On our Leading Hero gaz'd,
His foremoft Guard cry'd, Arm!
Beat Drums, Sound Trumpets, all the Camp Alarm;
　　　　　　　　　　　　　　　　　　　　　　Hark

---

(4)

Hark! The Foes come. See, fee, they March along,
In dire Array, a Hundred Thoufand ftrong.
Their threat'ning Legions View!
Advance, and Fame purfue!
What horrid Slaughter will enfue!
Rous'd by the dreadful Charm, the Warriors wake,
The Valiant glow, the Vulgar quake:
But nothing can our leading Hero fhake.
　　　Let 'em come on, he cry'd!
Let Fate the War decide;
The Foes thus num'rous on us call,
But to be worthy by our Arms to fall.
　Chorus. Honour calling,
　　Warriors raging,
　　Thoufands falling,
　　　All engaging,
Horror Reigns, with boundlefs fway.
　　Honour calling,
　　Warriors raging,
　　Thoufands falling,
　　All engaging,
Mars with *Memnon* wins the Day.

　　A Boy *and* Girl.
Let gentle Notes fucceed your Noife;
Our Youth and Peace love calmer Joys.
Sure, tho' we're little, we may claim
A Right to Lifp the Conqu'ror's Name,
His Praife fhould bufy ev'ry Tongue,
But moft the Innocent and Young;
　The Young can beft Preferve the Fame
Of Deeds accomplifh'd moft for Them.

　　A Sheperdefs.
Let all be gay, let Pleafure Reign;
Peace and *Memnon* cheer the Plain.
　　Both Arriving,
　　Sports Reviving,
None but Lovers now fhall Mourn,
None but Hearts who Rage and burn,
　　Soon with Cooing,
　　Or with Ranging,
　　　　　　　　　　　　With

---

(5)

　　With Purfuing,
　　Or with Changing,
All their Pain to Joy fhall turn.

*A Dance of Marriners as returning home after Victory. Their
Miftreffes with them, and* African Slaves.

　　Grand Chorus.
Rejoyce, rejoyce, our Sorrow now muft ceafe,
For Conqueft Crowns our Ifle with lafting Peace. ［*Exeunt.*

WINE and LOVE

A

MASQUE

I N

The Third Act.

After a humorous Symphony, expreffing the reeling of Drunkards
Bacchus *is difcover'd Sitting on a Golden Tun, in a Vine-Ar-
bor, Crownd with Grapes, and Vine-Leaves, a Cup in one hand and
a Bottle in the other.* Satyres, *and* Bacchanals.

Chorus of Bacchanals.

SEE great *Bacchus*, fee
　How we Worfhip thee.
Here we Laugh and Sing
Till the Vallies Ring.
B　　　　　　　　　　　　　　　　　　　　　　All

*Title page and opening pages from the unique copy of the interludes Motteux wrote for a 1701 semi-operatic adaptation of a play
by John Fletcher (by permission of the University Library, Cambridge)*

with Graces misapply'd to almost every Sentiment, and with Action, lifeless and unmeaning, through every Character." Yet despite Cibber's disdain and its own obvious flaws, *Arsinoe* created a sensation with Londoners, who found it a refreshing change from the stifling insularity of the native theater's increased reliance on revivals of old plays and dramatic operas to vary the general dullness of the few new plays that appeared. The success of *Arsinoe* gave immediate encouragement to other operas by other hands–the unsuccessful *Loves of Ergasto* (1705), the smash hit *Camilla* (1706), and Joseph Addison's solidly English failure *Rosamond* (1707).

After *Arsinoe*, Motteux concocted *The Temple of Love* (1706) and *Love's Triumph* (1708), pastoral fantasies based on the intrigues of amorous Arcadians; Motteux provided an original libretto for *The Temple of Love*, with music by Giuseppe Saggione, and loosely translated Cardinal Pietro Ottoboni's *La Pastorella* (1705) for *Love's Triumph*. Both works were staged at the Haymarket, which had been built especially for opera performances; however, neither achieved any great or lasting success. Between these two failures came Motteux's more-ambitious *Thomyris, Queen of Scythia* (1707), received with enthusiasm by the town: the music was by Alessandro Scarlatti and Marc Antonio or Giovanni Bononcini, with recitatives by Christopher Pepusch, but Motteux made it clear in his preface that "Neither the words, the Thoughts, nor the Design owe anything to Italy, except the Advantage of the Musick." However, *Thomyris* was further indebted to Italy for one of its performers, the castrato Valentino Urbani, who sang in his native language while the rest of the cast sang in English; the audience, far from minding the incongruity, was enchanted. Besides the sensation created by this exotic innovation, *Thomyris* included bits of Motteux's characteristically racy low comedy in addition to its heroics and thus succeeded wonderfully in appealing to all levels of its audience, from side box to upper gallery.

Motteux's retirement from the stage coincided with the lord chamberlain's decree (1708) that only two dramatic genres–straight English plays without musical embellishments, and foreign operas–were to be staged in London, the former at Drury Lane, the latter at the Haymarket. English-language musical entertainments of the type in which Motteux specialized–semi-opera, interlude, Italianate opera–were banned, and apparently as a result Motteux ceased writing for the

theater altogether. He seems to have lived peacefully and well after he forsook writing for the more lucrative rewards of business; his comfortable circumstances, however, met an abrupt and violent end on the night of 18 February 1718 when he died suddenly in a manner that mystified London and was never officially explained. According to town rumor, he was killed in a brothel near Temple Bar, where he had gone with a prostitute; the coroner's inquest declared that he had been willfully murdered, but the ill-famed suspects involved in the death were all acquitted of wrongdoing. The mildness of the verdict surprised Londoners, and the viewpoint of at least one of them comes down in a scrawled note in the margin of a British Museum copy of Charles Gildon's *Lives of the Poets*, which succinctly and explicitly observes that "Mr. M---x is suppos'd to have been strangled by Whores, who forgot to cut the cord They ha[d] ty'd abt. hi[s] Neck to provok[e] venery." Apparently Motteux's strivings after novelty went considerably further than the stage.

Any assessment of Motteux's works must take into consideration the essentially mercantile nature of his inspiration. Motteux, like virtually every other playwright of his day, considered his works as commercial ventures and wrote accordingly. Unconcerned with the judgments of posterity, he aimed to please his audience and, in general, met with success. His works all too often substitute erratic and undisciplined novelty for originality, windy effusion for high inspiration, and Grub-Street coarseness for wit; however, they offer the student of theater a lively and unvarnished portrait of their time. More important are his ventures in the field of opera, which despite their paucity of intrinsic worth had considerable influence on the fortunes of the English theater at the onset of the eighteenth century.

References:

F. W. Bateson, "Motteux and *The Amorous Miser*," *Review of English Studies*, 3 (July 1927): 340-342;

Colley Cibber, *An Apology for the Life of Colley Cibber*, edited by B. R. S. Fone (Ann Arbor: University of Michigan Press, 1968);

Robert Newton Cunningham, *Peter Anthony Motteux, 1663-1718: A Biographical and Critical Study* (Oxford: Blackwell, 1933);

John Downes, *Roscius Anglicanus* (1708), edited by Montague Summers (London: Fortune Press, 1928);

Lucyle Hook, Introduction to *The Rape of Europa by Jupiter (1694) and Acis and Galatea (1701)* (Los Angeles: William Andrews Clark Memorial Library, 1981);

Hook, "Motteux and the Classical Masque," in *British Theatre and the Other Arts,* edited by Shirley Strum Kenney (Washington, D.C.: Folger Books, 1984), pp. 105-115;

Robert D. Hume, *The Development of English Drama in the Late Seventeenth Century* (Oxford: Clarendon Press, 1976);

Hume, "Opera in London, 1695-1706," in *British Theatre and the Other Arts,* pp. 67-91;

Carolyn Kephart, "The Uses of Song in English Drama, 1680-1700," *Theatre Studies,* 33 (Winter 1988): 59-78;

J. Merrill Knapp, "Eighteenth-Century Opera in London before Handel, 1705-1710," in *British Theatre and the Other Arts,* pp. 92-104;

Judith Milhous, "The Multimedia Spectacular on the Restoration Stage," in *British Theatre and the Other Arts,* pp. 41-66;

Curtis A. Price, "The Critical Decade for English Music Drama, 1700-1710," *Harvard Library Bulletin,* 26 (January 1978): 38-76;

Price and Robert D. Hume, eds., Introduction to *The Island Princess: A Semi-Opera,* series C, volume 2 of *English Opera and Masque* (Tunbridge Wells: Richard Macnutt, 1985);

Arthur Colby Sprague, *Beaumont and Fletcher on the Restoration Stage* (Cambridge, Mass.: Harvard University Press, 1926).

Thomas Otway

(3 March 1652-14 April 1685)

J. Douglas Canfield
University of Arizona

PLAY PRODUCTIONS: *Alcibiades,* London, Dorset Garden Theatre, September 1675;

Don Carlos, London, Dorset Garden Theatre, 8 June 1676;

Titus and Berenice, with *The Cheats of Scapin,* London, Dorset Garden Theatre, December 1676;

Friendship in Fashion, London, Dorset Garden Theatre, 5 April 1678;

Caius Marius, London, Dorset Garden Theatre, October 1679;

The Orphan, London, Dorset Garden Theatre, late February or early March 1680;

The Souldiers Fortune, London, Dorset Garden Theatre, June 1680;

Venice Preserved, London, Dorset Garden Theatre, 9 February 1682;

The Atheist; or, The Second Part of the Souldiers Fortune, London, Dorset Garden Theatre, circa July 1683.

BOOKS: *Alcibiades. A Tragedy, Acted at the Duke's Theatre* (London: Printed for William Cademan, 1675);

Don Carlos, Prince of Spain. A Tragedy. Acted at the Duke's Theatre (London: Printed for Richard Tonson, 1676);

Titus and Berenice, a Tragedy, Acted at the Duke's Theatre, with a Farce called the Cheats of Scapin (London: Printed for Richard Tonson, 1677);

Friendship in Fashion. A Comedy, As it is Acted at his Royal Highness the Dukes Theatre (London: Printed by E. F. for Richard Tonson, 1678);

The History and Fall of Caius Marius. A Tragedy. As it is Acted at the Duke's Theatre (London: Printed for Tho. Flesher, 1680);

The Orphan; or, The Unhappy-Marriage. A Tragedy, As it is Acted at His Royal Highness the Duke's Theatre (London: Printed for R. Bentley & M. Magnes, 1680); modern edition, edited by Aline Mackenzie Taylor (Lincoln: University of Nebraska Press, 1976);

The Poet's Complaint of his Muse; or, A Satyr Against Libells. A Poem (London: Printed for Thomas Norman, 1680);

The Souldiers Fortune. A Comedy. Acted by their Royal Highnesses Servants at the Duke's Theatre (Lon-

Thomas Otway, engraving based on a portrait by Mary Beale

don: Printed for R. Bentley & M. Magnes, 1681);

Prologue. By Mr. Otway to his Play call'd Venice preserv'd, or the Plot discover'd. Acted at his Royal Highness the Duke of Yorks Theater, the 9th of February, 1681 [1682] [single sheet, with epilogue–probably by Otway–on verso] (London: Printed for A. Green, 1681 [i.e., 1682]);

Venice Preserv'd; or, A Plot Discover'd. A Tragedy. As it is Acted at the Duke's Theatre (London: Printed for Jos. Hindmarsh, 1682); modern edition, edited by Malcolm Kelsall (Lincoln: University of Nebraska Press, 1969);

Prologue to a New Play, called Venice Preserv'd; or, The Plot Discover'd. At the Duke's Theatre; Spoken by Mr. Smith [single sheet with epilogue on verso] (London: Printed for A. Banks, 1682);

The Prologue to The City Heiress, or, Sir Timothy Treatall [by Aphra Behn] [single sheet with epilogue on verso] (London: Printed for J. Tonson, 1682);

Epilogue to Her Royal Highness, on Her Return from Scotland [broadside] (London: Printed for Jacob Tonson, 1682);

The Epilogue. Written by Mr. Otway to his Play call'd Venice Preserv'd, or a Plot Discover'd; spoken upon his Royal Highness the Duke of York's coming to the Theatre, Friday, April 21 1682 [single sheet] (London: Printed for Joseph Hindmarsh, 1682);

The Prologue and Epilogue, to the Last New Play; Constantine the Great [by Nathaniel Lee] [single sheet], prologue by Otway, epilogue by John Dryden (London: Printed for C. Tebroc, 1683);

The Atheist; or, The Second Part of the Souldiers Fortune. Acted at the Duke's Theatre (London: Printed for R. Bentley & J. Tonson, 1684);

Windsor Castle, in a Monument to our Late Sovereign K. Charles II. of ever Blessed Memory. A Poem (London: Printed for Charles Brom, 1685).

Collections: *The Works of Mr. Thomas Otway*, 2 volumes (London: Printed for J. Tonson, sold by W. Taylor, 1712);

The Works of Thomas Otway, 3 volumes, edited by Thomas Thornton (London: Printed for T. Turner, sold by B. McMillan, 1813);

The Works of Thomas Otway: Plays, Poems, and Love-Letters, 2 volumes, edited by J. C. Ghosh (Oxford: Clarendon Press, 1932).

OTHER: "Phaedra to Hippolytus. By Mr. Otway," in *Ovid's Epistles, translated by several hands* (London: Printed for Jacob Tonson, 1680);

"To Mr. Creech upon His Translation of Lucretius," in *T. Lucretius Carus . . . Done into English Verse*, by Thomas Creech, second edition (Oxford, 1683);

"Epistle to R. D. from T. O." and "The Sixteenth Ode of the Second Book of Horace," in *Miscellany Poems* (London: Printed for Jacob Tonson, 1684);

"The Complaint. A Song to a new Scotch Tune of Mr. Farmers, by Mr. T. O.," in *Miscellany, Being a Collection of Poems by Several Hands*, edited by Aphra Behn (London: Printed for J. Hindmarsh, 1685);

"A Pastoral on the Death of His Late Majesty written by Mr. Otway," in *Lycidus: or The Lover in Fashion. Being an account from Lycidus to Lysander, of His Voyage to the Island of Love. From the French. . . . Together with a miscellany of New Poems. By Several Hands,* by Aphra Behn and others (London: Printed for J. Knight & F. Saunders, 1688);

"Love-Letters, Written by the Late Most Ingenious Mr. Thomas Otway, Printed from the Original Copy," in *Familiar Letters: Written by the Right Honourable John late Earl of Rochester. . . . With Letters Written by the most Ingenious Mr. Thomas Otway* (London: Printed by W. Onley for Sam. Briscoe, 1697).

Thomas Otway is one of the most brilliant–and one of the most disturbed–of Restoration playwrights. His two most popular tragedies, *The Orphan* and *Venice Preserved*, held the boards for a century and a half and were second in popularity only to those of William Shakespeare. They spawned other tragedies focusing especially on women protagonists–plays by John Banks, Thomas Southerne, and Nicholas Rowe–and they influenced the development of bourgeois drama both in France and Germany. But the versions that remained popular acting vehicles for the great actors and actresses of the eighteenth century were expurgated. From the beginning

Otway's plays were disturbing, and his comedies, perhaps his greatest achievement, have never been popular after some initial success by the first two. They reveal that Otway's real bent is as a satirist who attacks the corruption and finally the absurdity of human existence.

The known facts of Otway's life are few, but they have tempted critics to romanticize him as the starving, lovelorn poet. Because some love letters attributed to Otway were published in a collection of letters by John Wilmot, earl of Rochester, in 1697, because they were "identified" some sixteen years later as having been written to Elizabeth Barry, and because Otway apparently really did die of poverty at the young age of thirty-three, his life has been interpreted accordingly. Supposedly, he fell in love with Mrs. Barry when she acted in his early tragedy, *Alcibiades*. But she did not requite his love; rather she was the mistress of Rochester, an early patron of Otway. Supposedly, Mrs. Barry's scorn was the reason why Otway's muse deserted him–as Otway complains in *The Poet's Complaint of his Muse* (1680)–after his early success with *Don Carlos* and the double bill, *Titus and Berenice* and *The Cheats of Scapin*, both produced in 1676. And that same scorn is said to be the reason why, in 1677 when Otway learned she was carrying Rochester's child, he left his new comedy, *Friendship in Fashion*, to fend for itself and joined the army. Mrs. Barry's scorn for him was compounded by his failure to get his soldier's pay, on the one hand, and any sustained patronage, on the other. So despite signal successes in 1679-1680 (*Caius Marius, The Orphan*, and *The Souldiers Fortune*) and again in 1682 (*Venice Preserved*), Otway's cynicism and pessimism fed off each other until he died. There are several romantic anecdotes describing the manner of his death, which are not worth recounting.

What is worth noting, however, is that Otway's works are filled with a misogyny that borders on the pathological, as in the veiled threats of rape in the love letters or his depiction of his muse as a whore that dallied with him only to betray him–or, even more, the portrayal, especially in his two greatest tragedies, of women as effeminizing and therefore destroying men. Also pervading his work, in the prologues and dedications, and in the plays as well, is a profound anger at patrons and other father figures who betray those dependent on them.

It is tempting to speculate that these pervasive hatreds have a biographical source, perhaps in a key moment in Otway's life, a clear vision of which still eludes the biographer. Otway's entire life was a series of successes that could not be sustained. Born in Milland, Sussex, the son of Humphrey Otway, Anglican priest and rector of All Hallows at Woolbeding, Sussex (except for a period during the civil war when Humphrey appears to have been an ousted loyalist), Thomas Otway had to fight his modest origins from the beginning. Records indicate that for several years Otway tried to get a scholarship at Winchester College, where he was finally admitted as a commoner but never did get the scholarship before he turned seventeen in 1669 and apparently went to try Oxford. He was admitted as a commoner of Christ Church on 12 May 1669, paid his caution money, and matriculated shortly thereafter. But Otway never took a degree, for, as he records in his *Poet's Complaint*, he was greeted in the midst of his "Happiness" with the "deadly Potion" of the news of his "good *Senander*'s"–that is, his father's–death.

The reason why his father's death was such a blow to Otway may be inferred, but not proved, from a few facts. On 28 September 1671 Otway returned his caution money and left Oxford. He could not afford to stay and take a degree. Humphrey Otway left a widow, Elizabeth, who did not die until 1703, and a daughter, Susanna, who had been born at least by 1671. Yet in *The Poet's Complaint* in 1680, Otway speaks of both his parents in the past tense and maintains he was the "onely" "pledge" of their "Marriagevows." J. C. Ghosh, Otway's best modern editor and biographer, suggested half a century ago that perhaps Thomas's mother was Humphrey's first wife and Elizabeth a second. And one of Ghosh's reviewers suggested that when his father died Otway was left out in the cold in favor of Susanna (*Times Literary Supplement*, 17 March 1932). Otway states in the epistle dedicatory to *Venice Preserved* that "*a steady Faith, and Loyalty to my Prince, was all the Inheritance my Father left me*," and his plays are filled with orphans or younger brothers who have no portion. Did Humphrey Otway leave everything to a second wife and Thomas's half sister? It is startling that Otway makes no mention, in an otherwise revelatory and accurate biographical poem, *The Poet's Complaint*, of this "mother" and "sister." Nor does he ever mention them anywhere else. It would appear that Otway himself was The Orphan, and he resented it.

After impecuniousness forced him to leave Oxford, Otway apparently went to London, became an actor, and began to write plays himself.

Though John Downes reports that in his first role–in Aphra Behn's first play (it must have been not the premiere in 1670 but a revival)–Otway was put into an agony and ruined as an actor, he must have continued as an actor, perhaps until the September 1675 production of his own first play, *Alcibiades*, a rhymed heroic play in the prevailing fashion.

The title character of Otway's first play is an orphan of sorts. His native Athens has disowned him in a sacrilegious uprising that left his deadly rival Theramnes in command. Alcibiades, then, is an orphan of ingratitude–a figure Otway returns to again and again. Alcibiades finds refuge with the Spartans, whose king knows how to value valor and nobility. But just as Theramnes, who has supplanted Alcibiades in Athens, views him as a supplanter with the fair Timandra, so now does the king's old general, Tissaphernes, view Alcibiades as a supplanter of his glories, for the king makes Alcibiades his champion. And the queen becomes a rival with Timandra for the love of Alcibiades. Of course, the entire play takes place within the context of deadly rivalry between Athens and Sparta. Thus Otway's first effort portrays what René Girard would call a sacrificial crisis precipitated by the endless reciprocal violence of rivalry. Tissaphernes, Theramnes, and the queen are Hobbist villains, nominalists who reject the social codes designed to avoid such a crisis. Tissaphernes unscrupulously plots first to poison the king and then, when that fails, to free the captured Theramnes and turn him against Alcibiades and Timandra. Finally, when Theramnes is killed, Tissaphernes turns the king against Alcibiades and warily plots with the queen to murder the king. But all of his wariness and hypocrisy prove to no avail when the queen turns on him and orders him tortured to death. He leaves the stage railing in satanic defiance.

Theramnes, bound by no code or law, would rape his rival's bride. As she calls on heaven for protection, Timandra is finally rescued from Theramnes and Tissaphernes by Alcibiades and by Tissaphernes's virtuous son Patroclus. Alcibiades kills Theramnes, who, unlike Tissaphernes (and like Shakespeare's Laertes), repents his sins, seeks atonement, and dies exchanging forgiveness with Alcibiades and Timandra. Since Patroclus has chosen honor over blood ties, Theramnes undergoes a deathbed conversion, and Timandra is saved. The implication seems to be that the Christian, chivalric code, invented to forestall endless reciprocal violence and to protect patrilineal genealogy, is vindicated. Even when cruelly poisoned by the queen, Timandra dies a martyr to that code, confident of an afterlife. And even though the queen commits a double parricide in killing her husband and her king, she is forced when overcome, rather than suffer the ignominy of a trial, to kill herself in defiance, and she dies descending to "Hell."

Yet Otway concludes his play with a twist that becomes characteristic. Driven mad by Timandra's murder, Alcibiades raves at the queen, threatening her with a dagger, then with tearing her piecemeal. But he is abruptly preoccupied by the bizarre thought that Timandra's ascending ghost will create him more rivals among the gods. So he stabs himself to "haste" after her and prevent them. The suffering of the innocent Timandra would seem to redeem the world from the sacrificial crisis of rivalry, but Alcibiades' paranoia would seem to indicate that on some level the rivalry will continue. And the play ends with a curious figure: Patroclus is proclaimed king of Sparta, but his closing thoughts are on how "wretched" he has been made by the loss of his friend, Alcibiades, his mistress, Draxilla (who has disappeared in the turmoil and who, interestingly, was played by Elizabeth Barry), and his father, Tissaphernes. In short, the play concludes with an orphan.

The prevailing fashion for noncomic plays in the early 1670s was the rhymed heroic play, which, even when the endings were unhappy for the protagonists, even when an Elkanah Settle or a Nathaniel Lee would litter the stage with bodies in an orgy of sadism, remains essentially within the world of romance with its exaggerated heroes and villains. Such plays focus on the problem of suffering innocence, and "tragedy," as the pseudo-Aristotelianism of the twentieth century means the term, was virtually nonexistent. But Lee in *Sophonisba* (1675) and especially Otway in *Don Carlos*—though both plays are in heroic couplets—begin to focus on protagonists who are essentially good but lose control of their passions and make fatal errors. The influence of the great French playwright Jean Racine is probably crucial in this movement. By the end of 1677 Otway had written *Titus and Berenice*, an abbreviated version of Racine's *Bérénice* (1670); Lee had abandoned rhyme in *The Rival Queens* (1677); Dryden had followed suit in *All for Love* (1678); and the Restoration tragedy of passion had seized the fashion from the Restoration rhymed-heroic play. Just as Lee and Dryden were to produce some of their

best work in this genre (the two plays just mentioned, plus Lee's *Mithridates*, 1678), so also would Otway in *The Orphan*.

Don Carlos is a fine initial movement; first produced on 8 June 1676, it won Otway immediate success and continued in the repertoire into the eighteenth century. The story itself is a great one for tragedy, and Friedrich von Schiller used it for one of his finest plays, certainly employing the same source as Otway, if he did not actually employ Otway's play directly. Again, Otway focuses on a figure who is metaphorically orphaned. Don Carlos, prince of Spain, is in love with and betrothed to a princess of France. Supposedly for purposes of state, she is married instead to Don Carlos's father, King Philip II. Yet the queen knows that the king was attracted to her as an object of mimetic desire, that his "pride" in his own sexual potency asserted itself in rivalry with his son. The queen and Don Carlos still love each other passionately, but she guards her virtue and tries to control his rebellious spirit, which sees his father as having cruelly robbed him of his right. Otway portrays their parting—their forgoing all intimate contact after the wedding—as excruciating and never fully accomplished, even when Don Carlos moves perilously close to open rebellion by planning to go lead the rebels in Flanders. Banished by his father, yet refusing to abandon his hopes for the crown, Don Carlos rationalizes that the rebels are really "Friends" and that "their Cause is just." But when he adds that his presence will *make* it just, he reveals that he has become an Oedipal rival. When the king goes so far as to place Don Carlos under arrest, the latter proclaims, "He's not my Father."

Although Don Carlos has powerful friends at court (his uncle, Don John of Austria, and the marquiss of Posa), their influence is counterbalanced by the Machiavellian statesman, Rui-Gomez, who hates Don Carlos for scorning him. Like Iago, he builds a raging fire of jealousy in Philip, who, out of his own sexual insecurity, leaps to misogynistic distrust of his queen and Oedipal rivalry with his son. The king's jealousy is also abetted by Gomez's wife, Eboli, a much more interesting character than the stock Restoration villainness. Rather than a diabolical, ranting termagant, Eboli is a seductive, sensual woman portrayed as nearly pure appetite. Having been disappointed in her desire to become queen herself, she has married Gomez only to further her ambition and her revenge. She is Don John's mistress, and although she employs the conventional language of fidelity, she is as thoroughgoing a libertine as he and attempts to seduce Don Carlos. If she were to succeed with him, she would probably murder her husband and plot with Don Carlos to murder the king so they might become king and queen. But Eboli's plotting never gets this far, for Don Carlos remains faithful to the queen and rejects Eboli's advances. Enraged, she arranges for the king to catch Don Carlos and the queen together after the latter had sworn never to see the former again, and she carries out the king's revenge by poisoning the queen.

Eboli and Don John are Otway's most interesting creations in this play. She has depth, albeit evil, beyond mere caricature, and he is a portrait of the Rochestrian libertine par excellence. They are central to Otway's play because they represent the anarchy of appetite unrestrained by a code of honor, fidelity, and obedience. Since Don Carlos is tempted throughout to break the bonds of filial loyalty and obedience—the play opens with his nominalistic questioning of this very concept—when the second act opens with Don John's rejection of the same concept, espousing instead libertine nature over chivalric law, we can see Don John as an extension of Don Carlos's rebellion. When Don John employs the traditional language of love and constancy, his rhetoric is merely performative, the currency he spends to obtain the object of his desire, which shifts from Eboli to the queen's lady-in-waiting, Henrietta. The most extraordinary scene in the play occurs when the king and Gomez sneak into the queen's chambers expecting to find her with Don Carlos. Instead, in an antechamber they discover Don John and Eboli in close embrace, and while the voyeurs express their dismay, the lovers leisurely stroll off the stage.

When the queen and Don Carlos enter momentarily, we realize that their own failure to control their desires, however essentially innocent they remain, has endangered their lives and threatened the peace of the kingdom. Although the queen has broken her word in order to see Don Carlos again, she has done so to try to restrain his headlong leap into open rebellion. Ironically, she recalls him to "true obedience," but it is too late. The king has not only been told Don Carlos is with the queen, he has discovered Don Carlos's dispatches to Flanders on the body of Posa, whom he has had Gomez murder. When the king accosts the couple in the queen's chambers, Don Carlos, struggling with his passionate

temper—first kneeling to his father then rising boldly when his father attacks his mother, drawing his sword on Gomez then relinquishing it in filial respect—finally submits to his father's rage. Concluding this inner scene that began with Eboli and Don John's embrace, Otway has Don Carlos catch the swooning queen in his arms in the only embrace they ever take. The queen fondly believes that since this sole embrace takes place before the king he will at last conclude them chaste, but of course the embrace serves only to further enrage him, and his guards' momentary failure to break the embrace exacerbates his growing sense of impotence in the face of a castrating, Oedipal rival. In the ultimate act of disinheritance, the king threatens to kill his son. And this amazing scene of passion and pathos ends with his plotting to murder his queen.

The last act opens with the king ironically lamenting his loss of control over his passions, for which control he has been famous. Don John tells him he has become a slave both to his passions and his corrupt advisers. But the king has planned for himself a scene of excitation to rival his wedding night as he displaces his potency from sex to sadistic murder: he intends to supplant his supplanter by disguising himself as his son, coming to the queen in her chambers, tricking her into an embrace, then watching her slowly die in agony from the poison Eboli has administered. The fact that she recognizes him immediately upon their embrace increases the king's sense of impotence, so he madly gloats over her expected agony. But she meets his assault with protestations of her innocence, an innocence that Eboli, stabbed by her avenging husband, runs in to witness in the face of heaven's judgment. The king pathetically complains, "Heav'n where is now thy sleeping providence, / That took so little care of Innocence?" But of course, his own sexual rivalry with his son and his fears of inadequacy have precipitated the catastrophe, which quickly worsens. For Don Carlos slashes his wrists in a bath poisoned by Gomez. Don Carlos and the queen die together in one last embrace, predicting their souls shall meet in transcendence, and the king madly stabs Gomez and attempts to mount the sky in pursuit of the lovers he has destroyed and in whose final embrace he cannot share.

Providence seems to have asserted itself after all in the poetical justice of the ending. Eboli is killed for her adultery, Gomez for his treachery, the king driven mad for his failure to

Otway in his twenties, engraving attributed to W. Faithorne, Jr., based on a portrait by Soest

control his passion. Don Carlos dies maintaining his innocence against the charge of incest but abjuring his rebelliousness. The queen's essential innocence, despite her well-intentioned errors in judgment, seems at last rewarded in a transcendent union with Don Carlos. But the play disturbingly ends with Don John's final comments:

> No more in Loves Enervate charms I'le ly,
> Shaking off softness, to the Camp I'le fly;
> Where Thirst of Fame the Active Hero warms,
> And what I've lost in Peace, regain in Arms.

It is as if the entire tragedy has been caused by man's effeminate attraction to weakening women. Don John's libertine exaltation of woman as an object of desire is finally as misogynistic as King Philip's precipitate distrust of his wife and his generalization of her supposed wickedness to all women. A man needs to free himself from these enervating creatures and immerse himself in the manly world of martial pursuits. Yet even as he says these lines, Don John orders the guards to watch Henrietta and keep her from her professed inten-

tion to follow her queen. It would appear that Don John wants her preserved as a treat for dessert after his military exploits. The play concludes, then, with no ringing celebration of traditional values of constancy and self-control but with libertine homosocial ambivalence.

Otway's success with his second play was followed later in the same year with another success, the performance in December of a double bill, *Titus and Berenice* and *The Cheats of Scapin*, the former adapted from Racine, the latter from Molière. His success must have been made headier by the fact that he beat two other playwrights to the draw—John Crowne, who was working on his massive ten-act version of the story of Titus and Berenice, and Edward Ravenscroft, who was working on his adaptation of part of the same material from Molière. Otway's dedication of the play to Rochester indicates that he had become the latest of that lord's protégés. He appears to have won Dryden's scorn (or jealousy) with *Don Carlos*, as one might expect in the rivalry between the chief writer for the King's company and a rising star for the Duke's—and as one might also expect between Dryden and a friend of Dryden's emerging nemesis, Thomas Shadwell. Shadwell lampooned Dryden in the 1676 *Virtuoso*, and most scholars now date that event as the origin of Dryden's great answering lampoon, *Mac Flecknoe*. Otway alludes to the rivalry between him and Dryden at the end of his preface to *Don Carlos*, published in the second half of 1676.

Otway may well have been attracted to Racine's play not only because Racine was the contemporary master at tragedy of passion but also because one of the major themes of Racine's version of the story of Titus and Berenice is ingratitude. Racine's Antiochus brands Bérénice "ingrate" for failing to reward his years of service to her with reciprocal love. In turn Bérénice brands Titus "ingrat" for failing to fulfill his repeated promises to wed her despite the Roman prohibition against marrying royalty. As we have already seen in *Alcibiades*, Otway was attracted to this theme, and he would return to it repeatedly.

In Racine's play Titus has been in mourning for several days after the death of his father, Tiberius. Bérénice had redeemed him from an early wicked life, so he is under great obligation to her. But the descending mantle of Tiberius carries with it a new aura of consciousness for Titus, who now must rise to the occasion of the consequent "gloire." His duty to Roman law becomes part of his essence as emperor, and he must break his vows to Bérénice and send her home to Judea. Antiochus, who has loved her long, hopes for a while that Titus's desertion of her will draw her to him. But when he realizes that she is absolutely constant to Titus, he plans instead to die. Bérénice calls on the two men, as well as herself, to live in misery, to bear their misfortunes with dignity as an example to the universe. She remains the teacher of aristocratic values to the last.

Otway retains the plot but not the tragic dignity. His characters are more self-indulgent than Racine's. Antiochus has none of Racine's restraint, resents Berenice's unrequiting of his love, blames her for breaking prior vows to him, and confesses his love to Titus in the middle of the play instead of the end, when Racine's Antiochus confesses it only, he supposes, at the point of death. Otway's Antiochus momentarily contemplates triumphing over Berenice's misfortune out of a spirit of revenge. And both Antiochus and Berenice take cheap shots at each other, revealing a pettiness that Racine's neoclassical decorum would never allow. Otway's Berenice, distracted

and disheveled, raves wildly in typical Otwavian fashion. And his Titus vacillates more passionately than his counterpart. Most important, Otway's play ends with no ringing call to transcendence, punctuated with Antiochus's tragically pathetic "Hélas!" One assumes Racine's Titus remains Bérénice's pupil to the last. But Otway's last lines are a violent outburst by Titus, who plans to return to his early wickedness and cruelly persecute the entire world in order to make it as "wretched" as he.

In short, while Otway's play focuses on typical aristocratic themes of constancy, fidelity, friendship (between Antiochus and Titus), gratitude, duty versus love; and while his ending ostensibly reaffirms those values, he creates characters who, even when they are essentially positive, fall short of the aristocratic ideal. None of his first three plays ends in a way that reaffirms values and grants a kind of comfort, even after tragic loss, to an aristocratic audience. Instead his plays increasingly vector toward a satiric portrait of human character and possibility. Alcibiades and King Philip achieve no transcendent wisdom but remain fundamentally paranoid. Patroclus and Don John are no magnanimous spokesmen for the reestablishment of order. And at the end of this third of Otway's tragedies, Titus does not ascend to a higher plane of nobility but instead descends into the bitter and sardonic tantrum of an orphaned tyrant.

In *The Cheats of Scapin*, from Molière's *Les Fourberies de Scapin* (1671), Otway addresses not so much the theme of ingratitude as other themes that are preoccupations of his work: rebellion and disobedience (as in *Don Carlos*), especially as they manifest themselves in secret marriage with the attendant threat of disinheritance (as in *Caius Marius, The Orphan, Venice Preserved*). Two young Town wits have secretly married two witty, young women. All four are thus rebels against patriarchal parental control (their mothers are hardly mentioned). The women escape their governess to follow the men just on their declarations of love. The men fall in love and marry in the absence of their fathers. Otway stresses the economic consequences of their actions: the sons risk disinheritance, the daughters their dowries. In a remarkable anticipation of Jaffeir's words to Belvidera in *Venice Preserved*, Octavian says to Clara, "How can you bear those wants to which we must be both reduc'd?" And in an even more remarkable insight into Otway's own biographical preoccupations, Scapin, in lines not in Otway's source, advises Octavian to take an insouciant pose with his father: "Tell him you can live without troubling him; threaten him to turn Souldier; or what will frighten him worse, say you'll turn Poet." Is Otway defying the ghost of his father? Could he have been glancing at his infatuation with Mrs. Barry and her being kept by his own patron, Rochester, when Scapin mockingly rehearses Octavian's father's fears that his son has married "some Waiting-Woman corrupted in a Civil Family, and reduc'd to one of the Play-Houses, remov'd from thence by some Keeping Coxcomb"? Otway added these lines to his source, but we will never know why. Finally, Otway added to his source an attack on wits who are no match for fools, because wits may have intelligence but fools win "Patrons" and succeed. So far in his life, none of Otway's appeals for patrons had resulted in financial security. He was plagued by persistent poverty.

Again, what is more important is the insight we gain into the meaning of Otway's canon. Otway repeatedly portrays a world of tyrannical fathers and orphaned sons and daughters, of rebellion against patriarchal authority. From Thrifty and Gripe, the tyrannical fathers in this play, to Priuli, Belvidera's father in *Venice Preserved*, Otway satirizes society's warped priorities: in what would come as a great shock to Dante, Gripe says, "For a Son to marry impudently without the Consent of his Father, is as great an Offence as can be imagin'd." Is it a greater offense than disinheritance? betrayal of friendship? ingratitude?

Typically, the sociopolitical problem of rebellion against the patriarchal system designed to exercise strict genealogical control and therefore the control of the transmission of power and property—that problem is not solved in this play, as it is not in most aristocratic comedies and romances. The rebellious couples turn out to have married not only within their class but within the families for which they were designed. Octavian's wife is his best friend Leander's sister and Gripe's daughter, the one he was designed to marry. Leander's wife is Octavian's sister. Accidents have concealed identities. All's well that ends well.

Otway's great contribution to the history of the theater in adapting this play by Molière is not so much that he wrote the first afterpiece and thus spawned a new genre. Nor is it that he provided a great acting vehicle for one of the great, established comic actors of his time, the inimitable

Nokes. It is that he provided an acting vehicle for the greatest comic actor of the new generation, Anthony Leigh. Leigh specialized in portraying disgusting, lubricious, vile, despicable—yet paradoxically lovable—antiheroes, from Scapin to Dryden's Pandarus (*Troilus and Cressida*, 1679), to Southerne's Abbé (*Sir Anthony Love*, 1690). Perhaps Otway created for him his greatest roles: Malagene, Sir Jolly Jumble, and Antonio. What is so interesting about Otway and Leigh's parasites is not so much that they are outrageous tricksters but that they are so antiheroic, antiaristocratic, antichivalric. They are perhaps the English theater's great contribution to the evolution of a type between Falstaff and the title character in Denis Diderot's *Le Neveu de Rameau* (written between 1761 and 1774, published in 1823). Otway's Scapin is still the creature of Molière, a slapstick trickster, master of the mask, the countenance, the cudgel. But in Otway's next comedy, he made for Leigh a role that was his own.

Despite his success in 1676 Otway appears to have fallen out of favor with Rochester, who may well be the author of the satire on him in *A Session of the Poets* (circulated 1677; published in *Poems on Several Occasions* . . . [1680]). At least Otway appears to have received no sustained patronage from Rochester, despite his acknowledgment of his aid in the preface to *Don Carlos* and his dedication to him of his double bill. Nor does Otway appear to have received any sustained patronage from the duke of York, to whom he dedicated *Don Carlos* and who apparently liked the play. In *The Poet's Complaint* Otway blames Fortune's desertion of him for his inability to write during this period. If he means that he ran out of money and could find no steady patronage, then we might infer that Otway continued the style of living that exceeded his means which he appears to have begun when he came to London. For whatever reason, Otway had no play produced in 1677 and, even though he finally regained enough inspiration to write one that would be produced in 1678, apparently decided to try an alternative career in the army. This choice would seem to accord with Otway's pugnacious personality. It is obvious from *The Poet's Complaint* that Otway deeply resented being lampooned in *A Session of the Poets* (among others we may not know), and he connects such lampoons with the libel that characterized the pamphlet warfare of the later Exclusion Crisis. Some of those pamphlets reveal that Otway blamed Settle for the lampoon and challenged him to a duel, a challenge the cowardly Settle refused to accept, swallowing the insults to his mother and (incorrectly) owning authorship of the satire in *A Session of Poets*. An even more delicious anecdote reports that Otway challenged to a duel and wounded young John Churchill, later duke of Marlborough, because Churchill had beaten an orange wench in the Duke's theater.

Otway's military career brought him no more financial security than play writing. Although he gained a commission as ensign in a new regiment under the command of the duke of Monmouth and another commission as lieutenant later in 1678, the regiment never saw action, was disbanded, and Otway was paid a virtually worthless debenture. He would reflect bitterly on the experience in *The Souldiers Fortune*, where the soldiers lament the ingratitude of their country.

While Otway was in Flanders in April 1678, the Duke's company produced his first full-fledged comedy, *Friendship in Fashion*. It is subversive comedy in the tradition of William Wycherley (even borrowing a character's name, Lady Squeamish, from *The Country Wife*, 1675), and it includes elements from three other great Restoration comedies, Sir George Etherege's *The Man of Mode* (1676), Sir John Vanbrugh's *The Relapse* (1696), and William Congreve's *The Way of the World* (1700). *Friendship in Fashion* ranks with these other comedies in terms of quality and ought to be as well known. Perhaps it remains obscure because of lingering Victorian sensibilities. Modern liberalism celebrates the sexcapades of a Dorimant or a Horner, but maybe a double standard still obtains. For Otway has given us a character very rare on not just the Restoration but the entire English stage—a witty, attractive, successful female libertine. Mrs. Goodvile is married to a libertine for whom marriage is no restraint upon desire. As in *The Relapse*, her husband has seduced her friend and cousin, named Victoria in this play, in their very house. Typically, he has tired of his mistress especially since she is pregnant and (shades of Edward Mirabel and Arabella Languish) plots to pass her off on his "friend" Truman, while he pursues the witty and attractive Camilla. Not only is this kind of friendship in fashion, but Mrs. Goodvile cynically jokes that this kind of incest is de rigueur: " 'tis almost the onely way Relations care to be kind to one another now a days." She decides to serve her husband in kind, and the play opens with Truman reading an unsigned billet-doux from her. For, as she says hilariously and blasphemously to her maid, "Oh, if I would ever consent to wrong my Husband (which Heav'n forbid, *Lettice*!) it should be, to choose, with his Friend. For such a one has a double Obligation to secrecy, as well for his own Honour as mine." And when the libertine Goodvile ironically becomes jealous of his wife and Truman and plots to catch them in flagrante delicto, she turns for approval to the audience: "Now if I plague not this wise jealous Husband of mine, let all Wives curse me, and Cuckolds laugh at me!" Again appropriating the religious language designed to sanction the sexual politics of feudal aristocracy, she exults, "And let the World know how dull a Tool a Husband is, compar'd with that triumphant thing a Wife, and her Guardian Angel Lover."

Mrs. Goodvile's rebellion is different from that of a Lady Fidget or a Margery Pinchwife, for she cuckolds no fool but a Town wit, the type in Stuart comedy almost always portrayed as dominant—over country boobies, cits, and uppity women. A more typical conflict is portrayed between the young Town wit Valentine and his aging cast mistress, Lady Squeamish. However angry she is, however much she plots to be revenged, her very name undercuts her power, and she becomes an unwitting pawn in frustrating Goodvile's designs on Camilla and abetting his cuckolding by Truman. For in a wonderful garden scene in the dark, while Goodvile is being cuckolded, he and Lady Squeamish copulate in a corner, each believing the other to be part of the Valentine-Camilla couple, a couple becoming romantically entwined in the midst of this adulterous garden of delights.

Like Wycherley's Harcourt and Alithea, Valentine and Camilla stand out as the only traditionally virtuous characters in the play. Camilla has a great scene with Goodvile, who is pursuing her as his new game. No naïf, Camilla sees him for what he is, sees that he has spent his verbal credit with all his broken vows: "How must I then suspect your love to me, that can so soon forget your faith to ["your Lady"]?" his "Lady" being at once his wife and his cast mistress. As in a typical Restoration comedy, the gay couple marries at the end. But their union is upstaged by the triumph of the gayer, adulterous couple, and the hymeneal celebration is marred by Goodvile's sardonic warnings to Valentine and to the audience not to trust wives.

Goodvile is perhaps most upset at the end because his plot to catch Truman and his wife has been betrayed by Victoria. Goodvile concludes ironically, "there is no Trust nor Faith in the Sex." In a world dominated by Don Juan Machiavels, to trust anyone is absurd. Yet out of the midst of this collective distrust emerges not only the mutual love and trust between Valentine and Camilla, but also an exchange of pledges of constancy between Truman and Mrs. Goodvile. They are a comic version of the chivalric courtly lovers, as they appropriate the words of the very code their love violates. Truman proclaims that his possessiveness would drive him to be anything, "except the very Husband himself, rather then lose you." Such possessiveness, on the part of Truman, Mrs. Goodvile, Lady Squeamish, and Goodvile himself gives the lie to the libertine ethic. Otway's play wants to have it both ways, true love *and* promiscuity.

Another bond of mutual trust apparently ruptured in this play–friendship–seems reaffirmed in two relationships: Truman and Valentine, and Victoria and Mrs. Goodvile. The former produces typical male bonding in mutual revenge on Goodvile. The latter produces less typical female bonding in a similar cause. Victoria, publicly sneered at by Mrs. Goodvile for her adultery with her husband, reveals that she was not the woman Goodvile caught with Truman in the garden, cementing his suspicion that it was his wife. Goodvile pledges to return his "heart" to Victoria and plots revenge against his wife. But Victoria decides to betray him to Mrs. Goodvile, and upon receipt of a note from Victoria, Mrs. Goodvile proclaims, "This is generously done." They thus forge a friendship of sisterhood, a league against "that false perjur'd Man." But the key word of the feudal aristocratic ethos, *generously*, has been employed in the service of adultery, the greatest threat to the aristocratic *gens*.

As in *The Way of the World* a great deal of stage action is taken up by two witwouds, Caper and Saunter, and a boozy country booby, Sir Noble Clumsey. Their main thematic function is to provide occasion for their dominance by the Town wits, who deserve success because of their superior urbanity and intelligence. (In the light of the discussion of the superior success of fools in *The Cheats of Scapin*, this motif reveals more clearly than in the typical Stuart comedy its nature as the poet's wish fulfillment.) Like Sir Wilful Witwoud, Sir Noble proves to be not altogether despicable (being a member of the gentry, perhaps, and no nouveau riche) and therefore is a fit match to save what is left of the reputation of Victoria through marriage.

The most interesting of these minor characters is Malagene, played by Leigh. Like Etherege's Medley, he is a purveyor of scandal; but Otway has expanded the character into a loose-tongued slanderer, liar, hypocrite. He is a thoroughly despicable parasite, the consummate actor: "I am a very good Mimick; I can act *Punchinello, Scaramouchio, Harlequin*, Prince *Prettyman*, or any thing. I can act the rumbling of a Wheelbarrow. . . . Nay, more than that, I can act a Sow and Piggs, Sausages a broiling, a Shoulder of Mutton a roasting: I can act a Fly in a Honey-pot." However ridiculous he is and however much a coward (he is afraid of Goodvile throughout but becomes even more afraid of Truman and finally lies to protect him and Mrs. Goodvile), Malagene is a kind of figure for all the characters in the play, who are all actors, masking their desires while plotting to achieve them. Success in the main is a matter of class.

But the final success is perhaps best viewed as a matter of naked phallic power in a reassertion of patriarchal dominance. Goodvile is no coward; he and Truman draw on each other once and nearly do so again toward the end. Finally, however, he is forced to adopt this submissive posture: "*Truman*, if thou hast enjoyed her [Mrs. Goodvile], I beg thee keep it close, and if it be possible let us yet be friends." And the play finally does not allow women freedom from male oppression. Lady Squeamish is humiliated. Victoria cannot have her baby out of wedlock and is forced to marry Sir Noble. Mrs. Goodvile cannot leave Goodvile and must continue to try to outmanipulate him in a power struggle over "possession of her Priviledges." She has cuckolded him, at least in spirit if not yet in fact, and will continue her liaison with Truman. Yet she herself articulates one of the subtlest forms of patriarchal oppression, stereotyping: "Now all the Malice, Illnature, Falshood and Hypocrisie of my Sex inspire me. . . . Now, once more let me invoke all the Arts of affectation, all the Revenge, the counterfeit Passions, pretended Love, pretended Jealousie, pretended Rage, and in sum the very Genius of my Sex to my assistance." Otway has written a brilliant comedy of subversive rebellion, but the subversion is within the context of a patriarchal master text.

If the cynicism of *Friendship in Fashion* is somewhat mitigated by the celebration of the triumph of Valentine and Camilla as lovers or at least Truman and Mrs. Goodvile as tricksters, by October 1679 and the production of *Caius Marius*

Otway's cynicism had become unmitigated. The play is a satire on civil war written after the Popish Plot and during the ensuing Exclusion Crisis. Otway mixes the history of Marius and Sylla with several of Shakespeare's plays, most notably *Romeo and Juliet*. Sulpitius, Otway's Mercutio, concludes his Queen Mab speech with this piece of gratuitous cynicism, emerging perhaps from Otway's own disturbed psyche:

> Sometimes she tweaks a Poet by the Ear,
> And then dreams he
> Of Panegyricks, flatt'ring Dedications,
> And mighty Presents from the Lord knows who,
> But wakes as empty as he laid him down.

The play portrays mobs as fickle and politicians as buying their votes. Despite Otway's reputation for Tory sympathies, neither side is portrayed as just or in the right. The play opens with the patrician senator Metellus mouthing sentiments of Rights and Law and Justice and Liberty and proclaiming the cause of Sylla. Meanwhile, the plebeian Marius, who would be consul once more, curses Rome for its ingratitude. But the rhetoric of each side merely masks its essential self-interestedness, ambition, and especially cruelty. Right in the middle of the Forum, Sulpitius butchers the son of Quintus Pompeius before his father's face, then goes on a rampage, asserting Marius's "Rod of Pow'r" in wanton slaughter. When Marius and his party are chased into exile, Metellus contemplates Marius's being beheaded, and when he considers who must be consul, he chooses first Cinna, for his ability to manipulate the rabble and his hatred to Marius, and second Octavius, "An honest, simple, downright-dealing Lord: / A little too Religious, that's his fault." When Marius would seem to have learned a little tenderness from the daughter-in-law, Lavinia, who ministers to him in the wilderness, he makes a mockery of mercy by ordering Sulpitius to murder everyone he smiles on in their reentry into Rome and by sparing a submissive child only to butcher his grandfather.

Otway tries to do too much in this play, borrowing too much from Shakespeare, especially the Roman plays. The confrontation between Marius and Sylla reflects an aging Antony's contempt for the boy, Octavius, especially as Dryden had reworked the theme. Marius in the wilderness becomes the mad King Lear, who would seem to have learned the lesson of *sic transit gloria mundi*. (For a brief moment he is also Charles II looking for a hollow tree to hide in.) But in another minute he is an unappeasable Coriolanus outside his "Mother *Rome*." Then he is a railing malcontent like Timon. The entire play develops the anti-heroic atmosphere of *Troilus and Cressida:* a meaningless war fought by worthless participants.

In the midst of this bleak world Otway introduces the love of children from the two warring factions. Marius junior loves Metellus's daughter Lavinia, who is promised to Sylla. Their story roughly follows Shakespeare's version, except that, perhaps taking a hint from Dryden's *Conquest of Granada* (1670, 1671) and Ozmyn and Benzayda's conversion of their enemy parents, Otway has the faithful Lavinia pursue the exiled Marius senior, minister to him, and convert his hatred of Metellus's daughter into parental affection. But the ending of their story is no redemptive sacrifice. Like Romeo, Marius junior takes poison at Lavinia's grave. Otway lets him live while Lavinia awakens, and he dies amid transcendent rhetoric. The only lesson Lavinia draws she communicates thus: "Who fix their Joys on any thing that's Mortall, / Let 'em behold my Portion, and despair." Then, while she already begins to rave in Otway's typical terminal madness, Marius senior drives her father in and kills him before her eyes. Impaling herself upon his sword, she rails, "And now let Rage, Distraction and Despair / Seize all Mankind, till they grow mad as I am."

Just as Malagene is a kind of sign of the rampant hypocrisy of the world in *Friendship in Fashion*, so also is Otway's version of Shakespeare's Nurse a sign of an amoral energy force that underlies all the rhetoric of justice and transcendence in the play. In the earlier comedy Otway created the role for one half of his comic combination in *The Cheats of Scapin*, Leigh. Here he creates it for the other, Nokes, who was already known as Nurse Nokes for earlier transvestite roles. Otway's Nurse is more lubricious and despicable than Shakespeare's. She looks forward to Otway's great masochist, Antonio, in *Venice Preserved*. Witness the limits to which she takes her (Otway's?) self-indulgence: Concerning her charge to prepare Lavinia's body for burial, she bubbles and babbles, "It shall be done and done and overdone, as we are undone. And I will sigh, and cry till I am swell'd as big as a Pumkin. Nay, my poor Baby, I'll take care thou shalt not dy for nothing: for I will wash thee with my Tears, perfume thee with my Sighs, and stick a Flower in every part about thee...."

Opening pages of act 1 in a copy of the 1680 edition of Otway's Caius Marius *(by permission of the Folger Shakespeare Library). The annotations and deletions were made by prompter W. R. Chetwood, probably for a 22 August 1735 revival of the play. Abbreviations indicate doors through which actors were to enter and exit: "O.P." means opposite prompt; "M.D.P.S." stands for middle door, prompt side. Heavy cuts were necessary because the play was part of a double bill.*

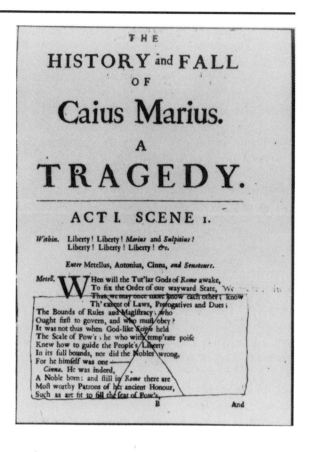

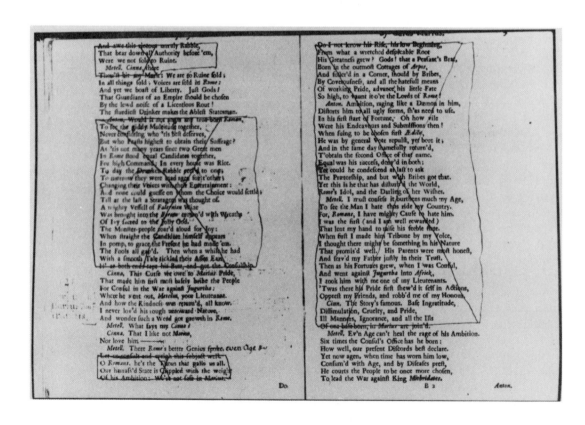

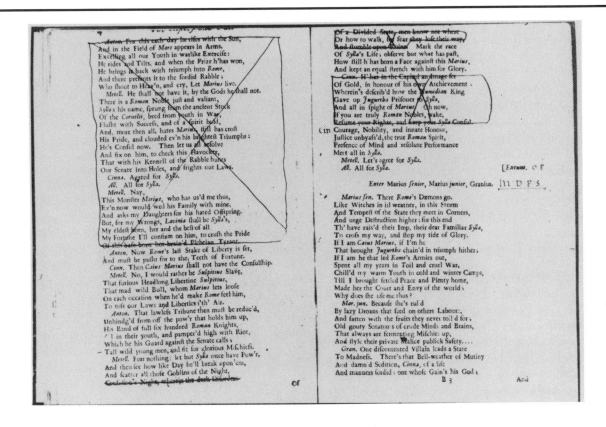

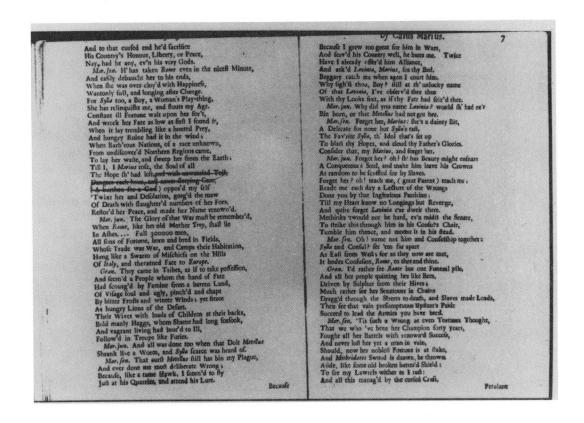

The play ends with Marius's attempting to read the audience a lesson against ambition, but the final lines are awarded to Sulpitius, who like the Nurse is totally amoral. Dying himself, he responds to Marius's moralizing thus: "A Curse on all Repentance! how I hate it! / I'd rather hear a Dog howl than a Man whine. . . . A Pox on all Madmen hereafter." Otway has postponed Mercutio's curse till the end of the play. No prince comes forward to heal. Instead, the last line are Sulpitius's cynical epitaph:

> Sulpitius *lies here, that troublesome Slave,*
> *That sent many honester men to the Grave,*
> *And dy'd like a Fool when h' had liv'd like a Knave.*

Otway has written not tragedy but bleak satire.

In *The Orphan* Otway wrote one of the best tragedies of passion of the Restoration, but his vision remains bleak. First produced in late February or early March 1680, the play is a tragedy in the modern sense of the term because the protagonists are more sinned against than sinning. Otway sets the play in a rural villa, where the brave old soldier Acasto has retired from a corrupt court and ungrateful army. Like Cymbeline, he raises his two sons to beware corruption and flattery. But right in the middle of his own pseudo-Eden, the crisis of society repeats itself. Polydore and Castalio, Acasto's twin sons, fall into deadly rivalry over an object of mimetic desire, Monimia, the orphan who has been raised by Acasto as part of his household. They confess their rival passions but pledge not to deceive each other. Fatally, however, Castalio conceals from his brother his secret marriage to Monimia. Hearing what he takes to be an assignation and therefore believing that both Castalio and Monimia, who has protested her chastity to him, have deceived him, Polydore, like Don John a libertine, determines to take revenge. On their wedding night he substitutes himself for his twin. When he comes to triumph over her and learns she is his brother's wife, all his libertinism goes out the window and he concludes they must exile themselves. But neither Polydore nor Monimia can stand the guilt, so she poisons herself, and he precipitates a duel with his brother so he might run upon his sword.

Two aspects of this tragedy seem nigh inexplicable to a modern audience. Why does Castalio conceal his marriage? And why the abrupt change in Polydore? Up until the moment Polydore discovers Monimia is his brother's wife, he has no bit of remorse. In his ethic she has played the wanton and deserves what she gets. But however unrealistic it might seem to us—or even to Mrs. Goodvile—Polydore is horrified by the truth. The key lies in the tapestry Monimia's brother Chamont pierces with his sword at the end of his dream concerning his sister's fate:

> I found my weapon had the arras pierc'd,
> Just where that famous tale was interwoven,
> How th' unhappy *Theban* slew his Father.

However unwittingly, Polydore and Monimia have committed incest. When he suggests he alone should go into exile, she protests, "Wouldst thou again have me betray thy Brother, / And bring pollution to his Arms?" If she were to get pregnant, how would she know whose child it is? Twins are dangerous figures in mythology, especially as René Girard has shown. Their identicalness collapses distinction, in this case distinction that is essential for the peaceful transmission of power and property through a patrilineal and primogenitive system of genealogy. Moreover, as still happens with domestic animals in the present day, a defiled pedigreed female can never again mother offspring that are formally recognized as pedigreed. Monimia is polluted, defiled, contaminated, adulterated. She is soiled goods and must be purified by the *pharmakon* that is both her poison and society's remedy. And Polydore must remove the confusion of identical twins, sacrificing himself for the survival of the other, who ostensibly would carry on patrilinearity.

The other question is more difficult to answer, though thanks to critics such as Derek Hughes and Laurie Morrow, we have come closer to an answer in recent years. Castalio keeps his marriage a secret, on one level, because for him to marry an orphan without his father's approval, since she is not an appropriate exchange item for building an estate, is likely to result in his disinheritance, as is hinted twice in the play and as Otway portrays elsewhere in his canon. On another level, he does not want to hurt his brother with news of his victory in their rivalry. But on a deeper level, his own father's attitude toward marriage—"Let Marriage be the last mad thing ye doe"—may threaten Castalio with the castration his name implies. In the libertine, homosocial world, marriage is a sin. It cheats man of his "Freedom," as Castalio himself protests to Polydore, insisting he would never marry

TO HER

Royal Highness

THE

DUTCHESS.

Madam,

AFTER having a great while wisht to write something that might be worthy to lay at your Highnesses Feet, and finding it impossible : Since the World has been so kind to me to Judge of this Poem to my advantage, as the most pardonable fault which I have made in its kind ; I had sinn'd against my self, if I had not chosen this Opportunity to implore (what my Ambition is most fond of) your Favour and Protection.

For though Fortune would not so far bless my endeavours, as to encourage them with your Royal Highnesses presence, when this came into the World : Yet, I cannot but declare it was my design and hopes it might have been your Divertisement in that happy season, when you return'd again to chear all those eyes that had before wept for your Departure, and enliven all hearts that had droopt for your Absence : When

A 2   Wit

The DEDICATION.

Wit ought to have pay'd it's Choicest Tributes in, and Joy have known no Limits, then I hop'd my little *Mite* would not have been rejected ; though my ill Fortune was too hard for me, and I lost a greater Honour, by your Royal Highnesses Absence, than all the Applauses of the World besides can make me Reparation for.

Nevertheless, I thought my self not quite unhappy, so long as I had hopes this way yet to recompence my disappointment past : When I consider'd also that Poetry might claim right to a little share in your Favour : For *Tasso,* and *Ariosto,* some of the best, have made their Names Eternal, by transmitting to after-Ages the Glory of your Ancestors : And under the spreading of that shade, where two of the best have planted their Lawrels, how Honoured should I be, who am the worst, if but a branch might grow for me.

I dare not think of offering at any thing in this Address, that might look like a Panegyrick, for fear lest when I have done my best, the World should Condemn me, for saying too little, and you your self check me, for medling with a Task unfit for my Talent.

For the description of Vertues, and Perfections so rare as yours are, ought to be done by as deliberate, as skillful a Hand ; the Features must be drawn very fine, to be like, hasty dawbing would but spoil the Picture, and make it so unnatural, as must want false lights to set it off :

And

The DEDICATION.

And your Vertue can receive no more Lustre from Praises, than your Beauty can be improv'd by Art ; which as it Charms the bravest Prince that ever amaz'd the World with his Virtue : So let but all other Hearts enquire into themselves, and then Judge how it ought to be prais'd.

Your Love too, as none but that great Heroe who has it could deserve it, and therefore, by a particular Lot from Heav'n, was destin'd to so extraordinary a blessing, so matchless for it self, and so wondrous for it's Constancy, shall be remembred to your Immortal Honour, when all other Transactions of the Age you live in shall be forgotten.

But I forget that I am to ask Pardon for the fault I have been all this while Committing : wherefore I beg your Highness to forgive me this presumption, and that you will be pleas'd to think well of one who cannot help resolving with all the Actions of Life, to endeavour to deserve it : Nay more, I would beg, and hope it may be granted, that I may through yours never want an Advocate in his Favour, whose Heart, and Mind, you have so entire a share in ; it is my only Portion and my Fortune ; I cannot but be happy, so long as I have but hopes I may enjoy it, and I must be Miserable, should it ever be my ill Fate to lose it.

This, with Eternal wishes for your Royal Highnesses Content, Happiness, and Prosperity, in all Humility is presented by

Your most obedient and devoted Servant,

THO. OTWAY.

The Persons Represented in the Tragedy.

MEN.

A*Casto,* A Nobleman retired from Court, and living privately in the Country. By Mr. *Gillow.*

Castalio, } His Sons.   By Mr. *Betterton.*
Polydore, }   By Mr. *Jo. Williams.*

Chamount, A young Souldier of Fortune.   By Mr. *Smith.*

Ernesto, } Servants in the Fa- By Mr. *Norris.*
Paulino, } mily.   By Mr. *Wiltshire.*

Cordelio, Polydore's Page.   By the little Girl.

Chaplain.   By Mr. *Percival.*

WOMEN.

Monimia, The Orphan, left under the Guardian-ship of old *Acasto.*   By Mrs. *Barry.*

Serina, Acasto's Daughter.   By Mrs. *Boteler.*

Florella, Monimia's Woman. By Mrs. *Osborn.*

SCENE, *BOHEMIA.*

Dedication and cast list for the first performance, from the 1680 edition of The Orphan. *The actress identified as "the little Girl" is Anne Bracegirdle in her first role.*

till he be old–too old to sow wild oats is the implication.

Yet on a deeper level still, Castalio cannot admit he is married because that would mark him as effeminate. All the sexual discourse in the play demonstrates that patriarchal society must, in order to control property through genealogy, inculcate from a very early age distrust of the opposite sex. Thus Monimia and Serina, Acasto's daughter, who is falling in love with Chamont, constantly betray a learned misandry, reinforced by Chamont, who warns Monimia to beware men for they are all false. On the other side–and far more serious for the outcome of the play–is the inculcation into young men of a fundamental misogyny. That which has wounded Acasto most is his whorish Fortune.

Throughout the discourse of his household, this supposed paradise free from the corruption of the court, woman is a metonymy for deceit, betrayal, frailty. We are not surprised at Polydore's repeated misogyny, for libertinism turns women into sex objects, instruments of male pleasure. But Castalio himself is thoroughly indoctrinated by the discourse. His insouciant pose with Polydore may be hypocritical, but as soon as he gets the first harsh look from Monimia, who is understandably upset that he loosed his brother on her, he concludes, "I am a Fool, and she has found my Weakness; . . . I am a doating honest Slave, design'd / For Bondage, Marriage bonds . . . Betray'd to Love and all its little follies." When he cannot gain admission to her chamber on their wedding night, he sits down outside and rails at "th' inconstant Sex." He considers being married tantamount to being effeminately chained, like Hercules, to a distaff. And he buys into the cultural stereotype of the relation between the sexes as a battle for dominance. When he finally learns the truth, he curses not his deceiving his brother but his engaging in heterosexual love: "My Fatal Love, alas! has ruin'd thee," he says to Polydore.

What is worse, like Mrs. Goodvile, Monimia herself buys into the patriarchal stereotype: when the page reports to her Castalio's affected libertine insouciance, she determines to "Be a true Woman, rail, protest my wrongs, / Resolve to hate him, and yet love him still." At the end, the dying Monimia asks Castalio, "Wilt thou receive pollution to thy Bosom, / And close the eyes of one that has betray'd thee?" Built into patriarchal discourse is not merely a rhetoric of sexual virtue that protects genealogy but a misogyny that reflects deep male fears that women might perform the ultimate castration of taking back the control of genealogy themselves.

Castalio dies cursing the world and its system of "trust," and Chamont reads a moral that does the opposite of the last lines of a typical Stuart tragedy: " 'Tis thus that Heaven it's Empire does maintain, / It may Afflict, but man must not Complain." Otway gives us no comforting rhetoric of providential justice or transcendence for the just. If there be a god, he is sheer Power. The world of *The Orphan* has collapsed because the discourse designed to enforce patriarchal control has done its job all too well. The men fundamentally distrust all women, and the women themselves accept the rhetoric of purity and pollution. Castalio's, Monimia's, Polydore's, Acasto's–all their personal tragedies are the tragedy of their patriarchal culture, revealing its essential tragic flaw.

Otway's dedication of *The Orphan* to the duchess of York maintains that the "share" she and the duke have in his heart is his "only Portion." In the prologue he complains that wit is out of fashion, and in the epilogue he wittily jokes that the poet may have to run away and be orphaned of his third-day's receipts. Earlier, Otway had dedicated *Friendship in Fashion* to the same dedicatee of his first play, Charles Sackville, then earl of Middlesex and by 1678 earl of Dorset as well. In 1679 Otway dedicated *Caius Marius* to his old school friend, the Viscount Falkland. And he dedicated *The Souldiers Fortune* to his bookseller, Richard Bentley. All these facts indicate that Otway could not maintain steady patronage. There were rumors that Dorset was offended by something in *Friendship in Fashion*. But Otway's fulsome praise of Falkland as his intellectual inspiration at Winchester, when Falkland was several years younger than he, and his repeated appeal on the grounds of loyalty to His and Her Highnesses appear not to have paid off either, at least not substantively (Falkland did contribute the prologue to *Souldiers Fortune*). By 1680, the year of publication of *The Orphan*, Otway had become cynical enough to mock the patronage system and to playfully substitute for it a business relationship with the bookseller. But not until the career of Alexander Pope would an author succeed in establishing a sound, bourgeois economic basis for his livelihood. Meanwhile, authors such as Otway would continue to have to grovel in humiliating flattery, often to no avail.

Miss Brunton as Monimia in an eighteenth-century production of The Orphan

The Souldiers Fortune seems to reflect a bitterness that goes beyond general to biographical satire. The title characters, Beaugard and Courtine, are younger brothers who have gone into the army for a living but have been precipitately disbanded with debentures, like Otway's own, that are virtually worthless. Moreover, a good deal of their stage time is given over to their complaining—and Courtine complains more bitterly—at the way of the world that rewards fools and parvenus rather than men of merit, even in the army. Here they sound like not only Otway's Acasto and Pierre but George Farquhar's Aimwell and Archer. This is a typical Stuart portrayal of class conflict, during what Lawrence Stone has called "the crisis of the aristocracy," between aristocrats, men of worth and wit and courage and good taste, and the nouveaux riches, men of money

and dullness and cowardice and bad taste. The conflict between Beaugard and Sir Davy Dunce over his wife is more specifically one between Cavalier and Roundhead, Tory and Whig: Beaugard has been loyal to his prince and served him well; Sir Davy has been "a common-Wealths-man" and now considers dining with the lord mayor of London tantamount to access to real power. Beaugard and Courtine complain that rebels have been rewarded, while Cavaliers have been poor ever since their fathers lost land and revenue during the civil war. The reference to Shaftesbury as rewarded rebel seems clear, but is Otway also glancing at his own impoverishment because of his father's royalism? Did Humphrey Otway not have enough to leave Thomas because he lost land and living during the war? However that may be, Otway wrote Beaugard a complaint that seems biographical:

In the mean while patience, *Courtine*, that is the *English* mans Vertue: Go to the man that ows you money, and tell him you are necessitated, his answer shall be, a little patience I beseech you, Sir: Ask a Cowardly Rascal satisfaction for a sordid injury done you, he shall cry, alas a day, Sir, you are the strangest Man living, you won't have patience to hear one speak: Complain to a great Man that you want preferment, that you have forsaken considerable advantages abroad in obedience to publick Edicts, all you shall get of him is this, you must have patience, Sir.

Beaugard remains essentially optimistic, however, and believes that he and Courtine can somehow strike their fortunes out of themselves. But Heathcliff's option—to make a fortune in America—is not yet available to them, and Courtine refuses to become a thief or a pimp. The play proceeds instead to two typical resolutions—but with atypical rhetoric. Courtine proves to be a Benedick, falling in love with his Beatrice, Sylvia. They both protest again and again that they are not in love and that marriage is the furthest thing from their minds. Yet they do finally marry; Courtine's libertine energy socializes into monogamy; and they engage in a typical gay-couple proviso scene. Yet when Sylvia tries to tame the Rover, converting his wonted performative into constative rhetoric, Courtine finally pledges his word as his bond in a fashion that transforms the idealism of that aristocratic trope into pragmatism: "Upon the word of a Gentleman, nay as I hope to get Mony in my Pocket." That is an oath Sylvia can bank on. And the rhetoric of their provisos amounts to an agreement that Courtine will remain faithful to Sylvia, in performance as well as promise, lest she take unwarranted tenants in revenge. Moreover, he will protect her as his property, provided that it is not already soiled. In other words they have rediscovered and reaffirmed the pragmatic basis of patriarchal sexual politics. Unlike his contemporaries, Otway does not employ religious language to reinvest the pragmatic with the idealistic. Before their "Covenant," when Sylvia is testing Courtine's fidelity with the affectation of her own libertinism, he starts off to pursue Lady Dunce. She says wittily, "What, commit Adultery Captain? fie upon't! What, hazard your soul!" and he responds even more wittily, "No, no, only venture my body a little, that's all." This ironic religious language is never redeemed even just for the sake of arbitrarily and artificially cloaking desire with traditional, conventional aristocratic rheto-

ric. At the end Courtine announces that Sylvia has had "no more Grace before her eyes" than to take him at his word and marry him. The language remains ironic, and Courtine's financial problem is solved not by any romantic devices but by the sheer phallic power of Beaugard's drawn sword, the fear of which has scared Sir Davy into hysterical acceptance of his fate, part of which is that his niece Sylvia "has five thousand to her Portion, and my Estate's bound to pay it." Sylvia and Courtine do not need Sir Davy's consent. Her portion is entailed to her, and the couple emerges financially independent.

The resolution to Beaugard's plight is even more pragmatic—and pagan. Early in the play he receives money from a strange woman, who turns out to be his beloved Clarinda, whom he had to leave for the wars and who in his absence has been forced to marry the senex, Sir Davy Dunce. By hilarious ruses they contrive to consummate their love and dupe the dunce as he deserves. At the end, when Beaugard is discovered not dead but quick and in his wife's arms, Sir Davy is cowed into compliance by Beaugard's sword and forced to keep his own wife and use her as if she were Beaugard's "Mistress." The "Covenants" of this comic resolution are no more traditionally idealistic than those of the other. The ending is pure aristocratic wish fulfillment.

Furthermore, all the civilities of the characters in the play are exposed as masking a desire that can be quite brutish and brutal. In a scene no more gratuitous than Etherege's similar scene in *The Man of Mode*, several whores and three bullies promenade as if to signify that the only difference between them and the wits is style. At one point Sir Davy interviews a ruffian named Bloody-Bones for the purpose of having Beaugard murdered according to his wife's ostensible wishes. While on one level the scene is a hilarious example of the way in which Sir Davy is made to cuckold himself, as he constantly plays into the hands of the young lovers, on another level the scene draws the curtain of social decorum back to reveal the savage behavior that lurks underneath, not in some underworld, but in one's own breast. When Bloody-Bones announces that he will bring Sir Davy Beaugard's heart the next morning for breakfast and asks, "did you never eat a Mans Heart Sir?" his discourse seems an invasion from a world that is totally Other than that of polite English society. But when Sir Davy requests only that Beaugard be beaten, knowing that beating was just as often fatal as not, and when after praying all night, supposedly out of repentance for the feigned death of Beaugard, he turns the Constable and the Watch against his own neighbor to charge *him* with the murder of Beaugard, then we see that violence is not *unheimlich* but *heimlich*, not foreign but domestic.

In this play Otway revived from *The Cheats of Scapin* the great comic team of Nokes and Leigh. Nokes must have made a great Sir Davy. But for Leigh, Otway created one of his greatest roles, Sir Jolly Jumble, a comic character that combines the tricks of Scapin with the amorality of Malagene. Sir Jolly is a pimp, a whoremaster, a voyeur, and a disgustingly, delightfully lubricious bisexual. He cannot keep his hands off the men's crotches and his fingers out of the women's bosoms. He is a totally amoral figure of sheer comic energy, an embodiment of a very unsentimental life force. And as he perverts all the key words of the conventional, Christian, chivalric ethos, he seems a perfect sign of the fundamental meaninglessness of his world. Otway creates a comic version of Hobbist society, where all man's systems, especially the language in which they are all embodied, are merely a veneer over desire. The celebration at the end of the play is positively Nietzschean.

In 1680 Otway was granted an M.A. degree from Cambridge; the documents speak of him as having a degree from Oxford. But from everything we know, he never received a degree from Oxford, and why he received this one from Cambridge, no one knows. It must have been, as it was typically, simply an honorary degree. Was it finally preferment of a kind? Was a patron responsible, perhaps powerful connections of Otway's friend Richard Duke, with whom Otway apparently stayed when he went up to receive the degree and who wrote to him later expressing the hope he would return? Could it have been the king himself or his brother, repaying Otway for his loyalty? Whatever happened, the only financial aid we are fairly certain Otway received in these years, in addition to the relative pittance he was paid for his plays, was payment from Nell Gwyn, who had played Otway's Lady Squeamish, for tutoring her bastard by Charles II, Charles Beauclerk. Roswell Ham, one of Otway's twentieth-century biographers, speculates that when this source of income ran out, Otway turned from Charles II's Protestant to his Catholic mistress, Louise de Kéroualle, duchess of Portsmouth, to whom he dedicated his next and now best-known play, *Venice Preserved*, and to whom he protests

again that his loyalty has been his only inheritance. Whether he received any support from her is unknown.

First performed on 9 February 1682, *Venice Preserved* has long been interpreted as a Tory play, and recent criticism has witnessed some elaborate arguments to prove it so. But *Venice Preserved* is essentially not political tragedy, advocating some clear ideology or judging corruption in the light of one. *Venice Preserved* is absurdist satire. And like *The Orphan*, it reveals a fundamental misogyny that is man's blight. The play is full of typical Otwavian resentment. Jaffeir and Belvidera are made orphans by her father, the senator Priuli, because she married Jaffeir, literally an orphan raised by her father, without his consent. Pierre has been orphaned by his country, as it were, because it has proved ungrateful to his military services by censoring him for threatening the senator Antonio, a rival for his mistress Aquilina. As Beaugard and Courtine join in homosocial bonding against the strumpet Fortune in the earlier play, Jaffeir and Pierre join in similar bonding here. Like Beaugard, Pierre gives his destitute friend money. But unlike Beaugard's essentially comic optimism, Pierre's prime motivation for his actions is revenge—against Antonio, against the entire senate by extension, against the whore Venice herself. And his gift to Jaffeir is, in effect, a bribe to get him to join in his revenge, which takes shape as rebellion against the government of Venice.

Jaffeir at first responds to his orphaned poverty with a brave *contemptus mundi,* and when he comforts Belvidera with promise of a pastoral retreat, he sounds like Dryden's Antony, who came at last to value his jewel Cleopatra more than all the world. But Pierre's altruistic rhetoric of revolution—and especially his rhetoric of revenge—wins Jaffeir back to the business of the world, and he joins the conspirators, offering his wife's life as his pledge of loyalty to his oath.

The discourse of altruism remains inextricably confused with that of self-interestedness throughout the play. Despite the rallying cries of liberty and freedom for the oppressed, the conspirators' motivations are tainted with selfish desire for power and, what is worse, a sadistic desire to murder, rape, and pillage. The total corruption of the senate is revealed when, despite their sacred oaths to Jaffeir not to harm the conspirators whom he turns in, they have them all tortured and executed. The ambitious, sadistic, rapist Renault, who would butcher women and children and rape his fellow conspirator Jaffeir's wife, is the badge of the rebels. The disgusting, masochistic, masturbatory Antonio is the badge of the "legitimate" government. The only viable political theory is the iron law of oligarchy: one group of supposed elites wants to dominate another and has no scruples about how it does so.

Belvidera would seem to provide an island of value in this sea of corruption. Indeed she recalls Jaffeir from his "Damning Oath," employing humanistic rhetoric to prevent him from such wanton slaughter. She uses the traditional rhetoric of filial piety: how can she, no matter how persecuted by her father, participate in a rebellion that will see him murdered? And at one point he seems to agree with the Christian, humanist position that an oath to thus wantonly shed blood is not binding but is damning indeed: "can there be a sin / In merciful repentance?" And yet Belvidera really wins Jaffeir over only by urging not altruism but revenge against Renault for trying to rape her.

Nor does Belvidera fully win Jaffeir over. He sees himself as having "In fond compassion to a Womans tears / Forgot his Manhood, Vertue, truth and Honour, / To sacrifice the Bosom that reliev'd him." Like Castalio, Jaffeir is caught not just between conflicting words and bonds but between homosocial and heterosexual codes. He shares with Pierre (who says to Aquilina, "How! a Woman ask Questions out of Bed?") a fundamental misogyny and views his yielding to Belvidera's erotic appeal as effeminate weakness. Again and again he tries to kill her to appease his friend and his conscience. He *lets* her live, charges her with raising their son "in vertue and the paths of Honour"—phrases that have lost their reference by this time in the play. Jaffeir can separate his rhetorics finally only by uncritically accepting Pierre not as the devil who tempted him on the Rialto but as a betrayed Jesus. Pierre postures on the scaffold, pretending that the conspirators all died "like men . . . , Worthy their Character"—a phrase their rapist rhetoric has belied. And in the end, unable to face the meaninglessness of all their language and their world, Jaffeir and Pierre write their last tragic act, attempting to inscribe their ending with the sense of heroic tragedy. Jaffeir stabs Pierre, then himself. The final use of the phallic dagger that has threatened throughout supposedly reaffirms phallic dominance. But Belvidera raves apocalyptically and Priuli, won over by his daughter's (erotically tinged) humanis-

tic rhetoric too late, sinks into abject despair. Again, no redemptive rhetoric saves the play from the bleakest vision.

Instead, again emerging in a character played by Leigh, the quivering masochist Antonio in effect has the last word. The speech he wrote for the senate is full of gibberish; yet he survives and prevails. Perverting the traditional rhetoric, he grovels before the enraged Aquilina muttering "faith and troth." As she whips him, he lies down and ejaculates on the stage, where he remains during Jaffeir's parting scene with Belvidera. Would not a good director have him leer knowingly at the audience? Would he not have Antonio return in the scaffold scene, an emblem, like William Faulkner's Jim Bond, that life is indeed a tale told by an idiot, full of sound and fury, signifying nothing?

In late 1682 the King's and Duke's companies merged into the United Company, which performed Otway's next and last play, *The Atheist; or, The Second Part of the Souldiers Fortune*, in 1683. This sequel to the successful *Souldiers Fortune* appears not to have met with success. Perhaps the reason is that such is the fate of most sequels. And the play is long, perhaps too full of characters (an accident of writing for the joint company?) and plot twists, and too short on rationale for character motivation, at least in the instance of Lucrece. Nevertheless, the play is remarkable for its subversion of patriarchal codes.

Courtine has returned to the Town desperate for libertine relief from his wife, Sylvia. Those who distrust the last-act conversion of the rake—in Otway's time and our own—have their doubts confirmed in Courtine's behavior. He despises his cloying wife and envies Beaugard's insouciant freedom. At points Otway appears to portray Sylvia's plight sympathetically. She follows him to town and rails at him for deserting her and her children. But Otway gives us a scene in which Sylvia's abject submissiveness to Courtine and their domestic baby talk make her appear a silly harmless household dove whom Courtine is well to be rid of. Still, Lucrece, apparently out of spite to Beaugard and by extension to his beloved Porcia and Porcia's cousin Sylvia, plots a bed switch so that instead of consummating his love for Porcia, Beaugard commits with Sylvia. How far he commits with her is unclear, for he protests to Courtine that he has not wronged him. Courtine is furious, however, convinced he has been cuckolded. There is no reconciliation between them, and he believes he now has the right

David Garrick as Jaffier and Susanna Arne Cibber as Belvidera in a scene from a 1762 production of Venice Preserved
(etching after a painting by Johann Zoffany; courtesy of the British Museum)

*Sarah Siddons as Belvidera in another eighteenth-century
production of* Venice Preserved

Eliza O'Neil as Belvidera in an 1814 production of
Venice Preserved

to cheat on her and to expect that she will never again complain. If this is poetical justice on Courtine, his part of the play ends with no more celebration than did that of Goodvile's part in *Friendship in Fashion*.

The play appears to follow a pattern typical of subversive comedy, however. If one plot ends with dissolution, the other ends with marriage and celebration. Despite his repeated, adamant insistence that he will never marry, Beaugard falls in love with Porcia, a wealthy widow. As in plays such as Aphra Behn's *Rover* (1677), Porcia tests the depth of Beaugard's love by proving his constancy. When he finds to his astonishment that he no longer desires promiscuous sex, Beaugard himself becomes the converted rake ready for marriage at the end of the play.

Moreover, Beaugard and Porcia have overcome blocking obstacles similar to those of such Spanish intrigue comedies as Behn's. Though she is a rich widow, Porcia's wealth is controlled by her dead husband's brother, Theodoret (whom she mistakenly calls an uncle; Otway was nodding). And the husband has bequeathed his widow to his old rival, Gratian. These two men are savage misogynists, whose motivation for forcing Porcia to marry Gratian becomes far less Gratian's old mimetic desire and far more the men's desire to teach this uppity woman a lesson. The extremity of their misogyny reminds one of that of the brothers of Webster's duchess of Malfi. In rebellion Porcia has established her house as a room of her own, an enchanted palace in which she may pursue her own desires.

Yet as usual, Otway has raised several deeply disturbing considerations that militate against the apparent fulfillment of the typical pattern of subversive comedy. First, Porcia justifies her rebellion against her sadistic male protectors in a way that keeps us from wholehearted embrace of that rebellion. She acknowledges to Sylvia that she is "transported . . . With hopes of Liberty": "it is an English Woman's natural Right. Do not our Fathers, Brothers and Kinsmen often, upon pretence of it, bid fair for Rebellion against their Soveraign; And why ought not we, by their Example, to rebel as plausibly against them?" Beaugard's resistance to marriage is based upon a cynicism with the whole system, best articulated in his complaint to his father that his uncle, who was the elder brother yet never married, was the one who left Beaugard enough money to be solvent, while his spendthrift father can give him nothing but comes to beg for himself. Therefore,

Beaugard's conversion, especially when seen also in the light of the sequel's treatment of the first play's fifth-act conversion, carries no real conviction but seems to belong to the enchanted, wish fulfillment of comedy alone. Moreover, Otway compounds this assault on patriarchy by having Beaugard's father, played by Leigh as a character similar to Otway's other parasites, join with Theodoret against his own son, despite the fact that Jackie, as he calls him, refuses to be irreverent to him and continues to give him money. Otway seems to be suggesting that there are no such things as natural bonds. They are instead a creation of language.

The most subversive aspect of the play is referred to in its title. Ostensibly, Daredevil is the atheist, and, because he recants in moments of fear and prays for his soul, the play appears to suggest that no thinking man can be an atheist. (Otway may well have been glancing at Rochester's deathbed repentance here, as Jessica Munns has recently argued.) But nothing in the play occurs to give the lie to Daredevil's indictment of even the plain-dealing libertines' hypocrisy in committing acts forbidden by the religion they seem to be defending in attacking his atheism. Moreover, as he has done so many times, instead of providing his audience with the comforting platitudes of poetical and providential justice at the end of the play, Otway has Beaugard attribute the denouement not to some metaphysical dynamic that underwrites patriarchal man's sociopolitical codes but strictly to "the Dominion of Chance." Beaugard is the real atheist in the play. He knows life is merely the pursuit of desire. And does not Otway suggest that he is one of those few poets Daredevil speaks of who "now and then stand up for the Truth manfully"–the truth of atheism?

Within two years, Otway was dead at thirty-three, apparently of poverty and starvation. Politically and economically, times were tough in the early 1680s. The only life records we have from the period are debts, as Otway apparently borrowed from his booksellers, from his actors, and from his vintner. He is reported to have been in debt to this last for four hundred pounds. And he began to be the subject of lampoons on the ironic juxtaposition of his corpulence and his poverty. One of these seems to tell it most cruelly but most truly:

Lift up your Heads ye Tories of the Age,
Lett Otway tumble Shadwell from the Stage,

Thomas Otway, engraving based on a portrait by John Ryley

Otway who long (leane Loyalty preserving)
Has showne a wonder and grown fat wth starving.

He died on 14 April 1685 somewhere on Tower Hill, and we really know no more than those bare facts, except that he continued to write up to the time of his death, publishing a eulogy to Charles II, among other minor poems. He may have been working on a play at the time of his death, for Thomas Betterton and William Smith, another actor, advertised to try to recover it. And Otway may have had a hand in *The History of the Triumvirates*, translated from the French and published in 1686, but Ghosh does not include it in his definitive edition. In short, however much Otway may have legitimately complained about his lack of preferment and patronage, he apparently continued in that life of debauched ease he describes in *The Poet's Complaint* and died of the consequences.

Despite their early rivalry, Dryden and Otway must have moved closer because of their simi-

lar political positions, and after Otway's death Dryden wrote Otway a generous brief eulogy in his "Parallel betwixt Painting and Poetry" (1695), praising him for that "greatest beauty" of all, "nature." Otway's credit with the critics thereafter rose and fell according to their political and ethical values, but his credit with audiences, especially after his plays were expurgated, continued strong on through the nineteenth century, as Aline Mackenzie Taylor has best shown. Otway's continuing fame rests partly on literary history—the success of his two great tragedies over the years—and partly on the critical attention those plays and others are beginning to receive. The greatness of his best plays, especially the comedies, lies in the extraordinary depth of his Nietzschean vision into the abyss of the human heart and the answering abyss of the cosmos. No other playwright of his time—and very few others of any time until our own—has portrayed that vision so relentlessly. The sadism and masochism, misogyny and misandry, and misogamy of his plays leave us with a vision of men and women as orphans and atheists in a universe of ingratitude and alienation. In such a Dominion of Chance one can only comfort oneself with the rhetoric of desire or else go mad and die.

Bibliography:

J. M. Armistead, *Four Restoration Playwrights: A Reference Guide to Thomas Shadwell, Aphra Behn, Nathaniel Lee, and Thomas Otway* (Boston: G. K. Hall, 1984), pp. 261-387.

Biographies:

Roswell Gray Ham, *Otway and Lee: Biography from a Baroque Age* (New Haven: Yale University Press, 1931);

J. C. Ghosh, Introduction to *The Works of Thomas Otway: Plays, Poems, and Love-Letters*, 2 volumes, edited by Ghosh (Oxford: Clarendon Press, 1932).

References:

Ronald Berman, "Nature in *Venice Preserved*," *ELH*, 36 (September 1969): 529-543;

Laura Brown, *English Dramatic Form, 1660-1760: An Essay in Generic History* (New Haven: Yale University Press, 1981), pp. 86-95;

David Bywaters, "Venice, Its Senate, and Its Plot in Otway's *Venice Preserv'd*," *Modern Philology*, 80 (February 1983): 256-263;

J. Douglas Canfield, *Word As Bond in English Literature from the Middle Ages to the Restoration* (Philadelphia: University of Pennsylvania Press, 1989), pp. 300-310;

Brian Corman, "Johnson and Profane Authors: The Lives of Otway and Congreve," in *Johnson after Two Hundred Years*, edited by Paul J. Korshin (Philadelphia: University of Pennsylvania Press, 1986), pp. 225-244;

Michael DePorte, "Otway and the Straits of Venice," *Papers on Language and Literature*, 18 (Summer 1982): 245-257;

Jack D. Durant, " 'Honor's Toughest Task': Family and State in *Venice Preserved*," *Studies in Philology*, 71 (October 1974): 484-503;

Jean H. Hagstrum, *Sex and Sensibility: Ideal and Erotic Love from Milton to Mozart* (Chicago: University of Chicago Press, 1980), pp. 90-98;

Phillip Harth, "Political Interpretations of *Venice Preserv'd*," *Modern Philology*, 85 (May 1988): 345-362;

David R. Hauser, "Otway Preserved: Theme and Form in *Venice Preserv'd*," *Studies in Philology*, 55 (July 1958): 481-493;

Derek W. Hughes, "A New Look at *Venice Preserv'd*," *Studies in English Literature*, 11 (Summer 1971): 437-457;

Hughes, "Otway's *The Orphan*: An Interpretation," *Durham University Journal*, 44 (1983): 45-54;

Robert D. Hume, "Otway and the Comic Muse," *Studies in Philology*, 73 (January 1976): 87-116;

Hume, "The Unconventional Tragedies of Thomas Otway," in *Du Verbe au geste: mélanges en l'honneur de Pierre Danchin* (Nancy: Presses Universitaires de Nancy, 1986), pp. 67-79;

Geoffrey Marshall, "The Coherence of *The Orphan*," *Texas Studies in Literature and Language*, 11 (Summer 1969): 931-943;

William H. McBurney, "Otway's Tragic Muse Debauched: Sensuality in *Venice Preserv'd*," *Journal of English and Germanic Philology*, 58 (1959): 380-399;

Judith Milhous and Robert D. Hume, *Producible Interpretation: Eight English Plays 1675-1707* (Carbondale: Southern Illinois University Press, 1985), pp. 172-200;

Laurie P. Morrow, "Chastity and Castration in Otway's *The Orphan*," *South Central Review*, 2, no. 4 (1985): 17-30;

Jessica Munns, "Daredevil in Thomas Otway's *The Atheist*: A New Identification," *Restoration: Studies in English Literary Culture, 1660-1700*, 11 (1987): 31-38;

Munns, " 'The Dark Disorders of a Divided State': Otway and Shakespeare's *Romeo and Juliet*," *Comparative Drama*, 19 (Winter 1985-1986): 347-362;

Munns, "Does Otway Praise Rochester in *The Poet's Complaint*," *Notes and Queries*, 231 (March 1986): 40-41;

Munns, " 'Plain as the light in the Cowcumber': A Note on the Conspiracy of Thomas Otway's *Venice Preserv'd*," *Modern Philology*, 85 (August 1987): 54-57;

Munns, "Thomas Otway's *Titus and Berenice* and Racine's *Bérénice*," *Restoration: Studies in English Literary Culture, 1660-1700*, 7 (Fall 1983): 58-67;

Katharine M. Rogers, "Masculine and Feminine Values in Restoration Drama: The Distinctive Power of *Venice Preserv'd*," *Texas Studies in Literature and Language*, 27 (Winter 1985): 390-404;

J. C. Ross, "An Attack on Thomas Shadwell in Otway's *The Atheist*," *Philological Quarterly*, 52 (October 1973): 753-760;

Eric Rothstein, *Restoration Tragedy: Form and the Process of Change* (Madison: University of Wisconsin Press, 1967), pp. 90-110;

Candy B. Schille, "Reappraising 'Pathetic' Tragedies: *Venice Preserved* and *The Massacre of Paris*," *Restoration: Studies in English Literary Culture, 1660-1700*, 12 (1988): 33-45;

Harry M. Solomon, "The Rhetoric of 'Redressing Grievances': Court Propaganda as the Hermeneutical Key to *Venice Preserv'd*," *ELH*, 53 (Summer 1986): 289-310;

Thomas B. Stroup, "Otway's Bitter Pessimism," in *Essays in English Literature of the Classical Period Presented to Dougald MacMillan*, edited by Daniel W. Patterson and Albrecht B. Strauss, *Studies in Philology*, extra series no. 4 (January 1967): 54-75;

Aline Mackenzie Taylor, *Next to Shakespeare: Otway's "Venice Preserv'd" and "The Orphan" and their History on the London Stage* (Durham: Duke University Press, 1950);

Eugene M. Waith, "Tears of Magnanimity in Otway and Racine," in *French and English Drama of the Seventeenth Century: Papers Read at a Clark Library Seminar March 13, 1971* (Los Angeles: W. A. Clark Library, 1971), pp. 1-22;

Kerstin Warner, *Thomas Otway* (Boston: Twayne, 1982);

Harold Weber, *The Restoration Rake-Hero: Transformations in Sexual Understanding in Seventeenth-Century England* (Madison: University of Wisconsin Press, 1986), pp. 83-90;

Matthew H. Wikander, "The Spitted Infant: Scenic Emblem and Exclusionist Politics in Restoration Adaptations of Shakespeare," *Shakespeare Quarterly*, 37 (Autumn 1986): 340-358.

Mary Pix

(1666-May 1709)

Linda R. Payne
University of Delaware

PLAY PRODUCTIONS: *Ibrahim, the Thirteenth Emperour of the Turks*, London, Theatre Royal in Drury Lane, May-June 1696;

The Spanish Wives, based on Gabriel de Brèmond's *The Pilgrim*, London, Dorset Garden Theatre, August 1696;

The Innocent Mistress, London, Lincoln's Inn Fields, June 1697;

The Deceiver Deceived (later *The French Beau*), London, Lincoln's Inn Fields, November 1697;

Queen Catherine; or, The Ruins of Love, London, Lincoln's Inn Fields, June 1698;

The False Friend; or, The Fate of Disobedience, London, Lincoln's Inn Fields, May 1699;

The Beau Defeated; or, The Lucky Younger Brother, anonymous, adapted from F. C. Dancourt's *Le Chevalier à la mode* and Molière's *Les Précieuses ridicules*, London, Lincoln's Inn Fields, March 1700;

The Double Distress, anonymous (Pix signed printed dedication), London, Lincoln's Inn Fields, March 1701;

The Czar of Muscovy, attributed to Pix, London, Lincoln's Inn Fields, March 1701;

The Different Widows; or, Intrigue à la Mode, attributed to Pix, London, Lincoln's Inn Fields, November 1703;

Zelmane; or, The Corinthian Queen, completion attributed to Pix, begun by William Mountfort, London, Lincoln's Inn Fields, 13 November 1704;

The Conquest of Spain, attributed to Pix, based on William Rowley's *All's Lost by Lust*, London, Queen's Theatre, May 1705;

The Adventures in Madrid, attributed to Pix, London, Queen's Theatre, June 1706.

BOOKS: *Ibrahim, The Thirteenth Emperour of the Turks: A Tragedy, As it is Acted by his Majesties Servants* (London: Printed for John Harding & Richard Wilkin, 1696);

The Spanish Wives. A Farce, As it was Acted by His Majesty's Servants, at the Theatre in Dorset-Garden (London: Printed for R. Wellington, 1696);

The Inhumane Cardinal; or, Innocence Betray'd. A Novel (London: Printed for John Harding & Richard Wilkin, 1696); facsimile, introduction by Constance Clark (Delmar, N.Y.: Scholars' Facsimiles & Reprints, 1984);

The Innocent Mistress. A Comedy. As it was Acted, by His Majesty's Servants at the Theatre in Little-Lincolns-Inn-Fields (London: Printed by J. Orme for R. Basset & F. Cogan, 1697); modern edition, in *The Female Wits*, edited by Fidelis Morgan (London: Virago, 1981);

The Deceiver Deceived: A Comedy, As 'tis now Acted by His Majesty's Servants, at the Theatre in Little-Lincolns-Inn-Fields (London: Printed for R. Basset, 1698); republished as *The French Beau: A Comedy, Acted by His Majesty's Servants At The New Theatre in Little-Lincolns-Inn-Fields* (London: Printed for William Brown, 1699);

Queen Catharine; or, The Ruines of Love. A Tragedy, As it is Acted at the New Theatre in Little-Lincolns-Inn-Field, by His Majesty's Servants (London: Printed for William Turner & Richard Basset, 1698);

The False Friend; or, The Fate of Disobedience. A Tragedy. As it is Acted at the New Theatre in Little-Lincolns-Inn-Fields (London: Printed for Richard Basset, 1699);

The Beau Defeated; or, The Lucky Younger Brother. A Comedy. As it is now Acted By His Majesty's Servants at the New Theatre in Lincolns-Inn-Fields (London: Printed for W. Turner & R. Basset, 1700);

The Double Distress. A Tragedy. As it is acted at the Theatre-Royal in Little Lincolns-Inn-Fields. By His Majesty's Servants (London: Printed for R. Wellington & Bernard Lintott, 1701);

The Czar of Muscovy. A Tragedy. As it is Acted at the Theatre in Little Lincolns-Inn-Fields. By His Majesty's Servants, attributed to Pix (London: Printed for B. B. Lintott, 1701);

The Different Widows; or, Intrigue All-à-Mode. A Comedy. As it is Acted at the New Theatre in Little Lincolns-Inn-Fields. By Her Majesty's Servants, attributed to Pix (London: Printed for Henry Playford & Bernard Lintott, 1703);

Violenta; or, The Rewards of Virtue: Turn'd from Boccace into Verse (London: Printed for John Nutt, 1704);

Zelmane; or, The Corinthian Queen. A Tragedy. As it is acted at the New-Theatre in Lincolns-Inn-Fields. By Her Majesties Servants, attributed to Pix (London: Printed for William Turner & John Nutt, 1705);

The Conquest of Spain: A Tragedy. As it is Acted by Her Majesties Servants at the Queen's Theatre in the Hay-Market, attributed to Pix (London: Printed for R. Wellington, 1705);

To the Right Honourable the Earl of Kent, Lord Chamberlain of Her Majesties Household, &c. (London, 1705?);

The Adventures in Madrid. A Comedy, As It Is Acted at the Queen's Theatre in the Hay-Market. By Her Majesty's Servants, attributed to Pix (London: Printed for William Turner and others, 1706).

Collection: *The Plays of Mary Pix and Catharine Trotter*, facsimiles, introduction by Edna L. Steeves (New York: Garland, 1982).

OTHER: Poem signed Clio, in *The Nine Muses. Or, Poems Written By Nine Severall Ladies Upon the Death of the late Famous John Dryden, Esq.*, possibly compiled by Delarivière Manley (London: Printed for Richard Basset, 1700);

Commendatory verses, in *A Collection of Poems on Several Occasions . . . To Which is Added a Pastoral . . . By Mrs. Sarah Fyge Egerton* (London: Printed & sold by the booksellers of London & Westminster, 1706).

Mary Pix was one of three women playwrights to debut in the London theatrical season of 1695-1696, but the only one to work consistently in the theater and to establish a serious career there over the next decade. Her six comedies and seven tragedies represent well the various trends of a difficult era for the stage, bridging the Restoration and Augustan ages. She consciously sought to emulate the first professional woman dramatist, Aphra Behn, and anticipated the strategies of the better-known Susanna Centlivre. Most of the little that is known about her has been gleaned from a few contemporary lampoons, and her life remains more obscure

than those of most of her more flamboyant contemporaries.

Although her work was a staple of Thomas Betterton's theater company at Lincoln's Inn Fields and later at the Queen's Theatre, Pix's plays have drawn scant attention. Her tragedies provided formulaic vehicles for the great acting triumvirate of Betterton, Elizabeth Barry, and Anne Bracegirdle, employing the spectacle and rant of the heroic mode. One major problem with Pix's choice of medium was that her talents lay more in stagecraft than in poetry; contemporary commentary nearly always deprecated her blank verse. Her plots and characterization, however, generally exploited passion and pathos in a crowd-pleasing manner.

Although Jeremy Collier's stage-reform movement somewhat confined her comedic writing within the awkward limbo between the "hard" comedy of manners and the cult of sensibility, she made exceptionally effective use of the latitude available in creating interesting and bold characters, particularly heroines. Again, Pix did not excel in writing witty dialogue, but her imagination was a fertile source for the popular intrigues and plot twists—which then had to be blunted or unconvincingly contorted to accomplish the requisite moralizing close.

Public records disclose very few facts about Pix. According to her marriage license, on 25 July 1684 eighteen-year-old Mary Griffith married merchant-tailor George Pix in London with the consent of her mother, the widow Lucy Griffith. The dating of that event places her birth to the Reverend Roger Griffith and Lucy Berriman Griffith in 1666. There is nothing else known about her childhood, although it is probable that the vicar's household provided an atmosphere more conducive than most for a young woman's education. No further documentary reference has been found about Pix's family after she and her husband buried a child at Hawkhurst in 1690.

Although her writing was subjected to the general condescension toward a woman's ability and proper position in society, Pix herself seems to have escaped the slanders usually heaped on the moral character of women daring to pursue public careers. Critics have speculated that she may have been known to be happily married, or that she was too unattractive physically to be a sexual threat, or that she was just generally amiable and well liked. In *The Female Wits*, the anonymous satire which appeared at Drury Lane the season following the triple debuts of Pix, Delarivière Manley, and Catharine Trotter, she is treated far more gently than her sister authors.

In fact, the caricature that emerges of her as Mrs. Wellfed–"a fat Female Author, a good, sociable, well-natur'd Companion, that will not suffer Martyrdom rather than take off three Bumpers in a Hand"–provides the basis for the personal allusions to her in contemporary commentaries. Her only notoriety was for enjoying good food, wine, and the lively company of the players; in the balance, she was considered generous and openhearted, although somewhat foolish.

Wellfed's self-deprecating sense of humor is shown in refreshing contrast to the inflated egos of her two colleagues. Pix displays the same quality in some of the dedications of her plays while making the conventional woman's apologies for venturing beyond her proper sphere and for lacking learning. Although humble ignorance was hinted in *The Female Wits* and exploited by later lampoonists, it seems likely that the caricature was a foil for the other two authors, particularly for Trotter, who was noted for vanity about her classical and theological reading. Pix's work evidences a respectable education, with more than the average woman's background in literature and languages.

The scanty contemporary data on Pix also provides a few glimpses of her professional relationships. She, Trotter, and Manley wrote verses praising each other's work, and several lampoons pair her with Trotter, who also wrote for the company at Lincoln's Inn Fields. She contributed to a collection of elegies on the death of John Dryden, *The Nine Muses*, which Manley also wrote for and may have compiled. Playwright William Congreve was considered her mentor and took her side when another writer plagiarized from her. Another successful writer, Peter Motteux, wrote two incidental songs for *The Innocent Mistress* (1697) and the prologue and epilogue to *The Deceiver Deceived* (1697).

By 1703 she was portrayed in a satire, *The Players Turn'd Academicks*, as the intimate friend of Susanna "Carroll" (Centlivre), with whom she contributed commendatory verses to *A Collection of Poems on Several Occasions* by feminist poet Sarah Fyge Egerton in 1706, the last year that anything is known of Pix. In 1709 two major London papers announced a performance of Centlivre's *The Busy Body* for the benefit of Pix's estate, claiming that Pix wrote "the Greatest·part"

both of that play and another Centlivre work, *The Gamester* (1705). Unfortunately, that notice is the only record of the alleged collaboration, and of Pix's death, as well.

Like her colleague Manley, Pix stormed London in 1696 with a comedy, a tragedy, and a novel. The tragedy, *Ibrahim, the Thirteenth Emperour of the Turks*, was her most popular work. The length of its original run, which began in May or June 1696, is unknown, but there were recorded revivals in 1702, 1714, and 1715. She referred in the prologue to her "dull Heroick Play," without "poignant Repartee, nor takıng Raillery," but based in "solid History" and the "Strict Rules of Honour." In the preface she credits her source as Sir Paul Rycaut's continuation of *The Turkish History* (1687) but apologizes for having erred in her title: Ibrahim was really the twelfth emperor of the Turks. To a story filled with lust and mayhem, well suited for the spectacular trappings of the heroic drama, she added a tragic romance and a rebellion. Her prologue is also notable for its appeal to the ladies to "protect one harmless, modest Play."

First produced in August 1696, her farce, *The Spanish Wives*, also enjoyed a long life, with revivals in 1705 and 1711, and possibly one as late as 1726. She used as a source *The Pilgrim* (1680), a translation of a French novel by Gabriel de Brèmond. In addition to the romantic intrigues of two couples, this play includes two of Pix's funniest low-comedy characters, a fruit seller and a corrupt friar who compete with each other as pimps. The characters of the elderly governor and his young wife are exceptionally amiable and share a rare, felicitous relationship.

Pix again turned to history for her only novel, *The Inhumane Cardinal; or, Innocence Betray'd* (1696), which apparently failed to appeal to readers. In 1696 she moved to Lincoln's Inn Fields with *The Innocent Mistress*, an engaging comedy which uses exceptionally charming characters to interweave gallantry with platonic love, a play marred only by its disappointingly creaky resolution turning on mistaken identity. First produced in June 1697, it was called a "good success" and has been marked as the earliest example of Congreve's influence on Pix's work. She never returned to Drury Lane after actor and playwright George Powell plagiarized parts of his *Imposture Defeated* (1697) from *The Deceiver Deceived*, which Betterton and Congreve brought out in November 1697. Pix's play was published in 1698 and republished as *The French Beau* in 1699. The leading

To the Honourable
RICHARD MINCHALL,
of *Bourton*, Esq;.

SIR,

THat sweetness of temper I have had the Happiness to discover in the honour of your Company in the first place , and your favourable Opinion of my Play in the next, gives me Incouragement to claim your Protection.

I am often told , and always pleased when I hear it, that the Works not mine ; but oh I fear your Closet view will too soon find out the Woman , the imperfect Woman there. The story was true, and the action gave it Life ; for I shou'd be very rude not to own each maintain'd their Character beyond my hopes. Then that pretty Ornament, the ingenious Dialogue, these might divert you at the Theatre, but these avail not me ; the reading may prove tiresome as a dull repeated tale : Yet I have still recourse to what I mention'd first, your good nature, that I hope

A 2   will

Dedication and preface to Pix's first play, from the 1696 edition

The Epistle Dedicatory.

will pardon and accept it. I only wish my self Mistress of Eloquence, Rhetorick, all the Perfections of the Pen, that I might worthily entertain Mr. *Minchall.*

Your Noble Family has been long the Glory of my Native Country, and you are what I think no other Nation equals , a true English Gentleman, kind to the distressed, a Friend to all. I dare not proceed----my Weakness wou'd too plainly appear in aiming at a Character which I can never reach : Therefore, I conclude, once more asking your Pardon , and leave to subscribe my self,

SIR,

Your most humble

and Obliged Servant,

Mary Pix.

THE
PREFACE.

I Did not intend to have troubl'd the Reader with any thing of a Preface ; for I am very sensible those that will be so unkind to Criticize upon what falls from a Womans Pen, may soon find more faults than I am ever able to answer. But there happens so gross a mistake, in calling it Ibrahim, the Thirteenth &c. that I cannot help taking notice of it. I read some years ago, at a Relations House in the Country, Sir Paul Ricaut's Continuation of the Turkish History ; I was pleas'd with the story and ventur'd to write upon it , but trusted too far to my Memory ; for I never saw the Book afterwards till the Play was Printed, and then I found Ibrahim was the Twelfth Emperour. I beg Pardon for the mistake, and hope the Good-Natur'd World will excuse that and what else is amiss, in a thing only design'd for their Diversion.

PRO-male character, a curmudgeon who tyrannizes both daughter and young second wife, is so thoroughly bad-natured and unattractive that some otherwise clever writing is wasted. The wife and daughter are also distasteful in their moral equivocations. Oddly, an inappropriate epilogue celebrates the new peace with France by hailing the second Augustan age and the ennobled offerings of the stage.

Pix's next play, *Queen Catherine; or, The Ruins of Love* (1698), was a historical tragedy, portraying incidents supposedly set around the battle of Mortimer's Cross (1461), which secured the reign of Edward IV from the usurped Henry VI. Disclaiming her presumption in following Shakespeare, she points out in the preface that she seeks instead to please the ladies by shunning the mighty martial themes to portray loves. However, she refers her audience to Shakespeare as the source for her characterization of Gloucester (later Richard III), and to discover the justice (albeit delayed) of his fate.

Ironically, while Pix shows competency in the dramatic structure and characterization of this genre, the greatest interest in the play has been that it fills the gap between Shakespeare's Henriad and *Richard III*. Yet Pix's manipulation of historical personalities and events is absurd: The plot evolves from the unrequited love of Edward IV for Catherine of Valois, who historically died before his birth. The play reportedly survived only four nights, but that was enough to provide one author's benefit performance.

The prologue for *The False Friend* (1699) claimed, "Amongst reformers of this Vitious Age, / Who think it Duty to Refine the Stage, / A Woman to Contribut, does Intend / In Hopes a Moral Play your Lives will Mend." The tragedy is an unsavory one that goes to great lengths to commend obedience to parents. Neither the villainess's parting admonition for women to shun "Black Revenge" and "Violent Passions" nor the viceroy's warning that children who "dare to disobey" may be "punished such a dismal way" is convincing.

Pix employed two new tactics in her next play, *The Beau Defeated; or, The Lucky Younger Brother* (first produced in March 1700). First, she admitted that it was "partly a translation from the French" and that she hoped to please her audience with the vogue for Continental entertainment. Her sources were F. C. Dancourt's *Le Chevalier à la mode* (1687) and Molière's *Les Précieuses ridicules* (1659). The resulting play is tighter than

those of her own design, and it presents exceptionally effective satire of pretended aristocracy juxtaposed against the true values of the rising middle class. However, it is somewhat lacking in Pix's usual good nature, for both the affected city widow and the ignorant country squire are tricked with less than fair play. Second, Pix not only published the play anonymously but represented its authorship in the prologue and epilogue with masculine pronouns. She did, however, sign the dedication in the printed edition.

In her next prologue, for *The Double Distress* (1701), she laments the eclipse of tragedy and the growing tedium of satire on the beaux. The play is unusual both for its time and also for the Pix canon: no blood-and-thunder spectacle; it has been called a tragicomedy. Two heroines face ethical choices, band together to renounce love for honor, and through predictable but skillfully handled plot twists are rewarded with their hearts' desires. Although there is no contemporary evidence about the reception of this play, it was the last that Pix ever signed.

Two more tragedies, *The Czar of Muscovy* (1701) and *Zelmane; or, The Corinthian Queen* (1704), are the most obscure of Pix's plays. Although they also bear the least certain attributions to Pix, each has a contemporary endorsement: *The Czar of Muscovy* in "A Criticism of Several Modern Plays" by Thomas Brown and *Zelmane* in a notice in the *Diverting Post* of 28 October 1704. Both are like *The Double Distress* in their happy endings, although *The Czar of Muscovy* reverts to Pix's more usual tone of oppressive menace. It is the only tragedy attributed to Pix that is written in prose rather than blank verse.

These two tragedies were separated by one of the playwright's brightest comedies, *The Different Widows; or, Intrigue à la Mode*, first produced in November 1703. The subtitle proves apt, with Pix demonstrating her versatility in navigating a tangle of romances to bring everyone to just rewards. The contrast between the two widowed sisters, Bellinda and Lady Gaylove, is particularly effective. The juxtaposition of the two distinct comic types dramatizes a moral worldview far more forcefully than the usual moralizations of sentimental conclusions. The comedy bustles with physical humor in the foiled assignations staged by Mrs. Gaylove—a nice counterpoint to the verbal repartée of the rake-taming by the sister widow and her young ward.

In the prologue Pix again bemoans the decline of tragedy, implying that she has returned

To the Honourable
Mrs COOK of Norfolk.

Madam,

DID not some of the brightest and best our Sex can boast of Incourage Attempts of this kind, the snarling Cynicks might prevail and cry down a diversion, which they themselves participate, though their ill Nature makes them grumble at their Entertainment, but when they shall see this Glorious name in the Front, when they shall know a Lady belov'd by Heaven and Earth, Mistress of all Perfections, the bounteous Powers give, or human nature is Capable to receive: when, I say they understand you protect, and like Innocent Plays, they must Acquiesce and be forc't to own so much goodness, cannot choose amiss. Queen *Catharine*, who tasted the Vicissitudes of Fate, will now forget her sufferings, and under such a Noble Patroness remain fixt in lasting Glory; and if my weak Pen has fail'd in the Character of that Great Princess : now I've made her an ample recompense, for where cou'd I have found a Lady of a more illustrious descent, or more Celebrated for her Vertues ? The name of *Cary* Graces all our *English* Chronicles and is adorn'd with the greatest Honours ; yet that Noble stock did ne'er produce a lovelier branch than your fair self, and as if Heaven Correspondent to our wishes, design'd you its peculiar blessings, you are given to a Gentleman, of whom we may venture to say, he merits even you ? Oh! may you appear many, many succeeding years, the bright Examples of Conjugal Affection, and shame that bare-fac'd Vice out of Countenance, which breaks the Marriage Vows without a blush : May you still remain blest in each other, pleas'd to see your Beauties and your Vertues renewed in your Charming Race, whilst the admiring World shall wonder at your happiness, and reform in hopes to obtain some of those blessings. May every thing contribute to your continual satisfaction, and amongst your more solid Joys, give me leave,

A 2   Madam,

Dedication and cast list for the first production from the 1698 edition of Queen Catherine

The Epistle Dedicatory.

Madam, to hope this trifle may find a vacant hour, when you will deign to peruse it, and be so good to forgive the Authors presumption in laying it at your feet.

I cou'd not, without a plain Contradiction to the History, punish the Instruments that made my Lovers unhappy ; but I know your Ladyship will trace *Richard* the Third into *Bosworth* Field, and find him there, as wretched as he made Queen *Catharine*.

I dare not add more, knowing how unworthy all I have said, or can say, is of you ; therefore shall only reiterate my Prayers for your lasting Happiness, and beg to subscribe my self,

Madam,

The humblest of your

Ladyships admirers, and

Most obedient Servant,

Mary Pix.

PRO.

THE

Actors Names.

Edward the Fourth.	Mr. *Scudamore.*
Duke of *Clarence*	Mr. *Verbruggen.*
Duke of *Gloucester*	Mr. *Arnold.*
Earl of *Warwick*	Mr. *Kynnaston.*
Malavill	Mr. *Bayly.*

Citizens, Guards, &c.

Owen Tudor	Mr. *Batterton.*
Lord *Dacres*	Mr. *Freeman.*
Sir *James Thyrrold*	Mr. *Thurmond.*

WOMEN.

Queen *Catharine*	Mrs. *Barry.*
Isabella her Ward	Mrs. *Bracegirdle.*
Esperanza Woman to *Isabella*	Mrs. *Martin.*
Ladies of Honour.	

ACT

TO THE

Right Honourable

JOHN,

Viscount *Fitz-Harding,*

Master of the HORSE to Her Royal
Highness, *&c.*

My LORD,

ROME, once Mistress of the World, her Nobles govern'd Tributary Nations, the Business and the Fate
of Mankind was theirs, yet they found leisure Hours
to entertain and encourage Poetry; and the greatest Heroes
were the Muses greatest Patrons; nor has their glorious Conquests, nor their stately Monuments, made their Memories so
immortal, as the grateful Pens of these they favour'd and pro-
tected. This Example of their Indulgence gives me boldness
to interrupt your Lordship, whose more important Affairs must
engross your Time. And tho' the Comparison will not hold,
when I reflect on the Meaness of this Trifle, and the worth of

A 2   their

The Epistle Dedicatory.

their elaborate Works, yet the Characters agree. Such Greatness of Soul, and such moral Virtues reigned in them, as we
now see conspicuous in your Lordship. The Parallel may justly be carry'd on, and the *English* Court for Politeness and re-
fin'd Gallantry vye with, if not outshine the *Roman*: In that
noble Circle your Lordship hath from your Youth appear'd, and
given as well as receiv'd Lustre from thence. There yet remains
and *Encomium* due to our Nobility, exceeding in Sweetness of
Temper all foreign Courts, which renders them belov'd by their
Inferiors. This Condescension, which blesses distant Admirers,
and takes off the Dread of approaching, is in a double Portion
posses'd by my Lord *Fitz-harding*. It is on this I ought to insist,
since 'tis on this I depend for a Pardon of this Presumption;
tho' I hope it may help to excuse me, when I say, the Play is
not wholly mine, because I thought it done and revised by
abler Hands, and therefore fitter to lay at your Lordships Feet:
The Success answered my Expectation, and this Honour fulfills
the Ambition of

My LORD,

Your Lordship's most Humble

and most Obedient Servant,

Mary Pix.

PROLOGUE.

A Serious Play in this Fantastick Age,
Without Ballad or Song upon the Stage,
Nor Wit nor Nature now can please alone,
When French Jack-pudding so delight the Town:
Instruction on the Stage is thrown away,
And Jegg does more then charming Dryden say:
Our Ancestors without Ragou's or Dance,
Fed on plain Beef, and bravely conquer'd France:
And Ben and Shakespear lasting Luirels made
With Wit alone, and scorn'd their wretched Aid:
Tho' our Play without a Villain's out of Fashion.
We hope no less to move your tender Passion;
Authors have worn so blunt those constant Tools,
That nothing is so dull as Knaves and Fools.
Why shou'd we paint the Vices of those Elves,
That take such care to represent themselves:
The Beaux in Person shews himself to all
Much better in Side-Boxes and the Mall,
In Dress and Mein so singular and vain,
In any Nation match him if you can,
He is indeed the True-born English Man.
Well, we've shew'n all we can to make you easie,
Tumblers and Monkeys, on the Stage to please you:
If all won't do we must to Treat incline,
And Women, rather than be starv'd, will join.
'Tis quickly done, the Racket Walls remain,
Give us but only time to shift the Scene,
And Presto, we're a Tennis Court again.
Yet we'll not of your wisht Applause despair,
Since faithful Lovers are again your Care;
Again the Tragick Scenes your soft Compassion share.
Our modest Muse no Fop nor Russian brings;
But treats of Heroiens and of sacred things:
Be kind, ye Fair, since of the Fair she sings.

These

---

*These Characters are for Examples drest;
Brave, like our Nobles, like our Ladies Chast;
Tho' not betray'd, pray pity them no less;
Like Heaven at last be kind to their Distress.*

EPILOGUE.

Spoken by Miss Porter.

THE Graver Bus'ness of the Day being past,
Perhaps you may expect to laugh at last;
That Epilogue shall bow, and break a Jest.
Faith we would please you in our own Defence,
But wish your Pleasures were ally'd to Sense.
We wish your Wits would suffer Reformation,
That Shrug, Grimace, and Farce were out of Fashion:
Satyr, they say, did once become the Stage,
But now w'have justly damn'd its useless Rage.
Since Fools and Knaves are Names unknown in this good Age,
This Play does no malicious Stories tell
Of Arts by which the Wise buy Stock, and sell.
For once be every Vice and Folly safe,
Censure shall have no cause to day to laugh:
But pray repay the Poet his good Nature,
Since 'tis at my Request he spares his Satyr.
If not------He knows such monstrous things of some,
Vices scarce known to Old or Modern Rome,
That if you damn the Play, let half the Town
Look to be publish'd in the next Lampoon.

E P I-

Dedication, prologue, and epilogue from the 1701 edition of The Double Distress

PROLOGUE,

Spoken by Mr. *BOOTH*.

WHAT Arts have we not try'd? What Labour ta'en,
To Reconcile You to Our House again?
One while, in Mournful Tragedy we strove,
T' Inspire You with the tender Thoughts of Love;
But never cou'd your drowsy Passions move.
You'r all of late such Rigid Stoicks grown,
Ev'n poor Monimia now might weep alone;
Whilst you most Thylosophically frown,
Since Flanders, and the Fighting Trade came up,
'Tis thought Effeminate one Tear to drop.
Damn Tragedys says one, I hate the strain,
I got a Surfeit of 'em last Campaign;
Come, prithee let's be gon to Drury-Lane.
Thither in Crouds ye flock'd to see, Sir Harry,
Or any Fop dress'd All-A-Mode de Paris;
So 'twas but Droll, it never could Miscarry.
Finding your Palates so much out of tast,
We fairly ventur'd for a lucky Cast;
And Wit being grown by Prohibition scarce,
Regal'd you here too with an Irish Farce.
'Twas Farce, and therefore pleas'd You; for a while,
Our Teague, and Nicodemus made you smile:
That Lure grown stale, we since are forc'd to fill,
With Supplemental Epilogue, our Bill:
For, having us'd you still to something new,
You now begin t' expect it as your due;
And ne'er reflect that these penurious Times,
Our Bards cannot afford to give us Rhymes.
How have I trudg'd about, from day, to day,
Barely to beg a Prologue to our PLAY.
Morn, after Morn, I've sought, yet could not get
(If Life had layn at Stake) one Drachm of Wit;
You'd swear I'd gon a Begging in the Pit.

From

From thence to the Old Exchange, and there I met
One of our Friends, who's turn'd a thrifty Cit:
At sight of me away the Poet Run,
Just as we sometimes a grim Serjeant shun;
Help, help, cry'd I, Sir, or We're all undone.
Begar, vid all my Art dit il, me'ave swore
Never to make the Englis Verses more;
But 'cause You be de Friend, if You vad know
Vad rate de Stock, or de Debenture go,
Me'll tell you dat. I thank You Sir, said I,
But, I have no Occasion now to buy.
From him, streight to St. Lawrence-Lane I went,
You mot Necessity knows no Restraint;
And there (most horrible to View) I saw
Such Magazines of Court-Hand, and the Law,
So nigh resembling those which cost us dear
(In Hall of Westminster) but the last Year,
I thought no Friend to th Play-House could live there;
But as the Proverb has't, do right to th' Devil;
The Kentish Yeoman, Faith, was very Civil:
It was Term-Time, and he was to attend
A Judge, so bid me not on him depend.
From thence, it being past the time of Noon,
With nimble Steps I hy'd to the Half-Moon:
Don Quixot had been there, but he was gon.
Yet speeding there, to Will's I took my round,
But not one Poet there was to be found,
Except the Author of the Country Wife,
But faith, I dur'st not Wake him for my Life:
Least his Plain Dealing Muse should let you hear
Such Stinging Truths, you'd not know how to bear,
And make you (in a Pet) our House forswear.

A D-

Prologue to The Different Widows, *from the 1703 edition*

to comedy because of the "penurious Times" in which "Our *Bards* cannot afford to give us *Rhyme*." The play opens, in fact, with a spoof on a poor poet seeking to dedicate a work to a rakish heir he has never met. Sir James declines the dubious honor and sends him off with a handout and the advice to cease groveling if he is serious about poetry or to give up "scribbling" if he would be either "rich or wise."

Interestingly, in Pix's last two plays she returned to the themes and moods of the first two. The tragic *The Conquest of Spain* (1705) was unsigned and represented the author as a man. Based on William Rowley's *All's Lost by Lust* (circa 1619), it was attributed to Pix by prompter John Downes. Although *The Conquest of Spain* has been called an adaptation, the plot was greatly altered and the dialogue almost entirely rewritten. With the addition of a new romantic hero, one of the two major plots resembles even more closely that of *Ibrahim*, to which Pix had made a similar addition. In both plays a decadent and unworthy ruler has been further corrupted by a strong, manipulative villainess. He betrays the exceptional service of one of his few loyal counselors by violently raping the friend's virgin daughter, who dies as her fiancé seeks to avenge her by rebellion. *The Conquest of Spain* is the only play by Pix after *Queen Catherine* for which there is evidence of an extended run, in this case six days.

Like *The Spanish Wives*, *The Adventures in Madrid* (1706) is a three-act farce, duplicating the Spanish setting and mixture of English and Spanish characters. Its action also centers on heroines confined by men obsessed with infidelity, but it is more complex, capitalizing on the techniques Pix had mastered in *The Different Widows* for juggling four romances instead of a mere two.

It would be interesting to know whether Pix's return to these materials was motivated solely by her early commercial success or whether their values had some other kind of appeal for her. Whatever the cause, she succeeded well in recapturing her early spark. The resulting quartet of plays, along with *The Different Widows* and *The Innocent Mistress*, are her strongest, with *The Double Distress* providing exceptional interest but less theatricality.

The few critics who have dealt with Pix have regretted that she bothered with tragedy instead of honing her greater talent for comedy. While this attitude is eminently sensible from a modern perspective that tends to dismiss both the decadent and Augustan strains of tragedy that her work spans, historically she appears as one of the more-successful tragedians of her era. Her taste for tragic plot lines, with the single exception of *The Double Distress*, is remarkably consistent, with even her choice of historical sources leading her into repeated horror stories of titanic villains threatening innocence and virtue with bloody death and sexual rapine. This basic formula provided for high drama: lust, obsession, fury, terror, and above all, pathos. The attitudes portrayed toward authority reflect the uneasiness of a generation who remembered regicide, restoration, and "glorious revolution" and who lived with a legal heir in exile: noble sentiments are expressed both in favor of and against rebellion, and rightful order is generally restored. The plays offered juicy parts to the best actors of the day and catharsis to their audiences.

Pix's comedies tend to repeat certain patterns as well, but demonstrate more imagination in recombining them with original ideas. While three plays feature plots involving the taming of a rake by a witty and virtuous woman, the counterplots show real variety: a true platonic relationship between a man and woman deeply in love (*The Innocent Mistress*), a mother-son relationship based on respect and love (*The Different Widows*), and the operations of a wise city merchant on the follies of both the decadent gentry and the affected middle class (*The Beau Defeated*).

Without portraying actual adultery, Pix manages to use the popular theme of cuckoldry, teasing the prurient interests of the traditional audience while assuaging the stage reformers and growing merchant-class theater clientele. In *The Deceiver Deceived*, *The Different Widows*, and *The Spanish Wives* she reverses the expected plot of the erring husband reclaimed by a forgiving wife, portraying instead an almost-erring wife prevented and reformed before actually yielding to temptation. Her comedies repeatedly dramatize the evils of forced marriages, deploring them while turning them to practical use in providing rationale for near adulteries or as a legal basis for elopements.

The other consistent theme that evolves from the troubled marriages Pix portrays is the confinement of women. In *The Spanish Wives*, *The*

Innocent Mistress, and *The Adventures in Madrid* women are kept prisoner by tyrannical men, while in *The Different Widows* a monstrous mother keeps her own grown offspring hidden from the world and locked in their childhood. This theme also forms a link between the comedies and tragedies, as in both Pix depicts women as victims. In *Ibrahim* and *The Conquest of Spain* a beautiful young virgin is brutally raped, and in *Queen Catherine*, *The Czar of Muscovy*, and *Zelmane* similar rapes are attempted. This dramatic portrayal of persecuted innocence was a tactic used extensively in the popular fiction of the day, even in the writing of women; Pix's novel is about rape and murder by a lecherous cardinal.

The titillation that must have been provided by these lovelies struggling with their ravishers is inescapable and disturbing. The rape itself is described graphically in *Ibrahim*, with the "savage Ravisher" tearing out by the root the "lovely Tresses" of the victim. When Morena was revealed "upon the ground disorder'd as before," according to one contemporary source it "never fail'd to bring Tears into the Eyes of the Audience." Similar responses were probably aroused in the comedies from the images of beautiful women confined to be enjoyed only by brutish and insensitive men.

It seems likely that by using sexual violence as a metaphor for victimization women authors were dealing with their own ambivalence toward the patriarchy that oppressed them but within which they had to survive. In Pix's tragedies the women who have been violated always choose death, usually remarking on the nobility of Roman heroines as their patterns for heroic honor. There are also an unusually large number of women who are the true movers and controllers not only of their own lives but of those around them. Her strong women, both virtuous and evil, are just as often agents as victims.

Although Pix's contemporary critics sometimes regarded her plays as obscene, they more often described them as dull; while they were not often outraged by her works, they tended to dismiss them as trifles. Theater historians have persisted in treating Pix as inoffensive but insignificant. Even today her plays are generally damned with faint praise, characterized by adjectives such as "workmanlike."

The fact that Pix somehow escaped the personal notoriety of many of her sister authors may ironically have helped to keep her in undeserved obscurity even longer. It is encouraging that her plays have now been collected in facsimile reprint, but modern editions are certainly called for. Although Mary Pix may not have created any one masterpiece, her dramatic canon is strong indeed, and particularly rich in comedies that may still be read with delight.

References:

Paula Louise Barbour, "A Critical Edition of Mary Pix's *The Spanish Wives*," Ph.D. dissertation, Yale University, 1975;

Herbert Carter, "Three Women Dramatists of the Restoration," *Bookman's Journal*, 13 (1925): 91-97;

Constance Clark, *Three Augustan Women Playwrights* (New York: Peter Lang, 1986), pp. 183-287;

Nancy Cotton, *Women Playwrights in England c. 1363-1750* (Lewisburg, Pa.: Bucknell University Press, 1980), pp. 88-90, 111-121;

Fidelis Morgan, Notes on Pix in *The Female Wits: Women Playwrights of the Restoration*, edited by Morgan (London: Virago, 1981), pp. 44-51, 263-264;

Edna L. Steeves, Introduction to *The Plays of Mary Pix and Catharine Trotter* (New York: Garland, 1982), pp. xi-xi.

Thomas Shadwell

(24 March 1641?-November 1692)

Eric Rothstein
University of Wisconsin–Madison

PLAY PRODUCTIONS: *The Sullen Lovers: or, The Impertinents*, adapted from Molière's *Les Fâcheux*, London, Lincoln's Inn Fields, 2 May 1668;

The Royal Shepherdess, adapted from John Fountain's *The Rewards of Virtue*, London, Lincoln's Inn Fields, 25 February 1669;

The Hypocrite (lost), adapted from Molière's *Tartuffe*, London, Lincoln's Inn Fields, 14 June 1669;

The Humourists, London, Lincoln's Inn Fields, 10 December 1670;

The Miser, adapted from Molière's *L'Avare*, London, Royal Theatre on Bridges Street, January 1672;

Epsom Wells, London, Dorset Garden Theatre, 2 December 1672;

The Tempest: or, The Enchanted Island, adapted from John Dryden and Sir William Davenant's adaptation of Shakespeare's play, London, Dorset Garden Theatre, 30 April 1674;

Psyche, adapted from Molière, Pierre Corneille, and Philippe Quinault's *Psyché*, London, Dorset Garden Theatre, 27 February 1675;

The Libertine, London, Dorset Garden Theatre, 12 June 1675;

The Virtuoso, London, Dorset Garden Theatre, 25 May 1676;

The History of Timon of Athens, the Man-hater, adapted from Shakespeare's play, London, Dorset Garden Theatre, January 1678;

A True Widow, London, Dorset Garden Theatre, 21 March 1678;

The Woman-Captain, London, Dorset Garden Theatre, September 1679;

The Lancashire Witches, and Tegue o Divelly, the Irish Priest, London, Dorset Garden Theatre, September 1681;

The Squire of Alsatia, London, Theatre Royal, Drury Lane, 3 May 1688;

Bury Fair, London, Theatre Royal, Drury Lane, April 1689;

The Amorous Bigotte: with the Second Part of Tegue o Divelly, London, Theatre Royal, Drury Lane, March(?) 1690;

The Scowrers, London, Theatre Royal, Drury Lane, December 1690;

The Volunteers: or the Stock Jobbers, London, Theatre Royal, Drury Lane, November 1692.

BOOKS: *The Sullen Lovers: Or, The Impertinents. A Comedy, Acted by His Highness the Duke of*

Thomas Shadwell (frontispiece to volume 1 of The Complete Works of Thomas Shadwell, *edited by Montague Summers, 1927)*

Yorkes Servants (London: Printed for Henry Herringman, 1668);

The Royal Shepherdess. A Tragi-comedy, Acted by His Highness the Duke of York's Servants (London: Printed for Henry Herringman, 1669);

The Humorists; A Comedy. Acted by his Royal Highnesses Servants (London: Printed for Henry Herringman, 1671);

The Miser, A Comedy. Acted by His Majesties Servants at the Theater Royal (London: Printed for Thomas Collins & John Ford, 1672);

Epsom-Wells. A Comedy, Acted at the Duke's Theatre (London: Printed by J. M. for Henry Herringman, 1673);

The Tempest, or The Enchanted Island. A Comedy. As it is now Acted at His Highness the Duke of York's Theatre (London: Printed by T. N. for Henry Herringman, 1674); modern edition, in *Five Restoration Adaptations of Shakespeare*, edited by Christopher Spencer (Urbana: University of Illinois Press, 1965), pp. 109-199;

Notes and Observations on the Empress of Morocco, by Shadwell, John Crowne, and John Dryden (London, 1674);

Psyche: A Tragedy, Acted at the Duke's Theatre (London: Printed by T. N. for Henry Herringman, 1675);

The Libertine: a Tragedy. Acted by His Royal Highness's Servants (London: Printed by T. N. for Henry Herringman, 1676);

The Virtuoso. A Comedy, Acted at the Duke's Theatre (London: Printed by T. N. for Henry Herringman, 1676);

The History of Timon of Athens, the Man-hater. As it is Acted at the Duke's Theatre. Made into a Play (London: Printed by J. M. for Henry Herringman, 1678);

A True Widow. A Comedy, Acted by The Duke's Servants (London: Printed for Benjamin Tooke, 1679);

The Woman-Captain: A Comedy Acted by His Royal Highnesses Servants (London: Printed for Samuel Carr, 1680);

The Lancashire-Witches, and Tegue O Divelly, the Irish Priest: A Comedy Acted at the Dukes's [sic] *Theatre* (London: Printed for John Starkey, 1682);

The Medal of John Bayes: A Satyr against Folly and Knavery (London: Printed for Richard Janeway, 1682);

Satyr to his Muse, by the Author of Absalom & Achitophel (London: Printed for D. Green, 1682);

The Tory-Poets: A Satyr (London: Printed by R. Johnson, 1682);

A Lenten Prologue Refus'd by the Players [single sheet printed on both sides] (London, 1683);

Some Reflections upon the Pretended Parallel in the Play Called The Duke of Guise. In a Letter to a Friend (London: Printed for Francis Smith, 1683);

The Tenth Satyr of Juvenal, English and Latin. The English by Tho. Shadwell (London: Printed by D. Mallet for Gabriel Collins, 1687);

The Squire of Alsatia. A Comedy, As it is Acted by Their Majesties Servants (London: Printed for James Knapton, 1688); modern edition, *Thomas Shadwell's "The Squire of Alsatia": A Critical Edition*, edited by J. C. Ross (New York: Garland, 1987);

Bury-Fair. A Comedy, As it is Acted by His Majesty's Servants (London: Printed for James Knapton, 1689);

A Congratulatory Poem on his Highness the Prince of Orange His Coming into England (London: Printed for James Knapton, 1689);

A Congratulatory Poem to the most Illustrious Queen Mary upon her Arrival in England (London: Printed for James Knapton, 1689);

The Address of John Dryden, Laureat to His Highness the Prince of Orange (London: Printed & sold by Randal Taylor, 1689);

The Amorous Bigotte; with the Second Part of Tegue o Divelly. A Comedy, Acted by Their Majesty's Servants (London: Printed for James Knapton, 1690);

Ode on the Anniversary of the King's Birth (London: Printed for James Knapton, 1690);

Ode to the King, on his Return from Ireland (London, 1690);

The Scowrers. A Comedy, Acted by Their Majesties Servants (London: Printed for James Knapton, 1691);

Votum Perenne: a Poem to the King on New-Years-Day (London: Printed for Samuel Crouch, 1692);

Ode on the King's Birth-Day (London: Francis Saunders, 1692);

The Volunteers: or the Stock-Jobbers. A Comedy, As it is Acted by Their Majesties Servants, at the Theatre Royal (London: Printed for James Knapton, 1693).

Collections: *The Works of Tho. Shadwell* (London: Printed for James Knapton, 1693);

The Dramatick Works of Thomas Shadwell, 4 volumes (London: Printed for James Knapton & Jacob Tonson, 1720);

The Complete Works of Thomas Shadwell, 5 volumes, edited by Montague Summers (London: Fortune Press, 1927).

An exceptionally skillful, thoughtful, and inventive comic playwright, Thomas Shadwell was a man of multiple misfortunes. By running afoul of one of the deadliest satirists in English, John Dryden, he found himself the butt of a poetic attack, *Mac Flecknoe*, that marked him as a pretentious dunce forever after: *Mac Flecknoe* is still read by everyone with more than a smattering of English literature, while only a few specialists now sample Shadwell's plays. Shadwell was highly successful at the time *Mac Flecknoe* appeared in late 1682, but he may already have been barred for political reasons from having new plays of his performed–the dedication to his *Bury Fair* (1689) refers to his having been "for near Ten years . . . kept from the exercise of that Profession which had afforded me a competent Subsistence"–and we, in fact, have no record of his plays being performed for six or seven years. He lapsed into severe financial difficulty, aided by patrons and exercising his dramatist's skills only, if at all, through giving anonymous help to a minor actor, Thomas Jevon (by one account, his brother-in-law), in preparing a first comedy. Starting shortly before the revolution of 1688-1689, Shadwell returned to the stage in a new bout of productivity and popularity and had the satisfaction of replacing as poet laureate the very Dryden who, he believed, had used the laureate's power to ban him from the stage. By this time, however, Shadwell was in ill health, and he cannot have been much over fifty when he died in 1692. Within a few years after his death, his comedies were eclipsed by the brilliance of William Congreve's and John Vanbrugh's, as well suited for the postrevolutionary age as his. They have never regained their due.

Shadwell was born on 24 March in 1640 or 1641 into the Norfolk gentry. His father, a Loyalist, was then suffering financially from support for the crown as the civil wars proceeded, so that Thomas later laid claim to "the Birth and Education without the Fortune of a Gentleman." Since

An anonymous portrait of Shadwell, circa 1690 (courtesy of the National Portrait Gallery, London)

his parents, John and Sarah, had eleven children, the penury is not surprising. After five years of tutoring at home, Thomas was sent to the King Edward VI Free Grammar School at Bury St. Edmunds, about fifteen miles south, where the headmaster, Thomas Stephens, was an ardent Royalist. The city was to be somewhat acidly remembered as part of the provinces in Shadwell's *Bury Fair*. From this school he followed his father's path, first to Cambridge, attending Gonville and Caius College for two years, and then, in 1658, to the Middle Temple, to train for the bar. (John Shadwell seems not to have practiced law but held various government positions, including some in Ireland.) During the early to mid 1660s he improved on the progression from school to university to London by a period of travel, with a four months' stay in Ireland, presumably with his father. Again, his life in the Middle Temple and his travel became dramatic material, as seen in his Belfond Jr. in *The Squire of Alsatia*.

Sometime between 1663 and 1667 Shadwell married Anne Gibbs, who had been one of the first actresses in the English theater, performing

as a principal at Oxford as early as July 1661. She was an actress for the Duke's company, which was to stage almost all Shadwell's plays before its union with the King's company in 1682. He must, finally, have made the acquaintance of wits about town and, still more important, of the patron and playwright William Cavendish, duke of Newcastle, who had suffered penury as a Royalist during the civil wars.

How Shadwell became interested in the theater remains unclear. His wife may have been the magnet, if he met her before he began to write. Newcastle liked some of his earliest writings, but we do not know if these were comedies or if the duke encouraged his protégé to write for the stage. (Montague Summers argues that, in fact, Shadwell served as a play doctor for Newcastle.) Shadwell may perhaps have owed the start of his theatrical career to the writing of songs or interludes; he was a highly skilled musician who played the lute or theorbo, having been taught by John Jenkins (1592-1678), musician in ordinary to Charles I and Charles II and a composer of both instrumental and vocal music. Whatever his stimuli to write for the theater, *The Sullen Lovers*, performed by the Duke's company at Lincoln's Inn Fields on 2 May 1668, made Shadwell's debut triumphant. The play responded to all three possible reasons for his theatrical involvement. Mrs. Shadwell enjoyed the best female part, and Shadwell had the chance to write music, if he wished, for some singing and dancing. He borrowed freely from Molière's *Les Fâcheux* (1661), just as his dedicatee, Newcastle, had borrowed freely from *L'Etourdi* (1655) in collaborating the year before with Dryden on *Sir Martin Mar-All*. *The Sullen Lovers* lampooned as an egomaniacal, drama-scribbling fool Sir Positive At-All (Sir Robert Howard, a member of the duke of Buckingham's parliament-centered political faction and therefore probably persona non grata to the Royalist Newcastle). Finally, the preface to *The Sullen Lovers* sounds a literary theme welcome to Newcastle, who had commissioned Ben Jonson's last two masques (1633-1634): adulation of Jonson and a claim to have imitated his "classical" construction and his characterization by humours. In the name of Jonsonian purity, too, his preface was politely severe toward Newcastle's rival protégé, Dryden, ten years Shadwell's senior and the enviable author of three successes in 1667, *Secret Love*, an adaptation of *The Tempest*, and *Sir Martin Mar-All*. Shadwell's insistence on his own Jonsonian spirit may have been due to the duke's persuasion or to a desire to flatter a generous patron by artistic means as well as in dedicatory epistles. He kept referring his own practice to Jonson's at least through *The Squire of Alsatia* (1688), where the prologue cites "the Rules of Master *Ben*" as his model, a dozen years after Newcastle's death.

The Sullen Lovers is a slight play, in which the grave couple, Stanford and Emilia, marry and flee the society of pestering fools whom Shadwell parades before them, while the gay couple, Carolina and Lovel, remain to be detachedly amused by the circus of impertinent antics in London. Obviously an audience of Londoners, paying to watch satiric comedy, must have come closer to the gay than the grave point of view, but the presence of Stanford and Emilia contributes a moral bite that adds to the customers' relish of their own superiority. That is quite Jonsonian, as are the personal lampoons on Howard and others, with Jonson's *Poetaster* (1601) as a legitimating model; much less so are the humourous characters, who serve as Molièrean foils to the lovers, and not at all Jonsonian is the relative plot-

lessness of this play. What Shadwell especially claimed to owe Jonson was an insistent morality: Jonson's and Shadwell's moral force, however, remains–somewhat differently for each–in question. In the preface to *An Evening's Love* (1671) Dryden points out how far Jonson is from any sort of poetic justice, and so, often, was Shadwell. He followed Jonson less dubiously in his precise portrayals of London follies, so precise that later George Etherege, off in Ratisbon, was to ask for a copy of *The Squire of Alsatia*, "that I may know what follies are in fashion."

Trying to duplicate the box-office success of *The Sullen Lovers*, Shadwell tried a brief, baffling foray into pastoral with a tragicomedy, *The Royal Shepherdess* (1669), rewritten from an earlier play by John Fountain. Its lukewarm reception brought him back to Jonsonian rough-and-tumble, including lampoons, in *The Humourists* (first produced on 10 December 1670); the lampoons vanished before the first night, probably under duress, and the play vanished from the boards shortly thereafter. Having done well with materials from Molière in *The Sullen Lovers*, he turned to *Tartuffe* (1664) and *L'Avare* (1668), respectively, for *The Hypocrite* (1669; now lost) and *The Miser* (1672). This second play, written for the King's company in haste and put on anonymously, probably suffered as the result of the company's theater's burning down shortly thereafter. *The Miser* joins a version of *L'Avare* to a coarse, lively underworld subplot that provides color and moral counterpoint to a greed more socially pernicious and widespread than in Molière: for cash the London miser Goldingham stands ready to conspire against his king, a crime not too appalling for comedy as the memory of the Commonwealth receded but one that can hardly have been casually chosen by John Shadwell's son or Newcastle's protégé. In keeping with his darkening of his source, Shadwell allows Goldingham's son Theodore to treat the old man with some of the callous abandon typical of parental-filial relations in comedies of the late 1660s and 1670s. Unlike Theodore, Cléante in *L'Avare* returns the stolen gold to his father so that Harpagon, obsessed with his money, accedes to his children's marriages; Theodore, cursed by his father with "invincible impotence," "raging Lust," and "tormenting jealousie," remarks blandly at the close of the play: "My passion will a just excuse be thought: / What is urg'd on by love, can be no fault." The shady characters who aid him end up unpunished, well rewarded.

PREFACE.

I N a good Natur'd Countrey, I doubt not but this my first Essay in Rhime would be at least forgiven; especially when I promise to offend no more in this kind: But I am sensible, that here I must encounter a great many Difficulties In the first place (though I expect more candour from the best Writers in Rhime) the more moderate of them (who have yet a numerous party, good Judges being very scarce) are very much offended with me, for leaving my own Province of Comedy, to invade their Dominion of Rhime: But me-thinks they might be satisfi'd, since I have made but a small incursion, and am resolv'd to retire. And were I never so powerful, they should escape me, as the Northern People did

did the Romans, their craggy barren Territories being not worth the Conqu'ring. The next sort I am to encounter with, are those who are too great Admirers of the French *Wit*, who (if they do not like this *Play*) will say, the French *Psyche* is much better; if they do, they will say, I have borrow'd it all from the French. Whether the French be better, I leave to the Men of *Wit* (who understand both Languages) to determine; I will onely say, Here is more Variety, and the Scenes of Passion are wrought up with more Art; and this is much more a Play then that. And I will be bold to affirm that this is *as much a Play, as could be made upon this Subject.* That I have borrow'd it all from the French, can onely be the objection of those, who do not know that it is a Fable, written by Apulejius, *in his Golden Ass;* where you will find most things in this Play, and the French too. For several things concerning the Decoration of the Play, I am oblig'd to the French, and for the Design of Two of the onely *moving Scenes* in the French, which I may say, without vanity, are very much improv'd, being wrought up with more Art in this, then in the French Play, without borrowing any of the thoughts from them.

In a thing written in five weeks, as this was, there must needs be many Errours, which I desire true Criticks to pass by; and which perhaps I see my self, but having much bus'ness, and indulging my self with some pleasure too, I have not had leisure to mend them, nor would it indeed be worth the pains, since there are so many splendid Objects in the Play, and such variety of Diversion, as will not give the Audience leave to mind the Writing; and I doubt

doubt not but the Candid Reader will forgive the faults, when he considers, that the great Design was to entertain the Town with variety of Musick, curious Dancing, splendid Scenes and Machines: And that I do not, nor ever did intend to value my self upon the writing of this Play. For I had rather be Author of one Scene of Comedy, like some of Ben. Johnsons, then of all the best Plays of this kind that have been, or ever shall be written: Good Comedy requiring much more Wit and Judgment in the Writer, then any Rhiming, unnatural Plays can do: This I have so little valu'd, that I have not alter'd six lines in it since it was first written, which (except the Songs at the Marriage of Psyche in the last Scene) was all done Sixteen moneths since. In all the words which are sung, I did not so much take care of the Wit or Fancy of 'em, as the making of 'em proper for Musick; in which I cannot but have some little knowledge, having been bred for many years of my Youth to some performance in it.

I chalked out the way to the Composer (in all but the Song of Furies and Devils in the Fifth Act) having design'd which Line I would have sung by One, which by Two, which by Three, which by four Voices, &c. and what manner of Humour I would have in all the Vocal Musick.

And by his excellent Composition, that long known able and approved Master of Musick, Mr Lock, (Composer to His Majesty, and Organist to the Queen) has done me a great deal of right; though, I believe, the unskilful in Musick will not like the more solemn part of it, as the Musick in the Temple of Apollo, and the Song of the Despairing Lovers, in the Second Act; both which are pro-
(b)   per

per and admirable in their kinds, and are recommended to the judgment of able Musicians: for those who are not so, there are light and ayery things to please them.

All the Instrumental Musick (which is not mingled with the Vocal) was composed by that Great Master, Seignior Gio: Baptista Draghi, Master of the Italian Musick to the King. The Dances were made by the most famous Master of France, Monsieur St. André. The Scenes were Painted by the Ingenious Artist, Mr. Stephenson. In those things that concern the Ornament or Decoration of the Play, the great industry and care of Mr. Betterton ought to be remember'd, at whose desire I wrote upon this Subject.

POSTSCRIPT.

I Had borrow'd something from two Songs of my own, which, till this Play was Printed, I did not know were publick; but I have since found 'em printed in Collections of Poems, viz. part of the Song of the Despairing Lovers, in the Second Act, and about Eight lines in the First Act, beginning at this line, 'Tis frail as an abortive Birth. This I say, to clear my self from Thiev'ry, 'tis none to rob my self. The Reader may please to take notice of several Errata's, as,

Page 2, for, bright Sun exhales, read, gross Earth exhales. p.6. after, where you shall be adorn'd by me, insert, with all the Treasures of the East and West. p.15. l. 5. for, upon the Tripod, read, before which stands the Tripod. p. 18. before, it Thunders, insert, As the Priestess Pythia is mounting the Tripod. p 42. read, Great Statues of Gold standing upon Pedestals, with small Figures of Gold sitting at their feet. Several other Errors there are, which the sense will help you to correct,

PRO-

Preface to Psyche, *from the 1675 edition*

Before British politics forced Shadwell from the stage in 1681, he wrote or adapted a full-length play annually, all but *The Miser* for the Duke's company at Dorset Garden. To read them in sequence is to have a clear sense of changing modes of comedy during an especially brilliant theatrical decade, for Shadwell took up and gave a highly individual stamp to an increasingly cynical, tonally complex series of plays, beginning with *Epsom Wells* (produced on 2 December 1672). His first hit after *The Sullen Lovers*, *Epsom Wells* helped introduce a new theme to the Restoration stage, the young, married rake, with an equally roving wife. Dryden's airy treatment of this theme in *Marriage A la Mode* had preceded *Epsom Wells* by about a year, but the embittered conflict and eventual separation of Shadwell's Mr. and Mrs. Woodly give the issue of marriage—the thematic focus of the play—a bite foreign to Dryden though increasingly common in later Restoration comedy. As is common in most Restoration comedy from the mid 1660s on, the values of *Epsom Wells* lie in freedom and pleasure, but Shadwell makes visible the instability in these supposedly natural ideals, which in fact continued to be redefined and differently hedged as the social and theatrical environment changed. He does so through setting his comedy in a "natural" spot, physically outside the city, socially a vacation spot, medically a spa. As in *The Miser*, subplots about duping and cuckolding give a thematic setting to the main action, but here they turn on inversions, marriages that are no marriages, and courage that is no courage. The Woodlys' marriage, at once plausible (both partners are wholly egoists) and unnatural (both are perfidious), gives a thematic setting in turn to the rapprochement of two couples: Lucia and Carolina, Bevil and Raines. Carolina is also wooed by Woodly; Bevil and Raines have or plan affairs with Mrs. Woodly. In such a world, where "nature" makes a bit too much visible, the ingenues require a period of trial before they will marry witty men-about-town: they do not easily trust either recent libertines or any husbands. The moral position is obviously prudential, and from it one might extrapolate a rule of prudence that is the only moral rule in Shadwell's plays of the 1670s.

Two flights into operatic adaptation intervened between *Epsom Wells* and Shadwell's next play, *The Libertine* (first produced on 12 June 1675): he decked out *The Tempest*, as wickedly improved by Dryden and Sir William Davenant, for musical and scenic effects (30 April 1674); and

having done that well, he wrote *Psyche* (27 February 1675), a version of a then hugely successful mythological *tragédie-ballet* with a book by Pierre Corneille and Molière and lyrics by Philippe Quinault. *The Libertine* also borrows from the French, from Molière's *Dom Juan* (1665) as well as a play by Claude la Rose, sieur de Rosimond. *Timon of Athens* (first produced in January 1678) again borrowed from Shakespeare. It was preceded by an original comedy, perhaps Shadwell's best, *The Virtuoso* (first produced on 25 May 1676), which has some affinities with *Epsom Wells*. Shadwell called his *Timon of Athens* and *The Libertine* tragedies, the only ones of his career. The generic label fits *Timon of Athens*, where Shadwell acted largely as skillful play doctor for Shakespeare's original, adding a love plot and tying up loose ends. Besides being good for Shadwell's wallet and reinforcing an inference that he liked to be thought a stern, austere satirist, *Timon of Athens*, through its love plot, attacks the libertine ethos that *Epsom Wells* at once employs and puts into question. Such an attack is the whole concern of *The Libertine*, a raucous, bloody, sadistic extravaganza filled with murders and rapes, even to the Oedipally tabooed parricide and incest which should mark the play a tragedy. Here, as Robert D. Hume says, "Shadwell imports the moral code of contemporary libertine comedy into a tragic structure, and the result is a soberfaced burlesque." Some of *The Libertine* even inhabits Don John's mind and values enough to induct one into this code at times and occasionally to be funny or mordant. It is a play of tonal complexity as well as originality. The comedy of the 1670s had developed superb techniques for proposing the code of the emancipated rake and at the same time for protecting the audience from its full Nietzschean consequences; Shadwell, later followed by Dryden, Thomas Otway, and Nathaniel Lee, made the consequences vivid. *Timon of Athens* and *The Libertine* are tragedies of excess, the ugly results of taking a code—liberality/misanthropy in the one, libertine freedom in the other—and pushing it to a logical extreme. In this sense they are, so to speak, tragedies of humours.

In his comedy *The Virtuoso* Shadwell returned to the themes of nature and freedom for which Epsom Wells had been a metaphor. It complements *The Libertine* in particular, for the heroes' libertinism harks back to the skeptical freethinking of the French *libertins* rather than to the cynical freedom from all standards that marks

To the Moſt

ILLUSTRIOUS PRINCE

GEORGE

DUKE of *BUCKINGHAM*, &c.

May it pleaſe your Grace,

NOthing could ever contribute more to my having a good opinion of my ſelf, than the being favour'd by your Grace: The thought of which has ſo exalted me, that I can no longer conceal my Pride from the World; but muſt publiſh the Joy I receive in having ſo noble a Patron, and one ſo excelling in Wit and Judgment; Qualities which even your Enemies could never doubt of, or detract from. And which make all good men and men of ſence admire you, and none but Fools and ill men fear you for 'em. I am extreamly ſenſible what honour it is to me that my Writings are approved by your Grace; who in your own

A.2   have

The Epiſtle Dedicatory.

have ſo clearly ſhown the excellency of Wit and Judgment in your Self, and ſo juſtly the defect of 'em in others, that they at once ſerve for the greateſt example, and the ſharpeſt reproof. And no man who has perfectly underſtood the *Rehearſal*, and ſome other of your Writings, if he has any *Genius* at all, can write ill after it.

I pretend not of an Epiſtle to make a Declamation upon theſe and your other excellent Qualities. For naming the Duke of *Buckingham* is enough: who cannot have greater commendations from me than all who have the honour to know him already give him. Amongſt which number I think it my greateſt happineſs to be one, and can never be prouder of any thing can arrive to me, than of the honour of having been admitted ſometimes into your Graces Converſation, the moſt charming in the World. I am now to preſent your Grace with this Hiſtory of *Timon*, which you were pleaſed to tell me you liked, and it is the more worthy of you, ſince it has the inimitable hand of *Shakeſpear*

in

The Epiſtle Dedicatory.

in it, which never made more Maſterly ſtrokes than in this. Yet I can truly ſay, I have made it into a Play. Which I humbly lay at your feet, begging the continuance of your Favour, which no man can value more than I ſhall ever do, who am unfeignedly,

My Lord,

Your Graces

Moſt Obedient,

humble Servant,

THO. SHADWELL.

Pro:

Perſons Names.

Timon *of Athens*	Mr. *Betterton.*
Alcibiades, *an Athenian Captain.*	Mr. *Smith.*
Apemantus, *a Rigid Philoſopher.*	Mr. *Harris.*
Nicias.	Mr. *Sandford.*
Phæax.	Mr. *Underhill.*
Ælius.	Mr. *Leigh.*
Cleon. } *Senators of* Athens.	Mr. *Norris.*
Iſander.	Mr. *Percival.*
Iſidore.	Mr. *Gillo.*
Thraſillus.	
Demetrius, Timons *Steward.*	Mr. *Medburne.*
Diphilus, *Servant to* Timon.	Mr. *Bowman.*
Old *man.*	Mr. *Richards.*
Poet.	Mr. *Jevon.*
Painter.	
Jeweller.	
Muſician.	
Merchant.	
Evandra.	Mrs. *Betterton.*
Meliſſa.	Mrs. *Shadwell.*
Chloe.	Mrs. *Gibbs.*
Thais. } *Miſtreſſes to* Alcibiades.	{ Mrs. *Seymor.*
Phrinias.	{ Mrs *Le-Grand.*
Servants.	
Meſſengers.	
Several Maſqueraders.	
Souldiers.	

Scene *Athens.*

Timon

Dedication and cast list for the first production in the 1678 edition of Shadwell's Timon of Athens, *which adds a love plot to Shakespeare's tragedy*

Don John. Shadwell seems to endorse these Epicurean heroes, whose aloof god leaves them space to act and uncommitted except to the pursuit of their natural passions. Despite Shadwell's claim to be a moralist, his Bruce and Longvil decry reform—"the Beastly, Restive World will go its way; and there is no so foolish a Creature as a Reformer"—and fornicate unpunished. Of course by the end of the play they are committed to love, and each, furthermore, to the woman whom the other has courted at the start. Still, they never lose their witty panache. Their commitment, once the right woman appears, only suggests the hedonistic basis for attachment. They are not foolish lovers (especially in the context of the other folly that Shadwell parades on the stage), and they never have a reason to repent the life they have led. In contrast, the titular virtuoso, Sir Nicholas Gimcrack, tries to control nature through science; to do so is unnatural, and his betrayal of his proper nature as a human being leads to his being controlled by his humour and by other characters.

If in *The Virtuoso* Shadwell's moral position seems to be based on good sense (as understood in the 1670s) rather than on Christian duty, he is much more like his contemporaries than he sometimes protested. The same holds for his way of constructing a play, which owes less to his revered Jonson than to the central legacy of Restoration comedy, descending from John Fletcher with some later Molièrean assets. Both Fletcher and Molière relish humours characters as much as Jonson; unlike Jonson but like Shadwell, they often supplement the humours plot with a strong love plot; and Fletcher, like Shadwell, shapes his comedies through symmetry of characters and repeated peripeteias. Symmetry and peripatetic action give formal pleasure, of course, but also the illusion of comprehensiveness over a whole world, rather than a Jonsonian limitation to a typology of fools and knaves. The symmetry of *The Virtuoso* is virtually total. Two gentlemen, Bruce and Longvil, love two ladies, Miranda and Clarinda, each of whom loves the gentleman who does not at the start love her. Each of the ladies has a second, foolish lover, one of whom is a windy, solemn orator and the other, a brisk joke-cracking witwoud. The older men are the virtuosos, Sir Nicholas Gimcrack, who strives to be forever new with his scientific discoveries, and his uncle Snarl, who strives to be forever old with his lamentations about the present age; each of these men keeps a whore. The older woman is Lady Gimcrack, who lusts after (and has quick sex with) both Bruce and Longvil and who keeps a gigolo. Her gigolo maintains an affair with Sir Nicholas's whore. Shadwell exploits this self-enclosed, doubling group of characters through an equally self-enclosed kind of plot—even from the cast and situation one can imagine the opportunities he had for reversals and discoveries of the sort in which Fletcher and Restoration comedians after him specialized. Although once he hit his stride with *Epsom Wells*, Shadwell was always a highly accomplished playwright, the complicated intrigue and striking figures in *The Virtuoso* brought out the best in him. In it he produced his funniest play, which is saying a good deal.

Shadwell's career just before and during the Exclusion Crisis began with his most complex comedy (which is also saying a good deal), the badly received but brilliantly mordant *A True Widow* (1678). It was too complex for the author's good, so he followed it with an announced potboiler, *The Woman-Captain* (1679), and then with a comedy too political for its author's safety, *The Lancashire Witches* (1681). These three fell into a pattern typical of their time: first, in *A True Widow*, a corrosive, individualistic cynicism before the Exclusion Crisis; next, in *The Woman-Captain*, a drawing back and toning down as the nation was swept with patriotic fervor; and finally, in *The Lancashire Witches*, a thorough problematizing of authority. These plays share a focus on women's action, bringing to the fore a theme noted by Michael W. Alssid: in this first phase of his career nearly "all of Shadwell's women (whether promiscuous or innocent, silly or wise, malicious or tender) triumph in a world presumably dominated by the male." By the mid 1670s the number of star actresses had grown; the vogue for pathetic "she-tragedy" and for sex comedy had developed their careers (and vice versa); and the war between the sexes was flourishing on stage as traditional hierarchies, on and off stage, were aggressively challenged. Women in comedy were as witty, accomplished, lustful, and conscious of their rights as were men, so that plays insistent on meritocracy, like these, had to give them their due. In particular, the skepticism about marriage exposed so plainly in *Epsom Wells* led to a political treatment of ties once thought to be knotted in heaven, but now taken as a social contract with a risk-reward ratio. English comedies written during Shadwell's lifetime present virtually no happy marriages, although marriage nearly always affords these same comedies a putatively happy end. This contradiction did not remain unnoticed as women, who risked most in marriage, gained more voice.

In *A True Widow* Shadwell makes much of these possibilities by displaying the highly successful wiles of a smart, ruthless confidence woman (who, for example, has legal papers signed in invisible ink): Lady Cheatley weds a rich husband and marries her daughters, even the stupid slut Gartrude, to eligible bachelors. Since the other plot in this play takes up the theme of libertinage developed in *The Libertine*, *The Virtuoso*, and even, to some extent, *Timon of Athens*, one can see Lady Cheatley's connivances as a kind of feminist reprisal. Unlike the Jonsonian predecessors one might imagine for her, Volpone and the alchemical plotters, she gets away scot free and darkly splendid. One can surely see feminist reprisal in the actions of Mrs. Gripe in *The Woman-Captain;* for this abused wife disguises herself as her soldier brother and humiliates not only her miserly despot of a husband but also other flaunters of masculinity, a gang of libertine bravos who flock around one Sir Humphrey Scattergood. Sir Humphrey himself, a tawdry Timon, ends up trapped into marriage with his whore, a fate usually reserved for fools but here allotted to the rakish prodigal who in so many other plays is the comic hero. *The Lancashire Witches*, finally, displays and analogizes two female types, witty ingenues and witches. Witches represent the powerful, lust-driven, mature females whom males fear, and the strong-minded, headstrong ingenues represent in turn a threat of female dominance. Both threats are held in check, without force, and, because without force, by the exemplary young male suitors of this play. Unbelievers as to witches, they snag the heiresses through virtue and fidelity, while the foolish men, including Irish-Catholic and Anglican priests, end up hag ridden. The witches thus depict the war between the sexes as institutionalized, since the priests, willful parents, and unwanted suitors stand for worthless social authority as against the rival diabolical authority of the witches.

Political references in *The Lancashire Witches*, especially those bearing on the hypocritical Anglican clergyman Smerk, brought Shadwell into trouble with the Master of the Revels, who made him expunge a good many lines. Nonetheless, the Whig partisanship it displayed was a good deal tamer than that expressed by Shadwell elsewhere, for example in his virulent, anonymous attack on Dryden, defender of the Stuart succession and enemy of the Whigs, in *The Medal of*

John Bayes (May 1682). As the Whiggery of *The Lancashire Witches* may have made Shadwell persona non grata to the theaters, the personal attack on Dryden may have occasioned the public appearance of *Mac Flecknoe* in September or October. Still, the first edition is so faulty that it may well have been unauthorized or authorized by Dryden's spoken "Yes" to a suggestion that a version be let spring into print. Allusions to Shadwell's plays of the mid 1670s are so many in *Mac Flecknoe*, abruptly stopping in 1676, as to imply that Dryden wrote the poem then, perhaps angered by some of Shadwell's on-and-off sniping at him. He let it circulate in manuscript among the cognoscenti, holding it back prudently or with aristocratic nonchalance. The conflict between the two had for many years featured Dryden's reticence but Shadwell's sneers toward those who adored Jonson too little and won success in an inferior mode. Despite some compliments and favors between the two, various social alliances in time aggravated hostility: Shadwell, a fine drinking companion who sparkled in conversation, won favor from aristocrats such as John Wilmot, earl of Rochester, men who were sometime friends and later enemies of Dryden's. Of course the turn of politics made an attack on Shadwell safe, and, in fact, by roasting Shadwell the playwright, *Mac Flecknoe* simply completed the job begun by Dryden on Shadwell as the political poet in *The Second Part of Absalom and Achitophel*, written with Nahum Tate in the summer of 1682. There he had flayed Shadwell as poet and politico and had discovered a monstrous mass of foul, corrupted matter rolling home from a treason tavern, accursed and incoherent. *Mac Flecknoe* was an unusually successful coup de grâce.

With his plunge into heated political controversy, Shadwell found himself outmanned as a Whig, outmaneuvered as a dramatist (hence his long absence from the stage), and outdone as a poet. He was, of course, to keep in the public eye as a poet for the remaining ten years of his life, first in quiescent opposition and then as laureate. As a playwright he was a capable producer of prologues, epilogues, and songs. As to more ambitious verse, his friend Charles Sackville, earl of Dorset, assessed his talents accurately when, being asked about them, he replied that Shadwell was an honest man. Shadwell's satiric verse makes do with energy of vituperation, as for example in the final anti-Dryden triplet in *The Medal of John Bayes:*

*The marriage of Belfond Jr.'s former mistress, Mrs. Termagant, to Belfond Sr. is stopped by Belfond Jr., who brings with him
a constable and a group of musketeers, in act 5, scene 5, of* The Squire of Alsatia *(frontispiece to the 1715 edition)*

Pied thing! half Wit! half Fool! and for a Knave,
Few Men, than this, a better mixture have:
But thou canst add to that, Coward and Slave.

One can allow that his panegyrics as laureate are
no more dreadful than the run of such odes and
addresses, and his translation of Juvenal's Tenth
Satire no windier than necessary in Englishing
the terse, forceful Latin into rhymed couplets.
He had the misfortune of writing satire, odes,
and translations at the same time and on the
same subjects as the greatest practitioner in his lifetime, Dryden; and, by being Dryden's rival and

successor as laureate, of inviting comparison between them. As a playwright, though Dryden was
a superb playwright, he could come far closer to
holding his own.

When Shadwell resumed his métier in 1688
with *The Squire of Alsatia*, he had immediate financial and artistic success, and he followed it in
April of the next year, as the new laureate, with
a comedy of similar merit, *Bury Fair*. Two much
weaker comedies, *The Amorous Bigotte* (a sequel to
The Lancashire Witches) a season later (March
1690) and *The Scowrers* the season after that (December 1690), were to be the last in his lifetime;

a spirited patriotic comedy, *The Volunteers* (November 1692), appeared posthumously, with an epilogue bearing tribute to Shadwell's "mighty *Genius* and discerning *Mind*, [that] Trac'd all the various *Humours* of Mankind." Though Shadwell continued to draw for ideas or plot from his favorite source, Molière, these last five comedies differ from their predecessors. In particular, they openly assert community values in their humours satire. *The Squire of Alsatia*, for example, features a benevolent, tolerant, humanely educated guardian and ward who set affairs right for their respective brothers, teaching good sense in everything, even in sowing one's wild oats. *Bury Fair* includes male friends, rivals in love, who end their abortive duel with an embrace, and a page who turns out to be a young woman disguised so as to be with the gentleman she loves. *The Scowrers*, like *The Squire of Alsatia*, ridicules those who roister violently ("scour"); it has a blank-verse lecture from a father to his son on drinking and whoring. Modern critics pinch such plays between disapproval as too moralized–"sentimental"–and disapproval as not rigorously moral enough. (One suspects that in dealing with their own children, say, the critics themselves would be open to the same criticisms; late-twentieth-century bourgeois Americans would rarely choose to live among a generation of Victorian men of duty or of Dorimants.) However one values such mellower, more humane comedy, it in fact was to become more prevalent toward the end of the seventeenth century and, of course, in the eighteenth. As the new laureate, Shadwell may also have felt added social responsibility and tailored his plays accordingly.

Of these last comedies, *The Squire of Alsatia* was the biggest hit at the time and held the boards the longest; it may serve to exemplify Shadwell's late work. His main source here was the *Adelphi* of Terence, a poet whom Justus Lipsius called "every where so Modest, so Chaste, and so Bashful, that even a *Vestal* need not be afraid of his Company," and particularly noted for his elegance of style. Shadwell's inspiration was to graft onto this plot, immediately recognizable to any man who had been a fourth-form schoolboy (aged ten or eleven), a stylistic foreignness through the scandalous actions and exotic English argot of the London thugs and swindlers who inhabited the Whitefriars district, "Alsatia." As in Terence (and Molière following him), two brothers–here Sir William and Sir Edward Belfond–each bring up one of Sir William's two sons. Sir William keeps the elder under strict

rein in the country and makes him learn only what is useful, while Sir Edward gives the younger his head and educates him as an urban gentleman. The younger, Belfond Jr., has a bastard by a termagant mistress and seduces a sweet, credulous girl, but he has a *bon fond* of good sense and decency that lets him make amends. The older, Belfond Sr., escapes to London as a credulous rustic booby, where he falls in with the "Alsatians," acquires their cant and habits, whores, swears, swaggers, gets cheated, defies his father, and needs rescue by his brother. Through leavening and spicing Terence with realism, Shadwell offers an exceptionally witty, fresh translation from Rome to London. He also underlines his play's larger social dimension, in generalizing the Terentian problem of governance from sons to a diverse body politic needing different, proper uses of tolerance and force. Instead of having the disciplinarian turn the tables on his indulgent brother, as in Terence, Shadwell incorporates the rights of force into his play by having it exercised against the Alsatians, in the public rather than the private sphere. Theatergoers were ready to see these issues of proper government raised, as the imminence of the revolution in six months suggests. James II's policies were widely resented as here too lax, there too coercive. Shadwell's play, no political document, nonetheless caught a topic to which the public responded as it had never responded to the overt, controversial politics of *The Lancashire Witches*.

The new, mellower tone of *The Squire of Alsatia* derives not so much from changes in the way Shadwell structured a play as in the way he redeployed familiar elements. From Terence, he inherited his favored character pattern, a symmetrical distribution with two pairs of brothers and, for the younger-generation brothers, one woman apiece, a seduced maiden and a girl of dubious reputation respectively. As a descendant of Fletcher, he adds two more women, an heiress proposed as a bride for both younger-generation brothers and a termagant who has been the mistress of one of these brothers and becomes the near-bride of the other; he adds a friend for Belfond Jr. and mock-friends, two bullies and two sharpers, for Belfond Sr.; Belfond Sr.'s servant, Lolpoop, is a country lout whose northern dialect is played off against the Alsatians' cant. In *The Virtuoso* and here, such an arrangement gives formal pleasure and also a sense of comprehensiveness, but here the comprehensiveness is made personal. That is, the "real world" is within the im-

The Shadwell monument in Westminster Abbey

mediate experience of Belfond Jr. in particular and it is undiscerned by his brother; Shadwell's earlier plays, such as *The Virtuoso*, simply exhibited the "real world" as a social tableau. A direct knowledge of the world through experience, so important for the educational theme in *The Squire of Alsatia*, leads to a morality tied to engagement, personal knowledge, rather than the aloofness of Bruce and Longvil. Their position as at once participants and observers allowed them both social and reflective language of wit, shared observation; such verbal wit is missing from Belfond Jr.'s conversation. Instead, Shadwell gives him the appeal of a youth whose understanding has helped make him a decent person. In showing him on the cusp between feisty adoles-

cence and adulthood, however, Shadwell lets him retain some of the fascination that the rake heroes in Shadwell's and, still more, other dramatists' heroes of the 1670s had had; they are heroes who acted out on stage the fantasies of the audience. Especially in his treatment of Lucia, an innocent whom he sweet-talks, seduces, and jilts (with a large purse of money and a false oath as to her innocence to ease the pain), he is not a morally exemplary character. Nonetheless, we are meant to believe that he can become one through knowledge and the cultivation of his understanding.

A knowledge of the "real world" now implies for Shadwell a knowledge of socially created types, not simply individuals, and this change is reflected in his treatment of attention-catching language. The linguistic inventiveness in *The Virtuoso* marks humours characters and wits, individuals who may approximate certain social types; in *The Squire of Alsatia* such language no longer marks humours but types generated by society, whether the country clown or the canting Alsatians. For example, in *The Virtuoso* figures from the same social class and setting are divided from one another in language practice. The fop Sir Samuel Hearty flaunts new-fangled oaths ("whip-slap," "slap-dash," "in the twinkling of a Bed-staff," "Whip Stich, your Nose in my Breech"), while Sir Nicholas Gimcrack mouths the Latinate terms beloved of Royal Society scientists: in "Respiration, or Breathing," the lungs expel air "to elaborate the Blood, by refrigerating it, and separating its fuliginous steams" (act 2). Sir Formal Trifle, the orator, sometimes speaks in similar terms, sometimes not, but always styles them in Ciceronian periods: "I observ'd, not far from the scene of my Meditation, an excellent Machine, call'd a Mouse-trap (which my Man had plac'd there) which had included in it a solitary Mouse; which pensive Prisoner, in vain bewayling its own misfortunes, and the precipitation of its too unadvised attempt, still strugling for liberty against the too stubborn opposition of solid Wood, and more obdurate Wyer: at last, the pretty Malefactor having tir'd, alas, its too feeble Limbs, till they became languid in fruitless endeavours for its excarceration" (act 3). By comparison, the Alsatians' argot—"prigster," "putt," "porker," "prog"—solidifies their existence and exclusion as a group from the rest of society, so that its delight for Belfond Sr. is precisely its esotericism. Lolpoop's accent ("Yeowst be run agraunt soon and you takken this caurse, Ise tell a that" [I.i]) also sets him apart as a member of a social class. By these means, Shadwell emphasizes the way in which characters are made what they are, in keeping with his theme of education but also, more generally, with a social bias that affects his drama from then on. Similarly, in *Bury Fair*, which does not have a theme of education, the provincial fop Trim, rural squire Sir Humphrey Noddy, and other butts of humor are set off by their speech and behavior as types in the broad portrait of a country community. It would be a vast exaggeration to talk of the sociological force behind this reconceiving of humours roles, but it would be to point in the right direction.

"Shadwell is always a bell-wether," writes Robert D. Hume, and with this last turn in his drama Shadwell led the dramatic flock toward the social, consensual, humane forms that became progressively more popular—although in the hands and to the literary credit of others—after his death. After *Bury Fair*, Shadwell's invention began to flag, maybe because of the ill health that plagued him. His posthumous *The Volunteers* is a good play that seems to have had moderate success in supporting a widow and children. For some years Shadwell apparently had been taking opium, which doctors prescribed as a tranquilizer and painkiller as well as a medicine for specific disorders (catarrh, gastrointestinal bleeding), and that he may have needed for his chronic "gout," whatever painful disorder that may have been. In November 1692 either disease, by way of a major vascular accident, or remedy, by way of overdose, killed him. His dramatic and medical battles were carried on by two sons: Charles became a professional playwright with at least one success, *The Fair Quaker of Deal* (1710), and other comedies produced in London and/or Dublin, while John became a royal physician, knighted in 1715. Their father, who had lost two sons to death during his lifetime, would have been pleased.

References:

Michael W. Alssid, *Thomas Shadwell* (New York: Twayne, 1967);

David S. Berkeley, "The Penitent Rake in Restoration Comedy," *Modern Philology*, 49 (May 1952): 223-233;

Ronald S. Berman, "The Values of Shadwell's *Squire of Alsatia*," *ELH*, 39 (September 1972): 375-386;

Albert S. Borgman, *Thomas Shadwell: His Life and Comedies* (New York: New York University Press, 1928);

Laura S. Brown, *English Dramatic Form, 1660-1760: An Essay in Generic History* (New Haven: Yale University Press, 1981);

Stephen D. Cox, "Public Virtue and Private Utility in Shadwell's Comedies," *Restoration and Eighteenth-Century Theatre Research*, 16 (1977): 1-22;

John Dryden, *The Works of John Dryden*, volume 2, edited by H. T. Swedenberg, Jr. (Berkeley: University of California Press, 1972);

Alan S. Fisher, "The Significance of Thomas Shadwell," *Studies in Philology*, 71 (April 1974): 225-246;

John T. Harwood, *Critics, Values, and Restoration Comedy* (Carbondale: Southern Illinois University Press, 1982);

Robert D. Hume, *The Development of English Drama in the Late Seventeenth Century* (Oxford: Clarendon Press, 1976);

Hume, "Formal Intentions in *The Brothers* and *The Squire of Alsatia*," *English Language Notes*, 6 (March 1969): 176-184;

Hume, *The Rakish Stage: Studies in English Drama, 1660-1800* (Carbondale: Southern Illinois University Press, 1983);

Don R. Kunz, *The Drama of Thomas Shadwell* (Salzburg: Institut für Englische Sprache und Literatur, 1972);

Claude Lloyd, "Shadwell and the Virtuosi," *PMLA*, 44 (June 1929): 472-494;

John Loftis, *The Spanish Plays of Neoclassical England* (New Haven: Yale University Press, 1973);

The London Stage, 1660-1800, part 1: 1660-1700, edited by William Van Lennep (Carbondale: Southern Illinois University Press, 1965);

William B. Ober, "Thomas Shadwell: His Exitus Revisited," *Annals of Internal Medicine*, 74 (January 1971): 126-130;

Richard Oden, ed., *Dryden and Shadwell, the Literary Controversy and "MacFlecknoe": Facsimile Reproductions* (Delmar, N.Y.: Scholars' Facsimiles & Reprints, 1977);

Jocelyn Powell, *Restoration Theatre Production* (London: Routledge & Kegan Paul, 1984);

Eric Rothstein and Frances M. Kavenik, *The Designs of Carolean Comedy* (Carbondale: Southern Illinois University Press, 1988);

Ben Ross Schneider, Jr., *The Ethos of Restoration Comedy* (Urbana: University of Illinois Press, 1971);

John Harrington Smith, "Shadwell, the Ladies, and the Change in Comedy," *Modern Philology*, 46 (August 1948): 22-33;

Hazelton Spencer, *Shakespeare Improved: The Restoration Versions in Quarto and on the Stage* (Cambridge, Mass.: Harvard University Press, 1927);

Susan Staves, *Players' Scepters: Fictions of Authority in the Restoration* (Lincoln: University of Nebraska Press, 1979);

Thomas B. Stroup, "Shadwell's Use of Hobbes," *Studies in Philology*, 35 (July 1938): 405-432;

Tom H. Towers, "The Lineage of Shadwell: an Approach to *Mac Flecknoe*," *Studies in English Literature, 1500-1900*, 3 (Summer 1963): 323-334;

P. F. Vernon, "Social Satire in Shadwell's *Timon*," *Studia Neophilologica*, 35 (1963): 221-226;

James Anderson Winn, *John Dryden and His World* (New Haven & London: Yale University Press, 1987);

Rose A. Zimbardo, *A Mirror to Nature: Transformations in Drama and Aesthetics, 1660-1732* (Lexington: University Press of Kentucky, 1986).

Thomas Southerne

(12 February 1660-26 May 1746)

Anthony Kaufman

University of Illinois, Urbana-Champaign

PLAY PRODUCTIONS: *The Loyal Brother, or, The Persian Prince*, London, Theatre Royal in Drury Lane, February 1682;

The Disappointment, or, The Mother in Fashion, London, Theatre Royal in Drury Lane, April 1684;

Sir Anthony Love, or, The Rambling Lady, adapted from Aphra Behn's *The Lucky Mistake*, London, Theatre Royal in Drury Lane, September or October 1690;

The Wives' Excuse, or, Cukolds Make Themselves, London, Theatre Royal in Drury Lane, December 1691;

The Maid's Last Prayer, or, Any Rather Than Fail, London, Theatre Royal in Drury Lane, February 1693 or slightly later;

The Fatal Marriage, or, The Innocent Adultery, based on Behn's *The History of the Nun; or, the Fair Vow-Breaker*, London, Theatre Royal in Drury Lane, February 1694;

Oroonoko, adapted from Behn's *Oroonoko; Or the Royal Slave*, London, Theatre Royal in Drury Lane, November 1695;

The Fate of Capua, based on Livy's *Roman History*, London, Lincoln's Inn Fields, April 1700;

The Spartan Dame, based on Plutarch's *Life of Agis*, London, Theatre Royal in Drury Lane, December 1719;

Money The Mistress, based on "La Marquise de los Rios" from Marie-Catherine Comtess d'Aulnoy's *Relation du Voyage d'Espagne*, London, Lincoln's Inn Fields, February 1726.

BOOKS: *The Loyal Brother, or, The Persian Prince. A Tragedy As it is Acted at the Theatre Royal by their Majesties Servants* (London: Printed for William Cademan, 1682);

The Disappointment, or The Mother in Fashion, A Play as it was Acted at the Theatre Royal (London: Printed for Jo. Hindmarsh, 1684);

Sir Anthony Love: or, The Rambling Lady. A Comedy. As it is Acted at the Theatre-Royal by Their Majesties Servants (London: Printed for Joseph Fox & Abel Roper, 1691);

The Wives' Excuse; or, Cuckolds Make Themselves. A Comedy. As it is Acted at the Theatre-Royal, By Their Majesties Servants (London: Printed for Samuel Brisco, 1692); modern edition, edited by Ralph R. Thornton (Wynnewood, Pa.: Livingston, 1973);

The Maid's Last Prayer, or, Any Rather Than Fail. A Comedy. As it is Acted at the Theatre Royal. By Their Majesties Servants (London: Printed for R. Bentley & J. Tonson, 1693);

The Fatal Marriage: or, The Innocent Adultery. A Play, Acted at the Theatre Royal, By Their Majesties Servants (London: Printed for Jacob Tonson, 1694);

Oroonoko: A Tragedy As it is Acted at the Theatre-Royal, By His Majesty's Servants (London: Printed for H. Playford, B. Tooke & S. Buckley, 1696); modern edition, edited by Maximillian E. Novak and David Stuart Rodes (Lincoln: University of Nebraska Press, 1976);

The Fate of Capua. A Tragedy. As it is Acted at the Theatre In Lincolns-Inn-Fields. By His Majesty's Servants (London: Printed for Benjamin Tooke, 1700);

The Spartan Dame. A Tragedy. As it is Acted at the Theatre-Royal in Drury-Lane By His Majesty's Servants (London: Printed for W. Chetwood, 1719);

Money The Mistress. A Play, as it is Acted at the Theatre-Royal in Lincoln's-Inn-Fields (London: Printed for J. Tonson, 1726).

Collections: *The Works of Mr. Thomas Southerne, Volume the First. Containing, The Loyal Brother: Or, The Persian Prince. The Disappointment; Or, The Mother in Fashion. Sir Anthony Love: Or, The Rambling Lady. The Wives' Excuse: Or, Cukolds make Themselves* (London: Printed for Jacob Tonson, Benjamin Tooke & Bernard Linott, 1713);

The Works of Mr. Thomas Southerne. Volume the Second. Containing, The Maid's Last Prayer: Or, Any, Rather than Fail. The Fatal Marriage: Or, the Innocent Adultery. Oroonoko. The Fate of

Thomas Southerne Esq.

Capua (London: Printed for Jacob Tonson, Benjamin Tooke & Bernard Linnott, 1713);

The Works of Mr. Thomas Southerne, 2 volumes (London: J. Tonson, Benjamin Tooke & Bernard Linnott, 1721);

Plays Written by Thomas Southerne, Esq. Now First Collected. With An Account of the Life and Writings of the Author, 3 volumes (London: Printed for T. Evans & T. Becket, 1774);

The Works of Thomas Southerne, 2 volumes, edited by Harold Love and Robert Jordan (Oxford: Clarendon Press, 1988).

OTHER: John Dryden, *Cleomenes, The Spartan Heroe. A Tragedy, As it is Acted at the Theatre Royal. Written by Mr. Dryden. To which is prefixt the Life of Cleomenes*, completed by Southerne (London: Printed for Jacob Tonson, 1692);

Preface to *Pausanias The Betrayer of His Country. A Tragedy, Acted at the Theatre Royal, By his Majesties Servants. Written by a Person of Quality*, by Richard Norton (London: Printed for Abel Roper, E. Wilkinson & Roger Clavell, 1696);

"On the Poets and Actors in King Charles II's Reign," *The Gentleman's Magazine and Historical Chronicle*, 15 (February 1745).

Thomas Southerne was a popular and influential playwright, a contemporary during his most productive years of John Dryden, William Congreve, Colley Cibber, and Sir John Vanbrugh. His two best tragedies, *The Fatal Marriage* (1694) and *Oroonoko* (1695), appealed to the imagination of his time and continued the tradition of "pathetic" tragedy, exemplified in the 1670s and early 1680s by Thomas Otway, John Banks, and Nathaniel Lee. This type of play, in which the sympathies of the audience are strongly moved by the sufferings of a worthy hero or heroine, foreshadows later playwrights, such as Nicholas Rowe and George Lillo, who worked within the tradition. Southerne was considered especially talented at developing female characters, such as Isabella of *The Fatal Marriage* and Imoinda of *Oroonoko*, who in distressed circumstances suffer mightily and, in the hands of a talented actress such as Elizabeth Barry, moved audiences to tears. Most recently, Southerne's comedies *Sir Anthony Love* and especially *The Wives' Excuse* have been recognized as considerable accomplishments. Southerne lived long; he was a protégé of Dryden, he assisted Congreve and Cibber to enter the theater, and he lived to enjoy the friendship of Alexander Pope and Jonathan Swift. At a time of fierce rivalry and competition in the theater world, Southerne was valued for his good nature, friendship, and generosity, as well as his undoubted achievement on the London stage.

Southerne was born in Ireland on 12 February 1660. He was the son of Francis Southerne, a Dublin brewer, and his wife, Margaret. Like Congreve and Swift, he attended Trinity College, Dublin. Like them he sought a wider scene in London, and in 1680 he entered the Middle Temple presumably to study law. But like Congreve and William Wycherley (who also started out as law students), he was drawn to the theater, and, guided by the greatest man of letters of the day, poet laureate John Dryden, in February 1682 he saw produced his first play, *The Loyal Brother, or, The Persian Prince*. This was the time of the Popish-Plot and Exclusion-Bill crisis, a time of great political and social turmoil, and Southerne's play was written in praise of James, duke of York, the established successor to King Charles II. Dryden, who supplied the prologue and epilogue, was the leading spokesman for the Tory cause, and Southerne thus allied himself with a group of Tory playwrights which included Aphra Behn, Thomas Otway, and John Crowne. Southerne bought his prologue and epilogue from Dryden, who made extra income from his ability to turn such pieces. Despite his friendship with the new playwright, Dryden raised his prices for Southerne, writing him that he did so "not, young man, out of disrespect to you, but the players have had my goods too cheap."

The Loyal Brother is a product of its time and does not today interest the general reader. It is one of a number of political propaganda plays, both Whig and Tory, produced during this peri-

od. The best of them is Otway's nearly contemporary *Venice Preserved* (first produced on 9 February 1682), where the tragedy of Jaffeir, Pierre, and Belinda takes precedence over the political subject matter. Dryden's prologue and epilogue for *The Loyal Brother* are politically charged, blasting the Whigs as he did in his celebrated poem *Absalom and Achitophel* (1681). Like Dryden's poem, *The Loyal Brother* is an allegory, with the villains Ismael and Arbanes representing the Whig leaders Anthony Ashley Cooper, earl of Shaftesbury and James Scott, duke of Monmouth. Seliman represents Charles II and the heroic Tachmas the duke of York. Few plays succeeded in this difficult time, and Southerne smilingly suggests in the dedication of his next play that with *The Loyal Brother*, he had "hardly escaped the venture of the stage."

At the center of *The Loyal Brother* is the love of Prince Tachmas and Semanthe. This love is threatened by the schemes of Ismael, adviser to the Sophy; Arbanes, a general resentful of Tachmas's military skill; and Sunamire, Arbanes's sister, who loves Tachmas but whose love is not reciprocated. Their machinations cause Seliman to doubt the loyalty of his brother and to resent his popularity with the people. At the conclusion Seliman's faith in his loyal brother is restored, the villains are punished, and Semanthe and Tachmas are united. The play is typical of several in the period in centering on a love relationship within the framework of contemporary politics. Southerne writes in the well-established tradition of heroic and pathetic tragedy; here, recalling Lee and especially Otway, the emphasis in tone is on the pathetic. Semanthe is the first example of a character important in Southerne's drama: the distressed heroine.

In April 1684 he brought out his second play, *The Disappointment, or, The Mother in Fashion*. Little is known of its reception. Southerne called *The Disappointment* a "play" rather than a tragedy, and indeed it is difficult to label this work securely within the context of Restoration drama. It is a serious play with comic characters and situations, akin perhaps to the tragicomedies of Beaumont and Fletcher. Set in Florence, the play features a striking libertine-villain, Alberto, a jealous husband, Alphonso, himself a would-be seducer, and his long-suffering wife, Erminia.

Alphonso is a strange character, now suspicious of his wife's virtue, now generous and understanding. There are echoes of Shakespeare in *The Disappointment*, in the murderous jealousy of

Sarah Siddons and her son, Henry Siddons, as the title character and her child in a 1782 production of Isabella, *David Garrick's adaptation of* The Fatal Marriage, *which Southerne had based on* The History of the Nun, *a novel by Aphra Behn*

Alphonso (which recalls Othello), and in his odd stratagem, reminiscent of *Measure for Measure* (1614), of pretending to leave Florence, only to enable him to observe her secretly. His anxiety concerning Erminia leads him to force her to receive Alberto so that he may observe how the libertine acts with her. *The Disappointment* twice uses the dramatic device of the "bed trick," once more recalling *Measure for Measure*, and Alphonso's obsession with his wife's virtue and his determination to test it recalls the "curious impertinent" story in *Don Quixote* and elsewhere. The multiple misunderstandings are resolved happily at the play's conclusion. The subplot offers an overtly comic character, old Rogero, whose daughter is the target of Alberto's desires.

A year later Southerne enlisted as an ensign in Princess Anne's Regiment of the Duke of Berwick's Foot, eventually gaining the command of a company. His good service in the cause loyal to the crown was not profitable, however, for in 1688 the Glorious Revolution saw the de facto abdication of King James II and the coming of William and Mary. Southerne left the army in 1688. In 1687 he had written four acts of another political allegory, *The Spartan Dame*, but had laid the play aside. After his return to the theater, he turned from political allegory to comedy, and in autumn 1690 he enjoyed great popular and financial success with *Sir Anthony Love, or, The Rambling Lady*.

The major source of this good-natured comedy is *The Lucky Mistake* (1689), a novel by Aphra Behn, although the various characters are familiar from earlier English comedy, and the idea of a girl who disguises herself as a boy to follow her lover is an old one. Here Lucia, "sold" by a grasping aunt to a wealthy fool, Sir Gentle Golding, has fled from England to France after robbing him. In France she disguises herself as a man, Sir Anthony Love, to gain the friendship, and ultimately the love, of Valentine. She plays the part of the swaggering gallant to perfection: fighting duels, seducing women (she turns over the "drudgery" of sex to others), playing witty jokes on the various fools and tricksters she encounters. The play presents an unusual twist at the conclusion. Where we may expect the disguised girl to reveal herself and thus gain the hand of her love, as does Viola in Shakespeare's *Twelfth Night* (1601), Lucia, after revealing herself to Valentine, rejects marriage, cynically observing that since most marriages fail it is better to remain a mistress than a wife. Through her wit and audacity she forces a financial settlement from her former keeper, Sir Gentle, and at the end of the play it appears that Lucia and Valentine will together continue their career of witty exploits.

The great success of *Sir Anthony Love* depended, as Southerne acknowledged, on the attractive and charming Mrs. Susanna Mountfort, who played the breeches role, and on the continual amusement provided by Sir Anthony's witty commentary and tricks on a variety of conventional fools and villains. "I made every line for her, she has mended every word for me; and by a gaiety and air, particular to her action, turned every thing into the genius of the character." The contemporary theater observer and historian Gerard Langbaine recorded the success of the play: "This Play was acted with extraordinary Applause; the Part of *Sir Anthony Love* being most Masterly play'd by Mrs. *Montfort:* and certainly, who ever reads it, will find it fraught with true Wit and Humour." The wit and charm of this comedienne were formidable, and the playwright smiled at his audience's willingness to "hear with Patience a dull scene, to see/ . . . The Female Montfort bare above the knee." Southerne profited well from the play's success, and indeed, the play, while having little or nothing to say, and being perhaps too long, offers a bustling plot, witty dialogue, and engaging comic characters. Moreover, with this, his first entirely comic piece, Southerne helped to revive the older satiric tradition of comedy of the 1670s as represented by George Etherege and William Wycherley.

With the great success of this comedy Southerne may have thought he had found his métier. But his next play, *The Wives' Excuse, or,* *Cuckolds Make Themselves*, produced at Drury Lane in December 1691 with an all-star cast, failed on the stage, apparently having only one performance. But a few did like the play, and in his commendatory verses printed with the first edition of the play, Dryden suggests that, although the play was "with a kind Civility, dismiss'd," the judicious had admired it. Scholars note that, with this play, Southerne shifted the focus of comedy from the pursuit of the beautiful and witty heiress to marital incompatibility, and indeed, the play is a serious study of the moral dilemma of its central character, Mrs. Friendall.

This beautiful heiress finds after only three months of marriage that she has married an impossible husband. Mr. Friendall keeps open house the better to attract the women of the town. The play begins with an unusual scene at the Friendalls', where a music meeting is taking place. The servants of the fashionable people within dice and gossip about their employers, revealing as they do so the personalities of their betters and the follies and vices of fashionable London. Some of the audience objected to this scene, as satire of a popular and fashionable activity. But Southerne disclaimed any intention to attack music meetings: "I introduc'd it as a fashionable Scene of bringing good Company together, without a Design of abusing what every body likes; being in my Temper so far from disturbing a publick Pleasure, that I wou'd establish twenty more of 'em, if I cou'd. . . ." But the scene, which opens to reveal the fashionable company at gossip and intrigues, remains a witty send-up of contemporary folly.

Mr. Friendall, "an impertinent, nonsensical, silly, entrigueing, cowardly, good-for-nothing Coxcomb," has already grown tired of his wife. Indeed, he married her for her fortune and to carry on his sexual affairs with greater opportunity and convenience. One regular visitor to the Friendalls' is the libertine Lovemore, who is determined to seduce Mrs. Friendall. Knowing the husband to be a coward, he hires a ruffian to challenge him to a duel, knowing Friendall will reveal his cowardice. But Mrs. Friendall, who believes that her own honor is associated with that of her husband, pretends to hold Friendall back, allowing him to escape for the moment from public disgrace. Mrs. Friendall has the wives' excuse: she knows her husband is a pretender to wit, a philanderer, and a coward, but out of a sense of responsibility and self-respect, she will not give in to the blandishments of the seducer, Lovemore, although she is strongly attracted to him. Her dilemma then is to come to terms with her husband's disgusting behavior, and also with the enticements of an attractive suitor.

In another plot the virtuous Mrs. Sightly is pursued by two quite different men, the honorable Wellville and the rakehell Wilding. Wilding gains the assistance of a disreputable female adventuress, Mrs. Witwoud, who agrees to help him to gain Mrs. Sightly. She tells him that she will arrange for him to get Mrs. Sightly at a masquerade; in fact she herself plans to pose as Mrs. Sightly and, masked, receive Wilding in an inner room. But Wilding learns of the impersonation, and together with Wellville, he sends the eager Mr. Friendall in to Witwoud. While making love, they are surprised by the company. Mrs. Sightly is revenged on her false friend Witwoud: Mr. Friendall must agree to a separation from his wife. But the situation is unequal. Friendall is pleased with his liberty, while Mrs. Friendall regrets that "I must be still your Wife, and still unhappy."

In Mrs. Friendall, Southerne presents a psychological study of a serious and intelligent woman, married–at a time when divorce was most difficult–to an intolerable husband. She is rejected by her husband and attracted to her suitor. And yet, although she has ample justification for betraying her husband, she refuses to do so. Here Southerne may have subverted his audience's expectations; he complains in his dedication of the play that some of the men "were Affronted at Mrs. *Friendall*: For those Sparks who were most offended with her Virtue in Publick, are the Men that lose little by it in Private. . . ." Southerne attacks in *The Wives' Excuse* the male sexual predator and the whole practice of "free gallantry." He rejects the mentality of those, like Wilding and Lovemore, who view women as potential fortunes and sexual conquests. He shows "This hard Condition of a Woman's fate," for at the end of the play, although she has acted honorably, she must remain married, while none of the men in the play is really damaged or even terribly inconvenienced by his reckless actions.

The Wives' Excuse is the earliest of several interesting plays of the 1690s which concern the problem of a wife trapped in a bad marriage. Indeed *The Wives' Excuse* turns the subject of comedy from the pursuit by the rake of the witty, free-speaking heiress, the great subject of the earlier period of Restoration comedy, to the problem marriage, later to appear in Cibber's *Love's Last Shift* (1696) and *The Careless Husband* (1704), Vanbrugh's *The Relapse* (1696) and *The Provoked Wife* (1697), Congreve's *The Double Dealer* (1693) and *The Way of the World* (1700), and Farquhar's *The Beaux' Stratagem* (1707). In *The Wives' Excuse* Southerne works in the tradition of satire of Wycherley, but moves beyond it to dramatize the moral predicament of an intelligent, serious woman, surrounded by a superficially elegant, but in reality sordid and corrupt, society. It may be that the satire of the play was too harsh for the audience of the 1690s, who may have felt uneasy at Southerne's exposé of contemporary folly. Dryden in his commendatory verse, "To Mr. Southerne on his comedy, call'd *The Wives' Excuse*," noted the play's failure at the box office: "*But rest secure, the* Readers *will be thine.*" And so it has proved: *The Wives' Excuse* today is thought the best of Southerne's comedies.

Although *The Wives' Excuse* was not a popular success, Southerne produced in early 1693 another comedy, with the teasing title *The Maid's Last Prayer, or, Any Rather Than Fail*. The play was brilliantly cast with Susanna Mountfort once again in a chief comic role, and Anne Bracegirdle and Elizabeth Barry in important parts. The farceur Cave Underhill took the role of Captain Drydrubb. Peter Anthony Motteux's *The Gentleman's Journal*, in January 1693, reported that the play "was acted the 3d time this evening, and is to be acted again to morrow. It discovers much knowledge of the Town in its Author; and its Wit and purity of Diction, are particularly commended." Motteux also reported that the play offered a song by young Mr. William Congreve, whose own comedy, his first, *The Old Bachelor*, was about to be presented. Southerne himself, with witty mock deference, wrote in the dedication of *The Maid's Last Prayer* that "a play once a year, looks very like turning into the profession," but says, "let it be the defence of my writing, that I have nothing else to do."

The play is the third and last of Southerne's important comedies, and it offers variety in the way of plots. There are four strands: the first of the old maid, Lady Susan Malepert, "a youthful virgin of five and forty, with a swelling rump, bow legs, a shining face, and colly'd eyebrows. . . ." This role was designed for Susanna Mountfort, who played quite different roles in Southerne's three successive comedies: the boyish, sexy Sir Anthony, the bitter and sordid Witwoud, and now an unattractive man-chasing old maid. Here she sets her cap for Granger, a

*Isabella faints in Villeroy's arms at the entrance of the dying Biron, "bloody, leaning upon his sword";
frontispiece to the 1808 edition of* Isabella, *David Garrick's adaptation of* The Fatal Marriage

man-about-town, but when she is rejected, she is willing to settle for the silly Sir Symphony: any man rather than none. A second play concerns the connubial bickering of Mrs. Siam and her husband, Captain Drydrubb. The captain, a braggart soldier, is ridiculously jealous of his plain wife, who lives by raffling Indian goods to fashionable London. He is very much under foot, and Mrs. Siam is happy to provide him with a separate maintenance, to keep him out of the way.

In a third story Granger desires the sordid, yet attractive, Lady Trickett, a mercenary woman who makes money through gambling and selling herself to high bidders. Granger despises yet desires her. Angered because Granger will not pay for her favors at a high enough rate, Trickett decides to humiliate him. She agrees by letter to meet him at a notorious London place of assignation, Rosamond's Pond, but tricks Lady Susan

into going in her place. When Granger encounters Lady Susan, Trickett is nearby to make much of his discomfiture. Finally, the main plot concerns the curious story of Lady Malepert, married to a foolish husband, but actually an upmarket prostitute. She is run by her middle-aged procuress, Wishwell, who sells her to wealthy men. Since her latest customer, Lord Lofty, has grown weary of Malepert, Wishwell desires to transfer her commodity to the idiotic Sir Ruff Rancounter, who is willing to pay well. But she has cause to fear Gayman, whom Lady Malepert herself desires. Wishwell sets up an assignation with Sir Ruff, but through a stratagem, Gayman substitutes himself in the darkened bedroom. Here again is the "bed trick," which Southerne loved so much, and Lady Malepert does not discover the imposture until after the encounter. She is not angry; indeed, she had fantasized during her lovemaking that her lover was Gayman. Lord Malepert nearly discovers his wife's true career, but she is saved by Gayman's witty devices. Still Gayman, despising Malepert for her unsavory and mercenary tricks, proposes to an innocent girl, Maria, thus revenging himself on Malepert.

Southerne portrays in *The Maid's Last Prayer* a mercenary, intriguing society made up of unpleasant, contriving people. Once again his play may have been too harsh for the contemporary audience of the mid 1690s; for, although not a failure, the play did not equal the success of *Sir Anthony Love*. Once again Southerne attacks free gallantry and greed. None of the characters, except perhaps for the relatively minor character Maria, act in a disinterested or generous manner. The men embody Southerne's attack on the libertine ethic; the women are venal and greedy.

The play is interesting for certain of its characterizations. Lady Trickett may be sordid, but she shows a vigorous sense of independence and a rejection of conventional social roles as she disdains the institution of marriage, which makes women merely slaves. Lady Malepert's sordid career is qualified by her real feeling for Gayman, and her rejection by him at the conclusion wounds her. Wishwell, like Witwoud of *The Wives' Excuse*, is a study in malice and ruthlessness, but we understand the sources of her anger in the loss of her youth and beauty and her resentment of the male-dominated world. In both *The Wives' Excuse* and *The Maid's Last Prayer* Southerne shows considerable skill in delineating the psychology of his major characters as well as in satirical force. And in Drydrubb he created a highly successful variation of a stock character. He once more explored a subject that concerned him in his best plays: the difficulties of marriage in an inadequate society. Southerne was disappointed by the cool reception of *The Maid's Last Prayer* and turned in his next play to another genre.

Between these two plays Southerne had been asked to complete Dryden's tragedy on a classical subject, *Cleomenes*, and it was performed in mid April 1692 and later at Westminster School by the students (1695). In February 1694 Southerne's tragicomedy *The Fatal Marriage, or, The Innocent Adultery* was produced at the Drury Lane theater. With this play Southerne scored an enormous success. His reputation as a tragic dramatist was made, and years later there were still references to his ability to provoke tears from audi-

ences. The starring role of Isabella was played by Elizabeth Barry, who was especially effective in tragic roles. Southerne acknowledged her part in the play's success in his dedication: "I made the play for her part, and her part has made the play for me." The play has echoes of Otway's powerful tragedy *Venice Preserved*, and Barry, Otway's favorite actress, had played the role of Belvidera in that play, as well as Monimia in his pathetic tragedy *The Orphan* (1680). Anne Bracegirdle played the role of Victoria, Thomas Betterton played Villeroy, and the great comic actor Underhill played the role of Sampson, the porter. The play was a great success. Peter Motteux reported in his *Gentleman's Journal* that *The Fatal Marriage* "has deservedly ingross'd all the Applause which the Town can well bestow." With *The Fatal Marriage* Southerne had surpassed even his success in comedy with *Sir Anthony Love*.

In accordance with the taste of the times the play has two plots, tragic and comic. In the serious plot, based on Aphra Behn's novel *The History of the Nun; or, the Fair Vow-Breaker* (1689), Isabella's husband, Biron, is reported dead after being captured by the Turks at the siege of Candia. He lives, however, and returns to Brussels after seven years of enforced absence only to find that his wife has remarried. The honorable Villeroy has pursued Isabella for seven years. She has withstood his courtship and agreed to marry him only because her situation is intolerable. She has no reason to think her husband alive, her creditors pursue her, and her father-in-law, Count Baldwin, spurns her pleas for assistance. Moreover she is drawn to Villeroy. The marriage is promoted by the villainous Carlos, Biron's brother, who is anxious to clear his path to the inheritance. Carlos has intercepted Biron's letters, warning Biron in return to stay away from home. But Biron does return, and he reveals himself to his wife. The situation is tragic: all three persons of the triangle are innocent, honorable people. The play ends with the treacherous murder of Biron by Carlos and the madness and suicide of Isabella. Carlos is exposed through the confession of an accomplice and punished, and Count Baldwin must see his fatal error.

This dark story is joined somewhat loosely to a comic plot in which Victoria escapes from her foolish father, Fernando, and elopes with her suitor. She is aided by her brother, Fabian, who wishes to inherit the family fortune. The old father is married to Julia, a young wife, who is res-

Miss Miller as Imoinda and Savigny as Oroonoko in a 1770 production of one of the plays Southerne adapted from novels by Aphra Behn

tive under his jealous scrutiny. The old man is given a sleeping potion, and when he awakens he is made to believe that he has died and was revived by a miracle. He is astonished and renounces his jealous and suspicious ways.

The emphasis in *The Fatal Marriage* is on the dilemma of Isabella, who wishes to mourn her lost husband and who finds herself alone, victimized by her unsympathetic father-in-law and deceived and betrayed by her false, scheming brother-in-law. Her "adultery" is undertaken with reluctance; Villeroy is portrayed as a sympathetic and admirable man. Southerne altered his source to emphasize Isabella's innocence. In Behn's novel Isabella's breaking of her sacred vows as a nun is fatal, and subsequently her career includes her murder of her two husbands and ends with her death on the scaffold. Southerne changed this; he was careful to avoid any hint of Isabella's guilt. Her only accuser is Count Baldwin, whose coldness and anger toward her are based on his

son's failure to marry a wealthy woman. Thus Southerne recast his source to emphasize her dilemma, victimization, and passive suffering.

Southerne varied from the practice of *Venice Preserved*, a play much echoed in *The Fatal Marriage*, in his inclusion of the comic plot, and he was uneasy about this violation of what some thought necessary practice. In his dedication he protested, "I have given you a little taste of comedy with it, not from my own opinion, but the present humour of the town." Although the comic scenes are conventional in character and situation, they are energetic and humorous, and it is curious that some of Southerne's best comic scenes are embedded within a work most famous for its strong appeal to our sympathy.

Southerne called *The Fatal Marriage* "a play." His conception of tragedy is similar to Otway's: although the play concerns people of consequence, it is essentially domestic–the tragedy of Biron, Villeroy, and Isabella–much as *Venice Preserved* is the tragedy of Jaffeir, Pierre, and Belvidera. At the center is Isabella; her sufferings are the play; the other characters of the tragic plot exist largely in relation to her. Her actions are guiltless; yet she suffers and dies. Isabella, like Mrs. Friendall, acts out of complex motives. She is drawn to Villeroy, but wishes to retain her self-respect and to fulfill her responsibilities. She is hesitant and distressed concerning her predicament.

In 1757 David Garrick adapted the play as *Isabella; or, The Fatal Marriage*. He removed the comic subplot, by then thought inappropriate and too ribald, while retaining almost intact the tragic portion. What sold the play originally was the character of Isabella, and Garrick's version is an intense theater piece. To a favorable reception he himself appeared as Biron and Mrs. Cibber as Isabella. Southerne's play was translated into French in 1749 and Garrick's version into German. The role of Isabella became a great favorite of actresses and was played by almost every contemporary actress of consequence: Elizabeth Barry, Mary Porter, Mary Ann Yates, Susanna Cibber, Ann Crawford, Sarah Siddons, and Fanny Kemble. Mrs. Siddons was especially effective: on 11 October 1782 a London newspaper noted that "the best panegyric we can make upon this Lady's performance of the pathetic scenes, is to remark, there was scarce a dry eye in the whole house, and that two Ladies in the boxes actually fainted." Introduced into the United States, it was first acted in Annapolis in April 1783. Later it was produced in Baltimore, New York, Philadelphia, Boston, Hartford, and Providence.

The high reputation of *The Fatal Marriage* with contemporary audiences has been partially restored by modern critics, who have noted Southerne's psychological acuity and power to dramatize intense situations. His use of the comic subplot, questioned by Southerne's contemporaries, is praised today as functional, in that comic relief heightens the pathos of Isabella's story.

After his success with his split-plot drama, Southerne undertook to repeat this formula with a play similar in emotional appeal. He found his subject once again in a novel by his colleague Aphra Behn. Her *Oroonoko, or The Royal Slave*, published in 1688, sets out the passionate love story of distressed lovers, most appropriate for Southerne's purposes. He acknowledged his debt to Mrs. Behn's work, but, as in *The Fatal Marriage*, Southerne's alteration of his source was substantial. He compressed Behn's rambling novel

into an effective theatrical structure. He emphasized the pathos of the Royal Slave and his beloved Imoinda. While Behn's Oroonoko is a fierce, ranting, violent man, Southerne's is philosophical, articulate, and civilized. (The violence of Behn's savage hero is suggested when, desperate, he attempts to commit suicide. Surprised by his enemies, he cuts off a piece of his own neck to hurl at them as a gesture of defiance.) There is another important change. In Behn, Imoinda is a "black Venus." Southerne changes her pigmentation: she is portrayed as white, the daughter of a European.

The play opened in November 1695 at the Theatre Royal in Drury Lane. It was an immediate success; a contemporary critic said, "It had indeed uncommon Success, and the Quality of both Sexes were very kind to the Play, and to the Poet." The success was much needed by the Theatre Royal: earlier the leading actor of the day, Thomas Betterton, had revolted against the management and led a group of actors out to establish a new theater at Lincoln's Inn Fields. The remaining company at Drury Lane was shaken, and the success of *Oroonoko*, as well as Vanbrugh's *The Relapse* and *Aesop* a year later, helped them maintain themselves. Since Betterton was gone, the part of Oroonoko fell to Jack Verbruggen, who advanced his reputation enormously in this part. "By doing the Author Right, [he] got himself the Reputation of one of the best Actors of his time," according to a contemporary source. Mrs. Rogers played Imoinda and Susanna Mountfort, who had married Verbruggen after the death (by murder) of her husband, played the breeches role of Charlotte Welldon. Once again this great comedienne served Southerne well, as she had in *Sir Anthony Love* and *The Wives' Excuse*.

The play is set in the English colony at Surinam. Oroonoko, a prince, is captured through the duplicity of the mercenary and heartless Captain Driver, who gives him to Blanford, representative of the governor of the colony. Oroonoko is reunited in captivity with his wife, Imoinda. Their joy is short-lived. The wicked lieutenant governor lusts after Imoinda, and Aboan, Oroonoko's faithful servant, urges him to lead a slaves' rebellion against the heartless colonists. Oroonoko demurs but finally, after considering that his own child will be born into slavery, consents. The uprising is betrayed by the treacherous slave Hottman, and the rebellion is crushed. In the fighting Oroonoko kills Captain Driver. Offered amnesty and honorable treatment,

Oroonoko lays down his sword but is once again betrayed by the Europeans. He is seized and taken from Imoinda. The lieutenant governor attempts to ravish Imoinda, but she is rescued by Blanford, who has freed Oroonoko. The couple is once more reunited, and in despair, they plan to commit suicide. Imoinda dies by her own hand. Discovered by the opposing factions of Blanford and the lieutenant governor, Oroonoko kills the latter before killing himself.

As in *The Fatal Marriage*, Southerne provides a comic plot. The Welldon sisters, Charlotte and Lucy, have failed to find husbands in London. Desperate, they venture their luck in Surinam, where husbands are said to grow "thick as oranges." Charlotte disguises herself as a man in order to make a false claim to an inheritance. She wins the lustful attentions of the rich Widow Lackitt and through trickery hands this prize over to an acquaintance. Through witty contrivance, very much in the manner of Sir Anthony Love, she wins the affection of Stanmore, while contriving to marry sister Lucy off to the booby son of the rich widow. Thus both sisters are married to some advantage. The two plots are loosely joined: the characters of the comic plot are in sympathy with Blanford's party, and Stanmore himself assists the honorable Blanford.

Oroonoko was a mainstay of the repertoire for nearly one hundred fifty years. It was often produced in America between 1792 and Junius Brutus Booth's revival in 1832. It has been republished in the twentieth century in several anthologies and remains perhaps Southerne's best-known play.

Its success parallels that of *The Fatal Marriage* in that the contemporary appeal seems to have been Southerne's ability to bring his audience to tears. In the prologue to Southerne's later play *The Spartan Dame*, the minor litterateur Elijah Fenton wrote of Southerne, "His Oroonoko never fail'd to engage/The radiant Circles of the former Age:/Each Bosom heav'd, all Eyes were seen to flow,/And sympathize with Isabella's Woe." This suggestion, that Southerne appealed especially to women in the audience, was much repeated in later accounts of Southerne. Isabella and then Imoinda and Oroonoko are Southerne's great creations in tragedy. They have about them a human quality and a dignity that demands our response.

There is a suggested parallel between the tragic and comic plots of *Oroonoko*. A prince in his own country, a man of intelligence and dignity, Oroonoko is enslaved through trickery. Similarly, in the comic plot, the Welldon sisters are also treated in London as commodities. They are dehumanized and treated without respect for their individual worth. Southerne does not show them as victims, but it is clear that the situation of women in England and the institution of slavery in Surinam have provocative parallels.

The tragedy of Oroonoko is of additional interest today in its presentation of the question of slavery. Although Southerne's attitude to slavery is debated, it seems clear that the play as a whole forms an indictment of slavery. John Ferriar, who revised *Oroonoko* into a clearly antislavery play in 1788, complained that Southerne provided a "grovelling apology for slave-holders." But Southerne shows clearly the greed and inhumanity of the planters, of Captain Driver, and of the lieutenant governor, in regard to the slaves. The debate over slavery was to become loud after the middle of the eighteenth century, but at the time of Southerne's play there was already awareness of the inequities of the trade. Southerne's own beliefs may have been influenced by Thomas Tryon's *Friendly Advice to the Gentleman-Planters of the East and West Indies* (1684). Here the barbarity of the slaveholders is criticized. Although it is possible to view *Oroonoko* through the filter of modern sensibilities as an antislavery play, this would be misleading. It is clear that Southerne detests the cruelty of the planters but does not object to the institution of slavery as such. Indeed, Oroonoko himself captures and sells black slaves to the Europeans. Blanford, approved of in the play, suggests that the majority of slaves are inferior, hardly worthy of another fate. Yet the overall effect of the play is to condemn the inhumanity of the practice, and, as Wylie Sypher has pointed out, Southerne's theme is the depravity of the white man.

Oroonoko is an example of the "noble savage" much portrayed in eighteenth-century literature. His true nobility dwarfs the other characters of the play, excepting Imoinda. Echoes of *Othello* (1604) reinforce our feelings of him as tragic hero. Even the worthy Blanford is of lesser stature. Oroonoko and Imoinda are treated heroically, although their passions are domestic–those of husband and wife. Yet it is possible to see in him, just as we see in certain portrayals of the heroic play, flaws: an egotism and innocence that are finally fatal. *Oroonoko* follows the pattern of Southerne's drama: innocence and nobility are beleaguered by cynicism, greed, and lust.

Elizabeth Hartley, an actress at Covent Garden during the 1770s, as she was depicted in the frontispiece to the 1777 edition of Oroonoko

Southerne plays on the opposition of Christian and heathen, dramatizing the familiar satirical proposition that the heathen is a better Christian: more humane and honest than the nominal Christian. As Robert L. Root, Jr., points out, through the innocent eyes of Oroonoko, the Christianity of the Europeans is horrendous; they fail to live by their professed principles.

The fatal error of Oroonoko is his failure to realize that he is in the hands of men entirely without his own sense of honor and decent practice. His death and Imoinda's, like those of Antony and Cleopatra, are a condemnation of a world too small and too sordid for them. The comic plot reinforces this perception: the Europeans' greed, cynicism, and capacity for double-dealing are seen in both plots as the essence of the European colonists. In the tragic plot the sordid world destroys the truly noble characters; in the comic the witty trickster, Charlotte, wins through her ability to disguise and dissemble, to act ruthlessly in her own interest.

The success of *Oroonoko* was great enough to make Southerne famous and, it seems, financially secure. After *Oroonoko*, his involvement with the theater was occasional. In 1696

Southerne was awarded an M.A. degree by Trinity College, and he assisted Cibber in getting *Love's Last Shift* accepted for performance at Drury Lane. At about this time Southerne married Agnes, the daughter of Sir Richard Atkyns, Bt., and the widow of Edward Atkyns of Sapperton, Gloucestershire. She had two children by her first marriage and bore Southerne a daughter, Agnes, who was baptized at St. Nicholas's Church, Gloucester, on 15 August 1699.

The Fate of Capua was produced in Lincoln's Inn Fields in April 1700. It failed, despite the presence of Betterton and Elizabeth Barry in leading roles. The prompter Downes wrote, "*The Fate of Capua,* wrote by Mr. *Southern,* better to Read then Act; 'twas well Acted, but answer'd not the Companies Expectation." The play departs from the split-plot format of *The Fatal Marriage* and *Oroonoko,* possibly in reaction to the criticism of those plays for joining risqué comedy to tragedy, and Southerne may also have been reacting to Collier's fierce blast in 1698 at the so-called immorality and profaneness of the English theater. Collier put the playwrights very much on the defensive, and Southerne, who was sensitive to the pulse of the times, may have chosen to take no risks. There was interest at the time in drama with "classical" settings and subjects, and Southerne himself had earlier assisted Dryden with *Cleomenes, The Spartan Hero.*

Southerne found his story in Livy's *Roman History,* books 23, 25, and 26. It takes place in Capua during the second Punic War. The Capuans, long allied with Rome, are persuaded by one of their senators to transfer their allegiance to Carthage and the recently victorious Hannibal. The mob concurs and rises against the senate and its leader, the noble Decius Magius. As is usual in Southerne, the mob is contemptuously portrayed as mindless and dangerous. The senate agrees to support Hannibal but quickly regrets its decision, for the Carthaginian soldiers enter the city only to plunder. Hannibal soon withdraws his troops, and the Romans, eager to punish their erring ally, lay siege to Capua. Decius Magius pleads with the Romans for mercy, but although they respect him they refuse to spare the city. Decius refuses their offer of life and returns to the doomed city to join the senators in death by suicide. The Romans destroy the city.

A lesser but important plot concerns the love triangle of Virginius, his wife, Favonia, and the husband's best friend, Junius. Although wife and friend love each other, they refuse to act dishonorably. Under the mistaken impression that Favonia has betrayed him, Virginius encourages her suicide, only to be interrupted by the furious Junius, who forces Virginius to fight. Both are killed, although not before the mistaken husband learns of his tragic error.

The Fate of Capua is a serious attempt at high tragedy. A short redaction of the plot cannot do justice to the serious questions it dramatizes nor to the complexity of certain of its characters. Once again, Southerne offers the portrait of an honorable, wronged woman, troubled by strong feelings for a man other than her husband, but able to resist her suitor out of a sense of duty and responsibility. Like Mrs. Friendall, her sense of honor is futile; there is no remedy for her situation. The political and domestic plots, both serious, reinforce each other. Unfortunately, the play is talky at the expense of action and the moralizing is too overt. The play failed. *The Fate of Capua,* somewhat like Joseph Addison's later and finer *Cato* (1713), is best admired from a distance.

Nearly twenty years passed before Southerne brought forth his next play. His reputation as comic and especially as tragic playwright was secure. Yet he was thought of as a figure from the past. His colleagues were either dead or no longer active. Otway and Dryden were gone; Wycherley and Congreve had retired from the stage. Southerne was nearly sixty-one in December 1719, when his *The Spartan Dame* was produced at Drury Lane and proved a great success. Betterton, Barry, and Mountfort were dead, but younger actors such as Robert Wilks and Anne Oldfield were equal to them in skill and brilliance.

Southerne had begun *The Spartan Dame* in 1687, in a time of great social and political turmoil. He had completed four acts, but such were the difficulties of those times that he found it necessary to lay the play aside. It was not until many years later that Southerne, with the help of certain friends (including Congreve, whom Southerne had assisted with *The Old Bachelor* in 1693), was able to see the play produced. Southerne's difficulties were caused by the perceived parallels between the plot of the play and the situation of Queen Mary, daughter of an exiled father and wife to the king who succeeded him. Southerne disclaimed any such parallels, but his actual loyalties and intention were not entirely clear.

Southerne's source for *The Spartan Dame* was Plutarch. The story concerns King Leonidas, deposed through popular revolution. In his place comes his own daughter, Celona, and her husband, the usurper Cleombrotus. The parallel with Queen Mary and King William is too obvious to be ignored. Southerne's sympathies are obviously with the deposed king; those who oppose him are self-interested opportunists, and the mob is seen as mindless and degraded. The new king ignores his worthy wife and pursues her sister, Thelamia, wife of Eurytion, a supporter of the old king. The lustful usurper is aided by his agent, Crites, who by trickery (once more the playwright uses the "bed trick") gets Thelamia to admit the king to her bed. But the imposture is discovered and Cleombrotus is exposed. At the center of the play are the two contrasted women. Both suffer: Celona is torn between her loyalty to her father and to her unjust husband; Thelamia is loyal to her husband and abused by the trickery of wicked friends.

There are parallels here to Thomas Otway's *The Orphan* (1680) and Nathaniel Lee's *Lucius Junius Brutus* (1680), but, as Root notes, overall the play does not succeed in eliciting Otway's intense emotion nor Lee's political heightening. Nor does it match Southerne's *The Fatal Marriage* as domestic tragedy. The ending of *The Spartan Dame* is puzzling and unsatisfactory: much is made of a minor character, Euphemia, who has little to do with the play overall, and the death of the archvillain Cleombrotus is offhand. What remains is a reminder of Southerne's power to dramatize the "hard condition of a woman's fate," his central concern.

At age sixty-seven Southerne offered one last play, *Money The Mistress*, produced at Lincolns Inn Fields, in February 1726. It is a weak conclusion to an honorable career. Southerne was known and honored as a playwright, "In works of wit, the *Nestor* of our land," but his friends were dubious about this late project. Even the prologue, by Leonard Welsted, admits that the old playwright: "Is wasted of his fire and wonted strength./The suns decay; the brightest lustre wains;/Nor is he all he was in former reigns." Nevertheless Southerne was hopeful of the play's chances. But *Money The Mistress* failed, and the story goes that the audience on opening night hissed the play. The manager of the theater, John Rich, "who was standing by Mr. *Southern*, asked him, if he heard what the Audi-

ence were doing? His Answer was, '*No, Sir, I am very deaf.*'"

Southerne calls *Money The Mistress* "a play," and it is an attempt at comedy in the new mode of moralism. Mariana, daughter to a miserly old man, runs away with her witty but treacherous friend Harriet to join her beloved, Mourville. Harriet, armed with jewels dishonestly obtained from her friend, convinces Mourville to marry her. Mariana, who has offered herself in Mourville's place as prisoner, is rescued by an older man, Warcourt, also in love with Mariana. The treacherous friend and weak former lover are exposed. There is a farcical subplot of Don Manuel, a Spanish officer, who tries to seduce the wife of an English officer.

The play attempts to demonstrate the destructive power of money. Southerne had long been interested in the evils of mercenary marriages and their deleterious effects on the women. Mariana is presented as an exemplary, distressed heroine. The love of sententious moralizing comes easily to such one-dimensional characters. Neither they nor the play is memorable, and in the prologue Welsted can only remind the audience of Southerne's honorable efforts in the theater for many years: "Nor let the Wreath from his grey Head be torn;/For half a Century, with Honour worn!"

Thomas Southerne was yet to live many years, long enough to win the friendship of Jonathan Swift and Alexander Pope, who in his "Epistle to Augustus" praised the elderly dramatist as skilled in expressing "the passions," citing him along with Jonson, Shakespeare, Beaumont and Fletcher, Wycherley, and Rowe as great English playwrights. Southerne died on 26 May 1746 at age eighty-seven. He was a successful man of the theater, a working playwright for forty-four years. His best plays, *The Wives' Excuse*, *The Fatal Marriage*, and *Oroonoko*, reveal a competent, indeed interesting, playwright. He experimented in a variety of dramatic forms. His contemporaries valued him for his ability to portray intensely emotional scenes and for his "pure" language. He worked in the tradition of Otway, and his tragedies point the way to his successor, Nicholas Rowe. In comedy his subject is the distressed wife, and here he offered a pattern for such playwrights as Vanbrugh, Cibber, Congreve, and Farquhar. Today readers are interested in his psychological realism, his portraits of complex characters, often women in the throes of domestic distress, and his coldly realistic, often harsh, analysis of corrupt societal relations.

Bibliography:

J. M. Armistead, "Thomas Southerne: Three Centuries of Criticism," *Bulletin of Bibliography*, 41 (December 1984): 216-237.

References:

John Wendell Dodds, *Thomas Southerne, Dramatist*, Yale Studies in English, no. 81 (New Haven: Yale University Press/London: Oxford University Press, 1933);

Anthony Kaufman, " 'This Hard Condition of a Woman's Fate': Southerne's *The Wives' Ex-*

cuse," *Modern Language Quarterly*, 34 (March 1973): 36-47;

Kenneth Muir, *The Comedy of Manners* (London: Hutchinson, 1970);

Robert L. Root, Jr., *Thomas Southerne* (Boston: Twayne, 1981);

James Sutherland, *English Literature of the Late Seventeenth Century* (Oxford: Oxford University Press, 1969), pp. 82-84, 144-146;

Eugene M. Waith, "Admiration in the Comedies of Thomas Southerne," in *Evidence in Literary Scholarship: Essays in Memory of James Marshall Osborn*, edited by René Wellek and Alvaro Ribeiro (Oxford: Clarendon Press, 1979), pp. 89-103.

Nahum Tate
(circa 1652-30 July 1715)

Brian Corman
Erindale College, University of Toronto

PLAY PRODUCTIONS: *Brutus of Alba*, London, Dorset Garden Theatre, circa June 1678;

The Loyal General, London, Dorset Garden Theatre, circa December 1679;

The History of King Richard the Second [first performed as *The Sicilian Usurper*], adapted from *Richard II* by William Shakespeare, London, Theatre Royal in Drury Lane, January 1681;

The History of King Lear, adapted from *King Lear* by Shakespeare, London, Dorset Garden Theatre, circa January 1681;

The Ingratitude of a Commonwealth, adapted from *Coriolanus* by Shakespeare, Theatre Royal in Drury Lane, circa December 1681;

A Duke and No Duke, adapted from *Trappolin Supposed a Prince* by Aston Cokain, London, Theatre Royal in Drury Lane or Dorset Garden Theatre, August 1684;

Cuckold's Haven, adapted from *Eastward Ho!* by Ben Jonson, George Chapman, and John Marston, London, Dorset Garden Theatre, circa July 1685;

The Island Princess, adapted from an anonymous adaptation of *The Island Princess* by John

Fletcher, London, Theatre Royal in Drury Lane, circa April 1687;

Dido and Aeneas, libretto by Tate, music by Henry Purcell, Chelsea, Josias Priest's Boarding School, December 1689.

SELECTED BOOKS: *Poems* (London: Printed by T. M. for Benj. Tooke, 1677); enlarged as *Poems Written on several Occasions* (London: Printed for B. Tooke, 1684);

Brutus of Alba: Or, The Enchanted Lovers. A Tragedy, Acted at the Duke's Theatre (London: Printed by E. F. for Jacob Tonson, 1678); modern edition, edited by Robert Russell Craven (New York: Garland, 1987);

The Loyal General, A Tragedy. Acted at the Duke's Theatre (London: Printed for Henry Bonwicke, 1680);

The History of King Richard the Second, Acted at the Theatre Royal, Under the Name of the Sicilian Usurper (London: Printed for Richard Tonson & Jacob Tonson, 1681); republished as *The Sicilian Usurper: A Tragedy, As it was Acted at the Theatre-Royal* (London: Printed for James Knapton, 1691);

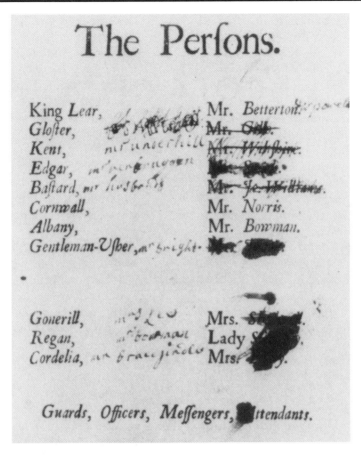

Page from a copy of the 1681 edition of Tate's King Lear, *in which the cast list for the first performance has been revised with names of actors who appeared in a later seventeenth-century production (by permission of the British Library)*

The History of King Lear, Acted at the Duke's Theatre. Reviv'd with Alterations (London: Printed for E. Flesher, sold by R. Bentley & M. Magnes, 1681); modern edition, edited by James Black (Lincoln: University of Nebraska Press, 1975);

The Ingratitude of a Common-wealth: Or, the Fall of Caius Martius Coriolanus, As It Is Acted At The Theatre-Royal (London: Printed by T. M. for Joseph Hindmarsh, 1682); modern edition, edited by Ruth McGugan (New York: Garland, 1987);

The Second Part of Absalom and Achitophel, by Tate and John Dryden (London: Printed for Jacob Tonson, 1682);

A Duke and no Duke. A Farce. As it is Acted by Their Majesties Servants (London: Printed for Henry Bonwicke, 1685); republished, with "A Preface Concerning Farce" (London: Printed for Henry Bonwicke, 1693); modern edition, in *Ten English Farces*, edited by Leo Hughes and A. H. Scouten (Austin: University of Texas Press, 1948);

Cuckolds-Haven: Or, An Alderman No Conjurer. A Farce. Acted at the Queen's Theatre in Dorset Garden (London: Printed for J. H. & sold by Edward Poole, 1685);

On The Sacred Memory Of Our Late Sovereign: With a Congratulation to His Present Majesty (London: Printed by J. Playford for Henry Playford, 1685);

Syphilis: or, A Poetical History of the French Disease, by Girolamo Fracastoro, translated by Tate (London: Printed for Jacob Tonson, 1686);

The Island-Princess: As it is Acted At the Theatre Royal, Reviv'd with Alterations (London: Printed by R. H. for W. Canning, 1687);

A Pastoral in Memory of His Grace the Illustrious Duke of Ormond, Deceased July the 21st. 1688 (London: Printed & sold by Randal Taylor, 1688);

An Opera Perform'd at Mr. Josias Priest's Boarding-School at Chelsey [Dido and Aeneas] (London, 1689); edited by Curtis A. Price (New York: Norton, 1986); edited by Ellen T. Harris (Oxford: Oxford University Press, 1987); revised and edited by Benjamin Britten and Imogen Holst (London: Boosey & Hawkes, 1960);

The Prolouge [sic] *to King William & Queen Mary at a Play Acted before Their Majesties at Whitehall, on the 15th of Nov. 1689* [single sheet printed on both sides] (London: Printed for F. Saunders & published by R. Baldwin, 1689);

A Pastoral Dialogue (London: Printed for Richard Baldwin, 1690); also published as *A Poem Occasioned by the Late Discontents & Disturbances in the State. With Reflections Upon the Rise and Progress of Priest-Craft.* (London: Printed for Richard Baldwin, 1691);

A Poem, Occasioned by His Majesty's Voyage to Holland, The Congress at The Hague, and Present Siege of Mons (London: Printed for Richard Baldwin, 1691);

Characters of Vertue and Vice, Attempted in Verse from a Treatise of the Reverend Joseph Hall, Late Lord Bishop of Exeter (London: Printed for Francis Saunders, 1691);

A Present for the Ladies: Being an Historical Vindication of the Female Sex. To Which Is Added, The Character of an Accomplish'd Virgin, Wife, and Widow, in Verse (London: Printed for Francis Saunders, 1693);

An Ode upon Her Majesty's Birth-Day, April the thirtieth. Set to Musick by Mr. Henry Purcell, and Perform'd before Her Majesty at Whitehall, Monday May the 1st. 1693 (London: Printed for Richard Baldwin, 1693);

The Life of Lewis of Bourbon, Late Prince of Conde. Digested into Annals. With Many Curious Remarks on the Transactions of Europe for These Last Sixty Years, by Pierre Coste, translated by Tate (London: Printed for Tim. Goodwin, 1693);

A Poem On The Late Promotion of Several Eminent Persons in Church and State (London: Printed for Richard Baldwin, 1694);

In Memory of Joseph Washington, Esq.; Late of the Middle Temple, An Elegy (London: Printed for Richard Baldwin, 1694);

The Four Epistles of A. G. Busbequius, Concerning His Embassy into Turkey, translated by Tate (London: Printed for J. Taylor & J. Wyat, 1694);

An Ode upon the Ninth of January 1693/4 the First Secular Day Since University of Dublin's Foundation by Queen Elizabeth [broadside] (Dublin: Printed by J. Ray, 1694);

Mausolaeum: A Funeral Poem On Our Late Gracious Sovereign Queen Mary of Blessed Memory (London: Printed for B. Aylmer, W. Rogers & R. Baldwin, 1695);

An Elegy on the Most Reverend Father in God, His Grace, John, Late Lord Archbishop of Canterbury (London: Printed for B. Aylmer & W. Rogers, 1695);

An Essay of a New Version of the Psalms of David (London: Printed for the Company of Stationers, 1695);

A New Version of the Psalms of David, Fitted to the Tunes Used in Churches, by Tate and Nicholas Brady (London: Printed by M. Clark for the Company of Stationers, 1696);

The Anniversary Ode for the Fourth of December, 1697. His Majesty's Birth-Day. Another for New-Year's-Day, 1697-8 (London: Printed for Richard Baldwin, 1698);

A Consolatory Poem to the Right Honourable John Lord Cutts, Upon the Death of His Most Accomplish'd Lady (London: Printed by R. R. for Henry Playford, 1698);

Elegies on I. Her Late Majesty of Blessed Memory. II. Late Arch-Bishop of Canterbury. III. Illustrious Duke of Ormond and Earl of Ossory. IV. Countess of Dorset. V. Consolatory Poem, &c. Together with A Poem on the Promotion of Several Eminent Persons, &c. (London: Printed for J. Wild, 1699);

An Essay of a Character of The Right Honourable Sir George Treby Kᵗ., Lord Chief Justice of His Majesty's Court of Common-Pleas (London: Printed by R. Roberts & sold by A. Baldwin, 1700);

Funeral Poems (London: Printed by J. Gardyner & sold by J. Nutt, 1700);

Panacea: A Poem Upon Tea: In Two Canto's (London: Printed by & for J. Roberts, 1700); revised as *A Poem Upon Tea* (London: Printed for J. Nutt, 1702);

An Elegy In Memory of the Much Esteemed and Truly Worthy Ralph Marshall, Esq.; One of His Majesty's Justices of Peace, &c. (London: Printed by R. Roberts for the Author, 1700);

A Congratulatory Poem On the New Parliament Assembled on This Great Conjuncture of Affairs (London: Printed for W. Rogers, 1701);

The Kentish Worthies. A Poem (London: Printed for A. Baldwin, 1701);

A Monumental Poem in Memory of the Right Honourable Sir George Treby Kᵗ. Late Lord Chief Justice of His Majesty's Court of Common-Pleas: Consisting of His Character and Elegy (London: Printed for Jacob Tonson, 1702);

Portrait-Royal. A Poem upon Her Majesty's Picture Set Up in Guild-Hall, by Order of the Lord Mayor and the Court of Aldermen of London (London: Printed by J. Rawlins for J. Nutt, 1703);

The Song for New-Years-Day, 1703. Perform'd before Her Majesty (London: Printed for J. Nutt, 1703);

The Triumph, or, Warriours Welcome: A Poem on the Glorious Successes of the Last Year. With The Ode for New-Year's-Day, 1705. (London: Printed by J. Rawlins for J. Holland, 1705);

Britannia's Prayer for the Queen (London: Printed for John Chantry, 1706);

Majestas Imperii Britannici. The Glories of Great Britain Celebrated in Latin Poems by Mr. Maidwell, translated by Tate (London, 1706);

A Congratulatory Poem, to the Right Honourable Earl Rivers, Upon His Lordship's Expedition (London: Printed & sold by B. Bragge, 1706);

The Triumph of Union: With the Muse's Address for the Consummation of it in the Parliament of Great Britain (London, 1707);

The Muse's Memorial of the Recovery of the Right Honourable Richard Earl of Burlington, From a Dangerous Sickness, In the Year 1706, A Congratulatory Poem. With an Account of the Present State of Poetry (London: Printed for Tho. Osborne & sold by B. Bragge, 1707);

Injur'd Love: Or, The Cruel Husband. A Tragedy, Design'd to be Acted at the Theatre Royal (London: Printed for Richard Wellington, 1707);

A Congratulatory Poem To His Royal Highness Prince George of Denmark, Lord High Admiral of Great Britain, Upon the Glorious Successes at Sea (London: Printed by H. Meere for J. B. & sold by R. Burrough & J. Baker, 1708);

The Celebrated Speeches of Ajax and Ulysses, for the Armour of Achilles. In the 13th Book of Ovid's Metamorph, translated by Tate and Aaron Hill (London: Printed for William Keble & Tho. Bickerton, 1708);

An Essay for Promoting of Psalmody (London: Printed for J. Holland & sold by J. Morphew, 1710);

The Muse's Memorial, Of the Right Honourable Earl of Oxford, Lord High Treasurer of Great Britain (London: Printed by E. Berington, and sold by J. Baker & B. Berington, 1712);

The Muse's Bower, an Epithalamium on the Auspicious Nuptials of the Right Honourable the Marquis of Caermarthen, With the Lady Elizabeth Harley, Daughter of the Right Honourable Earl of Oxford and Mortimer, Lord High Treasurer of Great Britain (London: Printed for the author & sold by J. Morphew, 1713);

The Triumph of Peace. A Poem, on the Magnificent Publick Entry of His Excellency the illustrious Duke of Shrewsbury, Ambassador Extraordinary from Her Majesty of Great Britain, to the Most Christian King. And the Magnificent Publick Entry of His Excellency the illustrious Duke D'Aumont, Ambassador from His Most Christian Majesty, to the Queen of Great Britain. With the Prospect of the Glorious Procession for a General Thanksgiving at St. Paul's (London: Printed for James Holland & sold by J. Morphew, 1713);

A Congratulatory Poem, On Her Majesties Happy Recovery, and Return to Meet her Parliament (London: Printed for James Holland & sold by John Morphew, 1714);

A Poem Sacred to the Glorious Memory of Her Late Majesty Queen Anne (London, 1716).

OTHER: Thomas Flatman, *Poems and Songs.... The 2d ed. with Additions and Amendments,* includes a congratulatory poem by Tate (London: B. Took & J. Edwin, 1676);

"Leander to Hero," "Hero to Leander," and "Medea to Jason," in *Ovid's Epistles, Translated by Several Hands* (London: Printed for Jacob Tonson, 1680);

Poems by Several Hands, And on Several Occasions, collected, with contributions, by Tate (London: Printed for J. Hindmarsh, 1685);

J. D., *A Memorial for the Learned: Or, Miscellany of Choice Collections from the Most Eminent Authors. In History, Philosophy, Physick, and Heraldry,* edited by Tate (London: Printed for George Powell and William Powle, 1686);

The Æthiopian History of Heliodorus. In Ten Books, books 6-10 translated by Tate (London: Printed by J. L. for Edward Poole, 1686); republished as *The Triumphs of Love and Constancy* (London: Printed by J. Leake for Edward Poole, 1687);

The Third Part Of the Works of Mr. Abraham Cowley, being his Six Books of Plants, Never before Printed in English, books 4 and 5 translated by Tate (London: Printed for Charles Harper, 1689);

Quintus Curtius Rufus, *The Life of Alexander the Great,* translated by several "Gentlemen in the University of Cambridge," edited by Tate (London: Printed for Francis Saunders, 1690);

Sir William Petty, *The Political Anatomy of Ireland*, edited by Tate (London: Printed for D. Brown & W. Rogers, 1691);

Satires 2 and 5, in *The Satires Of Junius Juvenalis. Translated into English Verse. By Mr. Dryden, And Several other Eminent Hands. Together with the Satires Of Aulus Persius Flaccus Made English by Mr. Dryden. With Explanatory Notes at the end of each Satire. To which is Prefix'd a Discourse concerning the Original and Progress of Satire. Dedicated to the Right Honourable Charles Earl of Dorset, &c.* (London: Printed for Jacob Tonson, 1693);

Miscellanea Sacra: Or, Poems on Divine & Moral Subjects, collected by Tate (London: Printed for Hen. Playford, 1696);

Sir John Davies, *The Original, Nature, and Immortality of the Soul*, edited by Tate (London: Printed for W. Rogers, 1697);

J. S., *The Innocent Epicure: Or, The Art of Angling. A Poem*, edited by Tate (London: Printed for S. Crouch, H. Playford & W. Brown, 1697);

An Essay on Poetry; Written by the Marquis of Normanby, and the Same Render'd into Latin by Another Hand. With Several Other Poems, edited by Tate (London: Printed by F. Saunders, 1697);

Most of book 4, in *Ovid's Metamorphosis. Translated by Several Hands. Vol. 1. Containing the First Five Books* (London: Printed for W. Rogers, F. Saunders & A. Roper, 1697);

"Ovid's Remedy of Love," in *Ovid's Art of Love. In Three Books. Together with his Remedy of Love. Translated into English Verse By Several Eminent Hands. To which are added, The Court of Love, A Tale from Chaucer. And The History of Love* (London: Printed for Jacob Tonson, 1709);

"Dialogues of the Gods: To Ridicule the Fables about them," in *The Fourth and Last Volume of the Works of Lucian* (London: Printed & sold by James Woodward, 1711);

The Monitor. Intended for the Promoting of Religion and Virtue, and Suppressing of Vice and Immorality, edited by Tate and M. Smith, nos. 1-21 (March and April 1713); collected as *An Entire Set of the Monitors* (London: J. Baker, 1713);

Most of book 7, in *Ovid's Metamorphoses In Fifteen Books. Translated by the most Eminent Hands* (London: Printed for Jacob Tonson, 1717).

It is one of the minor ironies of literary history that Nahum Tate's small claim to fame is for having the audacity to attempt to "improve" Shakespeare's plays, most egregiously *King Lear*. His contemporaries found him anything but audacious; Charles Gildon is typical in his referring to "a Person of great Probity of Manners, Learning, and good Nature," whose relative lack of success in the world came from being "guilty of Modesty," since "it is the noisy pushing Man in Poetry, as well as other things, that prevails with Fame as well as Fortune." Modest in manners, Tate possessed abilities to match. The "life" published under the name of Theophilus Cibber in *Lives of the Poets* (1753) repeated concisely the commonplace view of Tate's limitations: He was "a man of learning, courteous and candid, but was thought to possess no great genius, as being deficient in what is its first characteristic, namely, invention." Tate came to terms with his limitations early in his career; Gerard Langbaine (1691) pointed out that "generally he follows other Mens Models and builds on their Foundations: for of eight Plays that are printed under his Name, Six of them owe their Original to other Pens." His greatest success came as a translator (most notably of Ovid and Juvenal, and, with Nicholas Brady, of a metrical version of the Psalms of David, parts of which are still included in many hymnals) and adapter (most notably of *King Lear;* his version held the stage for more than 150 years). Tate was a pioneer of English farce; his *A Duke and No Duke* (1684) had a long and influential history on the stage. He was also a fine librettist, providing the text for Henry Purcell's *Dido and Aeneas* (1689) as well as many shorter pieces. He was appointed poet laureate in 1692 and held the position until his death twenty-three years later.

Nahum Tate was probably born in Ireland in 1652, the son of Faithful Teate and Katherine Kenetie Teate. His father and both of his grandfathers were Irish clergymen. His family had suffered considerably during the Catholic rebellion of 1641, and their lives over the next twenty years were predictably unstable. Tate's father and grandfather both held livings in England as well as in Ireland, and the lack of precise dates makes it impossible to know with certainty where Tate spent his childhood. His father was also a writer—of sermons, an epithalamium, and a long metaphysical poem on the doctrine of the trinity called *Ter Tria* (1658).

Tate entered Trinity College, Dublin, in June 1668 along with his brother Faithful; they gave their place of birth as Dublin. He seems to

Tate's version of **King Lear,** *with its happy ending, in which Lear does not die and Cordelia lives on to marry Edgar, held the stage for more than a century and a half after its premiere in 1681. Susanna Arne Cibber (top), who played Cordelia in a 1754 production, is depicted on the heath in a scene that Tate added to the play. David Garrick (bottom), who first played Lear in 1747, is shown in a 1760 performance with William Havard as Edgar and Astley Bransby as Kent.*

have enjoyed his years at Trinity, happily accepting an invitation years later to write an ode for its centenary, which was set to music by Henry Purcell and performed on 9 January 1694. Tate's earliest acquaintance with the theater would have been at Smock Alley, Dublin, where at least one-third of the Shakespeare canon, including *King Lear*, formed part of the repertoire.

Tate had been in London long enough to establish a friendship with the poet and miniaturist Thomas Flatman by 1676, when he contributed a congratulatory poem (signed "N. Teat") to Flatman's revised *Poems and Songs*. His own first book, *Poems* (1677), was published under the signature "N. Tate," the spelling he continued to use throughout his career. (Since several of his contemporaries refer to him as Nathaniel or Nat, it is likely that he answered to those names as well as Nahum.)

Tate's first play, *Brutus of Alba*, opened in the late spring of 1678 at Dorset Garden. In the preface to the 1678 quarto, Tate confirms that his primary source is "the Fourth Book of the *Aeneids*," adding that he "had begun and finished it under the Names of *Dido* and *Aeneas*." Not wishing to "appear Arrogant" by "improving" Virgil, Tate superimposed the legendary history of Brutus, the eponymous hero of Britain (by a false etymology) and builder of New Troy (London), onto his Virgilian model. According to his secondary sources (Geoffrey of Monmouth and probably Raphael Holinshed and John Milton), Brutus, the great grandson of Aeneas, was forced to leave Italy and, after heroic exploits, fulfilled a destiny like his grandfather's, the founding of a great nation, Britain. In Tate's version, Brutus stops in Syracuse and has an affair with a queen strikingly similar to Dido, a widow who has vowed never to love again. Brutus, too, resisted love, but when a storm drives them into a cave by themselves, under the influence of a philter, they succumb to the inevitable.

The skeletal love plot is fleshed out with several related subplots. The principal opposition to Brutus's stay in Syracuse comes from his loyal friend, the honest soldier Asaracus. The Syracusan lord Soziman plots with the neighboring Agrigentines to turn the queen over to their lustful king in exchange for the Syracusan crown. Soziman resents Brutus because his son Locrinus has killed Soziman's son Hylax, and he shares with Asaracus a love for Amarante, the queen's maid. To help him achieve his ends, he turns to the sorceress Ragusa, who provides both the phil-

ter and the storm. Brutus is returned to his duty by Asaracus, who, when suicide fails to achieve the required result, returns as a ghost to urge Brutus, this time successfully, on his way. The queen dies of grief, and Amarante joins her through suicide. Soziman is poisoned by Ragusa just at his moment of triumph, and even Ragusa is denied pleasure from her villainy by being recalled to the underworld, her powers expired.

Tate's plot, then, is a full one, contrived with care and competence, albeit mechanically. Like many first plays, it is a pastiche of theatrical clichés, very much a representative play of the transition between the heroic play and the affective, blank-verse tragedy that replaced it in the mid to late 1670s, complete with classical subject. The influence of John Dryden is particularly strong. The Queen-Brutus-Asaracus triangle recalls that of Cleopatra-Antony-Ventidius in *All for Love* (1677) too closely for coincidence, and the queen of Syracuse shares much in common with her Sicilian counterpart in *Secret Love*. Soziman is a stock character from the heroic play. And in Ragusa and her attendants, Tate incorporates the spectacular tradition of stage witchcraft, most immediately from Sir William Davenant's operatic adaptation of *Macbeth* (1664) and from Charles Davenant's opera *Circe* (1677). The most important legacy of *Brutus of Alba* is operatic: the George Powell-John Verbruggen operatic adaptation (1696) and, of course, Tate's own reworking for *Dido and Aeneas* in 1689. The first production was probably a failure, and there are no records of subsequent revivals. A lack of critical attention confirms the judgment *Brutus of Alba* met in the theater.

Tate's next play, *The Loyal General*, probably appeared eighteen months later, in December 1679, but even with a vintage Dryden prologue, it was no more successful than *Brutus of Alba*. It is made up of a similar mix of heroic and affective elements and reveals the increasing influence of Shakespeare on the Restoration stage. Tate's dedication to Edward Taylor, especially interesting as an early testimony of his "Reverence four our *Shakespear*," echoes Dryden's early criticism, just as the play's text reflects the Restoration appropriation of Shakespeare by, most notably, Dryden, Thomas Otway, and Nathaniel Lee. *The Loyal General* shows Tate working, without an apparent major source, toward the kind of plays he would shortly make from three of Shakespeare's best.

An old king has surrounded himself with self-serving courtiers, who look the other way while his second queen foments rebellion to install her daughter, Edraste, on the throne ahead of the king's two sons and daughter, Arviola. When the sons are killed, Edraste, who lacks her mother's ambition, goes into hiding to protect her friend Arviola and the object of both their affections, the loyal general Theocrin. The queen's discarded lover, Escalus, and his sister, Myrrhoe, match her in evil ambition and are more clever. Their many plots and counterplots produce nearly universal suffering as the lovers are deceived into doubting each other while the king is tricked into taking Theocrin for a traitor. The truth ultimately emerges and the villains are punished, but not before the deaths of the three virtuous principals, the reconciled lovers by premature suicides (again recalling *All for Love* or, more closely, *Romeo and Juliet*). (Otway employed elements from *Romeo and Juliet* in *Caius Marius*, one of the great successes of the fall season of 1679.) John Genest's capsule summary, "a poor play with some good lines in it," is not unjust, although the mechanics of plot are again well executed while the good lines are far too few.

The Loyal General was Tate's last attempt at an "original" play; he spent the remainder of his career as a dramatist adapting earlier plays, a task at which he was far more successful, both artistically and commercially. According to Tate himself, the first Shakespeare text he attempted was the one that would win him much fame—and more notoriety. His adaptation of *King Lear* (circa January 1681) was Tate's biggest hit (although there is little evidence about its initial run) and the version of Shakespeare's masterpiece that held the stage for more than 150 years. Because Tate had the audacity to tamper with the play that has since come to be viewed as the greatest play by the greatest of playwrights, he has subsequently (since the Romantics) been accused of everything from rank hubris to gross insensitivity to errant stupidity. Tate's version is anything but an "improvement" to be sure; rather, it is a skillful reworking of a great play into a competent, workmanlike, minor piece for the theater. It also reflects the tastes and attitudes of the late 1670s.

Adapting Renaissance plays was a standard source of new texts for the Restoration theater. If an earlier play kept its audience with minimal change, Restoration playwrights normally found little motivation to "improve" it. But good plays, including Shakespeare's, that did not suit the tastes of Restoration audiences were likely targets for

the improvers. *Hamlet* and *Othello* played relatively unscathed, while *Macbeth* (Davenant, 1664), *The Taming of the Shrew* (John Lacy's *Sauny the Scot*, 1667), and *The Tempest* (Dryden and Davenant, 1667) were among the early Restoration remakes of Shakespeare's plays. In the late 1670s Dryden's *All for Love*, based upon *Antony and Cleopatra*, initiated a renewed interest in Shakespeare's tragedies and tragic histories: Edward Ravenscroft's *Titus Andronicus* (circa 1678), Otway's *Caius Marius* (1679), and John Crowne's *The Misery of Civil War* (1680) and *Henry the Sixth*, part 1 (1681)–both derived from Shakespeare's *Henry VI*–followed soon after Dryden's success. It is in this context that Tate joined in the search for Shakespeare plays to rewrite. Nor was his choice of *King Lear* surprising, since it had not been a very popular play after the Restoration.

In his dedication to *King Lear*, Tate credits Thomas Boteler with suggesting that he attempt to rework Shakespeare's text. Tate shared Boteler's admiration for parts of the play, especially "Lear's real and Edgar's pretended madness" and "the images and language, . . . so odd and surprising, and yet so agreeable and proper." Tate also shared Boteler's objections to the play: "I found the whole to answer your account of it, a heap of jewels, unstrung and unpolished, yet so dazzling in their disorder that I soon perceived I had seized a treasure." The first principle behind the alteration was moral: Shakespeare's particular violation of poetic justice in *Lear* was as intolerable to Tate as it was later to Samuel Johnson (though their reasons were probably not quite the same). A second principle was Tate's sense of a need to regularize Shakespeare: his language, to bring it in line with the more refined norms of Restoration England; his characterization, to clarify motives for action; and his plot, to free the tragic structure from the pollution of such indecorous, comic figures as the Fool and to insure that it effects the kind of emotional purgation enjoyed by audiences at the Duke's Theatre and sanctioned by critics (such as Thomas Rymer, whose *Tragedies of the Last Age Considered* [1677] had provoked a rethinking of the principles of tragedy by Dryden and most other tragic writers).

Tate was able to satisfy his objections by a single shift in the story. As he explains to Boteler:

> 'Twas my good fortune to light on one expedient
> to rectify what was wanting in the regularity and
> probability of the tale, which was to run through

the whole a love betwixt Edgar and Cordelia, that never changed word with each other in the original. This renders Cordelia's indifference and her father's passion in the first scene probable. It likewise gives countenance to Edgar's disguise, making that a generous design that was before a poor shift to save his life. The distress of the story is evidently heightened by it; and it particularly gave occasion of a scene or two, of more success (perhaps) than merit. This method necessarily threw me on making the tale conclude in a success to the innocent distressed persons: otherwise I must have encumbered the stage with dead bodies, which conduct makes many tragedies conclude with unseasonable jests.

If for twentieth-century readers Tate's entire project remains one of madness, it is certainly not without method.

Tate's many changes also contribute to extraliterary concerns he chose to ignore in his dedication, but they never violate his stated aesthetic design. The admission of women to the acting companies after the Restoration encouraged dramatists to expand female roles in their plays. All three of Lear's daughters play more prominent roles in Tate's version, and Cordelia is given a companion, Arante, but none of these changes breaks the coherence of a play that is nearly a she-tragedy with a happy ending. And like most of the Shakespeare adaptations of the late 1670s and 1680s, Tate's Lear responds to the highly politicized decade that begins with the Popish Plot and Exclusion Crisis and ends with the Glorious Revolution. Shakespeare's tragedies and histories, with their treatment of the importance of legitimate and proper succession to the throne and the civil wars that result from usurpation or alteration offered easy, oblique commentaries on Restoration politics to Tate and his contemporaries. Lear's restoration and settling of the succession on Cordelia and Edgar superimpose a Royalist fable onto Tate's plot. Shakespeare's politics, like his story, are simplified and regularized, and the result is again in perfect harmony with the reconceived plot.

Like Dryden and Otway, Tate rewrote Shakespeare under the influence of the heroic play. Tate's characters are motivated by the same conflicts of love and honor that energize the plots of the heroic drama with the idealized feudal and patriarchal values that served so well the Tory cause in 1680. Edmund, Goneril, and Regan all become Hobbesian villains who sacrifice virtue and honor in their self-indulgent pursuit of power.

Their ultimate defeat aligns the happy ending with the traditional endings of the earlier heroic plays, providing an additional context for Edgar's oft-ridiculed closing lines:

> Our drooping Country now erects her Head,
> Peace spreads her balmy Wings, and Plenty blooms.
> Divine *Cordelia*, all the Gods can witness
> How much thy Love to Empire I prefer!
> Thy bright Example shall convince the World
> (Whatever Storms of Fortune are decreed)
> That Truth and Vertue shall at last succeed.

Had Tate chosen to adapt a play less revered by later generations or had he been less successful in his adaptation, his *King Lear* would be no better known today than his other plays. But since it was to keep Shakespeare's play off the stage for so long, Tate's *Lear* has had a perverse appeal for Shakespeareans and theater historians alike. Bardolatry led to the coining of phrases such as "Tatification" to facilitate the mindless rejection of efforts like Tate's. The extensive treatment by theater historians, however, especially in the past generation, has been far more fruitful. Not only has it provided a necessary context for understanding what Tate was doing, but by showing the continuity in the performance history of both Tate's and Shakespeare's versions of *Lear*, it has forced complacent twentieth-century interpreters to recognize that their *Lear*s are hardly more pure than Tate's. They probably even retain some contamination from the 150-year performance tradition that altered ineluctably future perceptions of Shakespeare's masterpiece.

Tate himself was merely following Dryden's lead in searching for his first success in the theater. The result was a competent effort that garnered fame beyond its merits. Also as a result, Tate's reputation has suffered disproportionately. He was guilty of little more than lacking the talent of his mentor Dryden.

In his epistle dedicatory to George Raynsford, Tate explained that he had written his *Lear* just before *The History of King Richard the Second*, his adaptation of Shakespeare's *Richard II*. The two plays have much in common in all but their fates. *Richard the Second* was banned in December 1680. It was staged the following month as *The Sicilian Usurper* but again banned after two performances. The "revised" title was justified by providing Sicilian names for Richard, Gaunt, York, Bullingbrook, Northumberland, and the queen (but not the other characters), so it is not surprising that the Theatre Royal was temporarily closed in response to its defiance of the original ban. Since the play was never revived, it has been dismissed generally as a failure.

Revealing the same thoughtful self-consciousness he showed in discussing his *Lear*, he calls his dedication to *The Sicilian Usurper* a "Vindication" and in it attempts to justify the play he "expected . . . wou'd have found Protection from whence it receiv'd Prohibition." What emerges is a story of gross miscalculation. Tate claims that he was "charm'd with the many Beauties" in his source and that in adapting it had "as little design of Satyr on present Transactions, as *Shakespeare* himself that wrote this story before this Age began." His disingenuousness escalates as he claims: "I am not ignorant of the posture of Affairs in King *Richard* the Second's Reign, how dissolute then the Age, and how corrupt the Court; a Season that beheld *Ignorance* and *Infamy* preferr'd to *Office* and *Pow'r* exercis'd in Oppressing, Learning and Merit; but why a History of those Times shou'd be supprest as a Libel upon Ours, is past my Understanding."

It is precisely his awareness of the likelihood of earlier history being seen allegorically in terms of current events that motivates Tate's alterations: "My Design was to engage the pitty of the Audience for him in his Distresses, which I cou'd never have compass'd had I not before shown him a Wise, Active and Just Prince. . . . Every Scene is full of Respect to Majesty and the dignity of Courts, not one alter'd Page but what breaths Loyalty, yet had this Play the hard future to receive its Prohibition from Court." Tate's description of the premise upon which he based his adaptation is accurate, but the obvious application of Richard's life to Charles II's (especially his pleasure-seeking court and his childlessness) and of his death to Charles I's (Tate's characterization emphasizes the parallel) was seen as more than adequate cause for censorship in the turbulent days of the Exclusion Crisis.

If Tate's *Lear* was unduly rewarded, his *Richard the Second* deserved better treatment. It shares the same, typical strengths and weaknesses. Like Lear, Richard is made a more sympathetic character, by providing him with motivation to excuse the weakness Shakespeare portrays in his deposition (he sacrifices himself to spare his people the misery of civil war) and by removing from Bullingbrook all justification for his rebellion (the future Henry IV proclaims his naked ambition early in the play; Richard merely borrows Gaunt's estate from Bullingbrook, with the con-

sent of Gaunt's executor, the Duke of York; Bullingbrook is presented as a Shaftesburian rabble-rouser, building his power base by manipulating the mob). Richard's courtiers are mentioned only in passing; instead, his military prowess in containing both Watt Tyler and the Irish is emphasized. Even John of Gaunt treats him with respect to the end (satire against his court comes mainly from the unequivocally loyal Duke of York).

Other changes also reveal similarities to *Lear*. The role of the queen is expanded considerably to provide a love interest and to evoke the kind of pity in adversity that Edgar and Cordelia garner on the heath. And Richard, like Lear, kills his antagonists when surprised by them in prison (four die, twice the number slain in Shakespeare's version) before being killed himself by Exton. Shakespeare's ambiguities and ambivalences are systematically and effectively resolved to maximize pity for the royal martyr and his queen. Once again, Tate's often mediocre, if not bathetic, blank verse intrudes upon–even clashes with–Shakespeare's. *Richard the Second* is neither more nor less faithful to its source than Tate's *Lear*; and like *Lear*, it is well conceived but greatly inferior to Shakespeare.

For the last of his Shakespeare adaptations, Tate chose the especially unpopular *Coriolanus* (*The London Stage* records only one Restoration performance before Tate's version). The play's modern editor, Ruth McGugan, points out that sixty percent of the lines in *The Ingratitude of a Commonwealth* are word-for-word from Shakespeare (compared to forty-six percent in *King Lear* and fifty percent in *Richard the Second*). And the changes follow the same pattern Tate established in his earlier reworkings of Shakespeare.

His dedication to Charles Somerset, lord Herbert, again pays tribute to his source: "Much of what is offered here, is Fruit that grew in the Richness of his Soil; and what ever the Superstructure prove, it was my good fortune to build upon a Rock." Having miscalculated the effect of the political implications of *Richard the Second*, Tate was reluctant to repeat his earlier error. Not only did he acknowledge the "no small Resemblance with the busie Faction of our own time" but claims to have "set the *Parallel* nearer to Sight." Many of the alterations of Shakespeare's plot sharpen the satire directed at the Whig "*Troublers* of the State." Nor does Tate leave his moral in doubt, "to Recommend Submission and Adherence to Established Lawful Power, which in a word, is *Loyalty*."

Tate follows Shakespeare fairly closely for the first four acts of *The Ingratitude of a Commonwealth*, cutting lines and rearranging scenes to regularize and to focus attention more clearly on his own interpretation. Ambiguities and ambivalences are once again removed in favor of simpler characterization and a more coherent plot. Tate's Coriolanus is a heroic figure whose similarities of character to James, duke of York, are repeatedly emphasized. Shakespeare's mixed presentation of the citizens of Rome and their tribunes is made wholly negative, in part to insure that the London mob and its Whig leaders receive no sympathy. Aufidius, too, is altered into another representative of Tate's version of the Hobbesian villain, a mirror image of Coriolanus in his willingness to sacrifice his country to fulfill his personal ambitions. And he shares in his villainy with Nigridius, Tate's development of Shakespeare's unnamed lieutenant, to offer a composite rendition of Anthony Ashley Cooper, first earl of Shaftesbury not unlike the one Otway was to construct in Renault and Antonio in *Venice Preserved*. He also turns Shakespeare's Valeria into a patrician version of Dryden's Melantha (*Marriage A la Mode*, 1671), but this insensitive comic social butterfly seems strangely out of place among Coriolanus and his family.

Tate also continued his pattern of imposing an affective aesthetic on Shakespeare. Coriolanus's wife and young son are both given larger profiles in *The Ingratitude of a Commonwealth;* Virgilia is portrayed as a tenderhearted heroine and made the object of Aufidius's lust. And in his most extravagant alteration of a Shakespearean plot, Tate rewrote the fifth act completely, adding to the death of the hero the attempted rape of Virgilia, which provokes her suicide, the death of Aufidius at Coriolanus's hand, the torture and subsequent death (onstage) of Young Martius, the resulting madness of Volumnia, and her killing of Nigridius. This effusion of blood and pathos effaces entirely the power of Shakespeare's ending by removing the focus from the tragedy of Coriolanus himself. Tate's vision of the horrific consequences of a commonwealth is no doubt the clearer for his changes, but the result, despite its success in handling a political theme without offense to the government, no more pleased its contemporary audience than it has interested subsequent audiences or critics.

After mounting his three Shakespeare adaptations within a year, Tate did not have another play staged for nearly three years. He had accepted and honored the commission to write *The Second Part of Absalom and Achitophel* (1682)–with some memorable contributions by Dryden–but his activities do not otherwise seem to have been literary. It is likely that he was discouraged from theatrical efforts by the amalgamation of the two acting companies and subsequent decline in interest in new plays by the now United Company. His next play, *A Duke and No Duke*, was one of very few new plays produced in 1684.

With *A Duke and No Duke*, Tate turned his attention for the first time to the adapting of comedy. His source, this time, was the little-known *Trappolin Supposed a Prince* (1633) by the minor Caroline poet, playwright, and "Son of Ben" Sir Aston Cokain. Cokain's play is in turn a rendition of the performances he saw by a commedia del l'arte troupe in Venice in 1632-1633. (It is one of the earliest recorded influences of commedia del l'arte on an English playwright.) Tate's approach to his source text here is not unlike his approach to his Shakespearean texts: he cuts, simplifies, and clarifies. The result is less than half the length of its original with a significant reduction in the number of characters, acts, and scenes.

Again, Tate is forthcoming with his thoughts about his work, stating them most clearly and forcefully in the expanded "Preface concerning Farce," which he added to the 1693 edition of *A Duke and No Duke*. Farce as a genre was generally held in contempt by Restoration critics, most notably Tate's own mentor Dryden. With considerable help from Agesilao Mariscotti's 1610 treatise on farce, Tate attempts to answer the critics, first by claiming an honorable lineage for farce and then by arguing that good farce is very difficult to write and thus worthy of increased respect. He devotes several pages to an unconvincing discussion of the origin and history of farce, but becomes more persuasive when he points to the importance of farce in the work of Aristophanes, Plautus, Shakespeare, Fletcher, Jonson, Molière, Shadwell, and even Dryden himself (Tate singles out Dryden's *The Spanish Friar* [1680] and *Sir Martin Mar-All* [1667]).

Still more interesting is Tate's attempt to define the genre by distinguishing it from comedy. Comedy, for Tate, is "an Imitation of Humane Life . . . and subsists upon Nature; so that whosoever has a genius to coppy her, and will take the Pains, is assured of Success." Farce, on the other hand, "extends beyond Nature and Probability." Since "so few Improbabilities . . . appear pleasant in the Representation," it is a more difficult form in which to succeed. Recognizing the close relationship between farce and satire, Tate argues that "Farce is not inconsistent with good Sence, because 'tis capable of Satyr, which is Sence with a Vengeance." He also explores the psychological effects of farce by distinguishing between acceptable and unacceptable degrees of improbability: "Extravagant and monstrous Fancies are but sick Dreams, that rather torment than divert the Mind; but when Extravagancy and Improbability happen to please at all, they do it to purpose, because they strike our own Thought with greatest Surprise." Tate's preface is an impressive, if unoriginal early English defense of farce, one that has rarely been improved upon by later critics.

In *A Duke and No Duke* Tate follows Cokain's plot with a few key alterations. The basic structure is provided by two love plots, one high, one low. In the high plot Horatio, prince of Savoy, disguised as Brunetto, is captured in battle by Lavinio, duke of Tuscany. He promptly falls in love with the duke's sister Prudentia and is cast into prison when the duke hears of it. In the low plot Trappolin, "a Parasite, Pimp, Fidler, and Buffoon," is loved by Flametta but has a well-born rival in Barberino, the duke's counselor, who has Trappolin banished. The duke goes to Milan to marry the Milanese princess Isabella, leaving Barberino and Brunetto's enemy Alberto in charge. The banished Trappolin is transformed into Lavinio's look-alike by the conjurer Mago and returns to Florence to the great confusion of all the concerned parties. The duke, too, returns and after a round of mistaken identities is in turn transformed into Trappolin's look-alike. Mago, Trappolin's father, appears to resolve the chaos he has created, and the lovers are happily united. Most of the action focuses on Trappolin's adventures as duke of Tuscany; physical comedy and crude jests abound. Tate's contributions are mainly a coarsening of Trappolin-as-Duke and the addition of the ambassadors from Savoy. It is likely that he was attempting to bring Cokain's play closer to comedy by increasing its probability and realistic detail. In any event the result, a great success, was performed throughout the eighteenth century and into the nineteenth. It was Tate's most successful play after *King Lear* and an important early attempt at farce in English.

Tate attempted to repeat his success in farce with his next play, *Cuckold's Haven* (1685), an adaptation of Ben Jonson, George Chapman, and John Marston's city comedy *Eastward Ho!* (1605). Hoping to capitalize on the name, Tate credits the play to "that great Master *Ben*." Once again, Tate adapted by heavy cutting: five acts become three, whole scenes and parts of scenes are eliminated, and the many long speeches—extended conceits, jokes, parodies, and burlesques—of the original are pared down to more dramatic scale. Fewer lines than usual were salvaged from the source because so much of its humor depended on satirizing social conditions no longer of interest to Tate's audience or on various topical and literary allusions no longer recognizable by that audience.

Tate's choice of source text, then, was not a promising one. But since he intended to turn it into "A Farce," he could safely eliminate most of the topical material, retaining only the basic plot structure: Alderman Touchstone has two apprentices, the virtuous "sober" Golding and the "debauch'd" Quick-silver, and two daughters, the virtuous, "sober" Mildred and the "affected cittess" Girtrud. With his wife's encouragement, Girtrud marries the impecunious, foolish Sir Petronell Flash, while Mildred follows her father's advice, marrying Golding. Sir Petronell finances a get-rich-quick scheme in Virginia with Girtrud's money, aided by Quick-silver and the "bawd and usurer" Security. Sir Petronell and Quick-silver then abscond with Security's wife Wynifred, but their boat is wrecked in a storm on the Thames. After much physical humor and the predictable cuckolding jokes (many from *Eastward Ho!*), the play ends in a round of reconciliation that disposes of all the characters happily. In transforming his source into a farce, Tate removed both the bite and the ambiguity of its satire, along with the temptation to question the values or ponder the issues it raises. He insured the frivolity of *Cuckold's Haven* by saving his major alterations for the end, resolving his version with a scene borrowed from Jonson's *The Devil Is an Ass* (1616). Golding is no longer the principal agent of the comic resolution; instead, it is achieved by the rogues accusing Touchstone of bewitching them.

Tate complained that "the principal Part (on which the Diversion depended) was, by Accident, disappointed of Mr. *Nokes*'s Performance, for whom it was design'd, and only proper." Nokes's absence, he added, led to some rewriting that fur-

The dedication that Tate called his "Epistle in Vindication of the Author" and the prologue from the 1681 edition of his adaptation of Shakespeare's Richard II

TO
My Esteemed FRIEND
George Raynsford, Esq;

SIR,

I Wou'd not have you surpriz'd with this Address, though I gave you no warning of it. The Business of this Epistle is more Vindication than Complement ; and when we are to tell our Grievances 'tis most natural to betake our selves to a Friend. 'Twas thought perhaps that this unfortunate Off-spring having been stifled on the Stage, shou'd have been buried in Oblivion ; and so it might have happened had it drawn its Being from me Alone, but it still retains the immortal Spirit of its first-Father, and will survive in Print, though forbid to tread the Stage. They that have not seen it Acted, by its being silenc't, must suspect me to have Compil'd a Disloyal or Reflecting Play. But how far distant this was from my Design and Conduct in the Story will appear to him that reads with half an Eye. To form any Resemblance between the Times here written of, and the Present, had been unpardonable Presumption in Me. If the Prohibiters conceive any such Notion I am not accountable for That. I fell upon the new-modelling of this Tragedy, (as I had just before done on the History of King Lear) charm'd with the many Beauties I discover'd in it, which I knew wou'd become the Stage ; with as little design of Satyr on present Transactions, as Shakespear himself that wrote this Story before this Age began. I am not ignorant of the posture of Affairs in King Richard the Second's Reign, how dissolute then the Age, and how corrupt the Court ; a Season that beheld Ignorance and Infamy preferr'd to Office and Pow'r, exercis'd in Oppressing, Learning and Merit ; but why a History of those Times shou'd be suppress as a Libel upon Ours, is past my

A   Under-

The Epistle Dedicatory.

Understanding. 'Tis sure the worst Complement that ever was made to a Prince.

O Rem ridiculam, Cato, & jocosam,
Dignámque Auribus, & tuo Cachinno.
Ride, quicquid amas, Cato, Catullum
Res est Ridicula, &c.

Our Shakespear in this Tragedy, bated none of his Characters an Ace of the Chronicle ; he took care to shew 'em no worse Men than They were, but represents them never a jot better. His Duke of York after all his busy pretended Loyalty, is found false to his Kinsman and Sovereign, and joyn'd with the Conspirators. His King Richard Himself is painted in the worst Colours of History. Dissolute, Unadviseable, devoted to Ease and Luxury. You find old Gaunt speaking of him in this Language

——Then there are found
Lascivious Meeters, to whose Venom sound
The open Ear of Youth do's always Listen.
Where doth the World thrust forth a Vanity,
(So it be New, there's no respect how Vile)
That is not quickly buzz'd into his Ear?
That all too late comes Counsel to be heard.

without the least palliating of his Miscarriages, which I have done in the new Draft, with such words as These.

Your Sycophants bred from your Child-hood with you,
Have such Advantage had to work upon you,
That scarce your Failings can be call'd your Faults.

His Reply in Shakespear to the blunt honest Adviser runs thus.

And Thou a Lunatick Lean-witted-fool, &c.
Now by my Seat's right Royal Majesty,
Wer't Thou not Brother to great Edward's Son.
The Tongue that runs thus roundly in thy Head
Shou'd run thy Head from thy unreverent Shoulders.

On the contrary (though I have made him express some Resentment) yet he is neither enrag'd with the good Advice, nor deaf to it. He answers Thus ——

—— Gentle Unkle ;
Excuse the Sally's of my Youthfull Blood.
We shall not be unmindfull to redress
(However difficult) our States Corruptions,
And purge the Vanities that crowd our Court.

I have

The Epistle Dedicatory.

I have every where given him the Language of an Active, Prudent Prince. Preferring the Good of his Subjects to his own private Pleasure. On his Irish Expedition, you find him thus bespeak his Queen

Though never vacant Swain in silent Bow'rs
Cou'd boast a Passion so sincere as Mine,
Yet where the Int'rest of the Subject calls
We wave the dearest Transports of our Love,
Flying from Beauties Arms to rugged War, &c.

Nor cou'd it suffice me to make him speak like a King (who as Mr. Rhymer says in his Tragedies of the last Age considered, are always in Poëtry presum'd Heroes) but to Act so too, viz. with Resolution and Justice. Resolute enough our Shakespear (copying the History) has made him, for concerning his seizing old Gaunt's Revennues, he tells the wise Diswaders,

Say what ye will, we seize into our Hands
His Plate, his Goods, his Money and his Lands.

But where was the Justice of this Action ? This Passage I confess was so material a Part of the Chronicle (being the very Basis of Bullingbrook's Usurpation) that I cou'd not in this new Model so far transgress Truth as to make no mention of it ; yet for the honour of my Heroe I suppose the foresaid Revennues to be Borrow'd onely for the present Exigence, not Extorted.

Be Heav'n our Judge, we mean him fair,
And shortly will with Interest restore
The Loan our suddain Streights make necessary.

My Design was to engage the pitty of the Audience for him in his Distresses, which I cou'd never have compass'd had I not before shewn him a Wise, Active and Just Prince. Detracting Language (if any where) had been excusable in the Mouths of the Conspirators : part of whose Dialogue runs thus in Shakespear ;

North. Now afore Heav'n 'tis shame such Wrongs are born
In him a Royal Prince and many more
Of noble Blood in this Declining Land :
The King is not Himself, but basely led
By Flatterers, &c.

Ross. The Commons He has pil'd with grievous Taxes
And lost their Hearts, &c.

Will. And daily new Exactions are devis'd
As Blanks, Benevolences, and I wot not what ;

A 2   But

The Epistle Dedicatory.

But what o' Gods Name doth become of This?
North. War hath not wasted it, for warr'd he has not;
But basely yielded upon Comprimize.
That which his Ancestours atchiev'd with Blows
More has He spent in Peace than they in War, &c.

with much more villifying Talk; but I wou'd not allow even Traytors and Conspirators thus to bespatter the Person whom I design'd to place in the Love and Compassion of the Audience. Ev'n this very Scene (as I have manag'd it) though it shew the Confederates to be Villains, yet it flings no Aspersion on my Prince.

Further, to Vindicate ev'n his Magnanimity in Regard of his Resigning the Crown, I have on purpose inserted an intirely new Scene between him and his Queen, wherein his Conduct is sufficiently excus'd by the Malignancy of his Fortune, which argues indeed Extremity of Distress, but Nothing of Weakness.

After this account it will be askt why this Play shou'd be supprest, first in its own Name, and after in Disguise? All that I can answer to this, is, That it was Silenc'd on the Third Day. I confess, I expected it wou'd have found Protection from whence it receiv'd Prohibition; and so questionless it wou'd, cou'd I have obtain'd my Petition to have it perus'd and dealt with according as the Contents Deserv'd, but a positive Doom of Suppression without Examination was all that I cou'd procure.

The Arbitrary Courtiers of the Reign here written, scarcely did more Violence to the Subjects of their Time, then I have done to Truth, in disguising their foul Practices. Take ev'n the Richard of Shakespear and History, you will find him Dissolute, Careless, and Unadvisable: peruse my Picture of him and you will say, as Æneas did of Hector, (though the Figure there was alter'd for the Worse and here for the Better) Quantum mutatus ab illo! And likewise for his chief Ministers of State, I have laid Vertues to their Charge of which they were not Guilty. Every Scene is full of Respect to Majesty and the dignity of Courts, not one alter'd Page but what breaths Loyalty, yet had this Play the hard fortune to receive its Prohibition from Court.

For the two days in which it was Acted, the Change of the Scene, Names of Persons, &c. was a great Disadvantage: many things were by this means render'd obscure and incoherent that in their native Dress had appear'd not only proper but gracefull. I call'd my Persons Sicilians but might as well have made 'em Inhabitants
of the

The Epistle Dedicatory.

of the Isle of Pines, or, World in the Moon, for whom an Audience are like to have small Concern. Yet I took care from the Beginning to adorn my Prince with such heroick Vertues, as afterwards made his distrest Scenes of force to draw Tears from the Spectators; which, how much more touching they would have been had the Scene been laid at Home, let the Reader judge. The additional Comedy I judg'd necessary to help off the heaviness of the Tale, which Design, Sir, you will not only Pardon, but Approve. I have heard you commend this Method in Stage writing, though less agreeable to strictness of Rule; and I find your Choice confirm'd by our Laureat's last Piece, who confesses himself to have broken a Rule for the Pleasure of Variety. *The Audience (says he) are grown weary of melancholly Scenes, and I dare prophesie that few Tragedies (except those in Verse) shall succeed in this Age if they are not lightned with a course of Mirth.

* Epst. Ded. to the Span. Fryar.

And now, Sir, I fear I have transgrest too far on your patience. Distress was always Talkative: be pleas'd to call to Mind your beloved Virgil's Nightingall when rob'd of her young.

Qualis populeâ mœrens Philomela sub Umbrâ,
Amissos queritur Fœtus, quos durus Arator
Observans, Nido implumes detraxit; at Illa
Flet noctem, ramoque sedens, miserabile Carmen
Integrat, & mœstis late loca Questibus implet.

This Simile you know, Sir, is occasion'd by Orpheus his lamenting the Loss of Euridice, which the Mythologists expound the Fruit of his Labours. You find Virgil himself elsewhere condoling his Oppression by Arrius. Such are the Complaints of our Spencer defrauded by Cecill. With these, the melancholly Cowley joyns his Note; and, as Mr. Flatman says, 'tis the Language of the whole Tribe.

I heard 'em Curse their Stars in ponderous Rhymes,
And in grave Numbers grumble at the Times.

Poetry and Learning, ev'n in Petronius his time, was a barren Province, when Villany of any sort was a thriving Trade.

Qui Pelago credit magno, se fœnore tollit,
Qui pugnat & Castra petit præcingitur Auro;
Vilis Adulator picto jacet Ebrius ostro;
Et qui sollicitat Nuptas, ad præmia peccat:
Sola pruinosis horret Facundia pannis.

Or

The Epistle Dedicatory.

Or to go a step higher in Antiquity ———
Qui'd est, Catulle, quod moraris emori?
Sellâ in Curuli Struma Nonius sedet,
Quid est, Catulle, quod moraris emori?

Aristotle himself confesses Poetry a better School of Vertue than Philosophy. Our own Sir Philip Sidney's learn'd Defence of it, is Demonstration what rewards are due, and our late incomparable Author of Hudibras, is no less Demonstration what returns are made to the best Masters of it. Not Greece or Rome can boast a Genius like His; yet after all, his Poverty was a greater Satyr on the Age than his Writings.

Once more, Sir, I beg your Pardon for digressing, and dismiss you to the following Poem, in which you will find some Master Touches of our Shakespear, that will Vie with the best Roman Poets, that have so deservedly your Veneration. If it yield you any Diversion I have my Desire, who covet all Opportunities of shewing my self gratefull for your Friendship to me, which I am proud of, and amongst the many whom your ingenious and obliging Temper has devoted to you, there is none that more prizes your Conversation, than

Your obliged Friend

and humble Servant,

N. Tate.

PRO-

PROLOGUE.

To what a wretched state are Poets born,
    Split on the Rocks of Envy or of Scorn?
Ev'n to the best the promis'd Wreath's deny'd,
And just Contempt attends on all beside.
This one wou'd think shou'd lessen the Temptation,
But they are Poëts by Predestination.
The fatal Bait undaunted they persue;
And claim the Laurel as their Labour's Due.
But where's the Use of Merit, or of Laws,
When Ingnorance and Malice judge the Cause?
'Twixt these, like Æsop's Husband, Poëts fare.
This pulls the black and that the silver Hair,
Till they have left the Poëm bald and bare.
Behold the dreadfull spot they ought to fear,
Whole Loads of Poët-bane are scattered here.
Where e'er it lights the sad Effects we find,
Tho' on the tender Hearts of Woman-kind.
The Men (whose Talents they themselves mistake,
Or misapply, for Contradiction sake.)
Spight of their Stars must needs be Critiques still,
Nay, tho' prohibited by th' Irish Bill.
Bless Age! when all our Actions seem design'd,
To prove a War 'twixt Reason and Mankind!
Here an affected Cocquet perks and prunes,
Tho' she's below the Level of Lampoons,
Venting her Fly-blown Charms till her Own Squire
Is grown too nice and dainty to Admire.
There a pretending Fop (a Man of Note
More for his thread-bare Jest than Gawdy Coat)
Sees every Coxcomb's Mirth, yet wants the Sense
To know 'tis caus'd by his Impertinence.
Nor rests the Mighty Grievance here alone;
For not content with Follys of our own,
We plunder the fair Sex of what we can,
Who seldom miss their dear Revenge on Man.
Their property of Falshood we invade,
Whilst they usurp our Mid-night Scouring Trade.

SONG

ther weakened his play. The result was a failure, and there are no recorded attempts at reviving it. *Cuckold's Haven* was an unhappy ending to Tate's brief career as a farceur.

After the failure of *Cuckold's Haven*, Tate returned to adapting serious drama, turning next to that most reliable source of popular stage material, the plays of Francis Beaumont and John Fletcher. Tate's choice, Fletcher's *The Island Princess* (circa 1621), had been adapted by an unknown playwright with some success in 1669. Tate certainly worked from this predecessor's text, and it is possible that he constructed his version entirely without recourse to Fletcher's original. But his dedication to Henry, lord Walgrave acknowledges only his "Obligation" to "*Beaumont* and *Fletcher*," along with his usual rationale for altering a play by a Jacobean master: "Those Defects in Manners, that were too palpable through the Work, must be imputed to the Age in which they Wrote; but still there are so many transcending Beauties in all their Writings, that I judg'd it safest to Rob their Treasure for a Tribute to your Lordship."

Fletcher's play is typical of his tragicomic romances, a love and honor spectacular, full of startling surprises and rhetorical tours de force. The play is made up of three nearly distinct, linear actions. The King of Tedore has been kidnapped by the wicked governor of Ternata. His sister Quisara, the island princess, promises to marry her brother's rescuer, expecting that hero to be her Portuguese lover Ruy Dias. She rejects with contempt the offer of the governor. Before Ruy Dias can screw up his courage, the newly arrived Portuguese Armusia surprises the governor and rescues the king. The middle of the play is structured around the love triangle between Quisara, Ruy Dias, and Armusia, resulting in the transfer of the princess's affections from Ruy Dias to Armusia. The play concludes with the moral reformation of Ruy Dias and the defeat of the governor, disguised as a "Moorish priest," in a climactic triumph of love, honor, and Christianity.

Tate's adaptation again follows his standard procedure. Fletcher's twenty-five-hundred lines are reduced to sixteen hundred, and his plot and language are simplified and purified. Tate claimed that "the design of my Authors in this Poem, was to show transcendent Vertue, Piety and Constancy successful." If so, it is a design that has escaped the attention of most subsequent critics, but it is a key to understanding the changes Tate systematically imposes upon Fletch-

er's text. Fletcher's Ruy Dias fails to attempt to rescue the king because of cowardice. He then urges his nephew Piniero to assassinate Armusia. Piniero, a witty, even caustic and worldly satirist, instead serves as the agent of his uncle's reform; he is given a large number of the best lines in the play. Tate not only eliminates the satire and most of the bawdy from the play but never calls his Ruidias's motives into question, thus reducing his Pymero to a very minor character. Similarly, in Fletcher's version, Quisara's conversion to Christianity seems to follow at least as much from her love for Armusia as from any newfound faith or belief. Tate moves the conversion from act 5 to act 4 and separates it from the resolution of the love plot, thereby insuring that the triumph of Christianity is not undermined by the triumph of love.

Fletcher's *The Island Princess* is a play full of spectacle. Tate maintained the theatrical spectacle, including such special effects as the fire Armusia sets in Ternata that so impressed Samuel Pepys in the 1669 version. But the fiery moral spectacle that is so much a part of the typical Fletcherian tragicomedy is purified beyond recognition, resulting in a play that failed to appeal to its or any subsequent audience. In rhyming couplets it would have had the makings of a popular heroic play ten or fifteen years earlier. With substantial musical settings, it served Peter Anthony Motteux considerably better in 1699. It was to be Tate's last new play to receive professional staging in London.

Although few are aware that Tate wrote it, the libretto for Purcell's *Dido and Aeneas* is, next to *King Lear*, his best-known work today. Purcell's short opera, an occasional work that was little known during his lifetime, has long since been recognized as one of his finest masterpieces. Recent Purcell scholarship credits Tate for his exemplary skills as a librettist; in this area alone he can be considered Dryden's superior, perhaps because his characteristic modesty allowed him to accept the secondary role that greater poets refuse. The verse for *Dido and Aeneas* consists of simple, short, flexible lines with an interesting and varied rhyme scheme. It is also free from tongue-twisting phrases so that it is as suitable for singing as for setting to music.

Purcell had provided music for two songs for Tate's *Richard the Second* (including the well-known "Retir'd from any mortal's sight") and another for *Cuckold's Haven*, so that the two would have been familiar with each other's work before collaborating on the opera commissioned by Josias Priest for performance by the girls at his boarding school in Chelsea. Priest was best known as a dancing master and choreographer who frequently worked for the theater. A number of constraints were no doubt imposed on Tate and Purcell by the circumstances of the school and its master. *Dido and Aeneas* contains seventeen dances in a work of just over an hour; almost all of the roles can be sung by women (two male singers were probably brought in for the original performance); the text calls for minimal scenery and spectacle; because Purcell's score comprises only five parts (two violins, viola, bass, and continuo), it may be played by a small number of musicians.

Most Purcell scholars now agree that the opera was presented in celebration of the coronation of William and Mary in April 1689. The prologue compliments the new monarchs in the tradition of the court masque. If the main action should also be read allegorically, Tate again miscalculated the effect of his application of a traditional story to the political situation around him. But it seems more likely that the Dido and Aeneas story was intended as a moral allegory for the schoolgirls who first performed it, since the most noteworthy departures from the Virgilian source that also provided the plot of *Brutus of Alba* include the separation of the lovers by the storm, the de-emphasis and virtual elimination of any reference to a sexual relationship between the principals, and the death of Dido from heartbreak rather than suicide. All of these changes point to a lesson for the girls about passion and chastity. Most of the other alterations from *Brutus of Alba* follow the pattern of Tate's adaptations of other writers' texts: a reduction in the number of characters, in the length of speeches, and in the total length. In this case, the result is far more successful than its source.

An entirely sung, Italian-style opera of the sort that was to have great success in London in the early eighteenth century was virtually unknown in England in 1689. Purcell was no doubt aware of at least some of the Continental developments in opera, but most of his theatrical writing is within the native traditions of the masque and of the spoken play with songs (sometimes called "English opera" and resembling twentieth-century musical comedy in its mixture of spoken dialogue and song). The most likely models for *Dido and Aeneas* are thus John Blow's masque *Venus and Adonis* (1685), Davenant's *Macbeth*, and

Thomas Shadwell's *The Lancashire Witches* (1681). Davenant's and Shadwell's plays are both in most ways fairly typical music dramas, but they capitalize on the musical possibilities (and spectacle) of witches; Tate's final major change from the Virgilian text is carrying over from *Brutus of Alba* the use of witches rather than deities as agents of the supernatural.

Aeneas, in Tate's version, is sent from Carthage by a false Mercury provided by the witches, a change that contributes to the overall shift in emphasis and sympathy from Aeneas to Dido. Aeneas is even weaker than Tate's Brutus or Dryden's Antony; his weakness is underscored in his transformation by Tate from a hero obedient to the divine will into the victim of a witch's vindictive mischief. The legendary honor and duty that Aeneas traditionally represents is thus called into question in a world in which the public virtues no longer command the respect accorded them in the heroic play. Instead, Tate's more Ovidian treatment renders Dido's love more heroic than Aeneas's sacrifice; it becomes a love too noble for this world.

Dido and Aeneas was not seen again in Purcell's lifetime and did not receive its first professional production until it was incorporated into Charles Gildon's adaptation of *Measure for Measure* (1700) as a masque for Angelo's entertainment. Gildon's version transformed an unusual opera into a typically English musical drama. It was revived on its own in the late eighteenth century but was not accepted into the standard concert repertoire until the twentieth.

Although Tate had more or less given up writing for the theater after 1687, his literary output did not slow down appreciably for another fifteen years. Most of his energy went into translations, editions, and compilations of classical authors, of the Psalms, and of a wide range of more contemporary writers. It is possible that he taught school between 1687 and 1692. At the death of Thomas Shadwell he was appointed poet laureate, probably through the patronage of the lord chamberlain, Charles Sackville, earl of Dorset. Tate was the first laureate to feel the need to produce official birthday poems and other occasional verse, and he did so dutifully—if without distinction—for twenty-three years. His laureate poems are noted for their loyalty and for their high moral tone.

Except for a brief response to an attack by Sir Richard Blackmore in the postscript to *Panacea* (1700) and support of the Kentish Petition in *The*

Kentish Worthies (1701), Tate avoided controversy in his late poetry. His support of Jeremy Collier in the form of an unpublished proposal to regulate the theaters calling for strict government supervision of what was to be performed and of the behavior of both actors and audience, as well as for the elimination of passages from old and new plays that offended the new moral standards, demonstrates Tate's commitment to the reformation of manners movement of the 1690s.

Sometime after 1702, that is, at least fifteen years after the failure of *The Island Princess*, Tate began work on his final adaptation, *Injur'd Love: Or, The Cruel Husband*, his version of John Webster's *The White Devil* (1612). Webster's play had not been very popular on the post-Restoration stage (*The Duchess of Malfi* [1614] was far more successful); Tate felt no need to acknowledge Webster (as he had Shakespeare, Jonson, and Beaumont and Fletcher) except for a passing reference in his epilogue to having "chose a Vessel that would bear the shock/of Censure; Yes, old Built, but Heart of Oak."

Tate's adaptation is largely an attempt to remold Webster's play into a post-Collier she-tragedy of the sort perfected by Nicholas Rowe. The most startling alteration is in the representation of Vittoria herself, largely transformed into a model of virtue besieged. When Flamineo first proposes that she meet with Brachiano, she turns to the audience to ensure all in aside, "Yes I will meet him, but for other Ends/Than their vile Purposes," setting the tone for this very different Vittoria. Tate's character is far more dignified and noble, with few apparent yearnings for political or sexual power. She does not cuckold her husband or urge his death. She is deferential to Brachiano's duchess Isabella, her mother, and, in fact, most of the other characters Occasionally Tate allows Webster's Vittoria to remain in his play, as when she and her servant Zanche stamp on the body of her apparently dead brother. This lapse in consistency of characterization only reminds an audience familiar with Webster's original of what has been lost in the process of purifying the white devil.

In keeping with early-eighteenth-century demands, Tate has cleaned up his source even more than he had in his earlier plays. Webster's exposure of the worldly Italian clergy is removed almost entirely, along with much of the sexual wordplay. The endemic moral corruption of the Rome of the Medicis and Orsinis is altered into a more neutral environment in which individuals are clearly good or evil. Poetic justice is violated but moral values are presented with clarity and certainty. There is little room for objection from the Colliers or the Blackmores among the critics.

Like Tate's earlier adaptations, *Injur'd Love* is considerably shorter and has fewer characters than its source. Motivation is clarified, as is Webster's complex, metaphysical language. Simplification and purification are, in short, again the watchwords for Tate. But since *The White Devil* is a play about a corrupt society, a world with no room for heroes or heroic values, the changes Tate imposes do more violence to his original than ever before. *Injur'd Love* extends the dangers of his approach to Jacobean plays to their logical extreme; the result is so unsatisfactory that the aging laureate was unable to find out if the play would succeed with an audience. The title page indicates that it was "Design'd to be Acted at the Theatre Royal," but it was not. As the play has found few if any subsequent defenders, it is probable that it has never been staged.

Tate's output finally caught up with his contemporary reputation for slowness during Queen Anne's reign, when he averaged about one official poem per year, along with the occasional translation. His last major endeavor was editing the periodical *The Monitor* with "M. Smith." Tate contributed a number of poems on religious and moral subjects to this short-lived poetry journal "for the Promoting of Religion and Virtue." He was plagued with financial worries and poor health in his last years and died in the Mint, the part of London in which debtors were legally safe from arrest, on 30 July 1715.

Nahum Tate never enjoyed a high reputation as a writer during his lifetime. Since his best work, except for the translation of the Psalms, was done before he was awarded the laureateship, he became a highly visible symbol of literary mediocrity for the generation of Jonathan Swift and Alexander Pope, and his *Lear* insured that his reputation declined as bardolatry grew. A modest man with modest talents, it is unlikely that his reputation will ever improve considerably. But he was a competent, workmanlike writer and translator who deserves an honorable place in literary history as a minor writer who made a few important contributions to the English theater.

References:

Doris Adler, "The Half-Life of Tate in *King Lear*," *Kenyon Review*, 7 (Summer 1985): 52-56;

James Black, "An Augustan Stage-History: Nahum Tate's *King Lear*," *Restoration and 18th Century Theatre Research*, 6 (May 1967): 36-54;

Black, "The Influence of Hobbes on Nahum Tate's *King Lear*," *Studies in English Literature*, 7 (Summer 1967): 377-385;

J. S. Bratton, Introduction to *King Lear*, by William Shakespeare, edited by Bratton, Plays in Performance (Bristol: Bristol Classical Press, 1987);

Nicholas Brooke, "The Ending of *King Lear*," in *Shakespeare 1564-1964: A Collection of Modern Essays by Various Hands*, edited by Edward A. Bloom (Providence: Brown University Press, 1964), pp. 71-87;

John Buttrey, "Dating Purcell's 'Dido and Aeneas,' " *Proceedings of the Royal Music Association*, 94 (1967-1968): 51-62;

J. Douglas Canfield, "Royalism's Last Dramatic Stand: English Political Tragedy, 1679-89," *Studies in Philology*, 82 (Spring 1985): 234-263;

Samuel A. Golden, "An Early Defense of Farce," in *Studies in Honor of John Wilcox*, edited by A. Dayle Wallace and Woodburn O. Ross (Detroit: Wayne State University Press, 1958), pp. 61-70;

Lawrence D. Green, " 'Where's My Fool?'—Some Consequences of the Omission of the Fool in Tate's *Lear*," *Studies in English Literature*, 12 (Spring 1972): 259-274;

Antony Hammond, " 'Rather a Heap of Rubbish Then a Structure': The Principles of Restoration Dramatic Adaptation Revisited," in *The Stage in the 18th Century*, edited by J. D. Browning (New York & London: Garland, 1981), pp. 113-148;

Alfred Harbage, "The Fierce Dispute," in his *Conceptions of Shakespeare* (Cambridge, Mass.: Harvard University Press/London: Oxford University Press, 1966), pp. 77-98;

Ellen T. Harris, *Henry Purcell's "Dido and Aeneas"* (Oxford: Clarendon Press, 1987);

Philip Hobsbaum, " 'King Lear' in the Eighteenth Century," *Modern Language Review*, 68 (July 1973): 494-506;

Geoffrey Hodson, "The Nahum Tate 'Lear' at Richmond," *Drama*, no. 81 (Summer 1966): 36-39;

A. K. Holland, *Henry Purcell: The English Musical Tradition* (London: G. Bell, 1932);

Norman N. Holland, "How Can Dr. Johnson's Remarks on Cordelia's Death Add to My Own Response?," in *Psychoanalysis and the Question of the Text*, edited by Geoffrey H. Hartman (Baltimore: Johns Hopkins University Press, 1978), pp. 18-44;

Imogen Holst, "Purcell's Librettist, Nahum Tate," in *Henry Purcell 1659-1695: Essays on His Music* (London: Oxford University Press, 1959), pp. 35-41;

Lucyle Hooke, "Shakespeare Improv'd, or A Case for the Affirmative," *Shakespeare Quarterly*, 4 (July 1953): 289-299;

Frank Kermode, "Survival of the Classic," in his *Shakespeare, Spenser, Donne: Renaissance Essays* (London: Routledge & Kegan Paul, 1971), pp. 164-180;

Maynard Mack, *King Lear in Our Time* (Berkeley: University of California Press, 1965; London: Methuen, 1966);

Wilfrid Mellers, "The Tragic Heroine and the Un-Hero; Henry Purcell: *Dido and Aeneas*," in his *Harmonious Meeting: A Study of the Relationship between English Music, Poetry and Theatre, c. 1600-1900* (London: Dobson, 1965), pp. 203-214;

W. Moelwyn Merchant, "Shakespeare 'Made Fit,' " in *Restoration Theatre*, edited by John Russell Brown and Bernard Harris, Stratford-upon-Avon Studies, 6 (London: Arnold, 1965), pp. 195-219;

Robert Etheridge Moore, *Henry Purcell & the Restoration Theatre* (Cambridge, Mass.: Harvard University Press/London: Heinemann, 1961);

Kenneth Muir, "Three Shakespeare Adaptations," *Proceedings of the Leeds Philosophical and Literary Society*, 8 (November 1957): 233-240;

Robert Müller, "Nahum Tate's 'Richard II' and Censorship during the Exclusion Bill Crisis in England," *Poetic Drama and Poetic Theory*, Salzburg Studies in English Literature, 26 (Salzburg: Institut für Englische Sprache und Literatur, Universität Salzburg, 1975), pp. 40-51;

Dorothy E. Nameri, *Three Versions of the Story of King Lear Studied in Relation to One Another*, Salzburg Studies in English Literature, 50 and 51 (Salzburg: Institut für Englische Sprache und Literatur, Universität Salzburg, 1976);

George C. D. Odell, *Shakespeare from Betterton to Irving*, 2 volumes (New York: Scribners, 1920; London: Constable, 1921);

Harry William Pedicord, "Shakespeare, Tate, and Garrick: New Light on Alterations of *King Lear*," *Theatre Notebook*, 36, no. 1 (1982): 14-21;

Curtis Alexander Price, *Henry Purcell and the London Stage* (Cambridge: Cambridge University Press, 1984);

Moody E. Prior, *The Language of Tragedy* (New York: Columbia University Press, 1947);

Mark A. Radice, "Tate's Libretto for *Dido and Aeneas*: A Revaluation," *Bach*, 7 (January 1976): 20-26;

David Rostron, "John Philip Kemble's 'King Lear' of 1795," in *Essays on the Eighteenth-Century Stage*, edited by Kenneth Richards and Peter Thomson (London: Methuen, 1972), pp. 149-170;

Eric Rothstein, *Restoration Tragedy: Form and the Process of Change* (Madison, Milwaukee & London: University of Wisconsin Press, 1967);

Max F. Schulz, "*King Lear*: A Box-Office Maverick among Shakespearean Tragedies on the London Stage 1700-1 to 1749-50," *Tulane Studies in English*, 7 (1957): 83-90;

H. F. Scott-Thomas, "Nahum Tate and the Seventeenth Century," *ELH*, 1 (December 1934): 250-275;

A. H. Scouten, "An Italian Source for Nahum Tate's Defence of Farce," *Italica*, 27 (September 1950): 238-240;

Peter L. Sharkey, "Performing Nahum Tate's *King Lear*: Coming Hither by Going Hence," *Quarterly Journal of Speech*, 54 (December 1968): 398-403;

Christopher Spencer, *Nahum Tate* (New York: Twayne, 1972);

Spencer, "A Word for Tate's *King Lear*," *Studies in English Literature*, 3 (Spring 1963): 241-251;

Hazelton Spencer, "Tate and *The White Devil*," *ELH*, 1 (December 1934): 235-249;

Spencer, "Tate's Adaptations," in his *Shakespeare Improved: The Restoration Versions in Quarto and on the Stage* (Cambridge, Mass.: Harvard University Press, 1927), pp. 241-273;

Arthur Colby Sprague, "Nahum Tate, *The Island Princess*," in his *Beaumont and Fletcher on the Restoration Stage* (Cambridge, Mass.: Harvard University Press, 1926), pp. 139-146;

George Winchester Stone, "Garrick's Production of *King Lear*: A Study in the Temper of the Eighteenth-Century Mind," *Studies in Philology*, 45 (January 1948): 89-103;

J. A. Westrup, *Purcell*, revised by Nigel Fortune (London: Dent, 1980);

Erick Walter White, "New Light on *Dido and Aeneas*," in *Henry Purcell 1659-1695: Essays on His Music*, edited by Imogen Holst (London: Oxford University Press, 1959), pp. 14-34;

Matthew H. Wikander, "The Spitted Infant: Scenic Emblem and Exclusionist Politics in Restoration Adaptations of Shakespeare," *Shakespeare Quarterly*, 37 (Autumn 1986): 340-358;

T. D. Duncan Williams, "Mr. Nahum Tate's *King Lear*," *Studia Neophilologica*, 38 (November 1966): 290-300.

Papers:
Tate's unpublished "Proposall for Regulating of the Stage & Stage-Plays" is in the Lambeth Palace Library. "The Constant Gallant or Truth found out at Last. A Comedy Being a Loose Translation of Terence's Andr[ia] Adapted to the humour of the English Stage a[s] farr as is Consistent with keeping the Origin[al] in View. Revised and Corrected by Nahum Tate Esq. late Poet Laureate to his Majesty," an unpublished manuscript, circa 1765, is in the Folger Shakespeare Libary.

Sir John Vanbrugh

(January 1664-26 March 1726)

Eric Rothstein
University of Wisconsin-Madison

PLAY PRODUCTIONS: *The Relapse,* London, Theatre Royal in Drury Lane, 21 November 1696;

Aesop, part 1, adapted from Edmé Boursault's *Les Fables d'Esope,* London, Theatre Royal in Drury Lane, December 1696; part 2, London, Theatre Royal in Drury Lane, March 1697;

The Provok'd Wife, London, Lincoln's Inn Fields, April 1697;

The Country House, adapted from Florent Carton Dancourt's *La Maison de campagne,* London, Theatre Royal in Drury Lane, January 1698;

The Pilgrim, adapted from John Fletcher's *The Pilgrim,* London, Theatre Royal in Drury Lane, 29 April 1700(?);

The False Friend, adapted from Alain-René Lesage's *Le Traître puni,* London, Theatre Royal in Drury Lane, February 1702;

Squire Trelooby, adapted from Molière's *Monsieur de Pourceaugnac,* by Vanbrugh, William Congreve, and William Walsh, London, Lincoln's Inn Fields, 30 March 1704;

The Confederacy, adapted from Dancourt's *Les Bourgeoises à la mode,* London, Queen's Theatre, 30 October 1705;

The Mistake, adapted from Molière's *Le Dépit amoureux,* London, Queen's Theatre, 27 December 1705;

The Cuckold in Conceit, adapted from Molière's *Sganarelle, ou le cocu imaginaire,* London, Queen's Theatre, 22 March 1707;

The Provok'd Husband, by Vanbrugh and Colley Cibber, London, Theatre Royal in Drury Lane, 10 January 1728.

BOOKS: *Aesop. A comedy. As it is acted at the Theatre-Royal in Drury-Lane,* part 1 (London: Printed for Thomas Bennet, 1697); parts 1 and 2 (London: Printed for Thomas Bennet, 1697);

The Provok'd Wife: A Comedy, As it is acted at the New Theatre, in Little Lincolns-Inn-Fields (London: Printed by J. O. for Richard Wellington & Samuel Briscoe, 1697);

The Relapse; or, Virtue in Danger: Being the sequel of The Fool in Fashion. A Comedy. Acted at the Theatre-Royal in Drury-Lane (London: Printed for Samuel Briscoe, 1697);

A Short Vindication of "The Relapse" and "The Provok'd Wife," from Immorality and Profaneness by the Author (London: Printed for Herbert Walwyn, 1698);

The Pilgrim, A Comedy: As It Is acted at the Theatre-Royal, in Drury-Lane Written Originally by Mr. Fletcher, and now very much Alter'd, with several Additions (London: Printed for Benjamin Tooke, 1700);

The False Friend, a comedy. As it is acted at the Theatre-Royal in Drury-Lane (London: Printed for Jacob Tonson, 1702);

The Confederacy. A comedy. As It Is Acted at the Queen's Theatre in the Hay-Market. By Her Majesty's Sworn Servants. [By the author of The Relapse.] (London: Jacob Tonson, 1705); modern edition, *A Critical Edition of Sir John Vanbrugh's "The Confederacy,"* edited by Thomas E. Lowderbaugh (New York: Garland, 1987);

The Mistake. A comedy. As It Is Acted at the Queen's Theatre in the Hay-Market. By Her Majesty's Sworn Servants [By the Author of The Provok'd Wife] (London: Jacob Tonson, 1706);

The Country House. A Farce. As Acted at Both Theatres with Great Applause (London: Printed for W. Meares & Jonas Browne, 1715);

The Provok'd Husband; or, a Journey to London. A comedy, as It Is Acted at the Theatre-Royal, by His Majesty's Servants, by Vanbrugh and Colley Cibber (London: Printed for J. Watts, 1728).

Collections: *The Plays of Sir John Vanbrugh,* 2 volumes (London: Printed by J. D. for Jacob Tonson and M. Wellington, 1719);

The Complete Works of Sir John Vanbrugh, 4 volumes, edited by Bonamy Dobrée and Geoffrey Webb (London: Nonesuch, 1927-1928).

Sir John Vanbrugh (engraving based on a portrait by Sir Godfrey Kneller)

With two brilliant stage successes in the same season, 1696-1697, John Vanbrugh won sudden fame in a most challenging arena: in a dramatic repertory that featured the works of John Dryden, George Etherege, William Wycherley, Thomas Otway, and William Congreve. As the architectural historian John Summerson wrote of him, "If he was deep, the depths were flood-lit by a wit which had few equals in his time and has had few since." For more than a decade Vanbrugh wrote for, built, and managed London theaters. At about the same time, he began to win equal fame as an architect, working with Sir Christopher Wren and Nicholas Hawksmoor. No other figure in British cultural history has won such acclaim in his or her own time as litterateur and artist; few have maintained their early fame, whatever it was, in both endeavors. But Vanbrugh's two original plays, *The Provok'd Wife* and *The Relapse,* still hold the stage along with those of his somewhat younger contemporaries Congreve and George Farquhar in revivals of "Restoration comedy," while the best-known of his great buildings, Blenheim Palace and Castle Howard, remain among the principal glories of a sublime, public style in British architecture.

John Vanbrugh–he was knighted in 1714–was the London-born eldest son of Elizabeth Barker Vanbrugh, who had close aristocratic connections, and Giles Vanbrugh, the son of a Flemish immigrant who fled religious persecution. (From spellings of the name it would seem that the guttural Flemish pronunciation of the *-gh* was retained in simplified form, as a hard *g* or *k;* the last syllable was never *broo* or *bruh*.) Giles Vanbrugh became a wealthy sugar refiner, following a luxury trade that flourished after the English took over Jamaica under Oliver Cromwell, and so, when John was a small child, the family moved to Chester, then an important harbor town to which sugar was shipped from the American colonies. There he presumably attended the King's School, and he may have gone to France for architectural training in 1683. By 1685 he was back in Chester, for a letter of his, dated December 1685 and written from there, asks his distant kinsman the earl of Huntingdon for some kind of place; his reward was a military commission that he soon resigned. Vanbrugh must have soon returned to France, for we know that he spent at least the period from late 1688 to late 1692 in French prisons. His next extant letter (1692), written from the Bastille, related his long arrest for voicing strong sympathies for the English revolution then in progress. No doubt he was echoing his family's zealously Protestant sentiments. What he said may have been rendered more suspicious if he had had architectural training and was seen prowling about buildings, scanning ramparts, and estimating the thickness of walls. After nearly four years of imprisonment in Calais, Vincennes, and Paris, John Vanbrugh was paroled and returned to England. Tradition has it that he brought his first literary efforts in his baggage. He found himself his now-deceased father's chief heir among the thirteen surviving children (of nineteen siblings born), and, as a man of some means, he began to serve the government in both civil and military roles. It was while a captain of marines, as of the very end of 1695, that he made his first, victorious foray into the theater, in 1696.

According to the actor and dramatist Colley Cibber, Vanbrugh had contracted some obligation to a slight acquaintance of his, the theatrical proprietor and manager Sir Thomas Skipwith of the Theatre Royal in Drury Lane. At this time, Skipwith and his partner, Christopher Rich, found themselves in dire straits because in the spring of 1695 sixteen of their most-experienced and best-known actors, led by the great Thomas Betterton, had angrily defected from their company to begin another, in a small Lincoln's Inn Fields theater. As a result, wrote the anonymous author of *A Comparison between the Two Stages* (1702), " 'twas almost impossible, in *Drury-Lane,* to muster up a sufficient number to take in all

the Parts of any Play; and of them so few were tolerable, that a Play must of necessity be damn'd that had not extraordinary favour from the Audience." The "very despicable Condition" into which "the *Theatre-Royal* was then sunk" may have prompted Vanbrugh to help Skipwith by contributing a sequel to a newly popular play, *Love's Last Shift* (first produced in January 1696), written by the fledgling Colley Cibber and featuring his nonpareil performance as a fop. Together with Thomas Southerne's *Oroonoko* (first produced in November 1695), Cibber's play had barely buoyed the Drury Lane company through its first season of competition with its proficient, glamorous rivals. By ten weeks or so into the next season, 1696-1697, Skipwith and Rich's callow band was on the verge of bankruptcy: "unless a new play [that] comes out on Saturday revives their reputation, they must break," wrote an observer on Thursday, 19 November. "The 'new play' was Vanbrugh's *The Relapse,* and its triumph," so Judith Milhous notes, "may indeed have saved the company."

In the wake of this triumph, Drury Lane's last shift, Vanbrugh's dramatic talents were in demand. He had produced *The Relapse* in under three months' time; now, with equal speed, he was adapting a French comedy, Edme Boursault's *Les Fables d'Esope* (1690), that had appeared during his imprisonment in the Bastille, so that he could bring his *Aesop* to Drury Lane in December, January at the latest, of the same season. No good figures exist for the number of productions *Aesop* and *The Relapse* enjoyed in the mid-to-late 1690s, but the author of *A Comparison between the Two Stages* singles them out with *Oroonoko* as "Masterpieces" that "subsisted *Drury-lane* House, the first two or three Years." Having sauced the goose, Vanbrugh next sauced the gander. One of the three plays that *A Comparison between the Two Stages* mentions as having "kept up" the *other* company "at the same time" was still another of Vanbrugh's comedies, *The Provok'd Wife,* first performed at Lincoln's Inn Fields in April 1697. It had gone to the competition rather than to Skipwith and Rich because of noble intervention. After the earl of Halifax had heard scenes read from a draft of this play, he prevailed on Vanbrugh to revise it for Betterton's troupe, whom the earl greatly admired. Before it was performed, Vanbrugh provocatively added to *Aesop,* a brief part 2 in March 1697, a scene satirizing the renegades from Drury Lane. Perhaps he did so to recompense Skipwith and Rich for the

Colley Cibber as Lord Foppington in the first production of The Relapse, *Vanbrugh's sequel to Cibber's* Love's Last Shift

loss of his new play, and perhaps to tweak the noses of the company to whom he was obliged to present it. Whatever his motives and their displeasure, Betterton's players must have held their peace when dealing with the author of *The Provok'd Wife*, for this second and last of Vanbrugh's original comedies, perhaps partly written in the Bastille, was once again immediately successful. Like *The Relapse*, it stayed in the active repertory for the next seventy-five years–*Aesop* had a somewhat shorter, poorer life–and maintained a popularity more or less equal to the comedies of Vanbrugh's friend and slight junior, Congreve.

Of Vanbrugh's two roughly contemporaneous original plays, *The Provok'd Wife* has a claim to be not only the earliest, "writ many years ago, and when I was very young," according to Vanbrugh in 1698, but also the most original and the best. Like many comedies in the 1680s and 1690s, it starts with a bad marriage, here between the surly, drunken Sir John Brute, sick of

a spouse to whom he was drawn by lust, and his witty, pretty, and lively wife, who has been trying to make the best of what was for her a mercenary marriage. The more attractive men are two gallants, Lady Brute's long-beseeching but unrequited suitor Constant and Heartfree, who during the play becomes suitor and at last fiancé of her niece Bellinda. To fill out the symmetrical pattern, the disaffected, coarse Sir John is balanced by Lady Fancyfull, a vain, Frenchified flirt interested in Heartfree.

As *The Provok'd Wife* resembles other plays of its period in the formal organization of its persons, so it adapts the three-part structure that Restoration comedy inherited from John Fletcher. Although Vanbrugh uses it more diffusely than some of his predecessors, one can break the action into an opening section that in some sense frees each character; a middle section that contrasts the freedom of the egoists, Sir John and Lady Fancyfull, with others' new relationships;

David Garrick as Sir John Brute, drunk and dressed in his wife's clothing, being arrested by the Watchman (far right), played by Watkins, in a 1763 production of The Provok'd Wife. *The other actors depicted in this engraving based on a painting by Johann Zoffany are Henry Vaughan, Hullet, Thomas Clough, William Parsons, and Thomas Phillips.*

and a final section of discovery and resolution. In the first two acts, then, Sir John and Lady Fancyfull create freedom by alienating those who might be close to them, Sir John through his maltreatment of Lady Brute and Lady Fancyfull by a show of affectation sufficient to confirm the misogyny of Heartfree. By the middle of the play new relationships have moved into focus. Lady Brute has accepted Constant, and Heartfree learns to love Bellinda; Sir John, infuriated by his wife's (sometimes mischievous) intentions, goes off to drink, and Lady Fancyfull, infuriated by Heartfree's neglect, goes off to "study revenge" (III.i). Both the egoists then assert their prior rights. Lady Fancyfull's revenge, after she finds the lovers trysting in the park in act 4, is to claim to be Heartfree's wife; her claim parallels that of Sir John, who says he is Lady Brute's husband—as he is in law only—when he finds the lovers trysting in his house in act 5. In the resolution both egoists are shown up. Sir John, appearing bloody and violent from his street rioting while drunk, is forced to accept an ongoing affair (or so he believes; the play is discreet about the facts) to avoid having to challenge Constant. Similarly the supposedly irresistible Lady Fancyfull must accept the equivalent for her,

Heartfree's marriage to Bellinda, when her perjury—her pretense to be a desired wife and mother—is made clear.

What is distinctive structurally about Vanbrugh's play is the ease and fluidity with which he develops this apparently schematic story, and the intricacy with which he weaves the characters together. The two plots have more interconnection than those of earlier double-plot plays, an effect intensified by his use of analogy and contrast to develop his principals. Alike in their distaste for each other after marrying for reasons other than love, the sodden husband carouses, and the clever wife teeters on cuckolding him; alike in their amorous bachelorhood, one suitor, Constant, admires women and has for two years courted adultery, while the other, Heartfree, a professed misogynist, suddenly falls for an available virgin. One woman who cares for Heartfree, Bellinda, is ingenuous and open; the other, Lady Fancyfull, brims over with affectation. The two mocked egoists whom the love action will exclude, Sir John and Lady Fancyfull, display lust (he as a whoremonger, she as a coquette) in their own modes, he recklessly uncouth and she calculatingly refined. So closely are these character pairings developed that every principal stands in paired relationship with every other, and only one of these pairings–Sir John and Bellinda–is dramatically uninteresting. Otherwise, Sir John deals with his wife, his would-be cuckolder, his fellow misogynist, and his fellow egoist. Lady Brute similarly deals with her husband, a niece (Bellinda) to whom she is an example, a lover (Constant), a fellow satirist (Heartfree), and a deceitful coquette (Fancyfull) to whom she stands in contrast but also begins to resemble as she nears cuckolding Sir John. Much of the strength and complexity of the play comes from these interlockings, reinforced not only by the often reflective, reflexive dialogue but also by the action, where Vanbrugh designed the encounters to throw analogous and contrasting characters together and to turn on impostures and substitutions in which one character takes the place of another.

Most visible to Vanbrugh's audience was a level of wit, of energy, and of dexterity in developing a scene which few new London comedies since the 1670s had provided. "His Wit, and Humour, was so little laboured, that his most entertaining Scenes seem'd to be no more, than his common Conversation committed to Paper," wrote an admiring Colley Cibber. From the combination of this seeming naturalness and the use of analogy to illustrate personality, Vanbrugh achieved brilliant characterization: a succession of star performers clung happily to these roles through the eighteenth century. He could also manage the illusion of emotional complexity, most notably in Sir John and Lady Brute, complementing his direct development of their characters with frank, often thoughtful soliloquies, and, still more, with a sense of realism which encourages one to invest them with a fuller range of emotion than had been common in Restoration plays. Part of Vanbrugh's realism grows from his "natural" dialogue and part from an uncynical but illusionless tone so typically worldly that the ingenue Bellinda is sniping gently at husbands as she trundles off to the altar at the end of the play.

Most of the same virtues mark Vanbrugh's second and last completed original comedy, *The Relapse,* his sequel to Cibber's *Love's Last Shift.* Cibber had ended his play with a straying and impoverished husband, Loveless, reclaimed by the loyalty and sexiness of his long-estranged wife, Amanda, with whom his friend Young Worthy contrives that he unknowingly spend what turns out to be an ecstatic night. *The Relapse* presents the same couple when Loveless has been plumped out by comfort and marital bliss, and so is ready to fall for more show of sex appeal and interest in him, this time from Amanda's widowed cousin, Berinthia. Berinthia's old lover, Worthy, again a reclaimed character from Cibber's play, eggs her on to open conquest so that he can seduce the outraged Amanda, but although Amanda is indeed outraged when she witnesses her husband's relapse, her virtue keeps her as chaste in Vanbrugh's play as she had been in Cibber's. Some of this plot, especially the scene where the aroused Loveless carries Berinthia over the threshold of her bedroom, while she utters "Help, help, I'm Ravish'd, ruin'd, undone" very softly (IV.iii), is extremely clever, but still funnier is the other plot, for which Vanbrugh created the greatest fop in British drama, Lord Foppington. Foppington flounces around *Love's Last Shift* as Sir Novelty Fashion; in the interval between plays he has acquired a title and a penurious brother, Tom, to whom he denies any help. Most of the action takes place in the country, where Tom, now posing as his brother, not only courts and weds an adolescent bumpkin heiress, Hoyden Clumsey, but also manages to discredit the real Lord Foppington as an imposter and have him set, bound, in the dog kennels. Though Foppington, properly identified at last, marries Hoyden too, her lust makes her avow her previous marriage to Tom, obviously a marriage that has as much chance of success as that of Amanda and Loveless.

The Relapse, so the prologue claims, was "Got, Conceiv'd, and Born in six Weeks space," and, as was recognized at the time, it is a much more carelessly put together play than either *Love's Last Shift* or *The Provok'd Wife.* This affects one's pleasure more now than when an audience who knew Cibber's comedy well could view *The Relapse* as an exercise in extravagant disintegration– in form as well as content–of a familiar arrangement that had seemed closed and stable. Very likely Vanbrugh was doing the best with what he had: Betterton's troupe, which was to perform *The Provok'd Wife,* had more polish than the company at Drury Lane, except in skilled buffoons; each of the two plays makes superb use of its human resources. Nevertheless, the characters of *The Relapse* also suffer from a loss of depth because their interrelations are less finely worked out than in *The Provok'd Wife,* and the extreme vividness of some of them–chiefly Foppington, Hoyden and her father Sir Tunbelly Clumsey, and

Sir John Vanbrugh

Berinthia–does not quite compensate for this shallowness. Nor is *The Relapse,* with its reliance on farcical action and allusion to Cibber, anywhere nearly so thoughtful as *The Provok'd Wife,* although it sounds some of the same themes, such as the transitoriness of human emotion, the closure that leaves the main issues unresolved, the need for worldly knowledge, and the liberating force of alienation–here made visible in Loveless's betrayal of Amanda and Foppington's rejection of his brother, Tom. In *The Relapse* this theme is compounded still more than in *The Provok'd Wife,* since the marriage between Hoyden and Tom so plainly represents in its consummation the forthcoming alienation between her

and him, an alienation more coarse and candid than that in the marriage one sees dissolving.

A final word needs to be said about Vanbrugh's treatment of marriage. The philosopher Edmund Leites has remarked that "during the last forty years of the seventeenth century, English playwrights engaged in what amounted to a systematic analysis–hardly superseded–of marriages devoted to excitement or enjoyment"–the wildly erotic or the calmly joyful. In Vanbrugh, the conflict of these pleasurable ideals leads to skepticism that either can last long; and yet the alternative kind of marriage, being wedded to oneself like Foppington, Lady Fancyfull, or Sir John Brute (who has outlived the erotic marriage and cannot enter a joyful one), does not work at all. In most of the playwrights older than Vanbrugh, the ideal of a marriage both solid and sexy remains free from scrutiny; in most of those younger than he, including his friends Congreve and Cibber, joy wins over eros. He perhaps faces the alternative Leites mentions more clearly than any major dramatist of the late-seventeenth and eighteenth centuries, and the marked open-endedness of his plays comes from this conflict and the temperament that led him to explore it when, in the 1690s, he could.

One rapid result of Vanbrugh's new stature was that he found himself the object of moral attack, in particular by Jeremy Collier. A high Anglican, nonjuring clergyman—one who clung to the ousted James II's right to the throne despite the revolution of 1688—Collier took up cudgels against the theater, such as had usually been wielded by his theological foes, the "Puritans." In his first and best-known work, *A Short View of the Prophaneness and Immorality of the English Stage* (1698), published a year after the opening of *The Provok'd Wife* and a year and a half after that of *The Relapse,* Collier devoted a good bit of malign attention to Vanbrugh, dwelling at length on *The Relapse.* He was not the first to do so. "I am . . . insensible of those two shining Graces in the Play (which some part of the Town is pleas'd to Compliment me with)–Blasphemy and Bawdy," Vanbrugh had written in the preface to *The Relapse,* and there had sneered at those men "with flat plod Shooes, a little Band, greasy Hair, and a dirty Face" who "make Debauches in Piety, as Sinners do in Wine." By way of reply, therefore, Collier not only took up his continuing topic, "vicious" morality, by condemning the reward of profligacy and opportunism in *The Relapse,* he also tried to evade the social stigma of being among the greasy-haired, dirty-faced set. Much more heavily here than in his prolonged attacks on two other plays, Dryden's *Amphitryon* (1690) and Thomas Durfey's *The Comical History of Don Quixote* (1694), he demonstrates his gentlemanly skills of criticism upon the construction of Vanbrugh's comedy and its alleged improbabilities, so as to show it "dull," "monstrous and chimerical," low and bungled, "a Heap of Irregularities" that contradict Nature. He ends with a triumphant burst of arcane, secular learning, "The *Relapser* would do well to transport his Muse to *Samourgan* [an Academy in Lithuania for the Education of Bears]. There it is likely he might find Leisure to lick his *Abortive Brat* into

Shape; and meet with proper Business for his Temper, and Encouragement for his Talent."

Like the irritated Congreve, whom Collier had also attacked, in 1698 Vanbrugh quickly responded. So did numbers of others, pro and con, while Collier's own work went into three more editions in 1698 and 1699, and his *A Defence of the Short View of the Profaneness and Immorality of the English Stage* (1699), with an answer to Vanbrugh's answer, also appeared. The enemies of the stage took heart: on 10 May, with the combined stimulus of Collier's onslaught and at least one physical altercation in the theater, the diarist Narcissus Luttrell recorded that "the justice of Middlesex have presented the playhouses to be nurseries of debauchery and blasphemy," and added two days later that Congreve, Durfey, and two booksellers were presented on the same grounds. Spies entered the playhouses to note down whatever wicked words the actors might speak and to have them indicted on this evidence. One year after the publication of *A Short View,* Congreve's *The Double Dealer* was presented in a cleaned-up form, following a royal order for the reformation of the stage. The public stir that encouraged these and other actions was to some extent caused by and to some extent corollary to the offensive that Collier launched. One needs to weigh carefully the playwrights' responses, then, writing as they did to defend both their threatened livelihoods and their reputations as all-conquering wits and gentlemen. This is certainly true of Vanbrugh's *A Short Vindication of "The Relapse" and "The Provok'd Wife," from Immorality and Prophaneness* (1698).

"What I have done," Vanbrugh smoothly protested, "is in general a Discouragement to Vice and Folly; I am sure I intended it, and I hope I have performed it." Most of his arguments, apart from the witty abuse that maintains his superiority to his foe, blame Collier for either taking words and expressions out of context or assuming that he, Vanbrugh, admires characters whom in fact he is holding up to scorn. "The Business of Comedy" is in fact satiric or counter-exemplary, "to shew People what they shou'd do, by representing them on the Stage, doing what they shou'd not. . . . The Stage is a Glass for the World to view itself in; People ought then to see themselves as they are; if it makes their Faces too Fair, they won't know they are Dirty, and by consequence will neglect to wash 'em." That comedy teaches by bad examples is old doctrine; and of course Vanbrugh would evoke no new doctrine,

Sir John Vanbrugh

since his strategy demands his assimilating his plays to those long known and accepted and representing the authority-citing Collier as, in fact, the upstart. The cleverest twist of Vanbrugh's argument comes in its reliance on the audience to recognize a dirty face without the playwright's or his *raisonneur*'s brandishing a soapy sponge. If Collier thinks that the rakes are in favor with their creator, so the implied and even explicit argument goes, he convicts himself of failing to put the action in a proper moral perspective. On the other hand, one might retort, if this indictment holds for Collier, an audience inclined to vice might also be blind to the deep ethical concerns that Vanbrugh assures that he had: to any eyes, Lord Foppington and Sir John Brute obviously do

what they should not, but only for certain members of the audience is this true of Young Fashion and Constant, the very members of the audience who do not need "reformation" in the first place. Only in a homogeneous society would the opposite be true, and as the clamor for ethical writing in the 1690s and much of the eighteenth century suggests, society was becoming less homogeneous, less willing to ground ethics in divine will or even social ukase, less able to contain ways of balancing between conflicting interests and values. Under these circumstances, as Collier insisted in rebuttal to Vanbrugh's response, "to shew a *Religious Person* ridiculous; to give Figure and Success to an ill Character, and make Lewdness modish and entertaining, is the way to mismark the Nature of Good and Evil, and confound the Understandings of the Audience." One may dismiss Collier as a shrill, dogged, and literal-minded vulgarian, as Vanbrugh tried to do, and dismiss Collier's concerns, as Vanbrugh did not dare do; but it is hard to help feeling that he would have liked to, for the answer he provided shows his ingenuity rather than his interest in morality onstage.

The only colliers whose labors Vanbrugh approved of in the years 1698-1699 and later were those who mined the fuel to keep buildings warm. Vanbrugh launched into his new career as an architect with the same suddenness that had marked his quite fresh *succès fou* as a playwright. We do not know how much architectural training he had had, but his contemporary Jonathan Swift suggested that it came from watching a small girl build a house of cards and boys "raking up mud to build a wall": "Van's genius, without thought or lecture, / Is hugely turn'd to architecture." If, as Swift might not have believed, originality is a mark of genius, the less training Vanbrugh had, the greater his triumph must be, for–except when their weighty baroque style has been too much out of fashion for them to be appreciated–his buildings have been lavishly admired since he first put them up. His first project, Castle Howard in Yorkshire, was begun for the earl of Carlisle during 1699, and, with the help of Sir Christopher Wren's brilliant, highly professional assistant Nicholas Hawksmoor, actual operations began in the spring of 1701. Through Carlisle, who briefly served as first lord of the Treasury, Vanbrugh was appointed comptroller of the Office of Works (1702) under the septuagenarian Wren and thus entered on a career as a chief architect for Queen Anne. He worked on many royal projects and, in addition, became sought after to design magnificent country houses for the magnates of England, including the conquering duke of Marlborough's Blenheim Palace.

Vanbrugh's architectural work was to dominate the rest of his life, far outweighing his contributions to the stage. Two points should be made about it. The first is that Vanbrugh's edifices–blocks of buildings, castles, palaces–are designed for theatrical, riveting effects, not for delicacy but for striking placements and interruptions: "Vanbrugh started with the two main elements of formal planning, axial vistas and symmetrical hierarchies, and dramatized them," as one architectural historian, Mark Girouard, says; the axial vis-

tas are "exquisitely interlocked . . . and vibrant with incident," the houses integrated into "an extended hierarchy that gradually builds up to the central crescendo." Thus, according to another student of architecture, John Summerson, "the main block [of Seaton Delaval] is comparatively small but comprises an astonishing number of disparate elements, and gives the impression of rapid movement arrested at a dramatic moment. . . . The different elements are worked together with a complete disregard for convention, enormous technical skill (which Vanbrugh is never supposed to have had), and a magical eye for sheer effect. The result is a superb, a breathtaking exaggeration." Earlier British architects emphasized a control of surfaces and harmonious volumes, but Vanbrugh and Hawksmoor made their effects through weight and mass, volumetric rhythms. As anyone who has visited Blenheim Palace or Castle Howard knows, their immense buildings domineer and are less to be seen as objects set apart from the viewer than as forces compelling an interaction. As Sir Joshua Reynolds told the students at the Royal Academy in 1786, "no Architect took greater care than he that his work should not appear crude and hard: that is, it did not abruptly start out of the ground without expectation and preparation"; because Vanbrugh's buildings participate in their landscape, they can take it over and subjugate nature, and they also control the viewer who moves in that landscape. Of course Vanbrugh's comedies, however compelling and interactive, naturalistic in dialogue, vivacious in texture, striking in theatrical effect, and coordinated as to plot, move one differently from his buildings, designed to exhibit greatness rather than to exploit wit, folly, and foibles. The theatrical mode in which greatness dominates is not comedy but the opera, which became the source of Vanbrugh's next deep involvement with the theater.

The second point that should be made about Vanbrugh's architecture follows from another of Reynolds's observations, that architecture can affect us through association of ideas, such as in the use of towers and battlements as indices of a venerable, therefore evocative past. Reynolds sees Vanbrugh's buildings as generally allusive, like much later-eighteenth- and some later-seventeenth-century poetry: "in the buildings of Vanbrugh, who was a Poet as well as an Architect, there is a greater display of imagination, than we shall find perhaps in any other; . . . For this purpose, Vanbrugh appears to have had re-

The Haymarket opera house designed by Vanbrugh and opened as the Queen's Theatre in 1705 (engraving based on a 1783 drawing by Capon). The building was destroyed by fire in 1789.

course to some principles of the Gothick Architecture, which, though not so ancient as the Grecian, is more so to our imagination, with which the Artist is more concerned than with absolute truth." One can extend this perception less with speculation about the influence on Vanbrugh of Gothic architecture in Chester, where he grew up, than by noting that the Gothic had quite specific political force. It symbolized liberty and property, the old British constitution as against Roman (and Roman Catholic) slavishness, a noble and indigenous strength. As Kerry Downes remarks, Vanbrugh's "ideas were simple and grand, and he believed that great architecture, exceeding in every way the products of the absolutist King Louis XIV and his minister Colbert, could be realized also under the constitutional monarchy of Whig liberty." Just as Vanbrugh adorned Blenheim with trophies of Marlborough's victory over the Sun King, so through allusion he marked his massive British buildings with the architectural signs of their heritage.

As Vanbrugh's architectural zest for the grand and gripping led him to the promotion of opera in England, so in the first decade of the new century his zeal for Englishing the symbols of Continental culture led him to bring London works of the French stage through a series of vivid dramatic translations. The operatic venture

fared the worse of the two. Seventeenth-century operas were, in the modern sense of the term, musicals spectacularly staged by the regular acting companies, first the Duke's at Dorset Garden and then, after 1682, the United Company: the company mostly acted, and specialized performers did the singing. These extravaganzas were so popular that Betterton's troupe, hampered by a tiny theater after their revolt in 1695, continued to produce masques and even an opera. With this market in mind, Vanbrugh in 1703 began to plan a new, grand theater in the Haymarket, fitted with an orchestra pit, and comfortably seating about 750. His hopes for merger between the two companies, which peacefully coexisted, fell through, and he found himself with Betterton's troupe to manage, Congreve as an inexperienced partner, and architectural duties that kept him from giving the theater its required attention. To show off the house, Vanbrugh seems to have commissioned a new opera in the Italian style (with sung recitative), Thomas Clayton's *Arsinoë*, but Rich at Drury Lane ended up with it (January 1705), a lucrative catch despite Dr. Charles Burney's judgment about it many Italianate and Italian operas later: "the English must have hungered and thirsted extremely after dramatic Music at this time, to be attracted and amused by such trash." Vanbrugh's operatic riposte, with imported Ital-

Vanbrugh after he was named Clarenceux King at Arms in the College of Heralds
(by permission of the National Portrait Gallery, London)

ian singers, was weak, and his first season thereafter ill-conceived; the new Queen's Theatre was also thought inconvenient in the Haymarket and acoustically bad. After failing in more attempts to unite the two companies on the old basis over 1705 and 1706, he tried several tactics with varying success–including hiring a more skilled manager, Owen Swiney–until in December 1707 he succeeded in a theatrical union along new lines, getting a monopoly on opera for himself and ceding all dramatic performances to Christopher Rich at Drury Lane. The change was a disaster. Not only did opera gobble up money for singers and sets, the repertory was also dangerously tiny in comparison to that of the acting companies, especially so in that operas in the English style, which combined spoken parts with singing, demanded the actors Vanbrugh no longer had available. Within four months he had so impoverished himself that he was delighted to have Swiney lease the whole enterprise from him. "I

have no money to dispose of," he wrote to the publisher Jacob Tonson in 1719; "I have been many years at hard Labour, to work thorough the Cruel Difficultys, that HayMarket undertaking involv'd me in; . . . Nor are those difficultys, quite at an end yet." Despite this sour experience, Vanbrugh for many years kept an interest in the theaters and promoted opera, G. F. Handel's in particular, through the Royal Academy of Music, of which he was a director.

A series of translations from the French during these same years took up nearly all Vanbrugh's energies as a playwright. The one exception was his enlivening of John Fletcher's *The Pilgrim* to offer the aged Dryden, who considered Vanbrugh a "good friend," an honorarial benefit not quite in the nick of time: Dryden, who contributed his "Secular Masque" to this production, died on 1 May 1700, which may have been its third night, the night from which the profits would have been his. Most other plays of

Memorandum by Vanbrugh, probably written in early 1708, suggesting that expenses at the Queen's Theatre could be reduced if the principal singers, composers, and musicians took shares of the theater's profits in lieu of salaries (by permission of the Pierpont Morgan Library)

Vanbrugh's, even his 1704 collaboration with Congreve and William Walsh on the lost *Squire Trelooby* (from Molière's *Monsieur de Pourceaugnac*, 1669), represent a spicing up, speeding up, and polishing up of French plays. This sometimes is a considerable accomplishment: for example, Molière's "I'm at least as angry as you, and I'd rather stay a virgin the rest of my life than show favor again to that fat traitor of mine" (*Le Dépit amoureux*, 1656) turns into Vanbrugh's "I'm charg'd to the Mouth with Fury, and if ever I meet that Fat Traytor of mine, such a Volley will I pour about his Ears–Now Heav'n prevent all hasty Vows; but in the Humour I am, methinks I'd carry my Maiden-Head to my cold Grave with me, before I'd let it simper at the Rascal" (*The Mistake*, 1705). Racy prose, vivid exchanges, shrewdly conceived stage business, often new satiric characters–these are the marks of Vanbrugh's Englishing of the Continental staples he brought to London.

The best of his adaptations, the most often performed in the eighteenth century, and the most original, is *The Confederacy*, a brilliantly cyni-cal reworking of Florent Carton Dancourt's *Les Bourgeoises à la mode* (1692) with which Vanbrugh launched his first complete season in his new theater in the Haymarket on 30 October 1705. In this acid comedy two rich, miserly, middle-class husbands despise their extravagant, unscrupulous, arriviste wives, and each husband loves the wife of the other. The women league to bilk the men. Furthermore, the adolescent daughter of one of these couples lusts after an alleged colonel who is in reality the son of a doting peddler woman from whom he thieves; because he lusts after the girl's money, his supposed manservant blackmails him with the threat of exposure as a social nobody. In tune with all this, the maidservant in the girl's family capitalizes on nearly everyone else's deceitful concealment to fatten her own purse. No one's motives, except perhaps the fond mother's, go beyond lust and acquisitiveness. Even more than in *The Provok'd Wife* and *The Relapse*, Vanbrugh avoids moral judgments, though he mocks those stock exemplars of comic failure, the wealthy, retentive, citizen husbands. The women, who triumph fully at the end of the

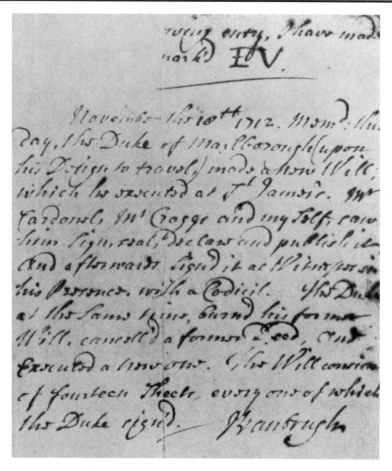

Vanbrugh's record of his having witnessed John Churchill, duke of Marlborough, signing of his will
(Richard Garrett and Edward Gosse, History of English Literature, *volume 3, 1903)*

play, have more than enough self-reflective brazenness to keep them from being laughed at during it. The servants and seedy imposters all get exactly what they want, including the pleasures of being willfully aggressive, and get it scot free.

With the opera disaster Vanbrugh closed his active life in the theater. His last adaptation, *The Cuckold in Conceit* (if, indeed, he was responsible for this play, as Cibber says but no other evidence confirms), appeared on 22 March 1707; the opera fiasco ended in 1708. His deep involvement with the London theater had lasted about a dozen years. Two decades later it was to have one last, glorious revival. At his death in 1726 Vanbrugh left behind an incomplete, enormously energetic play of indeterminable date, *A Journey to London,* whose comic and main plots his friend Cibber remodeled. Cibber brought it to the Drury Lane stage triumphantly in January 1728 as *The Provok'd Husband.* During the intervening years Vanbrugh pursued his other careers, most significantly architecture. Here his fortunes fluctuated,

as court positions did, with changes in British politics, and also with changes in British taste, for the massive, rugged palaces that he planned so generously were by the mid 1710s starting to go out of fashion in favor of Palladian simplicity. The decades 1700-1720 were scarred, too, by an epic squabble over Blenheim with the tempestuous duchess of Marlborough. As a political appointee, starting in 1703, he also enjoyed the prestige and income of being Clarenceux King at Arms, the second in importance in the College of Heralds, till in 1725, some months before his death, he was allowed to sell the position to the next unqualified incumbent for twenty-four hundred pounds.

A charming and affable man, Vanbrugh had a large group of friends, which centered from about 1700 in the Kit-Cat Club, made up of the chief Whig aristocrats and literati. With them Vanbrugh could be fashionably convivial, and some of them were to become his architectural clients and political protectors. On one of his visits

Sir John Vanbrugh (engraving by J. Faber, based on a 1725 portrait by J. Richardson)

to a client or friend, some time before 1713, he met the members of the Yarburgh family in Yorkshire, and finally married the twenty-five-year-old Henrietta Maria, second cousin of the duchess of Newcastle, in January 1719. Vanbrugh, whose plays frequently snipe at matrimony, was fifty-four. Charles Vanbrugh, the only one of three children to have lived long enough to be baptized, was born in May 1720. Vanbrugh's marriage seems to have been happy, and he had the satisfaction of receiving all the money owed him for Blenheim before an attack of quinsy, a severe tonsillitis with swelling and abscesses, caused his death on 26 March 1726.

Biographies:

Laurence Whistler, *Sir John Vanbrugh, Architect and Dramatist, 1664-1726* (London: Cobden-Sanderson, 1938);

Kerry Downes, *Sir John Vanbrugh. A Biography* (New York: St. Martin's Press, 1987).

References:

Sr. Rose Anthony, *The Jeremy Collier Stage Controversy, 1698-1726* (Milwaukee: Marquette University Press, 1937);

Gerald M. Berkowitz, "Sir John Vanbrugh and the Conventions of Restoration Comedy," *Genre*, 6 (September 1973): 346-361;

Madeleine Bingham, *Masks and Façades: Sir John Vanbrugh, the Man in His Setting* (London: Allen & Unwin, 1974);

Laura S. Brown, *English Dramatic Form, 1660-1760: An Essay in Generic History* (New Haven: Yale University Press, 1981);

Colley Cibber, *An Apology for the Life of Colley Cibber*, edited by B. R. S. Fone (Ann Arbor: University of Michigan Press, 1968);

Jeremy Collier, *A Short View of the Profaneness and Immorality of the English Stage: A Critical Edition*, edited by Benjamin Hellinger (New York: Garland, 1987);

Lincoln B. Faller, "Between Jest and Earnest: The Comedy of Sir John Vanbrugh," *Modern Philology*, 72 (August 1974): 17-29;

Bernard A. Harris, *Sir John Vanbrugh*, Writers and Their Work, no. 197 (London: Longmans, 1967);

Robert D. Hume, *The Development of English Drama in the Late Seventeenth Century* (Oxford: Clarendon Press, 1976);

Hume, "The Sponsorship of Opera in London, 1704-1720," *Modern Philology*, 85 (May 1988): 420-432;

Arthur R. Huseboe, *Sir John Vanbrugh* (Boston: Twayne, 1976);

Judith Milhous, *Thomas Betterton and the Management of Lincoln's Inn Fields, 1695-1708* (Carbondale: Southern Illinois University Press, 1979);

Paul Mueschke and Jeanette Fleisher, "A Reevaluation of Vanbrugh," *PMLA*, 49 (September 1934): 848-889;

Alan Roper, "Language and Action in *The Way of the World*, *Love's Last Shift*, and *The Relapse*," *ELH*, 40 (Spring 1973): 44-69;

Ben Ross Schneider, Jr., *The Ethos of Restoration Comedy* (Urbana: University of Illinois Press, 1971);

Arthur Colby Sprague, *Beaumont and Fletcher on the Restoration Stage* (Cambridge, Mass.: Harvard University Press, 1926);

Susan Staves, *Players' Scepters: Fictions of Authority in the Restoration* (Lincoln: University of Nebraska Press, 1979);

John Summerson, *Architecture in Britain, 1530 to 1830*, The Pelican History of Art Series (Harmondsworth: Penguin, 1953);

Staring B. Wells, ed., *A Comparison between the Two Stages*, by Charles Gildon(?) (Princeton: Princeton University Press, 1942);

Rose A. Zimbardo, *A Mirror to Nature: Transformations in Drama and Aesthetics, 1660-1732* (Lexington: University Press of Kentucky, 1986).

Papers:

Many of Vanbrugh's letters are at the British Library and the Public Record Office. His letters, published and unpublished, are calendared in Appendix B of Downes's *Sir John Vanbrugh*.

George Villiers, Second Duke of Buckingham

(30 January 1628-16 April 1687)

John H. O'Neill
Hamilton College

PLAY PRODUCTIONS: *The Chances*, by John Fletcher, revised by Buckingham, London, Theatre Royal on Bridges Street, summer 1664;

The Rehearsal, by Buckingham, Martin Clifford, Samuel Butler, and Thomas Sprat, London, Theatre Royal on Bridges Street, 7 December 1671.

BOOKS: *The Declaration of the Right Honourable The Duke of Buckingham, and the Earles of Holland, and Peterborough, and other Lords and Gentlemen now associated for the King and Parliament, the Religion, Laws, and Peace of His Majesties Kingdomes* (London, 1648);

The Duke of Buckingham's Speech in a Late Conference (London: Printed for M. I., 1668);

An Epitaph upon Thomas late lord Fairfax. Written by a person of honour [single sheet] (London?, circa 1671);

A Letter to Sir Thomas Osborn, one of His Majesties Privy council, upon the Reading of a Book called, The Present Interest of England stated (London: Printed for Henry Brome, 1672);

The Rehearsal, as it was acted at the Theatre-Royal (London: Printed for Thomas Dring, 1672); modern edition, edited by D. E. L. Crane (Durham: University of Durham Press, 1976);

Two Speeches. I. The Earl of Shaftesbury's Speech in the House of Lords, the 20th. of October, 1675. II. The D. of Buckingham's Speech in the House of Lords, the 16th of November, 1675 (Amsterdam, 1675);

The Duke of Buckingham's Speech: Spoken in the House of Lords. Feb. 15th. 1676. Proving that the Parliament is Dissolved (Amsterdam, 1677);

The Chances, a Comedy: As it was Acted at the Theatre Royal. Corrected and Altered by a Person of Honour (London: Printed for A. B. & S. M. and sold by Langley Curtis, 1682);

A Short Discourse upon the Reasonableness of Men's having a Religion, or Worship of God. By George Duke of Buckingham (London: Printed by John Leake, for Luke Meredith, 1685);

The Duke of Buckingham His Grace's letter, to the unknown author of a paper, entituled, A short answer to His Grace the Duke of Buckingham's paper concerning religion, toleration, and liberty of conscience (London: Printed by J. L. for Luke Meredith, 1685);

The Battle of Sedgmoor: betwixt King James's forces and Duke of Monmouth, rehears'd at White-Hall. A Farce. By George late duke of Buckingham (London, 1714);

The Restauration: or, Right will take place. A tragic-comedy. Written by George Villiers, late Duke of Buckingham. From the original copy, never before printed (London, 1714);

The Country Gentleman, by Buckingham and Sir Robert Howard, edited by Arthur H. Scouten and Robert D. Hume (Philadelphia: University of Pennsylvania Press, 1976);

Sir Politick Would-Be: Comedie à la manière des Anglois, edited by Robert Finch and Eugene Joliat, Textes Littéraires Français (Geneva: Droz, 1978).

Collections: *Miscellaneous Works, Written by His Grace, George, Late Duke of Buckingham. Collected in One Volume from the Original Papers. . . . Never Before Printed* (London: Printed for & sold by J. Nutt, 1704);

The Second Volume of Miscellaneous Works, Written by George, Late Duke of Buckingham, Containing a Key to the Rehearsal, and several Pieces in Prose and Verse; Never before Printed. . . . Collected and Prepar'd for the Press, by the Late Ingenious Mr. Tho. Brown (London: Printed for Sam. Briscoe & sold by J. Nutt, 1705);

The Works of his Grace, George Villiers, Late Duke of Buckingham. In two volumes. . . . The third edition with large additions, adorn'd with cuts (London: Printed for Sam. Briscoe & sold by Fardinando Burleigh, 1715);

Buckingham: Public and Private Man: The Prose, Poems and Commonplace Book of George Villiers,

George Villiers, second duke of Buckingham (by permission of the Earl of Jersey)

Second Duke of Buckingham (1628-1687), edited by Christine Phipps, The Renaissance Imagination, volume 13 (New York: Garland, 1985).

OTHER: *Sir Politick Would-Be,* by Buckingham (?), Louis d'Aubigny, and Charles de Saint-Evremond, in *Oevres meslées,* by Saint-Evremond, edited by P. Silvestre and des Maizeaux (London, 1705).

The Court Wits of the Restoration were men of extraordinary talents, energies, and accomplishments. In the history of English literature, no other group of writers has ever had such wealth, power, and celebrity; or to put the matter differently, no other group of statesmen, courtiers, and politicians has ever been so involved in literature. Among this group, George Villiers, the

second duke of Buckingham, was in some ways the most distinguished. As a duke, he held the highest rank and had the greatest income outside the royal family. As the king's first minister, he was at one time directly responsible for all affairs of the government; and later, as one of the principal leaders of the opposition, he was much more popular and nearly as influential. As a wit, rake, and courtier, he was "the most accomplished man of the age," according to Francis Lockier, a contemporary observer: "When he came into the presence chamber, it was impossible for you not to follow him with your eye as he went along, he moved so gracefully." As an advocate of religious toleration, he was a pioneer in a movement too young even to have a name, one which would wait over a century for its fulfillment. And as a playwright, Buckingham was the author of two successful comedies, his revision of John Fletch-

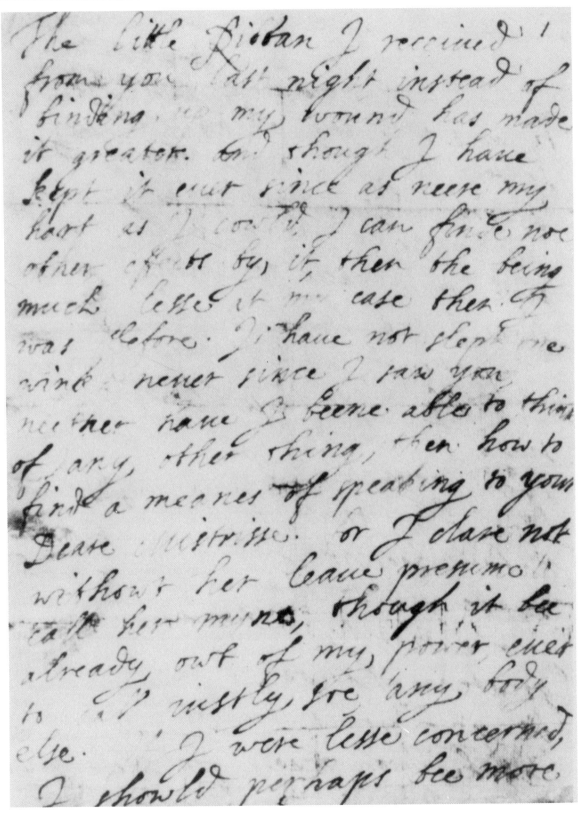

Page from a 1657 letter from Buckingham, probably to Mrs. Worsnam, a friend of Mary Fairfax, whom Buckingham married on
15 September 1657 (MS Add. 27872, fol. 1; by permission of the British Library)

George Villiers, second duke of Buckingham (engraving based on a portrait by Verelst)

er's *The Chances* and his burlesque farce *The Rehearsal*.

Our critical estimate of Buckingham's accomplishments may suffer in part from differences between our ideas of individual authorship and those of his circle. The Court Wits seldom wrote for publication; they were their own audience, and they circulated their poetic works in manuscript within their group. Because the Wits often did not sign their names to their works and because they often wrote collaboratively, the authorship of an individual poem or play is often impossible to determine. It may be difficult for us to reconcile the flamboyant personality of the duke of Buckingham with the idea of his effacing his literary identity in anonymous or collaborative work, but all of Buckingham's full-length dramatic works are either the products of collaborations with living contemporaries (*The Rehearsal, The Country Gentleman*) or revisions of plays by Jacobean playwrights (*The Restauration, The Chances*). Except for the poems in his commonplace book,

which appear in his autograph and are found nowhere else, none of his poems can be attributed to him with certainty. Only his prose works of political propaganda appeared in print during his lifetime with his name signed to them.

George Villiers, the second duke of Buckingham, was born on 30 January 1628 into a family of preeminent wealth, power, and fame. His father, George Villiers, first duke of Buckingham, was the principal favorite of King James I. He owned a huge fortune; a glorious palace, York House; and an art collection unequaled by any but those of kings. On 23 August 1628 the first duke was assassinated, leaving a five-year-old daughter, Mary; the seven-month-old infant George, now the second duke; and his widow, Lady Katherine Manners, pregnant with their third child, Francis. The duchess of Buckingham soon remarried, reconverted to Catholicism (she had been a Catholic until her marriage), and relinquished her children to the care of the royal family, who brought them up and educated them as

Mary Villiers, second duchess of Buckingham

companions to their own children.

The fact that he spent virtually all of his childhood in the company of the princes, Charles and James, made George Villiers one of the first and closest friends of the two men who in adult life became his sovereigns. It engendered a relationship with King Charles which was strengthened by the hardships of war, revolution, and power politics—all the great events of seventeenth-century history. It accustomed him to expect to exercise civil and military leadership and to accept personal sacrifice as inevitable. But it also led him to believe himself superior to considerations which ruled the lives and actions of other people, even of other noblemen. And it taught him to think of the two royal brothers with the familiarity which breeds contempt. Bishop Gilbert Burnet reports, "The duke of Buckingham gave me once a short but severe character of the two broth-

ers; it was the more severe, because it was true. The king [Charles] could see things if he would, and the duke [James, then duke of York] would see things if he could."

At the age of twelve, Buckingham was sent with his brother, Francis, to Cambridge and enrolled in Trinity College, but in 1642, soon after the civil war began, the brothers left the university (where George had just received the largely ceremonial Master of Arts degree) and joined the Royalist forces. On 7 July 1648, in a skirmish at Surbiton Common, Francis, then aged nineteen, was killed. George fled to France. King Charles was executed in January 1649, and Buckingham, together with the princes Charles and James, was officially banished as a traitor. Over the nine years between Francis's death and Buckingham's marriage, the young duke lived a restless, unsettled life on the Continent, working to subvert the

Commonwealth and to engineer Charles's return to power. He intrigued with Scottish Puritans, with French Catholics, and with exiled English Levellers; he made at least one (and probably more) dangerous clandestine visit to England as a secret agent; he accompanied the king on his ill-fated attempt to invade England from the north in 1651; and he served in the French army under Henri de la Tour d'Auvergne, vicomte de Turenne, against the Spanish. Since Charles in exile could not reward the service of his courtiers with the customary pensions and sinecures and since the Parliament had seized the Villiers estates with their large annual income, Buckingham supported himself primarily by selling his father's art collection. In 1657 Buckingham returned openly to England and, on 15 September 1657, was married to Mary Fairfax, daughter of Thomas, third baron Fairfax, a Parliamentary general who had received a large portion of the confiscated Buckingham estates. Fairfax, commander in chief of the Parliamentary armies from 1645 to 1650, had resigned his commission in June 1650 and retired to Nun Appleton House, his estate in Yorkshire. Buckingham held Fairfax in high esteem. His elegy, *An Epitaph upon Thomas late lord Fairfax* (circa 1671), praises the general for courage, honesty, and modesty, but especially for the greatness of his spirit in renouncing power.

Buckingham was too intimate with the exiled king to be tolerated in close alliance with an important figure in the Parliamentary party. Oliver Cromwell's agents watched him constantly, and in October, less than a month after his marriage, Buckingham was arrested. He was held in the Tower of London until April, released to house arrest, and in August again seized and sent to the Tower. Had not Cromwell himself died, on 3 September 1658, Buckingham would have been executed.

After the Restoration Buckingham's life changed dramatically. Whereas his economic condition during his exile was always precarious, after the Restoration his income, at twenty-six thousand pounds a year, was the highest in England. Whereas other Royalists were prevented by the Act of Indemnity from regaining their lost property, Buckingham's marriage had already restored most of his estates to him. Having been loyal to King Charles in his exile, Buckingham received rewards now that the king was again in a position to bestow them. Politics became Buckingham's primary activity after the Restoration. As a high-ranking peer of the realm, the son of King James's powerful first minister, and a lifelong intimate of the king, Buckingham played a major role in the affairs of his country. By 1662 he was admitted to the Privy Council. As lord lieutenant of the West Riding in Yorkshire, he commanded a troop of cavalry volunteers to quell sporadic rebellions of Puritan sympathizers disaffected from the restored monarchy. And he assumed a position of leadership in the House of Lords.

At the same time the Restoration and the establishment of his wealth and his social and political position led to an exuberant flowering of his intellectual curiosity and artistic creativity. Around Buckingham developed a circle of wits—some professionals, others gentleman amateurs—who discussed the arts and sciences: Abraham Cowley, Matt Clifford, Thomas Sprat, Charles Sackville, Charles Sedley, Sir John Denham, Edmund Waller, Christopher Wren, Samuel Butler. Buckingham joined the Royal Society in 1661 and conducted chemical experiments. He played the violin and composed music for strings. Together with his intellectual and artistic friends, he composed and circulated the poems and plays which are today the basis of his literary reputation. Around 1663 or 1664 Buckingham apparently collaborated with Charles Saint-Evremond and Louis d'Aubigny on *Sir Politick Would-Be*, a comedy written in French but "à la manière des Anglois" and loosely based on Ben Jonson's *Volpone* (1606). The play was written to be read, rather than performed; it was not published during the lifetimes of any of its authors.

In the spring of 1663 one of Buckingham's servants, Abraham Goodman, attempted to assassinate him. At one o'clock in the morning, Goodman rushed into Buckingham's chamber with a sword. Buckingham seized a table knife and napkin and, with these weapons, took Goodman's sword from him. This incident, recalling the assassination of his father, must have shaken the duke, though he behaved with his customary resolution.

Buckingham's revision of John Fletcher's *The Chances*, first performed in the summer of 1664, helped to establish the popularity of split-plot plays featuring "gay couples." Fletcher's version of the play, written about 1617, does not exploit the comic possibilities of the characters of Don John and the Second Constantia, whom Buckingham makes the central interest. The heroic

*David Garrick as Don John in a 1754 production of his version of Buckingham's adaptation
of* The Chances, *by John Fletcher (engraving by Hall, from a portrait by Edwards)*

plot concerns Constantia, sister of the governor of Bologna. She loves the duke of Naples (of Ferrara in Fletcher's version) and has borne a son by him. The two seek to elope, but Petruchio, her brother, believing his honor irreparably damaged, has confined Constantia and seeks to kill the duke in a duel. His desire for revenge threatens war between Bologna and Naples. Don Frederick and Don John, young Spanish gentlemen, are brought into the plot through a series of coincidences (the "chances" of the title). Constantia, in flight from her brother's house, blunders into Don Frederick. After she charges him in the name of honor to help her, he commits himself to her defense. Don Frederick and Don John arrange a meeting between Petruchio and the Duke and effect a reconciliation, but Constantia, in terror, has again fled. After the men disperse to search for Constantia, Don John finds another

woman named Constantia, the mistress of Antonio, one of Petruchio's attendants. She has run away from Antonio at the same time the first Constantia has fled from her brother. Prompted not by honor but by sexual desire, Don John promises to help her. As she seeks to avoid Antonio, and the first Constantia flees from Petruchio, the various men and women blunder into one another's way, and the identity of the two women's names contributes to the comic confusion.

Parallels between the comic and heroic plots underline the themes of the work. Each of the two parts of the plot has an unmasking scene, in which the beauty of each Constantia strikes her rescuer with awe and in which her appeal for the help of a stranger is answered. Most important to the fabric of the play is the recurrence in different contexts of key words, particularly *love* and *honor,* so as to cause the audience to reconsider the meanings of the ideas they denote. Don Frederick is a man of honor. His intrepidity, decisiveness, and selflessness constitute the masculine ideal of the heroic plot, and the first Constantia displays the feminine versions of the same qualities. For Petruchio, Constantia's brother, the concept of honor is a kind of social straitjacket, confining him in rigid views of himself and his duty and forcing him to violate his ethical beliefs. Don John regards himself as a man of honor, too. But he is too much a libertine to be strictly honorable. Though danger cannot frighten him from his duty, sexual desire diverts him from it. The idea of honor is reduced to its most absurd extreme in the Second Constantia's mother, an affected fool.

The split-plot play permits us to see the limitations of the heroic character, the rigidity of the concept of honor which forces Petruchio and the Duke toward a senseless combat they do not want but cannot honorably decline. But it also permits us to see the limitations of libertine skepticism. Thus Buckingham places two dominant ideologies of the Restoration court in a productive, unresolved tension. Each reveals the limits of the other; neither holds the final or total truth. If libertine skepticism reveals the inhuman rigidity of too heroic a view of human nature, the heroic sense of honor shows the boundless sea of valuelessness which is a danger of the libertine view. Buckingham's version of *The Chances* was immediately popular in its first performance, with Nell Gwyn, in her earliest known role, as the Second Constantia and with Charles Hart as Don John. Popular revivals took place in 1667, in 1690-1691, and at frequent intervals throughout the eighteenth century, when *The Chances* in Buckingham's version became a stock play in the repertoire of the dramatic companies. *The Chances* was published in six editions between 1682 and 1800.

For several years after the fall of Edward Hyde, earl of Clarendon, in 1667, Buckingham was the most powerful member of the Privy Council and of the inner circle of the government, the Cabal. In 1665, at York, Buckingham began a flirtation with Anna-Maria, countess of Shrewsbury, then twenty-three. Anna-Maria had been married since 1659 to Francis Talbot, eleventh earl of Shrewsbury, nineteen years her senior, and had borne him two sons. Buckingham's flirtation with her led to a notorious affair. In January of 1668 the earl of Shrewsbury sent Buckingham a challenge to a duel. The men met on 16 January at Barn Elms. Buckingham quickly ran Shrewsbury through the body. The earl was carried from the field to a house in Chelsea, where the surgeons pronounced him seriously wounded but likely to recover. He convalesced for two months and then, on 16 March, when his doctors supposed him out of danger, he died. Public opinion condemned Buckingham. Although he could not have refused Shrewsbury's challenge, he was now infamous for killing the husband of his mistress. In April, Samuel Pepys recorded in his diary, "I am told that the Countesse of Shrewsbery is brought home by the Duke of Buckingham to his house; where his Duchess saying that it was not for her and the other to live together in a house, he answered, 'Why, Madam, I did think so; and therefore have ordered your coach to be ready to carry you to your father's;' which was a devilish speech, but they say true; and my Lady Shrewsbry is there it seems."

Buckingham's next work for the stage was *The Country Gentleman,* an intrigue comedy written in collaboration with Sir Robert Howard and prepared for production in 1669. Like most of the intrigue comedies of the late 1660s, *The Country Gentleman* emphasizes the clever plots by which the heroes and heroines triumph over the fops and the pretentious idiots. It has some mildly witty "gay couple" scenes of banter among the young leads, but these have little real sexual tension, let alone any hint of impropriety. The vogue for sex comedy was not to come until the middle 1670s. Two characters in the play, Sir Cautious Trouble-All and Sir Gravity Empty, are easily recognizable caricatures of two of Buckingham's enemies on the Privy Council, Sir William Coventry and Sir John Duncomb. In one scene in the play, Sir Cautious shows Sir Gravity his worktable, round with a hole in the middle, so that he can arrange his papers in a circle about him and use a swivel stool to turn from one matter to another. Court insiders knew that Sir William Coventry took great pride in having invented a table precisely like the one in the play. The similarity was devastating. Grammont said of Buckingham, "His particular talent consisted in turning into ridicule whatever was ridiculous in other people, and in taking them off, even in their presence, without their perceiving it."

The late 1660s had seen the beginning of a vogue for personal satire in stage comedies, beginning with caricatures of Sir Robert Howard in Thomas Shadwell's *The Sullen Lovers* in May 1668 and of Sir Charles Sedley in William Cavendish,

Anna-Maria Talbot, countess of Shrewsbury, circa 1670 (portrait by Sir Peter Lely; by permission of the National Portrait Gallery, London). Buckingham's affair with her led to a duel in which he killed her husband.

duke of Newcastle's *The Heiress* in January 1669. But Buckingham's imitation of Coventry and Duncomb in *The Country Gentleman* was not only part of the theatrical fashion; it was a political move to dislodge Coventry from the Privy Council. Buckingham knew that Coventry could not permit this attack without making some response. When the play was in rehearsal, Coventry sent a challenge to Buckingham. King Charles, hearing of the planned duel, stopped it by sending Coventry to the Tower of London on the charge that he had conspired the death of a Privy Councilor. He ordered the performance of the play, scheduled for 27 February, canceled and the play suppressed; it has never been performed, and until a decade ago no copy of it was known to exist. Coventry lost all his offices under the Crown, and, once he was released from the Tower, retired from public life.

Buckingham had used the play to destroy a political enemy and to weaken the duke of York's faction in the Council, but it had been a risky tactic. If the king had not stopped the duel, Buckingham's position might have been impossible. He could not have killed Coventry, just a year after killing the earl of Shrewsbury in the most infamous duel in Restoration history, and still have survived in public life. Contemporary reports seem to suggest that Buckingham simply inserted the "oyster-table scene" into a play which Howard had already nearly completed. But parallels between *The Country Gentleman* and *The Chances* suggest that Buckingham may have collaborated with Howard on the entire composition. The character of Mistress Finical Fart, the scheming landlady of *The Country Gentleman*, very much resembles that of the mother of the Second Constantia in *The Chances*, a character we know Buckingham invented. Both strive vainly to imitate the manners of the fashionable beau monde, particularly by affecting French phrases and manners. Such Frenchified fools are recurring characters in Restoration comedy, but the commonest version is a member of the upper-middle or upper class,

One of the plays parodied in The Rehearsal *was John Dryden's* Tyrannic Love, *in which Valeria, as her corpse is about to be carried offstage, rises to speak the epilogue (frontispiece to* The Key to the Rehearsal, *1714).*

rather than the lower class, like these two.

The ideological slant of the play, like its personal satire, seems calculated to serve political ends. Not only Sir Richard Plainbred, the country gentleman of the title, but also his witty and attractive daughters, Isabella and Philadelphia, and their equally witty and handsome suitors, Worthy and Lovetruth, all despise London and prefer their home in the country. The city characters, by contrast, include the pompous "men of business," Sir Cautious and Sir Gravity; the vain, cowardly fops, Vapour and Slander; and the affected and avaricious landlady, Mrs. Finical. In this re-

spect *The Country Gentleman* differs markedly from the London comedies which dominated the stage in the 1660s and 1670s, in which a love of the town (at least the fashionable part of it) and a distaste for the country are almost articles of faith. But by reinforcing the values of the "Country Party" in Parliament, the play would have bolstered Buckingham's and Howard's standing with the opposition.

In 1670 King Charles sent Buckingham to France to negotiate an alliance between the two countries in opposition to the power of the Dutch. This was the public version of the now-

Prince Volseius "goes out hopping with one Boot on, and the other off " *in act 3, scene 4, of* The Rehearsal *(frontispiece to the 1734 edition)*

infamous Treaty of Dover, the secret version of which provided for Charles's conversion to Catholicism in return for £375,000 per year in subsidies from Louis XIV. Since it would be necessary to account publicly for the money he received, Charles needed a "public" version of the treaty, without the conversion clause. He selected Buckingham as his negotiator because the duke's ties to the Protestant left and the Parliamentary opposition were strongest of any of the Cabal. In December of 1670 the sham treaty was concluded, binding England to declare war on Holland.

For Buckingham the year 1671 was filled with events and sudden shifts of fortune. In February of that year, Lady Shrewsbury bore him a son. Buckingham's delight in this, his only child (he had no children in his marriage to the duchess), was cut short a few days later, when the boy died. In June Buckingham was installed as chancellor of Cambridge University. In October he suffered a bitter disappointment: King Charles bestowed the command of his army in Holland, which he had promised to Buckingham at the time of the Treaty of Dover, upon his oldest illegitimate son, James Scott, duke of Monmouth, and upon Thomas Butler, earl of Ossory, the brother-in-law of Henry Bennet, baron Arlington. In December Buckingham's most successful play, *The Rehearsal*, was produced at the Theatre Royal on Bridges Street.

255

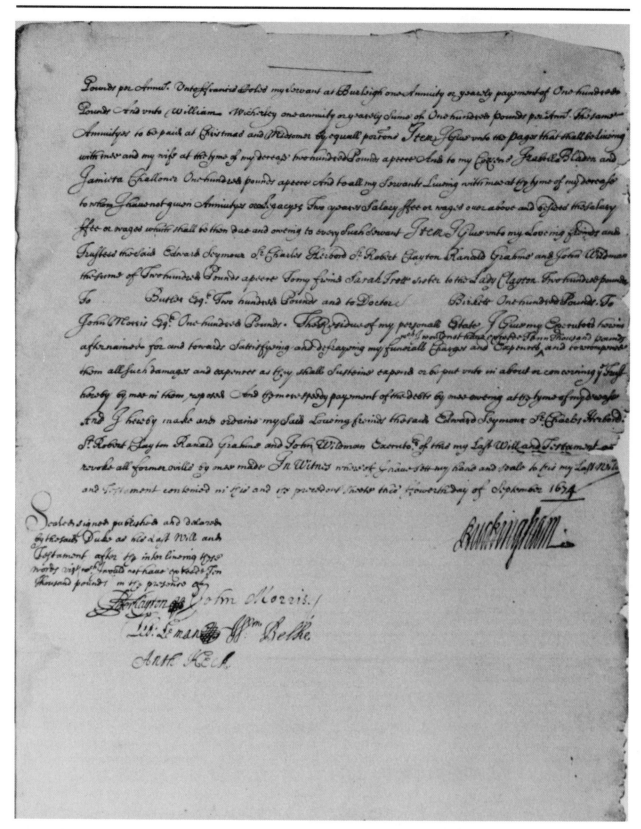

Second page of a will dated 4 September 1674 and signed by Buckingham (by permission of the Pierpont Morgan Library; MA 3386, purchased as the gift of Mr. David Pleydell-Bouverie)

Like all Buckingham's original plays, *The Rehearsal* is a collaborative work; the duke's chief collaborators were Martin Clifford, Buckingham's personal secretary and later master of the Charterhouse School; Thomas Sprat, Buckingham's chaplain, later Bishop of Rochester and the historian of the Royal Society; and Samuel Butler, the author of *Hudibras* (1663-1678), who also served Buckingham as a secretary. The group completed one version of the play for production in June 1665, but the closing of the theaters that summer because of the plague made its presentation impossible.

Political considerations may well have been the main reason why Buckingham's interest in *The Rehearsal* revived in 1671. According to tradition, the primary target of the critical burlesque and the personal satire in the 1665 version of the play was Sir Robert Howard, whose *The Indian Queen*, written in collaboration with John Dryden and first performed in January 1664, began the vogue for rhymed heroic drama. Between 1665 and 1671, Buckingham and Howard had become political allies. As we have already seen, they collaborated on *The Country Gentleman*. Perhaps their success in destroying Coventry's career with *The Country Gentleman* encouraged Buckingham to try the same tactic again. Whatever the reason, the burlesque in the 1671 version focuses on the plays of Dryden, and the personal satire consists of references to Arlington and to others among Buckingham's enemies in court intrigue.

The burlesque elements in *The Rehearsal* are contained in the inner play, an untitled heroic drama supposedly written by Mr. Bayes. The audience observes the rehearsal of scenes in which the thrones of the two kings of Brentford are usurped by their Physician and their Gentleman-Usher, in which two princes proclaim their love for two maidens, and in which the fierce hero Drawcansir frightens the two usurpers by interrupting their banquet. There is little logic or continuity to the scenes, and the rhetoric burlesques the heroic style. Many passages are direct parodies of memorable sections of plays by Dryden—including *The Rival Ladies* (1664), *The Indian Emperor* (1665), *Secret-Love* (1667), *Tyrannic Love* (1669), and *The Conquest of Granada* (1670-1671)—and by many of his fellow Restoration playwrights, including Roger Boyle, earl of Orrery, Aphra Behn, Sir William Davenant, all four Howard brothers, Thomas Killigrew, and Elkanah Settle. The outer farce of *The Rehearsal* presents Mr. Bayes, the foolish, hyperimaginative, self-ad-

miring playwright, directing the dress rehearsal of his heroic drama and commenting on its action to Mr. Smith and Mr. Johnson, two gentlemen whom he hopes to impress. Mr. Smith, like Sir Richard Plainbred in *The Country Gentleman*, has just arrived in London from the country. Like Sir Richard he values frankness (his first name is Frank) and honesty. Although at first he expresses curiosity about "the strange new things we have heard in the country," he is quickly disgusted with Bayes and his play. Mr. Johnson, whose name calls to mind the great Jacobean playwright and critic Ben Jonson, is a man of the town, coolly detached and mockingly ironic. Together the two gentlemen make comments on the inner play which both guide the audience in understanding the burlesque and provide a standard of taste for judging it.

Traditionally Bayes has been taken as a caricature of Dryden. Dryden was the leading author of heroic drama in 1671, and more of his plays than of any other playwright are burlesqued or alluded to in *The Rehearsal*. At one point in the play there is apparently an allusion to Dryden's mistress, Anne Reeve, and Bayes's claim that he has "talkt bawdy" to her anticipates John Wilmot, earl of Rochester's charge in his "Allusion to Horace" that Dryden could not achieve the decorum of obscenity. But it seems more likely that any personal strokes at Dryden are isolated than that the character of Bayes is intended for a full-length portrait. In addition, *The Rehearsal* follows *The Country Gentleman* in making repeated personal allusions to Buckingham's political enemies. As George McFadden has pointed out, the patch Bayes places on his nose after he injures himself (II.v) precisely duplicates the one worn by the earl of Arlington, Buckingham's archrival in the Privy Council, who, in the summer of 1671, had helped to cheat the duke of his promised command of an English army in the Netherlands. The Physician and the Gentleman-Usher, "two grand, sober, governing persons" and "men of business," resemble Sir William Coventry and Sir John Duncomb, whom Buckingham had already satirized in *The Country Gentleman*. Prince Pretty-Man, the son of a king who is thought to be the son of a fisherman and who fears that "he should be thought no bodies Son at all," resembles James Scott, duke of Monmouth, best known for his good looks, his lack of intelligence, and his aspirations to the throne. Monmouth and Buckingham were later to be political allies, but in 1671 Buckingham's resentment over losing to

George Villiers, second duke of Buckingham, circa 1675 (portrait by Sir Peter Lely; by permission of the National Portrait Gallery, London)

Monmouth and Ossory the command of the English army in the Netherlands found comic expression in this caricature. None of these references is as unambiguous as those to Coventry and Duncomb in *The Country Gentleman*. As Margarita Stocker has demonstrated, in *The Rehearsal* Buckingham and his collaborators mingled literary and political satire with such delicacy that they forestalled the kinds of scandal and censorship which had attended the earlier play.

The Rehearsal was Buckingham's most popular work. After the success of the initial performance, with John Lacy in the role of Bayes, there were frequent revivals, often with allusions to new plays. It continued to be popular well into the eighteenth century. The role of Bayes was played by such great eighteenth-century actors as Colley Cibber and David Garrick. The play went through five separate quarto editions, each with revisions and additions, before Buckingham's death, and twelve editions were published in the eighteenth century. Critics since the Restoration have professed themselves surprised that, notwithstanding the popularity of *The Rehearsal*, the rhymed heroic drama remained as popular as ever–indeed, even grew in popularity in the 1670s. But Buckingham's farce is not really a satire of the heroic drama as a genre–certainly not

Pages from Buckingham's commonplace book, in which he wrote an unfinished play (top left), poems, and epigrams (by permission of the Earl of Jersey)

Drawing of the house at Kirkby Moorside where Buckingham died

of the ideology of the heroic drama, of its belief in the necessity of honor to heroic love, of its implicit belief in the transcendent significance of the actions of heroic individuals. It does not even, as *The Chances* does, juxtapose the heroic ideals against libertine materialism to show the limitations of each. Rather, it satirizes the ways in which poor playwrights and plays fail to give coherent and convincing form to those heroic ideals. The enduring value of *The Rehearsal* lies not in its political references or even in its critical strictures against the contemporary stage. In its core of meaning, it satirizes the creative imagination run wild. As Sheridan Baker has said, "The quintessential fact of comedy is human ineptitude mistaking itself for omnipotence. Authorship, by nature, assumes an omnipotence it must disguise. And Bayes is authorship laid comically bare, and never more thoroughly and comically so."

In the early 1670s the Cabal ministry, never more than an alliance of convenience, became increasingly unstable. In January of 1674 the House of Commons impeached Buckingham, blaming him for the unpopular alliance with France and the war with Holland. At the same time the House of Lords charged him with adultery with Lady Shrewsbury. By the end of the month, the Lords had ordered Buckingham "not to converse or cohabit with the said Anna-Maria, countess of Shrewsbury, for the future," and had required him to put up a bond of ten thousand pounds as a security of good behavior. And the Commons had voted to request that the king dismiss Buckingham from all his employments. For a year after his fall from power, Buckingham lived in retirement in Yorkshire. In the spring of

1675 he returned to London and, together with Anthony Ashley Cooper, earl of Shaftesbury, who had also left the Cabal, he led the Country party, the parliamentary opposition. When he was briefly imprisoned in February 1677, at the order of Lord Treasurer Thomas Osborn, earl of Danby, Buckingham's popularity reached its greatest height. Having pursued heroic glory throughout his life, he was now at last a popular hero, cheered by crowds as he rode through the streets.

In 1681 Buckingham again retired from public life, but he continued to write actively. In 1683 he completed *The Restauration: or, Right will take place,* a revision of Beaumont and Fletcher's circa 1609 tragicomedy, *Philaster: or, Love Lies a-Bleeding.* In this revision Buckingham seems to have worked to separate the comic from the heroic elements more thoroughly than they had been in the original and to purge from its language the kinds of stylistic excesses he had satirized in *The Rehearsal.* But the result is the duke's least successful play, and it has never been performed. In 1685 Buckingham published *A Short Discourse upon the Reasonableness of Men's having a Religion, or Worship of God,* his most sustained argument in favor of religious toleration. He also wrote a brief farce, *The Battle of Sedgmoor . . . Rehearsed at Whitehall,* an attack on Louis de Duras, earl of Feversham, the commander of King James's forces at Sedgmoor. The piece, humorous but slight, imitates the accent and personal mannerisms of Feversham and portrays him as boasting of his success in crushing Monmouth's rebellion. First published in 1714, it probably was not intended for performance.

During his last years at Castle Helmsley, his estate in Yorkshire, Buckingham worked on an autograph fair-copy manuscript collection of his unpublished works. This book, generally but inaccurately known as his commonplace book, was actually in his pocket when he died, so he must have been working on it or reviewing it on his deathbed. It is our only source for the works it contains. One of these is a fragment of an untitled blank-verse tragedy devoted to Theodoric, prince of the Ostrogoths. The surviving fragment occupies the first thirty-seven pages of the "commonplace book" and includes the first act and the first scene of the second. Since almost all of the first act is exposition, it is impossible now to judge the quality of the action of the play, but the blank verse is better than in *The Restauration*.

On 14 April 1687 while Buckingham was foxhunting with tenants and friends, his horse fell dead. As he waited for a fresh horse to be brought to him, he sat on the cold, wet ground and contracted a chill. He was taken to the house of a tenant at Kirkby Moorside and put to bed. He died two days later, on 16 April 1687.

Like Lord Byron or Oscar Wilde, the duke of Buckingham made his life his most successful work of art. Like them, Buckingham showed in his work a rich ambivalence between a passionate commitment to and a detached, satirical perspective on the same set of ideals. Buckingham combined, in his life and in his best work, a belief in the heroic ideology of his time and class with a libertine skepticism about all beliefs, including that ideology. As a witness to many of the greatest events of his turbulent century, he knew that the actions of an individual—a Cromwell, a Fairfax, or a Buckingham—could change history. He also knew, from his intimacy with the king and the highest-ranking statesmen of his time, how empty all pretensions to greatness could be. In his two most successful dramas, *The Rehearsal* and *The Chances*, Buckingham found a way of giving theatrical form to the full complexity of that ambivalence.

Biographies:

Winifred Gardner, Lady Burghclere, *George Villiers, Second Duke of Buckingham, 1628-1687: A Study in the History of the Restoration* (London: John Murray, 1903);

Hester W. Chapman, *Great Villiers: A Study of George Villiers, Second Duke of Buckingham, 1628-1687* (London: Secker & Warburg, 1949);

John Harold Wilson, *A Rake and His Times: George Villiers, Second Duke of Buckingham* (New York: Farrar, Straus & Young, 1954).

References:

Emmett L. Avery, "The Stage Popularity of The Rehearsal, 1671-1777," *Research Studies, State College of Washington*, 7 (December 1939): 201-204;

Sheridan Baker, "Buckingham's Permanent Rehearsal," *Michigan Quarterly Review*, 12 (Spring 1973): 160-171;

Douglas R. Butler, "The Date of Buckingham's Revision of *The Chances* and Nell Gwynn's First Season on the London Stage," *Notes and Queries*, new series 29 (December 1982): 515-516;

Victor Clinton Clinton-Baddeley, *The Burlesque Tradition in the English Theatre After 1660* (London: Methuen, 1952);

Richard Elias, " 'Bayes' in Buckingham's *The Rehearsal*," *English Language Notes*, 15 (March 1978): 178-181;

John P. Emery, "Restoration Dualism of the Court Writers," *Revue des langues vivantes*, 32 (1966): 238-265;

Alan S. Fisher, "The Significance of Thomas Shadwell," *Studies in Philology*, 71 (April 1974): 225-246;

Garland Jack Gravitt, "The Modernity of *The Rehearsal*: Buckingham's Theatre of the Absurd," *College Literature*, 9 (Winter 1982): 30-38;

Robert D. Hume, *The Development of the English Drama in the Late Seventeenth Century* (Oxford: Clarendon Press, 1976);

Hume, *The Rakish Stage: Studies in English Drama, 1660-1800* (Carbondale: Southern Illinois University Press, 1983);

Phillip K. Jason, "A Twentieth-Century Response to *The Critic*," *Theatre Survey*, 15 (May 1974): 51-58;

Pierre Legouis, "Buckingham et Sheridan: ce que le *Critique* doit à la *Répétition*," *Revue anglo-américaine*, 11 (1934): 423-434;

Peter Lewis, "*The Rehearsal*: A Study of Its Satirical Methods," *Durham University Journal*, new series 31 (March 1970): 96-113;

Samuel L. Macey, "Fielding's *Tom Thumb* as the Heir to Buckingham's *Rehearsal*," *Texas Studies in Literature and Language*, 10 (Fall 1968): 405-414;

George McFadden, "Political Satire in *The Rehearsal*," *Yearbook of English Studies*, 4 (1974): 120-128;

John H. O'Neill, "Edward Hyde, Heneage Finch, and the Duke of Buckingham's Commonplace Book," *Modern Philology*, 83 (August 1985): 51-54;

O'Neill, *George Villiers, Second Duke of Buckingham* (Boston: Twayne, 1984);

John Orrell, "Buckingham's Patronage of the Dramatic Arts: The Crowe Accounts," *Records of Early English Drama Newsletter*, 2 (1980): 8-17;

William R. Orwen, "Marvell and Buckingham," *Notes and Queries*, 196 (1951): 10-11;

Annabel Patterson, "*The Country Gentleman*: Howard, Marvell, and Dryden in the Theatre of Politics," *Studies in English Literature*, 25 (Summer 1985): 491-509;

Ken Robinson, "Two Cast Lists for Buckingham's *The Chances*," *Notes and Queries*, new series 26 (October 1979): 436-437;

Dane Farnsworth Smith, *The Critics in the Audience of the London Theatres from Buckingham to Sheridan: A Study of Neoclassicism in the Playhouse, 1671-1779*, University of New Mexico Publications in Language and Literature, no. 12 (Albuquerque: University of New Mexico Press, 1953);

Smith, *Plays About the Theatre in England from "The Rehearsal" in 1671 to the Licensing Act in 1737* (London: Oxford University Press, 1936);

John Harrington Smith, "Dryden and Buckingham: The Beginnings of the Feud," *Modern Language Notes*, 69 (April 1954): 242-245;

Smith, *The Gay Couple in Restoration Comedy* (Cambridge, Mass.: Harvard University Press, 1948);

Gunnar Sorelius, "Shadwell Deviating Into Sense: Timon of Athens and the Duke of Buckingham," *Studia Neophilologica*, 36 (1964): 232-244;

Arthur Colby Sprague, *Beaumont and Fletcher on the Restoration Stage* (Cambridge, Mass.: Harvard University Press, 1926);

Margarita Stocker, "Political Allusion in The Rehearsal," *Philological Quarterly*, 67 (1988): 11-35;

Robert F. Willson, Jr., *"Their Form Confounded": Studies in the Burlesque Play from Udall to Sheridan* (Paris: Mouton, 1975);

John Harold Wilson, *The Court Wits of the Restoration: An Introduction* (Princeton: Princeton University Press, 1948).

Papers:

A scribal manuscript for *The Country Gentleman* is at the Folger Shakespeare Library. The commonplace book of the duke of Buckingham is in the library of the earl of Jersey at Radier Manor. The manuscript biography of Buckingham by Brian Fairfax is in British Library (MS. Harl. 6862, "An Account of the Family of Fairfax"). Most other manuscripts relating to Buckingham's life and career are in the British Library; a few are in the Bodleian Library.

William Wycherley

(March or April 1641-31 December 1715)

Rose A. Zimbardo
State University of New York at Stony Brook

PLAY PRODUCTIONS: *Love in a Wood*, London, Theatre Royal on Bridges Street, March 1671;

The Gentleman Dancing Master, London, Dorset Garden Theatre, 6 February 1672;

The Country Wife, London, Theatre Royal in Drury Lane, 12 January 1675;

The Plain Dealer, London, Theatre Royal in Drury Lane, 11 December 1676.

BOOKS: *Hero and Leander, in Burlesque* (London, 1669);

Love in a Wood, Or, St. James's Park. A Comedy. As it is Acted at the Theatre Royal, by his Majesties Servants (London: Printed by J. M. for H. Herringman, 1672);

The Gentleman Dancing-Master. A Comedy, Acted at the Duke's Theatre (London: Printed by J. M. for H. Herringman & T. Dring, 1673);

The Country-Wife, A Comedy, Acted at the Theatre Royal (London: Printed for Thomas Dring, 1675);

The Plain-Dealer. A Comedy. As it is Acted at the Theatre Royal (London: Printed by T. N. for James Magnes & Rich. Bentley, 1677);

Epistles to the King and Duke (London: Printed for Thomas Dring, 1683);

Miscellany Poems: as Satyrs, Epistles, Love-Verses, Songs, Sonnets, & c. (London: Printed for C. Brome, J. Taylor, B. Tooke, 1704);

The Folly of Industry; or The Busy Man Expos'd, A Satyr (London: Printed for A. Baldwin, 1704); republished as *The Idleness of Business* (London: Printed for B. Bragg, 1705);

On His Grace the Duke of Marlborough (London: Printed for John Morphew, 1707).

Collections: *The Works of the Ingenious Mr. William Wycherley, Collected into One Volume* (London: Printed for Richard Wellington, 1713);

The Posthumous Works of William Wycherley, esq. in Prose and Verse. Faithfully publish'd from His Original Manuscripts, by Mr. Theobald. In Two Parts. To which are Prefixed. Some Memoirs of Mr. Wycherley's Life. By Major Pack, edited by L. Theobald (London: Printed for A. Bettesworth, 1728);

The Posthumous Works of William Wycherley, Esq; in Prose and Verse. Vol. II. Consisting of Letters and Poems Publish'd from Original Manuscripts, edited by Alexander Pope (London: Printed for J. Roberts, 1729);

The Dramatic Works of Wycherley, Congreve, Vanbrugh, and Farquhar. With Biographical and Critical Notices by Leigh Hunt, edited by Hunt (London: Moxon, 1840);

William Wycherley, edited by W. C. Ward (London: Vizetelly, 1888);

The Complete Works of William Wycherley, 4 volumes, edited by Montague Summers (Soho: Nonesuch Press, 1924);

The Complete Plays of William Wycherley, edited by Gerald Weales (Garden City, N.Y.: Doubleday, 1966);

The Plays of William Wycherley, edited by Arthur Friedman (Oxford: Clarendon Press, 1979).

OTHER: "The Answer to A Letter from Mr. Shadwell, to Mr. Wicherley," in *Poems on Affairs of State, Part 3* (London, 1689);

"To My Friend Mr. Pope, on his Pastorals," in *Poetical Miscellanies: The Sixth Part* (London: Printed for Jacob Tonson, 1709);

"An Epistle to Mr. Dryden, from Mr. Wycherley. Occasion'd by his Proposal to write a Comedy together," in *Poems on Several Occasions* (London: Printed for Bernard Lintott, 1717).

Satyre lashes Vice into Reformation, and humour represents folly so as to render it ridiculous. Many of our present Writers are eminent in both these kinds; and particularly the Author of the *Plain Dealer*, whom I am proud to call my Friend, has oblig'd all honest and vertuous Men, by one of the most bold, most general, and most useful Satyres which has ever been presented on the English Theatre.

William Wycherley (portrait by Sir Peter Lely; by permission of the National Portrait Gallery, London)

—so John Dryden wrote in his preface to *The State of Innocence* (1677). Nevertheless, Wycherley's reputation as a playwright and his place in the literary tradition have always been problematic because the history of Wycherley studies hinges upon a bitter paradox. In his own day Wycherley was considered to be a moral satirist of the seriousness and stature of Juvenal; yet from the nineteenth century to the present he has been thought successively to be: a monster of moral depravity; a writer of artificial comedies of manners that are "holidays from the sublime . . . and the real"; a closet Savaranola, who restrained his neurotic rage while he was writing his first three plays only to have it burst forth in his "truly disturbing" last play; and, most recently, a writer of sex farces.

There was no doubt in the minds of his contemporaries that Wycherley was one of the greatest practitioners of moral satire since the ancient Roman masters, Horace and Juvenal. The diarist John Evelyn, a man of education and taste, expressed the critical consensus of his day when he wrote in his prefatory verse to the 1678 edition of *The Plain Dealer,*

> As long as Men are false and Women vain,
> While Gold continues to be Virtue's bane,
> In pointed Satire Wycherley shall reign.

Dryden, poet laureate during the reigns of Charles II and James II and the greatest literary theorist of his age, used Wycherley's practice to illustrate the delicate balance between satire and humor that must be obtained in moralistic writing. In "The Original and Progress of Satire" (1693) one of the best and most comprehensive examinations of that elusive genre that has ever been written, Dryden argues a similarity between Wycherley and Juvenal, and he uses Wycherley's style to illustrate the "abundance" and *ira* of Juvenal. In 1678, when Charles II offered Wycherley the post of tutor to his son, Charles Lennox, duke of Richmond, he made the offer in the conviction that Wycherley was the greatest moralist and teacher of the day. The poet, Charles said, had particular "skill in Men and Manners"; he could "pull off the Mask which [men's] several Callings and Pretenses cover them with, and make his Pupil discern what lies at the Bottom of such Appearances." To teach "the Son of a King," Charles believed, he "could make Choice of no Man so proper . . . as Mr. Wycherley." Even Jeremy Collier, in his famous attack upon "the Immorality and Profaneness of the English Stage," exempted Wycherley from his fury and "own[ed] the *Poet* to be an Author of good Sense." Late in his life, when Wycherley was recovering from a near fatal illness, the young Alexander Pope wrote to their friend Henry Cromwell that if Wycherley had died "our nation would have lost in him as much wit and probity as would have remained . . . in the rest of it." And, in 1709, when "sentiment" was well on the way to replacing satire in English comedy, the father of sentimental comedy himself, Richard Steele, wrote in *The Tatler* no. 3 that the "Moral" of *The Country Wife* was that "there is no Defence against Vice, but Contempt of it," and he called the play a "very pleasant and instructive satire."

It is hard to imagine that so widespread and firmly established a reputation for morality and skill in teaching moral values as Wycherley's could ever be toppled; yet that is precisely what happened. In the two hundred years following his death, gradually but steadily, Wycherley's image changed from that of a stern, fearless moralist to that of a monster of moral depravity whose works were infectious to all who approached them.

In the first half of the eighteenth century Wycherley's two best plays, *The Country Wife* and *The Plain Dealer*, still held the stage steadily–*The Country Wife* hit two high points of popularity: in 1725-1729 when the two theaters staged thirty-three performances of it, and in 1742-1743, when it was shown twelve times. *The Plain Dealer* played perhaps sixty-eight times from the time of its first performance, but printed editions of the play were even more frequent than those of *The Country Wife.* However, in the mid-eighteenth century a change began. It occurred first in performance, in bowdlerized versions of the plays, such as David Garrick's *The Country Girl*, which cut Horner and the "ladies of honour" from the script. In order "to clear one of our most cele-

brated Comedies from immorality and obscenity," Garrick said, he was put "to the necessity of lopping off a limb to save the whole from putrefaction." Although the critical reputation of *The Plain Dealer*, always greater than that of *The Country Wife*, remained high in the latter part of the eighteenth century, the play met with much the same fate as *The Country Wife* in performance. Isaac Bickerstaff staged a much-cut version in 1765, and the famous actor John Philip Kemble put his revised version on for three performances in 1796. In all cases revision pulled the satiric teeth from the plays and reduced them to harmless, and, indeed, pointless slapstick farces.

Ironically enough, growing opinion that the plays were "immoral" soon rubbed off on the playwright. In his "Life of Pope" Samuel Johnson, the most highly influential critic of his period, dismissed Wycherley the *man* on moral grounds, saying that he had "had among his contemporaries his full share of reputation, to have been esteemed without virtue, and caressed without good-humour." This strange opinion was taken up and greatly intensified in the nineteenth century. In 1840 Leigh Hunt, in an attempt to reclaim Wycherley and his contemporaries, published *The Dramatic Works of Wycherley, Congreve, Vanbrugh, and Farquhar.* The edition drew the fiery wrath of Thomas Babington Macauley, influential critic for the *Edinburgh Review.* In Macauley's view the works of all four Restoration playwrights were "the most profligate and heartless of human compositions," but among them he singled out Wycherley as the greatest offender, a man depraved in his work, in his life, and in his mind. For Macauley the Restoration period as a whole was "the nadir of national taste and morality," but, in his Bosch-like picture of the age, he conjured no devil more monstrous than Wycherley. Wycherley's plays, Macauley said, were like skunks, safe from critics because they were too filthy to touch. So widely was Macauley's judgment adopted that by the end of the century Wycherley had become a standard against which the relative depravity of other writers of his period was measured. For example, John Doran, writing of Aphra Behn, said, "There is no one that equals this woman in downright nastiness, save Ravenscroft and Wycherley."

From the mid-nineteenth to the mid-twentieth century, the history of Wycherley criticism was one long contention between critics who dismissed the plays as immoral and those who sought to clear them of that charge. Detractors often damned the plays without granting them the objective consideration that allows a work of art to reveal its moral position in terms of its own aesthetic, while, on the other hand, admirers, in trying to prove the plays harmless, rendered them trivial. Constructing their approaches upon grounds foreign to the plays' aesthetic, they made them either pointless–"holiday[s] from the sublime and the beautiful, from the coarse and the real"–or mindless, photographically realistic reproductions of that carnival of rakes and wenches that "good King Charles's golden days" were supposed to be. Bonamy Dobrée's *Restoration Comedy* (1924) excepted, it was not until the 1950s, in works such as Thomas Fujimura's *The Restoration Comedy of Wit* (1952), Norman Holland's *The First Modern Comedies* (1959), and Dale Underwood's *Etherege and the Seventeenth Century Comedy of Manners* (1957), that objective critical re-evaluation of Wycherley's drama was undertaken in earnest, and it was not until 1965, in Rose Zimbardo's *Wycherley's Drama: A Link in the Development of English Satire,* that a serious, book-length study was devoted to placing Wycherley, the satirist, firmly back into English literary history.

How are we to explain so radical a change as that which Wycherley's reputation underwent? Major transformations in epistemology, aesthetics, and social history took place in the centuries following Wycherley's death that caused the changes in critical attitudes toward him. Primary among these was a change in the understanding of how a drama *functions* in relation to its audience. In the Restoration and very early eighteenth century a satiric play was thought to operate by *displaying* vice and folly and *exposing* them to make them ridiculous in the sight of the audience. The play, it was thought, *holds up* images of vice, and the spectator, recognizing them, laughs them to scorn and contempt. The underlying assumption in this kind of moralistic writing was, as Pope put it, that "Vice is a monster of so fearful mien / As, to be hated, needs but to be seen."

However, as the eighteenth century progressed, theories of associationism that had been formulated by John Locke and popularized by Joseph Addison led playwrights and critics to hold an entirely different view of how drama operates upon the minds and sensibility of an audience. From the eighteenth century, we have thought that audiences *imitate* in their own behavior what they see on a stage. Therefore, if we see on stage attractive characters who behave immorally, we are drawn to emulate their behavior with the con-

sequence that we become immoral. We commonly hold this view still, for we think that watching violence in a film makes us violent, or that merry little housewives in television commercials induce passivity and submissiveness in female soap-opera fans.

Concomitant with the notion that audiences identify with dramatic characters was the identification of playwrights with the characters in their plays. As this line of reasoning goes, if Horner is sexually promiscuous and Horner equals Wycherley, or, at the very least, is the spokesman of Wycherley's moral attitudes, then it follows that Wycherley the man was sexually promiscuous–and, indeed, that he wrote his plays in order to seduce *us* into adopting his immoral attitudes.

Wycherley's contemporaries and immediate successors, of course, could never have predicted such a radical transformation in aesthetics, and, most certainly, they could not have imagined that "Manly" Wycherley would one day be accused of encouraging immorality. On the contrary, they saw it as their task to persuade us that a satirist so unflinchingly hard on vice as Wycherley could, in his personal behavior, be an amiable man. In his *Memoirs of the Life of William Wycherley, Esq.; With a Character of his Writings* (1718) one of Wycherley's earliest biographers, George Granville, baron Lansdowne, felt obliged to reconcile the moral severity of Wycherley the poet with the genial disposition of Wycherley the man:

> As pointed and severe as he is in his writings, in his Temper he has all the softness of the tenderest disposition; gentle and inoffensive to every man in his particular character; he only attacks Vice as a public Enemy, compassionating the wound he is under necessity to probe.

From his earliest appearance on the London scene in 1671 to his last days, when the young poet whose career he helped to launch, Alexander Pope, declared him supreme among his age in "Wit, Probity, and Good Nature," Wycherley was universally valued for his judicious and penetrating wit, for his warm heart, and for his generosity of spirit.

We know very little that is verifiable about Wycherley's life before the success in 1671 of his first play, *Love in a Wood,* rocketed him into the arms of Charles II's then reigning mistress, Barbara Villiers, the duchess of Cleveland, and from thence into the charmed and enviable circle

Clive Hall, near Shrewsbury, may have been the birthplace of William Wycherley or his father

of the court wits. And, curiously enough, disagreement about Wycherley begins over his very birth. His earliest biographers call him "a Shropshire gentleman" who was born on 28 May 1640; his most-recent biographers disagree about whether it was William Wycherley or his father, Daniel, who was born at Clive Hall near Shrewsbury in Shropshire, and they date the son's birth in March of 1641. The firmest evidence indicates that William Wycherley was baptized in Whitchurch, Hampshire, in April 1641, and that the family into which he was born had lived comfortably in Shropshire for more than two centuries. The playwright's father is much easier quarry for a biographer than William because he was a singularly litigious man, and court records make it easier to track him than it is to follow his dazzling son. Daniel Wycherley was high steward in the household of John Paulet, marquess of Winchester at Basing House in Hampshire. There he met and married Bethnia Shrimpton, lady-in-waiting to the marchioness. William was the eldest of their six children. Less than two years after William Wycherley's birth, civil war broke out, and in 1645 Basing House was invaded by the parliamentary forces under Oliver Cromwell. The marquess was arrested and imprisoned for the duration of the interregnum. During the absence of the marquess Daniel Wycherley remained his steward and his deputy, and he did very well not

only for the marquess but also for himself. He was able to set aside a good deal of money, with which he later bought substantial lands in Shropshire. Daniel Wycherley's two great passions—for land buying and for law suits—date from the time of his service to the absent marquess. His passions for litigation, social climbing, and money became prime targets of satire in his son's plays. It is generally accepted that the litigious Widow Blackacre in *The Plain Dealer*, whose passion for the law courts surpasses all other passions and who is ready on the spot to declare her son, Jerry, a bastard to preserve her freedom to sue, is patterned after Daniel Wycherley. More subtle mockery of Daniel's type can be found in Sir Simon Addleplot of *Love in a Wood*, the character who bought his title "of a Court laundress" and who attempts to imitate aristocratic values that he cannot understand, or Sir Jasper Fidget of *The Country Wife*, whose sole "pleasure" is "business." So strong was the playwright's reaction against his father's behavior that, according to B. Eugene McCarthy, his most recent biographer, it formed the mainspring of his characters. In the portrait McCarthy draws, William Wycherley emerges as a decidedly unworldly and certainly unbusinesslike man, a person too easily led by others and too readily duped by them. Wycherley's mocking contempt for "business" and "industry"—the qualities most highly valued by the class that became the ruling class in England in the centuries following his death–is amply demonstrated everywhere in his work, but most pointedly in his poem *The Folly of Industry; or The Busy Man Expos'd* (1704). It is hard to say whether Daniel Wycherley was "the dominating figure in William's life" that McCarthy thinks he was, but certainly self-important, money-hungry social upstarts of the kind that Daniel was are prominent butts in Wycherley's satire.

Predictably, the son of an ardently Royalist family who sent money to the exiled king was sent to France for his education. At the age of fifteen Wycherley was sent to Angoulême in the Charante district, where he became closely associated with Julie d'Angennes, marquise de Montausier. He had the good fortune–good for any young man, but inestimably valuable for a prospective literary artist–to be "often admitted to the Conversation" of this brilliant intellectual. The marquise de Montausier, the wife of the provincial governor, was the daughter and the disciple of the celebrated Catherine de Vivonne, marquise de Rambouillet, in whose salon the cult of exquisitely refined manners, morals, and literary brilliance, *préciosité*, was born and flourished. Kathleen M. Lynch, in her seminal study, *The Social Mode of Restoration Comedy* (1926) has demonstrated the formative influence which *préciosité* exercised upon the philosophical and moral attitudes of the English in the Restoration period. Charles II's mother, Henrietta Maria, herself had had strong connections with the salon de Rambouillet, and it was she who had imported the précieuse cult of "platonic love" into the English Caroline court. The values upheld by this code formed part of the Restoration's inheritance from "before the Flood." Primary among these inherited attitudes was the idea that a generous, passionate love refines the soul and lifts it above the binding coils of commercially contracted marriage and the idea of the ideal of equality and free converse between the sexes. Not only did Mme de Montausier, "the incomparable Julie," introduce the adolescent Wycherley to the brilliant world of French intellectual and social life, but we may also assume that she taught him properly to value women, for "he was equally pleas'd with the Beauty of her Mind, and with the Graces of her Person." Her husband, Charles de Sainte-Maure, marquis de Montausier, was an equally formative influence upon the young Wycherley. Molière patterned the rigidly honest protagonist of *Le Misanthrope* (1666) Alceste, upon de

Montausier, and the latter was pleased to own his resemblance to the character. A strange anomaly in the court of Louis XIV, de Montausier was a highly successful courtier whose pride it was always to tell the truth despite the social consequences. Gilbert Burnet describes him as "a pattern of virtue and sincerity, if not too cynical in it. He was so far from flattering the King, as all the rest did most abjectly, that he could not hold contradicting him." Whether or not we can say with surety that the young Wycherley patterned his own behavior upon that of this remarkable man, there can be little doubt that aspects of his character went into the making of the protagonist of *The Plain Dealer*.

Between his fifteenth year, when the conversation of Julie d'Angennes polished him into a gentleman, and his thirtieth, when the more raucous voice of the duchess of Cleveland called him "a Son of a Whore" and catapulted him into fame, we lose sight of Wycherley. It is generally believed that during his early twenties he spent some time in Madrid in the household of the poet-ambassador Sir Richard Fanshawe. Wycherley's borrowings from the Spanish drama in his first two plays have been used as evidence for a stay in Spain (J. N. Rundle believes that part of the high plot of *Love in a Wood* is taken from Pedro Calderón de la Barca's *Mañanas de abril y mayo*, and the title of his second play is obviously taken from Calderón's *El Maestro del Danzar*), but Spanish influence upon Wycherley's drama seems negligible. It is well for us to keep in mind that our own provinciality in matters of nationalistic encapsulation and literary borrowing did not obtain in the seventeenth century.

All that is verifiable about Wycherley's life in this vast gap of time is that he returned to England early in 1660 some months before the Restoration of Charles II and began his formal education at Queen's College, Oxford. During his time in France, probably under the influence of the de Montausiers, Wycherley had converted to Roman Catholicism. In his few months at Oxford, he reconverted to Protestantism, probably under the influence of Thomas Barlow, the head of his college, in whose house he lived. Barlow was a distinguished Anglican divine, who had flourished during the Commonwealth period as he did after the return of the king. Wycherley's stay at Oxford was very short. In November of 1660 he enrolled as a student in the Inner Temple. It is doubtful, however, that he ever com-

Joseph Haines, who played Sparkish in the first production of The Country Wife *and Lord Plausible in the premiere of* The Plain Dealer, *was known for speaking the epilogue in the July 1696 production of Thomas Scott's* The Unhappy Kindness *while seated on a live ass*

pleted his legal training either, and it is extremely unlikely that he ever practiced the law.

Although we cannot prove it, we may be fairly confident that Wycherley took some part in the naval battle against the Dutch in 1665. Certainly it is true that throughout his writing career he associates aristocratic bravery with heroism at sea. For example, in the epilogue to *The Gentleman Dancing Master* Wycherley mocks the citizens, the "good men o' th'Exchange," who will be the only audience left, for all true "Gentlemen must pack to Sea." More pointedly in *The Plain Dealer*

he describes Manly in the list of dramatis personae as being "of an honest, surly, nice humour, suppos'd first, in the time of the *Dutch* War, to have procur'd the Command of a Ship, out of Honour, not Interest."

We resume sure contact with Wycherley in 1669 when his first work was published anonymously. The poem, *Hero and Leander, in Burlesque* is a mock-heroic burlesque that is much indebted to the puppet play in Ben Jonson's *Bartholomew Fair.* Although the piece has not much intrinsic value, it does demonstrate that from the beginning of his poetic career Wycherley had a penchant for mock-heroic, that is, for the nice tension between hypsos and bathos that forms the tightrope upon which great satire dances.

Wycherley's first play, *Love in a Wood,* made him famous. It was first performed in 1671 by the King's Company at the Theatre Royal on Bridges Street. A reference to Lent in the dedication (the poet says that his enviers will say the duchess of Cleveland favored the play because it was part of her Lenten self-mortification) leads us to believe that the play premiered in the spring, possibly in March, but it is listed in the *Stationers' Register,* 6 October 1671, and in the *Term Catalogues,* 20 November 1671.

The story of how *Love in a Wood* made Wycherley a star and a member of the charmed company of court wits is so wonderful that, whether or not it is precisely true, it is worth retelling. What is more, the anecdote comes best in the words of the man who first set it down, John Dennis:

> The writing of that Play (*Love in a Wood*) was likewise the Occasion of his becoming acquainted with one of King *Charles's* Mistresses after a very particular manner. As Mr. *Wycherley* was going thro' *Pall-mall* toward *St. James's* in his Chariot, he met the foresaid Lady in hers, who, thrusting half her Body out of the Chariot, cry'd out aloud to him, *You,* Wycherley, *you are a Son of a Whore,* at the same time laughing aloud and heartily. Perhaps, Sir, if you never heard of this Passage before, you may be surpris'd at so strange a Greeting from one of the most beautiful and best bred Ladies in the World. Mr. *Wycherley* was certainly very much surpris'd at it, yet not so much but he soon apprehended it was spoke with Allusion to the latter End of a Song in the foremention'd Play.

> *When Parents are Slaves*
> *Their Brats cannot be any other,*
> *Great Wits and great Braves*
> *Have always a Punk to their Mother.*

> As, during Mr. *Wycherley's* Surprise, the Chariots drove different ways, they were soon at considerable Distance from each other, when Mr. *Wycherley* recovering from his Surprise, ordered his Coachman to drive back, and to overtake the Lady. As soon as he got over-against her, he said to her, *Madam, you have been pleased to bestow a Title on me which generally belongs to the Fortunate. Will your Ladyship be at the Play to Night? Well,* she reply'd, *what if I am there? Why then I will be there to wait on your Ladyship, tho' I disappoint a very fine Woman who has made me an Assignation. So,* said she, *you are sure to disappoint a Woman who has favour'd you for one who has not. Yes,* he reply'd, *if she who has not favour'd me is the finer Woman of the two. But he who will be constant to your Ladyship, till he can find a finer Woman, is sure to die your Captive.* The Lady blush'd, and bade her Coachman drive away. As she was then in all her Bloom, and the most celebrated Beauty that was then in *England,* or perhaps that has been in *England* since, she was touch'd with the Gallantry of that Compliment. In short, she was that Night in the first Row of the King's Box in *Drury Lane,* and Mr. *Wycherley* in the Pit under her, where he entertained her during the whole Play. And this, Sir, was the beginning of a Correspondence between these two Persons, which afterwards made a great Noise in the Town. ("To the Honourable Major Pack," 1 September 1720).

Although Dennis's anecdote no doubt embroiders the past, it gives us a window on the world in which Wycherley lived during the whole of his career as a playwright. It was a world that delighted in elegant, playful talk and in sprightly courtship, a world in which men and women alike enjoyed the so-called innocent pleasures of the Town. It was a world in which women were freer in their manners—and only *perhaps* in their morals—than they were to be for the next two hundred years. What is more, it was a world in which women were *valued* for their brains as highly as for their bodies, for their ability to think quickly and to talk wittily as well as for their ability to breed. A great nobleman of the time, the earl of Halifax, advised his daughter that unless wit is *combined* with virtue in a woman's character "the first is so empty and the other so faint, that they scarce have right to be commended." It was a society that held something of the same values as G. B. Shaw's Mrs. Warren, who thinks that it is better to be brave, generous, free, and "immoral," than it is to be respectable and be a slave. Lastly, it was a world in which, literally and figuratively, the playhouse was an important center.

The question has been raised, if Wycherley the man was so swimmingly successful in such a world (as indeed he was until sickness and penury made him too tired to swim), how could he have been a satirist. The very reason that we are led to ask such a question is that we have lost sight of what satire, as the seventeenth century understood it to be, is. For the ancient Romans, as well as for writers, readers, and spectators of the Restoration period, satire "did not . . . denote a specific attitude of mind involving the contemporary scene, but was a term used for an independent literary genre of a particular kind with well-defined limits and a unique profile" (Ulrich Knoche, *Roman Satire* [1975]). In Wycherley's age, satire did not reflect the "real" feelings of an author toward his realistically portrayed society; rather it was a recognized literary genre, just as tragedy, comedy, or epic was. As Maynard Mack showed in his essay "The Muse of Satire," the satiric perspective is a lens which a writer takes up in order to practice his delicate and demanding art. Therefore, it is as irrelevant to ask how a writer who so loved his world and was so well loved by it as Wycherley could write satire as it is to ask how Shakespeare could have written as dark a tragedy as *Hamlet* and as glorious a comedy as *Twelfth Night* in the same year (1600). The inconsistency, if indeed there is one, lies not in the practice of the seventeenth-century writer but in the expectations of a twentieth-century critic, most especially the kind of critic who cannot accept that there has ever been a conception of artistic imitation different from our own. The conceptual design of satire from Ancient Rome to seventeenth-century England and France consisted in a collision and interplay between contradictory *literary* perspectives upon our timeless human condition. A multivalent mode, satire mocks us for the high-blown heroic, noble, glittering images of ourselves that we spin out of our own feverish imaginations, but, ironically, it also mocks us for not living up to those ideals. It laughs at us for being goats and monkeys, but it also jeers at us for making goats and monkeys of ourselves. It simultaneously elevates what we should be and denigrates what we are. Moreover, satire mocks the satirist himself for the most egregious of follies, that is, thinking that satire can reform anybody. As Wycherley says in *The Plain Dealer* (V.ii) "You [the satirist] rail, and nobody hangs himself: And thou has nothing of the Satyr, but in thy face." Until the eighteenth century, when it came to be thought that the aim of literary art was to draw readers or spectators into good moral behavior by making them emulate the good-natured, virtuous characters it portrayed, satire did not portray a standard of good behavior for emulation. It directed its audience to the good only very obliquely and always by indirection. Those of us who have called Wycherley's plays satires have done so in the understanding that Restoration satire does not provide models of good behavior, and that it is, above all, funny. Those who have argued that Wycherley's plays cannot be satires have done so because they think that satirists should be more serious than Wycherley is in "lashing vice" and "ridiculing folly" and   in showing us how to behave ourselves.

How can we be sure that Wycherley thought himself to be a satirist? After all, Dryden's essay, which was the first attempt to describe the generic form of satire and trace its development, was written in 1692, almost twenty years after brain fever and consequent loss of memory prevented Wycherley from ever writing another play, and Wycherley, a supreme ironist, would never, of course, condescend to justify his art in literary criticism, except self-mockingly, as when he quotes Tertullian to the famous brothel keeper, Mother Bennett, to whom *The Plain Dealer* is dedicated, and adds:

> *There's* Latin *for you again, Madam; I protest to you, as I am an Author, I cannot help it; nay, I can hardly keep my self from quoting* Aristotle *and* Horace, *and talking to you of the Rules of Writing (like the French Authors,) to show you and my Readers I understand 'em, in my Epistle, lest neither of you should find it out by the Play.*

The message is clear. If we want to understand the satire of this elusive joker, we have to look to his plays, not to critical speculations about them.

In his first play, *Love in a Wood,* Wycherley is light-handed in his satire; he uses it to mock the highly flattering perspective upon our human nature that pastoral romance affords us. The epigraph to the play, "Excludit sanos helicone poetas Democritus" (Democritus excludes those poets who are in their right senses from Helicon), comes from a section of the *Ars Poetica* (296) in which Horace is urging a young poet to try his wings, but also cautioning him to be aware always of the tradition in which he is writing. The epigraph itself is a delicious joke because in this play Wycherley is using for *satiric* purposes one of the most popular plays of the Caroline period, one of the first plays to be revived when the theaters were reopened in 1660, and one of the most traditional and rarified pastoral romances ever written, John Fletcher's *The Faithful Shepherdess* (circa 1608).

Like allegory, satire always "speaks of the *other*"; that is to say, just as it exaggerates *downward* to grotesque effect, a satire must also posit the existence of an equal and opposite *upward* perspective. In a great many satires the indirectly expressed but indispensable upward, *other* perspec-

To my LADY B——

Madam,

THO I never had the Honour to receive a Favour from you, nay, or be known to you, I take the confidence of an Author to write to you a Billiet doux Dedicatory; which is no new thing, for by most Dedications it appears, that Authors, though they praise their Patrons from top to toe, and seem to turn 'em inside out, know 'em as little, as sometimes their Patrons their Books, tho they read 'em ont; and if the Poetical Daubers did not write the name of the Man or Woman on top of the Picture, 'twere impossible to guess whose it were. But you, Madam, without the help of a Poet, have made your self known and famous in the world; and, because you do not want it, are therefore most worthy of an Epistle Dedicatory. And this Play claims naturally your Protection, since it has lost its Reputation with the Ladies of stricter lives in the Play-house; and (you know) when mens endeavours are discountenanc'd and refus'd, by the nice coy Women of Honour, they come to you, To you the Great and Noble Patroness of rejected and bashful men, of which number I profess my self to be one, though a Poet, a Dedicating Poet; To you I say, Madam, who have as discerning a judgement, in what's obscene or not, as any quick-sighted civil Person of 'em all, and can make as much of a double meaning saying as the best of 'em; yet wou'd not, as some do, make nonsense of a Poet's jest, rather than not make it baudy: by which they show they as little value wit in a Play, as in a Lover, provided they can bring t'other thing about. Their sense indeed lies all one way, and therefore are only for that in a Poet which is moving, as they say; but what do they mean by that word moving? Well, I must not put 'em to the blush, since I find I can

           †   do't.

The Epistle

do't. In short, Madam, you wou'd not be one of those who ravish a Poet's innocent words, and make 'em guilty of their own naughtiness (as 'tis term'd) in spight of his teeth; nay, nothing is secure from the power of their imaginations; no, not their Husbands, whom they Cuckold with themselve; by thinking of other men, and so make the lawful matrimonial embraces Adultery, wrong Husbands and Poets in thought and word, to keep their own Reputations; but your Ladyship's justice, I know, wou'd think a Woman's Arraigning and Damning a Poet for her own obscenity, like her crying out a Rape, and hanging a man for giving her pleasure, only that she might be thought not to consent to't; and so to vindicate her honour forfeits her modesty. But you, Madam, have too much modesty to pretend to't; tho you have as much to say for your modesty as many a nicer she; for you never were seen at this Play, no, not the first day; and 'tis no matter what Peoples lives have been, they are unquestionably modest who frequent not this Play: For, as Mr. Bays says of his, that it is the only Touchstone of Mens Wit and Understanding; mine is, it seems, the only Touchstone of Womens Vertue and Modesty. But hold, that Touchstone is equivocal, and, by the strength of a Lady's Imagination, may become something that is not civil; but your Ladyship, I know, scorns to misapply a Touchstone. And, Madam, tho you have not seen this Play, I hope (like other nice Ladies) you will the rather read it; yet, lest the Chambermaid or Page shou'd not be trusted, and their indulgence cou'd gain no further admittance for it, than to their Ladies Lobbies or outward Rooms, take it into your care and protection; for, by your recommendation and procurement, it may have the honour to get into their Closets: For what they renounce in publick often entertains 'em there, with your help especially. In fine, Madam, for these and many other reasons, you are the fittest Patroness or Judge of this Play; for you shew no partiality to this or that Author; for from some many Ladies will take a broad jeast as chearfully as from the watermen, and sit at some downright filthy Plays (as they call 'em) as well satisfy'd, and as still, as a Poet cou'd wish 'em elsewhere; therefore it must be the doubtful obscenity of my Plays alone they take exceptions at, because it is too bashful

Dedicatory.

ful for 'em; and indeed most women hate men, for attempting to halves on their Chastity; and Baudy I find, like Satyr, shou'd be home, not to have it taken notice of. But, now I mention Satyr, some there are who say, 'Tis the Plain-dealing of the Play, not the obscenity, 'tis taking off the Ladies Masks, not offering at their Pettycoats, which offends 'em: and generally they are not the handsomest, or most innocent, who are the most angry at being discover'd:

    —Nihil est audacius illis
Deprehensis; iram, atq; animos a crimine sumunt.

Pardon, Madam, the Quotation, for a Dedication can no more be without ends of Latine, than Flattery; and 'tis no matter whom it is writ to; for an Author can as easily (I hope) suppose People to have more understanding and Languages than they have, as well as more Vertues: But why, the Devil! shou'd any of the few modest and handsome be alarm'd? (for some there are who as well as deserve those Attributes, yet refrain not from seeing this Play, nor think it any addition to their Vertue to set up for it in a Play-house, lest there it shou'd look too much like acting.) But why, I say, shou'd any at all of the truly vertuous be concern'd, if those who are not so are distinguish'd from 'em? For by that Mask of modesty which women wear promiscuously in publick, they are all alike, and you can no more know a kept Wench from a Woman of Honour by her looks than by her Dress; for those who are of Quality without Honour (if any such there are) they have their Quality to set off their false Modesty, as well as their false Jewels, and you must no more suspect their Countenances for counterfeit than their Pendants, tho, as the Plain-dealer Montaigne says, Els envoy leur conscience au Bordel, & teinnent leur contenance en regle: But those who act as they look, ought not to be scandaliz'd at the reprehension of others faults, which they tax themselves with 'em, and by too delicate and quick an apprehension not only make that obscene which I meant innocent, but that Satyr on all, which was intended only on those who deserv'd it. But, Madam, I beg your par-

        † 2   don

Dedication to The Plain Dealer, *from the 1677 edition. Lady B—— was Mother Bennett, a well-known brothel keeper*

The Epistle

...on for this digreſſion, to Civil Women and Ladies of Honour, ſince you and I ſhall never be the better for 'em ; for a Comic Poet, and a Lady of your Profeſſion, make moſt of the other ſort, and the Stage and your Houſes, like our Plantations, are propagated by the leaſt nice Women ; and as with the Miniſters of Juſtice, the Vices of the Age are our beſt buſineſs. But, now I mention Publick Perſons, I can no longer defer doing you the juſtice of a Dedication, and telling you your own ; who are, of all publick-ſpirited people, the moſt neceſſary, moſt communicative, moſt generous and hoſpitable ; your houſe has been the houſe of the People, your ſleep ſtill diſturb'd for the Publick, and when you aroſe 'twas that others might lye down, and you waked that others might reſt ; The good you have done is unſpeakable ; How many young unexperienc'd Heirs have you kept from raſh fooliſh Marriages ? and from being jilted for their lives by the worſt ſort of Jilts, Wives ? How many unbewitched Widowers Children have you preſerv'd from the Tyranny of Stepmothers ? How many old Dotards from Cuckoldage, and keeping other mens Wenches and Children ? How many Adulteries and unnatural ſins have you prevented ? In fine, you have been a conſtant ſcourge to the old Lecher, and often a terrour to the young ; you have made concupiſcence its own puniſhment, and extinguiſh'd Luſt with Luſt, like blowing up of Houſes to ſtop the fire.

*Nimirum propter continentiam, incontinentia
Neceſſaria eſt, incendium ignibus extinguitur.*

There's Latin for you again, Madam ; I proteſt to you, as I am an Author, I cannot help it ; nay, I can hardly keep my ſelf from quoting Ariſtotle and Horace, and talking to you of the Rules of Writing, (like the French Authors,) to ſhew you and my Readers I underſtand 'em, in my Epiſtle, leſt neither of you ſhould find it out by the Play ; and, according to the Rules of Dedications, 'tis no matter whether you underſtand or no, what I quote or ſay to you, of Writing ; for an Author can as eaſily make any one a Judge or Critick, in an Epiſtle, as an Hero in his Play : But, Madam, that this may prove to the end a true Epiſtle Dedicatory, I'd have you know 'tis not

Dedicatory.

not without a deſign upon you, which is in the behalf of the Fraternity of Parnaſſus, that Songs and Sonnets may go at your Houſes, and in your Liberties, for Guinneys and half Guinneys ; and that Wit, at leaſt with you, as of old, may be the price of Beauty, and ſo you will prove a true encourager of Poetry, for Love is a better help to it than Wine ; and Poets, like Painters, draw better after the Life, than by Fancy ; Nay, in juſtice, Madam, I think a Poet ought to be as free of your Houſes, as of the Play-houſes ; ſince he contributes to the ſupport of both, and is as neceſſary to ſuch as you, as a Ballad-ſinger to the Pick-purſe, in convening the Cullies at the Theatres, to be pick'd up, and carry'd to Supper and Bed at your houſes. And, Madam, the reaſon of this motion of mine is, becauſe poor Poets can get no favour in the Tiring Rooms, for they are no Keepers, you know ; and Folly and Money, the old Enemies of Wit, are even too hard for it on its own Dunghill : And for other Ladies, a Poet can leaſt go to the price of them ; beſides, his Wit, which ought to recommend him to 'em, is as much an obſtruction to his Love, as to his wealth or preferment ; for moſt Women now adays, apprehend Wit in a Lover, as much as in a Husband ; they hate a Man that knows 'em, they muſt have a blind eaſie Fool, whom they can lead by the Noſe, and as the Scythian Women of old, muſt baffle a Man, and put out his Eyes, ere they will lye with him, and then too, like Thieves, when they have plunder'd and ſtript a Man, leave him But if there ſhou'd be one of an hundred of thoſe Ladies, generous enough to give her ſelf to a Man that has more Wit than Money, (all things conſider'd) he wou'd think it cheaper coming to you for a Miſtreſs, though you made him pay his Guinney ; as a Man in a Journey, (out of good husbandry) had better pay for what he has in an Inn, than lye on freecoſt at a Gentlemans Houſe.

In fine, Madam, like a faithful Dedicator, I hope I have done my ſelf right in the firſt place, then you, and your Profeſſion, which in the wiſeſt and moſt religious Government of the World, is honour'd with the publick allowance ; and in thoſe that are thought the moſt unciviliz'd and barbarous, is proteſted, and ſupported by the Miniſters of Juſtice ; and of you, Madam, I ought to ſay no more here, for your Vertues deſerve a Poem rather than an Epiſtle, or

The Epistle

or a Volume intire to give the World your Memoirs, or Life at large, and which (upon the word of an Author that has a mind to make an end of his Dedication) I promiſe to do, when I write the Annals of our Britiſh Love, which ſhall be Dedicated to the Ladies concern'd, if they will not think them ſomething too obſcene too ; when your Life, compar'd with many that are thought innocent, I doubt not may vindicate you, and me, to the World, for the confidence I have taken in this Addreſs to you ; which then may be thought neither impertinent, nor immodeſt ; and, whatſoever your Amorous misfortunes have been, none can charge you with that heinous, and worſt of Womens Crimes, Hypocriſie ; nay, in ſpight of misfortunes or age, you are the ſame Woman ſtill ; though moſt of your Sex grow Magdalens at fifty, and as a ſolid French Author has it,

*Apres le plaiſir, vien't la peine,
Apres la peine la vertu ;*

But ſure an old ſinner's continency is much like a Gameſter's forſwearing Play, when he has loſt all his Money ; and Modeſty is a kind of a youthful dreſs, which, as it makes a young Woman more amiable, makes an old one more nauſeous ; a baſhful old woman is like an hopeful old man ; and the affected Chaſtity of antiquated Beauties, is rather a reproach than an honour to 'em, for it ſhews the mens Vertue only, not theirs. But you, in fine, Madam, are no more an Hypocrite than I am when I praiſe you ; therefore I doubt not will be thought (even by your's and the Play's Enemies, the niceſt Ladies) to be the fitteſt Patroneſs for,

Madam,

Your Ladyſhip's moſt obedient,
faithful, humble Servant, and

The Plain-Dealer.

tive is that of pastoral romance. As E. M. Waith, writing about pastoral, puts it in *The Pattern of Tragi-Comedy in Beaumont and Fletcher* (1959), "The satirist . . . portrays with awful vividness the very conditions from which the pastoral poet longs to escape." Looking at the matter from the other side of the coin and writing about satire, Alvin Kernan says in *The Cankered Muse* (1959), "Somehow the satirist seems always to come from a world of pastoral innocence and kindness; he is the prophet come down from the hills to the cities of the plain . . . abroad in the cruel world." Wycherley, the trickster, makes the connection in his work itself and laughs at us while he is making it. There are direct references to Fletcher's play in *Love in a Wood*; for example the suprasensuous Cristina, who mourns for her absent Valentine as though he were dead, is twice called "the Faithful Shepherdess." The connection, of course, is to Fletcher's title character, Clorin, who is so elevated of soul and so refined in love that she is married to a dead man, beside whose grave she keeps her bower. There are also direct echoes of Fletcher's play, as when Lady Flippant, a citizen's widow, ranging the park in search of any man who will satisfy her raging sexual appetite, uses words similar to those of Fletcher's Cloe as she ranges the Arcadian wood; Cloe says, "It is impossible to ravish me, / I am so willing." However, the most obvious device Wycherley employs to achieve the necessary satiric-pastoral collision of perspectives is to transfer the pastoral meadows and forests of Arcadia to the middle of Restoration London, to make the pastoral "wood" the most fashionable trysting place in the dear, distracting town, St. James's Park—and then to go a step further and pun on the contradiction in his title. *Love in a Wood* means *both* love in the nowhere-nowhere wood of a wash-tint pastoral landscape *and* love in the mad, muddled whirligig of life in here-and-now fashionable London. The word *wood* is a romantic word for a forest, but it is also a common Restoration word for madness or confusion.

As numerous prefaces and prologues of the 1660s and 1670s testify, the two most powerful influences upon comic and satiric playwrights of the time were "Fletcher" and "Ben" (Jonson). In his first play the fledgling playwright Wycherley follows the Horatian precept that he quotes in his epigraph rather closely. He takes the frame and the high romance plane of his structure from Fletcher, but he takes his downwardly exaggerated humours characters and his low plane of

action from Ben. The frame of the play is a pastoral romance ladder of love that stretches from apex in the highly romantic attachment of Cristina and Valentine, where stately postures of the soul and refinements of the debate between love and honor dominate, to nadir in the lecherous Alderman Gripe and the Crossbites, where prurience and greed drive action and hypocritical Puritan cant dominates discourse. One degree less perfect in love and more contemporary in action than the faithful Cristina and her heroic Valentine are Ranger and Lydia. Ranger is a Restoration libertine and Lydia the female wit who cleverly snares him. Their action is typical love chase and their discourse witty banter. The next step down on the Fletcherian scale of love is a step down in social class as well. Dapperwit, a fop and would-be wit, who mistakes backbiting for satire, takes as his partner Martha, the daughter of Alderman Gripe. As is always the case both in pastoral romance and in three-tiered early Restoration comedy, descent into the world is descent into confusion and duplicity—and the further the descent the greater the confusion. Dapperwit is the lover of Martha, but he is also the keeper of Lucy Crossbite, who expects to be elevated by him to success on the stage "where [she] might have had as good luck as others . . . good Cloaths, Plate, Jewels." Martha, on the other hand, is pursued by a newly made knight, Sir Simon Addleplot. In the interchanges of Martha and Sir Simon, Wycherley mocks a *real* social phenomenon—the new upstart class that has bought its nobility with money—and a *literary* mode—romance—at the same time:

SIR SIMON: . . . I have freed the Captive Lady, for her longing Knight. . . .

SIR SIMON: I wou'd have kept the Maiden-head of your lips, for your sweet Knight. . . .

MARTHA: My sweet Knight, if he will be Knight of mine, must be contented with what he finds, as well as other Knights.

SIR SIMON: . . . your Worthy Noble, Brave, Heroick Knight; who loves you only, and only deserves your kindness.

One rung from the bottom of the scale is Wycherley's rendering of Cloe. Lady Flippant, the widow of a Citizen and sister of Alderman Gripe (and consequently among the social climbers and pretenders who are Wycherley's prime targets), nudges her brother's servants into sexual play, relentlessly pursues Dapperwit, who she knows despises her, and hires Mrs. Joyner, the bawd, to get her a husband. When all expedients fail she ranges the park like a predator: "Unfortunate Lady, that I am! I have left the Herd on purpose to be chas'd, and have wandred this hour here; but the Park affords not so much as a Satyr for me, (and that's strange) no Burgundy man, or drunken Scourer will reel my way" (V.i). The discourse of such a passage reveals the subtlety of Wycherley's satire. Language parodies the elevated discourse of pastoral romance; action parodies pastoral action. The Citizen-Lady, a combination oxymoronic in itself, ranges St. James's Park, the favorite site for illicit sexual encounters at that time, in parodic imitation of pastoral's shepherds and shepherdesses who meet at midnight in Arcadian woods to pledge their innocent, platonic loves. The highly literary romantic past collides with the all too tarnished present "reality" in the formation of that complex disjunctive unity that is the hallmark of satire.

At the absolute nadir of the scale, exaggerated downwardly to the same degree as Cristina and Valentine are upwardly idealized, are the Jonsonian humours characters, Alderman Gripe, Mrs. Crossbite and her daughter, Lucy, and Mrs. Joyner, the bawd. Their lechery and avarice create the impression of impenetrable materialism to counterbalance the translucent atmosphere of the high plane. However, even their materialism is not simple; it is distorted into grotesque deformity by hypocrisy. "Peace, Plenty, and Pastime be within these Walls!" Alderman Gripe cants upon entering the house of a young wench he means to buy at the lowest possible price. Following Jonson's lead, Wycherley makes his lowest figures–the lecher, the whore, and the pimp–Puritans. It is, in fact, highly probable that his most grossly ridiculous characterizations were created with particular actors in mind, for each of the roles was played by an actor famous for some interpretation of a Jonsonian character. Mrs. Joyner, for instance, was played by Katherine Mitchell Corey, who is referred to by theatrical chroniclers of the time as "Doll Common" because of the excellence of her portrayal of that character in *The Alchemist*. Gripe was played by John Lacey, famous for Sir Politic Would-be, Ananias, and Otter, and Dapperwit was played by Michael Mohun, the Face and Volpone of the Restoration stage.

The geography of *Love in a Wood*, then, is Fletcherian in its heights and Jonsonian in its depths. The new poet has followed the advice of Horace to perfection; he has tried his wings, and yet kept his eye steadily trained upon the traditions in which he was writing.

In composing his second play Wycherley was writing a potboiler, and, what is more, he knew it. Appropriately, the epigraph he chose for this play is "Non satis est risu diducere rictum/ Auditoris; et est quaedam tamen hic quoq; virtus" (It is not enough to make your reader laugh, though there is something even in that). It is taken from Horace's *Satires* I,x,7-8, and when we go to the Horatian context, we find that in it the Roman theorist-poet is discussing the proper manner of writing moral satire. In choosing the particular passage that he does, Wycherley is apologizing for writing so flimsy a play as *The Gentleman Dancing Master*, acknowledging that it is not worthy work for a satirist, but arguing, almost with a grin, that simply raising a laugh has some merit in it. Nevertheless, even this trifle of a play enjoyed considerable popularity in its time; after its premiere on 6 February 1672, it appeared in three separate editions, in 1673, in 1693, and as late as 1702.

Strictly considered, *The Gentleman Dancing Master* may well by Wycherley's only comedy. Borrowing his central plot device from Calderon's *El Maestro del Danzar*, Wycherley stretches it into a structure, admittedly thin and obvious, that answers the demands of the classic comic formula: the outwitting of a *senex iratus* by a clever innocent, and the triumph of love in an end-scene wedding that unites not just the lovers but all the members of the human community whatever their nature or their initial deviation from the ideal. Perhaps because it so obviously fulfills our expectations of comedy, and Wycherley's drama has so often been labeled "Restoration Comedy," the play has found favor with many critics in this century and even in the last decades of the last century. A. C. Ward thought the play "less exceptionable and more uniformly pleasing than *The Country Wife*." Montague Summers preferred it to *Love in a Wood*, and in more recent times Virginia Birdsall and Norman Holland considered the play worthy of close critical attention.

In *The Gentleman Dancing Master* the ideal is the same in *kind* as that in Wycherley's first play (that is, love and virtue), but the ideal does not exist on a high plane of romantic, literary abstraction. The anti-ideal is also the same in kind as

Agnes Lauchlan as Lady Fidget and Lesley Wareing as Mrs. Margery Pinchwife in a 1934 production of The Country Wife
(photographs by Sasha)

that in *Love in a Wood* (hypocrisy and materialism) but whereas in the first play the anti-ideal is exaggerated downward to grotesque satiric effect, in the second it is realized in lightly drawn caricatures of stock comic types—the fop, the prude, the jealous father, the music-hall "foreigner." The play's action is the simplest of one-turn comic plots. Don Diego, an Englishman turned Spaniard, with the caution of his adopted nationality, has locked up his daughter to preserve her virtue, and, by extension, his honor. He intends to marry her to her cousin, Monsieur de Paris, who affects French manners to the same ridiculous degree as his uncle affects Spanish. Hippolita, the bride-elect, is determined not to marry her foolish cousin, but to find means to get herself a husband more to her liking. Playing upon Monsieur's vanity she tricks him into sending Gerrard, the finest gentleman of the town, to her window. Gerrard and Hippolita fall in love at once, but they are surprised in their first interview by the arrival of Don Diego, who has just returned from Spain, and Mrs. Caution, Hippolita's prudish aunt and duenna. To save

Hippolita's honor and her life, Gerrard goes along with her deception that he is a dancing master sent by Monsieur de Paris to instruct his future bride. The rest of the play revolves around the efforts of the lovers to come to an agreement while at the same time maintaining their deception. A subplot concerns the efforts of Don Diego to turn his nephew, the would-be Frenchman, into a would-be Spaniard like himself. Discourse in this play has none of the double-edged parodic subtlety that we found in *Love in a Wood*. It is the nearest that Wycherley comes in any of his drama to "dialogue," to simulation of contemporary parlance. Similarly, there is very little complexity in character. Characters in satire, of course, are types, but these are not the carefully constructed types of satire. They are simple, stock comic figures. Hippolita is the stock heroine of comedy, whose cleverness is sufficiently transparent to reveal the old-fashioned modesty in which it is rooted. For example, she blushes and stutters at her own audacity when she speaks to her lover. Gerrard is a robust, honest Englishman. He cannot dance; he cannot sing any but old English catches; and his speech is plain English, unadorned by foreign locutions. Wycherley is certainly not concerned with lashing vice into reformation in this play, and the folly he ridicules is too preposterous and too simply drawn to have any satiric impact upon an audience. The play may have been intended as a propaganda piece extolling everything that is good, old-fashioned, and English and despising whatever is foreign; and it may have been inspired by the general patriotic enthusiasm that prevailed in preparation for the impending Third Dutch War. We have some historical evidence that Wycherley fought in that war. George Villiers, duke of Buckingham, author of *The Rehearsal* (1671), a rollicking parody of the heroic drama of the 1660s, was one of the courtiers in the circle of which Wycherley's success as a playwright and a wit had made him a member. Buckingham was given a regiment on 20 June 1672, and commissioned Wycherley as a captain-lieutenant, a position which would have put the playwright into close association with his friend, the colonel. The Third Dutch War was, of course, a naval war, but it is very doubtful that Wycherley saw sea duty in it, because we know that Buckingham spent most of 1673 raising troops in Yorkshire and preparing them for ground combat in the event of invasion on Blackheath Common, just outside of London. Given Wycherley's rank and his friendship with Buckingham, it is likely that he was involved in these activities during the war. When the regiment disbanded at the end of the war Wycherley was a captain in Buckingham's company. He resigned his commission on 26 February 1674.

Wycherley's two great plays, *The Country Wife* and *The Plain Dealer*, are the works upon which his importance in the history of English drama must be judged. In this writer's opinion, they are among the greatest satires in English, and one of the reasons that we have not generally thought of them in relation to works such as Pope's "To a Lady; On the Character of Women" (1735) or "Verses on the Death of Dr. Swift" (1731) is that we tend to think of satire as a verse or prose form. As we can see in the quotation from Dryden, which calls *The Plain Dealer* "one of the most bold, most general, and most useful Satyres which has ever been presented on the English Theatre," the seventeenth century made no distinction between verse and drama as suitable media for the expression of the distinct *genre* satire. Both *The Country Wife* and *The Plain Dealer* are satires, but they are quite different from one

another in style and in intensity. *The Country Wife* is a comical satire; indeed, most critics would not accept that it is a satire at all, but would rather classify it "Restoration Comedy." *The Plain Dealer* is a darker, more deeply disturbing work, which verges on that end of the satiric spectrum that skirts nihilistic irony. In the former play Wycherley is putting a *particular* Roman model into Restoration dress, Juvenal's *Satire Six*; in the latter he has abstracted the classical structural design of satire, which he fleshes to the contours of his own invention.

Between the beginning and ending of the verse paragraph in Horace from which Wycherley drew epigraphs for his most trivial, second play and his most serious, last play, Horace tells us what style is demanded by moral satire: "You need terseness.... You also need a style now grave, often gay, in keeping with the role, now of orator or poet, at times of the wit who holds his strength in check and husbands it with wisdom" (*Satires* I,x,10-14). Wycherley has been faulted by some twentieth-century critics for not bringing his prose "within the range of realistic conversation." But Wycherley's aim was not to write comic dialogue nor to create naturalistic characters with the interiority and psychology that we novel-conditioned readers expect to find in drama. At his satiric best Wycherley writes almost no dialogue; his discourse is satiric declamation. His style consciously follows the guidance of his theoretical mentor, Horace, for his aim was to write dramatic satire in the classical Roman mode. This he accomplished admirably.

The Country Wife was performed on 12 January 1675, by the King's Company at the Theatre Royal in Drury Lane. It was entered in the *Stationers' Register*, 13 January 1675, and listed in the *Term Catalogues*, 10 May 1675. In the prologue Wycherley calls himself "the late so baffled Scribler," referring to the cold reception which *The Gentleman Dancing Master* had so justly received. *The Country Wife* restored his reputation immediately; it passed at once into the repertory, where–if we discount the nineteenth-century hiatus as an aberration–it has remained. It is the only one of Wycherley's plays that still enjoys occasional performance.

The epigraph to *The Country Wife*, Wycherley's transcreation of Juvenal's *Sixth Satire* in contemporary dress, is most ingenious, for in it Wycherley makes clear that he is returning to an ancient model and also that he is taking liberties with it, experimenting with its form. The epi-

Iris Hoey, Edith Evans, and Eileen Peel in a 1936 Old Vic production of The Country Wife *(photograph by Angus McBean)*

graph is taken from the Horatian epistle that concerns itself with the proper approach of a "modern" poet to the ancients: "Indignor quicquam reprehendi, non quia crasse / Compositum illepideve putetur, sed quia nuper: / Nec veniam Antiquis, sed honorem et preamia posci" (I am impatient when any work is censured not because it is coarse or inelegant in style, but because it is modern. What we owe the Ancients is not indulgence but honor and rewards [*Epistles*, II,i,76-78]). Employing a new approach to an ancient model, Wycherley *becomes* Juvenal, and, transversely, Imperial Rome *becomes* Restoration London. Many of Wycherley's characters and scenes–ironically enough, those which have been thought to be particularly "Restoration"– grow from germ ideas and suggestions he found in Juvenal. For example, Pinchwife, the typically Restoration jealous husband is the shape that Wycherley gives to Juvenal's Ursidius, the old whoremaster, who, despite his knowledge of the world, is driven at last to marry in order to keep a woman to himself (*Satire Six*, 38). Lady Fidget,

so adept at acquitting herself when she is surprised by her husband in Horner's arms, finds her origins in Juvenal's women who can employ "the colors of Quintilian" in such a situation. The character of the country wife herself and the pivotal question she presents of whether ignorance and rusticity are any insurance of chastity are Juvenal's (55-59). Margery's goggling over the "player men" comes from Juvenal (63-66), and, in fact, when Dryden translated Juvenal's *Satire Six* in 1693, it is clear that he was remembering Wycherley's Margery:

> The Country Lady in the Box appears,
> Softly she warbles over all she hears;
>   And sucks in Passion, both at Eyes and Ears.

Mrs. Squeamish's keeping a "little tragedian" appears in Juvenal (73-75), as does the drinking party wherein the "virtuous crew" finally drop their masks and openly acknowledge their sexual voraciousness. However, most striking is the appearance in Juvenal of Horner himself. In Rome, of course, a Horner-figure has a somewhat differ-

A scene from a 1936 production of The Country Wife *starring Ruth Gordon*

ent way of disguising himself, but he is the same Horner at heart, and he uses his disguise for the same purpose:

> [The cinaedi] do women consult about marriage and divorce, with their society do they relieve boredom, from them do they learn lascivious motions and whatever else the teacher knows. But beware! that teacher is not always what he seems; true he darkens his eyes and dresses like a woman, but adultery is his design. Mistrust him the more for his show of effeminacy; he is a valiant mattress-knight; there Triphallus drops his disguise of Thais.

It would have been impossible to present a sexual stallion disguised as a homosexual transvestite on the Restoration stage, and, therefore, Wycherley re-creates the homosexual disguise of Juvenal's Triphallus as Horner's pretended impotence. Nonetheless, Horner's trick upon husbands is present in the Juvenalian passage, as indeed is the psychology of the Sir Jasper Fidgets of the world, who, too busy to tend to their wives, supply them with sexually disabled male companions as a relief from boredom and a preventive against sexual adventuring.

In *Satire Six,* Juvenal does not follow the usual surface design of Roman verse satire—in which a satiric spokesman and an adversarius survey a "background," the panorama of fools and knaves in satire's fallen city. Rather the satiric spokesman is the narrator's voice and the adversarius is the reader-audience. The design was, therefore, relatively easy to translate into a dramatic medium. The satirist-persona does not appear in the play (as he will in *The Plain Dealer*); the adversarius is the audience; and the scenes presented before us are the satiric background. *The Country Wife* has neither a central character nor a central action. Horner is most often used as a mouthpiece for directly spoken satire, but he is not even present in the majority of scenes. The play's action itself speaks Wycherley's satire and is only occasionally interspersed with scenes of direct satiric commentary. Horner is not sufficiently detached from the scene to be the satirist's persona. He is distinguished from the other characters by his cleverness, but he is morally of their number. All the characters, including Horner, serve as butts and instruments of satire, examples used by Wycherley, the poet-satirist, to illustrate his vision of the "falling city" of the plain.

The play opens, as a verse satire does, with a declaration of the satiric "thesis" to be argued. The vice in question is lust, which from the middle ages to the eighteenth century does not mean sexual activity or even sexual excess, but rather means sexual *exploitation*. However, the vice here is not merely lust; it is lust that disguises itself, assumes one or another mask, not out of deference to morality nor out of shame, but that under the protection of a disguise, it may enjoy greater freedom to operate. The thesis is not directly declared because there is no central satiric persona here; it is presented in the exchanges of Horner and Quack wherein Horner discloses his plan to pretend that he has been rendered sexually impotent in order to ferret out his prey, women who "love the sport," and to fool their husbands and guardians. Horner is less a character than an emblem, a grotesquely exaggerated "sign" of the moral defect for which we are to watch. In effect, Horner is in himself a graphic declaration of the satiric thesis.

The thesis declared, the argument begins–just as in Roman verse satire. There are three separate actions, of equal importance and maintaining a degree of independence from each other, that attract our attention by turn to the various aspects of the vice under consideration "in something of the way premises are turned about in the octave of a sonnet" (Mary Clare Randolph, "The Structural Design of Formal Verse Satire," *Philological Quarterly*, 21 October [1942]). This enables the satirist to turn the vice under consideration around on all sides, to attack it from as many angles as possible. Scene after scene is presented in which some new face of the vice is presented, or some aspect already presented is more deeply probed. The movement is circular and continues until what Dryden calls the "members" of the central vice have all been explored to the fullest extent.

The four faces of disguised lust in *The Country Wife* have all made their first appearance by the end of the second act. First Horner is introduced to present lust in the mask of an impotence which secures it freedom. Then Sir Jasper appears with the "ladies of honour," who flaunt their masks of modesty and virtue; Horner sounds their virtue and reveals it to be hollow.

The exposure of vice disguised as honor is followed by a brief interlude of satiric commentary. Horner and the company of wits observe and comment upon the lust-hypocrisy that pervades the contemporary social scene. Into this commentary a new aspect of disguised lust is introduced in the person of Pinchwife, who hides and indulges his sexual exploitation under the façade of marriage (I.i):

> HORNER: But prithee, was not the way you were in better, is not keeping better than Marriage?
> PINCH: A Pox on't, The Jades woud jilt me. I coud never keep a Whore to my self.
> HORNER: So then you only marry'd to keep a whore to youself.

Pinchwife's "honor" as a husband is as false as Lady Fidget's virtue or Horner's impotence. In reality Pinchwife is not a husband for he neither trusts, esteems, nor protects his wife; he is the legally sanctioned keeper of a whore, a piece of property that he is anxious to preserve to his exclusive enjoyment. Just like Lady Fidget, he desires to indulge his lust under the cover of a carefully sustained respectability, marriage.

The last face of the vice that is presented to us is lust disguised as innocence. Perhaps *lust* is too strong a word to describe Margery's emotion, as *innocence* is too imprecise to define her ignorance. Her innocence is at first genuine. However, once she has fallen in love with Horner, she develops guile, and she feigns innocence to disguise her passion from Pinchwife in the hope that she will thereby find freedom to satisfy it.

In their first appearance, all four aspects of the vice are purely comic–Horner's knavery, Fidget's affectation, Pinchwife's jealousy, and Margery's rusticity, are all at first glance simple follies. However, as the vice is turned around and around, at each successive appearance they assume more serious proportions, and by gradual steps the comic tone fades to be replaced by the more deeply satiric. For example, consider lust disguised as virtue. Fidget and her company are wholly comic in their first appearance. They are objects of satire only in their exaggeration; theirs is the "humour" of virtue which is exposed by Horner's wit. In act 2 a new dimension of their vice is revealed; their hidden lust, until now only suspected, is uncovered and with it their whole perverted system of morality. Their next appearance in the famous "china scene" is so uproariously funny and so perfectly sustained in its double entendre that we might almost miss its satiric point. The "virtuous gang," who in their first appearance affected exaggerated virtue and in their second appearance could still discuss sexuality only in heroic periphrasis, in their third reverse roles with Horner and become voracious predators upon *him*. (The china scene should remind us that in the seventeenth century the first requirement for satire was to be funny; we must be made to *laugh* our vices to contempt.) In the penultimate appearance of the women (act 4), which Wycherley models closely on Juvenal's description of Roman wives who throw off all restraint in performing the rites of the *Bona Dea*, comic tone vanishes. The women drop their masks and do not bother to pretend virtue. The stylistic tension between heroic/romantic surface of discourse and its underlying satiric intention–which was present in their earlier appearances–is gone. Wine loosens the women's tongues; their tone coarsens and becomes sluttish. They damn their husbands openly, comparing them to "old keeper[s]." They describe themselves as whores, commodities–"women of quality, like the richest Stuffs, lye untumbled and unask'd for." At the climax of the scene, when each of them acknowledges that she has enjoyed Horner, their lust is fully exposed and with it the extent of their hypocrisy. They will form a conspiracy of silence to insure that the "counterfeit" "Jewel," their reputation for virtue, still shines as though it were real.

The same progress from comic to deeply satiric is described in the successive appearances of the other three aspects of the vice. Pinchwife's jealousy is merely ridiculous when he is the butt of the wits' teasing. It becomes a more serious defect when we see him abusing his wife. In his next appearance, when he threatens "Write as I bid you, or I will write Whore with this Penknife in your Face," it has darkened into cruel sadism. At last it is aggravated into a frenzy that makes him draw his sword on Margery. Her death is averted only when *his reputation* as a husband is rescued by the public assurance that Horner is sexually incapable. Pinchwife's last lines in the play make it clear that *he* knows he has been cuckolded, but, like the "ladies of honor," he is less concerned that his wife has been false than that, false though she is, she has been socially cleared, and, therefore, the false jewel of his "honor" as a husband still shines as though it were real.

Following exactly the same pattern, Margery's disguise, at first so charming, leads to her willingness to sacrifice Alithea's reputation in order that, by saving her own, she may indulge her passion for Horner; and Horner's knavery, at first so devilishly clever and beguiling that it escapes our censure, degenerates into mean duplicity when at last he sacrifices Alithea's true honor to the preservation of his false disguise.

The satiric thesis is complete when we see that in this fallen world of knaves and gulls the gulls are not a jot more sympathetic than the knaves. Sir Jasper as a husband bears resemblance to Pinchwife; it is not his wife he loves but his public image. Sparkish is the male counterpart to Lady Fidget; as she is a would-be lady, he is a would-be man. Her disguise is false modesty; his disguise is false wit and false broadmindedness.

The satiric antithesis of the play (the upward perspective toward the ideal) is presented in Alithea and Harcourt. Antithesis, at first sight, seems stronger here than in most satires, for virtue is presented in the action of the piece, as a human possibility, not, as it would be in *The Plain Dealer*, as a quaint remnant of a mythic literary past. Alithea and Harcourt figure the twin virtues that oppose the double vice of the satiric thesis. Alithea, as her name indicates, is the truth that opposes hypocrisy; Harcourt is the generous, self-sacrificing love that stands against exploitative lust. For every aspect of the vice we are shown, the opposing virtue is held up for comparison in Alithea and Harcourt. For Margery's dishonesty clothed in ignorance is Alithea's sophisticated honesty. For Pinchwife's jealousy is Harcourt's absolute faith that defies social opinion in spite of the most damning evidence. Scenes of vice are underscored by corresponding scenes of virtue. For example, Horner and Fidget's "as perfectly, perfectly?" exchange, in which the two plan an adulterous encounter in the language of heroic romance, is immediately followed by a scene in which Harcourt tries to express his honorable passion for Alithea under the disguise of a double-faced discourse. Even though Harcourt's romantic love is the very opposite of Horner's and Fidget's indiscriminate sexual appetites, Alithea will not allow even honorable love to go masked. Horner, Margery, or Fidget will do harm to others to protect themselves. Alithea sacrifices her own feeling for Harcourt to keep a promise to Sparkish even though she knows he is unworthy of her. Pinchwife will threaten to kill his wife to protect his reputation, and Horner will sacrifice Alithea to preserve his disguise, but Harcourt will stand firm against the "combination against [Alithea's] honour" to prove that his love is stronger and his generosity of spirit greater than his desire for public approval. Alithea and Harcourt end by marrying because it is not marriage that is the object of the satirist's scorn. Quite the contrary, we the audience are made by indirection to *admire* true marriage. What we are made to scorn is marriage as commercial contract (Sparkish's view), marriage as social accoutrement (the view of Sir Jasper and Lady Fidget), and marriage as legalized prostitution (Pinchwife's view).

Nevertheless, great satirists, because their mockery extends even to their own art, would seem to agree with W. H. Auden that "poetry makes nothing happen." In *The Country Wife* the ideal still exists as a possibility in the Restoration present; Harcourt and Alithea survive in the corrupt mob scene of cuckolds, knaves, and fools, but they are hard-pressed. Truth (Alithea) is not only threatened by falsity from without, but it works to its own confounding. (Alithea clings to her contract with Sparkish long after she knows that he is not even aware of the meaning of the contract.) But more important than that, presumably Alithea and Harcourt will live happily ever after in their virtue, but *so will* Horner, Sparkish, the Fidgets, and the Pinchwifes, live happily ever after in their vice. Horner has learned nothing more than not to trust his secret with a fool. And to crown this moral ambivalence, the play ends with an ironic twist. Wycherley depends upon our familiarity with the end-scene, stately pairing-dance, and Hymeneal blessing that brings *As You Like It* (circa 1599-1600) to comic closure when he stages his final "Dance of the Cuckolds." He distinctly parodies Shakespeare's *romantic* point-counterpoint choral finale, in which Rosalind sorts out the green world couples ("Good shepherd, tell this youth what 'tis to love . . . "), with his *ironic* choral point-counterpoint commentary offered by each of the cuckolds, prospective cuckolds, and cuckold makers in the dance. "There's doctrine for all Husbands Mr. *Harcourt*," the commentary begins, and, in descending order it moves step by step from Harcourt's idealistic "I edifie Madam so much, that I am impatient till I am one," to Pinchwife's final, bitter "But I must be one—against my will to a Country-Wife, with a Country-murrain to me." Wycherley pairs ill-matched city couples to lifelong bondage in satiric parody of the Arcadian harmony to which he alludes.

Wycherley's last play, *The Plain Dealer*, is his most classically perfect, as well as his darkest, satire. It was the composition of this "most bold, most general, and most useful satyre" that earned him the name "Manly Wycherley" and the reputation for fearless, incorruptible honesty. *The Plain Dealer* was performed on 11 December 1676 by the King's Company at the Theatre Royal in Drury Lane, in what might have been its premiere performance. The title page of the first quarto edition, dated 1677, lists the official licensing of the play as 9 January 1676, and it is listed in the *Term Catalogues*, 28 May 1677. Even the nimblest critics have always been hard put to fit *The Plain Dealer* into the category "Restoration Comedy," for it is, as James Sutherland calls it in *English Literature of the Late Seventeenth Century* (1969), "much the grimmest of Wycherley's four plays." As a satire in the Ancient Roman mold, it is also much the most perfect, for it not only fulfills in every detail the basic tri-elemental classical verse structure of satirist, adversarius, and background, but it also contains a parody substructure, so that it is at once a satire and a satiric commentary on satire itself. The epigraph, drawn from the verse paragraph in *Satires* I. x in which Horace lays down the rules of composition for moral satire, forcefully underscores Wycherley's intention in this play. The lines he chooses are "Ridiculum acre / Fortus et melius magnas plerumque secat res" (Ridicule often deals more forcefully and more effectively with great matters than severity does). Once again the playwright is pointing to the "rules" that govern the unique genre in which he writes. Once again he is reminding us that it *is* a literary genre, that as a satirist he is not a self-flagellating malcontent with a personality defect that makes him vacillate between love and hatred of his fellow human beings but a quite self-conscious poet who is wrestling with the demands of a difficult and exacting poetic form.

The epistle dedicatory of *The Plain Dealer* is itself a masterly piece of prose satire. In it Wycherley mocks the dedication style of his day, one empty of meaning and crammed with fulsome flattery. He also mocks those playwrights who write critical prefaces by explaining to reader / audiences what they are doing in their works and how closely they are conforming to the trendiest theories of their time. Finally it jeers at those pretenders to virtue who had been shocked by *The Country Wife*. They are Fidget-like hypocrites, scandalized by *words* but not half so

Ernest Thesiger as Sparkish in a 1924 production of The Country Wife *(photograph by Bertram Park)*

put off by the acts they describe–provided they are done in secret.

The play begins with a crashing declaration of thesis. The vice under consideration is hypocrisy. It is ubiquitous, poisoning every sphere of human life, and even a plain dealer, who attacks, or tries to flee from it, is in danger of being overtaken. The thesis is declared both directly, in Manly's spoken rebuke of Lord Plausible, and emblematically: Manly, a personification of the plain dealer is pursued by Lord Plausible, a personification of the hypocrite. The former figure lashes out at the latter but finds that he is fighting a shadow; the more fierce his attack, the more elaborate the flattery it evokes.

The thesis declared, Wycherley sets the traditional contestants of verse satire, the satirist-persona and the adversarius, to argue it. There has been much critical controversy about these figures. Some critics believe that Manly is a hero

and Freeman an opportunist (Dobrée); some believe that Manly is a repressed neurotic and Freeman is a hero (Norman Holland), full of "wild civility" (Birdsall). However, it is well to remember the generic mode in which Wycherley is very consciously and obviously writing. There are no "characters"–in our modern novel-conditioned sense of the term–in satire. Neither Manly nor Freeman, nor indeed any other character in any of Wycherley's plays, has interiority or "psychology." They are not meant to simulate "real" people; they are rather meant to designate certain rhetorical positions determined by the poetic form. Manly cannot be a "hero," for his very position as satiric persona requires a certain moral dubiousness (as we have seen, satire mocks satirist-reformers too). As adversarius, Freeman need not have any consistent morality; all that the form requires is that he maintain a rhetorical position opposite to that of the satirist-persona.

Freeman's is a type of adversarius common in Roman satire; he is one of the very number that the satirist hates, one who detaches himself from the crowd and draws near to the satirist, where he plays the role of devil's advocate. Freeman does not want to convince Manly that the world is *not* full of hypocrites; rather he argues that hypocrisy is the way of the world and the only course of action available to a man of sense. He is in the play, in effect, to reason the satirist to the side of unreason, to win him to the very vice he stands most firmly against.

In act 1 Wycherley closely adheres to the form of verse satire. Having established the necessary antagonism between satirist and adversarius, he must provide a satiric "background." His first "background" is presented as it is in verse satire, in the conversation of his adversaries. If we examine one of the key act 1 exchanges between Manly and Freeman we discover that it is a classical satire in little. It employs all the rhetorical devices used in verse satire and also figures the pattern of the larger satiric design in miniature. Freeman provokes an attack from Manly with an argument designed to draw the satirist's fire—that is, everybody does it, so it must be right. Then Manly launches his counterargument. To illustrate the rationality of his disgust with the world, he describes a scene that is the usual, moving "background" in verse satire. In it he sketches caricatures of the hypocrites of the world, falling upon every level of society from the bishop to the fishmonger. Finally this minisatire is clinched with a recapitulation of the basic opposing positions of satirist and adversarius (I.i):

> FREEMAN: . . . Observe but any Morning what people do when they get together on the *Exchange*, in *Westminster-hall*, or the Galleries of *Whitehall.*
> MANLY: I must confess, there they seem to rehearse *Bays's* grand Dance: here you see a *Bishop* bowing to a gaudy *Atheist*; a Judge, to a Door-keeper; a great Lord, to a Fishmonger, or a Scrivener with a Jack-chain about his neck; a Lawyer, to a Serjeant at Arms; a velvet *Physician*, to a threadbare *Chymist*: and a supple Gentleman Usher, to a surly Beef-eater; and so tread round in a preposterous huddle of Ceremony to each other, whil'st they can hardly hold their solemn false countenances.
> FREEMAN: Well, they understand the World.
> MANLY: Which I do not, I confess.

Manly's attack is upon a simple, harmless kind of flattery, the light oil that keeps the social gears

turning. The ferocity of it clearly marks him a humorous character; his attack is overkill, too hot a fire for the harmless folly that provokes it. Wycherley the poet's attack is more complex than his character's. He uses Manley's description of the seats of power—Westminster, Whitehall, and the Exchange—not primarily to ridicule affected manners, but to expose deep-seated social decay. The poet-satirist must not be confused with his character, the satirist-persona. As the play progresses the distance between them widens. Manly, the exposer, will be exposed, first as being a pigheaded fool, mistaken in his judgment, and then, as a practitioner of the very vice he most strongly attacks. Wycherley uses Manly as his primary instrument for satiric exposure, but he widens the scope and intensifies the depth of satire in his play beyond his character-persona's limitations.

In act 2 Wycherley proves the spoken satire of act 1 in the scene he sets before us. He broadens our venue to include a new class of society, aristocratic idlers, and he intensifies our focus to reveal the distortions hypocrisy effects in personal life. In act 3 he broadens his scope still further to the widest extent possible, and he intensifies the severity of his attack. The hypocrisy which appeared in act 1 as a simple glossing over of the emptiness of social forms, and deepened in act 2 to become a cover for personal exploitation and spiteful backbiting, is enlarged in act 3 to become the perversion of justice itself. Here hypocrisy is a methodized, culturally determined mechanism for justifying and legitimizing the most brutish self-seeking. When we look back from act 3, we discover that Wycherley has been shaping a perverse platonic progression, tracing hypocrisy from falsity in personal relations, to a poisoning of social and class relations and responsibilities, and finally, to corruption of the principle upon which the government of nations depends, justice. His satire reveals a whole world dancing a Bays's dance to its ruin.

Having widened the scope of satire to the fullest dimension possible in a drama, Wycherley turns our attention in the last two acts to the process by which hypocrisy corrupts the soul of a single man, the plain dealer himself.

The deterioration of Manly has been prepared from the beginning of the play. As we have seen, in act 1 his ferocity is such that we rather think him a crank. Act 2 not only reveals how far off Manly's judgment of his beloved mistress, Olivia, and his trusted friend, Vernish, is

The seventh plate in William Hogarth's The Rake's Progress (1735), *showing Tom Rakewell in Fleet debtors' prison, where Wycherley was probably confined in 1682-1686*

but it also introduces a parody satiric substructure. Olivia's opening words, "Ah, Cousin, what a World 'tis we live in! I am so weary of it" reveal her to be a tin pot imitation Manly. This mock-satirist-persona engages Eliza, a mock-adversarius, but their moral roles are reversed—that is, Eliza is a plain dealer and Olivia a hypocrite. The parody renders the original suspect. Moreover, Manly's image is further tarnished when we discover that Olivia has tricked him into loving her by playing on his own self-love: "I knew he lov'd his own singular moroseness so well, as to dote upon any Copy of it." We begin to find Manly's, or any satirist's, position questionable. In raging against vice in others, we ask, does not the satirist claim by implication to be above censure? May it not be that his ferocious honesty is founded in pride and self-love?

Wycherley hinges the final deterioration of Manly on these questions. Manly's fall into the vice he detests is pride's fall. When Manly is disenchanted by Olivia, his love turns to ungovernable lust. However, he tries to hide what he feels, especially because he fears Freeman's scorn. At first

he finds deception a difficult game—he reflects, "How hard it is to be a Hypocrite!" However, as his lust (hatred combined with sexual desire) is thwarted and becomes increasingly difficult to bear, he falls into greater and greater deceit. He lies to Freeman, pretending to be above a woman's scorn. He lies to Fidelia, pretending that his grotesque efforts to bed Olivia are his way of punishing the wrong she has done him. He lies to Vernish, claiming he has enjoyed Olivia's favors when he has not, in order to enhance his male pride. Finally, Manly reaches the depth of degradation when, since his threat to kill Fidelia if she does not get Olivia for him proves ineffectual, he bribes her with the promise that if she lures Olivia to him, he will allow her to stay with him. Manly has come full circle; he is what he accused Lord Plausible of being at the very beginning of the play, "like common Whores . . . dangerous to those [he] embraces."

Because the satiric thesis of *The Plain Dealer* is so dark and so pervasive that it even undermines itself as an instrument of moral reformation, satiric antithesis is correspondingly more remote, improbable, and literary-romantic, an ideal that could exist only in the imagination of poets. The satiric antithesis exists in a lone emblematic figure, a Morality play "Faithful" tricked out in Shakespearean garb: a girl named Fidelia, who dresses up as a boy to follow her beloved and woos an Olivia for him, even though it breaks her heart. The ending of the play, which unites Manly and Fidelia and elicits Freeman's supposition that the Plain Dealer has married for money, is as ironic as the Dance of the Cuckolds that closes / but does not really close *The Country Wife*.

The Plain Dealer was Wycherley's last play. Though he lived on for another forty years, he never wrote another. His brilliant career as a dramatist lasted only five short years. Nevertheless, his fame, his virtues, and the nickname derived from his most famous character, "Manly," lived on with him. John Dennis wrote that the honesty, loyalty, and sincerity of Manly Wycherley were "long and . . . peculiarly his own." Certainly the poet demonstrated these qualities against his own interests in 1677. His friend the duke of Buckingham was sent to the Tower in February of that year for attempting to force the king to prorogue Parliament. The poetic epistle which Wycherley wrote and circulated in Buckingham's defense began "Your late Disgrace, is but the Court's Disgrace"–and this in spite of the fact that Wycherley's only hope for support depended on the favor of the king. It is, on the other hand, a measure of the real goodness of "Good King Charles" that he not only overlooked the attack but continued to admire and support the poet who launched it. When Wycherley fell sick with the brain fever that was to shatter his memory and rob him of his creative powers, the king visited him in his lodgings in Bow Street, a demonstration of "Esteem and Affection," as Dennis tells us, "which never any Sovereign Prince before had given to an Author who was only a private Gentleman." Moreover, the king gave him five hundred pounds to pay for a rest cure at the famous health resort, Montpelier, and proposed that, on his return, Wycherley should become tutor to the duke of Richmond.

Wycherley spent the winter and spring of 1678 in France, but he never fully recovered his health nor his creative ability. In describing his own state of mind in a letter to Etherege, Dryden mentions Wycherley's symptoms and the long trial under which he suffered them: "In short, without apoplexy, Wycherley's long sickness, I for-

got everything to enjoy nothing–that is myself." The young Pope later complained that Wycherley "would repeat the same thought sometimes in the compass of ten lines, did not dream of its being inserted but just before. . . . His memory did not carry above a sentence at a time. These single sentences were good, but the whole was without connexion and good for nothing but to be flung into maxims."

The ravages of brain fever were not Wycherley's only problem after 1679. From the time of his first success he had lived the life of a London gentleman, a life which centered around the court, the theaters, the coffeehouses, and all the other places "where youth and wit and bravery keep cost." But, alas, the life of a London wit took money, and Wycherley despised "busy" money brokers and "industrious" country land grabbers with equal asperity. In an age when it was considered ungentlemanly to write for money (only Aphra Behn had the courage to admit that she "wrote for bread"), there were few acceptable ways to get it. One might inherit it, and Wycherley could not do that because Daniel Wycherley was still alive and vigorously spending all his available capital on law suits. One could honorably receive a royal appointment or annuity. This Wycherley *almost* did. The king's offer of the position as tutor to his illegitimate seven-year-old son carried a salary of fifteen hundred pounds a year with a liberal annuity after the office terminated. Finally, one could marry it. This Wycherley *thought* he had done, but he proved to be mistaken. On the contrary, it was his marriage that brought on his final financial ruin.

After Wycherley had received the king's offer of a tutorship, he unfortunately took a trip to the fashionable watering place Tunbridge Wells. In a bookstore there he overheard a young widow–noble, beautiful, and reputedly rich–asking for a copy of *The Plain Dealer*. The friend who accompanied him, Mr. Fairbeard, stepped forward and said, "*Since you are for the* Plain Dealer, *there he is for you,* pushing Mr. *Wycherley* towards her." Wycherley, who seems not to have lost his charm with his memory, complimented the lady in the same sprightly manner he had used on the duchess of Cleveland in his youth. So elegantly witty was the courtship, John Dennis tells us, that Mr. Fairbeard was moved to declare "*Madam . . . you and the* Plain Dealer *seem design'd by Heaven for each other.*" Mr. Fairbeard was wrong. Whether by the design of a just providence or not, Wycherley's September 1679 marriage to Lady Laetitia-Isabella, countess of Drogheda, led him to hell. To begin with, it lost him the king's favor as well as the offered post because he rushed into marriage (by his father's command, according to Dennis) without informing the king of his intention. Then, as it turned out, the countess had been living on credit and was deep in debt, even to her maid, when Wycherley met her (a state of affairs that led eventually to the maid's suing the countess and Wycherley). Finally, the estates left to the countess by her late husband were contested by his brother. Henry, the new earl, charged that the late earl had been coerced by his wife into leaving his lands out of his own family. The litigation arising from this suit lasted fifteen years longer than the countess, Mrs. Wycherley, did. At the time of her death the legal dispute, which was to bring Wycherley to final ruin, had only just entered its preliminary stages.

We might chalk off Wycherley's loss of royal patronage and the failure of his expectations in the widow's fortune as among the "little disturbances of man" with which fortune plagues us, but the character of Lady Laetitia-Isabella, countess of Drogheda, seems to have been designed especially for the torment of William Wycherley, for she was possessed by temperament with the two qualities he most hated. She was fiercely litigious and even more fiercely jealous. Dennis tells us that "she could not endure that [Wycherley] should be one Moment out of her Sight." When he went with his friends from their lodgings in Bow Street to a next door tavern, the *Cock,* "he was oblig'd to leave the Windows open, that the Lady might see there was no Woman in Company, or she would be immediately in a downright raving Condition." Wycherley's willingness to endure her jealousy was part of his code of honor; as Dennis puts it, he "thought that he was oblig'd to humour" his wife because she "had bestow'd her Person and her Fortune on him." He believed this even in the teeth of the financial disaster she brought upon him. Wycherley added to his own debts the debts he inherited from her in addition to the staggering costs that accrued constantly from her case in Chancery.

As Wycherley's financial situation grew more desperate, he wrote epistles "To the King" and "To the Duke" in the hope of regaining royal favor. But these were the days of the Popish Plot, the Rye House Plot, and the Exclusion Crisis, and neither of the royal brothers had attention to spare for a destitute playwright, no matter

how much they might have liked and admired him. There is no reason to believe that the sentiments expressed in Wycherley's *Epistles to the King and Duke,* published in 1683, were mere flattery designed to curry favor. There can be no doubt that Wycherley was a royalist born and bred, and he remained loyal to the Stuart monarchy to his dying day. In fact the poem "To the King My Master; After His Mercy to a Fault, shown to some Conspirators against his Power and Life," which was written on the occasion of Charles's clemency to the perpetrators of the Rye House Plot, was not published until 1704, long after it could have done Wycherley any material good.

Wycherley's creditors had him arrested and committed to Newgate Prison in 1682. He very probably had himself transferred to Fleet Prison, which was a common practice of imprisoned debtors at the time, but we cannot be certain of this, since prison records were not kept before 1685. He remained in debtor's prison for four years, almost the length of time that he was a practicing playwright. None of the friends from his days of glory came to his aid. John Wilmot, earl of Rochester, was dead, and Charles Sackville, earl of Dorset, was suffering severe illness. Buckingham and John Sheffield, earl of Mulgrave, who had given themselves to poetry and criticism in the 1660s and 1670s, were thoroughly involved in the feverish, and sometimes fatal, political machinations of the 1680s. Daniel Wycherley was still alive, but being, as he always was, involved in expensive litigation, he did not feel obliged to come to the rescue of his impecunious son. Wycherley's most recent biographer, McCarthy, has attempted to rescue Daniel from the cliché identity of "stingy and tyrannical senex iratus" imposed on him by earlier biographers, but a man of wealth who allowed two of his sons to languish in debtor's prison at the same time–William and his brother, George, who, it has been said, was committed on his father's complaint and who died in prison–may justly be said to be somewhat wanting in fatherly feeling.

It has been said that the Fleet in the late-seventeenth and early-eighteenth centuries was no more intolerable than an overcrowded, frowsy inn. Prisoners could bring their furniture, their servants, and their families with them; they could be visited by their tradesmen, their doxies, and their friends. For a price, they could even have their manacles adjusted to a comfortable fit–as in Hogarth's engraving. It was only dreadful, John

William Wycherley in the 1690s

Strype, the eighteenth-century surveyor of prison conditions, said "to such poor Men as have parted with their All to their Creditors." We must assume that Wycherley was such a one, for he found life in the Fleet greatly depressing. In a poem he wrote while he was there, "In Praise of a Prison, call'd by its Prisoners their College; and written there," he described himself and his fellow prisoners as "Carcasses of Skin and Bone,/ From which, Life, Soul, Spirit, are dead and gone." He was released from prison in 1686, when the new king, James II, helped to clear his debts and promised him a pension after influential friends had arranged a performance of *The*

Plain Dealer at court. Alas, Wycherley was no luckier in his kings than in his wives; when James fled the country less than three years later Wycherley was once again left penniless.

After this Wycherley lived very modestly, partly in London and partly in Shropshire, with occasional visits to Bath. When he was in London, he was still at the center of the literary world. He was an accepted and admired leader among the poets, critics, and wits who gathered at Will's Coffee House. Dryden remained his constant friend throughout all his misfortune, and he was also much admired by the foremost writers and critics of the younger generation, Congreve, Southerne, Dennis, and Pope.

He had been writing poems off and on throughout his life, and sometime before 1696 he decided to bring out a collection, consisting mainly of new verse. The volume was ready by 1699 but difficulties arose with the publisher. Briscoe advertised it in 1696, but he neither published the book nor gave Wycherley the money he had received in subscriptions. Wycherley had to sue for the return of his manuscript in 1700. The book was finally brought out by Broome, Taylor, and Tooke in 1704 as *Miscellany Poems*. The poet introduced the work in his usual ironic style. The preface was addressed "To my Criticks . . . Who were my *Criticks*, before they were my *Readers*" and the book was dedicated "To The Greatest Friend of the Muses, Vanity." The collection was generally condemned. There is no question that for the most part the failure rests with the uneven quality of the poems themselves; Wycherley was no longer capable of the sustained concentration of satiric energy that marked his plays. However, there may be another reason the miscellany had so unfavorable a reception, one which has not been taken sufficiently into account. Wycherley wrote cutting, ironic satire; in style, theme, and tone, he was an artist of the 1670s. The ascension of William and Mary brought a new, decorous, and very bourgeois respectability into fashion. In the miscellany, Wycherley's poems were addressed to an audience thirty years gone.

At about this time Wycherley met the sixteen-year-old Alexander Pope and was much impressed by the elegance of his early pastoral poems. The old "lion of the satire," as Pope called him, took the fledgling poet under his wing and greatly promoted his reputation in literary circles. Pope, who was at first greatly honored to be invited by the famous Mr. Wycherley to help him revise the *Miscellany Poems* that had had such ill success when it appeared in 1704, was soon driven to distraction by Wycherley's incapacity. He finally told Wycherley to undertake the revision himself and advised him to cut the poems into epigrams in the manner of Rochefoucault. For a time the friendship cooled, but Wycherley's great generosity of spirit, which had never left him, revived it.

Wycherley's end could have been written by him in a play; it has all the bitter-sweet satiric ambiguity of one of his end-scenes. His first wife having died in 1685, he married again at the age of seventy-four. In 1715 his cousin, Captain Thomas Shrimpton, advised him to marry a young woman who could bring with her a cash dowry sufficient to pay off his debts. The woman, for her part, would receive the jointure provided in old Daniel's will should his son remarry. The woman, Elizabeth Jackson, was Captain Shrimpton's mistress, and some biographers, looking at the scene from a romantic perspective, have drawn a dark picture of the wicked Shrimpton and Jackson getting the poor old Wycherley drunk and threatening him with debtor's prison if he did not go along with their nefarious scheme. Yet Wycherley "had often told [Pope], as I doubt not he did all his Acquaintance, that he would Marry as soon as his life was despair'd of." Wycherley could well have been in on the scheme from the first, and he may have found it a wonderful joke–especially on the ghost of old Daniel. Pope visited him on the day of his death, eleven days after his wedding day (19 December 1715), and found him "less peevish in his Sickness than he used to be in his Health, neither much afraid of dying, nor (which in him had been more likely) much ashamed of Marrying." His last request of his young wife seems to be perfectly in keeping with the sensibility of this great satirist who was withal a most gentle and amiable man. He asked her to make him a single, simple promise: "My Dear, it is only this; that you will never marry an old Man again." The second Mrs. Wycherley, a young widow with a rich jointure, kept her promise. She married the young Captain Shrimpton a few months after the poet's death.

Letters:

Letters Upon several Occasions: Written by and between Mr. Dryden, Mr. Wycherly, Mr. ----, Mr. Congreve, and Mr. Dennis, edited by John Dennis (London: Printed for Sam Briscoe, 1696);

The Correspondence of Alexander Pope, edited by George Sherburn, volume 1 (Oxford: Clarendon Press, 1956).

Biographies:

Charles Gildon, ed., *Memoirs of the Life of William Wycherley, Esq.; with a Character of his Writings. By the Right Honourable George, lord Lansdowne. To which are added, Some Familiar Letters, written by Mr. Wycherley, and a True Copy of His Last Will and Testament* (London: Printed for E. Curll, 1718);

John Dennis, "Letters on Milton and Wycherley," "Letter 'To the Honourable Major Pack. Containing some remarkable Passages to Mr. Wycherley's Life,'" in *The Critical Works of John Dennis*, 2 volumes, edited by E. N. Hooker (Baltimore: Johns Hopkins University Press, 1939, 1943); II:221-235, 409-412;

Gerald Weales, "William Wycherley," *Michigan Quarterly Review*, 12 (1973): 45-58;

B. Eugene McCarthy, *William Wycherley: A Biography* (Athens: Ohio University Press, 1979).

References:

Emmett L. Avery, *"The Country Wife* in the Eighteenth Century," *Research Studies of the State College of Washington*, 10 (June 1942): 141-172;

Avery, *"The Plain Dealer* in the Eighteenth Century," *Research Studies of the State College of Washington*, 11 (September 1943): 234-256;

Avery, "The Reputation of Wycherley's Comedies as Stage Plays in the Eighteenth Century," *Research Studies of the State College of Washington*, 12 (September 1944): 131-154;

Virginia Ogden Birdsall, *Wild Civility* (Bloomington: Indiana University Press, 1970);

Bonamy Dobrée, *Restoration Comedy* (London: Oxford University Press, 1924);

William Freedman, "Impotence and Self-Destruction in *The Country Wife," English Studies*, 53 (October 1972): 421-431;

A. M. Friedson, "Wycherley and Molière; Satirical Point of View in *The Plain Dealer," Modern Philology*, 64 (February 1967): 189-197;

Thomas Fujimura, *The Restoration Comedy of Wit* (Princeton: Princeton University Press, 1952);

Charles A. Hallett, "The Hobbesian Substructure of *The Country Wife,* " *Papers on Language and Literature*, 9 (Fall 1973): 380-395;

Philip A. Highfill, Kalman A. Burnim, and Edward A. Langhans, eds., *A Bibliographical Dictionary of Actors, Actresses, Musicians, Dancers, Managers, and other State Personnel in London, 1660-1800*, 12 volumes to date (Carbondale: Southern Illinois University Press, 1973-);

Norman Holland, *The First Modern Comedies* (Cambridge: Harvard University Press, 1959);

Peter Holland, *The Ornament of Action* (Cambridge, Mass.: Cambridge University Press, 1979);

Robert D. Hume, *The Development of English Drama in the Late Seventeenth Century* (London: Oxford University Press, 1976);

Anthony Kaufman, "Idealization, Disillusion, and Narcissistic Rage in Wycherley's *The Plain Dealer," Criticism*, 21 (Spring 1979): 119-133;

John Loftis, Richard Southern, Marion Jones, and A. H. Scouten, *The Revels History of Drama in English*, volume 5: 1660-1750 (London: Methuen, 1976);

Kathleen Lynch, *The Social Mode of Restoration Comedy* (New York: Macmillan, 1926);

Cynthia Matlack, "Parody and Burlesque of Heroic Ideals in Wycherley's Comedies; A Critical Reinterpretation of Contemporary Evidence," *Papers in Language and Literature*, 8 (Summer 1972): 273-286;

Maximillian E. Novak, "Margery Pinchwife's London Disease; Restoration Comedy and the Libertine Offensive of the 1670's," *Studies in the Literary Imagination*, 10 (Spring 1977): 1-23;

Anne Righter, "William Wycherley," in *Restoration Theater,* edited by J. R. Brown and B. Harris (New York: Capricorn, 1967);

Katharine M. Rogers, *William Wycherley* (New York: Twayne, 1972);

Eric Rump, "Theme and Structure in Wycherley's *Love in a Wood," English Studies*, 54 (August 1973): 326-333;

P. F. Vernon, *William Wycherley* (London: Longmans, Green, 1965);

John Harold Wilson, *A Preface to Restoration Drama* (Boston: Houghton Mifflin, 1965);

Rose A. Zimbardo, *Wycherley's Drama; A Link in the Development of English Satire* (New Haven: Yale University Press, 1965).

Appendix

Playwrights on the Theater

Restoration and eighteenth-century dramatists used prologues, epilogues, prefaces, and dedications to comment on their plays, their audiences, and every aspect of the theater of their time. Within these witty pieces can be found literary criticism, topical commentary, and above all, efforts to enlist audience support.

On the Prologue Form

Prologue to *The Vestal Virgin*, by Sir Robert Howard

From Sir Robert Howard, Four New Plays *(London: Printed for Henry Herringman, 1665). The Vestal Virgin was first performed by the King's Company at the Theatre Royal on Bridges Street, probably by February 1665 but perhaps as early as October 1664.*

Prologues, like Forlorn-hopes, first face the Stage,
Before the main Battalions do engage:
Just so our Poet, doubtful of the day,
Ventures his Prologue first and next his Play.
But stay, I fancy that I hear one call;
I'le step but to the door, and tell you all.
'Troth 'tis the Poets voice, now danger's near;
He sends me back as his Commissioner,
To treat that he might fairly march away,
If you wou'd be content to have no Play.
He offers fair: Shou'd it prove very bad,
As like enough it will, you'd wish you had:
He has been wounded, proofs there need no more
Than what you know, that he has writ before;
For sure none ever scap'd that ever writ;
There's no being shot-free in the Wars of Wit:
Poets by dangers like old Souldiers taught,
Grow wise, and shun the fame which once they sought.
    But if we must proceed---
Wou'd you wou'd tell him which of all the ways
You like in Prologues, us'd to help out Plays.
Some tell you stories of the former Age,
And swear that Faction now undoes the Stage;
Sure such believe you'l do as you are bid,
And that you paid your money to be chid.
Some craftier Poets at each other hit,
Knowing grave Rudeness has been took for Wit;
This does a wretched dearth of Wit betray,
When things of Kind on one another prey.
Some Prologues are more modestly address'd,
Just like Petitions, those he thinks are best;
For such a one he means that this shall be,
And therefore *humbly shews* as you shall see.

Prologue to *The Surprisal*, by Sir Robert Howard

From Sir Robert Howard, Four New Plays *(London: Printed for Henry Herringman, 1665). The first recorded performance of* The Surprisal *was mounted by the King's Company at the Vere Street Theatre on 23 April 1662.*

Since you expect a Prologue, we submit:
But let me tell you, this Excise on Wit,
Though undiscern'd, consumes the Stock so fast,
That no new Phancy will be left at last.
Wit's not like Money; Money though paid in
Passes about, and is receiv'd agen:
But Wit when it has once been paid before,
There it lies dead, 'tis currant then no more.
Nor must we plead for what we do present,
As in Law-Cases, by a President:
Poets and Mountebanks in this strange Age
Practise with equal hopes upon the Stage;
For 'tis expected they shou'd both apply
To every Humour some new Remedy:
And one's as likely every man to please,
As t' other to cure every mans Disease.
—But you are welcome all; and what men say
Before a Feast, will serve before a Play:
Here's nothing you can like: Thus he that writes
Or makes a Feast, more certainly invites
His Judges than his Friends; there's not a Guest
But will find somthing wanting or ill-drest.

      The Proverb but thus varied serves I fear;
      Fools make the Plays, and Wise-men come to hear.

Prologue to a Play Acted Privately, by Thomas Duffett

From Thomas Duffett, New Poems, Songs, Prologues and Epilogues *(London: Printed for Nicholas Woolfe, 1676). Because of its reference to the "Verestreet croud" listening eagerly to zealous preaching, this prologue must have been written after mid 1663. Thomas Killigrew, director of the King's Company, moved his actors from the Vere Street Theatre to the new Theatre Royal on Bridges Street on 7 May 1663, and by June the Vere Street playhouse was in use as a Nonconformist meetinghouse.*

Prologues, those pleasing and successful ways,
To gain protection for ill written Plays,
Most useful are in our ingenious times,
To cloud brisk nonsense and amazing rimes;
Th'are interpos'd like flashy glaring light,
For they the judgment cheat, as that the sight.
Now Poets like the worst Mechanicks grown,
Do rail at others ware to sell their own.
The last new Play still th' other house does huff,
To set some newer mess of folly off.
    Poor harmless Punck they fiercely do abuse,
Because she did Heroick love refuse,
Or made the running Nag out-strip the Muse.
Finding that Gallants now do Spaniel like,
Fawn most on those whose Satyrs deepest strike.
Fop, Critick, Flaxen Wig, the Miss and Cit,
Are daily massacr'd by Prologue Wit,
A modish wheedle to amuse the Pit;
With dropping follyes of their own they drive them in,
That their great showr's of dogrel stuff may fall unseen;
    From all this mighty pother we are free'd,
Our Play does no excuse or Prologue need.
He, who all other Poets would devour,
Who swells with Poyson suck'd from ev'ry flowr,
Who rakes up dirt and lays it by his door,
To make his glitt'ring dross seem golden Ore;
Ev'n he, when his Satyrick humor reign'd,
Permitted this rare Play to pass unstain'd.
    Now to our selves—
By railing first your censures which we fear,
We may prevent or make them less severe;
But to oblige you rather we'l believe,
None will so rudely take what we so freely give.
If any should condemn our harmless sport,
We will not plead high presidents from Court:
But with an equal rashness we'l maintain,
If serious, he's a formal Fop, whose brain
Does envy what it never could attain.
    The brisker Criticks we'l debauch'd proclaim,
Mere noise and froth without or salt or flame.
    How patiently the *Verestreet* croud do stay,

And for loud zealous nonsense weep and pray,
So eager are they to be led astray.
Had you but half their zeal for no expence,
With sounder reason and far better sense,
You all may go much more reform'd from hence.

Prologue, Spoken by Mr. Smith, to *The Siege of Babylon*, by Samuel Pordage

From Samuel Pordage, The Siege of Babylon: As it is Acted at the Dukes Theatre *(London: Printed for Richard Tonson, 1678). The play was first performed in September or October 1677 by the Duke's Company at the Dorset Garden Theatre. William Smith, who played Perdicas in this production, spoke the prologue. "Mugletons of Wit" alludes to Lodowicke Muggleton, a puritanical religious zealot who was tried for his blasphemous writings in January 1677, was pilloried for three days, and confined to Newgate Prison until July.*

Prologues of old, as learned Authors say,
Us'd, to have some Coherence, with the Play,
Were not so much, for Ornament, as use;
Like necessary Porches, to a House;
They, to the Inner Rooms, did introduce.
But now, such is the custom of the Age,
A rough hewn Satyr, enters first, the Stage.
Who barks, bites, pushes, and at all does hit,
Pelts Men, and manners, with his wicked witt,
Grinns at the Court, the Country, and the Citt,
And sometimes snaps, you Criticks, in the Pitt.
Such is the Rage, that one Poetick Brother,
Falls foul with, and downright, rails at another,
And tho, the play, be moving, soft, and sweet,
And Verses run, on smooth, and even feet,
And tho it does of Love, and Honour treat,
And shews a body, soft, fair, gay, and neat,
The Prologue still, has a rough Satyr's face,
Which does the moving, sweet, soft, thing, disgrace:
What e're the Play be, Custom does prevail,
It must be Satyr, in its Head, and Tail.
But Gentlemen, our Author bid me say,
He'd have no Satyrs face, before his Play,
Nor should it have, tho it be much in Vogue,
A swinging Tail, a lashing Epilogue.
Ladys, to you, he does himself address,
From you, he would receive, his happiness,
If your fair hands, shall his endeavours bless,
He will not fear, the Criticks of the Pit,
Those Cursing, Damning, *Mugletons* of Wit.

Prologue to *The Atheist*, by Thomas Otway

From Thomas Otway, The Atheist; or, The Second Part of the Souldiers Fortune. Acted at the Duke's Theatre *(London: Printed for R. Bentley & J. Tonson,
1684).* The Atheist *was first performed at the Dorset Garden Theatre in July 1683 or
earlier by the United Company, created through the 1682 merger of the Duke's and
King's companies, the "Two Houses" mentioned below.*

Though *Plays* and *Prologues* ne'er did more abound,
Ne'er were *good Prologues* harder to be found.
To me the Cause seems eas'ly understood:
For there are *Poets* prove not *very good,*
Who, like base Sign-Post Dawbers, wanting Skill,
Steal from Great Masters Hands, and Copy ill.
Thus, if by chance, before a Noble Feast
Of Gen'rous Wit, to whet and fit your Taste,
Some poignant *Satyr* in a *Prologue* rise,
And growing *Vices* handsomly chastise;
Each *Poetaster* thence presumes on *Rules,*
And ever after calls ye downright *Fools.*
    These Marks describe him.-----
Writing by rote; Small Wit, or none to spare;
Jangle and Chime's his Study, Toil, and Care:
He always in One Line upbraids the *Age;*
And a good Reason why; it Rymes to *Stage.*
With *Wit* and *Pit* he keeps a hideous pother;
Sure to be damn'd by One, for want of T'other:
But if, by chance, he get the *French* Word *Raillery,*
Lord, how he fegues the Vizor-Masques with *Gallery!*
    'Tis said, Astrologers strange Wonders find
To come, in two great *Planets* lately joyn'd.
From our *Two Houses* joyning, most will hold,
Vast Deluges of *Dulness* were foretold.
Poor *Holborn-Ballads* now being born away
By Tides of *duller Madrigals* than they;
Jockeys and *Jennyes* set to *Northern Airs,*
While Lowsie *Thespis* chaunts at Country Fairs
Politick Ditties, full of Sage Debate,
And Merry Catches, how to *Rule the State.*
Vicars neglect their Flocks, to turn *Translators,*
And Barley-water Whey-fac'd *Beau's* write *Satyrs;*
Though none can guess to which most Praise belongs,
To the Learn'd *Versions, Scandals,* or the *Songs.*
For all things now by Contraries succeed;
Of *Wit* or *Vertue* there's no longer need:
Beauty submits to him who loudliest rails;
She fears the sawcie Fop, and he prevails.
Who for his best Preferment would devise,
Let him renounce all *Honesty,* and rise.
Villains and *Parasites* Success will gain;

But in the Court of *Wit*, shall *Dulness* Reign?
No: Let th' angry 'Squire give his *Iambicks* o're,
Twirl Crevat-strings, but write *Lampoons* no more;
Rhymesters get *Wit*, e'er they pretend to shew it,
Nor think a Game at *Cramboe* makes a *Poet:*
Else is our Author hopeless of Success,
But then his Study shall be next time less:
He'll find out Ways to your Applause, more easie;
That is, write worse and worse, till he can please ye.

On the Audience

Prologue for the Stage, with Additions for the Court, to *Erminia*, by Richard Flecknoe

From Richard Flecknoe, Erminia; or, The Fair and Vertuous Lady *(London: Printed for the Author, 1661). According to its preface this play was not performed before Flecknoe had it printed for private circulation. There is no record of any subsequent production.*

You'd have new Playes, & when you have them, you
Do by them, as Children by their Trifles do,
Slight and dislike them, and then cry for more,
And use them just as you did those before:
And this you think fine sport now, so do'nt they,
(I tell ye Gentlemen) who make the Play.
Notwithstanding, our Author gives you one
This once, and comes with resolution,
To try whether or no, t' be a Disease
That reigns amongst you, no new Playes can please.
And if he finde it so, he bid me say,
All th' harm they'l do him who condemn his Play;
They'l bring him off oth' Stage, into the Pit,
To judge with them, of others Playes and wit.
    Additions for the Court
To others this. But to Your Majesty,
Our Author here with all humility,
Offers his Labours: chiefly he' underwent,
Most Royall Sir, for Your Divertisement.
Counting it highest Happiness can befall,
To delight Him, who's the Delight of all.

Prologue to a Restoration Revival of *The Wits*, by Sir William Davenant

From The Works of Sᴿ William D'avenant Kᵗ *(London: Printed by T. N. for Henry Herringman, 1673). This prologue is a revised version of the one in Davenant's* The Witts *(London: Printed by A. Matthewes for R. Meighen, 1636) and may have been the prologue spoken at the 15 August 1661 production of the play by the Duke's Company in Lisle's Tennis Court at Lincoln's Inn Fields. This Restoration performance of* The Wits, *which premiered in 1634, is notable because, according to Samuel Pepys, it was being acted for the first time "with Scenes."*

Bless me you kinder Starrs! How are we throng'd?
Allass! whom hath our harmless Poet wrong'd,
That he should meet together in one day
A Session, and a Faction at his Play,
To judge, and to condemne? It cannot be
Amongst so many here, all should agree.
Your expectation too, you so much raise
As if you came to wonder, not to praise.
And this Sir-Poet (if I e're have read
Customes, or Men) strikes you, and your Muse dead!
Conceive now too, how much, how oft each Ear
Hath surfeited in this our Hemisphear,
With various, pure, eternal Wit; add then
Young Comick-Sir, you must be kill'd agen.
But, to out-doe these miseries a sort
Of cruel spies (we hear) intend a sport
Among themselves; our mirth must not at all
Tickle, or stirre their Lungs, but shake their Gall.
So this, joyn'd with the rest, makes me agin
To say, you and your Lady Muse within
Will have but a sad doom; and your trim Brow
Which long'd for Wreaths, you must wear naked now;
Unless some here, out of a courteous pride,
Resolve to praise what others shall decide.
So they will have their humour too; and we,
More out of dulness then Civility,
Grow highly pleas'd with our success to night,
By thinking both, perhaps, are in the right.
Such is your pleasant judgements upon Plays,
Like Par'lels that run straight, though sev'ral ways.

Prologue to *Irena*

From Irena *(London, 1664). This play by an unknown author may have been per-formed during the 1663-1664 season, but no record of such a production exists.*

If by your faces I can guess; to day,
I fear but ill success attends our Play.
Your looks me-thinks to me seems so severe,
As if that none but Criticks now were here.
And we've small hopes our Play should take; There sits
So many here, that are, or would be, Wits.
Y're lately grown so critically wise,
There's scarce a Play that's writ, but you despise.
And to speak truth, Nothing almost can be
From your dislik, or from your censure, free.
Such Fate our Authour fears; I heard him guess,
And swear his Play would have the like success;
But yet he say's, He cares not; for he writ
Not to gain praise, or to be call'd a wit:
The motives which induc'd him for to write
This Play, he say's, was most for your delight.
He hopes for that, if for no other cause,
(Though undeserv'd) you'll give him your Applause.
And hopes you'll pardon all the faults you find,
Since that to recreate you 'twas design'd.

Prologue to *Herod the Great*, by Roger Boyle, Earl of Orrery

From Roger Boyle, Earl of Orrery, Herod the Great. A Tragedy *(London: Printed by Tho. Warren for Francis Saunders & Thomas Bennet, 1694). Written in 1671, this play was prepared for the stage by the King's Company, but their Theatre Royal on Bridges Street was destroyed by fire on 25 January 1672, before* Herod the Great *could be performed.*

How various are the Humours of this Age!
Sermons at first were follow'd, then the Stage;
But that they neither are frequented now,
Is a variety we owe to you:
One would have thought Extreams which were so vast,
As pleas'd the Soul and Sense, might longer last.
⠀⠀⠀Your Fathers other methods did pursue,
Yet some Fops swear they were as wise as you:
They left not Stage nor Pulpit in the lurch;
Week-Days they went to Plays, Sundays to Church:
And judged the Muses gratious did appear,
Presenting them one new Play every Year.
⠀⠀⠀But without daily new ones you are cloy'd,
And slight Plays seem as Mistresses enjoy'd,
For we must say---we'll give the Devil his due,
In Wit, as Love, you daily gape for new.
⠀⠀⠀Rare Scenes like Opera's, nay She-Actors too,
Though they less often Act with us, than you;
Whereby---will none here blush when it is said,
Some with great Bellies Virgin's parts have plaid?
Yet a good Play once acted, you're so nice,
You'll go to Church as soon as see it twice.
s' Death, Gentlemen, this usage we'll not bear,
You are not better than your Fathers were;
And if we are not as well us'd by you,
We'll shut up House, nay worse, our Women too.
Then with Street Cruzors you must have to do,
'Mongst which, you'll sometimes board a Fireship too.
When thus in your Chief Pleasures you are crost,
You'll value us, like Health, most when 'tis lost.

Prologue, Spoken by Mr. Haines, to *The Tragedy of Nero*, by Nathaniel Lee

From The Tragedy of Nero, Emperour of Rome: As It Is Acted at the Theatre-Royal, by His Majesties Servants *(London: Printed by T. R. & N. T. for James Magnus & Richard Bentley, 1675). Acted by the King's Company,* The Tragedy of Nero *was first produced at the Theatre Royal in Drury Lane on 16 May 1674, with comic actor Joseph Haines speaking the prologue.*

Good Playes, and perfect Sense as scarce are grown,
As civil Women in this damn'd lewd Town.
Plain Sense, is despicable as plain Cloaths,
As English Hatts, Bone-lace, or woollen Hose;
'Tis your brisk fool that is your Man of Note;
Yonder he goes, in the embroider'd Cote;
Such wenching eyes, and hands so prone to ruffle;
The gentile fling, the Trip and modish shuffle;
Salt soul and flame, as gay as any Prince
Thus Taggs and Silks, make up your Men of Sense.
I'm told that some are present here to day,
Who e're they see, resolve to Dam this Play,
So much wou'd interest with ill nature Sway;
But Ladies, you we hope, will prove more civil,
And charm these witts that Dam beyond the Devil:
Then let each Crittick here, all Hell inherit,
You have attractions that can lay a Spirit.
A bloody fatal Play you'l see to night,
I vow to Gad, 'thas put me in a fright.
The meanest waiter huffs, looks Big, and struts,
Gives brest a blow, then hand on hilt he puts;
'Tis a fine Age, a tearing Thund'ring age,
Pray *Heav'n*, this Thund'ring does not crack the Stage:
This Play I like not now ---------
And yet for ought I know, it may be good,
But still I hate this fighting wounds, and blood,
Why, what the devil have I to do with honour,
Let *Heroes* Court her, I cry, Pox upon her;
All *Tragedies* i' Gad to me sound odly,
I can no more be serious, than you *Godly*.

Prologue, by Sir Carr Scrope, to *The Man of Mode*, by George Etherege

From George Etherege, The Man of Mode, or, Sr Fopling Flutter. A Comedy. Acted at the Duke's Theatre *(London: Printed by J. Macock for Henry Herringman, 1676). The first recorded performance of this play was staged by the Duke's Company on 11 March 1676 at the Dorset Garden Theatre.*

Like Dancers on the Ropes poor Poets fare,
Most perish young, the rest in danger are;
This (one wou'd think) shou'd make our Authors wary,
But Gamester like the Giddy Fools miscarry.
A lucky hand or two so tempts 'em on,
They cannot leave off Play till they're undone.
With modest Fears a Muse does first begin,
Like a young Wench newly entic'd to Sin:
But tickl'd once with praise by her good Will,
The Wanton Fool wou'd never more lie still.
'Tis an old Mrs. you'll meet here to night,
Whose charms you once have lookt on with delight.
But now of late such dirty Drabs have known yee,
A Muse o'th'better sort's asham'd to own you.
Nature well drawn and Wit must now give place
To gawdy Nonsence and to dull Grimace;
Nor is it strange that you shou'd like so much
That kind of Wit, for most of yours is such.
But I'm afraid that while to *France* we go,
To bring you home Fine Dresses, Dance, and Show;
The Stage like you will but more Foppish grow.
Of Foreign Wares why shou'd we fetch the scum,
When we can be so richly serv'd at home?
For Heav'n be thankt 'tis not so wise an Age,
But your own Follies may supply the Stage.
Tho' often plow'd, there's no great Fear the soil
Should Barren grow by the too frequent toil;
While at your Doors are to be daily found
Such loads of Dunghil to manure the ground.
'Tis by your Follies that we Players thrive
As the Physicians by Diseases live.
And as each year some new distemper Reigns,
Whose friendly poison helps to increase their gains:
So among you, there starts up every day,
Some new unheard of Fool for us to Play.
Then for your own sakes be not too severe,
Nor what you all admire at home, Damn here.
Since each is fond of his own ugly Face,
Why shou'd you, when we hold it, break the Glass?

Prologue, Spoken by Mr. Clark, to *The Country Innocence*, by John Learned

From John Learned, The Country Innocence; or, The Chamber-Maid Turn'd
Quaker *(London: Printed for Charles Harper, 1677). When this play was produced by
the King's Company at the Theatre Royal in Drury Lane, probably in March 1677, the
prologue was spoken by Thomas Clark.*

> As a young Girl that's newly come to Town
> And in her Russet wanders up and down,
> Ventures her Maiden-head for half a Crown,
> So our young Poet with his first Design
> Hazards his Credit for a Pint of Wine.
> Honour's grown wondrous cheap, as well as Plays;
> Igad, both are worth nothing, now adays,
> Since ev'ry Fop presumes to wear the Bays.
> Never was Wit so much abus'd before;
> The Trade's grown common, and the Jilting Whore's
> Debauch'd in ev'ry Street, at ev'ry Door.
> You men of Wit, of Honour, and Renown,
> Those little Fops, the Monsters of the Town,
> To be thought witty, with their Noise cry down.
> But let that pass; Damn all those men of sense,
> Whose Wit consists in Noise and Impudence.
> Our Fate's so hard, and you are so severe,
> To hiss and rail, is all your Bus'ness here.
> The Visor-Masks you mind, and not the Wit;
> Talk Bawdy, and Debauch your selves i' th' Pit.
> Then in a rage, as if your Wit was scar'd,
> You damn the Play, though scarce a Word you heard.
> Pray let Good Nature, now that slighted Miss,
> Whisper the Wits, and beg 'em not to hiss.
> For those whose Wit consists in gawdy Cloaths,
> In vamping Old, and studying New Oaths,
> Ile leave, until their want of Noise and Sense
> Damn 'em beyond their own Impertinence.

On the Players

"A Prologue to introduce the first Woman that came to Act on the Stage in the Tragedy, call'd *The Moor of Venice*."

From Thomas Jordan, A Royal Arbour of Loyal Poesie *(London: Printed by R. Wood, 1663). The King's Company production of* The Moor of Venice *(a revival of William Shakespeare's* Othello*) on 8 December 1660 at Vere Street Theatre was the first in which the part of Desdemona was played by an actress.*

I Come, unknown to any of the rest
To tell you news, I saw the Lady drest;
The Woman playes to day, mistake me not,
No Man in Gown, or Page in Petty-Coat;
A Woman to my knowledge, yet I cann't
(If I should dye) make *Affidavit* on't.
Do you not twitter Gentlemen? I know
You will be censuring, do't fairly though;
'Tis possible a vertuous woman may
Abhor all sorts of looseness, and yet play;
Play on the Stage, where all eyes are upon her,
Shall we count that a crime *France* calls an honour?
In other Kingdoms Husbands safely trust 'um,
The difference lies onely in the custom;
And let it be our custom I advise,
I'm sure this Custom's better then th'Excise,
And may procure us custom; hearts of flint
Will melt in passion when a woman's in't.
    But Gentlemen you that as judges sit
    In the Star-Chamber of the house the Pit;
Have modest thoughts of her; pray do not run
To give her visits when the Play is done,
With dam me, your most humble Servant Lady,
She knows these things as well as you it may be:
Not a bit there dear Gallants, she doth know
Her own deserts, and your temptations too.
    But to the point, in this reforming age
    We have intents to civilize the Stage.
Our women are defective, and so siz'd
You'd think they were some of the Guard disguiz'd;
For (to speak truth) men act, that are between
Forty and fifty, Wenches of fifteen;
With bone so large, and nerve so incomplyant,
When you call *Desdemona*, enter Giant;

We shall purge every thing that is unclean,
Lascivious, scurrilous, impious or obscene;
And when we've put all things in this fair way
Barebones himself may come to see a Play.

Prologue, spoken by Mrs. Lee, to *The Constant Nymph*

From The Constant Nymph; or, The Rambling Shepheard, A Pastoral *(London: Printed for Langley Curtis, 1678). This play by an unknown author was first produced by the Duke's Company at the Dorset Garden Theatre no later than July 1677. Mary Lee, who played Astatius, spoke the prologue dressed in man's clothing.*

Gallants, to Night I'm to be one of you,
As Brisk, as Amorous, as Inconstant too;
A Spark that has Debauch'd e'ne half the Town,
Been kind to all the Sex, but true to none.
And t' Act that part to th' life
Suppose me now walking in *Lumbarstreet*:
Here I an old cast Citty Mistress meet.
Madam, your humble Slave; I can't express
My joy for this surprizing happiness:
How does your Husband, the good Alderman?
I Wonder at your impudence; how can   } *In a Womans*
You ask that question, false, ungrateful Man,   } *Voyce.*
And know how much you have abused him?
---I
Abused him; Heaven forbid-----I hope you joy,   } *In his voyce.*
My little Godson grows a dainty Boy.
Yes Sir, I thank you,
He grows a pace, a very precious Bud,   } *In her Voyce.*
But he's too like the Father to be good.
Thanks t' Heaven, that Thunder clap is at an end,
And now I meet a *Covent-garden*-Friend.
Madam, my old Acquaintance-----   } *In his Voyce.*
------------------------------------Old, (cryes she) } *In her Voyce.*
Why Sir, is it so long agoe since we-------
Oh Madam, no old storyes: I must own,
I once was th' happy Man, but you are grown   } *In his voyce.*
Acquainted since with half the Blades o' th' Town.
Well, if I am: the greater Villain you,
You are the first my frailty ever knew.   } *In her Voyce.*
And when
Her honour's lost, her Fortunes, mind too.
What would you have a poor weak Woman do?
Another cryes, you're a fine Gentleman!

Well, if *I* ever trust a man again------
Did you not Swear, and tell me you would dye,
Before you'd wrong me: Oh the more Fool *I*.
'Tis well you tired me out, teas'd me whole dayes,
Hurryed, and haunted me from Park to th' Plays;
Then kept me up whole Nights twixt sleep and waking,
Or else, I am sure, I had ne're been so o'retaken.
This is a man of Mode, and should I spin ye
Your Crimes at length, lay all your sins again' ye;
Raile at ye, say how many Devils are in ye,
T' abuse poor Woman-kind, the work were easie,
But that I fear 'twould rather tire than please ye:
For how can that divert you in a Play,
That's your old constant Musick every day.

Prologue, by John Dryden, to *The Mistakes*, by Joseph Harris

From Joseph Harris, The Mistakes, or, The False Report: A Tragi-Comedy.
Acted by their Majesties Servants *(London: Printed by Jo. Hindmarsh, 1691). This*
play was first performed by the United Company at the Theatre Royal in Drury Lane, prob-
ably in December 1690. George Bright, William Bowen, and Joseph Williams spoke the
prologue.

Gentlemen, we must beg your pardon; here's no Prologue to be
had to day; Our New Play is like to come on, without a Frontispiece;
as bald as one of you young Beaux, without your Perriwig.
I left our young Poet, sniveling and sobbing behind the Scenes, and
cursing some body that has deceiv'd him.

Enter Mr. Bowen.

Hold your prating to the Audience; Here's honest Mr. *Williams,* just
come in, half mellow, from the *Rose-Tavern*. He swears he is inspir'd
with Claret, and will come on, and that *Extempore* too, either with a
Prologue of his own or something like one: O here he comes to his
Tryal, at all Adventures; for my part I wish him a good Deliverance.

Exeunt Mr. Bright, *and Mr.* Bowen.

Enter Mr. *Williams.*

Save ye Sirs, save ye! I am in a hopefull way.
I shou'd speak something, in Rhyme, now, for the Play:
But the duce take me, if I know what to say.
I'le stick to my Friend the Authour, that I can tell ye,
To the last drop of Claret, in my belly.

So far I'me sure 'tis Rhyme---that needs no granting:
And, if my verses feet stumble---you see my own are wanting.
Our young Poet, has brought a piece of work,
In which, though much of Art there does not lurk,
It may hold out three days---And that's as long as Cork.
But, for this Play--(which till I have done, we show not,)
What may be its fortune--By the Lord--I know not.
This I dare swear, no malice here is writ:
'Tis Innocent of all things---ev'n of wit.
He's no high Flyer---he makes no sky Rockets,
His Squibbs are only levell'd at your Pockets.
And if his Crackers light among your pelf
You are blown-up: if not, then he's blown-up himself.
By this time, I'me something recover'd of my fluster'd madness:
And, now, a word or two in sober sadness.
Ours is a Common Play: and you pay down
A Common Harlots price--just half a Crown.
You'le say, I play the Pimp, on my Friends score;
But since 'tis for a Friend your gibes give o're:
For many a Mother has done that before.
How's this, you cry? an Actor write?--we know it;
But *Shakspear* was an Actor, and a Poet.
Has not Great *Johnsons* learning, often fail'd?
But *Shakspear's* greater Genius, still prevail'd.
Have not some writing Actors, in this Age
Deserv'd and found Success upon the Stage?
To tell the truth, when our old Wits are tir'd,
Not one of us, but means to be inspir'd.
Let your kind presence grace our homely cheer;
Peace and the Butt, is all our bus'ness here:
So much for that;--and the Devil take small beer.

On Authors

Prologue to *The Wild Gallant*, by John Dryden

From John Dryden, The Wild Gallant: A Comedy. As it was Acted at the Theater-Royal, By His Majesties Servants *(In the Savoy: Printed by Tho. Newcomb for H. Herringman, 1669). Dryden's first play,* The Wild Gallant *premiered on 5 February 1663 at the Vere Street Theatre, the home of the King's Company. Later that month Samuel Pepys attended a performance of the play at Court and recorded in his diary that "it was ill acted, and the play so poor a thing as I never saw in my life almost. . . . The King did not seem pleased at all, all the whole play, nor any body else. . . ."*

Is it not strange, to hear a Poet say,
He comes to ask you, how you like the Play?
You have not seen it yet! alas 'tis true,
But now your Love and Hatred judge, not You.
And cruel Factions (brib'd by Interest) come,
Not to weigh Merit, but to give their Doome:
Our Poet therefore, jealous of th' Event,
And (though much boldness takes) not confident,
Has sent me, whither you, fair Ladies, too
Sometimes upon as small occasions goe,
And from this Scheme, drawn for the hour and day,
Bid me inquire the fortune of his Play.
The Curtain drawn discovers two Astrologers;

   The Prologue is presented to them.
   First Astrol, reads. A Figure of the Heavenly Bodies in
their several Apartments, *Feb.* the *5th.* half an hour after
three after Noon, from whence you are to judge the success
of a new Play call'd the *Wild Gallant.*
2. Astrol. Who must Judge of it, we, or these Gentlemen?
We'l not meddle with it, so tell your Poet. Here are in
this House the ablest Mathematicians in *Europe* for his purpose.
   They will resolve the question e'r they part.
1. Ast. Yet let us judge it by the rules of Art.
   First *Jupiter*, the Ascendants Lord disgrac'd,
In the twelfth House, and near *Saturn* plac'd,
Denote short life unto this Play: ----------
2. Ast. --------------------*Jove* yet,
In his Apartment *Sagitary*, set
Under his own Roof, cannot take much wrong;
1. Ast. Why then the Lifes not very short, nor long;
2. Ast. The Luck not very good, nor very ill,

Prolo. That is to say, 'tis as 'tis taken still.
1. Ast. But, Brother, *Ptolomy* the Learned says,
'Tis the fifth house from whence we judge of Plays.
Venus the Lady of that House I find
Is *Peregrine*, your Play is ill design'd,
It should have been but one continued Song,
Or at the least a Dance of 3 hours long.
2. Ast. But yet the greatest Mischief does remain,
The twelfth apartment bears te Lord of Spain;
Whence I conclude it is your Authors lot,
To be indanger'd by a Spanish Plot.
Prolo. Our Poet yet protection hopes from you,
But bribes you not with any thing that's new.
Nature is old, which Poets imitate,
And for Wit, those that boast their own estate,
Forget *Fletcher* and *Ben* before them went,
Their Elder Brothers, and that vastly spent:
So much 'twill hardly be repair'd again,
Not, though supply'd with all the wealth of *Spain*:
This Play is *English*, and the growth your own;
As such it yields to *English* Plays alone.
He could have wish'd it better for your sakes;
But that in Plays he finds you love mistakes:
Besides he thought it was in vain to mend
What you are bound in honour to defend,
That *English* Wit (how e'r despis'd by some)
Like *English* Valour still may overcome.

Prologue to *The Forced Marriage*, by Aphra Behn

From The Works of Aphra Behn, *edited by Montague Summers, volume 3 (London: Heinemann/Stratford-upon-Avon: Bullen, 1915); first published in Aphra Behn,* The Forc'd Marriage, Or The Jealous Bridegroom. A Tragi-Comedy. As it is Acted at His Highnesse The Duke of York's Theatre *(London: Printed by H. L. & R. B. for James Magnus, 1671). The premiere of this play, staged by the Duke's Company at their Lincoln's Inn Fields theatre, took place on 20 September 1670.*

GALLANTS, our Poets have of late so us'd ye,
In Play and Prologue too so much abus'd ye,
That should we beg your aids, I justly fear,
Ye're so incens'd you'd hardly lend it here.
But when against a common Foe we arm,
Each will assist to guard his own concern.
Women those charming Victors, in whose Eyes
Lie all their Arts, and their Artilleries,
Not being contented with the Wounds they made,
Would by new Stratagems our Lives invade.
Beauty alone goes now at too cheap rates;
And therefore they, like Wise and Politick States,
Court a new Power that may the old supply,
To keep as well as gain the Victory.
They'll join the force of Wit to Beauty now,
And so maintain the Right they have in you.
If the vain Sex this privilege should boast,
Past cure of a declining Face we're lost.
You'll never know the bliss of Change; this Art
Retrieves (when Beauty fades) the wandring Heart;
And though the Airy Spirits move no more,
Wit still invites, as Beauty did before.
To day one of their Party ventures out,
Not with design to conquer, but to scout.
Discourage but this first attempt, and then
They'll hardly dare to sally out again.

PROLOGUE

The Poetess too, they say, has Spies abroad,
Which have dispers'd themselves in every road,
I'th' Upper Box, Pit, Galleries; every Face
You find disguis'd in a Black Velvet Case.
My life on't; is her Spy on purpose sent,
To hold you in a wanton Compliment;
That so you may not censure what she'as writ,
Which done, they face you down 'twas full of Wit.
Thus, while some common Prize you hope to win,
You let the Tyrant Victor enter in.
I beg to day you'd lay that humour by,
Till your Rencounter at the Nursery;

311

Where they, like Centinels from duty free,
May meet and wanton with the Enemy.

Enter an Actress.

How hast thou labour'd to subvert in vain,
What one poor Smile of ours calls home again?
Can any see that glorious Sight and say
A Woman shall not Victor prove to day?
Who is't that to their Beauty would submit,
And yet refuse the Fetters of their Wit?
He tells you tales of Stratagems and Spies;
Can they need Art that have such powerful Eyes?
Believe me, Gallants, he'as abus'd you all;
There's not a Vizard in our whole Cabal:
Those are but Pickeroons that scour for prey
And catch up all they meet with in their way;
Who can no Captives take, for all they do
Is pillage ye, then gladly let you go.
Ours scorns the petty Spoils, and do prefer
The Glory not the Interest of the War:
But yet our Forces shall obliging prove,
Imposing nought but Constancy in Love:
That's all our Aim, and when we have it too,
We'll sacrifice it all to pleasure you.

Prologue, Spoken by Mr. Hart, to *The Country Wife*, by William Wycherley

From William Wycherley, The Country-Wife, A Comedy, Acted at the Theatre Royal *(London: Printed for Thomas Dring, 1675). At the premiere of* The Country Wife *at the Theatre Royal in Drury Lane, probably on 12 January 1675, the prologue was spoken by King's Company actor Charles Hart, who also played the part of Horner.*

Poets like Cudgel'd Bullys, never do
At first, or second blow, submit to you;
But will provoke you still, and ne're have done,
Till you are weary first, with laying on:
The late so bafled Scribler of this day,
Though he stands trembling, bids me boldly say,
What we, before most Playes are us'd to do,
For Poets out of fear, first draw on you;
In a fierce Prologue, the still Pit defie,
And e're you speak, like *Castril*, give the lye;
But though our *Bayses* Batles oft I've fought,
And with bruis'd knuckles, their dear Conquests bought;
Nay, never yet fear'd Odds upon the Stage,
In Prologue dare not Hector with the Age,
But wou'd take Quarter from your saving hands,
Though *Bayse* within all yielding Countermands,
Says you Confed'rate Wits no Quarter give,
Ther'fore his Play shan't ask your leave to live:
Well, let the vain rash Fop, by huffing so,
Think to obtain the better terms of you;
But we the Actors humbly will submit,
Now, and at any time, to a full Pit;
Nay, often we anticipate your rage,
And murder Poets for you, on our Stage:
We set no Guards upon our Tyring-Room;
But when with flying Colours, there you come,
We patiently you see, give up to you,
Our Poets, Virgins, nay our Matrons too.

Prologue to *Psyche*, by Thomas Shadwell

From Thomas Shadwell, Psyche: A Tragedy, Acted at the Duke's Theatre *(London: Printed by T. N. for Henry Herringman, 1675). This semi-opera was lavishly produced by the Duke's Company at the Dorset Garden Theatre on 27 February 1675.*

As a young Wanton when she first begins,
With shame and with regret of Conscience sins;
So fares our trembling Poet, the first time,
He has committed the lewd sin of Rhime,
While Custom hardens others in the Crime.
It might in him that boldness too beget,
To lay about him without fear or wit:
But humbly he your pardon does implore;
Already he repents, and says he'll sin no more.
His bus'ness now is to shew splendid Scenes,
T' interpret 'twixt the Audience and Machines.
You must not here expect exalted Thought,
Nor lofty Verse, nor Scenes with labour wrought:
His Subject's humble, and his Verse is so;
This Theme no thundring Raptures would allow,
Nor would he, if he could, that way pursue.
He'd ride unruly Fancy with a Bit,
And keep within the bounds of Sense and Wit,
Those bounds no boystrous Fustian will admit,
And did not gentle Hearers oft dispence
With all the Sacred Rules of Wit and Sense;
Such tearing Lines, as crack the Writers Brain,
And the laborious Actors Lungs o'rstrain,
Wou'd, on our Stages, be roar'd out in vain.
In all true Wit, a due proportion's found,
To the Just Rules of heighth and distance bound.
Wit, like a Faulcon, tow'ring in its flight,
When once it soars above its lawful height,
Lessens, till it becomes quite out of sight.
But of such flights, there is no danger now;
He would not soar too high, nor creep too low:
Howe'r, he hopes you will excuse his haste,
For he this gawdy Trifle wrote so fast;
Five weeks begun and finish'd this design,
In those few hours he snatch'd from Friends and Wine;
And since in better things h' has spent his time,
With which he hopes ere long t'atone this Crime.
But he, alas! has several pow'rful Foes,
Who are unjustly so, and yet he knows,
They will, what e'r he writes, though good, oppose.
If he the honour has to please the best,
'Tis not his fault if he offends the rest:
But none of them yet so severe can be,
As to condemn this Trifle more then he.

Prologue to *Aureng-Zebe*, by John Dryden

From John Dryden, Aureng-Zebe: A Tragedy. *Acted at the Royal Theatre (London: Printed by T. N. for Henry Herringman, 1676). Dyrden's last rhymed tragedy,* Aureng-Zebe *was first produced by the King's Company at the Theatre Royal in Drury Lane on 17 November 1675.*

Our Author by experience finds it true,
'Tis much more hard to please himself than you:
And out of no feign'd modesty, this day,
Damns his laborious Trifle of a Play:
Not that its worse than what before he writ,
But he has now another taste of Wit;
And to confess a truth, (though out of time)
Grows weary of his long-lov'd Mistris, Rhyme.
Passion's too fierce to be in Fetters bound,
And Nature flies him like Enchanted Ground.
What Verse can do, he has perform'd in this,
Which he presumes the most correct of his:
But spite of all his pride a secret shame,
Invades his breast at *Shakespear*'s sacred name:
Aw'd when he hears his Godlike *Romans* rage,
He, in a just despair, would quit the Stage.
And to an Age less polish'd, more unskill'd,
Does, with disdain the foremost Honours yield.
As with the greater Dead he dares not strive,
He wou'd not match his Verse with those who live:
Let him retire, betwixt two Ages cast,
The first of this, and hindmost of the last.
A losing Gamester, let him sneak away;
He bears no ready Money from the Play.
The Fate which governs Poets, thought it fit,
He shou'd not raise his Fortunes by his Wit.
The Clergy thrive, and the litigious Bar;
Dull Heroes fatten with the spoils of War.
All Southern Vices, Heav'n be prais'd, are here;
But Wit's a luxury you think too dear.
When you to cultivate the Plant are loath,
'Tis a shrewd sign 'twas never of your growth.
And Wit in Northern Climates will not blow,
Except, like *Orange-trees,* 'tis hous'd from Snow.
There needs no care to put a Play-house down,
'Tis the most desart place of all the Town.
We and our Neighbours, to speak proudly, are
Like Monarchs, ruin'd with expensive War.
While, like wise *English,* unconcern'd, you sit,
And see us play the Tragedy of Wit.

Prologue, by Mr. Hodgson, to *The False Friend*, by Mary Pix

From Mary Pix, The False Friend, or, The Fate of Disobedience. A Tragedy *As it is Acted at the New Theatre in Little Lincolns-Inn-Fields (London: Printed for Richard Basset, 1699). This prologue by actor John Hodgson of Thomas Betterton's Company was spoken at the first performance of Pix's play, at the company's Lincoln's Inn Fields theater in May 1699.*

Amongst Reformers of this Vitious Age,
Who think it Duty to Refine the Stage:
A Woman, to Contribute, does Intend,
In Hopes a Moral Play your Lives will Mend.
Matters of State, she'l not pretend to Teach;
Or Treat of War, or things above her Reach:
Nor Scourge your Folly's, with keen *Satyrs* Rage;
But try if good Example will Engage.
For Precepts oft do fail from *Vice* to win,
And Punishments but harden you in Sin.
Therefore (*Male Judges*) She prescribes no Rules,
And knows 'tis vain to make Wise Men of Fools.
Lest all those Wholesom Laws that she can give,
You'd think too much below you to receive.
–That part then of the Reformation,
Which she believes the fittest for her Station;
Is, to shew *Man* the surest way to Charm:
And all those Virtues, *Women* most Adorn.

First then,—No *Beau* can e're Succesful prove,
Narcissus like, who's with himself in Love.
No wretched *Miser* must e're hope to find,
With Chest's Lok'd up, a Friend 'mongst Woman kind.
No *Drunkard, Fool, Debauchee,* or one that Swears,
Can Win a Woman, or beguile her Fears;
But He that's *Honest, Generous,* and *Brave,*
That's *Wise* and *Constant,* may his Wishes have.
But Hold, I'de forgot—
You must not be *Ill natur'd* and *Unkind,*
Moroseness Suits not with their Tender Minds.
They are all soft, as is the Down of *Doves,*
As Innocent and Harmless are their Loves;
And those Misfortunes which on *Men* do fall,
To their False Selves they Chiefly owe 'em all.
Did *Men* Reform, all *Women* wou'd do well:
In *Virtue,* as in *Beauty* they'd Excell.
But while each strive the other to Betray,
Both are to *Fears* and *Jealone's* a Prey.
Let not *Ill-nature* then Reign here to Night,
Nor think you shew most Wit, when most you Spite;
But Strive the Beauties of the *Play* to find,
The Modest *Scenes,* and Nicest *Actions* mind,
Then to your *Selves,* and *Authress* you'l be kind.

History of Theater

Prologue to the House, to *The Slighted Maid*, by Sir Robert Stapylton

From Sir Robert Stapylton, The Slighted Maid, A Comedy, Acted with Great Ap-
plause at the Theatre in Little Lincolns-Inn-Fields, by His Highness the Duke
of York's Servants (London: Printed for Thomas Dring, 1663). Acted by the Duke's
Company in Lisle's Tennis Court at Lincoln's Inn Fields, The Slighted Maid, *which pre-*
miered on 23 February 1663, caused Samuel Pepys to comment that there was "little
good in it" except the legs of actress Moll Davis, who danced "in boy's apparel."

Your looks are eager, Gentlemen; new Plays,
Like our new Beauties, expectation raise
So high, you promise to your selves a Feast
Of Wonders; alas, Miracles are ceas'd:
No working now by Supernatural means,
Beaumont and *Fletcher* have writ their last Scenes:
No *Johnson*'s Art, no *Shakespear*'s Wit in Nature:
For, Men are shrunk in Brain as well as Stature.
Little pure Wit is stirring, (I confess;)
And that's cri'd down by those that have much less;
And some by the Fanaticks have been taught
To conclude, All Gentlemen do, is naught.
When those Grave Criticks in their Cradles lay,
Good Plays grew faster than ill Weeds, than they:
Now, one would think, that our slow Writers play'd
A *Spanish* Mate at Chess, for Draughts are made,
Since meer Gambetters kept the Stage in aw,
For, (whoe'r sets the Men) they give the Law,
Tyrannically, to our cost we know it,
For (Right or wrong) they judge against the Poet.
From such (whom Spleen and Prejudice transport)
Th'Author refers himself to this just Court,
These Noble Ladies, Lords, and Gentlemen,
And humbly at your feet he lays his Pen:
If bad, it shall not write another Letter;
If 't please, he'l take it up, and please you better.
Incourag'd Poets heighten their Designes,
Like Painters, who at first draw ruder Lines.

From the Prologue for the Reopening of the Theatre Royal on Bridges Street

Quoted by J. Payne Collier in his manuscript Restoration Stage History, I:106 (Harvard Theatre Collection). London theaters were closed in June 1665 because of the plague, and acting did not resume until autumn 1666. The King's Company reopened the Theatre Royal on Bridges Street on 29 November 1666.

The Plague & Fire which half destroy'd the town
And people also, once more put us down,
As when old Noll usurp'd the realm & Crown.

Some of us trembling here were forc'd to stay;
Others to country quarters took their way,
To live or starve upon brown-bread & whey.

To day reviving from our trance-like state,
Struggling against the hard decrees of fate,
We once again for your approval wait.

After so long a fast, methinks, you all
Will hungrily on what we offer fall;
The welcome hearty though the cheer be small.

For though before the late too long distress,
You shunned our house as if you liked it less,
You'll now return with double eagerness.

"A Prologue Spoken at the opening of the Duke's New Play-House," by George Etherege

From A Collection of Poems Written upon several Occasions By several Persons *(London: Printed for Hobart Kemp, 1672). The Duke's Company opened their new Dorset Garden Theatre on 9 November 1671 with a performance of John Dryden's popular 1667 play* Sir Martin Mar-All, *for which Etherege wrote a new prologue.*

> 'Tis not in this as in the former Age,
> When Wit alone suffic'd t' adorn the Stage;
> When things well said an Audience cou'd invite,
> Without the hope of such a Gaudy Sight:
> What with your Fathers took wou'd take with you,
> If Wit had still the Charm of being New:
> Had not enjoyment dull'd your appetite,
> She in her homely dress wou'd yet delight;
> Such stately Theatres we need not raise,
> Our Old House wou'd put off our dullest Plays.
> You Gallants know a fresh Wench of sixteen
> May drive the Trade in honest Bombarine;
> And never want good Custom, shou'd she lie
> In a back Room, two or three stories high:
> But such a Beauty as has long been known,
> Though not decay'd, but to perfection grown,
> Must, if she mean to thrive in this leud Town,
> Wear Points, Lac'd Petticoats, and a rich Gown;
> Her Lodgings too must with her Dress agree,
> Be hung with Damask, or with Tapestry;
> Have Chyna, Cabinets, and a great Glass,
> To strike respect into an Am'rous Ass.
> Without the help of Stratagems and Arts,
> An old Acquaintance cannot touch your Hearts.
> Methinks 'tis hard our Authors shou'd submit
> So tamely to their Predecessors wit,
> Since, I am sure, among you there are few
> Wou'd grant your Grand-fathers had more then you.
> But hold! I in this business may proceed too far,
> And raise a storm against our Theatre;
> And then what wou'd the wise Adventurers say,
> Who are in a much greater fright to day
> Then ever Poet was about his Play?
> Our apprehensions none can justly blame,
> Money is dearer much to us then Fame:
> This thought on, let our Poets justifie
> The Reputation of their Poetry;
> We are resolv'd we will not have to do
> With what's between those Gentlemen and you.
> Be kind, and let our House have but your praise,
> You'r welcome every day to damn their Plays.

Prologue to a Restoration Performance of *Wit Without Money*, by John Fletcher, "being the first Play acted after the Fire"

From Covent Garden Drollery, *edited by Montague Summers (London: Fortune Press, 1927; first edition, London: Printed for James Magnes, 1672). After the Theatre Royal on Bridges Street was destroyed by fire on 25 January 1672, the King's Company moved temporarily to Lisle's Tennis Court in Lincoln's Inn Fields while a new playhouse was being built for them in Drury Lane. Their first performance at Lisle's Tennis Court, staged on 26 February 1672, was a production of John Fletcher's circa 1614 play* Wit Without Money, *with a new prologue.*

So shipwrack't Passengers escape to Land,
So look they, when on bare Beach they stand,
Dropping and cold; and their first fear scarce o're;
Expecting Famine from a desert Shore;
From that hard Climate, we must wait for Bread,
Whence even the Natives forc't by hunger fled.
Our Stage does humane chance present to view,
But ne're before was seen so sadly true,
You are chang'd to, and your pretence to see
Is but a nobler name of charity.
Your own provisions furnish out our Feasts
Whilst you the Founders make your selves our guests.
Of all mankind besides Fate had some care,
But for poor wit no portion did prepare,
Tis left a rent-charge to the brave and fair.
You cherish it, and now its fall you mourn,
Which blind unmanner'd *Zealots* make their scorn,
Who think the Fire a judgement on the Stage,
Which spar'd not *Temples* in its furious rage.
But as our new-built City rises higher,
So from old Theaters *may new aspire,*
Since Fate contrives magnificence by fire.

Dedication to *An Evening's Love*, by John Dryden

From The Works of John Dryden, *volume 10, edited by Maximillian E. Novak and George Robert Guffey (Berkeley, Los Angeles & London: University of California Press, 1970); first published in John Dryden,* An Evening's Love, Or, The Mock-Astrologer. Acted at the Theater Royal, By His Majesties Servants *(In the Savoy: Printed by T. N. for Henry Herringman, 1671).* An Evening's Love *was first performed on 12 June 1668, by the King's Company at the Theatre Royal on Bridges Street. Dryden's dedication of the published version to William Cavendish, duke of Newcastle, includes praise for Newcastle's wife, Margaret Cavendish, duchess of Newcastle, author of philosophical treatises, poems, essays, romances, and a biography of her husband. In defending her against critics of women writers he sounds a theme taken up by Aphra Behn in the preface and epilogue that follow.*

TO HIS GRACE, *WILLIAM*, DUKE of *NEWCAS-TLE*, One of his Majestie's most Honourable Privy Council; and of the most noble Order of the Garter, &c.

May it please your Grace,
AMONGST those few persons of Wit and Honour, whose favourable opinion I have desir'd, your own vertue and my great obligations to your Grace, have justly given you the precedence. For what could be more glorious to me, than to have acquir'd some part of your esteem, who are admir'd and honour'd by all good men; who have been, for so many years together, the Pattern and Standard of Honor to the Nation: and whose whole life has been so great an example of Heroick vertue, that we might wonder how it happen'd into an Age so corrupt as ours, if it had not likewise been a part of the former? as you came into the world with all the advantages of a noble Birth and Education, so you have rendered both yet more conspicuous by your vertue. Fortune, indeed, has perpetually crown'd your undertakings with success, but she has only waited on your valour, not conducted it. She mas ministred to your glory like a slave, and has been led in triumph by it; or at most, while Honour led you by the hand to greatness, fortune only follow'd to keep you from sliding back in the ascent. That which *Plutarch* accounted her favour to *Cymon* and *Lucullus*, was but her justice to your Grace: and, never to have been overcome where you led in person, as it was more than *Hannibal* could boast, so it was all that providence could do for that party which it had resolv'd to ruine. Thus, my Lord, the last smiles of victory were on your armes: and, every where else, declaring for the Rebels, she seem'd to suspend her self, and to doubt, before she took her flight, whether she were able wholly to abandon that cause for which you fought.

But the greatest tryals of your Courage and Constancy were yet to come: many had ventur'd their fortunes, and expos'd their lives to the utmost dangers for their King and Country, who ended their loyalty with the War: and submitting to the iniquity of the times, chose rather to redeem their former plenty by acknowledging an Usurper, than to suffer with an unprofitable fidelity (as those meaner spirits call'd it) for their lawful Soveraign. But, as I dare not accuse so many of our Nobility, who were content to accept their Patrimonies from the Clemency of the *Conquerour*, and to retain only a secret veneration for their Prince, amidst the open worship which they were forc'd to pay to the Usurper, who had dethron'd him; so, I hope, I may have leave to extoll that vertue which acted more generously; and which was not satisfi'd with an inward devotion to Monarchy, but produc'd it self to view, and asserted the cause by open Martyrdome. Of these rare patterns of loyalty your Grace was chief; those examples you cou'd not find, you made. Some few *Cato's* there were with you, whose invincible resolution could not be conquer'd by *that usurping Cæsar:* your vertue oppos'd it self to his fortune, and overcame it by not submitting to it. The last and most difficult Enterprize he had to effect, when he had conquer'd three Nations, was to subdue your spirits: and he dy'd weary of that War, and unable to finish it.

In the mean time you liv'd more happily in your exile then the other on his Throne: your loyalty made you friends and servants amongst Forreigners: and you liv'd plentifully without a fortune; for you liv'd on your own desert and reputation. The glorious Name of the valiant and faithful *Newcastle* was a Patrimony which cou'd never be exhausted.

Thus, my Lord, the morning of your life was clear, and calm; and, though it was afterwards overcast; yet, in that general storm, you were never without a shelter. And now you are happily arriv'd to the evening of a day as serene, as the dawn of it was glorious: but such an evening as, I hope, and almost prophesie, is far from night: 'Tis the Evening of a Summer's Sun, which keeps the day-light long within the skies. The health of your body is maintain'd by the vigour of your mind: neither does the one shrink from the fatigue of exercise, nor the other bend under the pains of study. Methinks I behold in you another *Caius Marius,* who in the extremity of his age, exercis'd himself almost every morning in the *Campus Martius,* amongst the youthful Nobility of *Rome.* And afterwards, in your retirements, when you do honour to Poetrie, by employing part of your leisure in it, I regard you as another *Silius Italicus,* who having pass'd over his Consulship with applause, dismiss'd himself from business and from the Gown, and employ'd his age, amongst the shades, in the reading and imitation of *Virgil.*

In which, lest any thing should be wanting to your happiness, you have, by a rare effect of Fortune, found, in the person of your excellent Lady, not only a *Lover,* but a Partner of your studies: a Lady whom our Age may justly equal with the *Sappho* of the *Greeks,* or the *Sulpitia* of the *Romans:* who, by being taken into your bosome, seems to be inspir'd with your Genius; and by writing the History of your life in so masculine a style, has already plac'd you in the Number of the Heroes. She has anticipated that great portion of Fame which envy often hinders a living vertue from possessing: which wou'd, indeed, have been given to your ashes, but with a latter payment: and, of which you could have no present use, except it were by a secret presage of that which was to come, when you were no longer in a possibility of knowing it. So that if that were a praise or satisfaction to the greatest of Emperors, which the most judicious of Poets gives him,

Præsenti tibi maturos largimur honores, &c.

That the adoration which was not allowed to *Hercules* and *Romulus* till after death, was given to *Augustus* living; then certainly it cannot be deny'd but that your Grace has receiv'd a double satisfaction: the one, to see your self consecrated to immortality while you are yet alive: the other, to have your praises celebrated by so dear, so just, and so pious an Historian.

'Tis the consideration of this that stops my pen: though I am loath to leave so fair a subject, which gives me as much field as Poetry cou'd wish; and yet no more than truth can justifie. But to attempt any thing of a Panegyrick were to enterprize on your Lady's right; and to seem to affect those praises, which none but the Dutchess of *Newcastle* can deserve, when she writes the actions of her Lord. I shall therefore leave that wider space, and contract my self to those narrow bounds which best become my *Fortune and Employment.*

I am oblig'd, my Lord, to return you not only my own acknowledgements; but to thank you in the name of former Poets. The *manes* of *Johnson* and *D'avenant* seem to require it from me, that those favours which you plac'd on them, and which they wanted opportunity to own in publick, yet might not be lost to the knowledge of Posterity, with a forgetfulness unbecoming of the Muses, who are the Daughters of Memory. And give me leave, my Lord, to avow so much of vanity, as to say, I am proud to be their Remembrancer: for, by relating how gracious you have been to them, and are to me, I in some measure joyn my name with theirs: and the continu'd descent of your favours to me is the best title which I can plead for my succession. I only wish, that I had as great reason to be satisfi'd with my self, in the return of our common acknowledgements, as your Grace may justly take in the conferring *them:* for I cannot but be very sensible that the present of an ill Comedy, which I here make you, is a very unsuitable way of giving thanks for them, who themselves have written so many better. This pretends to nothing more than to be a foyl to those Scenes, which are compos'd by the most noble Poet of our Age, and Nation: and to be set as a water-mark of the lowest ebb, to which the wit of my Predecessors has sunk and run down in me: but, though all of 'em have surpass'd me in the Scene; there is one part of glory in which I will not yield to any of them. I mean, my Lord, that honour and veneration which they had for you in their lives; and which I preserve after them, more holily than the Vestal fires were maintain'd from Age to Age; but with a greater degree of heat and of devotion than theirs, as being with more respect and passion then they ever were,

Your GRACES most obliged, most humble, and most obedient Servant,

JOHN DRYDEN.

"An Epistle to the Reader," Preface to *The Dutch Lover*, by Aphra Behn

From The Works of Aphra Behn, *edited by Montague Summers, volume 1 (London: Heinemann/Stratford-on-Avon: Bullen, 1915); first published in* The Dutch Lover: A Comedy, Acted At The Dukes Theatre *(London: Printed for Thomas Dring, 1673). The first recorded performance of this play, staged by the Duke's Company, was on 6 February 1673 at the Dorset Garden Theatre.*

Good, Sweet, Honey, Sugar-Candied READER,

Which I think is more than anyone has called you yet, I must have a word or two with you before you do advance into the Treatise; but 'tis not to beg your pardon for diverting you from your affairs, by such an idle Pamphlet as this is, for I presume you have not much to do and therefore are to be obliged to me for keeping you from worse employment, and if you have a better you may get you gone about your business: but if you will misspend your Time, pray lay the fault upon yourself; for I have dealt pretty fairly in the matter, told you in the Title Page what you are to expect within. Indeed, had I hung a sign of the Immortality of the Soul, of the Mystery of Godliness, or of Ecclesiastical Policie, and then had treated you with Indiscerpibility and Essential Spissitude (words, which though I am no competent Judge of, for want of Languages, yet I fancy strongly ought to mean just nothing) with a company of Apocryphal midnight Tales cull'd out of the choicest Insignificant Authors; If I had only proved in Folio that Apollonius was a naughty knave, or had presented you with two or three of the worst principles transcrib'd out of the peremptory and ill-natur'd (though prettily ingenious) Doctor of Malmsbury undigested and ill-manag'd by a silly, saucy, ignorant, impertinent, ill educated Chaplain I were then indeed sufficiently in fault; but having inscrib'd Comedy on the beginning of my Book, you may guess pretty near what pennyworths you are like to have, and ware your money and your time accordingly. I would not yet be understood to lessen the dignity of Playes, for surely they deserve a place among the middle if not the better sort of Books; for I have heard the most of that which bears the name of Learning, and which has abused such quantities of Ink and Paper, and continually employs so many ignorant, unhappy souls for ten, twelve, twenty years in the University (who yet poor wretches think they are doing something all the while) as Logick

etc. and several other things (that shall be nameless lest I misspell them) are much more absolutely nothing than the errantest Play that e'er was writ. Take notice, Reader, I do not assert this purely upon my own knowledge, but I think I have known it very fully prov'd, both sides being fairly heard, and even some ingenious opposers of it most abominably baffl'd in the Argument: Some of which I have got so perfectly by rote, that if this were a proper place for it, I am apt to think myself could almost make it clear; and as I would not undervalue Poetry, so neither am I altogether of their judgement who believe no wisdom in the world beyond it. I have often heard indeed (and read) how much the World was anciently oblig'd to it for most of that which they call'd Science, which my want of letters makes me less assured of than others happily may be: but I have heard some wise men say that no considerable part of useful knowledge was this way communicated, and on the other way, that it hath serv'd to propogate so many idle superstitions, as all the benefits it hath or can be guilty of, can never make sufficient amends for; which unaided by the unlucky charms of Poetry, could never have possest a thinking Creature such as man. However true this is, I am myself well able to affirm that none of all our English Poets, and least the Dramatique (so I think you call them) can be justly charg'd with too great reformation of men's minds or manners, and for that I may appeal to general experiment, if those who are the most assiduous Disciples of the Stage, do not make the fondest and the lewdest Crew about this Town; for if you should unhappily converse them through the year, you will not find one Dram of sense amongst a Club of them, unless you will allow for such a little Link-Boy's Ribaldry thick larded with unseasonable oaths & impudent defiance of God, and all things serious; and that at such a senseless damn'd unthinking rate, as, if 'twere well distributed, would spoil near half the Apothecaries trade, and save the sober people of the Town the charge of Vomits; And it was smartly said (how prudently I cannot tell) by a late learned Doctor, who, though himself no great asserter of a Deity, (as you'll believe by that which follows) yet was observed to be continually persuading of this sort of men (if I for once may call them so) of the necessity and truth of our Religion; and being ask'd how he came to bestir himself so much this way, made answer that it was because their ignorance and indiscreet debauch made them a scandal to the profession of Atheism. And for their wisdom and design I never knew it reach beyond the invention of some notable expedient, for the speedier ridding them of their Estate, (a devilish clog to Wit and Parts), than other grouling Mortals know, or battering half-a-dozen fair new Windows in a Morning after their debauch, whilst the dull unjantee Rascal they belong to is fast asleep. But I'll proceed no farther in their character, because that miracle of Wit (in spite of Academick frippery) the mighty Echard hath already done it to my satisfaction; and whoever undertakes a Supplement to anything he hath discourst, had better for their reputation be doing nothing.

Besides this Theam is worn too thread-bare by the whiffling would-be Wits of the Town, and of both the stone-blind-eyes of the Kingdom. And therefore to return to that which I before was speaking of, I will have leave to say that in my judgement the increasing number of our latter Plays have not done much more towards the amending of men's Morals, or their Wit, than hath the frequent Preaching, which this last age hath been pester'd with, (indeed without all Controversie they have done less harm) nor can I once imagine what temptation anyone can have to expect it from them; for sure I am no Play was ever writ with that design. If you consider Tragedy, you'll find their best of Characters unlikely patterns for a wise man to pursue: For he that is the Knight of the Play, no sublunary feats must serve his Dulcinea; for if he can't bestrid the Moon, he'll ne'er make good his business to the end, and if he chance to be offended, he must without considering right or wrong confound all things he meets, and put you half-a-score likely tall fellows into each pocket; and truly if he come not something near this Pitch I think the Tragedy's not worth a farthing; for Playes were certainly intended for the exercising of men's passions not their understandings, and he is infinitely far from wise that will bestow one moment's meditation on such things: And as for

Comedie, the finest folks you meet with there are still unfitter for your imitation, for though within a leaf or two of the Prologue, you are told that they are people of Wit, good Humour, good Manners, and all that: yet if the Authors did not kindly add their proper names, you'd never know them by their Characters; for whatsoe'er's the matter, it hath happen'd so spightfully in several Playes, which have been prettie well received of late, that even those persons that were meant to be ingenious Censors of the Play, have either prov'd the most debauch'd, or most unwittie people in the Company: nor is this error very lamentable, since as I take it Comedie was never meant, either for a converting or a conforming Ordinance: In short, I think a Play the best divertisement that wise men have: but I do also think them nothing so who do discourse as formallie about the rules of it, as if 'twere the grand affair of humane life. This being my opinion of Plays, I studied only to make this as entertaining as I could, which whether I have been successful in, my gentle Reader, you may for your shilling judge. To tell you my thoughts of it, were to little purpose, for were they very ill, you may be sure I would not have expos'd it; nor did I so till I had first consulted most of those who have a reputation for judgement of this kind; who were at least so civil (if not kind) to it as did encourage me to venture it upon the Stage, and in the Press: Nor did I take their single word for it, but us'd their reasons as a confirmation of my own.

Indeed that day 'twas Acted first, there comes me into the Pit, a long, lither, phlegmatick, white, ill-favour'd, wretched Fop, an Officer in Masquerade newly transported with a Scarf & Feather out of France, a sorry Animal that has nought else to shield it from the uttermost contempt of all mankind, but that respect which we afford to Rats and Toads, which though we do not well allow to live, yet when considered as a part of God's Creation, we make honourable mention of them. A thing, Reader–but no more of such a Smelt: This thing, I tell ye, opening that which serves it for a mouth, out issued such a noise as this to those that sate about it, that they were to expect a woful Play, God damn him, for it was a woman's. Now how this came about I am not sure, but I suppose he brought it piping hot from some who had with him the reputation of a villanous Wit: for Creatures of his size of sense talk without all imagination, such scraps as they pick up from other folks. I would not for a world be taken arguing with such a propertie as this; but if I thought there were a man of any tolerable parts, who could upon mature deliberation distinguish well his right hand from his left, and justly state the difference between the number of sixteen and two, yet had this prejudice upon him; I would take a little pains to make him know how much he errs. For waving the examination why women having equal education with men, were not as capable of knowledge, of whatsoever sort as well as they: I'll only say as I have touch'd before, that Plays have no great room for that which is men's great advantage over women, that is Learning; We all well know that the immortal Shakespeare's Plays (who was not guilty-of much more of this than often falls to women's share) have better pleas'd the World than Johnson's works, though by the way 'tis said that Benjamin was no such Rabbi neither, for I am inform'd that his Learning was but Grammar high; (sufficient indeed to rob poor Salust of his best orations) and it hath been observ'd that they are apt to admire him most confoundedly, who have just such a scantling of it as he had; and I have seen a man the most severe of Johnson's Sect, sit with his Hat remov'd less than a hair's breadth from one sullen posture for almost three hours at *The Alchymist;* who at that excellent Play of *Harry the Fourth* (which yet I hope is far enough from Farce) hath very hardly kept his Doublet whole; but affectation hath always had a greater share both in the action and discourse of men than truth and judgement have; and for our Modern ones, except our most unimitable Laureat, I dare to say I know of none that write at such a formidable rate, but that a woman may well hope to reach their greatest heights. Then for their musty rules of Unity, and God knows what besides, if they meant anything, they are enough intelligible and as practible by a woman; but really methinks they that disturb their heads with any other rule of Playes besides the making them pleasant, and avoiding of scurrility, might much better be employed in studying

how to improve men's too imperfect knowledge of that ancient English Game which hight long Laurence: And if Comedy should be the picture of ridiculous mankind I wonder anyone should think it such a sturdy task, whilst we are furnish'd with such precious Originals as him I lately told you of; if at least that Character do not dwindle into Farce, and so become too mean an entertainment for those persons who are us'd to think. Reader, I have a complaint or two to make to you and I have done; Know then that this Play was hugely injur'd in the Acting, for 'twas done so imperfectly as never any was before, which did more harm to this than it could have done to any of another sort; the Plot being busie (though I think not intricate) and so requiring a continual attention, which being interrupted by the intolerable negligence of some that acted in it, must needs much spoil the beauty on't. My Dutch Lover spoke but little of what I intended for him, but supplied it with a great deal of idle stuff, which I was wholly unacquainted with until I had heard it first from him; so that Jack-pudding ever us'd to do: which though I knew before, I gave him yet the Part, because I knew him so acceptable to most o'th' lighter Periwigs about the Town, and he indeed did vex me so, I could almost be angry: Yet, but Reader, you remember, I suppose, a fusty piece of Latine that has past from hand to hand this thousand years they say (and how much longer I can't tell) in favour of the dead. I intended him a habit much more notably ridiculous, which if ever it be important was so here, for many of the Scenes in the three last Acts depended upon the mistakes of the Colonel for Haunce, which the ill-favour'd likeness of their Habits is suppos'd to cause. Lastly my Epilogue was promis'd me by a Person who had surely made it good, if any, but he failing of his word, deput'd one, who has made it as you see, and to make out your penyworth you have it here. The Prologue is by misfortune lost. Now, Reader, I have eas'd my mind of all I had to say, and so sans farther complyment, Adieu.

Epilogue, Spoken by Mrs. Quin, to *Sir Patient Fancy*, by Aphra Behn

From The Works of Aphra Behn, *edited by Montague Summers, volume 4 (London: Heinemann/Stratford-on-Avon: Bullen, 1915); first published in* Sir Patient Fancy: A Comedy. As it is Acted at the Duke's Theatre *(London: Printed by D. Flesher for Richard Tonson & Jacob Tonson, 1698). At the first recorded performance of* Sir Patient Fancy, *by the King's Company on 17 January 1678 at the Dorset Garden Theatre, actress Anne Quin, who played Lady Knowell, spoke the epilogue.*

I here and there o'erheard a Coxcomb cry,
Ah, Rot it–'tis a Woman's Comedy,
One, who because she lately chanc'd to please us,
With her damn'd Stuff, will never cease to teeze us.
What has poor Woman done, that she must be
Debar'd from Sense, and sacred Poetry?
Why in this Age has Heaven allow'd you more,
And Women less of Wit than heretofore?
We once were fam'd in story, and could write
Equal to Men; cou'd govern, nay, cou'd fight.
We still have passive Valour, and can show,
Wou'd Custom give us leave, the active too,
Since we no Provocations want from you.
For who but we cou'd your dull Fopperies bear,
Your saucy Love, and your brisk Nonsense hear;
Indure your worse than womanish Affectation,
Which renders you the Nusance of the Nation;
Scorn'd even by all the Misses of the Town,
A Jest to Vizard Mask, the *Pit-Buffoon*;
A Glass by which the admiring Country Fool
May learn to dress himself *en Ridicule:*
Both striving who shall most ingenious grow
In Leudness, Foppery, Nonsense, Noise and Show.
And yet to these fine things we must submit
Our Reason, Arms, our Laurels, and our Wit.
Because we do not laugh at you, when leud,
And scorn and cudgel ye when you are rude.
That we have nobler Souls than you, we prove,
By how much more we're sensible of Love;
Quickest in finding all the subtlest ways
To make your Joys, why not to make you Plays?
We best can find your Foibles, know our own,
And Jilts and Cuckolds now best please the Town;
Your way of Writing's out of fashion grown.
Method, and Rule–you only understand;
Pursue that way of Fooling, and be damn'd.
Your learned Cant of Action, Time and Place,
Must all give way to the unlabour'd Farce.
To all the Men of Wit we will subscribe:
But for your half Wits, you unthinking Tribe,
We'll let you see, whate'er besides we do,

How artfully we copy some of you:
And if you're drawn to th' Life, pray tell me then,
Why Women should not write as well as Men.

Books For Further Reading

Bateson, Frederick. *English Comic Drama (1700-1750)*. Oxford: Clarendon Press, 1929.

Braunmuller, A. R., and J. C. Bulman, eds. *Comedy from Shakespeare to Sheridan: Change and Continuity in the English and European Dramatic Tradition*. Newark: University of Delaware Press, 1986.

Brown, Laura. *English Dramatic Form, 1660-1760*. New Haven & London: Yale University Press, 1981.

Danchin, Pierre. *The Prologues and Epilogues of the Restoration*, 4 volumes. Nancy: Presses Universitaires de Nancy, 1981.

Fiske, Roger. *English Theatre Music in the Eighteenth Century*. Oxford: Oxford University Press, 1973.

Fujimura, Thomas H. *The Restoration Comedy of Wit*. Princeton: Princeton University Press, 1952.

Griswold, Wendy. *Renaissance Revivals: City Comedy and Revenge Tragedy in the London Theatre: 1576-1980*. Chicago: University of Chicago Press, 1986.

Holland, Norman N. *The First Modern Comedies: The Significance of Etherege, Wycherley, and Congreve*. Cambridge, Mass.: Harvard University Press, 1959.

Holland, Peter. *The Ornament of Action: Text and Performance in Restoration Comedy*. Cambridge: Cambridge University Press, 1979.

Hotson, Leslie. *The Commonwealth and Restoration Stage*. Cambridge, Mass.: Harvard University Press, 1928.

Hume, Robert D. *The Development of English Drama in the Late Seventeenth Century*. Oxford: Clarendon Press, 1976.

Hume. *The London Theatre World, 1660-1800*. Carbondale & Edwardsville: Southern Illinois University Press, 1980.

Kenny, Shirley S. *British Theatre and the Other Arts, 1660-1800*. Washington, D.C.: Folger Books, 1984.

Leach, Robert. *The Punch and Judy Show: History, Tradition and Meaning*. Athens: University of Georgia Press, 1985.

Leacroft, Richard. *The Development of the English Playhouse*. Ithaca: Cornell University Press, 1973.

Liesenfeld, Vincent J. *The Licensing Act of 1737*. Madison: University of Wisconsin Press, 1984.

Lindley, David, ed. *The Court Masque*. Manchester & Dover, N.H.: Manchester University Press, 1984.

Loftis, John. *Comedy and Society from Congreve to Fielding*. Stanford: Stanford University Press, 1959.

Loftis. *Politics of Drama in Augustan England*. Oxford: Clarendon Press, 1963.

Loftis, ed. *Restoration Drama: Modern Essays in Criticism*. New York: Oxford University Press, 1966.

Manifold, John S. *The Music in English Drama from Shakespeare to Purcell.* London: Rockliff, 1956.

Milhous, Judith, and Robert D. Hume. *Producible Interpretation: Eight English Plays 1675-1707.* Carbondale & Edwardsville: Southern Illinois University Press, 1985.

Mills, John A. *Hamlet on Stage: The Great Tradition.* Westport, Conn.: Greenwood Press, 1985.

Nicoll, Allardyce. *A History of English Drama, 1660-1900,* 6 volumes, fourth edition revised. Cambridge: Cambridge University Press, 1952-1959.

Powell, Jocelyn. *Restoration Theatre Production.* London & Boston: Routledge & Kegan Paul, 1984.

Price, Curtis A. *Henry Purcell and the London Stage.* London, New York & Cambridge: Cambridge University Press, 1984.

Price. *Music in the Restoration Theatre.* Ann Arbor, Mich.: UMI Research Press, 1979.

Prior, Moody. *The Language of Tragedy.* New York: Columbia University Press, 1947.

Rosenfeld, Sybil M. *A Short History of Scene Design in Great Britain.* Oxford: Blackwell, 1973.

Rothstein, Eric. *Restoration Tragedy: Form and the Process of Change.* Madison: University of Wisconsin Press, 1967.

Sawyer, Paul. *Christopher Rich of Drury Lane.* Lanham, Md.: University Press of America, 1986.

Southern, Richard. *Changeable Scenery: Its Origin and Development in the British Theatre.* London: Faber & Faber, 1952.

Staves, Susan. *Players' Sceptres: Fictions of Authority in the Restoration.* Lincoln & London: University of Nebraska Press, 1979.

Styan, J. L. *Restoration Comedy in Performance.* New York: Cambridge University Press, 1986.

Taney, Retta. *Restoration Revivals on the British Stage, 1944-1979: A Critical Survey.* Lanham, Md.: University Press of America, 1985.

Van Lennep, William, and others. *The London Stage 1660-1800: A Calendar of Plays, Entertainments, and Afterpieces,* 5 parts. Carbondale: Southern Illinois University Press, 1960-1968.

Waith, Eugene. *Ideas of Greatness: Heroic Drama in England.* New York: Barnes & Noble, 1971.

Weber, Harold. *The Restoration Rake Hero: Transformations in Sexual Understanding in Seventeenth-Century England.* Madison: University of Wisconsin Press, 1986.

Worthen, William B. *The Idea of the Actor: Drama and the Ethics of Performance.* Princeton: Princeton University Press, 1984.

Zimbardo, Rose A. *A Mirror to Nature: Transformations in Drama and Aesthetics, 1600-1732.* Lexington: University Press of Kentucky, 1986.

Contributors

Robert F. Bode ....*Tennessee Technological University*
Richard E. Brown ....*University of Nevada, Reno*
J. Douglas Canfield ....*University of Arizona*
Brian Corman ....*Erindale College, University of Toronto*
Anthony Kaufman ....*University of Illinois, Urbana-Champaign*
Carolyn Kephart ....*Nashville, Tennessee*
Frederick M. Link...*University of Nebraska–Lincoln*
Beth S. Neman..*Wilmington College*
John H. O'Neill ....*Hamilton College*
Linda R. Payne...*University of Delaware*
Katharine M. Rogers ....*American University*
Eric Rothstein...*University of Wisconsin–Madison*
James A. Winn...*University of Michigan*
David Wykes ....*Dartmouth College*
Rose A. Zimbardo.................................*State University of New York at Stony Brook*

Cumulative Index

Dictionary of Literary Biography, Volumes 1-80
Dictionary of Literary Biography Yearbook, 1980-1988
Dictionary of Literary Biography Documentary Series, Volumes 1-6

Cumulative Index

DLB before number: *Dictionary of Literary Biography*, Volumes 1-80
Y before number: *Dictionary of Literary Biography Yearbook*, 1980-1988
DS before number: *Dictionary of Literary Biography Documentary Series*, Volumes 1-6

A

C

D

G

H

K

L

M

N

O

P

Q

S

T

U

V

Y

Z

continued from front endsheets

71: *American Literary Critics and Scholars, 1880-1900,* edited by John W. Rathbun and Monica M. Grecu (1988)

72: *French Novelists, 1930-1960,* edited by Catharine Savage Brosman (1988)

73: *American Magazine Journalists, 1741-1850,* edited by Sam G. Riley (1988)

74: *American Short-Story Writers Before 1880,* edited by Bobby Ellen Kimbel, with the assistance of William E. Grant (1988)

75: *Contemporary German Fiction Writers,* Second Series, edited by Wolfgang D. Elfe and James Hardin (1988)

76: *Afro-American Writers, 1940-1955,* edited by Trudier Harris (1988)

77: *British Mystery Writers, 1920-1939,* edited by Bernard Benstock and Thomas F. Staley (1988)

78: *American Short-Story Writers, 1880-1910,* edited by Bobby Ellen Kimbel, with the assistance of William E. Grant (1988)

79: *American Magazine Journalists, 1850-1900,* edited by Sam G. Riley (1988)

80: *Restoration and Eighteenth-Century Dramatists,* First Series, edited by Paula R. Backsheider (1989)

Documentary Series

1: *Sherwood Anderson, Willa Cather, John Dos Passos, Theodore Dreiser, F. Scott Fitzgerald, Ernest Hemingway, Sinclair Lewis,* edited by Margaret A. Van Antwerp (1982)

2: *James Gould Cozzens, James T. Farrell, William Faulkner, John O'Hara, John Steinbeck, Thomas Wolfe, Richard Wright,* edited by Margaret A. Van Antwerp (1982)

3: *Saul Bellow, Jack Kerouac, Norman Mailer, Vladimir Nabokov, John Updike, Kurt Vonnegut,* edited by Mary Bruccoli (1983)

4: *Tennessee Williams,* edited by Margaret A. Van Antwerp and Sally Johns (1984)

5: *American Transcendentalists,* edited by Joel Myerson (1988)

6: *Hardboiled Mystery Writers,* edited by Matthew J. Bruccoli and Richard Layman (1988)

Yearbooks

1980, edited by Karen L. Rood, Jean W. Ross, and Richard Ziegfeld (1981)

1981, edited by Karen L. Rood, Jean W. Ross, and Richard Ziegfeld (1982)

1982, edited by Richard Ziegfeld; associate editors: Jean W. Ross and Lynne C. Zeigler (1983)

1983, edited by Mary Bruccoli and Jean W. Ross; associate editor: Richard Ziegfeld (1984)

1984, edited by Jean W. Ross (1985)

1985, edited by Jean W. Ross (1986)

1986, edited by J. M. Brook (1987)

1987, edited by J. M. Brook (1988)

1988, edited by J. M. Brook (1989)

Concise Series

The New Consciousness, 1941-1968 (1987)

Colonization to the American Renaissance, 1640-1865 (1988)

Realism, Naturalism, and Local Color, 1865-1917 (1988)

The Twenties, 1917-1929 (1989)